From the Library

RCA Institutes,
New York City

PROGRAMMING
BUSINESS COMPUTERS

PROGRAMMING BUSINESS COMPUTERS

DANIEL D. McCRACKEN
Consultant

HAROLD WEISS
Computer Department
General Electric Company
Phoenix, Arizona

TSAI-HWA LEE
Computer Department
General Electric Company
Phoenix, Arizona

New York · John Wiley & Sons, Inc.
London · Chapman & Hall, Ltd.

Copyright © 1959 by John Wiley & Sons, Inc.

All rights reserved. This book or any part thereof must not be reproduced in any form without the written permission of the publisher.

Library of Congress Catalog Card Number: 59-11804
Printed in the United States of America

To

Evelyn,
Marilyn,
and
Nai-Hsin

PREFACE

Programming Business Computers is written for the person who is involved (or expects to be) in the day-to-day application of electronic computers to business data processing problems, or whose work is so closely related to computer applications that he must have something more than a skimming of the highlights. Such a person might be an accounting or business administration student who wants to know how to use computers; a punched card man who wants to know what computers are all about; a programmer with a few months' or years' experience who wants to broaden his background; a procedures analyst or auditor who wants to understand the language of the computer people he deals with; a manager of finance who needs more concrete information about computers in order to make informed decisions about them. We feel that the book fills a long-standing need in the literature of electronic data processing. There have been books for the designer of computers, books for the engineer or scientist who wants to know how to apply computers to his problems, and books for the man who wants only a "top-level" introduction to the subject. But there has not been a book for the person who is interested in applying computers to business problems, and who may not have a mathematical background.

In writing about the use of electronic computers in business data processing, we have drawn on our experience in a variety of actual applications involving nearly all major computers and applications areas. Our cumulative background includes training and experience in accounting (one of us is a Certified Public Accountant), systems and procedures, engineering, and mathematics. Thus the text is based on actual experience with realistic problems, and this is reflected in the examples used to illustrate the principles.

The material in the book divides rather naturally into four parts:

1. Chapters 1–4 provide certain background information which is necessary to an understanding of almost all of the later topics: the nature of the data processing problem, the central concept of the file, flow charting, and the general characteristics of electronic computers.

2. Chapters 5–12 (along with parts of 14) deal with coding, covering

the minimum body of knowledge required by a person doing actual programming or coding. All of the standard coding techniques are presented, with numerous examples. The coding examples are written in terms of a hypothetical computer called DATAC (which stands for nothing), which is a compilation of features of many machines. A number of the features of DATAC are to be found on machines which are only coming on the market at the time of writing. It must be recognized, of course, that no such mythical computer can satisfy everybody; each computer man has his own ideas of how a "dream" computer should be built. We naturally were not trying to design a dream machine, but simply to come up with something which is reasonably representative, contains some of the more recent advances, and is not too difficult to learn. The reader or instructor can easily enough skip sections dealing with machine features which are not of interest in a particular situation, and he can also invent new features. The reader who understands the principles which are presented in terms of DATAC will find no difficulty in learning how to apply real computers.

3. Chapters 13–19 discuss a number of more advanced topics which are perhaps not essential to the beginning coder, but which are essential to anyone wanting a deeper grasp and a broader background. A number of the subjects in this section have heretofore been discussed either in terms of a specific machine or application, or have been available only in highly technical articles. For several of the topics, this is the first extended treatment in book form.

4. Chapters 20 and 21 present a summary of the steps involved in getting a computer application going, and a critical look at the accounting and auditing problems associated with electronic data processing.

The appendices present a summary of DATAC operating characteristics, a discussion of binary numbers and binary coding of decimal digits, and "A Data Processing Diary," which describes one person's experiences in the early stages of an actual application. The extensive glossary is oriented toward business data processing.

The book can be utilized in a variety of situations. The material in it has been taught to accounting majors as a two-semester course, divided between Chapters 12 and 13. It can be used as a text for a one-semester survey or "selected topics" course. In any case, the instructor has a choice as to whether to teach coding in terms of DATAC, or to teach a real computer and use the text material in the coding chapters for background reading and for the exercises.

For individual study, the book can be used by itself or in conjunction with a programming manual if studying a real machine. Programming manuals give the facts about a computer, but unfortunately cannot give much in the way of explanation, motivation, and interpretation.

PREFACE

It is felt that many people who have a "medium" amount of experience with computers will find the second half of the book of much help in developing depth and breadth. Finally, we feel that the person who does not expect to do any direct work with computers will still find it valuable to read the book for a "feel" of what computers can and cannot do, what the problems are, what the language is, etc.

It is almost impossible to give proper credit to everyone who helped in one way or another to make this book possible. The computer manufacturers were most helpful in providing material on their equipment. We wish to acknowledge the efforts of the following people who read the glossary and made suggestions for its improvement (although we accept responsibility for any shortcomings in it): Dr. Grace Murray Hopper, Remington Rand; Robert W. Bemer, IBM; Donald L. Shell, Charles E. Thompson, and Russell C. McGee, General Electric Company; and Fred J. Gruenberger, The RAND Corporation. Many thanks again to Fred Gruenberger, who also read the entire manuscript critically and made many valuable suggestions, and who wrote the diary reproduced as Appendix 3. Our thanks, for direct and indirect support in a variety of ways, to Dr. H. R. J. Grosch of IBM and C. C. Lasher of the Computer Department of the General Electric Company. To our various secretaries go our awe at their ability to read our handwriting, and our thanks for their untiring efforts. (Actually, they *did* get tired; what we appreciate is that they went on working anyway.)

Finally, we wish to express our gratitude to our wives for their moral support, patience, and general hard work. Even though, we suspect, they sometimes rued the day we decided to become authors, they backed us up all the way.

DANIEL D. MCCRACKEN
HAROLD WEISS
TSAI-HWA LEE

March, 1959

CONTENTS

CHAPTER
1 The Data Processing Problem ... 1
    1.0 Introduction ... 1
    1.1 The Need for Improved Methods ... 1
    1.2 Data Processing Functions ... 5
    1.3 The Improvement in Data Processing Methods ... 6
    1.4 Integrated Data Processing and the Systems Approach ... 7
    1.5 Summary ... 8
        Exercises ... 8

2 Files ... 10
    2.0 Introduction ... 10
    2.1 The Functions of Files ... 10
    2.2 The Organization of Files ... 12
    2.3 File Storage Media ... 16
    2.4 Sequential File Processing ... 21
    2.5 Summary ... 24
        Exercises ... 24

3 Flow Charting ... 26
    3.0 Introduction ... 26
    3.1 Types of Flow Charts ... 27
    3.2 A Flowing Charting Notation ... 28
    3.3 General Observations on Flow Charting Techniques ... 40
    3.4 Summary ... 42
        Exercises ... 42

4 The Data Processor ... 44
    4.0 Introduction ... 44
    4.1 Organization and Operation of the Data Processor ... 44

CONTENTS

CHAPTER

	4.2	DATAC	48
	4.3	History of Computing	52
	4.4	Summary	54
		Exercises	54
5	Coding Arithmetic and Shift Operations		56
	5.0	Introduction	56
	5.1	Word Structure and Memory Identification	58
	5.2	Instruction Format and Execution	60
	5.3	Multiplication and Division	69
	5.4	Shift Operations	77
	5.5	Decimal Point Location	84
	5.6	Coding Example	86
	5.7	Summary	89
		Exercises	90
6	Further Coding Operations		95
	6.0	Introduction	95
	6.1	Decision Instructions	95
	6.2	Other Jump Instructions	102
	6.3	DATAC Filters	106
	6.4	Tape Instructions	111
	6.5	Application and Coding Illustration	114
	6.6	Summary	121
		Exercises	122
7	Address Computation		125
	7.0	Introduction	125
	7.1	Grouped Tape Record Example	125
	7.2	Digit Selection	128
	7.3	Computation of Jump Addresses	130
	7.4	Summary	132
		Exercises	133
8	Loops and Index Registers		136
	8.0	Introduction	136
	8.1	Parts of a Loop	136
	8.2	A Tape Loop Example	142
	8.3	Index Register Functions and Applications	145
	8.4	Another Loop Example	151
	8.5	Indexers in DATAC Tape Functions	154
	8.6	Indexing in a Tape Application	156
	8.7	Summary	162
		Exercises	162

CONTENTS

CHAPTER
9 Subroutines ... 167
    9.0 Introduction ... 167
    9.1 Subroutine Linkage Methods ... 167
    9.2 Indexed Linkages ... 170
    9.3 Calling Sequences ... 171
    9.4 Subroutine Libraries ... 174
    9.5 Summary ... 175
        Exercises ... 175

10 Input and Output Devices ... 177
    10.0 Introduction ... 177
    10.1 The Computer Console ... 177
    10.2 Magnetic Tape ... 181
    10.3 Punched Cards ... 184
    10.4 Printing Devices ... 185
    10.5 Paper Tape ... 188
    10.6 Cathode-Ray Tube Output ... 190
    10.7 Keyboard Entry and Inquiry Devices ... 190
    10.8 Buffers ... 192
    10.9 Off-Line Tape Devices ... 194
    10.10 Summary ... 196
        Exercises ... 196

11 Input and Output Programming ... 198
    11.0 Introduction ... 198
    11.1 Planning for Input and Output ... 198
    11.2 Input and Output Instructions and Programming ... 201
    11.3 A Program for Loading Cards ... 211
    11.4 Input and Output Subroutines ... 216
    11.5 Summary ... 221
        Exercises ... 222

12 Verifying Program Accuracy ... 224
    12.0 Introduction ... 224
    12.1 Detecting Programming Errors Before Running the Program ... 226
    12.2 Using the Computer to Detect Programming Errors ... 230
    12.3 Procedural Checks ... 238
    12.4 Coding for Ease of Checkout ... 240
    12.5 Summary ... 241
        Exercises ... 242

CONTENTS

CHAPTER
13 Advanced Techniques in Magnetic Tape Programming — 244
    13.0 Introduction — 244
    13.1 Interior Labels and Label Checking — 245
    13.2 Sentinels — 245
    13.3 Run Locators — 247
    13.4 Dating Routines — 249
    13.5 Overlays — 250
    13.6 Alternation of Tape Units — 251
    13.7 Record Grouping — 253
    13.8 Variable Length Records — 254
    13.9 Effective Use of Tape Buffers — 256
    13.10 Summary — 257
    Exercises — 258

14 Machine-Aided Coding — 260
    14.0 Introduction — 260
    14.1 Relative Address Coding — 262
    14.2 An Assembly System — 266
    14.3 Symbolic Coding and Compiling — 273
    14.4 Interpretive Coding — 276
    14.5 Nonmachine-Language Compiling — 279
    14.6 Generators and the Report Generator — 289
    14.7 The Place of Machine-Language Coding — 295
    14.8 Summary — 296
    Exercises — 297

15 Sorting — 298
    15.0 Introduction — 298
    15.1 General Considerations — 298
    15.2 Sorting by Selection — 302
    15.3 Sorting by Exchanging — 306
    15.4 Sorting by Insertion — 308
    15.5 Radix Sorting — 310
    15.6 Straight Merge Sorting — 315
    15.7 Probability Merge Sorting — 320
    15.8 A Flow-Charted Example — 323
    15.9 Computer Considerations in Sorting — 327
    15.10 Sort Generators — 328
    15.11 Systems Considerations in Sorting — 329
    15.12 Summary — 331
    Exercises — 331

CONTENTS

CHAPTER

16 Economizing and Estimating Computer Time — 333
- 16.0 Introduction — 333
- 16.1 Timing Considerations in Systems Design — 335
- 16.2 Timing Considerations in Programming — 339
- 16.3 Timing Considerations in Coding — 341
- 16.4 Estimating Computer Time — 342
- 16.5 Summary — 343
- Exercises — 345

17 Rerun Techniques — 347
- 17.0 Introduction — 347
- 17.1 The Rerun Principle — 348
- 17.2 Rerun Procedures for Small Program Segments — 349
- 17.3 Program Reruns — 352
- 17.4 System Reruns — 355
- 17.5 Summary — 357
- Exercises — 358

18 Nonrandom Access Main Memories — 359
- 18.0 Introduction — 359
- 18.1 Optimum Placement of Data and Instructions — 360
- 18.2 Rapid-Access Loops — 363
- 18.3 Summary — 365
- Exercises — 365

19 Large Random Access File Storage — 367
- 19.0 Introduction — 367
- 19.1 Large Random Access Storage Devices — 368
- 19.2 Addressing of Records — 369
- 19.3 Uses of Large Random Access Storage — 371
- 19.4 Summary — 374
- Exercises — 374

20 Steps in Planning and Programming Computer Applications — 376
- 20.0 Introduction — 376
- 20.1 The Systems Study — 376
- 20.2 Preparation of Top-Level Flow Charts — 379
- 20.3 Design of Input and Output Forms and Records — 380
- 20.4 Tentative Layout of Memory and Allocation of Tape Units — 381

CHAPTER

20.5	Preparation of Detailed Flow Charts	381
20.6	Coding	382
20.7	Checking and Review	383
20.8	Getting the Coding into Machine Language	384
20.9	Preparation of Test Data and Accuracy Checking	385
20.10	Volume Test and Conversion	386
20.11	System Write-up	387
20.12	Program Maintenance	390
20.13	Training Activities	391
20.14	Evaluation	392
20.15	Summary	393
	Exercises	393

21 Accounting, Auditing, and Data Protection ... 395

21.0	Introduction	395
21.1	Some Characteristics of Accounting by Computer	395
21.2	Reliability of Computers	400
21.3	System Checks	405
21.4	Data Protection	411
21.5	Planning for Emergencies	415
21.6	Auditing Problems	417
21.7	The Role of the Accountant	425
21.8	Summary	426
	Exercises	427

Appendix 1 DATAC ... 429

A1.0	General	429
A1.1	Machine Characteristics	429
A1.2	Instruction Format	431
A1.3	Arithmetic and Control Registers	432
A1.4	Instruction Details	433

Appendix 2 Number Representation ... 444

A2.0	Binary Numbers	444
A2.1	Number Representation	445
A2.2	Binary Arithmetic	447
A2.3	Number Base Conversion	452
A2.4	Binary Coding of Decimal Digits	457

CONTENTS

CHAPTER
Appendix 3 A Data Processing Diary,
            by Fred Gruenberger   461

Glossary   469

Bibliography   489

Index   503

1 THE DATA PROCESSING PROBLEM

1.0 Introduction

Business today is faced with two pressing problems: a spiraling increase in the amount of paperwork, and the need to make managerial decisions faster and on the basis of more reliable information. The advent of electronic digital computers has made possible a decisive solution to these problems. The bulk of this book is devoted to the application of computers to business operations once the application has been defined. It may be instructive in this chapter to discuss the nature of the problems themselves. We shall also introduce, in very broad outline, the functions and methods of electronic data processing.

1.1 The Need for Improved Methods

The volume and complexity of business data processing has been growing in the last few decades at an almost spectacular rate, and shows no signs of slackening. As one concrete example of the increase in paperwork, consider the United States banking system. In 1935 the national banking system processed approximately 2.5 billion checks. In 1956 the figure reached about 10 billion. The American Bankers Association has estimated that in 1965 the total will be 20 billion.

Along with the growth in volume of clerical operations, there has been an increased complexity in the management of business. As businesses become larger, the problems of management grow out of proportion to the mere size increase. Geographical distance often creates difficulty. Diversification makes measurement of results hard. More and more, management decisions must be made before all the data is available, or as sometimes facetiously suggested, *in spite of* a mass of detailed information. One can sympathize with the harried executive who attributes his success to the ability to make correct decisions on the basis of out-of-date, misleading information.

The commonest solution to these problems in the past seems to have been to hire more clerks. The estimated size of this work force varies with the source of the estimate, but an indication of the magnitude and trend may be seen in Figure 1, which is a reproduction of a chart distributed at a recent International Systems Meeting. It has often been pointed out, as is apparent in the chart, that the amount of paperwork in the United States has been growing much faster than the economy as a whole or than clerical productivity.

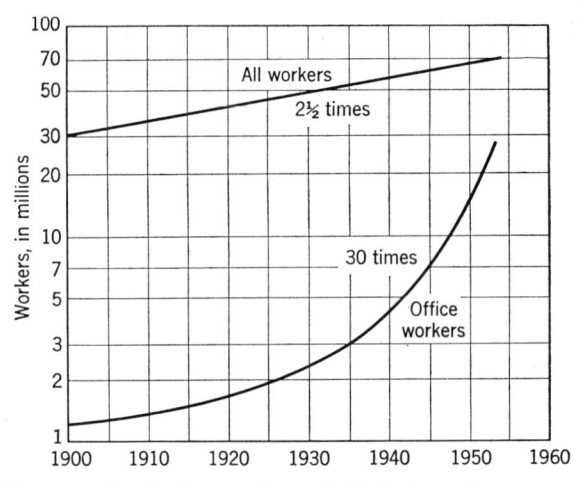

Figure 1. The growth of the number of clerical workers compared to all workers, in the United States. Courtesy of the Systems and Procedures Association of America.

Most computer applications are directed toward a *combination* of paperwork reduction and improved managerial control. As an example of this fact, and as a general introduction to some of the typical data processing problems in industry, consider a certain concern which manufactures major appliances—refrigerators, stoves, etc. This plant normally employs some 15,000 people, produces about 2,000,000 appliances a year, and is a typical mass-production type of operation.

The appliance industry makes products which are subject to widely fluctuating markets. The first thing a manager would like in running such a business is an analysis of sales, on as current a basis as possible. With such information the items which are moving well can be fully exploited, and the production rate can be reduced on items which are doing poorly. Better yet, the manager would like to have reliable forecasts of sales, well ahead of production, so that production can be better scheduled. Marketing research techniques may be applied in an attempt to correlate appliance sales with dozens of variables such as disposable income, new housing starts, automobile sales, weather, etc. The relationships vary for different product lines. Vast quantities of data must be analyzed over and over again to refine the relationships and techniques. Various mathematical techniques must be explored. Such a job alone can easily tax the capabilities of a large computer, but if successful, the payoff is very high. This type of project, which usually cannot be done economically or rapidly enough without a computer, can easily be justified on the basis of savings in overproduction.

Given a reasonably reliable sales forecast, the manager still has problems in deciding what to produce. Certain lines have a low gross margin but high volume, whereas others have higher margins but lower volumes. The manager has, within certain limits, a set of variable resources at his command—space, men, machines, and capital. What he would like to find is a product "mix" which will maximize his profits. It may take several months, however, to explore the impact of a single model mix on a business, which would be done by working out a forecasted budget (or profit and loss statement) from the top level all the way down the line of operations. By the time this has been done by manual methods, conditions have probably changed and the analysis is too late to be of much value. The concern we are discussing makes use of a computer program which allows a manager to submit several alternative product mixes and provides for him within a few hours a budget forecast of each of the alternatives.

By one method or another a production schedule is established. At this point an almost overwhelming shop scheduling problem develops. Hundreds of freight cars and trucks deliver raw materials and ship away finished goods; there are many miles of continually moving conveyor belts; there are literally thousands of machines; many different models may be in production on parallel lines, each model requiring hundreds of parts. What would ordinarily seem to be minor delays or unimportant failures in scheduling become amplified in such a large and complex system of interrelated activities. If just one part is missing when needed, an entire production line may have to be shut down. There is no room for storage of many partly finished machines, nor is there room in the plant for storing even a day's supply of a bulky item such as refrigerator insulation. It is not uncommon for critically short parts to be shipped in by air express, only to discover later that the needed parts were in the plant, but could not be located. The problem of conveyor belt optimization alone is staggering. Computers have been successfully applied to all of the types of manufacturing problems mentioned above, which usually go under such names as material control, production control, and vendor and distributor shipping schedules, to name a few. This is not to say that no problems remain to be solved, but the practicality of computers in these areas has been conclusively demonstrated.

It may be of interest to note a few details of one of the areas mentioned above, namely material control (inventory control). The purpose of any system of inventory control is to provide material when it is needed at the least possible cost. If inventory is too low, the result is costly expediting, idle manpower, production line shutdown, loss of sales, etc. Excessive inventory also costs money in storage space, capital which could be used otherwise, insurance, and obsolescence. Striking a balance between these two extremes is a matter both of mathematical techniques for minimizing total cost, and the handling of a great deal of detailed information. That a computer can handle a complex material control system is no longer a matter of conjecture. In its first year of operation, a computer system in one part of the appliance concern we have been describing increased the inventory turnover rate from 12.6 to 18.0, while absorbing a 64% increase in production. This improvement in turnover (44%) reduced the investment in inventory required (to support the *higher* production volume) by $2,000,000. At the same time personnel efficiency increased 100%; each clerk now handles double the number of parts previously assigned. This material control system has since been substantially revised and made even more efficient.

So far we have discussed briefly some of the data processing problems in the marketing and manufacturing areas. There are, of course, many good applications for electronic computing in the financial areas of a business also. One of the most common of these is payroll, in which a great many clerical operations are involved. Job tickets must be balanced to time cards. Some production workers may work in several different teams or groups in one week, where incentive pay has to be calculated separately for each group. A large variety of deductions may be made from gross pay, such as withholding tax, social security contribution, state income tax, pension plan, stock bonus plan, union dues, payroll savings plan, group insurance, safety shoes, community fund, garnishments, etc. In addition to simply calculating the net pay, many personnel records must be updated and labor costs distributed to show individual, section, and department costs and efficiencies. Tax reports must be made up. All of this, of course, must be done on a rather rigid time schedule for each of some 15,000 people, in the example above.

There is no need to prolong this discussion by describing the many other data processing functions such as accounts receivable, accounts

THE DATA PROCESSING PROBLEM   5

payable, capital investment in plant and equipment, stock transaction records, etc. In all of these areas and many others, computers are being employed, and their use, of course, is not limited to the manufacturing industry. They are in widespread use, or will be in the near future, in insurance companies, public utilities, department stores, the transportation industry, and the Government, to name some.

1.2 Data Processing Functions

There are a number of functions which must always be carried out in business data processing, whether done by manual, mechanical, or electronic methods.

1. Most business information must initially be *recorded*. The information may originate in many ways, such as the manufacture of a product, its sale, the payment for it, payment of the workers who made it, etc. The information may be recorded on any of a variety of media: paper, paper tape, punched cards, magnetic tape, etc. If the recording is done directly in a *machine language*, a *hard copy*, such as a typewritten sheet which is more readily comprehensible to human beings, is frequently also produced.

2. The information which has been recorded is usually needed at other physical locations, so some means of *communication* are required. This is commonly provided by the manual movement of documents, but the use of such techniques as teletype transmission is growing rapidly.

3. Information must be *stored*. It may be stored in the same form as originally recorded, or it may pass through several forms of storage during its processing. For instance, it may be manually recorded on a document initially, then punched into cards, then converted to magnetic tape, processed by a computer, and then converted to a printed report.

4. Information must usually be *processed* to put it in more useful form. Examples of this processing include: arithmetic operations such as the calculation of a man's pay from his hours worked and pay rate; sorting into some sequence; summarization. Other examples could be given but these are representative.

5. The processed information must be made available to the ultimate users. This *output* may be some form of report for operating or planning purposes, or it may be a punched card bill sent to a customer, to name two examples.

6 PROGRAMMING BUSINESS COMPUTERS

These functions are very general and apply to entirely different data processing systems. In Chapter 4 we shall see how a computer is organized with input, output, arithmetic, control, and memory devices, which accomplish these same functions, although the correspondence is not exact.

1.3 The Improvement in Data Processing Methods

There are three areas of data processing where major advances have been made in the last few years, and are being made now. The first concerns the initial handling of information. New equipment is available which provides increased accuracy, speed, and economy. Optical paper tape readers are a prime example. Since the same information is often needed in many areas for different purposes, and since it is expensive to record the same information several times, techniques have been developed which provide for automatic duplication after information has been recorded *once*. As a by-product of the preparation of a sales invoice, for example, paper tape or punched cards may be produced which record the information in a form which can later be read by another machine for production scheduling, sales analysis, and various accounting records. This is an illustration of the *common language* concept in data processing whereby different machines "communicate" with each other through some common storage medium. This requires an integration of the handling of the data, hence the term *integrated data processing* (IDP) to describe the automatic or semiautomatic flow of information in a business, and its manipulation, organization, and analysis. The development of devices which can optically or magnetically read ordinary printed numbers and/or letters (which is called *character reading*) is another advance which promises to ease the burden of getting information into machine language.

A second major development bearing on the clerical problem is the development of the electronic digital computer. For our purposes here a computer may be defined as a device which accepts *raw data*, manipulates it, makes calculations, and produces *reports* and *documents*. Computers are powerful because they are fast, accurate, automatic, and can make elementary *logical decisions*. Most computers can perform many thousands of operations, such as addition and multiplication, each second. They are inherently much more accurate than any human clerk and they can be set up so that when they do make mistakes they usually give an indication of the fact. Most data processing problems can be set up for a computer in such a manner that relatively little human intervention is required. The elementary decisions of which a computer is capable are vastly simpler than those which a human being can make, but computers can at least take over the completely routine quantitive decisions which do not make full use of a human being's powers. Furthermore, any decision which can be expressed completely in quantitive terms, no matter how complex, can be expressed as a combination of simple decisions, so that we sometimes find computers doing rather surprising things in this area of decision making. The limitation of this statement is that many decision making processes cannot be expressed in quantitive terms; the era of the automatic "push-button" office is many years off, if indeed it ever comes.*

The third area in which major advances are being made is the analysis of information. The field of *operations research* finds scientists of many different disciplines bringing to bear mathematical techniques of analyzing data to allow better decision making by management. The emphasis of this work, in this context, is on predicting the impact of different alternatives on the profit of a business. An attempt is also made to define better measurement techniques and to determine which of the many factors affecting the success of a business are the most significant.

1.4 Integrated Data Processing and the Systems Approach

Of the three areas discussed in the previous section, the emphasis in this book will naturally be upon the application of a computer after the job to be done has been defined. We must not overlook the fact, however, that a great deal of careful effort must go into the proper definition of the job—which, if anything, is more work than the programming and coding which we shall discuss. The point we wish to make here is that it is usually unwise to concentrate on an *isolated* area of data processing; rather, some attempt must be made to integrate the different areas of applications so that there is no duplication of source information or of basic files or results. This is what we mean in the general sense by integrated data processing.

The idea of the systems approach is closely related to integrated data processing. In this context a *system* is a collection of operations and procedures by which management gets the business activity performed. A broader definition includes men and machines. By a

---
* Neither do we expect millions of clerks to be laid off overnight. Some clerical positions will undoubtedly be eliminated, but history has shown that in the long run technological advances increase employment, not decrease it.

systems approach we mean taking a broad look at the business and its problems and trying to understand the *interrelationships* between the information requirements of the different parts of the business. Many organizations, unfortunately, pay only lip service to this ideal. The history of automation in the factory shows that only minor improvements generally result until the *basic* process or methods are considered, i.e., until a systems approach is followed. The concepts of integrated data processing and the systems approach require that consideration be given to the flow of information through the *entire* business. Even if only a restricted area is to be worked with, an attempt should be made to see how this area fits in with other areas.

1.5 Summary

The rapid growth of overhead costs in business is causing management to scrutinize closely one of its major costs, that of the office. As businesses have grown in size and complexity, piecemeal solutions to office problems have been characteristic: adding a few more clerks or using slightly faster machines here and there. It is becoming increasingly apparent that a systems approach, formal long-range planning, and scientific techniques must be applied to clerical problems, much as they have been applied to production problems. Labor-saving methods and machinery must be utilized more extensively than at present. Electronic digital computers may provide the required technological breakthrough in the business paperwork crisis.

Management control, however, should eventually prove to be the major contribution of electronic computers to business operations. Too often today, business computers are being used for routine record keeping, despite the fact that forecasting, planning, and scheduling offer the potential of far greater financial return on equipment investment than does clerical cost reduction. The oft-stated goal is after all to make money, not to save it. In the words of the Society for the Advancement of Management, "No war, no strike, no depression, can so completely destroy an established business or its profits, as new and better methods, equipment and materials in the hands of an enlightened competitor."

Exercises

1. Take a data processing problem that you are familiar with in school, business, government, club, etc., and show where a computer could make a contribution to its solution.

THE DATA PROCESSING PROBLEM

2. Comment on the statement, "Anything can be done on an electronic computer." How can the capabilities of an electronic computer be more accurately described?

3. Name several illustrations not given in the text of the need for improved clerical methods.

4. Is the advantage of the electronic computer primarily in clerical savings? Name some of the other advantages.

5. Discuss the limitations of electronic computers as applied to business data processing.

6. Discuss the systems versus the piecemeal approach. Show how the two might be different as applied to manual, punched card, and electronic data processing methods.

7. Give an example of how a systems approach could simplify an area of data processing with which you are familiar.

2 FILES

2.0 Introduction

The history of files is as old as the history of business. Since the day when the first owner of a one-man store realized that his records exceeded his memory capacity, visual records have been used to help people remember facts about customer sales and expenses. Later, when files became more extensive and complex, they were kept to be able to answer customer inquiries more quickly. For example, a customer might challenge the accuracy of his account statement or demand to examine the original invoice; the business concern must be able to provide the information. Still later, management learned to depend on information in files to help make decisions. For instance, sales analysis often provides clues on the performance of products or of salesmen's performances or on the effectiveness of advertising. Inventory records help to determine the cost of keeping inventory and allow for systematic ordering policies.

In all of these cases, we see that a file consists of a collection of *records* providing information about a group of related accounts, people, stock items, etc. We realize furthermore that each record in a file must be identifiable, i.e., part of the information in each record of a file must be an account number, or a stock number, or an employee's pay number, or some other such identification. This identification is usually called the *key* of the record, in the terminology of data processing.

In this chapter we shall discuss in a little more detail the functions of files, the organization of files, the media on which files are typically recorded, and the methods of systematically processing the information in files.

2.1 The Functions of Files

Files are maintained in business for a variety of purposes. The most fundamental purpose is to keep permanent records about the business or about functions which must be carried on as a part of the business. These are usually called *master files*. Typical examples are files of accounts receivable, master payroll information about employees, inventory files, Federal Government social security files, etc. Another important type of file is what we shall call a *transaction file*. This has to do typically with information which will result in some change in a master file. Examples are records of payments and purchases, records of stock disbursement, and payroll status change notices. Another type of file might be called a *report file,* which contains information excerpted from master files. Businesses in the United States are required to send to the Federal Government information on social security tax withheld from an employee's pay, for example.

It may be instructive to show some of the contents of a typical business file. The following items were extracted from a listing of the items contained in a master file of a payroll system which uses a large computer. The complete payroll file in this particular case contains about three times as much information; that shown is typical of the amount needed for each employee in most payroll systems.

    Department
    Payroll number
    Organization code
    Name
    Sex
    Marital status
    Social security number
    When first employed
    Birth date
    Where time card is located
    Where check is sent
    Number of dependents
    Job classification
    Pay rate
    Pension code
    Insurance code
    Savings bonds amount
    Union dues amount
    Community Service Fund (or similar) amount
    Credit union amount
    Shift worked
    Year to date gross earnings

Year to date gross earnings which are federal-taxable
Year to date withholding tax
Year to date social security
Year to date pension plan contribution
Year to date hours sick
Management club dues
Miscellaneous deduction code
Miscellaneous deduction amount

2.2 The Organization of Files

We defined a file as a collection of related information about some subject. We might have added, *directed toward some purpose*. For instance, a combination of a phone directory, a list of members of the Diners' Club, and a list of automobile license numbers of residents of New York City might conceivably be related in the sense of all being about the same broad group of people, but it would not be a file. Or at least not a very useful one. That is to say, files are *organized* with some eye toward their *use* or *purpose*.

For this reason we may find that the same body of related information may for different purposes be organized into several different files, or it may be broken up into several subfiles. For instance, a manual data processing system can seldom make good use of a completely centralized file of information about a business, but must rather break the information into many smaller files which can be located at various places, thus facilitating the work of the many different clerks who must have access to the information. The very *same* information might be one large combined file for use in electronic data processing systems. Furthermore, the same body of related information may be differently organized depending on how the information contained in it is to be processed. A file which is to be "updated" only once a month will typically be set up quite differently from one which is to be used to provide immediate answers to customer inquiries, even though the information contained might be the same.

All of the things that can happen to change or alter the contents of a master file are collected under the generic term of *activity*. Thus we might speak of the master file in a payroll application as having 98% activity, meaning that approximately 98% of the records are used every time the file is processed. On the other hand, the master file in an inventory accounting application which is processed daily might have an activity of only 5%, because only that fraction of the total number of items in the stockroom is used on a typical day. In a very general way we may classify activity under three headings: *additions, changes,* and *deletions*. Additions refer to the *insertion of new records in a file,* such as when new employees report for work, or when new customers open accounts at a department store. Changes usually represent the bulk of the file activity and represent merely a *change in some part of the information in the records.* Many examples could be cited: an increase in the number of dependents claimed by an employee; a change in the amount which a customer owes because of a purchase or a payment on his account; a change in the number of a particular stock item on hand when some of that item is sold to customers or received from vendors; a change in an employee's pension program status; an increase in a salesman's accrued commissions. Deletions occur when a *record is removed from a file.* Examples are the termination of a person's employment; withdrawal from a pension program, etc. It must be pointed out, however, that a record is usually deleted *only with respect to a certain file.* For instance, when a customer drops his account at a department store, his record will be deleted from the appropriate master file, but this may cause a corresponding addition to a file of dead accounts which the store may maintain for credit information purposes. This fact illustrates once again that we cannot ignore the *purpose* of a file; the active and inactive account files of a department store may contain almost exactly the same type of information, but they are used for entirely different purposes.

There are two very broad classifications of file organization, which, because of the way they have historically been processed in data processing applications, go under the names of *sequential files* and *random access files.* The sequential file, which is by far the more common at the present time, is one in which the records must be processed one after the other, and in which the records are almost always in sequence according to a key. A telephone directory is a sequential file: it is sequenced in ascending alphabetic order of the customer's name. (Incidentally, we have here an illustration of the fact that the same information may be the basis of more than one file. The telephone company for its purposes must maintain exactly the same information in two other sequences, namely, telephone number and customer's address.) The sequentially organized file is characterized by the fact that all we know about the location of the records in the file is that they are in sequence. If I want to find the telephone number of Richard A. Turner I have no way of knowing beforehand that I should look halfway down the third column of page **602**.

Instead, I open the book and determine which direction I am from the T's, then I narrow the field down to the Tu's, etc.; all I am able to do in each case is determine whether the page I am currently looking at is before or after the one I want. Typical techniques of processing sequential files with electronic equipment cannot even do as intelligent a job as the one outlined above.

Although some systems of organizing a problem are somewhat less cumbersome, the usual data processing approach to the problem of finding the phone number of Richard A. Turner would be to inspect every prior name in the book to determine whether it is Richard A. Turner, starting from the front of the book and proceeding in sequence. In a file the size of the New York telephone directory, this would be an extremely wasteful process. This has led to the practice of *batching* the activity to be processed against a master file. For instance, in this analogy I might wait until I had 200 phone numbers to look up; then I would sort all of them into alphabetic name sequence and look up the 200 telephone numbers *in order*. This would mean I would have to go through the master file only once, although it would still be wasteful because I would still be inspecting a great many names which I was not really interested in.

Although the situation is not usually so bad as this example might imply, we have here an example of three of the fundamental characteristics of a sequentially organized file:

1. All of the activity or transactions must be sequenced before the processing can be done.

2. All of the information in the master file must be inspected even though in many applications most of that information is of no interest.

3. In order to alleviate the inefficiency enforced by the second point, the activity must typically be batched. In some cases this is the natural method of operation, such as in a payroll application. In others it is not natural and sometimes becomes quite a burden.

These three characteristics, although they by no means make sequential files useless, do, in some cases, limit their usefulness. This has led to the second broad classification of file organization, namely the random access method. Basically, this term is meant to imply simply that it is possible to obtain any record in the file as quickly as any other, *approximately*. (It will be recognized that this most decidedly is not true of the type of sequential file processing in which it is necessary always to start at the beginning and run through the file in sequence until the record of interest is found.) Examples are a little difficult to find because files are not usually organized completely on one basis or the other. The general idea of the random access file might be illustrated by a technique of looking up telephone numbers in which one first goes to an auxiliary reference file with the first two letters of the desired name; this reference file in turn tells the page of the telephone directory on which to begin looking, with the assurance that one will never have to search through more than a few pages. This may seem like a rather small gain since some searching must still be done and since there is the additional burden of locating the correct place in the auxiliary reference file. It should be pointed out, however, that, first of all, there are techniques in electronic computing which make it fairly simple to find the correct place in the reference file and that, second, the total amount of searching required to find one record has been greatly reduced. Furthermore, techniques have been developed which make it possible, in some cases, to eliminate both the auxiliary reference file and all searching of the master file—even of a few records. These techniques will be discussed in Chapter 19 on random access memories.

The example given has perhaps left the incorrect impression that in a file organized according to the random access concept the records are still in sequence according to some key. This is usually not so. In fact, one of the advantages of the random access file is that it is usually no longer necessary to sequence the records. In comparison with the three characteristics of sequentially organized files mentioned above, we see in broad outline that random access files have the following characteristics:

1. The file no longer need be in sequence. This eliminates the sometimes burdensome task of sorting a file into sequence, and also somewhat simplifies the processing of the master file. It may not have been apparent to the reader that when an addition is made to a sequential file, new space must be created; with certain types of recording media this implies the necessity for creating an entirely new master file each time it is processed. This can impose a rather heavy burden of time on the processing.

2. It is now no longer necessary to inspect every record during the processing. With some types of random access file organization only a few need be inspected in order to find the correct one, and with others no irrelevant records need be inspected.

3. The requirement of batching the activity is now much less serious. For reasons not having to do with file organization, it may still be desirable to do some batching, but it is not mandatory. Some applications can now be carried out which would be almost impossible

From the Library

RCA Institutes,

New York City

with the sequential file: providing immediate answers to customer inquiries on, say, a large sequential insurance policy file, is next to impossible.

We see that the difference between sequential and random access file organization techniques may be characterized by the difference in *average access time*, which is defined as the average time required to retrieve any given record in a file. The extreme in random access organization is reached when any record in a file can be obtained in just the time required to read or transcribe the information from the file storage medium to the working medium. The extreme of sequential processing occurs, as it usually does, when the key for every record in the file must be compared with the key of the record being sought until the desired record is found. It can be seen that the average access time for this type of storage is approximately the time required to search halfway through the entire file. It is clear that with a sequential access file organization, we would rarely set up the processing so that we entered the file with only one transaction. Files in everyday use may actually fall into one of these extremes or almost anywhere in between.

This comparison of sequential and random access file storage may leave the impression that there is nothing to be said for sequential files and everything to be said for random access files. This is not true, partly because many applications do not need the flexibility of a random access file, and partly because with the presently available storage media and devices it is considerably more expensive to store the same information in random form; furthermore, in some cases the random access method actually leads to *longer* total processing times. It is worth noting also that in many problems both techniques are used, at different points.

2.3 File Storage Media

File information may be recorded on a great variety of media, the most important of which at present are paper forms, perforated paper tape, punched cards, photographic film, magnetic tape, and magnetic disks. Paper forms are by far the most common medium currently in use in the office. Many examples come to mind immediately. However, with the exception of the relatively new technique of reading printed forms directly from paper or cardboard, this medium is not in wide use for files which must be processed by electronic computers. This situation may well change in the future, but we shall have little to say about the technique in this book.

Perforated paper tape is in fairly wide use in diversified business operations. It may be produced as a distinct clerical operation or as a by-product of other business equipment such as typewriters, billing machines, desk calculators, and cash registers. It is also widely used as a data communication medium.

Punched cards, of course, have been in very wide use for many years as a file storage medium. Here, as everyone knows, information is represented by holes punched in pieces of postcard-size lightweight cardboard. These cards are usually originally prepared as a separate clerical operation but in some cases can be produced as a by-product of other operations. The superiority of punched cards over paper forms lies in the ability to operate mechanically on the information contained in them. (Once again this relative advantage may not be a permanent one; the equipment now under development for mechanically or optically reading printed information from paper forms may fairly soon challenge the superiority of punched cards.) The disadvantages of punched cards are:

1. the restriction of either eighty or ninety columns on each card;
2. the relatively bulky volume compared to newer forms of storage;
3. the relatively slow speed with which they can be processed compared with other file storage media, which is based on the fact that
4. all processing of punched cards is based on physical movement of the cards.

Information can be recorded on photographic film in much more compact form than on either paper or punched cards. However, it is somewhat more difficult to record and retrieve the information on film.

Magnetic tape is a relative newcomer to the business office, although it has been used to record sound for many years. Magnetic tapes in current use are made of thin strips of plastic or steel on which a magnetizable surface is coated. They are typically $\frac{1}{2}$ inch wide and perhaps 3000 feet long. Information is recorded on magnetic tape by passing it over small coils which can cause the surface to be magnetized at points along the tape. The information can then be retrieved by passing the tape over the same or different coils and electronically sensing the voltages induced in them. (A more complete discussion of this form of recording can be found on pages 111 and 181 and in references in the bibliography.) The primary advantage of magnetic tape over the other forms of file storage we have discussed is the speed with which information can be placed on them and retrieved from them, and the relative compactness of the recording.

For instance, a 10½-inch-diameter reel of tape at the present time can contain as many as 20 million digits or letters, and if the processing is extremely simple, be completely processed in less than 10 minutes. The primary disadvantage of magnetic tape is that it cannot practically be organized completely randomly. (We shall see in Chapter 19 that a large number of relatively short strips of tape can be organized for random access in the sense of the telephone directory analogy above, in which one first found the approximate location of the record of interest and then searched through a relatively small section of the file.)

The current use of magnetic tape may be broadly classified under three headings: *input/output files, on-line storage, and off-line storage*. Magnetic tape is used for input/output files when the transactions for a given data processing operation are entered into the computer on magnetic tape. This may be accomplished either by recording the information on the magnetic tape, using a keyboard designed for the purpose, or by first recording the information on cards, paper tape, or microfilm, and then converting this information to magnetic tape, again employing a special device. The information going onto the tape may or may not be already sequenced. In some cases, it is advantageous to sort the punched cards before the magnetic tape is produced. In other cases, there may be no need for sequencing, such as when the transactions are to be processed against a random access file or when it is more desirable to carry out the sorting process inside the electronic computer itself.

By on-line storage we mean temporary storage which is made necessary by the characteristics of the electronic computer being used. As we shall see in Chapter 4, an electronic computer typically has a relatively small, fast-access main storage and a much larger, relatively slower, auxiliary storage. This division of storage into two types is made necessary by the comparatively expensive nature of the fast-access storage devices currently available. In typical electronic data processing, records are frequently transferred between the main storage and the auxiliary storage; it is in this sense that we refer to on-line storage.

Off-line storage implies a large bulk of information which must be kept between processing runs. This is perhaps the most common use of magnetic tape, and corresponds most closely to our earlier discussion of what a file is. For the purpose of off-line storage a complete file may consist of one or many reels of magnetic tape. The complete policyholder files of the larger insurance companies (most of which are using electronic data processing) involve several million records and hundreds of reels of magnetic tape. The United States social security program, a sizable portion of which is being carried out using electronic data processing and magnetic tape files, involves individual records on some 75,000,000 persons. On the other end of the scale, it is possible to have a complete file consist of only a few dozen or a few hundred records; there is nothing in the file concept which implies bigness.

Information is recorded on magnetic tape in groups called *records*, or *blocks*. These may or may not correspond exactly to the records as defined previously. One tape record may in some cases contain just one file record. The processing is somewhat simpler if it is possible to set up the tape records this way. In other cases it is necessary to combine several file records into one tape record, because, in some machines, the tape records must always contain a fixed amount of information which is sometimes considerably greater than the amount of information in a file record. Or the situation may be just reversed, requiring that a file record be spread out over several tape records. There may be reasons other than fixed tape record lengths which make it desirable to group several file records into one tape record; these reasons will be discussed later (Chapter 13).

In any case, one of the tasks which must be carried out fairly early in the planning of any data processing application which uses magnetic tapes is to plan how the information in each file record will appear on tape. That is, it is necessary to decide how much space is to be allotted to each piece of information and in what order it will appear. In many computers the unit of information, for practical purposes, is a group of (typically) ten to twelve characters (numbers, letters, or special symbols) which are handled by the computer essentially as a unit, and are often referred to as a *word*. The pieces of information in the file record are in general not of this same length, so information must either be grouped into one word or spread out over several, just as file records may be grouped or spread. This problem of defining the appearance of the tape records is called *file design*, *file record design*, or *file layout*. Figure 1 shows a possible file record design for the payroll record information shown on page 11, with the number of characters being approximately typical, although this would of course vary with each application. In this illustration it is assumed that the computer word is eleven characters (as it is in the mythical computer to be used for illustrative purposes in this book), and that there are no computer characteristics which require

PROGRAMMING BUSINESS COMPUTERS

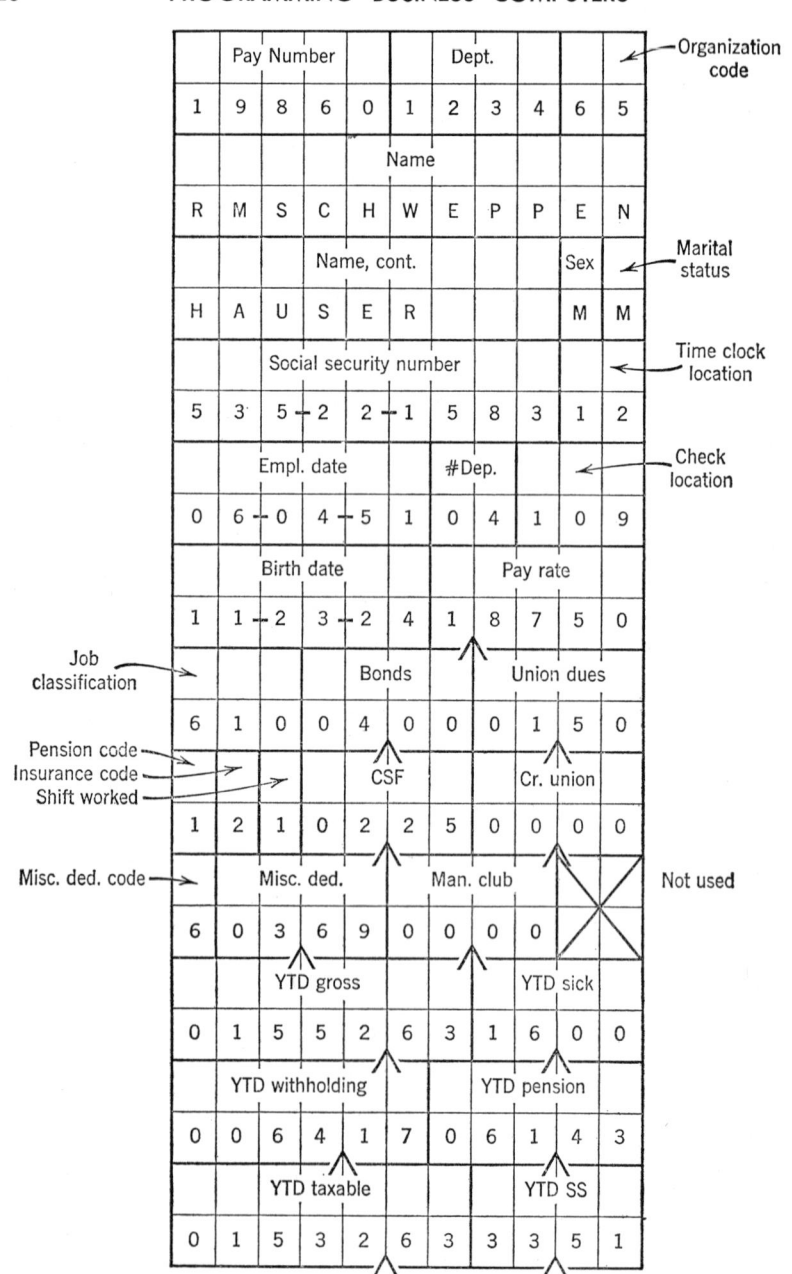

\multicolumn{5}{c	}{Pay Number}	\multicolumn{4}{c	}{Dept.}		← Organization code
1	9	8	6	0	1	2	3	4	6	5
\multicolumn{10}{c	}{Name}	
R	M	S	C	H	W	E	P	P	E	N
\multicolumn{6}{c	}{Name, cont.}			Sex		← Marital status
H	A	U	S	E	R				M	M
\multicolumn{9}{c	}{Social security number}		← Time clock location
5	3	5	2	2	1	5	8	3	1	2
\multicolumn{5}{c	}{Empl. date}		\#Dep.				← Check location
0	6	0	4	5	1	0	4	1	0	9
\multicolumn{5}{c	}{Birth date}		\multicolumn{4}{c	}{Pay rate}	
1	1	2	3	2	4	1	8	7	5	0
Job classification →				\multicolumn{2}{c	}{Bonds}	\multicolumn{4}{c	}{Union dues}	
6	1	0	0	4	0	0	0	1	5	0
Pension code → Insurance code → Shift worked →			→	\multicolumn{2}{c	}{CSF}	\multicolumn{4}{c	}{Cr. union}	
1	2	1	0	2	2	5	0	0	0	0
Misc. ded. code →				\multicolumn{2}{c	}{Misc. ded.}	\multicolumn{2}{c	}{Man. club}			Not used
6	0	3	6	9	0	0	0	0	\multicolumn{2}{c	}{✕}
\multicolumn{6}{c	}{YTD gross}	\multicolumn{4}{c	}{YTD sick}	
0	1	5	5	2	6	3	1	6	0	0
\multicolumn{6}{c	}{YTD withholding}	\multicolumn{4}{c	}{YTD pension}	
0	0	6	4	1	7	0	6	1	4	3
\multicolumn{6}{c	}{YTD taxable}	\multicolumn{4}{c	}{YTD SS}	
0	1	5	3	2	6	3	3	3	5	1

Figure 1. Illustration of a file record design.

that information which is part of the key be placed at the "front" or "top" of the record. In order not to split things over two words any more than necessary, it was essential to change the order of information considerably. This was done completely arbitrarily for Figure 1; in practice, there may be various restrictions on how such rearrangement may be done.

One of the more widely used random access file storage devices at present is based on a system involving a stack of rotating magnetic disks. These are all mounted on a single shaft and information is recorded on the disks in concentric tracks. The information is recorded on or read from these tracks by one or more *arms* which have coils or *reading heads* mounted on the ends of the arms. Under control of the data processor these arms move to the correct disk and to the correct track on the disk at speeds which are quite high considering the mechanical elements involved. This, it will be recognized, is not *completely* random access memory: the time required to obtain the record is somewhat dependent on whether the next record is on the same disk as the current one. Nevertheless, compared to the rather long access times of magnetic tapes when used for this purpose, the magnetic disk storage system may fairly be called random access.

2.4 Sequential File Processing

At this point it might be well to take an introductory look at the technique of processing file information. Since sequential files are at present in wider use than random access files, we shall consider only the former in this discussion. A treatment of random access file processing will be found in Chapter 19. The discussion that follows applies to sequential processing no matter what the medium; the same concepts apply to files on punched cards, magnetic tape, or any other file storage medium.

Assume that we begin with what will be called the *old master file;* information in it might pertain to payroll, material control, customer account status, or any of the many other areas of information of concern to a business. Assume that we have a *transaction file* containing records which are identifiable as consisting of additions, deletions, and changes. Both of these files are naturally in sequence according to some key which is the same for both files. Broadly speaking, the processing consists of inserting the addition records into the master file in correct sequence, deleting from the master file the records so indicated on the transaction file, and making the necessary changes in the appropriate master file records. As we saw, it is usually necessary using magnetic tapes to create a *new master file* during the processing; this may be desirable using punched cards even though it is sometimes not necessary.*

A number of names have been applied to this processing technique to signify different things about it. It is sometimes called the *expanding file* technique to imply that it is possible to increase the size of the file as new records are added to it. In some quarters it is called the *father-son* technique to imply that a new master file is created each time the processing is carried out. This name is also used because it ties in with another technique which is often utilized in sequential file processing. This latter has to do with the fact that it is usually wise to save the old master file until after the following processing cycle. Then if during that following processing cycle a master file is destroyed, such as by breakage of magnetic tape, the lost master can be reconstructed by reprocessing the previous cycle's master file which has been saved. The old master file that has been preserved through one cycle is referred to as the *grandfather* file.

After these preliminaries, we may now describe in broad outline the sequential file processing technique.

1. A record is read from the transaction file.
2. A record is read from the master file.
3. The master record key is compared with the transaction record key.
4. If the master record key is less than the transaction record key, then this master record is inactive and is simply written out unchanged onto the new master file. We then return to step 2 to bring in and test the next master record.
5. If the master record key is equal to the transaction record key, then the current transaction should either be a change or a deletion. If it is a change (which is determined by examining an identifying code in the transaction record), the appropriate change is made in the master record information and the altered record written out on the new master file. If it is a deletion, nothing is written on the new

---

* Some computers use a magnetic tape system in which it is not *necessary* to create a new master tape each time the file is processed, although if desired it *may* be done. This flexibility, which is available on an important segment of the machines now in operation, is made possible by the ability to place new information on a tape without disturbing the adjacent information. With most computers this is impossible, or at least very poor practice. Associated with this feature, in one machine, is a technique which in many cases greatly reduces the effort required to locate the desired record on a tape.

master file. In either case, we return to step 1 and bring in the next transaction record.

6. If the master record key is greater than the transaction record key, then the transaction should be an addition. The transaction record is written out onto the new master file. A new transaction record is read from the transaction file and we return to step 3. Observe that we cannot return to step 2 because we still have an old master record which has not yet been processed in this case.

In very broad outline we have here the heart of the sequential processing technique. Many other features could be added. A few of these are:

1. It is common practice not to trust the files to be in sequence; many errors are possible in the handling and preparation of files. Therefore, it is a good idea to insert tests to assure ourselves that the files are indeed in sequence and halt or take corrective action if they are not.

2. Although it may not have been apparent, we have tacitly assumed here that the transaction file would never have two records with the same key. This is hardly realistic; the same customer might make two purchases in one processing period, for instance. Additional steps could be added to handle this situation.

3. Some test should normally be made to determine whether the transaction code is consistent with the relationship between the transaction and master keys. Suppose, for instance, that through a clerical error a new account is assigned the same account number as an existing account. Such checking is a necessary part of all electronic data processing.

4. Some sort of test should be provided to determine when the processing is finished. Whereas a clerk has the good sense to quit when the job is ended, a machine typically has to be instructed rather explicitly on how to determine when it should quit. This is often, but not always, done by placing at the end of each file a *sentinel*, or *fence*, which is recognizable as denoting the end of the file. In multiple reel tape files using a sentinel, it is furthermore necessary to distinguish between the end-of-tape sentinel and end-of-file sentinel.

Many, many other elaborations could be mentioned. This discussion introduces us to the central ideas of sequential file processing, if not to all the necessary embellishments. An example of these techniques in terms of an accounts receivable application is given in Chapter 8.

2.5 Summary

It is hard to conceive of an extensive business data processing problem which would not involve files of some type. It is perhaps this characteristic which best distinguishes data processing from what is usually called engineering or scientific computation, more than the sometimes exaggerated disparity between the amounts of input and output in the two types of calculation. We have seen that the concept of a file is a very general one, being independent of both the storage medium used and the question of whether the file is in some sequence or not. We have seen finally that a great many data processing tasks can be reduced in broadest outline to the problem of updating a master file according to records contained in a transaction file.

It seems appropriate to close this chapter with the words of Sir Robert Watson-Watt, noted alike for his poetic expressions and for his pioneering in electronics:*

"Do we submit quietly to the prospect of going about the world festooned with miles of paper tape or loaded with stacks of stiff paper rectangles counted in megacards? There is basically one reason for cards, that they are not inconvenient for manual use. There is basically only one reason for a filing, to wit, subsequent retrieval. It is a semantic danger to concentrate on the passive and limited concept 'file' when what we really want is assured timely retrieval by selection. . . ."

Exercises

1. Discuss some of the reasons why files are kept in business.

2. Name all the files that the following businesses should keep. Discuss the similarities and the dissimilarities:
   (a) A drugstore with two employees.
   (b) A national distributor for foreign cars.

3. Discuss the purpose and functions of the following files. Suggest some possible ways of organizing them:
   (a) A technical library abstract.
   (b) U. S. Supreme Court decisions and rulings.
   (c) A handbook of medicine.

4. What is the difference between a master file and a transaction file? Give an example of each not mentioned in the text.

* Sir Robert Watson-Watt, "Are Computers Important?", *Proceedings of the Eastern Joint Computer Conference,* American Institute of Electrical Engineers, New York. December, 1956, page 68.

5. Would an electronic data processing system reduce or increase the amount of information stored in the master files of a business in comparison to manual or punched card methods? What about working files?

6. Name five file storage media and give the advantages and disadvantages of each.

7. In setting up a file is the selection of the key important? What are some of the factors affecting selection of the key? In practice, the keys sometimes used seem to be unnecessarily large, e.g., a ten-digit key may be used when there are only 50,000 items in the file. Does this *necessarily* mean they are inefficient?

8. Discuss the advantages and disadvantages of sequential versus random file processing.

3 FLOW CHARTING

3.0 Introduction

Business data processing problems and the computer programs which are proposed as solutions are characterized by extremely complex combinations of elementary steps. An involved payroll system, for example, may require 50,000 separate operations such as additions, tests for equality, and other simple operations. The present trend is toward even more complex data processing problems and programs.

The systems or procedures analyst must analyze and summarize existing methods and propose a computer solution which may or may not be based on the procedures which are currently in effect. The programmer, who is often also the analyst, must elaborate upon the broad outline of the proposed solution before it can be coded for a computer. Both individuals run the risk of becoming bogged down in an incomprehensible mass of details. The *flow chart,* or *block diagram,* helps to bring order out of chaos by allowing complex situations to be visualized.

The flow chart is a systematic graphic or pictorial representation of a program or procedure showing the sequence of operations on data, the logical steps in alternative paths of processing, and other relevant information. It helps to systematize the thinking of the analyst and to clarify intricate procedures. The flow chart is often used as a basis for coding and in that connection should contain enough detail to allow the discovery of logical errors, omissions, and unnecessary operations. However, the flow chart should not be so detailed as to become a graphic replica of the coding itself, for then the exact opposite of its function may result: the *loss* of clarity of the over-all picture because of a mass of extraneous details.

A flow chart, if properly prepared, becomes a valuable means of communication among the many individuals who work on or are affected by a data processing project. These may include the problem originator, a manager of a related function, the project leader, or the programmer whose work precedes or follows the part of the application under consideration. Because flow charts are used as a communication medium, it is important that some degree of standardization be required. This is particularly true when the person who draws the flow chart is not the one who will do the coding. A project may be interrupted or transferred to another programmer with much less effort if it is flow-charted than if no flow charts have been prepared. It may be noted that in a certain sense a flow chart allows a programmer to communicate with himself; it often happens that a programmer is called back to revise or correct his work months after the project had supposedly been completed. It is surprising how obscure and meaningless one's work in this area can be after a period of time. A properly drawn flow chart is of great assistance in obtaining a quick picture of the over-all nature of the application.

Once a complete flow chart has been drawn for an application, the over-all job is usually better than half done. Most of the time, the effort and creative work involved in setting up a computer application are required in the analysis and definition of the problem and the drawing of a good flow chart of the proposed solution. The translation of the flow-charted procedure into explicit computer instructions is relatively a simpler matter than the work which leads to that stage.

3.1 Types of Flow Charts

The purpose for which a flow chart is intended determines its scope and form. A general pictorial chart, for example, may be most useful in presenting a system to members of management who are usually not interested in details and do not have computer experience. The people who will use the system once it is completed, who also may not have computer experience, may require that the information be in nontechnical, although detailed, terms. The programmers and coders involved in a project generally need flow charts which are quite detailed and comprehensive.

In general, there are two levels of flow charting, which we shall call *top level* and *detailed*. Top level flow charts, which are also variously called *process, system, over-all,* and *gross* flow charts, show the sequence of major routines of a system in summary form without detailing the individual operations. The top level flow chart is the master plan of the system and is a graphic representation of the flow of data through it. Such a chart should be drawn for every data processing application and for every major segment of it, the latter usually being called *runs*. It is particularly useful at the beginning of a project to provide a comprehensive picture of the major routines which are later to be developed in detail.

The detailed flow chart, or simply flow chart, differs in intent from the top level chart. It shows in proper sequence all the steps to be followed by the data processor in order to provide the desired results. The detailed flow chart should show the complete analysis of the problem; the handling of every anticipated condition must be defined; each logical decision, group of arithmetic computations, transfer of data, and every other operation involved in the solution of the problem must be indicated on the detailed flow chart. It must be emphasized that we are discussing *logical* steps, not individual computer instructions. The detailed flow chart must contain sufficient detail, however, to allow the coder to work directly from it. The detailed flow chart should be referenced to the top level chart which it supports. In this book no distinction will ordinarily be made between top level and detailed flow charts. The context and the diagrams themselves will indicate which is intended.

3.2 A Flow Charting Notation*

Basically, a flow chart is simply a collection of boxes, lines, arrows, and comments which, taken together, indicate what is to be done. This being true, presumably any notation which is convenient for the people working on a project could be defended. It is desirable, however, to have a somewhat standardized system of symbols and method of writing comments. Most of the conventions which are presented here are simply short cuts which have been developed by experience. It must be admitted that any flow charting notation is rather arbitrary; the precise shape of the boxes used to symbolize certain operations is obviously merely a matter of personal preference. The important point, however, is that regardless of what arbitrary system is chosen or developed, it is very desirable that an organization be consistent within itself. It is also desirable, although perhaps less crucial, that all the users of one type of computer employ the same flow charting system so that programs can more readily be compared and exchanged. In the following paragraphs we shall present a relatively simple system of flow charting and give some examples of its use. It is not intended as an answer to the need for standardization of flow charting

---

* The notation presented here differs somewhat from that presented in Chapter 7 of *Digital Computer Programming*, D. D. McCracken, John Wiley, New York, 1957.

FLOW CHARTING

in the computer industry, but is simply one acceptable system which meets the needs of this book.

To begin with, it is desirable that wherever possible clear English words be used on flow charts rather than obscure symbols. There are a number of symbols, however, which are not obscure, either because they are very commonly used in the industry or because they have a well-understood meaning within an organization. An example of the latter is the abbreviation YTD for year to date. Some of the most commonly used abbreviations are:

$\quad :\quad$ Comparison (the nature of the comparison is indicated separately)
$\quad =\quad$ Equal to
$\quad \neq\quad$ Not equal to
$\quad >\quad$ Greater than
$\quad <\quad$ Less than
$\quad \geq\quad$ Greater than or equal to
$\quad \leq\quad$ Less than or equal to

The following flow charting symbols are suggested:

1. The direction of data flow or the next step in a procedure. In most cases a flow chart is read from left to right and/or from top to bottom. There are exceptions, however, as when a program uses a *loop* (Chapter 8). It is common practice to designate the direction of flow by connecting the various symbols with arrows (Figure 1). A broken line either designates a conditional path or shows that the output of the processing in one period becomes input to the processing in the next period. Where necessary for clarity, it may be desirable to avoid having more than one line entering a box by using a connector (see below).

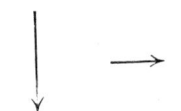

Figure 1. Arrows used to indicate direction of flow in a flow chart.

2. Input/output symbols (Figure 2). (The symbols written inside the various boxes are illustrations of the type of identification which might be used.)

3. Operation symbols. These are used to describe all operations for which special symbols are not designated. Figure 3 shows a number of examples of the type of operations which are so described. An operation box containing a circled number, as shown in one of the examples in Figure 3, is used to indicate in summary form a group of related operations. This may be done either to avoid cluttering

30   PROGRAMMING BUSINESS COMPUTERS

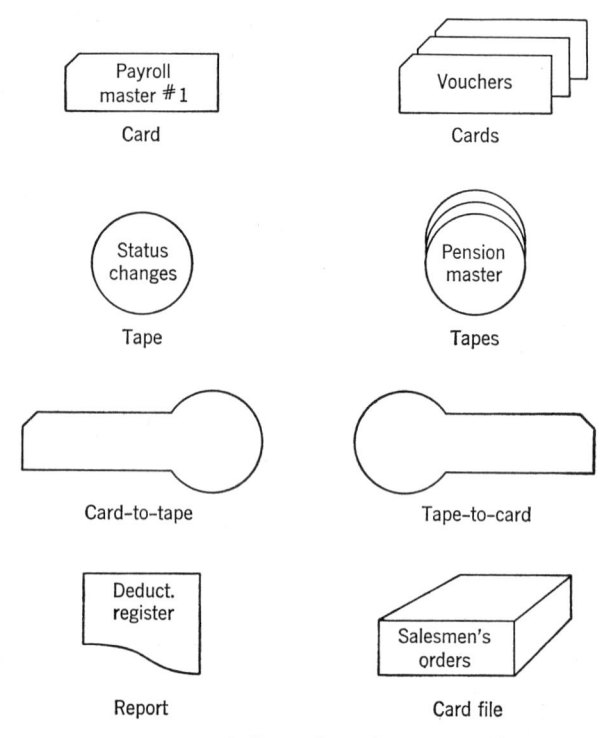

Figure 2. Symbols used to indicate input/output media and operations.

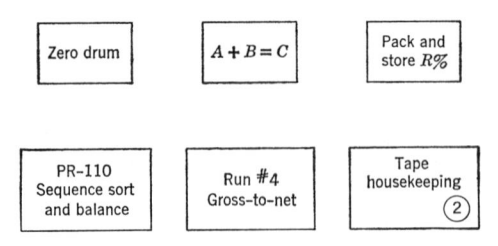

Figure 3. Examples of operation symbols.

up a diagram with excessive details or to indicate that the operations involved are a *subroutine* (Chapter 9). The corresponding subroutine charting is illustrated in Figure 6, and is discussed further under connectors, below.

4. Logical tests and branching. This type of box, which is illustrated in Figure 4, is used to indicate which of two or more paths is to be followed as a result of making a comparison or answering a question; hence it has a single entry and two or more exits. It is also called a *choice box* or a *decision box*.

FLOW CHARTING 31

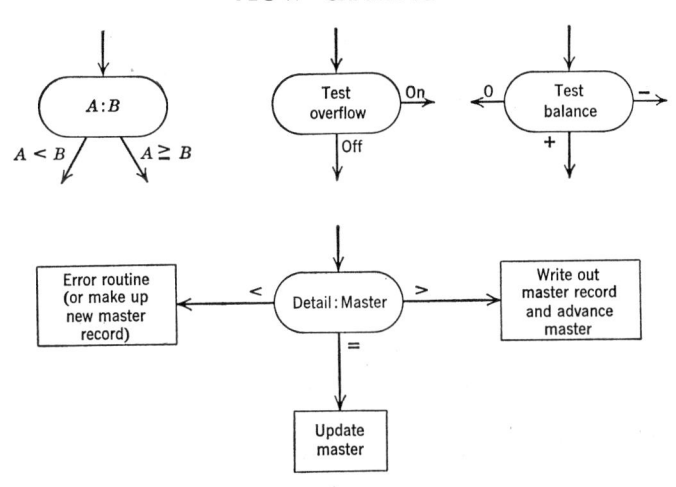

Figure 4. Examples of decision boxes.

5. Connectors. Connectors are used to connect remote portions of a flow chart with one another without the use of long or crossing lines and to avoid making a complex diagram into an unintelligible maze. They are also used to connect different levels of flow charts when there is a hierarchy of them. In this book connectors of all types will be designated by small circles. Any hard and fast rule for the identification of connectors is inevitably arbitrary. The one suggested here is that letters of the alphabet be used for corresponding entry and exit points. Connectors are often used to connect points which are on different pages of a flow chart. A number outside the circle may be used in this case to indicate the page number of the corresponding entry or exit, since flow charts very often require many pages. Examples of this use of connectors are shown in Figure 5 and in many of the flow charts later in the text, such as on page 159.

Connectors are also used for a detailed flow chart or a subroutine which is referenced by a circled number inside of an operation box. All operations to be performed in the subroutine indicated by the summary symbol are shown between two correspondingly numbered connectors. This is illustrated in Figure 6.

Figure 5. Examples of connectors.

32   PROGRAMMING BUSINESS COMPUTERS

6. Switches. A *switch,* also called a *variable connector,* appears frequently in most flow charts. It is used whenever the results of a decision made at one point in the routine must be used at some later point(s). We speak then of *setting* a switch, which usually implies that an instruction at some later point in the routine is modified. A switch obviously must have at least two possible settings but it may have many more, each of which leads to a different segment of the data processing routine. Once again, the notation used to designate switches and their settings must necessarily be arbitrary. It is suggested that *switches* be *numbered,* and that their *switch settings* be *lettered* with lower case letters. A switch is initially assumed to be in the "a" position until changed by the routine; it is wise, however, to indicate this fact explicitly on the flow chart. A switch is commonly set in its various positions many times during the operation of a program.

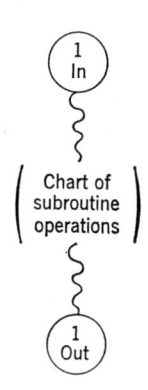

Figure 6. Example of the use of connectors in charting subroutines.

Figure 7 shows the conventions that are suggested for the use of switches. A medium-sized circle is used to show the switch itself with the word "switch" and the switch number written inside it. Small circles with the setting numbers written in them are used to show the start of the various paths. A small square is used to indicate the operation of setting a switch to a particular position. Inside of the square is written (1) a period to symbolize the operation "set," (2) the switch number, and (3) the desired switch setting. Thus ".6a" would be read: set switch 6 to the "a" position. This is illustrated in Figure 8.

7. Miscellaneous symbols. It is common practice to indicate the beginning and ending of an application or a major segment of it by circles with the words "start" and "stop" in them (Figure 9). It is sometimes desirable to have a graphic representation of the fact that a console operation is required of the machine operator at some point in the program. It is suggested that a diamond-shaped figure be used for this symbol. The

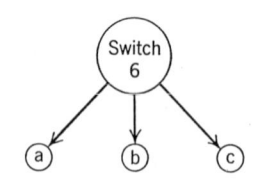

Figure 7. A flow charting "switch," showing the suggested convention for identifying the switch and the alternate paths.

| .6a | Set switch 6 to *a* | | .6b | Set switch 6 to *b* |

Figure 8. "Setting" a switch, showing the suggested convention for indicating the operation.

FLOW CHARTING

Figure 9. Start and stop symbols.

Figure 10. Symbols used to indicate error conditions and console operations.

same symbol is suggested for the presence of error conditions; the nature of the error should be written inside of the box (Figure 10). A *flag* or *assertion box* can occasionally add clarity by indicating that a certain condition is true at some point on a flow chart. It is especially useful for noting initial conditions such as the starting values of counters which are simply loaded into memory with the correct values (Figure 11).

8. Notes. The basic purpose of a flow chart is to simplify the understanding of a program or system. A short note can often add clarity to a flow chart. Two examples are shown in Figure 12, where numbers outside the two boxes represent a tape number in one case and in the other the starting address of a routine which carries out the indicated function. A little experience will indicate the type and extent of notes which are necessary and useful.

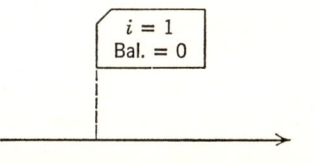

Figure 11. Example of an assertion box.

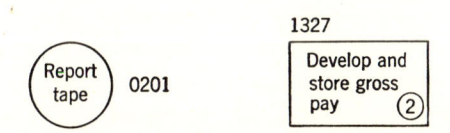

$i = 1$
Bal. $= 0$

Figure 12. Examples of notes.

It is quite essential that each computer organization have a rather rigid set of conventions on the way letters and numbers are to be made in handwriting. For instance, if no distinction is made between the number 1 and the letter I, confusion can result; a computer cannot know that SM1TH "obviously" means SMITH. Figure 13 shows the recommended form for writing numerals and letters; it gives some examples of easily misinterpreted numerals, and it emphasizes four pairs of numerals and letters which must be very carefully distinguished.

The concepts we have been discussing here are illustrated in Figures 14 through 18. Figure 14 is a classic illustration of a flow chart called How to Get to Work in the Morning. The source of the original version of this chart is unknown. Figures 15 and 16 comprise a section of a hypothetical flow chart for a punched card computer

34   PROGRAMMING BUSINESS COMPUTERS

	Good Form	Bad Form	
Numerals:	1	1	could be a seven
	2	2	could be the letter Q
	3	3	could be the letter B
	4	4	a check mark?
	5	5	could be the letter S
	6	6	
	7	7	
	8	8	zero?
	9	9	could be a seven
	0	0	could be the letter U

Letters: Should be written as capital letters:

A	F	K	P	U	Z
B	G	L	Q	V	
C	H	M	R	W	
D	I	N	S	X	
E	J	O or Ø	T	Y	

Particular care should be exercised in writing the following characters, which are frequently confused:

The number one:	1	The number two:	2
The letter "I":	I	The letter "Z":	Z
The number zero:	0	The number five:	5
The letter "O":	O or Ø	The letter "S":	S

Figure 13. Recommended form for writing numerals and letters.

system. Figure 16 is a detailed flow chart of one of the routines (number 3) shown in summary form in Figure 15. It is supposed that this much of the complete flow chart would be drawn on three pages, as indicated in the illustrations. The small numbers outside the connectors refer to the page numbers of the hypothetical chart. Thus the four connectors on "page 1" are shown as referring to correspondingly lettered connectors on "page 2." Figure 17 is a section of a top level flow chart for an electronic computer using magnetic tapes. Figure 18 is an example of a rather different flow chart style from that described here, called a *skeleton* flow chart. It has been adopted by the personnel of one computer manufacturer as especially suited to the logic of one of their machines. This computer has instructions which carry out more processing than do the instructions of most computers. The advantages claimed for this system of flow charting are: (1) it is simple and uniform; (2) the structure is shown more readily; and (3) one is free to write as much as desired about each operation instead of being limited to the rather small boxes usually drawn.

With this particular computer it is sometimes possible to draw flow charts so that each box corresponds to one instruction; with most computers where instructions are much more elementary, it is usually

FLOW CHARTING

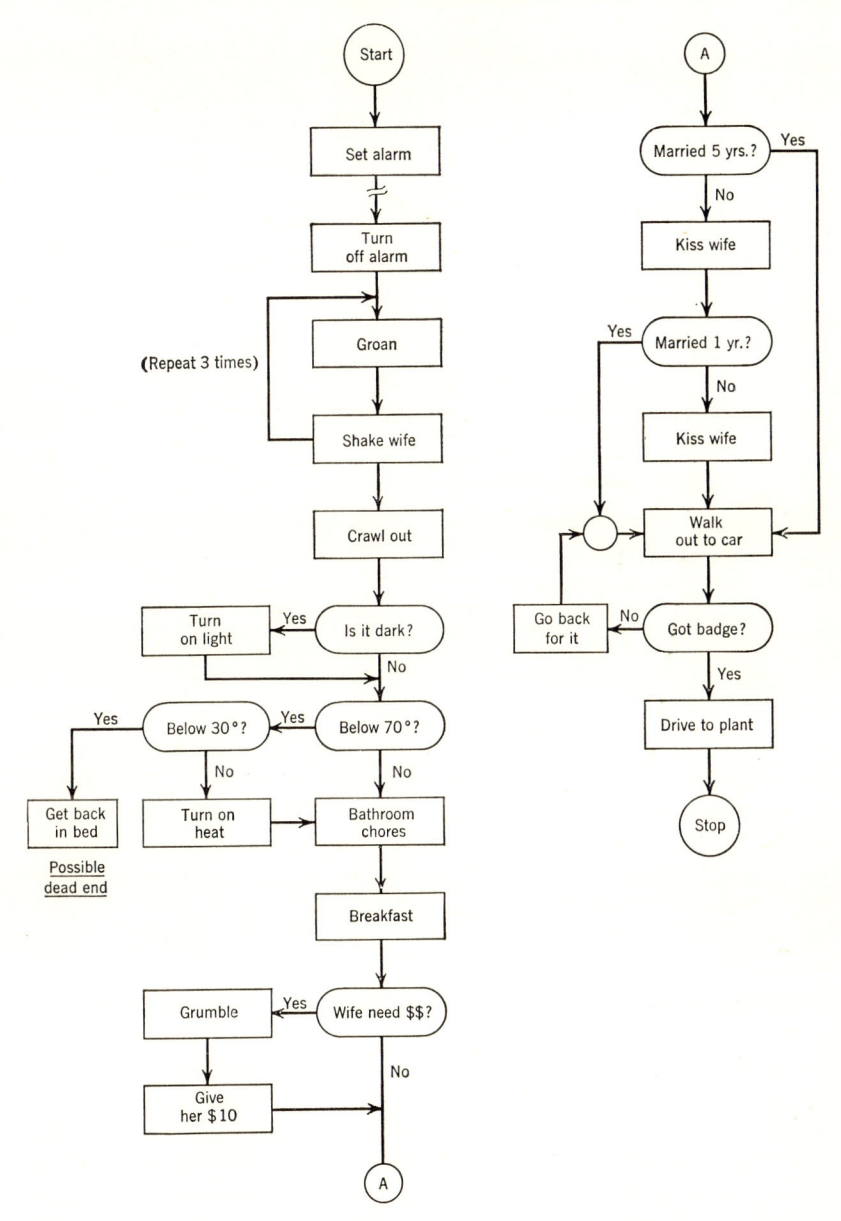

Figure 14. "How to Get to Work in the Morning." Original source unknown.

36 PROGRAMMING BUSINESS COMPUTERS

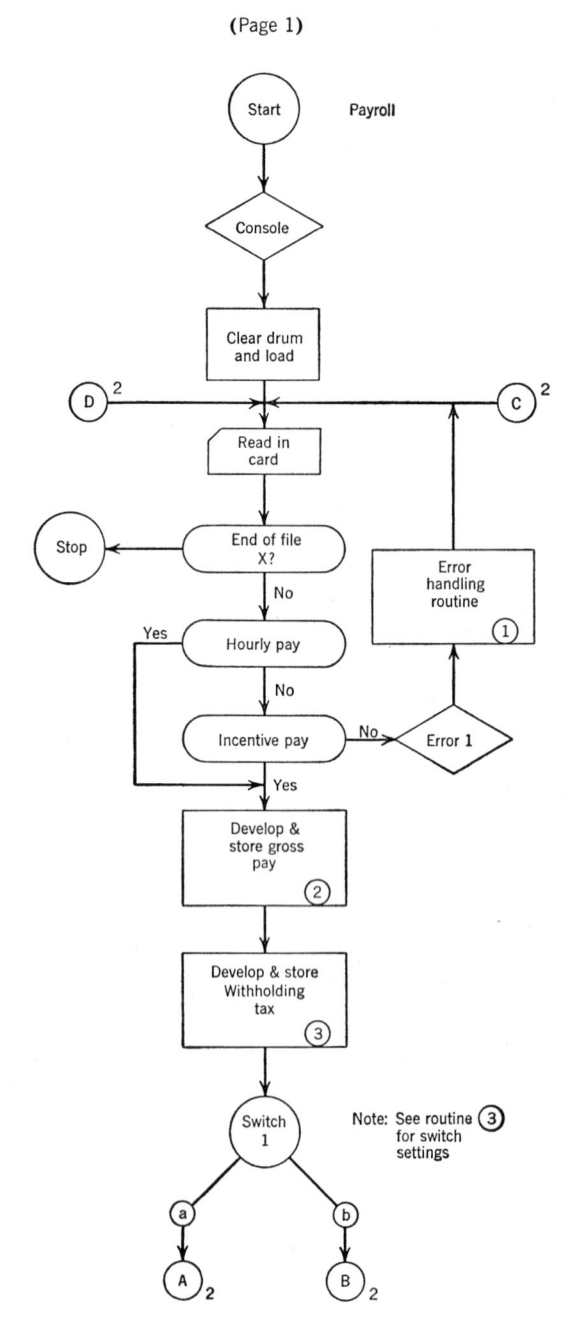

(Page 1)

Figure 15. Section of a hypothetical flow chart for a punched card computer system.

FLOW CHARTING

(Page 2)

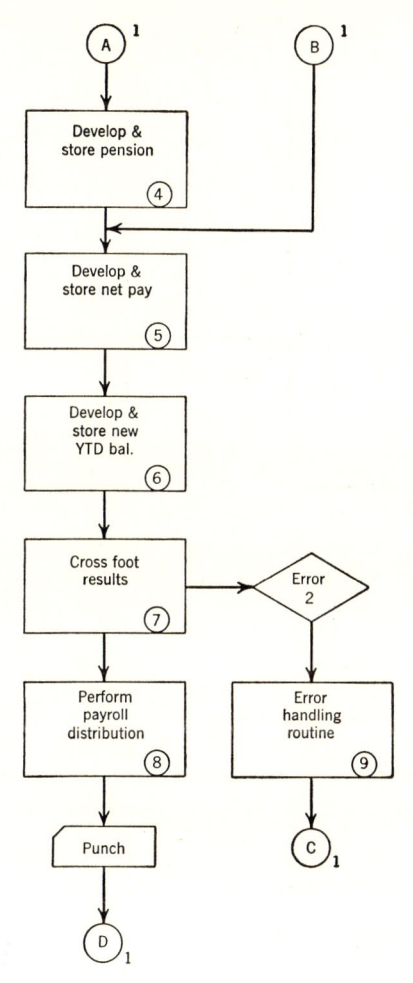

Figure 15 (*continued*)

(Page 3)

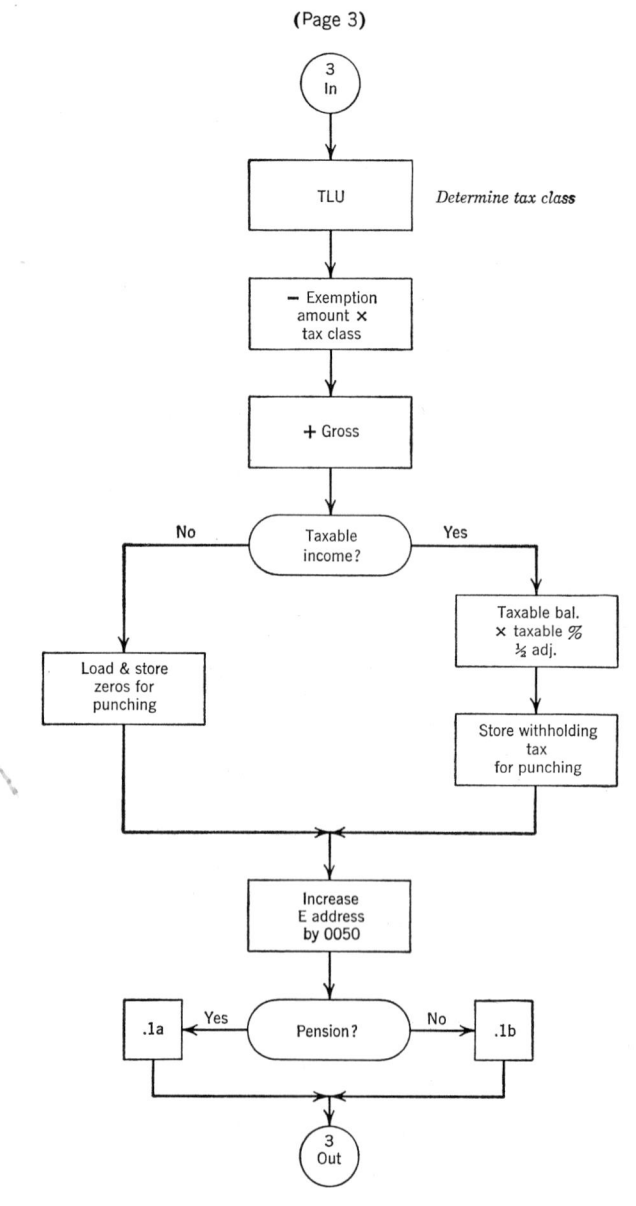

Figure 16. Detailed flow chart of one of the routines shown in summary form in Figure 15.

FLOW CHARTING

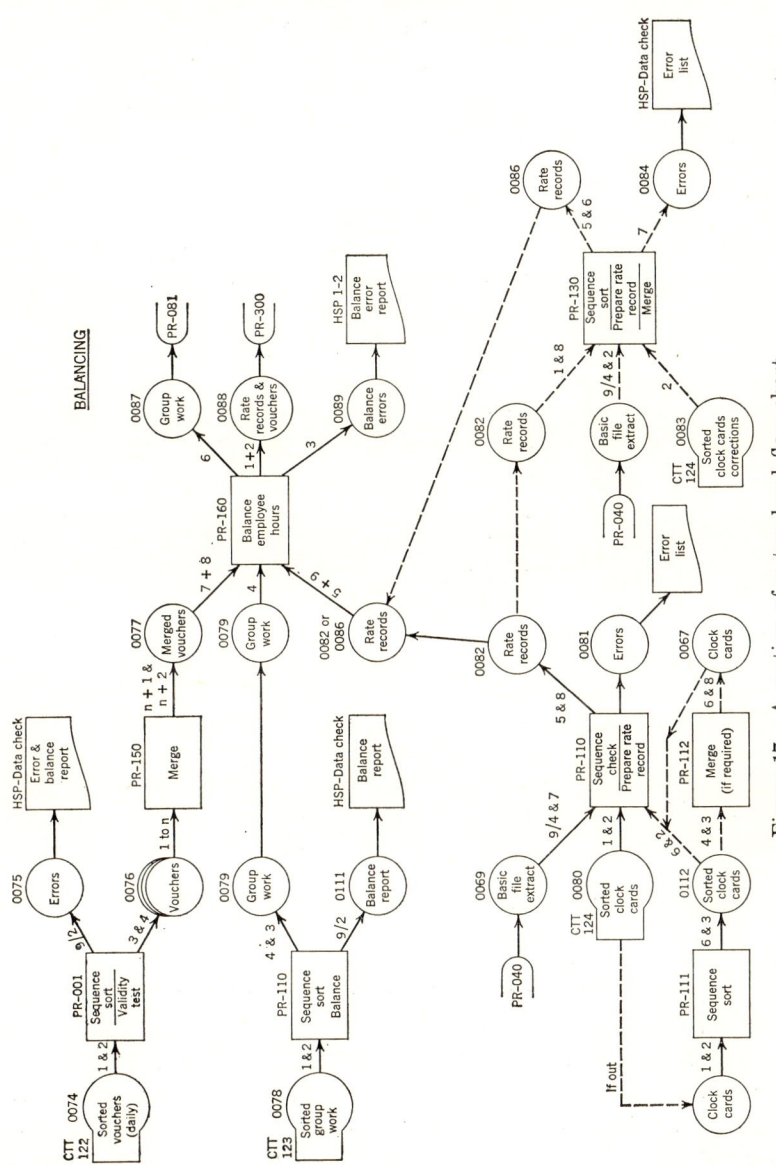

Figure 17. A section of a top level flow chart.

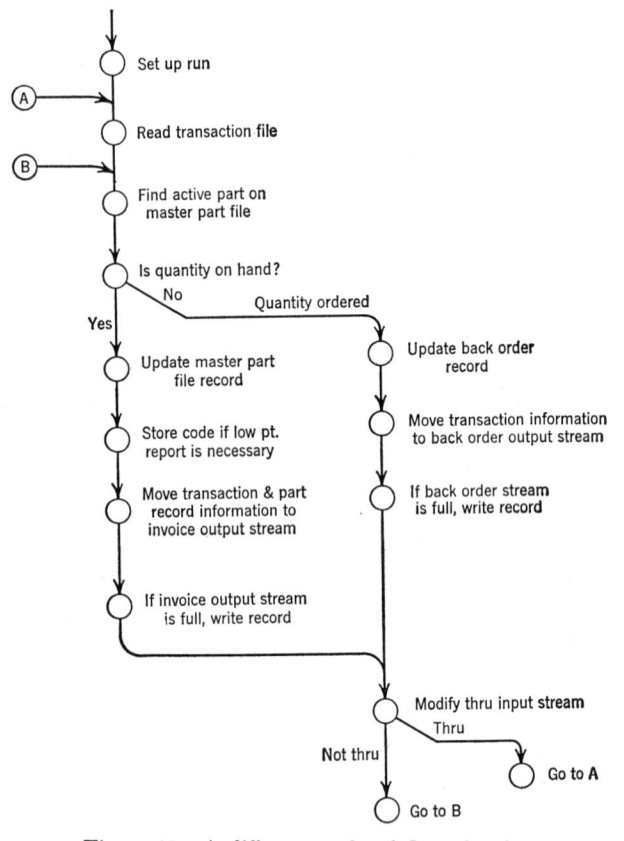

```
              ○ Set up run
    Ⓐ ───┐   │
         └──→○ Read transaction file
    Ⓑ ───┐   │
         └──→○ Find active part on
              │  master part file
              │
              ○ Is quantity on hand?
             ╱  No
          Yes╱       Quantity ordered
            │    ┌─────────────────┐
            ○ Update master part   ○ Update back order
            │  file record         │  record
            │                      │
            ○ Store code if low pt.○ Move transaction information
            │  report is necessary │  to back order output stream
            │                      │
            ○ Move transaction & part○ If back order stream
            │  record information to│  is full, write record
            │  invoice output stream│
            │                      │
            ○ If invoice output stream
            │  is full, write record│
            └──────────────┬───────┘
                           │
                           ○ Modify thru input stream
                          ╱ Thru
                    Not thru╲    →○ Go to A
                             ○ Go to B
```

Figure 18. A different style of flow charting.

poor practice to do so, as we have noted. We show an example of this system of flow charting primarily to illustrate that special conditions may dictate special flow charting systems. Probably no one method of flow charting will ever satisfy all needs.

3.3 General Observations on Flow Charting Techniques

For preliminary drafts of a flow chart any convenient paper may be used if it is large enough. For the final version (if a computer flow chart may ever be termed "final"), which may get widespread distribution, a hard-surfaced paper which erases easily and duplicates well is best. These are often preprinted with the name of the organization, space for date, title, name of person drawing the flow chart, page number, etc. Most computer manufacturers supply plastic templates which make it easier to draw the various flow charting symbols neatly.

FLOW CHARTING

Flow charting techniques are often very personal and vary greatly with individual temperament. Some individuals, like hikers in a strange terrain who smile disdainfully at a compass, prefer to code without a flow chart; if pressured, they will create one when the project is almost completed. Not only is this bad for the internal communications of an organization, but most individuals cannot code effectively without a flow chart. If possible, a "complete" flow chart should be attempted before coding begins. Coding generally provides insight into solutions which are superior to the original plan and also often shows up flaws in the logic of the solution. Therefore, frequent revisions of flow charts are usually necessary. Some individuals like to make a sketchy initial flow chart and work out the details as they code. Others want to be able to see all the details of a problem before they begin and paper their office walls with huge charts. Most, however, use standard-sized loose-leaf sheets, cross-referencing the entries and exits to other pages. With a little ingenuity, the smaller-sized sheets may be pasted together in accordion form, if desired, to enable the charts of the different parts of the system to be placed adjacent to each other; this gives a clearer picture of the relationships of the problem.

The preparation of flow charts for a large business system or for an involved computer run can be extremely complex and discouraging until experience in the art is developed. And an art it is; some of the techniques of the painter can be emulated with profit. The artist often makes preparatory sketches for his canvas, and, when ready with the rough outline, gradually fills in more and more details. The programmer may find it helpful to make a half dozen trials before an adequate flow chart is achieved. At first only a gross solution is attempted. With each revision more details are filled in area by area, with new problems becoming exposed. The flow chart gradually increases in depth, complexity, and subtlety, but in manageable proportions.

In developing computer flow charts, existing charts are frequently of little value, especially those affecting routines in manual systems which are to be mechanized. Often the existing charts are obsolete or do not fully reflect what is actually being done. In many cases the systems analyst must ferret out the elements of the routines which are recorded only in some clerk's head. These often turn out to be the procedures for handling exceptions, which present enough problems even when they are completely defined, let alone not even known.

3.4 Summary

Flow charts are frequently compared to road maps: they show the best route to take and how to save time with short cuts. A well-executed flow chart, however, is not a *picture* of the eventual coding, but rather is a graphic representation of the logical steps in solving a problem. A flow chart helps to prevent and/or detect errors in a proposed solution and aids in the discovery of labor- and time-saving short cuts. The basic elements of the method of solution are made much more understandable to anyone who has to participate in the work or review it. A most important secondary benefit of flow charting is that it assists a person to organize his thinking about a complex procedure; it might even be argued that this is the most important benefit.

With the extreme time pressures which confront many data processing installations, a strong effort must be made to resist the temptation to "save time" by eliminating some of the flow charting. This is decidedly a shortsighted and illusory approach in terms of the overall man-hours required to complete a project. Even when this mistake is not made, there is sometimes the temptation to slight the drawing of final versions of flow charts. It perhaps goes without saying that flow charts must be kept up to date when revisions are made in a system. It is often surprising how rapidly a flow chart can become obsolete, especially in the weeks and months following the introduction of a new system, when changes are most frequent.

The degree of flow charting standardization which should be established varies with the needs of each installation. In a situation where some people prepare detailed flow charts and others do the coding, it is obvious that fairly rigid conventions must be established. Where the same person does the flow charting and coding, standardization is still very desirable, but perhaps need not be as rigid.

Exercises

1. Discuss the reasons for flow charting in electronic data processing.

2. What other fields, disciplines, and technologies also use flow charts?

3. Flow-chart the following applications:
   (a) Setting up a portable typewriter for typing.
   (b) Investigating a table lamp that does not give light.

   Flow-chart these using the conventions suggested in the text, and using your own conventions. Discuss the differences.

FLOW CHARTING

4. Is it possible to do a certain amount of checking of a flow chart without knowing anything about the problem being solved? Suggest a list of errors in flow charts that can be checked for mechanically.

5. Discuss the statement, "The degree of detail should be consistent within a given flow chart."

6. What is the difference between a switch and a decision box?

4. THE DATA PROCESSOR

4.0 Introduction

In the previous chapters the emphasis has been on the problems to be solved. In this chapter we begin to explore the techniques of solving the problems. The first section is a general description of how any computer is organized and in broad outline how it operates (in terms of information flow, not electronics). The second section provides a preview of the hypothetical computer used for illustrative purposes in the following chapters. The third section is a very brief history of computers.

4.1 Organization and Operation of the Data Processor

The data processing problem was characterized in Chapter 1 as requiring *recording, storage, processing,* and *output.* In fairly standard computer terminology, the recording is called *input,* and the processing is conventionally called *arithmetic*—even though more than arithmetic is done in the "arithmetic" section of a computer. Besides these computer characteristics, which are dictated by the nature of the problem, a computer has a fifth function imposed by the way it operates, which is called *control.* This section in effect tells the rest of the machine what to do.

Figure 1 may be of assistance in visualizing the interrelationships between these five functions, and in reading the more detailed descriptions below.

The input section of a computer ordinarily consists of devices which take information from punched cards, paper tape, or other devices, and place it in memory. In technical language, this is called *reading.* The function of the input device(s) is essentially to translate from the external form in which the information is represented, such as holes in a punched card, to the form in which the same information is stored in memory. The *information* in question may be anything

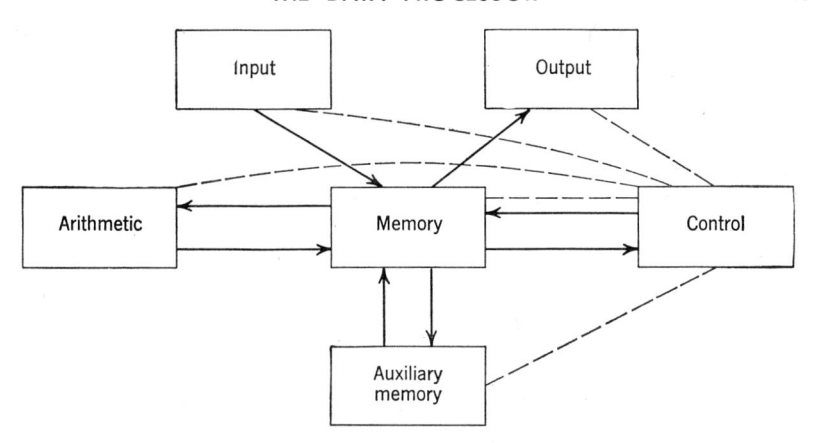

Figure 1. The functional parts of a stored program computer.

which can be stored in memory: numbers to be used in the calculation, *instructions* which tell the machine what to do, numbers or letters to be used later as column headings on the output, names and addresses, etc. The single arrow from the input box to the memory box in Figure 1 implies that the information goes only *to* memory; further operations must move the information from memory to the other sections of the machine.

It is difficult to find good analogies between large computers and things more familiar, and the analogies are apt to be misleading. Nevertheless, it may be helpful to characterize the input function as equivalent to the keyboard of a desk calculator. Of course, the difficulty with this analogy is that a desk calculator has no real internal memory.

The memory or storage (used interchangeably) of a computer is the nerve center of the machine. All information being processed must travel through it. All numbers must be in it before any arithmetic manipulations can be carried out. All the instructions which tell the machine what to do must be in memory before they can go over to the control section. The memory needs to be large and fast, i.e., it should be able to hold many numbers or instructions—from 1000 to 100,000 in present equipment—and be able to send these to the arithmetic or control sections with a minimum delay—as short as a fraction of a microsecond (millionth of a second) in the fastest machines at the time of writing. Since it is not technically or economically feasible to build a high-speed memory large enough to hold all the information required, a solution is to store the part not currently needed in a larger, but slower, auxiliary device. As indicated in Figure 1, the auxiliary memory "communicates" only with the main memory.

The present trend is for the main memory to be built around *magnetic cores* in large machines, and *magnetic drums* in the smaller ones. Auxiliary memory is most commonly magnetic tape, with magnetic drums and disks also being used. *Electrostatic* and *mercury-delay line* storage are still employed in some machines, but are being superseded in the newer ones. Descriptions of the operation of these devices will be found in works listed in the bibliography.

The arithmetic section of the computer does what its name implies. In addition to the four arithmetic operations, this section can *shift* numbers right and left, and can assist in certain operations which make it possible for the computer to make *decisions*. It corresponds in a desk calculator to the wheels and gears and shafts that actually do the calculation.

Register is a term commonly used in connection with the arithmetic and control sections; this is simply a device for temporarily storing a piece of information while or until it is used. A register corresponds quite closely to the dials on a desk calculator, which are wheels that temporarily store the numbers on which arithmetic is done. In our case, it is not only numbers which may be stored in a register but also instructions.

The control section of a calculator has the function of *interpreting* or *decoding* the instructions stored in memory, and then sending signals to the rest of the parts telling them what to do. In Figure 1 we see two solid lines, implying that instructions are sent to and from (usually *from*) memory to control; the dashed lines imply electric signals sent to the rest of the machine, based on these instructions.

The control section is equivalent to the buttons which are pushed to start the various arithmetic operations on a desk calculator, but the analogy is quite incomplete. The arithmetic and control sections are the hardest functions to point to in looking at a machine. The input and output devices are usually separate *frames*, or boxes, as are memory and the magnetic drums and tapes if any. The arithmetic and control sections, on the other hand, are made up of ordinary-looking electronic components, and the equipment constituting the two functions is usually in the same cabinet. Incidentally, there are usually one or more boxes to which no reference has been made here: the power supply. This omission simply implies that we are looking at a computer from the standpoint of what it does and how the information flows, not from the standpoint of electrical engineering.

THE DATA PROCESSOR   47

The output section has the obvious purpose of recording in convenient form the results of the processing, or anything else in memory. The media may be punched cards, printed pages, or paper or magnetic tapes. The chart shows that information may be recorded (or *written*, in the jargon) only *from* memory.

The word *instruction* should be amplified. Anyone who has used a desk calculator realizes that it is necessary to have some sort of pattern to the operations so that the operator can get into a routine. This pattern consists of a sequence of specified arithmetic operations on specified quantities. Analyzing the process further, we see that doing a desk calculation consists of doing a series of distinct steps, each step involving one arithmetic operation and one new piece of information.

The situation in the electronic computer is not so different. For a problem to be solved on a computer, it must be broken down into a series of precise steps, each involving one operation and one piece of information (two or three in some machines) in addition to the result of the previous step. The difference between this situation and the desk calculator is that with the desk calculator the sequence of operations is in the operator's head, whereas to satisfy the computer the sequence must be written down in a rigidly defined form and stored in the computer's memory. The appearance of these instructions will be elaborated on later; we may say here that they are usually stored in memory as ordinary numbers and/or letters.

Because the instructions are stored in memory, machines of this type are called *stored program* computers. A *program*, in this context, is simply a collection of instructions which carry out some desired function, whether it be a complete payroll calculation or an elementary part of it. This usage of the word "program" is the historical one. Many people in the field, including the authors, feel that it is better to use *routine* here, and reserve program for the planning that is done between the time the application is started and the time when detailed instructions are written, the latter being then called *coding*. To summarize this slightly confusing terminology: programming has to do with the planning required to determine how to go about solving the problem, including flow-charting it; coding is the writing of the detailed machine instructions; the end result of both together is a computer routine.*

---

* Terminology in the computer field is neither static nor completely satisfying. The definitions given here are the generally accepted ones, yet we always speak of a stored *program* computer not stored *routine*. Furthermore, the term "programming" is used by many to *include* coding.

Word is used in computing as a generic term to cover either a number or an instruction or a group of characters used for some other purpose, which is treated by the computer as a unit. It is equivalent (very roughly) to *piece of information* as used previously.

With these matters of definition out of the way, we may proceed to a very simple example of computer operation, namely, the addition of two numbers. The two numbers, and, in the type of machine to be considered in this book, three instructions, would first have to be loaded into memory using an input device. Actually, other instructions would normally be used to get the data and instructions into memory, as we shall discuss in Chapter 11. The question naturally arises: How does the *first* instruction get there? Without attempting to go into a complete description here, it may help to note that it is always possible to enter a few instructions "by hand," using the computer console. These few can be set up so that they "call in" the instructions of a *loading routine* which then loads the actual data and instructions of the routine which is of interest.

The first instruction moves from memory to the control unit, which analyzes the coded instruction to determine what operation is called for and where in memory to locate the first number. After this analysis or interpretation, the control unit sends out signals to the appropriate units, calling for the specified number to move to one of the arithmetic registers in preparation for the next operation. The second instruction is similarly interpreted and the control unit calls for the second of the two numbers to move from memory to the arithmetic unit and be added to the first number. The third instruction sends the sum back to memory. Finally, the sum is written on an output device. In Chapter 5 we shall discuss the same example in terms of the details of machine characteristics.

4.2 DATAC

Much of the material of later chapters will be illustrated by writing codes for DATAC, a hypothetical computer. This "machine" is a compilation of features of present and proposed computers, and, of course, exists only in this book. DATAC naturally does not correspond exactly to any actual machine, but it has characteristics which are representative of most of the trends in computer design.*

* It should be remembered, however, that the primary motivation in "designing" DATAC was not to propose a "dream" machine (an interesting pastime in itself), but to provide a *teaching tool*. No hypothetical computer will satisfy all readers; it is difficult to strike a compromise between a "design" which is easy to teach and one which has all the latest ideas in it.

THE DATA PROCESSOR 49

The input media of DATAC are assumed to include punched cards and magnetic tape. This last points up the dual use of magnetic tapes in many modern computers: as input/output media, and as auxiliary storage. When used as input, the tape would be prepared either with a special transcription device which puts information directly on magnetic tapes, or with a device which reads punched cards or paper tape and puts the information on magnetic tape. The same reels of tape and the same tape handlers may at different times be used either for input or auxiliary storage.

The main memory is taken to be 2000 words, each consisting of eleven *alpha-numeric* characters. A word can contain eleven arbitrary letters, digits, or special symbols; or an instruction; or a number—in which case the first character is a plus or minus sign and the other ten are the digits of the number. The exact physical form of storage is not important to us in this book, except that in most connections we assume *random access*. This means that any word in memory is available as quickly as any other word. The typical storage system in this category at the time of writing is magnetic cores. An example of nonimmediate access storage is magnetic drum storage, since it is necessary to wait some fraction of a drum revolution for each word to arrive at the "reading head" from where it may be transferred to the arithmetic or control section. Ten magnetic tape handlers are assumed as auxiliary memory or input/output devices.

The arithmetic unit in DATAC consists of four registers. The *filter* register is used when it is necessary to operate on only part of a word. (In actual computers which have such a register, it more commonly goes under the name *extract* register.) The *transfer-shift* register is used to shift numbers right or left as they are being transferred between memory and the L and R *registers*. The L and R registers (for left and right) are used in most of the actual processing.[*] Addition and subtraction involve primarily the R register, although in some cases the L register comes into play also. In multiplication, the multiplier is first placed in the R register; the product is developed in L and R combined, as we shall see in Chapter 5. In division, the dividend is in L and R combined; the quotient is developed in R. Either R alone or L and R together may be used in a variety of ways to *shift* words right or left. Most of the decision operations involve R.

The control section has three registers: the instruction register, the location counter, and the index register. As discussed in the previous

---

[*] In real computers these registers have names such as accumulator and multiplier-quotient, upper and lower accumulator, or simple letter designations such as A, X, and L.

section on general computer organization, each instruction from memory has to be placed in the control section before being interpreted and executed. The temporary storage register in which each instruction is held after being brought from memory, and while it is being decoded, is called the *instruction register*. The register which keeps a running record of the "location" in memory of the instruction of current interest is called the *location counter*. (The notion of location in memory has not been discussed yet; it will be clarified early in the next chapter.) The *index register* has to do mostly with the automatic modification of instructions. Chapter 8 is devoted to its operation and use.

In the main we are not concerned in this book with engineering questions of how a computer actually carries out the function described. There is one matter, however, which is of some slight interest to programmers and which is often not made clear in machine manuals. This is the fact that arithmetic is seldom actually carried out in the arithmetic registers themselves; in most computers these are simply storage registers. The arithmetic is done in a separate device called the *adder;* with proper auxiliary circuits, the adder can be made to serve for all arithmetic and decision operations. The programmer has no direct access to the adder, but if he knows the actual operation it can help him to avoid certain mistakes.

The output devices of DATAC consist of a line printer and magnetic tapes. The line printer is a device which prints one line of 120 characters at a time, under control of the computer. The use of magnetic tapes as output (remembering once again that the same tapes may at other times be used as auxiliary storage) assumes the existence of devices which can "read" a magnetic tape and print the information on paper, employing a line printer. Usually, the line printer utilized for this purpose is different from the line printer which is connected to the computer, but in some machines it is possible to use the *same* line printer for both purposes (at different times, obviously). It is always necessary to make a careful distinction between tapes for input and output and tapes for auxiliary storage. It is similarly necessary to distinguish between the use of card readers, printers, and card punches as computer input/output devices (which is called *on-line* operation) and the use of the same devices to translate from cards to magnetic tape or from magnetic tape to paper or cards (which is called *off-line, peripheral,* or *auxiliary* operation).

Figure 2 is an elaboration of Figure 1, showing the arithmetic and control registers and the information flow paths of DATAC. The details of operation of these devices are presented in later chapters.

THE DATA PROCESSOR

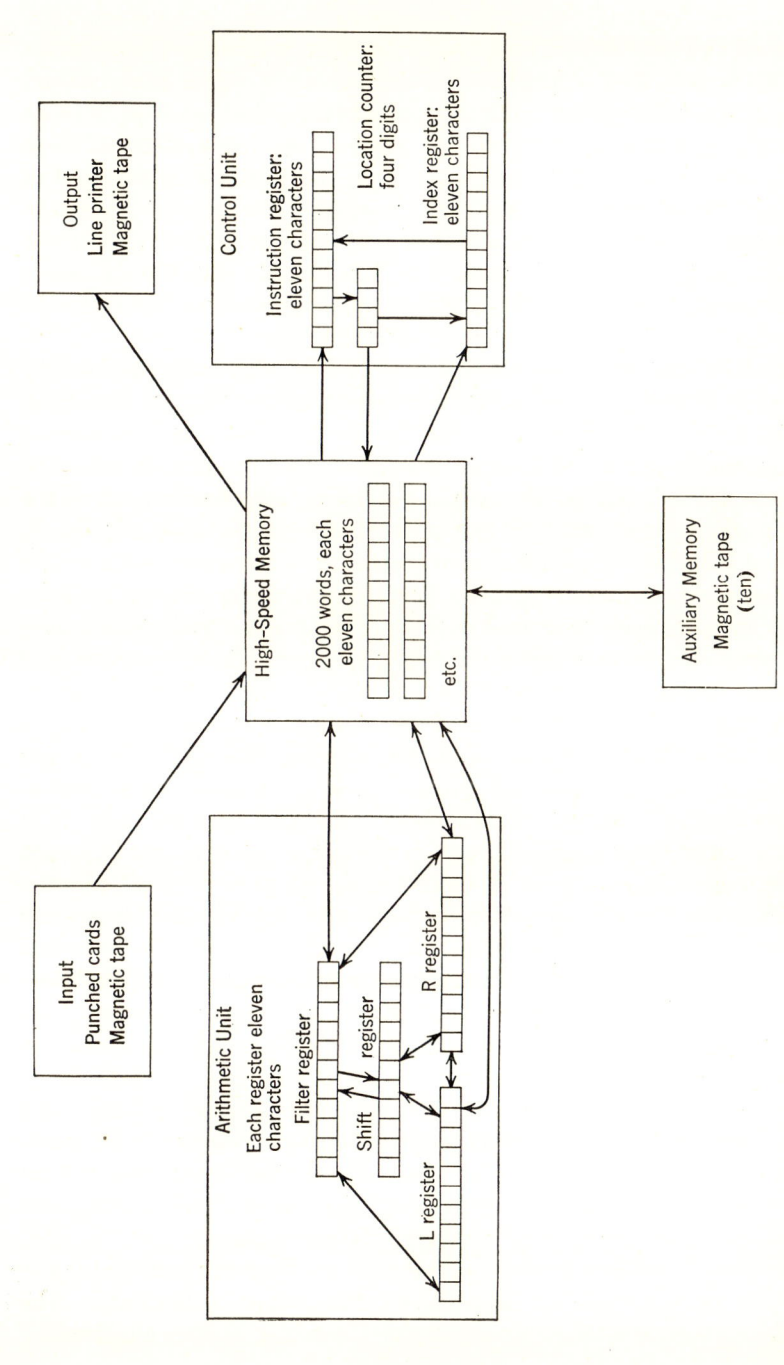

Figure 2. Organization of the parts of DATAC, the mythical computer used to illustrate coding principles in the text.

4.3 History of Computing

The characteristics of present computers have been arrived at through a process of development, most of which has occurred since 1945. It may be instructive to trace, in broad outline, the course of these developments.

Devices to assist in working with numbers have been in existence as long as there have been numbers. The first was the abacus, which made use of the bi-quinary number system some several thousand years before its application in several modern computers. The first mechanical computer was built by Pascal in 1642; a better device was built by Leibnitz in 1673. The first large computer was started in 1812 by Charles Babbage, a British mathematician. The machine was called the Difference Engine, from the mathematics it employed to calculate tables of mathematical functions. Babbage did not complete his machine, but others built a computer from his plans.

In 1833 Babbage conceived the Analytical Engine, which is the ancestor of all automatic computers. This machine can fairly be called a general-purpose computer, since it was to have flexible sequential control over the arithmetic operations it performed. *Sequential control* means that it was to be possible to specify in advance a sequence of arithmetic operations and the numbers to be operated on. Once the sequence had been specified by a punched card mechanism, developed earlier for use on the Jacquard loom, the machine would carry out the operations automatically. The sequence could be changed by altering the punched cards. It was to store numbers in mechanical wheels and use mechanical arithmetic elements. The input was to be either punched cards or hand-set dials, and the output was to be punched cards, a printed page, or a mold from which type could be set. Unfortunately, this brilliant conception was never translated into a working machine, partly because of financial difficulties and partly because of engineering problems which were at the time insurmountable.

The present application of punched cards began in 1889 when Dr. Herman Hollerith patented the Hollerith punched card. The equipment he invented and constructed was used in his work for the U. S. Census Bureau, and later became the basis for the International Business Machines Corporation which was organized in 1911.

The first modern machine to use Babbage's principle of sequential control was described subsequently by Dr. Howard Aiken of Harvard University in the 1930's. Called the Automatic Sequence Controlled

THE DATA PROCESSOR

Calculator, or more commonly the Mark I, it is remarkably similar in principle to the Analytical Engine. It does, however, make use of electromagnetic relays, and uses punched paper tape for sequence control rather than punched cards. It was completed in 1944 after several years' work by Harvard University and IBM. It is still in use.

The ENIAC (Electronic Numerical Integrator and Computer) represented a considerable advance in the computer building technology, since it is entirely electronic in internal operation. Designed by J. P. Eckert and Dr. J. W. Mauchly, then of the Moore School of Electrical Engineering at the University of Pennsylvania, it was completed in 1946. It was, of course, much faster than any previous machine. Sequence control is effected by means of many external wires running between holes in plugboards, and by external switches. Input and output are basically IBM cards, but dials may be used for the input of constants.

All these machines, and others along the same lines, use some external means of sequence control: punched cards, paper tape, wired plugboards. The memory is used only to store numbers. The fundamental idea of placing instructions in memory, which is basic to modern computers, did not emerge until 1945. This stored program idea, with which we shall have much contact, appeared in a report written by the late Dr. John von Neumann, proposing a computer quite different from the ENIAC. By storing the instructions internally and by using binary instead of decimal numbers (Appendix 3), much greater power could be achieved at considerably less expense of electronic equipment. The name EDVAC (Electronic Discrete Variable Automatic Computer) was suggested. In a further attempt to reduce the bulk of equipment, the memory of the EDVAC was built around the ultrasonic or mercury-delay line type of memory. The EDSAC (Electronic Delay Storage Automatic Computer) was built along similar lines at Cambridge University under the direction of Dr. M. V. Wilkes. It first operated in 1949.

The Univac, produced by what is now the Sperry Rand Corporation, was the first mass-produced computer placed on the market, in 1951. It is a decimal and alphabetic machine, has magnetic tapes, and uses mercury delay line memory. It and its successors are in wide use.

The IBM 701 appeared in 1953. It gained speed by using binary numbers and electrostatic storage.

The Whirlwind I, built at the Massachusetts Institute of Technology, was the first large machine to use magnetic cores for main memory.

This development represented a gain of a factor of 2 or more in speed, and a great increase in reliability, over electrostatic memory.

The foregoing is a sketch of the early developments in computers. Many advances have been made since these early days in such areas as memory speed and cost, system reliability, and speed of input and output devices.

4.4 Summary

This chapter has presented an outline of the parts of a computer, how they fit together, and how the concepts developed. It is intended only as a broad-brush treatment; later chapters will fill in the details.

The detailed material on DATAC, of course, applies only to this mythical machine. But the reader need not be unduly concerned that he is learning something that cannot be used in actual work. The basic principles of computer application and organization are the same for all stored program machines. The basic programming techniques we shall learn in this book are applicable to all computers. Experience shows that it is *much* easier to learn the details of programming a subsequent machine than to learn how to program in the first place. The reader who is thoroughly familiar with DATAC will have relatively little difficulty learning how to use actual equipment.

Exercises

1. What is a register in a computer?

2. Define the following:
   (a) On-line input/output equipment.
   (b) Off-line input/output equipment.
   (c) Auxiliary storage.
   (d) Peripheral equipment.
   (e) Arithmetic unit.
   (f) Control unit.

3. Name and state the functions of the seven DATAC registers.

4. What enables modern computers to operate in millionths of a second?

5. Why do digital computers use binary number systems internally?

6. Discuss the advantages and disadvantages of alpha-numeric versus numeric computers for business data processing.

7. Discuss the over-all organization of an electronic computer and the paths of information flow.

THE DATA PROCESSOR

8. Discuss the similarities and dissimilarities in the organization and paths of information flow, between an electronic computer and the following:
   (a) A small business.
   (b) The human nervous system.

9. List and explain three major differences between a stored program computer and an ordinary desk calculator.

10. List at least two examples of the following types of computers:
    (a) Manually controlled.
    (b) Control permanently wired in.
    (c) Externally programmed.
    (d) Stored program.

11. What is meant by an "unbalanced" computer organization? Does this question have any meaning apart from a specific application or class of applications?

5 CODING ARITHMETIC AND SHIFT OPERATIONS

5.0 Introduction

So far, we have only described the problem and seen in broad outline how to solve it; now we must learn in detail how to go about solving it. We have discussed the types of problems which data processing equipment can help with; we have seen that some kind of master file is at the heart of most data processing; we have seen some of the tools for representing data processing problems; we have had a brief introduction to the characteristics of computers and seen very sketchily how they operate.

Now we come to grips with the important problem of how to communicate to the computer what we want it to do: what information is to be processed, what is to be done with the information, how the results are to be presented. It is most important to realize that all of these "orders" to the computer must be presented to it in a precisely and rigidly defined form. We can walk up to a clerk and say, "Add these sales and give me subtotals by salesman." We can do no such thing with a computer, although, as we shall see in Chapter 14 on machine-aided coding, the task is not always so burdensome as it may appear in this chapter. For now, and to get a thorough understanding of how a computer basically operates (even when the machine helps us), we must realize that a computer accepts only the most elementary "instructions." A basic operation for a computer is merely to add two numbers, or "read" a card, or decide whether a number is positive or negative, or prepare a number for printing, for instance. Computers vary in how elementary their basic operations are; some older models, for instance, had no divide operation, requiring more elementary operations to be combined to effect a divide. Some recent machines have basic operations which under proper conditions will add a *group* of numbers, which ordinarily requires many instructions. It is safe to say, however, that by and large the operations which a computer can perform are essentially simple, and are

CODING ARITHMETIC AND SHIFT OPERATIONS 57

different in concept from the payroll or material control or utility billing functions that we as users are interested in.

The computer programmer has a dual function, then. He must know the application of interest (or have it described to him in precise language) and he must know in intimate detail how his computer operates. Even those who are reading only for general familiarity and do not expect to do any actual programming, however, will do well to read these next chapters carefully. It is almost impossible to appreciate what a computer is capable of, or to determine even in a general way what it ought to be applied to, without knowing how a computer operates "on the inside." People who do not have this appreciation have on occasion made rather fantastic claims or tried to promote applications or methods of solution which were totally inappropriate.

We may characterize programming and coding as a matter of *translation*. The problem is originally described in word procedures or in flow charts; the computer understands only things like "add," "shift," or "print." Perhaps it would be well at this point to outline the steps in this translation.

1. The problem in its earliest stage is described in words and mathematical formulas such as "We want a weekly list of all inventory items which fall below 25% of their average use for the past 3 months."

2. The first step in the translation is to put the problem statement into more precise form, usually using flow charts. This is necessary because most data processing applications involve a large number of combinations of choices, of alternatives, of exceptions and how to handle them. Trying to state all these in words becomes unduly complex.

3. The third step is to redraw the flow chart in more detail, showing now how the computer is to implement all the choices, the sequence in which it is to process the various pieces of information inside the machine, etc. It is at this stage also that the file layout job described in Chapter 2 is usually done.

4. The next step is to describe the detailed flow chart to the computer in *its* language, or in a language which it can translate into its language. This means writing the instructions mentioned in Chapter 4 and which will be explored in greater detail shortly. Often these are first written in a form which is not the same as the computer requires, but which is more convenient to the human being, and then the computer translates these "symbolic" or "relative" instructions to the correct form. This is part of the subject of Chapter 14. For our purposes here, it is necessary to learn the basic form before taking

up the short cuts. Step 4, as described here, is usually called *coding*.

5. These instructions are originally written on ordinary paper, which present computers cannot "read," so we next get the instructions into machine-understandable form. This consists of punching holes in a card or a strip of paper tape or preparing a magnetic input tape in a special machine.

6. The input medium is finally placed on some sort of reading device on the computer and the instructions are "read" electrically or photo-electrically or magnetically into the memory or storage of the computer. There they exist in the form of magnetization or sound waves or whatever the storage technique of the particular computer is. The instructions are then "executed," or carried out, one at a time, as we shall see, to accomplish the purpose of the program.

Instructions can be classified approximately into four groups. The first group includes the *arithmetic* operations: add, subtract, multiply, and divide (also sometimes shifting, as when a number is multiplied by ten by shifting one decimal place left). The second group consists of instructions which make *decisions,* such as testing whether a number is positive or negative, or whether a balance is exactly zero. These are frequently also called *logical* operations. The third group consists of operations whose purpose is to *rearrange* or *edit* data, such as inserting commas and decimal points, or combining two small numbers into one number in order to conserve tape or storage space. The fourth group includes instructions which involve getting information into the computer's memory from its card or tape readers and out to its printer or tape or punch. These are called *input/output* instructions. This chapter discusses the first of these four groups. A summary of all DATAC instructions will be found in Appendix 1. This should be used as a reference in reading the following chapters.

5.1 Word Structure and Memory Identification

DATAC has 2000 words of storage, which is roughly typical of present data processors, although the trend is to larger memories. Each word consists of eleven *characters,* where a character can be a numeric digit, a letter of the alphabet, one of several special symbols, or a "blank" character which will cause the printer not to print anything in a given position. The numbering of the eleven character positions of a word is shown in the diagram on page 61.

Each character is represented by a distinct combination of six *binary digits,*[*] i.e., digits which can only be zero or one. "Binary

---

[*] See Appendix 2 for a discussion of this subject.

CODING ARITHMETIC AND SHIFT OPERATIONS

digit" is commonly abbreviated to "bit." For historical reasons based on punched card terminology, it is common to call the left two bits of the six the *zone* bits, and the right four the *numeric* bits. With six binary digits, it is possible to represent $2^6 = 64$ distinct characters; only 45 of these are used in DATAC. The bit patterns assumed for DATAC are as follows:

CHARACTER	REPRESENTATION	CHARACTER	REPRESENTATION
blank	11 1010	M	10 0100
0	00 0000	N	10 0101
1	00 0001	O	10 0110
2	00 0010	P	10 0111
3	00 0011	Q	10 1000
4	00 0100	R	10 1001
5	00 0101	S	11 0010
6	00 0110	T	11 0011
7	00 0111	U	11 0100
8	00 1000	V	11 0101
9	00 1001	W	11 0110
A	01 0001	X	11 0111
B	01 0010	Y	11 1000
C	01 0011	Z	11 1001
D	01 0100	.	01 1010
E	01 0101	,	01 1011
F	01 0110	$	01 1100
G	01 0111	*	01 1101
H	01 1000	(	10 1010
I	01 1001	)	10 1011
J	10 0001	−	10 1100
K	10 0010	+	10 1101
L	10 0011		

For much coding work it is not necessary to know these binary codes, or their equivalent in a particular actual computer, but it is definitely worth knowing in general fashion how the information is represented inside the machine. It is the function of the circuitry of the computer to be able to recognize these bit patterns for what they are: to be able to print them correctly, to recognize that "9" and "R" cannot be added,* etc.

In DATAC if a given word in memory is alphabetic, such as a man's name or a part number, then all eleven characters may contain any symbol: numeric digit, letter, punctuation mark, or plus or minus sign. If a word is a number, then the first character, called the sign or "S" position, must contain the configuration for either a plus or a minus sign. The format for DATAC instructions is quite different and is described in the next section.

* If this is so in a particular machine; in some, they *can* be "added."

Since there are 2000 different locations where numbers or instructions can be located, some means must be provided for identifying each one uniquely. This is so that there will be some way of specifying the location of an instruction, where to find data, where to put answers, or where to find the next instruction. The problem is solved by giving each of the 2000 locations an identification number, from 0000 to 1999, which is called the *address* of the location. A common analogy is to compare the computer memory with pigeonholes in a post office. Pigeonholes have name plates on them which serve as a reference identification. It is important to note that the name plate does not tell anything about the contents. The name "Smith" on the name plate does not tell where a letter came from or what it says. All it does is this: if you put a certain letter in the box labeled "Smith," you should subsequently be able to find that same letter, whatever it may be about, by going back to the pigeonhole marked "Smith."

That is really all the address of a memory location does: if we put a certain number in location 1507, we should be able to go back to 1507 later and find that same number. The address 1507 certainly does not mean that we can find the number 1507 stored there—except by coincidence. This may seem painfully obvious, perhaps, but it is a perennial source of difficulty to new coders.

Memory has two additional characteristics which unfortunately do not fit into the post office analogy. First, a memory location can hold only one word at a time, and placing a word in the location automatically and finally destroys whatever was there previously. This means that there is no problem of making sure a location is empty before putting something there, but it also means that we must be sure a cell does not contain anything we wish to keep before something else is put in it. Second, it is possible to read a number out of memory without destroying or removing it. It is as though the postal clerk, instead of removing a letter, simply made a quick copy of it on another piece of paper.

5.2 Instruction Format and Execution

An instruction in DATAC consists of all eleven characters of a word. The first character from the left, designated the sign character, contains the *suboperation code*.* Its function is discussed later. The next, or *"ten,"* character, is called the *operation code;* this is the part of the instruction which tells DATAC whether to add or subtract or

---

* In real machines this is sometimes called the *variation designator*.

CODING ARITHMETIC AND SHIFT OPERATIONS   61

shift or read a card, or whatever. The control circuits of the machine *interpret* or *decode* the pattern of bits in the operation code and send signals to the other parts of the machine to carry out the function of the particular instruction. The next four characters, nine through six, contain the *address* part. The address characters most commonly specify a location in memory at which to find a word to be operated on, or where in memory to place a result. The address has different functions in other instructions, such as specifying the number of shifts to be performed, or where the next instruction should be found on decision operations. Characters five and four specify an *indexer*, which may be used to modify addresses or for other purposes.

Character →	S	10	9	8	7	6	5	4	3	2	1
	Sub-operation	Operation		Address			Indexer		Filter		Monitor

Figure 1. The six possible parts of a DATAC instruction. The numbering of the characters of a word is that used throughout the book.

Indexers are discussed in Chapter 8. Characters three and two specify a *filter*, which may be used to exclude some of the characters of the word being transferred between memory and the arithmetic unit or vice versa. We shall see how filters operate in the next chapter. The last, or "one," character, of an instruction is called the *monitor* digit. It is used in conjunction with certain switches on the console to provide alternative paths through the program and to assist in checking a completed program for correctness. We shall return to the monitor function in Chapters 10-12.

The six possible parts of an instruction are shown in Figure 1.

Not all of the six functions need be used on every instruction. There must always be an operation code, and there is usually an address; on some operations in DATAC a suboperation code is required by the machine specification. The indexer, filter, and monitor characters are almost always optional, depending on the requirements of the particular instruction. For the next few pages we shall have need only for the operation code and the address. When a particular part of an instruction is not required, we shall simply write nothing on that part of the coding sheet.

Let us now turn to the actual *execution*, or carrying out, of a small set of instructions. We shall need another diagram of the pertinent registers of DATAC, omitting those which will not concern us immediately. This is shown in Figure 2.

62 PROGRAMMING BUSINESS COMPUTERS

Suppose for an illustration that we are working with a salesmen's compensation calculation. The segment we wish to consider is adding a particular man's base pay to his commission to get his gross pay. Suppose that all the necessary data has already been entered into memory by previous sections of the routine. Suppose that a base pay of $45.75 is in memory in the location identified by the address

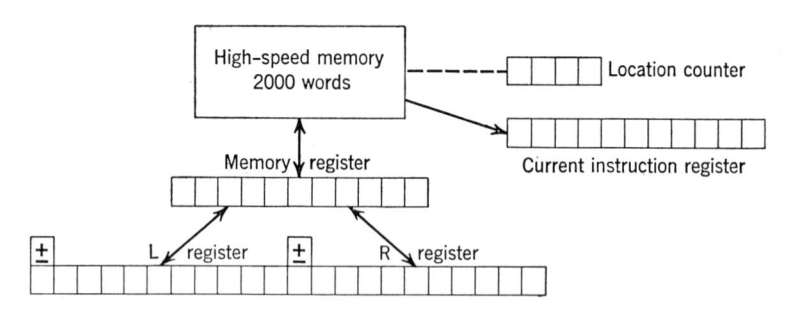

Figure 2. Simplified diagram of the DATAC arithmetic and control registers.

1307. A commission of $58.17 has been read in (or calculated, as the case may be) and is in location 1583; the total gross pay is to be stored in location 0789. All of these amounts and addresses were chosen arbitrarily. Suppose finally that the routine of three instructions required (in DATAC) to calculate the gross pay is stored in locations 1804, 1805, and 1806. The routine could be as follows:

INSTRUC- TION LOCATION	SUBOP- ERATION	OPERA- TION	ADDRESS	IN- DEXER	FIL- TER	MONI- TOR	REMARKS
1804		B	1307				Bring base pay to R
1805		A	1583				Add commission
1806		S	0789				Store gross pay in 0789

Recall that in memory these three instructions would appear as:

$$0B130700000$$
$$0A158300000$$
$$0S078900000$$

Note that we have left the suboperation code, indexer, filter, and monitor digits blank; these would be entered into memory by the loading routine (Chapter 11) or assembly routine (Chapter 14) as

CODING ARITHMETIC AND SHIFT OPERATIONS 63

zeros. This is necessary because the six-bit codes for zero and blank are different. It was an arbitrary choice to assume the program to be in 1804–1806.

Let us now assume that the computer is just ready to execute the instruction in 1804, and follow in detail the steps the computer would go through in carrying out these three instructions.

The execution of the first instruction would require five steps.

1. At the start of the cycle the location counter contains 1804, indicating that the instruction now to be performed is in location 1804 in memory.

2. The control circuits send electric signals to memory asking for the instruction in 1804 to be brought to the instruction register. This would be the coded instruction 0B130700000.

3. The control circuits analyze, or *decode*, the bit pattern making up the operation code B to discover what is to be done in this instruction. This would be found to be "Bring the word in memory identified by the address (1307 in this case) to the arithmetic section and replace the contents of the R register with it." The machine "discovers" all this in the sense that as a result of electrically analyzing the bit pattern making up the operation code B, electronic circuits are conditioned so that the following steps are executed in the proper order.

4. After analyzing the address part of the instruction register, the control circuits send a signal to memory asking that the number in location 1307 be sent to the R register, replacing whatever was there previously. As pointed out above in the discussion of memory, the word in 1307 would be left unchanged in memory after it is sent to R.

5. Since, in DATAC, instructions are taken from consecutively numbered locations in memory unless specified otherwise (by jumps, to be discussed later), the contents of the location counter are automatically increased by one. This means that the next instruction will come from location 1805. The control circuits proceed to deal with this instruction.

So far, the machine has merely brought the salesman's base pay from memory to the appropriate arithmetic register, where it may next be added to the commission.

The Add instruction at 1805 is analyzed and executed by a process similar to the steps outlined above; we will not spell them out in detail again. The result of this instruction is to add the commission, stored in location 1583 in memory, to the base pay now in the R register, and leave the sum (gross pay) in R.

The Store instruction at 1806 tells the machine to send the gross pay in R to location 0789 in memory, and hold the result in R. The action of storing the result in 0789 destroys any previous word which may have been in that location, but has no effect on any other storage location.

It may help to show the quantities as they would appear in memory and the R register during the execution of the three steps. The contents are shown on each line as they would appear *after* the execution of the corresponding instruction.

INSTRUCTION LOCATION	CONTENTS OF 1307	CONTENTS OF 1583	CONTENTS OF 0789	CONTENTS OF R
1804	+0000004575	+0000005817	Immaterial	+0000004575
1805	+0000004575	+0000005817	Immaterial	+0000010392
1806	+0000004575	+0000005817	+0000010392	+0000010392

Dollar signs and visual decimal points do not appear in memory—at least not at this stage. Later in the program when it is necessary to print the results, they can be inserted in the correct positions. The question of decimal points in the arithmetic sense is discussed in Section 5.5. For now, we are safe if we simply make certain we are consistent, i.e., we cannot add $45.75 stored in memory as +0000004575 to $58.17 stored in memory as +0005817000. That is, not if we expect to get meaningful results.

For another example of computer operation we may consider subtraction. Suppose that the following quantities are stored in memory as follows: gross pay of $103.92 in location 0789, withholding tax of $12.23 in 1050, FICA (Federal Insurance Contributions Act, or social security) of $2.60 in 0480, and pension deduction of $3.72 in 1313. It is required to subtract the various deductions from gross pay to get net pay and store it in 1350. (The amounts and addresses are, as usual, arbitrarily chosen.) The program could be a continuation of the previous one. The gross pay would still be available in the R register.

LOC.	S	O	ADDRESS	REMARKS
1807		M	1050	Subtract tax from gross pay
1808		M	0480	Subtract FICA
1809		M	1313	Subtract pension
1810		S	1350	Store net pay

The only new concept here is the Subtract instruction, which does exactly what one would expect: the word in memory specified by the address part of the instruction is subtracted from the number in the R

CODING ARITHMETIC AND SHIFT OPERATIONS 65

register. (The operation code "M" comes from "minus"; "S" for "subtract" would of course have been more logical, but we chose instead to use "S" for "store.") The usual considerations apply: the numbers subtracted must have a plus or minus sign in the sign character—in this case a plus sign—and the decimal points must "line up." Sign control in DATAC is algebraic, i.e., subtracting a number with a minus sign has the same effect as adding the same number with a plus sign. As another example, if the sum of the deductions had been greater than the gross pay (which can happen!), the "net pay" would have been negative. The contents of the R register after the execution of each instruction in the above routine:

INSTRUCTION LOCATION	R
1806	+0000010392
1807	+0000009169
1808	+0000008909
1809	+0000008537
1810	+0000008537

What would happen if the result of an addition or subtraction were too large to be contained in the R register? This could occur through an error in positioning the numbers in memory as illustrated above, or because the result of a calculation becomes larger than anticipated, or intentionally, in certain applications. The answer assumed for DATAC's operation is that the correct sum would appear in the L and R registers combined, assuming that L originally contained zeros. What this means is that if the sum or difference is greater than ten digits, the carry or borrow propagates to L. If L is not zero to start, the result will be mathematically correct, but it may not be meaningful to the coder. A few examples may help to clarify the point. The first line in each case is the original contents of L and R, the second is the positive or negative number added to R, the third is the result in L and R.

```
         L              R
   +0000000000   +0000000000
                 +1234567899
   +0000000000   +1234567899

   +0000000000   +9876000000
                 +4000000000
   +0000000001   +3876000000
```

(Continued on next page)

```
    +0000000000+9000000000
              -6000000000
    +0000000000+3000000000

    +0000000000+6000000000
              -9000000000
    +0000000000-3000000000

    +0000000000-6000000000
              -9000000000
    -0000000001-5000000000

    +1234567899+8900000000
              +4500000000
    +1234567900+3400000000

    +1234567899+1230000000
              -9876543210
    +1234567898+1353456790
```

Most of these cases of carry into or borrow from L, if not representing clear-cut errors in coding or number size, are at least exceptions; the coder wants to have a warning that they have occurred. And of course this warning must be built into the machine, since if it were possible to anticipate all cases where it would occur while doing coding, the error would be avoided. In DATAC we assume the existence of an *overflow trigger*. A trigger may be defined for our purpose as a device or circuit which can "remember" some condition. A trigger is also called a flip-flop. If a carry or borrow out of R occurs, which is called *overflow*, the overflow trigger is *set*. The Overflow jump instruction (to be discussed in Section 6.2) can be used to "test" the condition of the overflow trigger, and permits appropriate action to be taken.

The next question about addition or subtraction is: What happens if the operations are attempted on words which contain something other than numbers? What happens if through error one attempts to add a man's name and his pay number? The answer in DATAC is roughly that if it was planned that way it will work, otherwise probably not. More precisely, the rule is: addition and subtraction of words containing letters or special symbols are permitted as long as in each character position the letters and punctuation marks are added only to zeros, and as long as no carry or borrow into a nonnumeric position is attempted. In such an addition or subtraction, i.e., where there is a nonnumeric character anywhere in either word, the word from memory is taken to be positive, and the character in the sign position of R is unaffected by the operation. If this rule is violated, the *adder-alphabetic error* trigger is set; it may be tested

CODING ARITHMETIC AND SHIFT OPERATIONS 67

by the Alphabetic error jump instruction. Examples of permissible additions:

```
  J O N E S 0 0 1 2 3 5        R
+ 0 0 0 0 0 0 0 0 1 4 2        Memory
  ─────────────────────
  J O N E S 0 0 1 3 7 7        Result in R
```

```
+ 0 0 0 0 0 0 4 0 7 2          R
  S M I T H 0 0 1 1 2 6        Memory
  ─────────────────────
+ M I T H 0 0 5 1 9 8          Result
```

The second example shows an addition which is permissible, but would normally not be the desired result. It is based on the fact that the sign character of R dominates the result in this type of addition.

```
  1 2 F 9 8 6 7 0 1 9 1        R
− 0 0 0 0 0 0 0 0 1 6          Memory
  ─────────────────────
  1 2 F 9 8 6 7 0 2 0 7        Result
```

Remember that the sign position of the word in memory is ignored in this type of addition.

Subtraction operates similarly, with the same rules regarding signs.

Additions which would cause the adder-alphabetic error trigger to be set:

```
  F J B R O W N 1 2 3 2        R
+ 0 0 0 3 5 4 6 9 0 2          Memory
  ─────────────────────
  F J B R ? ? ? 8 1 3 4        Result
```

The "addition" of a letter and a number cannot be carried out in DATAC.

```
  G A L L O N 8 7 6 5 0        R
+ 0 0 0 0 0 3 1 1 1 8          Memory
  ─────────────────────
  G A L L O ? 1 8 7 6 8        Result
```

In this example, a "carry" into the N would be required to represent the arithmetic sum.*

---

*It may seem that these rules are unnecessarily arbitrary and complicated. This appears to be an unfortunate result of many of the design features which add power and flexibility to a computer. For instance, there would be no arbitrary rules regarding adding words containing letters or punctuation if the machine could directly represent *only* numbers. Many machines are built in such a fashion. But when it is necessary to represent letters in some indirect way in these machines, the programmer is faced with a much more complicated

68   PROGRAMMING BUSINESS COMPUTERS

A frequent requirement in data processing is to add one quantity in memory to another also in memory. An example is an inventory control application, where it is necessary (among other things) to add the quantity received to the previous quantity on hand. For an illustration suppose that for a certain item the old quantity on hand is stored in location 1000 in memory, and that the quantity received at the warehouse is in 1100; the sum should be stored back in 1000 as the "updated" quantity on hand. If the routine starts in 850:

850	B	1000	Bring quantity on hand to R
851	A	1100	Add quantity received
852	S	1000	Store updated quantity

We observe that in such instances, which are numerous, one of the addresses appears twice. Why not have an instruction which adds a number in R to a word in memory? This instruction, which is usually called *Add to memory*, is available in DATAC as in several real computers. The original contents of R are unchanged after the instruction is executed. The operation code for Add to memory is A, the same as plain addition. However, we write an X in the suboperation position.

850		B	1100	Bring quantity received to R
851	X	A	1000	Add old quantity on hand and return sum to memory

If there were 785 units on hand and 250 received, the pertinent quantities during the execution of this program would be:

INSTRUCTION LOCATION	1100 (RECEIVED)	1000 (ON HAND)	R
850	+0000000250	+0000000785	+0000000250
851	+0000000250	+0000001035	+0000000250

The *Subtract from memory* (operation code: XM) instruction results in the number in the R register being subtracted from the word specified in the address, with the R register left unchanged. Its operation is so similar to Add to memory that we need not provide an illustration.

---

task. As a rough generalization we may say that in designing computers there is a choice between providing powerful features that make programming simpler but imply arbitrary rules, and providing a few less powerful features that involve a more complex job of programming. Many real computers designed for business applications are much more arbitrary in their programming rules than DATAC is.

5.3 Multiplication and Division

There are fairly frequent instances in data processing in which two numbers must be multiplied. Examples: calculation of taxes from a rate table, extension of quantity and unit price to get total cost, calculation of commissions. Division is used less frequently than multiplication, and a great deal less often in business data processing than in engineering and scientific computation. One example is the calculation of averages, used in a variety of applications. For a clear understanding of how these instructions operate and to get an insight into later discussions of decimal point location, it is necessary to follow through some illustrations in detail.

In DATAC multiplication is effected by placing one factor in the R register (or having it there as a result of a previous instruction), and executing a Multiply instruction which has the address of the other factor. The operation code for Multiply is X ("times"). Since both multiplier and multiplicand can have as many as ten digits, the product may have as many as twenty, which appear in the L and R registers. The more significant half of the product appears in the L register, and the less significant half in the R register. (We shall see later that it often works out that the multiplier and multiplicand have few enough digits and are placed in the words in such a way that the product will have nothing but zeros in the L register. The phrase "more significant half" thus applies strictly only to products having more than ten digits.) During multiplication, the multiplicand is held temporarily in the memory register—so that the multiplicand need be obtained from memory only once, although it will ordinarily be needed many different times during the multiplication. In DATAC it is not possible to add the product to a number previously in the L register; L is cleared to zero at the start of execution of the Multiply order. With these factors in mind, the multiplication process may be explained by means of an example.

Suppose the number +1111111111 is to be multiplied by +9987654321, the latter being taken in this example as the multiplier which is already in R as we begin. (It would be somewhat untypical in business applications to find a multiplication with factors having so many digits. It is hoped that this choice makes the process simpler to follow. We shall consider more realistic examples later.) After the control circuits analyze the operation code and find that it is Multiply, the steps in DATAC are:

1. The number 1111111111 is brought from memory to the memory

register, and the L register is cleared. The picture is now:

+	Memory Register
1	1	1	1	1	1	1	1	1	1

+	L	+	R
0	0	0	0	0	0	0	0	0	0	9	9	8	7	6	5	4	3	2	1

L and R are drawn together since that is the way they operate in multiplication.

2. The multiplicand is added into L as many times as the value of the digit standing in the rightmost (or Least Significant Digit—LSD) position of R:

+	L	+	R
1	1	1	1	1	1	1	1	1	1	9	9	8	7	6	5	4	3	2	1

(The memory register is unchanged throughout and will not be redrawn.)

3. The entire contents of L and R, not including signs, are shifted right one place, as though the two were one register of twenty digits.

+	L	+	R
0	1	1	1	1	1	1	1	1	1	1	9	9	8	7	6	5	4	3	2

4. The multiplicand is added into L as many times as the value of the digit in the LSD position of R, which is now **2**:

+	L	+	R
2	3	3	3	3	3	3	3	3	3	1	9	9	8	7	6	5	4	3	2

5. L and R are shifted right one place:

+	L	+	R
0	2	3	3	3	3	3	3	3	3	3	1	9	9	8	7	6	5	4	3

6. The multiplicand is added into L as many times as the value of the digit in the LSD position of R, which is now **3**:

+	L	+	R
3	5	6	6	6	6	6	6	6	6	3	1	9	9	8	7	6	5	4	3

Following the same pattern, the successive contents of these two registers are:

Shift

+	L	+	R
0	3	5	6	6	6	6	6	6	6	3	1	9	9	8	7	6	5	4

CODING ARITHMETIC AND SHIFT OPERATIONS 71

Add |+| L |+| R
| 4 | 8 | 0 | 1 | 1 | 1 | 1 | 1 | 0 | 6 | 3 | 1 | 9 | 9 | 8 | 7 | 6 | 5 | 4 |

Shift |+| L |+| R
| 0 | 4 | 8 | 0 | 1 | 1 | 1 | 1 | 1 | 0 | 6 | 3 | 1 | 9 | 9 | 8 | 7 | 6 | 5 |

Add |+| L |+| R
| 6 | 0 | 3 | 5 | 6 | 6 | 6 | 6 | 6 | 0 | 6 | 3 | 1 | 9 | 9 | 8 | 7 | 6 | 5 |

Shift |+| L |+| R
| 0 | 6 | 0 | 3 | 5 | 6 | 6 | 6 | 6 | 6 | 0 | 6 | 3 | 1 | 9 | 9 | 8 | 7 | 6 |

Add |+| L |+| R
| 7 | 2 | 7 | 0 | 2 | 3 | 3 | 3 | 2 | 6 | 0 | 6 | 3 | 1 | 9 | 9 | 8 | 7 | 6 |

Shift |+| L |+| R
| 0 | 7 | 2 | 7 | 0 | 2 | 3 | 3 | 3 | 2 | 6 | 0 | 6 | 3 | 1 | 9 | 9 | 8 | 7 |

Add |+| L |+| R
| 8 | 5 | 0 | 4 | 8 | 0 | 1 | 1 | 1 | 0 | 2 | 6 | 0 | 6 | 3 | 1 | 9 | 9 | 8 | 7 |

Shift |+| L |+| R
| 0 | 8 | 5 | 0 | 4 | 8 | 0 | 1 | 1 | 1 | 0 | 2 | 6 | 0 | 6 | 3 | 1 | 9 | 9 | 8 |

Add |+| L |+| R
| 9 | 7 | 3 | 9 | 3 | 6 | 8 | 9 | 9 | 9 | 0 | 2 | 6 | 0 | 6 | 3 | 1 | 9 | 9 | 8 |

Shift |+| L |+| R
| 0 | 9 | 7 | 3 | 9 | 3 | 6 | 8 | 9 | 9 | 9 | 0 | 2 | 6 | 0 | 6 | 3 | 1 | 9 | 9 |

Add (1) |+| L |+| R
| 0 | 9 | 7 | 3 | 9 | 3 | 6 | 8 | 9 | 8 | 9 | 0 | 2 | 6 | 0 | 6 | 3 | 1 | 9 | 9 |

Shift |+| L |+| R
| 1 | 0 | 9 | 7 | 3 | 9 | 3 | 6 | 8 | 9 | 8 | 9 | 0 | 2 | 6 | 0 | 6 | 3 | 1 | 9 |

Add (1) |+| L |+| R
| 1 | 0 | 9 | 7 | 3 | 9 | 3 | 6 | 8 | 8 | 8 | 9 | 0 | 2 | 6 | 0 | 6 | 3 | 1 | 9 |

Shift |+| L |+| R
| 1 | 1 | 0 | 9 | 7 | 3 | 9 | 3 | 6 | 8 | 8 | 8 | 9 | 0 | 2 | 6 | 0 | 6 | 3 | 1 |

The 1's which appear in parentheses to the left of the L register on the last two additions are part of the product; it is assumed that DATAC has some way to store such a digit temporarily until the shifting takes place. Note also that the machine has to have circuits which determine when the adding-and-shifting scheme has been carried out ten times, and then stop the operation.

The multiplication is now complete. The product has been developed in L and R taken as one long register. The multiplier in R has been lost. The multiplicand is still in memory. If either or both numbers had been negative, algebraic sign control would have given the correct sign to the product, with the sign appearing in the sign positions of both L and R. All of this is effected by the single instruction, Multiply.

All of this may be seen to be simply a mechanization of the ordinary process of multiplying with paper and pencil. Details vary from one machine to the next, as regards the actual multiplication of the multiplicand by one digit of the multiplier and the placement of operands in arithmetic registers, but the adding-and-shifting scheme is generally the same.

In many, if not most, business applications the factors have few enough digits that the product would appear entirely in R. Suppose, for example, that $88.03 in location 1007 is to be multiplied by 18% which is in 0860. The routine could be:

```
0500   B   0860   Bring multiplier to R
0501   X   1007   Multiply
```

The contents of the pertinent registers after each instruction has been executed:

1007	0860	L	R
+0000008803	+0000000018	Immaterial	+0000000018
+0000008803	+0000000018	+0000000000	+0000158454

The same result would of course have been obtained if the $88.03 had been brought into R and the location of the 18% given as the address of the Multiply. However, the time required by the machine to execute the multiplication would have been different. It will be seen that the number of additions required in the multiplication is the sum of all the digits of the multiplier in R. As the multiplication of $88.03 by 18% was set up, nine additions were required (1 + 8); if the $88.03 had been placed in R, 19 additions would have been needed (8 + 8 + 3). The same is true of an ordinary desk calculator. Some computers, however, have circuitry which makes the multiplication time somewhat independent of the multiplier digits, or takes advantage of the fact that no addition is required for digits of the multiplier which are zero.

CODING ARITHMETIC AND SHIFT OPERATIONS 73

Multiplication is effected by using one digit of the multiplier in an *adding*-and-shifting routine; division is accomplished by building up the quotient one digit at a time in a *subtracting*-and-shifting system. The process is similar to multiplication and is almost exactly analogous to paper-and-pencil long division, except, as we shall see, that in paper-and-pencil division we shift the divisor right as we proceed whereas in the machine the dividend is shifted left; the result is the same.

We saw in multiplication that the product was always twenty digits —*as far as the machine was concerned*—even though we might be multiplying factors which had only a few nonzero digits, resulting in a product which had nothing but zeros in the L register. We are forced to accept this method of operation by the machine, and set up the routines to take the result from the correct register. Similarly, in division there are machine idiosyncrasies to contend with: the machine demands that the dividend always be twenty digits long, i.e., it takes the L and R registers together as containing the dividend. In some cases this is just what we want, but more frequently, in business calculations, the dividend is not in fact anywhere near that long. In such a case we simply clear the L register to zeros before dividing, and place the dividend in the R register. It will be noted below, also, that the machine is completely inflexible (almost stupid, in fact) in its approach to division: where you and I would make a guess as to how many digits there would be in the quotient and act accordingly, the machine ploddingly inspects every position of the potential quotient to see if it is anything but zero. Thus in the detailed example worked out below, the first half-dozen cycles of the subtracting-and-shifting scheme actually accomplish nothing but getting the dividend over where something can be done with it.

The operation code for Divide in DATAC is D, as might be expected. To state precisely the function of the instruction, the dividend is placed in the L and R registers (or R alone, and L cleared, depending on how we are looking at it) and the instruction Divide given; the location of the divisor is specified by the address part of the Divide instruction. The quotient is developed in the R register and the remainder in the L register.

Suppose that the total gross pay for a plant's weekly payroll is $120,746.87 for 1472 men. It is desired to calculate the average gross pay. We assume that at the start of the operation the L register contains zeros and the total gross pay is in R. After the Divide instruction (with the *address* of the number 1472) is analyzed by the control circuits, the steps would be:

1. The divisor is brought from memory and placed in the memory register. The picture:

+	Memory Register
0 | 0 | 0 | 0 | 0 | 0 | 1 | 4 | 7 | 2	

+	L	+	R
0 | 0 | 0 | 0 | 0 | 0 | 0 | 0 | 0 | 0		0 | 1 | 2 | 0 | 7 | 4 | 6 | 8 | 7	

2. The divisor is compared with the number in L. If the divisor is larger than L, the division continues. If not, i.e., if the divisor is equal or smaller, we have what is called the *divide overflow* condition. This turns on the overflow trigger as does overflow in addition or subtraction, and the division is not performed. A little experimentation with paper and pencil or a desk calculator will show that if the condition is not met the quotient will have at least eleven digits—and the R register, where the quotient must be developed, has room for only ten. In the type of division usually encountered in business calculation, however, divide overflow will seldom occur. We may observe that if L is zero and the divisor is not zero, divide overflow is impossible; if the divisor is zero, divide overflow will always occur. This divide overflow testing is naturally done only once.

3. The contents of L and R together are shifted left one place. If this is taken literally as a statement of internal machine operation, it implies the existence of some way of temporarily storing a digit which might be shifted out of the left end of L. We shall not concern ourselves with the *exact* way this is done in real machines; the concept is accurate, although details vary. (Memory register again omitted.)

+	L	+	R
0 | 0 | 0 | 0 | 0 | 0 | 0 | 0 | 0 | 0		1 | 2 | 0 | 7 | 4 | 6 | 8 | 7 | 0	

4. The divisor is subtracted from L (including the temporarily stored digit) as many times as possible without changing the sign of the L register. This is in effect the long division process of "seeing how many times it will go." The number of times, which will eventually be the leftmost digit of the quotient, is entered into the last position of R. This position is now zero because of the previous left shift:

+	L	+	R
0 | 0 | 0 | 0 | 0 | 0 | 0 | 0 | 0 | 0		1 | 2 | 0 | 7 | 4 | 6 | 8 | 7 | 0	

CODING ARITHMETIC AND SHIFT OPERATIONS

Of course the digit entered is also zero, since the quotient will have several zeros at the left.

Following the same pattern:

Shift |+| L |+| R
         | 0 | 0 | 0 | 0 | 0 | 0 | 0 | 0 | 0 | 0 | 1 | 2 | 0 | 7 | 4 | 6 | 8 | 7 | 0 | 0 |

Subtract |+| L |+| R
         | 0 | 0 | 0 | 0 | 0 | 0 | 0 | 0 | 0 | 0 | 1 | 2 | 0 | 7 | 4 | 6 | 8 | 7 | 0 | 0 |

Shift |+| L |+| R
         | 0 | 0 | 0 | 0 | 0 | 0 | 0 | 0 | 0 | 1 | 2 | 0 | 7 | 4 | 6 | 8 | 7 | 0 | 0 | 0 |

Subtract |+| L |+| R
         | 0 | 0 | 0 | 0 | 0 | 0 | 0 | 0 | 0 | 1 | 2 | 0 | 7 | 4 | 6 | 8 | 7 | 0 | 0 | 0 |

Shift |+| L |+| R
         | 0 | 0 | 0 | 0 | 0 | 0 | 0 | 0 | 1 | 2 | 0 | 7 | 4 | 6 | 8 | 7 | 0 | 0 | 0 | 0 |

Subtract |+| L |+| R
         | 0 | 0 | 0 | 0 | 0 | 0 | 0 | 0 | 1 | 2 | 0 | 7 | 4 | 6 | 8 | 7 | 0 | 0 | 0 | 0 |

Shift |+| L |+| R
         | 0 | 0 | 0 | 0 | 0 | 0 | 0 | 1 | 2 | 0 | 7 | 4 | 6 | 8 | 7 | 0 | 0 | 0 | 0 | 0 |

Subtract |+| L |+| R
         | 0 | 0 | 0 | 0 | 0 | 0 | 0 | 1 | 2 | 0 | 7 | 4 | 6 | 8 | 7 | 0 | 0 | 0 | 0 | 0 |

Shift |+| L |+| R
         | 0 | 0 | 0 | 0 | 0 | 0 | 1 | 2 | 0 | 7 | 4 | 6 | 8 | 7 | 0 | 0 | 0 | 0 | 0 | 0 |

Subtract |+| L |+| R
         | 0 | 0 | 0 | 0 | 0 | 0 | 1 | 2 | 0 | 7 | 4 | 6 | 8 | 7 | 0 | 0 | 0 | 0 | 0 | 0 |

Shift |+| L |+| R
         | 0 | 0 | 0 | 0 | 0 | 1 | 2 | 0 | 7 | 4 | 6 | 8 | 7 | 0 | 0 | 0 | 0 | 0 | 0 | 0 |

Subtract |+| L |+| R
         | 0 | 0 | 0 | 0 | 0 | 0 | 2 | 9 | 8 | 6 | 8 | 7 | 0 | 0 | 0 | 0 | 0 | 0 | 0 | 8 |

Shift |+| L |+| R
         | 0 | 0 | 0 | 0 | 0 | 2 | 9 | 8 | 6 | 8 | 7 | 0 | 0 | 0 | 0 | 0 | 0 | 0 | 8 | 0 |

Subtract

|+| L |+| R
|0|0|0|0|0|0|0|0|4|2|8|7|0|0|0|0|0|0|8|2|

Shift

|+| L |+| R
|0|0|0|0|0|0|0|4|2|8|7|0|0|0|0|0|0|8|2|0|

Subtract

|+| L |+| R
|0|0|0|0|0|0|0|4|2|8|7|0|0|0|0|0|0|8|2|0|

Shift

|+| L |+| R
|0|0|0|0|0|0|4|2|8|7|0|0|0|0|0|8|2|0|0|

Subtract

|+| L |+| R
|0|0|0|0|0|0|1|3|4|3|0|0|0|0|0|8|2|0|2|

The process has now been carried out ten times, developing the ten digits of the quotient. The quotient, which we interpret as $82.02, is in R; the remainder is in L. What is done with the remainder depends on the requirements of the application. In this illustration it means that the exact average is $82.02, plus 1343/1472 of a cent. We shall see later how it would be possible without much extra difficulty to get a quotient rounded to the nearest cent.

The question of divide overflow must be explored a little more fully. Stated formally, the rule is: divide overflow will occur if the divisor is not greater than the most significant (or L) part of the dividend. Signs are ignored, i.e., we do not mean "greater" in the algebraic sense.

Examples of permissible divisions:

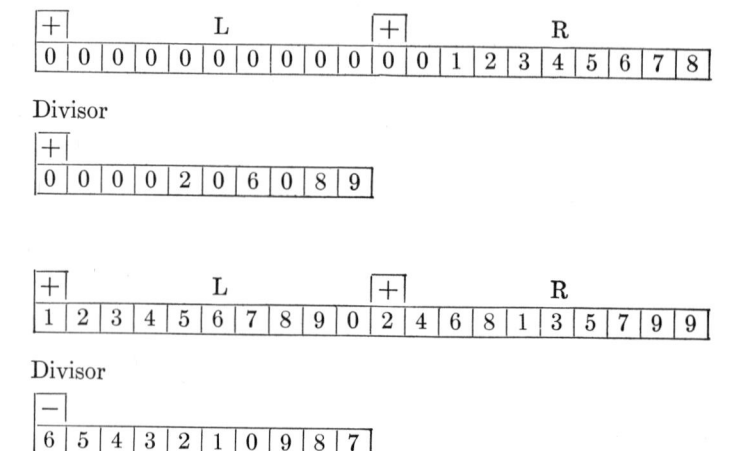

|+| L |+| R
|0|0|0|0|0|0|0|0|0|0|0|1|2|3|4|5|6|7|8|

Divisor

|+|
|0|0|0|0|2|0|6|0|8|9|

|+| L |+| R
|1|2|3|4|5|6|7|8|9|0|2|4|6|8|1|3|5|7|9|9|

Divisor

|−|
|6|5|4|3|2|1|0|9|8|7|

CODING ARITHMETIC AND SHIFT OPERATIONS

Illegal divisions:

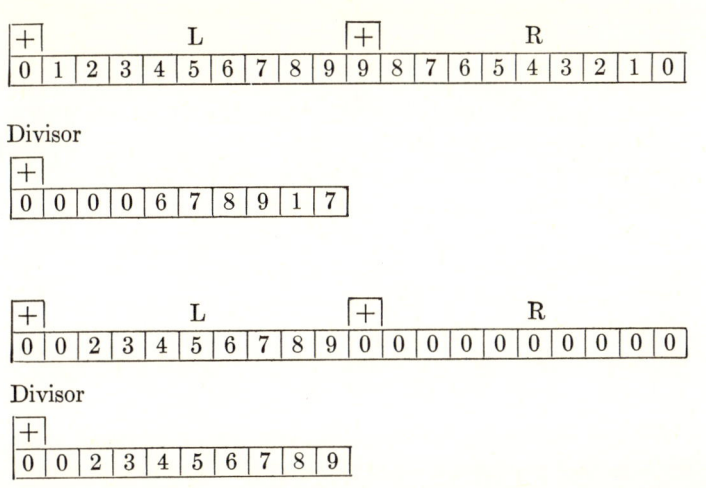

+				L						+				R					
0	1	2	3	4	5	6	7	8	9	9	8	7	6	5	4	3	2	1	0

Divisor

+									
0	0	0	0	6	7	8	9	1	7

+				L						+				R					
0	0	2	3	4	5	6	7	8	9	0	0	0	0	0	0	0	0	0	0

Divisor

+									
0	0	2	3	4	5	6	7	8	9

If the details of the Multiply and Divide instructions are a little hazy at this point, don't worry about it. All we are really trying to accomplish by this discussion is to take a little of the mystery out of digital computers, and to show that no matter how complex an operation may appear, it *can* be precisely defined. In fact, it is rather seldom that a coder needs to know this much detail about how his machine operates—but many coders *like* to know even if they do not *need* to know. And, as pointed out above, it may help in some cases to have a *general* idea of how multiplication and division work.

5.4 Shift Operations

It is very frequently necessary in data processing to shift numbers or alpha-numeric quantities in the arithmetic registers. We have seen briefly in Chapter 2 that it is often necessary to store more than one piece of information in a word, particularly on tape, to save space. When such a word is to be operated on, the parts must somehow be separated. This section presents one method of doing so; Section 6.3 presents a somewhat more convenient method. Similar problems arise in "packing" two or more pieces of information into one word preparatory to putting the word on tape. Another application of shifting is in arithmetic. One of our first examples will deal with producing the rounded quotient mentioned in the previous section. As a final example of the use of shifting, we may note that it is possible to multiply or divide by powers of ten by shifting. For instance, $123.45 shifted two places left becomes $12,345.00. When this trick applies, it can save a little machine time over multiplication.

In DATAC two methods of shifting are available. One is to use the ordinary shift instructions, which almost all real computers have. (Machines which do not have shift orders have an altogether different arrangement of the arithmetic registers.) The other is a system of shifting numbers as they are brought from memory to the arithmetic registers or vice versa. At the time of writing, the latter was available in somewhat different form on two machines.

There are basically only two types of ordinary shift instructions on DATAC, but variations specified by the suboperation code make seven distinct shifts. The two basic shifts are left and right, specified by operation codes of L and R. (The left and right here refer to the *direction of the shift*, not to the L and R registers.) The variations determine handling of the sign characters, whether both L and R or only R shift, and whether a rounding function is included with the shift.

Perhaps the simplest place to start is with Shift only R right (operation code: OR), which shifts the number in the R register only to the right, not including the sign character. The "only" R implies that the L register is completely unaffected. This is frequently used in arithmetic operations. For instance, suppose that a man's straight time pay of $78.50 and his total hours worked of 46.87 are packed into 1150 as follows:

$$+0078504687$$

In 1151 are his overtime earnings of $20.22 as +0000002022. It is necessary to shift the packed quantity in 1150 four places right before adding to get total gross pay; otherwise the sum has no meaning. This can easily be done with the Only R right instruction.

At this point we come to a new concept. How is the machine to know how many places it should shift R? The answer lies in a different interpretation of the "address" of an instruction. Heretofore the address has always specified where to get a word in memory or where to store a result in memory. In a shift instruction it has no such meaning, but rather specifies the *number of shifts to be performed*. In the routine which follows, we have the instruction OR 0004. This means to shift R *four* characters right, without affecting the sign character. The four characters initially at the right end of the R register are lost, and four zeros are entered at the left. The routine might be:

CODING ARITHMETIC AND SHIFT OPERATIONS

1600		B	1150	Bring straight time earnings to R
1601	O	R	0004	Shift four places right
1602		A	1151	Add overtime earnings

The contents of the pertinent memory locations and the registers after the execution of each instruction:

INSTRUCTION LOCATION	1150	1151	R
1600	+0078504687	+0000002022	+0078504687
1601	+0078504687	+0000002022	+0000007850
1602	+0078504687	+0000002022	+0000009872

The instruction Shift only R left (operation code: OL), not including sign character, is quite similar except that it of course shifts in the other direction. No example will be given here.

The instruction Shift R right and round (operation code: RR) is used to *round* a number in R. For instance, RR 0001 shifts the number in the R register right one place and adds *one* to the last position of R if the digit originally in position one of R was five or greater. The one is *subtracted* if R is negative, i.e., negative numbers are correctly rounded. All this is done automatically, a part of the instruction execution. The averaging illustration of the previous section could be coded to give a rounded average as follows.

Suppose the total gross pay of $120,746.87 is in 0500, and 1472, the number of men on this week's payroll, is in 0700. The average gross pay is to be stored in 0950. +0000000000 is in 0450. The Fetch instruction in the following routine is analogous to Bring, except that it operates on the L register instead of R.

1010		F	0450	Fetch plus zero to L
1011		B	0500	Bring total gross pay to R
1012	O	L	0001	Shift gross pay one place left to give an extra digit in quotient
1013		D	0700	Divide by number of men to get average
1014	R	R	0001	Shift and round quotient
1015		S	0950	Store average

The contents of L and R after the execution of the instructions:

INSTRUCTION LOCATION	L	R
1010	+0000000000	Immaterial
1011	+0000000000	+0012074687
1012	+0000000000	+0120746870
1013	+0000000182	+0000082029
1014	+0000000182	+0000008203
1015	+0000000182	+0000008203

80   PROGRAMMING BUSINESS COMPUTERS

It is sometimes necessary to shift both L and R together as though they made up one long register. In DATAC there are four instructions which operate in this fashion. The first we shall consider is Shift all characters of L and R, including sign characters, right (operation code: AR). Zeros are entered in the sign position of L; characters shifted out of the L register sign position enter position 10 of L; characters shifted out of L enter the sign character of R and move from there to position 10 of R; characters shifted out of the right end of R are lost. This instruction is used in what is generally called *editing*. Editing has to do with the manipulation of words and quantities in preparation for storing them on tape in condensed, or packed, form, or in preparation for printing. In these cases the "sign" character is usually not a sign at all, but simply another character, as for instance in a name and address.

For an example, suppose we have in 0507 a man's name, with the first two characters allotted to initials and nine to last name. An example might be ABSMITHbbbb. The lower case b's are used to indicate *blanks*, characters which will not print on the printer. It is required to split the name into the two words 1157 and 1158 to appear as bbbbbbbbAbBbSMITHbbbb. Using the instructions Shift all characters right and Shift only R right and assuming that the constants +b000000000 and bbbbbbbbbb are in memory in 0410 and 0411, the routine could be:

1000		F	0507	Fetch name to L
1001	A	R	0010	Shift name partially into R
1002	O	R	0001	Insert zero between second initial and name
1003		A	0410	Replace zero with blank
1004		S	1158	Store second word of edited name
1005		B	0411	Bring blanks to R
1006	A	R	0001	Shift first initial into R sign character
1007		F	0411	Fetch blanks to L
1008	A	R	0009	Shift first initial to correct position of R
1009		S	1157	Store first word of edited name

The contents of L and R after the execution of each instruction are shown below. 0507 contains ABSMITHbbbb throughout and is not shown.

INSTRUCTION LOCATION	L	R
1000	A B S M I T H b b b b	Immaterial
1001	0 0 0 0 0 0 0 0 0 A	B S M I T H b b b b ?

(Continued on next page)

CODING ARITHMETIC AND SHIFT OPERATIONS 81

1002	0 0 0 0 0 0 0 0 0 A	B 0 S M I T H b b b b
1003	0 0 0 0 0 0 0 0 0 A	B b S M I T H b b b b
1004	0 0 0 0 0 0 0 0 0 A	B b S M I T H b b b b
1005	0 0 0 0 0 0 0 0 0 A	b b b b b b b b b b
1006	0 0 0 0 0 0 0 0 0 0	A b b b b b b b b b
1007	b b b b b b b b b b	A b b b b b b b b b
1008	0 0 0 0 0 0 0 0 b b	b b b b b b b b A b
1009	0 0 0 0 0 0 0 0 b b	b b b b b b b b A b

The question mark in the last character of R after instruction 1001 indicates that we do not know what character might have been left there by previous operations, but it makes no difference since the character will be shifted out of R. The replacement of a zero by a blank at instruction 1003 is based on the addition of alphabetic characters, as discussed on page 66. If this seems like a rather lengthy process simply to prepare a name for printing, welcome to the club. We shall see that short cuts are available which can simplify the routine somewhat, but there is still much of such manipulation required in electronic data processing. Such details can easily be overlooked by someone familiar with an application but not with computers, resulting in consternation at the processing time required by the computer, fast as it is, and the programming time required.

The instruction Shift all characters of L and R left, including sign characters (operation code: AL), is exactly analogous to Shift all characters right.

The instructions Shift characters of L and R right, except sign characters (operation code: ER), and Shift characters of L and R left, except sign characters (operation code: EL), are used in some arithmetic operations, and to move numbers from L to R or R to L. These shifts are similar to Shift all characters left and Shift all characters right, except that the sign characters do not shift—which is what is needed in shifting signed numbers instead of alpha-numeric quantities. Also, they have an effect on the sign characters. In Shift right except signs, the sign of R is made the same as that of L; in Shift left except signs, the sign of L is made the same as that of R. This sign-controlling function is necessary because without it there would be difficulty in using the results of a Shift right except signs or a Shift left except signs instruction if the signs of L and R were different. Observe that since the sign characters do not shift, the number of shifts required must be counted differently than in Shift all characters right and Shift all characters left. Moving the L register to R using Shift all right requires an address of eleven; with Shift right except signs, ten.

The question is frequently asked: "What happens if a shift of more than ten is given, say on an Only R right?" The answer is simply that the machine keeps shifting, entering zeros at the left, until it has shifted as many times as specified in the address. The result would of course be to clear the R register to zeros. The question then is: "Why provide the possibility of a shift of more than ten places?" Some machines do not, of course, but in others it is provided either because there is occasional need for it, or to provide flexibility in certain operations where the address of a shift instruction is sometimes *computed* (see Chapter 7). We shall have no occasion to do the latter in this book. We shall, however, sometimes want to shift more than ten places on a Shift right except signs or Shift left except signs, in order to move a quantity between the L and R registers. (It may be noted that there is sometimes a use for a shift of *zero* with these last two instructions. The net effect of such an instruction is to transfer the sign of one of the registers to the other; for instance, a Shift right except signs of zero transfers the sign of the L register to the sign of the R register.) Real computers have a variety of limits on the maximum number of allowable shifts; in DATAC we say that the limit is ninety-nine, which is based on the assumption that the machine would "look at" only the right two digits of the address of a shift instruction.

In DATAC it is often possible to avoid using separate shift instructions by shifting as part of some other instruction, using DATAC's *shift register*. This was shown in Figure 2 on page 51; we need not show it again because the concept of its operation is simple. On certain instructions where it is allowed, the word being transferred between memory and the arithmetic unit can be shifted right or left *during the transfer*. The sign character does not shift; thus transfer shift is analogous *in this sense* to Shift only R right, and Shift only R left. Whether to perform this transfer shift, which direction, and how many characters, is specified (in the instructions where it is allowed) by the suboperation code. Recall that each character of a DATAC word is represented by six binary digits and that the left two are conventionally called the zone bits and the right four the numeric bits. If no transfer shift is to be performed, the suboperation code is zero, which in DATAC is represented by six binary zeros. If the transfer shift is *right,* the zone bits are 01; if *left,* 10. The number of shifts is contained in binary form in the numeric bits, which, although it may not be obvious, implies that the maximum number of characters of transfer shift is nine, which is all that could ever be needed. This is the *machine* representation, which obviously would be a bit unwieldy to write on a coding sheet. We shall, instead, show the transfer-

CODING ARITHMETIC AND SHIFT OPERATIONS

shift suboperation code as a plus or minus and one of the digits one through nine: the plus indicates a right shift, minus indicates left. The digit is the number of shifts. In Chapter 14 we shall learn how such a notation might easily be transformed into the form the machine requires.

Table 1 summarizes the possible shifts, the binary form in which the suboperation codes would appear in the instructions in the machine, the form in which we shall write the suboperation code in coding, and the letter of the alphabet which the binary form would represent if the suboperation code were taken as an ordinary DATAC character.

TABLE 1

NUMBER AND DIRECTION OF SHIFT	BINARY FORM	CODING FORM	DATAC LETTER
None	000000	Blank	Zero
Right 1 place	010001	+1	A
2	010010	+2	B
3	010011	+3	C
4	010100	+4	D
5	010101	+5	E
6	010110	+6	F
7	010111	+7	G
8	011000	+8	H
9	011001	+9	I
Left 1 place	100001	−1	J
2	100010	−2	K
3	100011	−3	L
4	100100	−4	M
5	100101	−5	N
6	100110	−6	O
7	100111	−7	P
8	101000	−8	Q
9	101001	−9	R

Transfer shifting is allowed in all arithmetic operations except Add to memory and Subtract from memory. It is of course not allowed on shift instructions, since there is no transfer of information between memory and the arithmetic unit. This is why there is no ambiguity in assigning the suboperation code a different meaning on shift instructions.

Two of the previous examples are shown below, rewritten to use transfer shifting. The first is the one shown on page 78, in which it was necessary to "discard" four characters at the right of the word in 1150 before adding the number in 1151. The routine is now:

LOC.	S	O	ADDRESS	REMARKS
1600	+4	B	1150	Bring straight time earnings to R, shifted
1601		A	1151	Add overtime earnings

The contents of R after each instruction:

INSTRUCTION	R REGISTER
1600	+0000007850
1601	+0000009872

The example shows that the word in 1150 was shifted four places right during the transfer from memory, which discarded the right four characters and moved the others into the desired position in R.

The second example is the rounded average problem shown on page 79.

LOC.	S	O	ADDRESS	REMARKS
1010		F	0450	Fetch plus zero to L
1011	−1	B	0500	Bring total gross pay to R, shifted
1012		D	0700	Divide by number of men to get average
1013	R	R	0001	Shift and round quotient
1014		S	0950	Store average

5.5 Decimal Point Location

With the previous parts of this chapter as background, it should not be too difficult now to understand the simple rules of decimal point location.* The rules are not much more complicated than those we learned in grade school, but they perhaps appear in a different light as applied to computers.

The rule for addition and subtraction is simplicity itself; the numbers added or subtracted must have their decimal points in the same position. This is so familiar as to need little elaboration: it is obvious that we cannot get meaningful results from an addition such as

$$12.34$$
$$+45.678$$

*It should perhaps be pointed out that the point location problem in business data processing is somewhat simpler than in scientific and engineering calculations. In the latter it is often difficult to predict, even approximately, the maximum and minimum sizes of intermediate and final results. Also, the approach is different in that in most scientific problems the calculations are realized to be at best approximate and subject to errors caused by the accumulation of rounding errors, etc. Complex and/or time-consuming procedures have been devised to handle these problems. See D. D. McCracken, *Digital Computer Programming*, John Wiley, New York, 1957, Chapters 4 and 10. This is not to say that the same problems do not sometimes cause trouble in business data processing, but they are at least less frequent.

CODING ARITHMETIC AND SHIFT OPERATIONS

In business data processing we are commonly dealing with quantities expressed in dollars, or dollars and cents, or hundredths of an hour, or whole numbers such as the number of a particular item currently in stock. Under such conditions, the only problems in addition and subtraction arise from packing or in using the results of multiplications or divisions. Where decimal points are not correct before addition or subtraction, they may be aligned by appropriate shift instructions or transfer shifts.

Multiplication is only slightly more complex. The rule may be stated thus: the number of places to the right of the decimal point of the product is the sum of the number of places to the right of the decimal points of the factors. As an example of this fairly obvious rule, suppose a man's hourly pay rate of $1.9862 is in 1000, his overtime hours of 8.00 is in 1001, and the constant 1.5 (time-and-a-half for overtime) is in 0800. A routine to calculate the man's overtime earnings, rounded to the nearest cent, and store it in 1002, might be:

LOC.	S	O	ADDRESS	REMARKS
1507		B	1000	Bring pay rate to R
1508		X	1001	Multiply by overtime hours
1509		X	0800	Multiply by 1.5
1510	R	R	0005	Shift and round overtime earnings
1511		S	1002	Store

Contents of pertinent registers with carets ($_\wedge$) used to indicate the assumed decimal point location:

INSTRUCTION LOCATION	1000	1001	0800	R
1507	+000001$_\wedge$9862	+00000008$_\wedge$00	+000000001$_\wedge$5	+000001$_\wedge$9862
1508	+000001$_\wedge$9862	+00000008$_\wedge$00	+000000001$_\wedge$5	+0015$_\wedge$889600
1509	+000001$_\wedge$9862	+00000008$_\wedge$00	+000000001$_\wedge$5	+023$_\wedge$8344000
1510	+000001$_\wedge$9862	+00000008$_\wedge$00	+000000001$_\wedge$5	+00000023$_\wedge$83
1511	+000001$_\wedge$9862	+00000008$_\wedge$00	+000000001$_\wedge$5	+00000023$_\wedge$83

The rule for division is the reverse of that for multiplication: the number of places to the right of the decimal point of the quotient is the number of places to the right of the decimal point of the dividend minus the number of places to the right of the decimal point of the divisor. Without writing programs, a few examples will show the application of this rule, as the results would be obtained in the computer, assuming L contains zeros to start.

$$\frac{+0120746_\wedge 870}{+0000001472_\wedge} = +0000082_\wedge 029$$

(Three places in dividend minus zero places in divisor equals three places in quotient.)

$$\frac{+12_\wedge 34567899}{+00001_\wedge 98023} = +000006_\wedge 234 \qquad (8-5=3)$$

$$\frac{+12_\wedge 34567899}{+00001980_\wedge 23} = +0000_\wedge 006234 \qquad (8-2=6)$$

It cannot be emphasized too strongly that the carets ($_\wedge$) shown in these examples do not exist in memory. In some machines there can be in memory what *amounts to* a decimal or binary point which the machine takes into account in arithmetic, but not in DATAC. The DATAC character "*.*" is used *only* for indicating decimal points or periods in printing, and has no relation whatsoever to the decimal point location problem. The word +00000019862 can mean $1.9862 per hour, $198.62, 19,862 items in stock, 0.019862 volt, or anything else, depending on the application. It is the responsibility of the coder to arrange the calculation so that decimal points are handled correctly. If one dollar amount is stored in memory as +000876$_\wedge$4100 and another as +00000017$_\wedge$82 and the two are added, the machine can give no warning of the error—since there is no decimal point indication in memory. The sum would appear in R as +0008765882; in this instance it *is* a totally meaningless number, but in another case it might be quite correct.

It may not be inappropriate to mention at this point a problem which is related to decimal points and rounding. Suppose two men both earn $1.8207 per hour. One worked 38.02 hours, the other 34.67 hours. Multiplying and rounding separately to arrive at earnings, we get $69.22 and $63.12 which add to $132.34. However, if we first add the hours worked to obtain 72.69 hours and then multiply and round, we get a figure of $132.35—which is one cent higher. This is a simple example of the *accumulation of round-off errors*, also called *breakage:* depending on the numbers, the sum of the two individual products may not be the same as the product obtained by adding before multiplying. On the average, round-off errors cancel each other: some round high and some low. But the "on the average" is misleading; it does not mean that the errors will always *exactly* cancel. Such problems must be very carefully considered in setting up accuracy-checking procedures and elsewhere.

Further examples of decimal point location problems appear in the next section.

5.6 Coding Example

For an illustration of how some of the instructions studied so far might be used in an application, we shall consider a small part of a

CODING ARITHMETIC AND SHIFT OPERATIONS

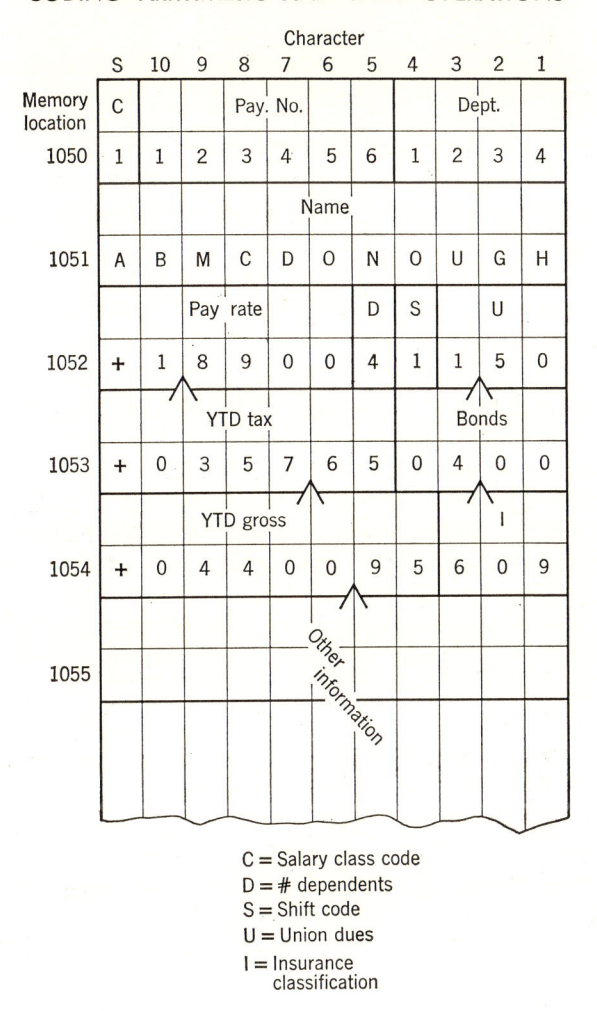

	S	10	9	8	7	6	5	4	3	2	1
Memory location				Pay. No.					Dept.		
1050	C	1	2	3	4	5	6	1	2	3	4
					Name						
1051		A	B	M	C	D	O	N	O	U	G	H
			Pay rate					D	S		U	
1052	+	1	8	9	0	0	4	1	1	5	0
					YTD tax				Bonds		
1053	+	0	3	5	7	6	5	0	4	0	0
					YTD gross					I
1054	+	0	4	4	0	0	9	5	6	0	9
				Other information							
1055											

C = Salary class code
D = # dependents
S = Shift code
U = Union dues
I = Insurance classification

Figure 3. Record format of an illustrative payroll master file. The sample values shown have no special meaning.

payroll calculation. We shall assume that we have in memory the master payroll file information for a man, plus his gross pay for the current week. We are required to compute his withholding tax, and his new year-to-date (YTD) gross earnings and tax. The current week's tax must also be edited for printing.

The United States withholding tax calculation may not be familiar to all readers. At the present time, an allowable calculation for weekly payrolls is 18% of the amount left after subtracting from the gross pay $13.00 for each dependent claimed by the employee. As a formula:

88 PROGRAMMING BUSINESS COMPUTERS

Tax = (0.18) × [gross pay − ($13.00) × (# dependents)]

In a real payroll problem, it would be most unwise to apply this formula blindly. A man who worked only a few hours could easily earn less than the amount allowed as exemption for dependents, which by the formula would give a negative tax! Testing for this possibility, however, would require instructions not yet introduced.

Suppose that the parts of the payroll master file we need are in memory with a partial record layout as shown in Figure 3. (This record layout is not intended to be representative, but simply to provide coding practice. See Chapter 2 for a discussion of record layout.)

It is required to add this week's gross pay to the figure for total YTD, and similarly update the YTD tax. The tax must be edited for printing, to appear as bbbbb$06.78 in 1650.

This week's gross pay is in 1207 as +00000089ʌ67. The constant 18% is in 0896 as +00000000ʌ18, the constant $13.00 as +00000013ʌ00 is in 0897, the editing constant bbbbb$00.00 is in 0910.

The routine could be:

LOC.	S	O	ADDRESS	REMARKS
0500	−5	B	1052	Bring number of dependents to R, transfer shifting to discard pay rate
0501	O	R	0009	Shift to position 1, discarding union dues
0502		X	0897	Multiply by $13.00
0503		S	1350	Store temporarily
0504		B	1207	Bring gross pay to R
0505		M	1350	Subtract exemptions
0506		X	0896	Multiply by 18% to get tax
0507	R	R	0002	Round to nearest cent
0508	O	L	0004	Shift to prepare to update YTD tax
0509	X	A	1053	Add to YTD tax
0510	E	L	0004	Shift dollars into L
0511	O	R	0008	Cents in position 2-1
0512		S	1351	Store temporarily
0513	E	R	0007	Dollars in position 5-4, cents discarded
0514		S	1650	Store temporarily in location of edited tax
0515		B	0910	Bring editing constant to R
0516		A	1351	Add in cents
0517	X	A	1650	Add in dollars, return edited tax to memory
0518	−3	B	1207	Bring gross to R. Shift to line up with master file
0519	X	A	1054	Update YTD gross

Assuming the values given previously, the contents of L, R, and the pertinent memory locations are:

CODING ARITHMETIC AND SHIFT OPERATIONS

INSTRUCTION LOCATION	MEMORY LOCATION	MEMORY CONTENTS	L	R
0500	1052	+1890041150	Immaterial	+4115000000
0501	No memory reference		Immaterial	+0000000004
0502	0897	+00000013$_\wedge$00	+0000000000	+00000052$_\wedge$00
0503	1350	+00000052$_\wedge$00	+0000000000	+00000052$_\wedge$00
0504	1207	+00000089$_\wedge$67	+0000000000	+00000089$_\wedge$67
0505	1350	+00000052$_\wedge$00	+0000000000	+00000037$_\wedge$67
0506	0896	+00000000$_\wedge$18	+0000000000	+000006$_\wedge$7806
0507	No memory reference		+0000000000	+00000006$_\wedge$78
0508	No memory reference		+0000000000	+0006$_\wedge$780000
0509	1053	+0364$_\wedge$430400	+0000000000	+0006$_\wedge$780000
0510	No memory reference		+0000000006	+7800000000
0511	No memory reference		+0000000006	+0000000078
0512	1351	+0000000078	+0000000006	+0000000078
0513	No memory reference		+0000000000	+0000006000
0514	1650	+0000006000	+0000000000	+0000006000
0515	0910	bbbbb$00.00	+0000000000	bbbbb$00.00
0516	1351	+0000000078	+0000000000	bbbbb$00.78
0517	1650	bbbbb$06.78	+0000000000	bbbbb$00.78
0518	1207	+0000008967	+0000000000	+00089$_\wedge$67000
0519	1054	+04490$_\wedge$62609	+0000000000	+00089$_\wedge$67000

Remember in following the program above that an Add to memory instruction leaves R unchanged, and that in an addition where nonnumeric characters are present, signs are ignored and the R sign character is unchanged.

It should be noted that some of the methods used in this program are more complicated than is necessary, but the instructions required to simplify the procedure have not been presented yet.

5.7 Summary

This chapter has described some of the basic concepts of coding, which is the process of telling a computer how to solve data processing problems. The reader at this point should know in detail how each of the instructions discussed so far works. We have not recounted how a machine would go about the execution of the various functions electronically. This may cause some feeling that the information presented so far has an insecure base, but it need not. The reader who has an interest in the internal operation of computers can find several readable books listed in the bibliography.

We have so far talked almost completely in terms of DATAC. This machine design, the authors feel, is representative of the major trends in computer building, but of course it cannot have all the characteristics of all available equipment. Some real computers have much more complex and powerful instructions; some cannot operate directly on alpha-numeric characters; some have markedly different main and auxiliary memories; a significant minority use instructions having more than one address per instruction. By and large, however, the fundamental principles of coding and of problem organization apply equally to all machines. The specific characteristics of a real computer must of course be known in order to be able to program for it, but we feel that the difficulty of learning the particulars of another machine after mastering the basic principles of DATAC or any real equipment is much smaller than the difficulty of learning the first machine.

It might be well to point out once again that the specific addresses and program locations in these and later examples are completely arbitrary. When we show a routine beginning at 1200, there is nothing significant about the 1200; it was picked at random to be able to show something specific. The program must of course be *somewhere* in memory before it can be executed, but exactly where it goes is at the option of the programmer and depends on memory allocation questions which are independent of machine operation. We shall look into these questions later, and shall find, for instance, that the exact memory assignment of data and instructions is often made by the machine itself under the control of a special program.

Exercises

In Exercises 1–8, assume that the following quantities are in the memory locations shown. In each case write a routine to calculate the quantity stated, and place the result in location 1200.

QUANTITY	VALUE	LOCATION
a	+0000001234	0900
b	+0000000901	0917
c	+0000000891	0918
d	+0000000605	0950
e	+0000088602	0951
zero	+0000000000	0960
one	+0000000001	0961
two	+0000000002	0962

1. a + b + c
2. a + c + d
3. b − d

CODING ARITHMETIC AND SHIFT OPERATIONS 91

4. $2(a + b + 1)$

5. $a \cdot b \cdot d$

6. $\dfrac{a + b}{2}$

7. $\dfrac{(a \cdot c) - (b \cdot d)}{a + b}$ (Will the values shown cause divide overflow?)

8. $\dfrac{a \cdot e^2}{2}$ (Divide overflow?)

In Exercises 9–13, assume the record layout shown in the adjacent figure. Without using transfer shifting, write routines to carry out the calculations indicated and store the sum in memory location 1601. For each calculation, draw a diagram showing the contents of the arithmetic registers after the execution of each instruction of your routine.

Memory location	S	10	9	8	7	6	5	4	3	2	1
1607			Nuts				Bolts				
	+	1	0	2	0	3	4	5	4	3	2
1608			Nails				Washers				
	+	9	7	5	3	1	2	3	4	5	6
1609			Pins		Keys			Locks			
	+	4	6	2	4	8	1	1	2	2	3

Character

9. Bolts + Locks.
10. Nuts + Nails + Pins.
11. Nuts + Bolts.
12. Pins + Keys + Locks.
13. Nuts + Washers + Keys.
14. Rewrite Exercises 9–13 using transfer shifting.

15. In memory location 0257 is the quantity xx535221583, where the x's represent irrelevant characters. This is actually a social security number; preparatory to printing, it must be placed in location 0270 in the form 535-22-1583. Write a routine to perform this editing. Assume locations for the minus sign(s) which will be needed, for the dashes in the number.

In Exercises 16–20, assume that the following quantities are in memory as shown. Write routines to carry out the calculation indicated, and in each case store the result in location 1995. Decimal points must be considered. In each case draw a diagram showing the contents of the arithmetic registers after the execution of each instruction of your routine.

PROGRAMMING BUSINESS COMPUTERS

QUANTITY	VALUE	LOCATION
g	+0000128∧907	1984
h	+00000096∧75	1985
k	+00000018∧95	1986
m	+0000000027∧	1987
two	+00000002∧00	1990
two	+0000000002∧	1991

16. $g + h - k$

17. $g \cdot m$

18. $\dfrac{h + k}{m}$

19. $2(h + k + 2)$

20. $g + h + k + m$, rounded to zero decimal places, i.e., the correct sum is +0000000272.

21. Given:

LOCATION	S 10 9 8 7	6 5 4 3 2 1
	Reg. Hrs.	Emp. No.
0398	+ 4 0∧0	7 6 5 4 3 2 1
	OT Hrs.	YTD Gross Earnings
0399	+ 0 6∧0	0 3 9 6 2∧4 0
	Reg. Rate/Hr.	Wk's Gross Earn.
0400	+ 2∧2 2 2	0 0 0 0∧0 0

(a) Compute week's gross pay and store, rounded to nearest cent, in the appropriate field of 0400. (Overtime is paid at time and a half.)

(b) Update YTD gross earnings to include this week's gross pay. You may use any constants you specify.

22. Do the example on page 79 without using the Shift right and round instruction.

23. Discuss and distinguish between the following:
(a) Problem definition.
(b) Flow charting.
(c) Coding.

24. Conceptually, there is little difference between the tasks of coding a general-purpose computer and engineering a special-purpose computer. The problem logic in the case of the stored program computer is in memory. The problem logic in the special-purpose computer is built into the actual hardware. Discuss the pros and cons of these two approaches.

25. Describe what is meant by the following terms:
(a) Memory location.
(b) Word.

CODING ARITHMETIC AND SHIFT OPERATIONS

(c) Instruction.
(d) Operand.
(e) Address.
(f) Register.
(g) Trigger.

26. Does the location of an instruction actually appear in memory?

27. Discuss the four groups of computer instructions. Give five DATAC examples of each group.

28. What is the difference between the location of a word and the contents of a word? Can the contents contain a location?

29. Describe the instruction format and the arithmetic operations of DATAC. Describe the same for two actual computers.

30. Describe the actual sequence of suboperations when DATAC executes these instructions:
(a) Add.
(b) Shift only R right.
(c) Divide.

31. List all the operation codes for DATAC discussed in this chapter that may turn on the overflow trigger.

32. Discuss the rules that help to locate the decimal point for division and multiplication.

33. Does shifting usually precede or follow multiplication? How about division? Why?

34. Does the computer know or distinguish whether a word stored in memory is a constant or instruction? Can arithmetic and other operations be performed on instructions?

35. The type of instructions DATAC offers are average in logic level. It the suboperations which make up the sequence of an operation are made accessible to programmers, this becomes micro-coding logic, i.e., a level of logic below the average. On the other hand, if we make accessible to programmers instructions which do the work of many average instructions, we have macro-coding logic, i.e., a level of logic above the average. Discuss.

36. Why is it desirable to pack more than one piece of information into a word? What are the disadvantages?

37. Why is it necessary to clear either L or R to zeros if only ten digits are used for the dividend?

38. How may the following be accomplished without using the multiply and divide instructions?
(a) Multiply by 2.
(b) Multiply by 54.
(c) Multiply by 100.
(d) Divide by 10.
(e) A number multiplied by itself.

39. Could it make a difference to DATAC'S calculating time which of two numbers to be multiplied was the multiplicand or multiplier? Explain.

40. Some computers use only four bits to represent a character. How many different characters could be represented in such a system? If two four-bit characters were used to represent alpha-numeric information, what would be the advantages and disadvantages compared to the DATAC representation?

6 FURTHER CODING OPERATIONS

6.0 Introduction

The previous chapter discussed only arithmetic and shift instructions. Now we proceed to the subject of decision instructions, which make it possible for the machine to choose between two or more alternative courses of action on the basis of data values or computed results. The chapter continues to the DATAC instructions which facilitate the preparation of results in an easily readable form, which is usually called *editing*. It concludes with a discussion of some of the operations used in working with magnetic tapes, and an example which uses most of the instructions presented so far.

6.1 Decision Instructions

It is very frequently necessary in electronic data processing to make choices. A good example is the calculation of U.S. Federal Insurance Contributions Act tax (social security) in a payroll application. This is currently $2\frac{1}{2}\%$ of gross salary, but it applies only to the first $4800 of annual salary. The "decision" which the computer must make is clearly: has a man earned $4800 yet this year? Then it must proceed into one of two alternative calculations on the basis of the decision. Dozens of similar examples could be cited. Another type of decision has to do with the problem organization of one common method of data processing. In this method all the "items" (information about one man in a payroll, for instance) are stored on a master file tape in ascending sequence according to some identifying code such as payroll number. The master file must be "read" in its entirety at least once, each time the problem is run. It is necessary to match the master file items with the new information coming into the system, such as hours worked. But not all master file items are "active" in a given run; for instance, some employees may be sick. How is the computer to make the match? It is unfortunately a bit more complicated than instructing a clerk to "pull from the file the payroll record corresponding to each time card." The heart of the matching process is usually the type of decision operation we are considering.

Probably the most typical situation is where we need to know whether one number is greater than, equal to, or less than another. The example coded below is the FICA calculation, in which it is necessary to know whether the gross pay earned to date in the current year is greater than $4800. In DATAC the decisions involved require the use of the *Compare* instruction and some of the *conditional jump* instructions.

The Compare R and memory instruction compares the word in the R register with the word in memory specified by the address of the instruction. If the word in R is greater than the word in memory, the *high* indicator is turned on; if equal, the *equal* indicator is turned on; if the word in R is less than the word in memory, the *low* indicator is turned on. These indicators, which are alternatively called triggers, flip-flops, or switches, may be thought of simply as electronic devices which can "remember" the result of a comparison. One of the three indicators is always turned on by the Compare instruction; the other two are turned off. The actual decision, in a sense, is made by the conditional jump instructions. A Compare instruction is followed, usually immediately, by a High jump, Equal jump, or Low jump, or some combination of them.

The various jump instructions are quite different from any studied in the previous chapter, which had to do with the manipulation of data. A conditional jump tests for the presence of some condition in the machine, and then if the condition does exist, "jumps" out of the normal one-after-the-other sequence in which instructions are usually taken. For instance a High jump tests whether the high indicator is on. If it is, the next instruction is taken from the location specified by the address of the High jump; if the high indicator is off, the next instruction is taken in normal sequence. (In either case, in DATAC, the indicator is unaffected.)

Consider the following example. Location 0800 contains +0000000008, 0700 contains +0000000007.

1000		B	0800	Bring 8 to R
1001		C	0700	Compare with 7
1002	H	J	1200	
1200				

FURTHER CODING OPERATIONS

Content of registers and condition of indicators:

INST. LOC.	MEMORY LOC.	MEMORY	R	\multicolumn{3}{c}{INDICATORS}
				High	Equal	Low
1000	0800	+0000000008	+0000000008	\multicolumn{3}{c}{Immaterial}
1001	0700	+0000000007	+0000000008	On	Off	Off
1002			+0000000008	On	Off	Off
1200						

In this example the word in the R register is greater than the word in memory specified by the Compare instruction, so the high indicator is turned on and the other two are turned off. The High jump causes the machine to inspect the high indicator, and since it was *on* the next instruction is taken from 1200 (the address of the High jump instruction) instead of 1003 as normally. If the comparison had been set up in reverse order, i.e., the 7 brought to R and compared with 8, the low indicator would have been turned on and the others off. The High jump would then have found the high indicator off and the jump would not have been executed, i.e., the next instruction would have been taken from 1003 as usual. This is the meaning of a "conditional" jump; it breaks out of the sequential execution of instructions if and only if some specified condition in the machine exists.

The example given above involved numeric quantities, i.e., the sign digits contained signs and the other ten characters of each word were decimal digits. If there are any alphabetic or punctuation characters in either word, DATAC will regard both words as eleven-character positive words. In such a case there must be a definition of what constitutes "greater"; for example, is the letter K greater or less than a dollar sign? Any sequence is somewhat arbitrary, especially the sequence arrived at by simply accepting the one that happens to be easiest for the machine designers. In DATAC we assume a sequence which we believe fairly well fits the needs of many applications. The sequence of the characters in ascending order is: blank, zero through nine, A through Z, decimal point (or period), comma, dollar sign, asterisk, left parenthesis, right parenthesis, minus sign, plus sign. This is called the *collation sequence* of the DATAC characters and is the same order as the allowable characters in DATAC listed on page 59. Thus K is less than $ in this sense. The comparison is made by applying this sequence to each character, but characters to the left carry more weight. For instance, RB is greater than KZ even though Z is greater than B—just as 42 is greater than 39 even though 9 is greater than 2. Thus it is possible to use the Compare instruction as part of a program to alphabetize information in memory. And since blank is at the low end of the sorting sequence,

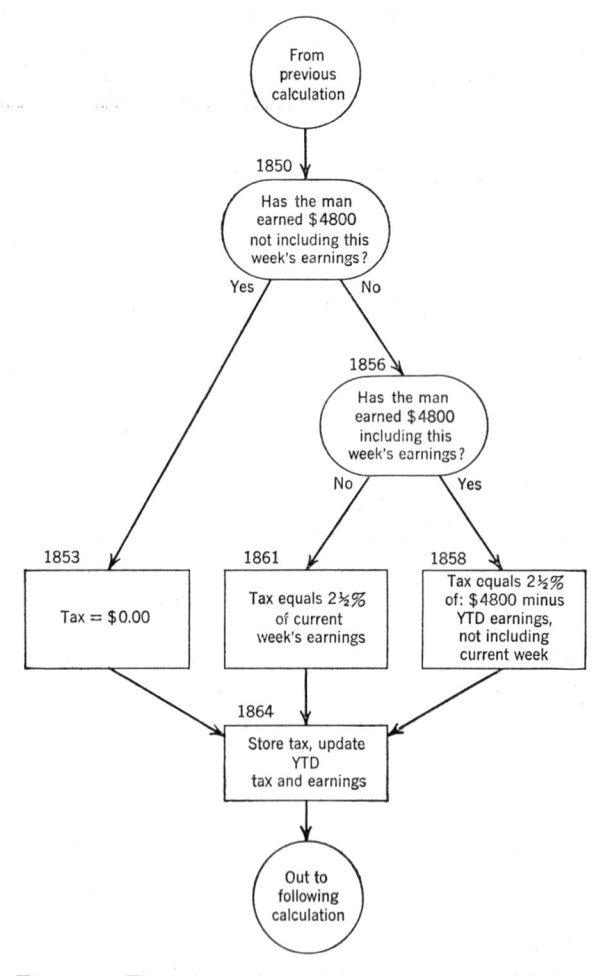

Figure 1. Flow chart of a social security tax calculation.

short names would be placed ahead of long names; for example, SMITH is "less" than SMITHSON according to the Compare instruction.

If there are no nonnumeric characters in the word and both the sign characters contain signs, the comparison is algebraic. That is, any positive number is greater than any negative number, and the comparison is "reversed" for two negative numbers. Examples:

FURTHER CODING OPERATIONS

$+50$ is greater than $+23$
$+50$ is greater than -79
$+00$ is greater than -00
-16 is greater than -40

Plus zero being greater than minus zero makes no sense mathematically, but the machine does have to put some sign on every result.

The FICA calculation requires us to define all the possible conditions and how each is to be handled—as do all decision situations. To repeat, the rule of calculation is that the tax is $2\frac{1}{2}\%$ of gross pay,* except that the maximum taxable earnings in any one year are $4800 (according to current law). In calculating the FICA deduction, we must consider three possibilities:

1. The man has earned $4800 or more before this week, in which case his FICA deduction is zero.

2. The man has not earned $4800 in the year including this week's pay, in which case his deduction is $2\frac{1}{2}\%$ of his current week's gross earnings.

3. Before this week he has not earned $4800, but including this week's pay he has, in which case his deduction is $2\frac{1}{2}\%$ of the difference between $4800 and his YTD earnings as of the previous week.†

This calculation is a very simple example of the many alternatives which are present in data processing. The *flow chart* (Chapter 3) of Figure 1 helps us to visualize these choices for this problem. The numbers above the boxes are the starting locations of the instructions in the computer routine (to follow) which carry out the functions specified by the boxes.

Assume the following storage assignments:

QUANTITY	MEMORY ADDRESS	ILLUSTRATIVE VALUE
Current week's earnings	0400	$+00000090\wedge 87$
YTD earnings, not including current week	0401	$+00004750\wedge 69$
YTD FICA tax, not including current week	0402	$+00000118\wedge 77$
Constant	0800	$+00004800\wedge 00$

(*Continued on next page*)

---

* More strictly, gross pay minus certain pay which is defined by law as not being taxable.

† In an actual payroll calculation, one would have to allow for the possibility that because of rounding errors the FICA tax accumulated week by week might not exactly equal $2\frac{1}{2}\%$ of $4800.

100 PROGRAMMING BUSINESS COMPUTERS

Constant	0801	+000000₍ₐ₎0250 (2½%)
Constant	0802	+00000000₍ₐ₎00
Current week's FICA tax	0403	To be computed
Updated YTD gross earnings	0401	To be computed and stored in original YTD earnings location
Updated YTD FICA tax	0402	To be computed and stored in original YTD FICA location
Temporary storage	0900	

With the preceding information we are almost ready to write a program. One more DATAC instruction is needed in the example: Unconditional jump (operation code: UJ). This instruction merely tells the machine to take the next instruction from the memory location specified in the address of the instruction. It is needed in conjunction with the conditional jumps, in situations where sections of a program do not follow each other in consecutive order.

LOC.	S	O	ADDRESS	INDEX	FILTER	MON.	REMARKS
1850		B	0401				Bring YTD earnings to R
1851		C	0800				Compare with $4800
1852	L	J	1855				Low jump if had not earned $4800 yet
1853		B	0802				Bring zero (no tax) to R
1854	U	J	1864				Unconditional jump to section which stores tax and updates
1855		A	0400				Add current week's earnings to get total earnings to date
1856		C	0800				Compare with $4800
1857	L	J	1861				Low jump if still has not earned $4800 yet
1858		B	0800				Bring $4800 to R
1859		M	0401				Subtract previous YTD to get taxable portion of this week's earnings
1860	U	J	1862				Unconditional jump to calculate FICA
1861		B	0400				Bring current week's earnings to R
1862		X	0801				Multiply by 2½%
1863	R	R	0004				Shift R to right and round
1864		S	0403				Store tax
1865	X	A	0402				Add to memory to update YTD FICA
1866		B	0400				Bring current week's earnings to R
1867	X	A	0401				Add to memory to update YTD earnings

FURTHER CODING OPERATIONS

Shown below are the contents of pertinent registers after the execution of each instruction under one of the three alternatives, namely the one which would be taken for the illustrative values listed on page 99. Note that not all the instructions are executed for any one alternative.

INST. LOC.	MEMORY LOC.	MEMORY CONTENTS	R
1850	0401	$+00004750_\wedge 69$	$+00004750_\wedge 69$
1851	0800	$+00004800_\wedge 00$	$+00004750_\wedge 69$
1852	No memory reference		$+00004750_\wedge 69$
1855	0400	$+00000090_\wedge 87$	$+00004841_\wedge 56$
1856	0800	$+00004800_\wedge 00$	$+00004841_\wedge 56$
1857	No memory reference		$+00004841_\wedge 56$
1858	0800	$+00004800_\wedge 00$	$+00004800_\wedge 00$
1859	0401	$+00004750_\wedge 69$	$+00000049_\wedge 31$
1860	No memory reference		$+00000049_\wedge 31$
1862	0801	$+000000_\wedge 0250$	$+0001_\wedge 232750$
1863	No memory reference		$+00000001_\wedge 23$
1864	0403	$+00000001_\wedge 23$	$+00000001_\wedge 23$
1865	0402	$+00000120_\wedge 00$	$+00000001_\wedge 23$
1866	0400	$+00000090_\wedge 87$	$+00000090_\wedge 87$
1867	0401	$+00004841_\wedge 56$	$+00000090_\wedge 87$

The reader will find it instructive to follow the calculation paths for the other two possibilities.

It should be pointed out, in case it is not obvious, that the routine shown here is by no means the only way to obtain the correct answer to the problem. And the same is true for all coding. Often, alternative programs which get the same answer are not equally desirable from other standpoints, however. We shall see repeatedly in later chapters that there are economic choices to be made; for example, is a program which requires little memory space for instructions and constants, but which is slow, better or worse than one which requires more space but which is faster? The answer depends on the circumstances of the application and the machine, and is not the central issue at the moment; the point is that whether the differences are important or not, many different programs can be written to accomplish a given purpose. Sometimes the differences are totally inconsequential: whether A is added to B or B added to A, the sum is the same. (This, incidentally, is one reason why it is difficult to write "solutions" to exercises in a book on programming. The student is apt to believe that the sample solution is the only possible one, or to think it is best—without knowing how to evaluate "best" in a given situation.)

6.2 Other Jump Instructions

We have so far discussed four of DATAC's jump instructions. The other five test various conditions in the machine and present no special conceptual problems.

The Jump if R is plus (operation code: PJ) instruction inspects the sign of the R register and takes the next instruction from the location specified by the address of the jump instruction if the R register is plus. The Jump if R is minus (MJ) instruction is the reverse. Jump if R is zero (ZJ) jumps if R contains zero. The sign character is completely ignored. Jump if R is not zero (NJ) is the reverse of Jump if R is zero. These four of course are redundant, in that some of them could be eliminated at the expense of only minor programming inconvenience. However, having assumed the existence of circuits to carry out Jump if R is plus, say, Jump if R is minus would require only a very little extra circuitry, so the assumption of the variety of jumps is not unreasonable. To illustrate that it is possible to "get by" with fewer jumps, and to show how they might be used, consider the following.

It is occasionally possible in a payroll application to arrive at a *negative* net pay! If large numbers of deductions such as taxes, bonds, union dues, salary advance repayments, insurance, etc., were to coincide with a pay period in which a man had been sick most of the time and was not eligible for sick pay, deductions could exceed the gross pay. (The solution is to have a priority for the various deductions, and postpone the least pressing deductions.) Although such a situation is not very common, it is definitely likely enough that it must be tested for to avoid occasionally printing a "deposit slip" instead of a check!

A possible method of testing for this eventuality would be to see if the R register is negative after subtracting each deduction. If the difference is negative, difficulty is signaled and a jump must be executed to a section of the program which corrects the situation and somehow stores the fact that the deduction should be taken from the *following* check. We shall not be concerned here with how the correction routine would be set up.

Suppose the following quantities have already been calculated and have been stored in memory as follows:

FURTHER CODING OPERATIONS

QUANTITY	LOCATION
Gross pay	1000
Withholding tax	1150
FICA	1151
Salary advance	1152
Bonds	1153
Union dues	1154
Insurance	1155

A possible routine is shown below. Observe that withholding and FICA cannot by themselves exceed gross pay, so a test need not be made after subtracting these.

LOC.	S	O	ADDRESS	INDEX	FILTER	MON.	REMARKS
1680		B	1000				Bring gross pay to R
1681		M	1150				Subtract withholding tax
1682		M	1151				Subtract FICA
1683		M	1152				Subtract salary advance repayment
1684	M	J	xxxx				If minus, jump out to corrective routine (location unspecified)
1685		M	1153				Subtract bonds
1686	M	J	xxxx				If minus, jump out
Etc.

If there were only a Plus jump and no Minus jump, the routine could be rewritten:

1680		B	1000				Bring gross pay to R
1681		M	1150				Subtract withholding tax
1682		M	1151				Subtract FICA
1683		M	1152				Subtract salary advance repayment
1684	P	J	1686				If plus, jump around next instruction (to correction)
1685	U	J	xxxx				Unconditional jump to correction
1686		M	1153				Subtract bonds
1687	P	J	1689				If plus, jump around
1688	U	J	xxxx				Unconditional jump to correction
Etc.

As a final observation, note that the function could be carried out with the Compare instruction.

1680		B	1000				Bring gross pay to R
1681		M	1150				Subtract withholding tax
1682		M	1151				Subtract FICA

(Continued on next page)

1683		C	1152	Compare with salary advance repayment
1684	L	J	xxxx	Low jump to correction if remaining pay is less than deduction
1685		M	1152	Subtract salary advance repayment
1686		C	1153	Compare with bond deduction
1687	L	J	xxxx	Low jump to correction if remaining pay is less than bond deduction
1688 Etc.		M	1153	Subtract bond deduction

The corrective program would be slightly different for this version, since the condition is found before subtracting the deduction.

To be thorough, consideration would have to be given to the possibility that the net pay could be exactly zero—which would require a policy decision on what to put in the pay envelope. In addition to illustrating the use of two new instructions and some alternative ways of doing the same thing, this example once again points up the very careful planning which must go into a major computer application. In a normal payroll, a negative pay would be caught by the payroll clerk, who, even though he might not know offhand what to do, would at least point out the situation to his superiors. A computer program, without some such tests as we have been discussing, would most likely print a check in the amount of the negative pay. And probably without a minus sign either, because if the possibility were overlooked in the calculation proper, no provision would probably have been made in the editing section for providing minus signs.*

The last jump instruction to be considered here is the Jump if over-

---

*The story is told of a utility company whose computer billing system once sent out a bill for exactly zero dollars. The customer chuckled and discarded the bill. In a few weeks, however, he received a delinquent payment notice! Nothing had been fed into the system to tell the computer that the "bill" had been paid. The customer once again laughed and threw away the notice. When he received a notice (produced automatically, of course) that his electricity service was about to be discontinued, he decided to talk things over with the utility company.

At this point the process became nonautomatic, and the clerk he spoke with should simply have laughed with him and apologized. Unfortunately, however, the clerk followed the rules rigidly and told the man that the computer could not handle the matter unless he actually "paid" the bill! According to the story, which may be apocryphal at this point at least, the customer eventually had to write a check for zero dollars.

FURTHER CODING OPERATIONS

flow (operation code: OJ). The condition tested in this instruction is whether there has been an overflow in the R register, or an improper division, since the last Jump if overflow. If the overflow indicator is on, it is turned off; if it is off, it is unchanged. Recall that overflow occurs in the R register when a sum or difference is too large to be contained in the register's ten digits. An improper division (in all computers) is one which, if attempted, would produce a quotient too large for the quotient register—in our case R. Two small routines will illustrate how the instruction operates.

It sometimes happens that some section of a routine can result in overflows which do not indicate errors, and are therefore not tested. After having gone through such a section of the program before coming to a section in which it will be necessary to use Jump if overflow, it is essential to turn off the overflow indicator. How can this be done when there is no way of knowing for sure whether it is on or off? One instruction inserted at the beginning of the section where it must be off to start will suffice:

LOC.	S	O	ADDRESS	REMARKS
1683	O	J	1684	Jump if overflow indicator is on
1684			Continuation	

If the overflow indicator is on, the jump to 1684 (the following instruction) will be executed and the overflow indicator turned off; if it is off, the jump will not be executed, but the next instruction in sequence taken—which is also 1684. The routine may be continued with absolute certainty that the overflow indicator is off.

Use of the Overflow jump instruction to test for the occurrence of an improper division is shown in the following illustration. Suppose that in an inventory control job it is necessary to divide a total cost figure by the number of items in stock to arrive at an average cost based on a predetermined costing system. But what if there happens to be none of a certain item in stock? Dividing by zero always is an improper division, regardless of the dividend. A test as shown in this program would detect the condition.

LOC.	S	O	ADDRESS	REMARKS
0407		F	"Zero"	Fetch zero to L to clear L
0408		B	"Total cost"	Bring total cost to R
0409		D	"Number items"	Divide by number of items
0410	O	J	"Correction routine"	Jump if improper division which indicates zero items

Continuation

The words in quotation marks written in the address parts of the instructions are meant to stand for the *addresses* of the quantities. In this example as in many others, we are not concerned with the *actual* address, but with a coding principle. The correction routine would place in the output some indication of the zero-items condition. (This method of solving the particular problem was chosen to be able to illustrate the use of the Overflow jump instruction, obviously. Another method, perhaps preferable, would be to use the Zero jump instruction to test the divisor before attempting to divide.)

Once again we have an illustration of a rather unlikely condition, which, if not anticipated, could cause an unscheduled machine stop or at least ambiguous results. Although it is not the authors' intention to belabor this point, it is one which experience has shown can cause missed deadlines and general grief. Even if it is not always desirable to attempt to determine in advance exactly how the machine should attempt to *deal with* every nonroutine situation, at least some provision must be made to *signal* the condition.

6.3 DATAC Filters

In commercial data processing, and to a lesser extent in scientific and engineering calculations, it is frequently necessary to operate only on *parts* of a word. A previous example, for instance, involved working with records which had been on tape in packed form, i.e., having more than one piece of information in each word. Actual computers have a variety of features for handling the situation in a less cumbersome manner than the shifting process shown in examples in the previous chapter. The method assumed for our illustrative machine does not exist in exactly the same form in any real computer, but it is different only in details of operation rather than in principle of application. In other computers which have it, the function usually goes under the name of *extracting*. In one machine the basic method of operation is somewhat similar to that shown below, but the way of specifying it in instructions is quite different.

In DATAC we assume the existence of a *filter register* through which words moving between memory and the arithmetic unit may be made to pass. This register may be thought of schematically as containing another word, called the *filter word*, which determines which characters of the word being transferred shall be allowed to "filter through" the register. This filter word, for our purposes, will be a word which contains only zeros and ones. Corresponding to each position where the filter word contains a one, the character of the

FURTHER CODING OPERATIONS

word being transferred is allowed to pass unchanged; where the filter word contains zeros, the corresponding character of the word being transferred is simply deleted. This has the *effect* that on a transfer from memory to the arithmetic section the characters which are "filtered out" are replaced by zeros; on transfers from the arithmetic section to memory the characters which are filtered out are not stored at all. Thus a filtered Store instruction stores only a partial word, leaving the character positions in memory which correspond to filtered-out characters completely unchanged. The following examples may help to make these operations clearer.

Examples of a filtered Bring instruction:

Memory	+1234567899	ABCDEF4529	+2X345FG17
Filter word	1111100000	0000011111	1000000001
R register	+1234500000	0000045329	+000000007

Examples of a filtered addition:

Memory	+1111111111	−1234567890	OABCDEFGHIJ
R before	+9861278514	+4567485962	LMNOPQ00000
Filter word	1000001111	1111000000	00000011111
R after	+9861279625	+3333485962	LMNOPQFGHIJ

Examples of a filtered Store operation:

R register	+0123400000	+1234567899	+0000873024
Memory before	0B198200000	+2222222222	bbbb$000.00
Filter word	00111100000	0101010101	00000111011
Memory after	0B123400000	+1232527292	bbbb$873.24

(The lower case b's in the last example stand for blanks.)

The filter word is obtained from memory as part of the execution of any instruction which calls for filtering. The two characters of each instruction called the *filter part* specify that filtering is to be performed and which word in a certain section of memory is to be used as the filter. Any of the words in memory locations 01–99* may be used as filters. This section of memory operates no differently than any other part, and may be used for any purpose desired. If filtering is to be used, however, the filter word must be somewhere in this section of memory. It would be placed there the same way any other word is placed in memory, by some type of loading routine. When the filter part of an instruction contains any digits except 00, the corresponding word from memory is brought to the filter register before the execution of a transfer to or from memory. If an attempt is made to filter an

---

*Locations 01–09 will ordinarily be reserved for another purpose, so we shall use only locations 10–99 for filters.

108 PROGRAMMING BUSINESS COMPUTERS

instruction which involves no transfer, such as a shift, the filtering has no effect. Figure 2 is a schematic representation of the registers that are involved in filtering.

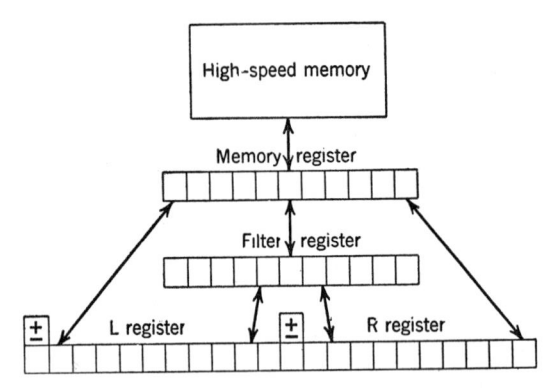

Figure 2. Schematic representation of the DATAC registers that are involved in filtering.

An illustration may clarify these ideas. Suppose there is in location 0787 a packed word consisting of three parts—pay number, department code, and shift-worked code:

S	10 9 8 7 6 5	4 3 2	1
	Pay Number	Dept.	Shift
+	1 2 3 4 5 6	7 8 9	1

A filter pattern, or word, consisting of 10000001110 is assumed to be in 0057. It is required to bring the department code into R in the same character position as it appears in the word in memory. This filtered instruction would accomplish the result:

LOC.	S	O	ADDRESS	FILTER	REMARKS
1907		B	0787	57	Bring department code (filtered) to R

The sequence of machine functions in executing the instruction is only slightly different from the sequence described on page 63.

1. The instruction, located at 1907 in this example, is brought to the instruction register. It consists now of three parts: operation code, address, and filter number.

2. The filter pattern, located in 0057 in the example, is brought to the filter register. It consists here of one's in the sign character and characters four, three, two. This means, in this case, that the char-

FURTHER CODING OPERATIONS

acters in the word coming from memory corresponding to one's in the filter pattern are to be "allowed" to pass into the R register; the others are simply replaced by zeros. The digit one in the sign character of the filter word allows the sign to pass through to R. If this had not been done, a zero would have gone to the sign character of R and succeeding arithmetic operations would have been on an "alphabetic" basis.

3. The operation code is decoded and the necessary circuits set up to bring a word from memory.

4. The R register is cleared to zeros.

5. The number in 0787 is brought to the memory register and the characters permitted to pass by the filter pattern are placed in the R register.

6. The location counter is advanced in preparation for execution of the next instruction.

The result of this instruction would be to place in R the characters:

$$+0000007890$$

The filtering function may be combined with transfer shifting. When this is done, we assume that DATAC performs the *filtering* first on a transfer from memory to the arithmetic section, and the *shifting* first on a transfer from the arithmetic section to memory. For instance, if it were required to place the department code in characters three through one instead of four through two, the instruction would be:

LOC.	S	O	ADDRESS	FILTER	REMARKS
1907	+1	B	0787	57	Bring department code to R, filtered, shifted

Since filtering is performed first, the same filter pattern can be used. The result in R would be:

$$+0000000789$$

Filtering may be used in conjunction with any instruction which involves a transfer of words between memory and the arithmetic unit.

It may also be used, in some fairly complex fashions, to reduce the number of instructions required to carry out a given function.

Suppose the following numbers are in memory:

LOCATION	QUANTITY	FORMAT
1000	Gross pay	+xx102∧86xxx
1001	Number of dependents	+xxxxx5xxxx
1380	Constants: $13.00 (exemption per dependent) and 18% (tax rate)	+x13∧00x∧18xx

(*Continued on next page*)

1381	Editing constant	bbbbb$00.00
50	Filter pattern	10011111000
51	Filter pattern	10000010000
52	Filter pattern	10111100000
53	Filter pattern	10000001100
54	Filter pattern	00000000011
55	Filter pattern	00000001100

The lower case x's represent other information which is not pertinent to this example. It is required to calculate the withholding tax and store it in 1600 in edited form as five blanks, dollar sign, two-digit dollars amount, decimal point and two-digit cents amount. Thus if the tax were $12.34, it would be stored as bbbbb$12.34. We worked out a routine for such a calculation earlier; now it can be done with less restrictive limitations as to format of words in memory and with fewer steps.

LOC.	S	O	ADDRESS	FILTER	REMARKS
0400	+4	B	1001	51	Bring number of dependents to R, filtered, shifted
0401	+5	X	1380	52	Multiply by exemption per dependent, filtered, shifted
0402	+3	M	1000	50	Subtract gross pay, filtered, shifted. Gives negative of taxable amount
0403	+2	X	1380	53	Multiply by 18%, shifted, filtered
0404	R	R	0002		Shift R right two places & round
0405		S	1400		Store temporarily
0406		B	1381		Bring editing constant to R
0407		A	1400	54	Add cents to R alphabetically, filtered
0408	−1	A	1400	55	Add dollars alphabetically to R, filtered, shifted
0409		S	1600		Store edited tax in 1600

Contents of pertinent memory location and R after execution of each instruction:

INSTRUCTION LOCATION	MEMORY REFERENCE	MEMORY CONTENTS	R
0400	1001	+xxxxx5xxxx	+0000000005$_\wedge$
0401	1380	+x13$_\wedge$00x$_\wedge$18xx	+00000065$_\wedge$00
0402	1000	+xx102$_\wedge$86xxx	−00000037$_\wedge$86
0403	1380	+x13$_\wedge$00x$_\wedge$18xx	−000006$_\wedge$8148
0404	No memory reference		−00000006$_\wedge$81
0405	1400	−00000006$_\wedge$81	−00000006$_\wedge$81
0406	1381	bbbbb$00.00	bbbbb$00.00
0407	1400	−00000006$_\wedge$81	bbbbb$00.81
0408	1400	−00000006$_\wedge$81	bbbbb$06.81
0409	1600	bbbbb$06.81	bbbbb$06.81

FURTHER CODING OPERATIONS

It will be noted that it happened to be more convenient to calculate the negative of the tax, but that in this isolated example it made no difference since all we were asked to do was to prepare the amount in edited form for printing. This is not to imply that the calculation would in practice be done twice, once for printing and once for updating YTD tax figures. It was done simply to emphasize the point that if you can take advantage of the limited requirements of a problem to save time or space, it is perfectly legitimate to do so. On the other hand, such a policy should be followed with discretion. It might be noted that the exemption per dependent, $13.00, could have been stored without the zeros since the multiplication could easily have been arranged to use the constant without the two zeros. But what if the tax law changes so that the exemption becomes $14.63? If space had not been allowed for the cents, a much more sizable revision of the program might be required than if the figures had been stored as $13_\wedge 00$. In this particular example the point may seem belabored, but the same general idea applies with great force to other situations. It is a common delusion of newcomers to the data processing field to assume that an application, once programmed, is finished. The ground rules in practice change continuously, so the wise programmer makes allowance for easy program maintenance.

6.4 Tape Instructions

Almost all data processing, as we have seen in earlier chapters, revolves around a master file. In this book we are concentrating on master files based on magnetic tapes. It will not be possible to present all DATAC tape instructions until after a discussion of index registers, but we may present some of the operations in order to be able to consider a fairly realistic example in the next section.

In Chapter 2 we discussed, to a certain extent, the use of magnetic tapes in electronic data processing. In Chapter 10, which is a collection of what little we say in this book about the physical hardware of which computers are built, we shall discuss a little more fully the physical side of magnetic tapes. A preview of Section 10.2 at this point will not hurt, although it is not necessary. For our purposes here, a magnetic tape record may be defined as a group of words on tape separated from adjacent records either by a gap in the recording or by magnetically recorded patterns which signify the beginning and end of the record. Suppose now that a record is positioned under the reading head of a tape handler, ready to be "read" into memory. What instructions must be executed to bring the record into memory?

In DATAC one instruction is required to bring a record from tape into memory, although for safety it would ordinarily be better to use a second instruction, as we shall see. The format of tape instructions is somewhat different from that of other types of instructions. The operation and suboperation codes are employed as usual to specify what the operation is. The address specifies where in memory the first word of the record is to be placed, in reading (or taken from, if writing) tape. Words following the first are located in sequential memory locations after the first. The indexer digits have a function which will be explained in Chapter 8, where we shall see that tape reading is actually more flexible than shown here. The filter digits have no significance as filter digits, since there is no reason to want partial word transfers between tape and memory. They are used in tape operations to specify which of the ten tape handlers* is involved in the operation.

We assume on DATAC that tapes are *buffered*. This sometimes means that there is in the machine an auxiliary storage through which all information being transferred between tape and memory must pass. The advantage of buffering is that, by proper program organization, it is possible to be executing instructions while the tape is being read and/or written. This is a very important consideration, since in many data processing applications the time required to read and write tapes is a significant fraction of the total time. If the internal processing of data can be carried out in less than "tape time," and if buffering is available, then the entire job can be carried out in just a little more time than that required to read and write tapes.

In some buffered machines (not all are buffered) there are instructions for transferring information between memory and the buffer and separate instructions for transfers between the buffer and tapes. In DATAC we assume a more advanced form of buffering in which no separate buffer storage is used. In this system, which may be called *direct memory buffering*, the movement of words between tape and memory usually interrupts temporarily the routine being executed. This method is considerably cheaper to build than one involving a separate buffer storage, but it has its own problems. A certain time elapses between giving an instruction to read tape and the completion of the reading. The time is considerably greater than that required for the execution of instructions which do not involve input or output. Suppose we read a record from tape into a section of memory, do a small amount of processing, then read another record into the same section of memory and process it, etc. After

---

* Also called tape units, tape frames, tape drives, and tape servos.

FURTHER CODING OPERATIONS

executing a tape read, is it safe to begin processing the record immediately? Clearly not, because the first word from tape may not get to memory until much later; with buffering, *interpretation* of the tape read instruction may require no longer than that of any other instruction, whereas the time required to get the tape moving and to transfer the first word may be fifty times as long as the instruction interpretation time. It may seem that this restriction makes buffering useless; we shall see in later chapters how to organize the program so that all the advantages of buffering are retained while avoiding this restriction. However, with this type of buffering it is fairly easy to allow for simultaneous reading, writing, and calculating, so overlapping is possible.

When the method to be described later cannot be used, it is possible at least to guarantee that the information has been moved from tape to memory or vice versa before any further operations are attempted. The Delay tape instruction (operation code: DT) causes the program to be delayed until the tape handler specified in the filter digits has completed its current operation, whatever that may be.*

The actual reading of tape is initiated by a Read tape instruction (RT). A Read tape followed by a Delay tape will move one record from the tape specified by the number in the filter digits to a section of memory beginning at the location specified by the address of the Read tape instruction, and delay the following instruction until the record actually is in memory. The length of the record need not be known except in planning for enough memory space to accommodate the largest record anticipated, since the computer will continue reading the tape until the end of the record is sensed by the tape handler. (On some computers the tape record is of fixed length and this comment does not apply.)

Suppose for a specific example that a ten-word record is in position to be read on tape handler number 6. We wish to bring the record into memory locations 1210–1219. If the first word of the record is +16098xxxxx (x's to be ignored in the comparison), a jump to 1850 should be executed; if not, the next record on tape handler 6 should be read and the process repeated. This is part of a search process which will find the next record on a master tape to be processed. The

---

* On some real machines which use this type of buffering, an alternative to the Delay tape instruction is used. There is an instruction which in effect determines if the tape unit is still busy, and if so, executes a jump. This allows the coder the freedom either to wait, as with Delay tape, or to perform alternate processing while waiting. This scheme is considerably more powerful than the Delay tape scheme.

constant +16098xxxxx is in 0589. The filter pattern 11111100000 is in 70. (All these numbers are, as usual, chosen completely arbitrarily and have no meaning in themselves.)

LOC.	S	O	ADDRESS	FILTER	REMARKS
1050	R	T	1210	06	Read a tape record from tape handler 6 into memory starting at 1210
1051	D	T		06	Delay until tape handler 6 is finished reading
1052		B	0589		Bring test constant to R
1053		C	1210	70	Compare first word of tape record with test constant, filtered
1054	E	J	1850		Jump, if equal, to process record
1055	U	J	1050		If not the correct record, repeat

The routine beginning at 1850 would carry out whatever processing of the tape record might be required. Observe that all records are read into the same section of memory, including the unwanted ones which must be tested in the process of finding the one desired.

6.5 Application and Coding Illustration

Consider an inventory control application. In one sentence, the task consists of keeping up-to-date records on magnetic tape on each type of part in a warehouse, showing such things as part number, description, quantity on hand, unit price, and sales to date. We shall describe and code a very small part of the total job, namely bringing the master file up to date as stock is received or shipped. As a matter of fact, we shall show the coding required to do this for only one order received or shipped. Various other tasks required in a realistic application will be omitted; some of these will be pointed out in the discussion.

Two tape files are involved in the segment of the application which will be described: the master file tape and the transaction tape. Either or both of these files could in practice be long enough to require more than one reel of tape—requiring programming which will be omitted here.

The master file contains a record for each type of part. In this condensed illustration, we assume that each master file record contains the following information:

FURTHER CODING OPERATIONS

1. The part number, which identifies the record in all processing.
2. A short word description, which is used only when certain types of reports are required.
3. Quantity on hand.
4. Price per unit.
5. Dollar amount of sales since beginning of the year.
6. Reorder point, i.e., the inventory level at which more stock should be ordered.
7. Reorder quantity, i.e., the quantity which should be ordered if the current quantity on hand reaches or falls below the reorder point.

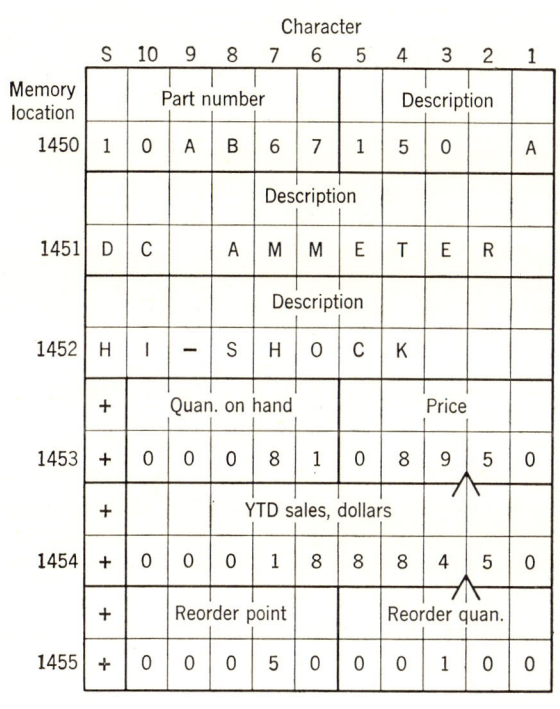

Memory location	S	10	9	8	7	6	5	4	3	2	1
			Part number					Description			
1450		1	0	A	B	6	7	1	5	0	A
					Description						
1451		D	C		A	M	M	E	T	E	R
					Description						
1452		H	I	—	S	H	O	C	K		
	+		Quan. on hand					Price			
1453	+	0	0	0	8	1	0	8	9	5	0
	+			YTD sales, dollars							
1454	+	0	0	0	1	8	8	8	4	5	0
	+		Reorder point					Reorder quan.			
1455	+	0	0	0	5	0	0	0	1	0	0

Figure 3. Item layout of the master file tape discussed in text.

The item layout of the master file tape is shown in Figure 3. The addresses at the left show the locations in memory into which the item is read.

The transaction tape items are shorter. Only three things are needed: the part number, the quantity shipped or received, and a code which identifies the transaction as a shipment or a receipt. The transaction tape also has fewer items on it than the master, since it is unlikely that there would be a shipment or receipt for every type of part. However, there is often more than one transaction for a given part—for instance, there could be many shipments of a certain part to different customers. A *realistic* program would of course have to process correctly the multiple-transaction-item case. And it would be necessary to process receipts before shipments; otherwise, the quantity on hand might appear incorrectly to have dropped below the reorder point. The preparation of the transaction tape is a problem in itself, since the data must be gathered from the warehouse and gotten onto the magnetic tape. The source document

Memory location	\multicolumn{10}{c	}{Character}
	S	10	9	8	7	6	5	4	3	2	1
	\multicolumn{2}{c	}{}	\multicolumn{3}{c	}{Part number}			\multicolumn{2}{c	}{Quantity}		Code
1712	1	0	B	D	1	4	0	0	1	2	1

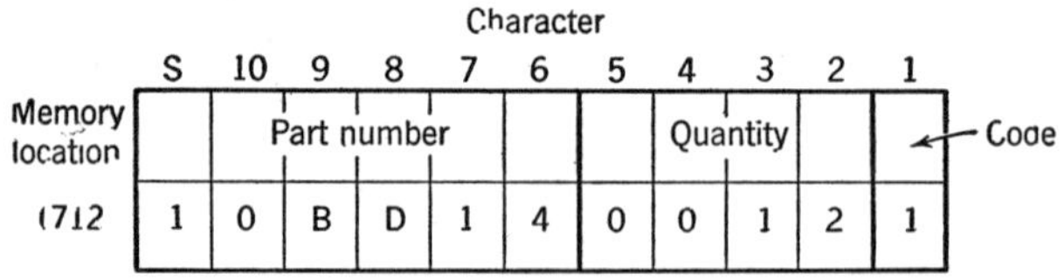

Figure 4. Item layout of the transaction file tape discussed in the text.

ment is an invoice or shipping notice; getting the information onto tape involves a process such as punching cards or paper tape, preparing magnetic tape, or reading the information directly with a magnetic or optical character reader. It is often possible to obtain this information on tape as a by-product of other clerical operations, in line with the integrated data processing concept mentioned in Chapter 1. In any case, we assume that by the time our routine begins, the tape has been prepared and is on a tape handler with the first record ready to be read.

The item layout for the transaction tape is shown in Figure 4. The "Code" shows whether the transaction is a shipment or a receipt; if the code is a zero, the transaction is a receipt; if a one, a shipment. If the code should be *anything but* zero or one, an error is indicated.

In the method of processing described here, both tape files must have been sorted into an ascending sequence according to part number. That is, the first item on the master tape must be the one for the part with the smallest part number, "smallest" being defined according to the collation sequence of the Compare instruction. The second item must be the one with the next "larger" part number, etc. (If the part numbers are numeric only, the sequence is simply the ascending sequence of the integers.)

The sequencing requirement poses another practical problem which

FURTHER CODING OPERATIONS 117

we shall ignore in the present illustration. The data for the transaction tape can hardly be expected to *arrive* in sequence. Therefore, the original transaction tape must be sorted by one of the methods to be discussed in Chapter 15. We shall assume that this has already been done.

The steps in the program segment to be shown may be listed. Compare with the flow chart shown in Figure 5.

1. Read one item from the transaction tape.

2. Search the master file tape for the master file item with the same part number, and test for missing master file items or master file out of sequence. This may be done quite simply by a very commonly used technique. When the part number from the transaction tape is compared with the part number of the item from the master tape, three conditions are possible:

    a. The two part numbers are equal, in which case the correct master file item has been found and the two may be processed.

    b. The transaction part number is greater than the master file part number, in which case the correct master item has not yet been found and another record should be read from the master file tape.

    c. The transaction part number is less than the master file part number, in which case the transaction part number is incorrect, a master file item is missing, or one of the files is out of sequence. Some corrective action must be taken.

This may be made clearer by examination of a sample set of part numbers.

TRANSACTION PART NUMBER	MASTER PART NUMBERS
	10 AB 67
	10 AB 80
	10 AB 81
	10 AB 97
10 BD 14	10 BD 14
	10 BD 17
	10 BD 60
	10 BD 62
	10 BD 63
	Etc.

3. When the correct master file item is found, the transaction code is first checked to determine whether the transaction is a shipment or a receipt. If it is a receipt, the transaction quantity is simply added to the quantity on hand. The processing of this record is then complete.

118 PROGRAMMING BUSINESS COMPUTERS

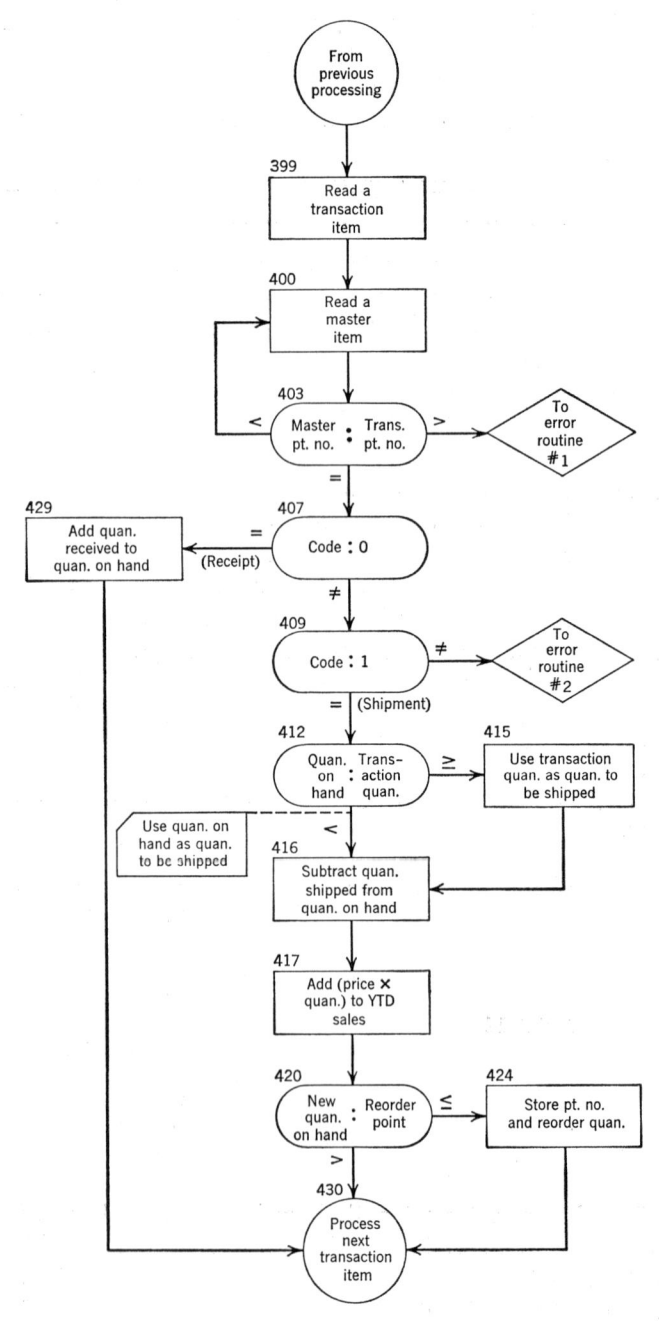

Figure 5. Flow chart of a simplified inventory control calculation.

FURTHER CODING OPERATIONS

4. If the transaction is a shipment, the transaction quantity is subtracted from the quantity on hand. If there should be insufficient parts on hand to ship the entire order, we shall assume that all on hand are shipped; we shall not consider a back-order procedure. The dollar amount of the shipment, i.e., quantity times unit price, is added to the YTD sales.

5. If the new quantity on hand is now equal to or less than the reorder point, an order must be placed with a vendor. In practice, some type of purchasing report would be part of the output of the program. We shall simply place the part number and the quantity to be ordered (reorder quantity) in memory; we shall ignore the need to keep a record of the quantity on order.

We have completely disregarded the question of what to do with the results, because tape writing in DATAC involves machine features not yet discussed. As a matter of fact, it would actually be necessary in almost all cases to prepare an entirely new master tape since the updated tape from this run would become the master file for the next run. Changes in the quantity on hand due to today's transactions must obviously be reflected in the next day's processing. Production of a new master file involves not only updating active items, but "copying" inactive master file items from the old tape to the new. Some computers have tape features which make the search-copy-update process very simple and fast.

This example, then, is very much simplified compared to the realistic situation. And it is, of course, not intended as a model of how an inventory control application should be organized, but merely as an *indication* of what must be done and as a programming illustration. To summarize, all we shall do here is read in the *first* transaction item, locate the corresponding master file item, and process that *one* item.

Assume the following locations for needed constants:

QUANTITY	LOCATION	FORMAT
Filter for part number, quantity on hand, and reorder point	40	11111100000
Filter for price and reorder quantity	41	00000011111
Filter for transaction quantity	42	00000011110
Filter for transaction code	43	00000000001
Filter to eliminate transaction quantity	44	11111100001
Filter for price, including sign	45	10000011111
Code testing constant	390	00000000001

120 PROGRAMMING BUSINESS COMPUTERS

LOC.	S	O	ADDRESS	FILTER	REMARKS
399	R	T	1712	01	Read a transaction item from the transaction file, assumed to be on tape handler 01
400	R	T	1450	02	Read a master item from the master file, assumed to be on tape handler 02
401	D	T		01	Delay until completion of reading tape 01
402	D	T		02	Delay until completion of reading tape 02
403		B	1450		Bring master part number to R
404		C	1712	40	Compare with transaction part number, filtered
405	L	J	0400		Low jump to read another master item
406	H	J	xxxx		High jump to error routine #1
407		B	1712	43	Bring transaction code to R, filtered (we are here only if master and transaction part numbers are equal)
408	Z	J	0429		Zero jump to receipt routine, if code is zero
409		C	0390		Compare code with one
410	E	J	0412		Equal jump if code is one, as it should be if we get here
411	U	J	xxxx		Unconditional jump to error routine #2 (if code is neither zero nor one)
412		B	1453	40	Bring quantity on hand to R, filtered
413	−4	C	1712	42	Compare with transaction quantity, filtered, shifted
414	L	J	0416		Low jump to use quantity on hand as transaction quantity
415	−4	B	1712	42	Bring transaction quantity to R, filtered, shifted
416	X	M	1453		Subtract from memory the actual quantity to be shipped from quantity on hand
417	O	R	0005		Shift only R right 5 places, not including sign, to prepare for multiplication
418		X	1453	45	Multiply quantity shipped by unit price, filtered
419	X	A	1454		Add to memory, to update dollar sales to date
420		B	1453		Bring (new) quantity on hand to R
421		C	1455	40	Compare with reorder point, filtered
422	H	J	0430		High jump to continuation
423		B	1455	41	Bring reorder quantity to R, filtered
424		S	xxxx		Store reorder quantity in memory preparatory to writing purchasing report
425		B	1450	40	Bring part number to R, filtered
426		S	xxxx		Store part number in memory, preparatory to writing purchasing report
427	U	J	0430		Unconditional jump around receipt routine
428	−4	B	1712	42	Bring transaction quantity to R, filtered, shifted
429	X	A	1453		Add to memory to add to quantity on hand
430		Continuation of processing			

A detailed example will not be given, but the student would do well to work through several examples which test all the branches of the program. A few notes may help to clarify some of the points.

On the flow chart (Figure 5), the arrow going back from the comparison box to the "read a master item" box indicates a *loop*, the subject of the next chapter. We assume that the comparison will at some point "break out" of this loop, either because a match between a transaction item and a master item is found or because an out-of-sequence file item is encountered. If the comparison between quantity on hand and transaction quantity shows that there are not enough parts on hand to ship the order, we take the path which is flagged "Use quantity on hand as quantity to be shipped." This simply says that we will ship all we have; in practice some notice would have to be given to the customer that we have *back-ordered* part of his order, but we are ignoring that requirement here in the interest of simplicity. There are other ways the flow chart could have been drawn to indicate the same operation. For instance, we could have two boxes coming out of the comparison box, one labeled "quantity shipped equals transaction quantity" (in case we had enough on hand to ship the entire requested amount) and the other labeled "quantity shipped equals quantity on hand." It happens that the way the flow chart is shown makes the coding of the calculation of dollar value of the sale a little easier.

In the coding, note that two Delay tape instructions are used. This is necessary because DATAC is assumed to allow simultaneous reading of several tapes at once, and we must be certain that both tapes have completed reading. The addresses of the instructions at 406 and 411 are shown as xxxx to indicate separate error correction routines somewhere else (we do not care where) in memory. Similarly, the addresses of the two instructions at 424 and 426, which have to do with the preparation of a report to purchasing (or production) of the items which went to or below the reorder point on this run, are shown as xxxx.

6.6 Summary

At this point, the serious reader would do well to pause for a review. It is fairly important to the further development that the material presented so far be well understood; not because any of the illustrations themselves are critical as regards details, but because the general way of thinking about the problems must be understood. As an illustration: the reader will never need to know, in actual programming situations, how the DATAC filters operate (since DATAC does not exist), but the attention to detail that is necessary to apply the filters properly will be important. Furthermore, unless the principles discussed so far are thoroughly understood, the next few chapters will be quite difficult to follow. The material beginning with Chapter 12 is not *quite* so dependent on the principles being discussed now, but the "feeling" for the ideas presented in the later chapters will be poorer if this part is skimmed.

Exercises

Write routines to carry out the following functions. Draw a flow chart for each exercise.

1. If either of the numbers in 0500 and 0501 is zero, place a zero in 0600; otherwise place a one in 0600.

2. Location 1010 contains either a one or a two; if it is one, bring the number in 1800 to the R register, but if it is two, bring the number in 1801 to R.

3. The words GREATER, EQUAL, and LESS are stored in 0597, 0598, and 0599 respectively. If the number in 0650 is larger than the number in 0750, bring the word GREATER to the R register, etc.

4. Three positive numbers are in 1100, 1101, and 1102. Place the *largest* of the three in 1103.

5. Assume the following simplified tax table:

ANNUAL EARNINGS	TAX
Less than $2000.00	Zero
$2000.00 or over but less than $5000.00	2% of the amount over $2000.00
$5000.00 or over	$60.00, plus 5% of the amount over $5000.00

A man's gross pay for a year is stored in 0150. Compute his tax and store it in 0157. Assume locations for all necessary constants.

6. Using the Overflow jump instruction, determine whether the sum of the numbers in 0657, 0659, 0661, and 0663 is greater than ten digits in length.

In Exercises 7–14, assume that the R register initially contains +0123456789 and that the memory locations shown contain the following quantities:

40	1 0 0 0 0 0 1 1 1 1 1
41	1 1 1 1 1 1 0 0 0 0 0
42	0 0 0 0 0 0 1 1 1 1 1
1000	+ 2 2 2 2 2 2 2 2 2 2
1001	A B C D E F G H I J K
1004	+ 9 8 7 6 5 4 3 2 1 0

In each exercise, state what the effect of the instruction would be. (Each

FURTHER CODING OPERATIONS

exercise is a separate problem, i.e., the R register *in each case* is assumed to contain +0123456789 initially.)

			FILTER	
7.	B	1000	40	
8.	B	1000	42	
9.	A	1000	40	
10.	A	1002	41	
11.	M	1000	40	
12.	A	1001	42	(Any special problems?)
13.	S	1000	40	
14.	S	1001	42	

15. Rewrite Exercises 9-13 of Chapter 5, using transfer shifting and filtering where beneficial. Assume locations for any necessary filter patterns.

16. Tape handlers 1 and 2 both contain 10 word records. Read one record from each tape into memory. If the first word of the record from tape 1 is *less* than the first word of the record from tape 2, jump to 1950; if they are *equal*, jump to 1975. If the first word of the record from tape 1 is *greater* than the first word of the record from tape 2, then jump back to the beginning of the routine to read *another* record from tape 2. Proceed with the same testing; if necessary, read another record from tape 2, etc., etc., until a record is found on tape 2 which causes a jump to either 1950 or 1975. Flow-chart and code.

17. Given the following 3 words in memory:

LOCATION

	S	10	9	8	7	6	5	4	3	2	1
1307	J	O	N	E	S	A	B	0	0	0	0
1308	W	E	I	S	S	H	X	0	0	0	0
1309	S	M	I	T	H	W	A	0	0	0	0

(a) Write a routine which will select the highest order (greatest according to the collation sequence of DATAC) name and place that name in location 1310.

(b) Edit that name and place it in location 1311 so that it looks as follows:

	S	10	9	8	7	6	5	4	3	2	1
1311	X	X	X	X	X	b	X	b	X	b	b

Use any editing constants necessary and show what was used.

(c) Flow-chart parts (a) and (b).

18. Show the contents of the appropriate memory location and the contents of the R register after each instruction in the routine on page 120.

19. List and discuss all the decision instructions of DATAC.

20. List and discuss all the decision instructions of two actual computers.

124   PROGRAMMING BUSINESS COMPUTERS

21. Describe the filtering operation.

22. If the Minus jump instruction were not available in DATAC, how might we test for a negative word (less than zero)?

23. Flow-chart and code a routine to determine which of the five numbers in locations 2043, 2044, 2045, 2046, 2047 is smallest, and place the number in the R register.

24. Flow-chart and code a routine to determine which number is larger than two of five numbers and smaller than two of five numbers. Use the same five numbers in Exercise 23 and place the *middle* number thus found in the R register. Assume none of the five numbers are equal.

25. Compute the average of the five numbers in Exercise 23. Sum all the numbers less than or equal to the average and store in 0514.

26. *Logical AND* is an operation which produces an output if and only if the inputs *A and B* are *on* (for two inputs); otherwise the output is zero. Filtering may be described as a digit-by-digit *logical AND* of the word selected from memory and the selected filter with the result in the accumulator. In this case, a digit that is nonzero will be considered as *on*. Discuss.

27. If filtering were not available in DATAC, how could packed words be handled?

28. Some actual computers use partial word operation instead of filtering to operate on packed words. The instruction specifies the digits to be operated on and only these are brought into the accumulator. Thus 27 would specify digits 2 through 7, 58 would specify digits 5 through 8. Discuss and compare with filtering.

29. The so-called variable word length computers can perform operations on data with virtually no limitations on the size of data. The length of the operand is determined by the preset length of accumulators, or by special characters in the data itself. Discuss and compare this with filtering.

30. (*a*) What does buffering mean to you?
    (*b*) What is its significance?
    (*c*) Give two noncomputer analogies of buffers.

31. Discuss the differences (in magnetic tape programming logic) in reading the master and change tapes in the following situations:

(*a*) The beginning records of each tape reel.
(*b*) Subsequent records.
(*c*) Last records.

32. Suggest a scheme to find the smallest of 10 characters where each character is stored in the low order position of a word. The collation sequence to be used in this comparison is some arbitrary one *other* than the collation sequence of DATAC. Flow-chart and code this.

33. Flow-chart and code a routine to compare two keys and place the smaller one in 0305, 0306. The two keys are each 18 digits long and each occupy one full word and the 7 high order positions of the next word in memory. The two keys are located in 0218–0219 and 1451–1452.

7 ADDRESS COMPUTATION

7.0 Introduction

Most of the operations discussed in the previous two chapters can be effected fairly adequately by punched card equipment. Punched card calculators and tabulators, like stored program computers, can do arithmetic, shift numbers, and make simple decisions—more slowly perhaps, but the principles are similar. There are two distinguishing features which take stored program computers out of the class of desk calculators and punched card equipment. One is the ease and flexibility of repeating a group of instructions, usually in order to perform a standard operation on different sets of data; this is the *loop* technique, which will be discussed in the next chapter. The other, which we shall describe in this chapter, is the power to perform arithmetic on the instructions which govern the machine's functions. (Some punched card calculators can be set up to do an equivalent thing, but only in a very awkward manner which is not a normal operating mode.)

A full chapter is devoted to address computation partly because it is so important and finds such wide application, and partly because, being peculiar to stored program computers, it is unfamiliar and often difficult to grasp. Three examples provide a representative set of illustrations of the technique.

7.1 Grouped Tape Record Example

As has been mentioned briefly in previous chapters, it is often necessary to place several file records in one tape record. This means that when one tape record is read, a number of file records come into memory, and similarly on writing. Some means must therefore be provided to deal appropriately with each of the file records. There are a number of ways of handling this common problem, as we shall see in Chapter 13; we shall discuss one of these methods here, not because it is necessarily the best in all circumstances, but because it illustrates address computation concepts.

To take a contrived example, suppose we have a tape on tape handler 6 which has many four-word records in each block. Suppose the Read tape instruction calls for the first word of the block to be placed in location 400. The records to be processed would be in 400–403, 404–407, 408–411, etc. Suppose finally—and this is hardly realistic—that it is required simply to add the first word of each record to the second and place the sum in the position occupied by the fourth word. A later operation would write the modified record on another tape. Our task is then to perform the following operations:

$$(400) + (401) \to (403)$$
$$(404) + (405) \to (407)$$
$$(408) + (409) \to (411)$$
$$(412) + (413) \to (415)$$
Etc.

where (0400) means "the contents of memory location 0400," etc., and the arrow means "replaces." Observe a characteristic of the calculation: the addresses in each column increase by four down the column. A routine such as the following would read a tape block and perform the required calculation on the first record. (We are completely ignoring the question of how long the tape record is, and how much memory space would have to be reserved for it. These are, of course, important questions, but we are not properly prepared to deal with them until the next chapter; attention is focused on the modification of the address only, not the complete task.)

LOC.	S	O	ADDRESS	FILTER	REMARKS
1099	R	T	0400	06	Read a block from tape handler 6 into 0400 and following
1100	D	T		06	Delay until reading complete
1101		B	0400		Bring first word of record to R
1102		A	0401		Add second word
1103		S	0403		Store sum in position of fourth word of record

Now if we could change the addresses of the instructions at 1101, 1102, and 1103 to have addresses 0404, 0405, and 0407 respectively, those three instructions could be repeated to process the second record. It is simple enough to do so, since the instructions are simply words in memory. Arithmetic may be performed on them as well as on any other word. The word in 1101 appears as 0B040000000. Adding the constant +0000400000 to this word changes it to 0B040400000, which is the instruction as it is needed to process the second record. Performing the addition on the other two arithmetic instructions in the program will change them similarly so that they will operate on the second record. Once the instructions have been modified, an Unconditional jump back to 1101 will cause the three instructions to be repeated, this time operating on the second record. Of course, the modification and the Unconditional jump are then repeated also, so that the program next processes the third record, etc. If the constant +0000400000 is in 0399, the routine becomes:

LOC.	S	O	ADDRESS	FILTER	REMARKS
1099	R	T	0400	06	Read a block from tape handler 6 into 0400 and following
1100	D	T		06	Delay until reading complete
1101		B	0400		Bring first word of record to R
1102		A	0401		Add second word
1103		S	0403		Store sum in position of fourth word of record
1104		B	0399		Bring modifying constant to R
1105	X	A	1101		Add 4 to address of instruction at 1101
1106	X	A	1102		Add 4 to address of instruction at 1102
1107	X	A	1103		Add 4 to address of instruction at 1103
1108	U	J	1101		Unconditional jump to 1101 to repeat

What we have here is a rudimentary loop, since the routine not only modifies the address of other parts of itself, but also repeats. *Very* rudimentary, however. A major failing of this routine as a loop is that it will not quit: there is no provision for testing to determine when the last record of the block has been processed. We shall see in the following chapter how this would be handled.

This first example of address modification shows how simple it is in concept to change an instruction by ordinary arithmetic, which is made possible by the fact that the instructions in a stored program computer are ordinary words. This is not to say that instructions *must* be indistinguishable from words which are not instructions; in some computers such is not the case, since instructions have some identifying characteristic which makes it impossible to attempt to interpret a data word as an instruction. All that is necessary for stored program operation is that arithmetic operations on instructions be possible. Note finally that the modification has of course changed the routine in memory. If the entire loop is to be used again, as it normally would be, the modified instruction addresses must somehow be replaced with their original values. This is the subject of *initialization* or *resetting*, also to be discussed in the following chapter.

7.2 Digit Selection

The next example of computation on addresses is quite different. In this case we shall use a part of the input to a problem to determine which of several constants in memory to employ in a calculation.

For a concrete example, consider the withholding tax calculation discussed previously, in which it is necessary to subtract from the gross pay a standard exemption for each dependent before multiplying by the tax rate. Under one method presently allowed by United States tax laws, the exemption is $13.00 per dependent on a weekly payroll. In the earlier examples we simply multiplied the number of dependents by $13.00 and subtracted the product from the gross pay, which is an entirely acceptable method. Here, however, a different method will be used in order to illustrate the digit selection principle, and also to bring out another point.

Suppose gross pay is in 1650 with the decimal point understood to be between characters three and two. For simplicity assume that the number of dependents is in 1683 as $+0000D00000$, that is, in position to "line up" with the least significant digit (LSD) of the address of an instruction. Finally, assume there is in memory a table as follows:

0900	$+00000000_\wedge 00$
0901	$+00000013_\wedge 00$
0902	$+00000026_\wedge 00$
0903	$+00000039_\wedge 00$
0904	$+00000052_\wedge 00$
0905	$+00000065_\wedge 00$
0906	$+00000078_\wedge 00$
0907	$+00000091_\wedge 00$
0908	$+00000104_\wedge 00$
0909	$+00000117_\wedge 00$*

It will be seen that there is a simple relationship between addresses and their contents. If D stands for the numbers of dependents, the relationship is:

Location (0900 + D) contains (D) × ($13.00)

Or, in other words, by adding the number of dependents to 0900 we

---
* The table as shown will handle up to nine dependents. If more are needed, the table can easily be extended.

ADDRESS COMPUTATION

get the address of a constant which is the exemption for that number of dependents. The pattern now is clear for a routine to use the scheme. It is only necessary to add the number of dependents to a constant which is in effect a Subtract instruction with the appropriate address for zero exemptions. The constant, 0M090000000, may be assumed to be in 1180.

LOC.	S	O	ADDRESS	REMARKS
1900		B	1180	Bring instructional constant to R
1901		A	1683	Add number of dependents
1902		S	1904	Store computed instruction in 1904
1903		B	1650	Bring gross pay to R
1904		M	090(x)	Subtract exemption

Continuation of calculation

The constant used in the first step is an example of what is often called an *instructional constant* since it has the *form* of an instruction, but is never *executed* as one. The next step of the routine would be to multiply by the tax rate, etc., as before.

The computation of the address of the instruction at 1904 is of course the heart of the concept under consideration. Since this concept is sometimes elusive at first contact, it may be helpful to give a numerical example. Suppose the gross pay is $68.04 and the man claims three dependents. Contents of pertinent registers after the execution of each instruction:

INSTRUCTION LOCATION	INSTRUCTION AS EXECUTED	R REGISTER
1900	B 1180	0M090000000
1901	A 1683	0M090300000
1902	S 1904	0M090300000
1903	B 1650	+00000068$_\wedge$04
1904	M 0903	+00000029$_\wedge$04

The crucial point is that by the time the instruction at 1904 is executed, its address has been computed by the three instructions at 1900–1902.

It may occur to some readers that there was no need to set up a separate instructional constant to use in computing the address. Why not write the routine as follows:

1900	B	1904
1901	A	1683
1902	S	1904
1903	B	1650
1904	M	0900

i.e., write the instruction at 1904 as we want it to appear as a constant, knowing that by the time it is executed it will have been appropriately modified? Such an approach will indeed work—*once*. But what happens if the same routine must be used again later, as it ordinarily would? The "constant" at 1904 has now been modified! Thus the need for the separate instructional constant.

7.3 Computation of Jump Addresses

The final example of address computation is somewhat similar to the second, but more complex. For an illustration this time we take a calculation of salesmen's commissions. It occasionally happens that there are a number of different methods of calculating commissions, depending on type of merchandise, and that these methods are so diverse that they cannot be compressed into one formula with different constants. We are not concerned here with the actual computations, but with how to choose the correct method. Suppose there are ten different commission formulas, and that the commission type is indicated somewhere in the master file record for each merchandise item by a digit between zero and nine. Suppose further that the commission calculations have already been coded and start in the following locations:

COMMISSION FORMULA CODE	COMMISSION COMPUTATION ROUTINE BEGINS AT
0	1000
1	1008
2	1019
3	1025
4	1039
5	1052
6	1058
7	1075
8	1083
9	1100

The table poses problems immediately: there is no pattern to the relationship between commission code and starting address of the corresponding calculation routine. If all the routines were the same length, the problem would be simple. A variation of the method of the previous section would suffice. Here, however, a more involved procedure is necessary.

The solution proposed is to set up in memory a *jump table*. It will consist in our example of ten Unconditional jump instructions, one for

ADDRESS COMPUTATION

each of the commission calculation routines. We may arbitrarily place this table in memory starting in 0453:

0453	UJ	1000
0454	UJ	1008
0455	UJ	1019
0456	UJ	1025
0457	UJ	1039
0458	UJ	1052
0459	UJ	1058
0460	UJ	1075
0461	UJ	1083
0462	UJ	1100

Now we have a pattern to work with: the relation between the commission code and an entry into the jump table. An Unconditional jump to

$$0453 + \text{commission code}$$

will cause the machine to jump to one of the ten locations in the jump table. At this location is found a second Unconditional jump, this time to the appropriate calculation routine. Assuming that the constant UJ045300000 is in 0387 and the commission code as +0000C00000 is in 0400, the routine could be:

LOC.	S	O	ADDRESS	REMARKS
0900		B	0387	Bring instructional constant to R
0901		A	0400	Add commission code
0902		S	0903	Store computed instruction in 0903
0903	U	J	[04xx]	Jump to jump table

For a numerical example, suppose the commission code is 8, which means that the correct calculation routine starts at 1083:

INSTRUCTION LOCATION	INSTRUCTION AS EXECUTED	R REGISTER
0900	B 0387	UJ045300000
0901	A 0400	UJ046100000
0902	S 0903	UJ046100000
0903	UJ 0461	UJ046100000
0461	UJ 1083	UJ046100000
1083	First step of commission calculation	

Again the important point is that although the address of the instruction at 0903 is variable, it has a relevant address by the time the routine gets that far. A little experimentation will show that the system works correctly for any of the ten commission codes.

7.4 Summary

This chapter, like the last, uses illustrations which are not important in themselves to serve as a framework for a discussion of concepts which are important. In a word, the idea that should be clear from this chapter is that it is possible to perform arithmetic on instructions, and that this possibility leads to useful and desirable approaches to problems.

Different computers have different characteristics which affect the carrying out of computations on addresses, some of which are carefully planned advantages, others of which are downright nuisances. In the latter category is the not uncommon fact that instructions are often *signed* numbers, which means that careful planning is necessary to avoid subtracting when you thought you were adding. There are, of course, systematic ways of avoiding trouble on this score, but the problem is still there. This is not to imply that the designers of such machines overlooked the difficulty, but simply that they felt that the disadvantages were outweighed by the gains, such as easier or cleaner design or the saving of space or a more flexible instruction list. Many such compromises must be made in computer design.

A characteristic of some of the more recent computers which has great potential power, although costing something in ease of learning, is called *indirect addressing*. With this technique, an "address" may refer to a memory location where what we have called "the address" is located. Thus the address of a Bring instruction might be 1200; this does not mean to bring the contents of location 1200 to the arithmetic unit, but to go to 1200 to find the address of what to bring to the arithmetic unit. This feature is optional on any given instruction, i.e., it is operative only if called for by placing certain digits in the instruction. A good example is the jump table calculation above. Using indirect addressing, we could have simply placed the address in a word in memory somewhere and then called for an indirectly addressed Unconditional jump.

Indirect addressing has great power in certain situations, in that it is possible to modify many instructions using only one constant. More generally, it allows great flexibility in the writing of routines—a flexibility which is not always needed but which is very valuable when it is required. One of the best applications is the modification of tape handler numbers when tape units are "alternated," which is discussed in Chapter 13.

It may be pointed out, finally, that in many machines it is perfectly

ADDRESS COMPUTATION

possible to do arithmetic on other parts of instructions than the address, in particular the operation code. This seems not to have as much usefulness, however, as the modification of addresses.

Russell C. McGee, Jr., of General Electric, has suggested that the subject of computer addressing in general, and indirect addressing in particular, may lead the beginning coder to sympathize strongly with Alice in the following passage from *Alice in Wonderland*.

"... The name of the song is called 'Haddocks' Eyes.'"

"Oh, that's the name of the song, is it?" Alice said, trying to feel interested.

"No, you don't understand," the Knight said, looking a little vexed. "That's what the name is *called*. The name really *is*, 'The Aged Aged Man.'"

"Then I ought to have said, 'That's what the *song* is called'?" Alice corrected herself.

"No, you oughtn't: that's quite another thing! The *song* is called 'Ways and Means': but that's only what it's *called*, you know!"

"Well, what *is* the song, then?" said Alice, who was by this time completely bewildered.

"I was coming to that," the Knight said. "The song really *is* 'A-sitting on a Gate': and the tune's my own invention."

Exercises

1. Suppose that in a department store sales statistics tabulation problem it is required to perform the following function. If the merchandise classification code number in 0753 is 1, the number of units sold (stored in 0754) must be added to the previous total for category 1 stored in 1080; if the code in 0753 is 2, the units sold must be added to the previous total for category 2 stored in 1081; if it is 3, the previous total is in 1082, etc., up to a previous total stored in 1099 for category 20. Write a routine to carry out the tabulation. The merchandise classification code appears in 0753 as +000CC00000.

2. Suppose that in a salesman's commission calculation there are five different commission formulas. One of the following five formulas is to be used, depending on a product classification code as follows:

PRODUCT CODE	COMMISSION FORMULA
1	$(0.15) \times$ (Sale price)
2	$(0.40) \times$ (Sale price $-$ Base price)
3	$(0.10) \times$ (Base price) $+ 0.50$ (Sale price $-$ Base price)
4	$\$10.00 + (0.05) \times$ (Base price)
5	$\$15.00$

The product code is stored in 1203 as XXXXXXXXXC, where the X's represent irrelevant characters which must be deleted. The base price of the product is in 1208 and the sale price in 1429, both in dollars-and-cents form with a decimal point assumed between character positions 3 and 2. The formulas apply to a sale of *one unit* of whatever product is involved; the number of units sold is stored in 1428 as +XXXXXXXXNN where again the X's are irrelevant characters which must be deleted. Write a routine to calculate the commission and store it in 1430. Assume locations for the necessary constants.

3. Suppose that in a certain application the records on the tape mounted on tape unit 7 are of variable length. They always consist of a key in the first word of the record, a word count as +00000000WW in the second word, and from one to ninety additional words. The word count specifies the number of *additional* words. Write a routine to read such a record, and then place the *last* word of that record in location 0575.

4. Set up the example of Section 7.3 to operate without actually jumping to a jump table.

5. Discuss the following types of computers. What meaning does *address* have in each of the types? Which types permit address computation?
   (a) Wired-in logic.
   (b) Plugboard or pinboard programmed.
   (c) Card or paper tape programmed.
   (d) Stored program.

6. Discuss the advantages of a stored program computer.

7. Can an instruction perform arithmetic on its own address? Discuss.

8. Can an instruction jump to itself? (A dynamic stop is one which consists of an unconditional jump instruction to itself.)

9. Suggest two other methods of doing the grouped tape record example discussed in the chapter. Code these and compare the speed and memory used with the code in the chapter.

10. Should constants which operate on instructions be regarded as distinct from other constants? Discuss.

11. If there is no simple relationship governing the code and the entry into the jump table, or the code and the constant selected, should the jump table or digit selection methods still be used?

12. Discuss and give some examples of each of the following types of address computation:
   (a) Compute the number of positions to be shifted.
   (b) Prepare the last instruction of a series of instructions to return to some point in the program.
   (c) Change a tape handler number.

13. In the two examples of digit selection and jump table discussed in the text, we see illustrations of how input data may affect the sequence (or course) of a program. Thus, the execution time is intimately related to the data and may vary from day to day as the nature (or mix) of the data varies. Discuss.

14. Discuss the auditing implications of electronic data processing where

ADDRESS COMPUTATION

the sequence of a program is controlled by codes punched on the input records. For example, a proper combination of codes (accidentally concocted or otherwise) may conceivably cause a $1,000,000 check to be printed out.

15. What is indirect addressing? Discuss some of its uses.

16. It is possible to have more than one level of indirect addressing. Discuss and suggest some uses for multilevel indirect addressing.

17. Some computers have a scheme where the address portion of the instruction is the operand and not the address; thus A0001 would add one to the accumulator in this scheme. This is sometimes called *zero-level* addressing. Discuss where this might be useful.

8 LOOPS AND INDEX REGISTERS

8.0 Introduction

Very often in data processing some function must be repeated a great many times. Many examples could be cited; one immediate illustration is the payroll application. For every man to be paid, a certain basic pattern of operations must be carried out. In some situations it is possible and even desirable to write out a separate routine to handle every case. In many others it is patently impossible to do so; in the payroll problem, for instance, it would be out of the question. In fact, it would be impossible to use computers without some repetition, because instructions can be executed much faster than they can be read into memory.

Our task in this chapter is to learn how to use the technique of repeating a section of a program, usually with some type of modification between repetitions. The repeated section, together with certain related parts, is universally called a *loop*. The second part of the chapter is devoted to *index registers*, which make the loop technique even more powerful.

Loops are the second distinguishing feature of the stored program computer, as was mentioned in the previous chapter. Because the loop concept is so close to the heart of the stored program principle, and because loops are so extensively used in all applications, it is safe to say that the concept is the most important single thing to be learned in coding. Powerful as the technique is, however, it is also one of the most frequent causes of coding errors.

For these reasons, the present chapter is fairly long. The reader will do well to understand this material thoroughly before continuing.

8.1 Parts of a Loop

It is convenient, in discussing loop techniques, to define four functions:

LOOPS AND INDEX REGISTERS

1. *Initialize.* It is ordinarily necessary to perform certain operations in order to get the repetition correctly started. These operations are, of course, executed only at the beginning and are not repeated.

2. *Compute.* This section of the loop actually performs the function required; the other sections are auxiliaries.

3. *Modify.* The basic purpose of a loop is to repeat the calculation on new data, or on the same data as modified by the loop. A process such as computing new addresses so as to operate on new data is a typical example.

4. *Test.* It is necessary somehow to determine when the repetition should be stopped. This may involve, for instance, using a decision instruction to determine whether the loop has been repeated a predetermined number of times.

Before proceeding to an example, it should be pointed out that the order of these four steps is often not the same as listed above. In particular situations it is frequently desirable to change the order of the last three. And depending on circumstances, machine characteristics, and personal preference, the initializing function may be replaced by a *resetting* function which *follows* the other three. Examples in this chapter and elsewhere will show some of the alternatives.

To illustrate the basic methods, we begin with a problem which is perhaps not the most realistic that could be found, but is quite simple and has become almost a classic illustrative loop problem. Suppose we have fifty numbers in memory, stored in 1000, 1005, 1010, etc., up to 1245. We are required simply to obtain the sum of the fifty numbers and store the sum in 1250.

The basic scheme to be used here is to accumulate the numbers in 1250 by a three-instruction computing part. The three steps initially will be:

LOC.	S	O	ADDRESS	REMARKS
		B	1250	Bring sum so far to R
		A	[1000]	Add next number from list
		S	1250	Store sum so far in 1250

One of the functions of the modification part will be to change the address of the Add instruction so that it successively calls for all of the numbers in the list from memory. The brackets around the address are used to indicate that the address is variable.

The test we shall use is to subtract 1 from a location which is initialized (or *preset*) to 50; when this *counter* has been reduced to

138 PROGRAMMING BUSINESS COMPUTERS

Initialize

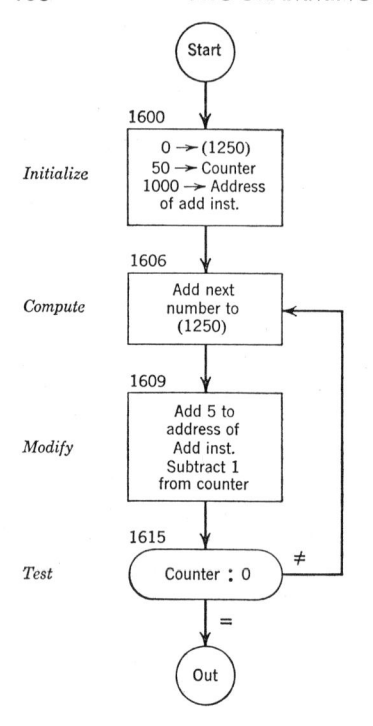

1600
0 → (1250)
50 → Counter
1000 → Address of add inst.

Compute

1606
Add next number to (1250)

Modify

1609
Add 5 to address of Add inst.
Subtract 1 from counter

Test

1615
Counter : 0
≠
=
Out

Figure 1. Flow chart of a loop to add fifty numbers.

zero the loop is finished. Subtracting the 1 from the counter each time through the loop is part of the modification. Location 1800 is the counter.

To understand the initialization shown below, it must be realized that a loop is ordinarily used many times. In our case, addition of the fifty numbers might be required *at several different points in the program*. The question is, What is the status of the address of the Add instruction, the counter, and location 1250—*after the loop has once been used?* In order to get the loop started correctly, it is necessary to place the correct values in these locations. If the loop were to be used only once, it would be possible to load the program into the machine in such a way that no initialization would be required.

The preceding description is of course not in the same order as the instructions which will be written, but it is perhaps fairly close to the sequence of thinking which a coder might go through. The flow chart of Figure 1 shows the order in which the parts of the routine are actually executed.

Assume constants:

	1789	+0000000000
	1790	0A100000000
	1791	+0000000050
	1792	+0000000001
	1793	+0000500000

The routine could be:

LOC.	S	O	ADDRESS	INDEX	FILTER	MON.	REMARKS
1600		B	1790				Bring Add instruction with correct address to R
1601		S	1607				Store in computing part. (Initialize address)
1602		B	1791				Bring 50 to R

(*Continued on next page*)

LOOPS AND INDEX REGISTERS 139

1603		S	1800	Store in counter at 1800. (Initialize counter)
1604		B	1789	Bring zero to R
1605		S	1250	Store in 1250. (Initialize storage location for sum)
1606		B	1250	Bring sum so far to R
1607		A	[1000]	Add next number from list to sum so far
1608		S	1250	Store sum so far in 1250
1609		B	1607	Bring Add instruction to R
1610		A	1793	Add 5 to address to get next number from list
1611		S	1607	Store instruction with modified address back in 1607
1612		B	1800	Bring counter to R
1613		M	1792	Subtract 1
1614		S	1800	Store modified counter
1615	N	J	1606	Nonzero jump back to compute, if counter not zero

1616 Program continuation

The workings of this routine may be made clearer by following its operation through the first few repetitions. The instructions at 1600 and 1601 initialize the address of the instruction which will later be modified. 1602 and 1603 put 50 in the counter which will be used to determine when the loop should stop repeating. 1604 and 1605 place zero in the location where the sum will be accumulated. All of these are done, as we saw, because previous use of the loop would have left incorrect starting values in some locations. The instructions at 1606–1608, the first time through, have the net result of simply moving the contents of 1000 to 1250. 1609–1611 add 5 to the address of the instruction at 1607, so that the next time through it will pick up the next number in the list. 1612–1614 subtract 1 from the counter and store the modified counter back in 1800. (The necessity of storing the modified counter back in memory may seem obvious, but it is often forgotten!) The Nonzero jump at 1615 tests whether the counter has yet been reduced to zero. After the first time through it obviously will not be zero, so the conditional jump to 1606 is executed. Execution of steps 1606–1608 the second time through has the net result of adding the first number from the list (which by now is in 1250) to the second (because of the modification of the address of the instruction at 1607), and storing the sum in 1250. Again the address of the instruction at 1607 is modified and the counter reduced, this time to 48. The jump is again executed. 1606–1608 the third time through result in the sum of the first *three* numbers being placed in 1250.

The fiftieth time this is done, the address of the instruction at 1607 will have been 1245 when the instruction was executed. Also, 1 will have been subtracted from the counter fifty times, reducing it to zero; the Nonzero jump will not jump and the routine will continue to the instruction at 1616—with the correct sum stored in 1250.

The routine above was set up as it was, not because the techniques are the best, but in the hope that it would be easy to follow. We may now explore possible improvements. In order to do so we should consider what makes a loop "good." A loop is basically a device for trading speed for memory space. The routine above would require the execution of 506 instructions: six initialization instructions and fifty times through the ten instructions in the part actually repeated. The same exercise could be coded in straight-line fashion to require only fifty-one instruction executions: one Bring, forty-nine Adds, and a Store, with the appropriate addresses. This would, of course, have been *much* faster, but it would require fifty-one memory locations versus twenty-one for the loop (including storage for constants). The comparison is intended not so much to justify loops as to point out what is important in "improving" a loop. In short, a reduction of steps in the compute, modify, or test sections can save much time, a reduction in the initialize section little. Adding two instructions in the initialize section while removing two elsewhere would leave memory requirements the same but would remove ninety-eight instruction executions. With this consideration in mind we may look into improvements in the form of the loop above.

One simple modification, which happens to save little execution time but removes one instruction from the memory required, is frequently applicable. Observe that there are two instructions in the program as written which are exactly the same, viz., Store 1800. A slight rearrangement will make it possible to use one instruction for both purposes, in this case initialization and modification.

LOC.	S	O	ADDRESS	INDEX	FILTER	MON.	REMARKS
1600		B	1790				Bring Add instruction to R
1601		S	1607				Store
1602		B	1789				Bring zero to R
1603		S	1250				Store in sum storage

(*Continued on next page*)

LOOPS AND INDEX REGISTERS

1604	B	1791	Bring 50 to R
1605	S		1800	Store counter in 1800
1606–1611	unchanged		
1612	B	1800	Bring counter to R
1613	M	1792	Subtract 1
1614 N	J	1605	Jump if nonzero to store modified counter and repeat loop

Note that the Store 1800 formerly at 1614 has been deleted, and that the address of the Nonzero jump is now 1605.

The second improvement saves more space and time. It may have been noticed that the counter is in this example redundant; another part of the routine is in effect also keeping a record of how far the loop has progressed. The modified address of the Add instruction at 1607 indicates unambiguously the stage of the calculation. If we can predict what the address of that instruction will be when the loop is finished, an appropriate instructional constant can be used to test for completion of the loop.

It is necessary to be quite careful in determining the address of the instructional constant. The last number in the list is at 1245, but is that the address which will be in the instruction when it is tested? As the program was set up, it will not, because by the time the test is made the address has been modified. The correct instructional constant is then 0A125000000.

The constant list is slightly different:

1780	+0000000000
1781	0A125000000
1782	+0000500000
1783	0A100000000

The routine is now:

LOC.	S	O	ADDRESS	REMARKS
1600		B	1780	Bring zero to R
1601		S	1250	Store to initialize sum
1602		B	1783	Bring Add instruction with correct initial address to R
1603		S	1605	Store to initialize (and modify) address of modified instruction
1604		B	1250	Bring sum so far to R
1605		A	[1000]	Add next number from list
1606		S	1250	Store sum so far in 1250
1607		B	1605	Bring Add instruction to R
1608		A	1782	Add 5 to address
1609		C	1781	Compare with instructional constant to test end of loop
1610	L	J	1603	Low jump back to 1603 if not completed

The test must now be made using a Compare instruction, because it is not possible in DATAC to do arithmetic on alphabetic characters such as operation codes. It should perhaps be obvious that the Add to memory instruction could have been used instead of the Bring-Add-Store combination; it was felt to be wise not to make exclusive use of a feature which many machines do not have.

8.2 A Tape Loop Example

Since the loop concept is so important, we shall devote a few pages to another example—this one a little more complex. Suppose a tape mounted on tape handler 8 contains an unknown number of blocks of information. All blocks contain twenty records of seven words each, but the last block may or may not be *filled* with data records since the number of records is not necessarily an exact multiple of twenty. The end of the information is signaled on the tape by what is usually called a *sentinel*. In our case we shall assume that the *first* word following the last record is all Z's. Such a sentinel can safely be used to signal the end of information only because we assume that the *first* word of a data record will never be eleven Z's. (For a further discussion of sentinels, see Chapter 13.)

To make the tape layout clearer, consider what would be on tape if the entire file consisted of twenty-three records. There would be first a full block of 140 words, consisting of twenty records of seven words each. The second (and in this case, final) block would consist of three data records of seven words each, followed by a word of Z's.

Since the routine must process only as many records of data as there are records on tape, and since the only indication of the end of data is the Z sentinel, a necessary part of the routine will be to test the first word of each record to determine if all data has been processed.

Suppose now that the calculation is simply to get the average of the third words of all those records in which the LSD ("Least Significant Digit," or rightmost character) of the first word is a 6. It would probably be unusual to find a computer run consisting of no more processing than this, but such a calculation is a fairly common *part* of a run. Such a calculation might, for instance, be required in order to obtain the average cost of a broad class of stock items. This problem will also illustrate a loop-within-a-loop: a major loop will be required to bring in successive blocks from tape, and another will be required to test each record in a block to determine if its first word contains a 6 in the LSD, and to add its third word to the sum location if so.

LOOPS AND INDEX REGISTERS 143

In the flow chart shown in Figure 2, we use a shorthand notation to indicate certain data and operations. The subscript n stands for the nth item in a sequence. B, R, and W stand respectively for Block, Record, and Word. Thus W_1 means the first *word* of a record. A

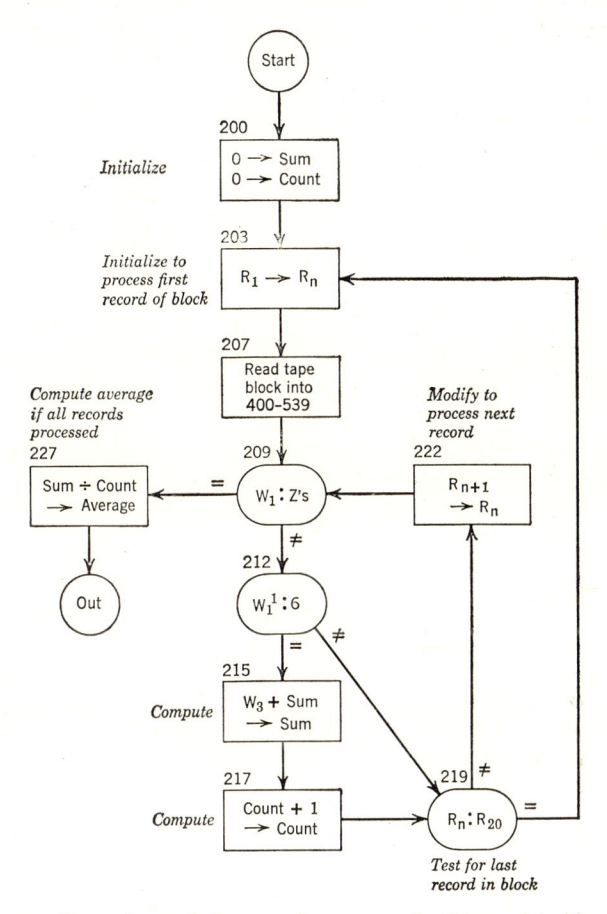

Figure 2. Flow chart of the tape loop example discussed in the text.

superscript is used to indicate the *character* of a word: W_1^1 means character 1 (the rightmost, or LSD) of the first word of a record. An arrow means either "replaces" or "goes to." $R_{n+1} \to R_n$ means "record n + 1 replaces record n," which implies modifying the necessary addresses so that the loop will process the next record when it is repeated. A colon is used to indicate a comparison, as we saw in Chapter 3. "$0 \to$ Sum" means that zero "goes to" or it "replaces the contents of" the location assigned to the sum.

144 PROGRAMMING BUSINESS COMPUTERS

A few notes may make the flow chart clearer. The first initializing box indicates that it is necessary to place zeros in the locations which hold the sum to be accumulated and the count of the number of records which have a 6 in the rightmost character of the first word. The comparison box "$W_1 : Z$'s" denotes the sentinel test. If the first word of the record is not equal ($\neq$) to the Z's, the processing continues. If the flow chart seems more complex than earlier examples, remember that two loops are involved and that the computation part of the minor loop itself involves a test—a test which is not part of the loop testing. The slight complexity of the application perhaps helps to emphasize the value of flow charting. Although some time and effort are of course required to draw the flow chart, coding is *much* simpler and more accurate having done so.

Constants:

700	+0000000000	
701	+0040000000	
702	+0040200000	
703	00000000006	
704	ZZZZZZZZZZ	
705	+0000000001	
706	+0000700000	
707	00053300000	
50	00111100000	address filter
51	00000000001	last character filter
600	Sum storage	
601	Count storage	

LOC.	S	O	ADDRESS	FILTER	REMARKS
200		B	0700		Bring zero to R
201		S	0600		Store in sum location
202		S	0601		Store in count location
203		B	0701		Bring initialized address for tests to R
204		S	0209	50	Store address, filtered
205		B	0702		Bring initialized address for summing to R
206		S	0215	50	Store address, filtered
207	R	T	0400	08	Read a block from tape 8 into 400–539
208	D	T		08	Delay tape until completion of reading
209		B	[0400]		Bring first word to R
210		C	0704		Compare with Z's
211	E	J	0227		Equal jump to compute average
212		C	0703	51	Compare with 6 in last character, filtered
213	E	J	0215		Equal jump to add third word of record to sum
214	U	J	0219		Unconditional jump to test whether last record of block

(*Continued on next page*)

LOOPS AND INDEX REGISTERS

215		B	[0402]		Bring third word of record to R
216	X	A	0600		Add to memory to get sum
217		B	0705		Bring 1 to R
218	X	A	0601		Add 1 to count
219		B	0209		Bring modified instruction to R
220		C	0707	50	Compare with address of final record, filtered
221	E	J	0203		Equal jump to reinitialize and read new tape block
222		A	0706		Add 7 to address
223		S	0209		Store modified instruction
224		B	0706		Bring 7 to R
225	X	A	0215		Add to memory to modify address
226	U	J	0209		Unconditional jump to process next record
227		F	0700		Fetch zero to L to set up division
228		B	0600		Bring sum to R
229		D	0601		Divide by count
230			Store average and continue		

The method of this routine takes no advantage of buffering. To be useful in real life, it would have to be modified to incorporate stand-by blocks, to be discussed in Chapter 13. Nevertheless, the routine as it stands is a fairly good introduction to the type of coding required very extensively in tape data processing applications. Both for a thorough understanding of loops and for the introduction to tape methods, the example should be carefully studied.

8.3 Index Register Functions and Applications

We have seen how frequently it is necessary in loops to modify addresses and to test for ending conditions. It may have been observed that often more instructions are used in the modification and testing functions than in the actual computation—which after all is the primary function of the loop.

It is in reducing this programming burden and wasted machine storage space and time that index registers are of primary value. They have three characteristics which constitute their power:

1. They make for much simpler address modification, including the ability to modify many addresses as easily as one.

2. They are easier to modify than instruction addresses and counters, because of certain powerful index instructions which perform several operations at once.

3. Modification can be combined with testing, again because of the availability of certain powerful index instructions.

In some real machines there are a small number of index registers, which are a part of the control section; information may be transferred between the index registers and memory or the arithmetic section. Other computers in effect have many index registers, since one control register may be loaded from any of many memory locations *as part of the execution of each instruction.* (And, of course, some machines have no index registers at all, although some of these have other loop-simplifying facilities.)

For DATAC we assume the many-register concept. All of the memory locations which can be used for filtering may also be used as index registers, or, as we shall say, *indexers.* When it is desired to apply an indexer to an instruction, it is necessary simply to specify the desired indexer location in the *indexer characters,* positions five and four of the instruction. Before the instruction is executed, the indexer is obtained from memory and placed in a control section register, and the appropriate characters of the indexer added to the address of the instruction. Then the instruction execution proceeds as usual, except that now the address used is the address as written *plus* the contents of the indexer, resulting in what we shall call the *effective address.*

We assume in DATAC that each indexer consists of three parts, called the *counter, modifier,* and *increment.* These are in a memory location as follows:

S 10 9	8 7 6 5	4 3 2 1
Counter	Increment	Modifier

The modifier is the part which is added to the address when an indexer is specified. The functions of the other parts will appear shortly.

To illustrate, suppose location 63 is an indexer containing 00000000040, and the instruction

0A123463000

is executed. The 63 in the indexer characters of the instruction specifies that the modifier part of the word at 63 should be added to the address 1234. The effective address of the Add instruction would thus be 1274. *The instruction remains unchanged in memory.*

It should be obvious that the ability to modify the addresses of instructions in this manner, particularly since the same indexer can be applied to any number of instructions, adds great power to a computer. But some means must be available for changing the contents of an indexer. In DATAC we have three special instruc-

LOOPS AND INDEX REGISTERS

tions for the purpose. All of them are actually jump instructions, partly because two of them are decision operations, but partly because, in "designing" DATAC, there would otherwise have been no function for the address.

The first index instruction is Raise index and jump (operation code: RI). The increment of the specified indexer is added to the modifier and a jump to the location specified in the Raise index instruction is executed. It is seen that the instruction is in concept a combination of a Bring, an Add to memory, and an Unconditional jump. It is used when it is desired merely to change the modifier of an indexer, without the testing function involved in the instructions discussed in the next paragraph.

The Zero index jump instruction (operation code: ZI) is in concept a combination of a Bring, a Subtract from memory, a Zero jump, another Bring, and an Add to memory. Its function is as follows: 1 is first subtracted from the counter part of the specified indexer, where the counter is three digits since it includes the sign character. If the counter is now zero, a jump to the address of the Zero index jump instruction is executed. If the counter *is not* now zero, the increment part is added to the modifier and the next instruction in normal sequence is executed. The Nonzero index jump instruction (operation code: NI) is similar. A 1 is subtracted from the counter as before. If the counter *is* now zero, the next instruction in sequence is executed. If the counter is not now zero, the increment is added to the modifier and the jump executed. These two instructions represent a very powerful combination of modify, test, and jump functions.

In all three, it is possible to get the effect of *subtracting* the "increment" from the modifier by use of *complement subtraction*. This is a technique which is fairly commonly used in computing devices (including the familiar Comptometer), especially in the internal arithmetic operations. The basis of the technique may be shown with an example.

$$1234 - 0012 = 1234 + (10{,}000 - 0012) - 10{,}000$$
$$= 1234 + 9988 - 10{,}000$$
$$= 1222$$

Presented thus, complement subtraction looks more complicated than it is in practice. The quantity in parentheses is called the *ten's complement* of 0012, and may be formed by subtracting each digit from nine except the last which is subtracted from ten. (If the last digit is zero, the *next-to-last* character is subtracted from ten, etc.)

Subtraction of the 10,000 (in this case) is effected by simply ignoring the 1 which will be the leftmost digit of the sum. Stated another way, the 10,000 may be subtracted by accepting only a *four-digit* sum.

To illustrate:

$$\begin{array}{r} 8876 \\ -0034 \\ \hline \end{array} \quad \text{is equivalent to} \quad \begin{array}{r} 8876 \\ +9966 \\ \hline (1)\ 8842 \end{array}$$

$$\begin{array}{r} 0400 \\ -0007 \\ \hline \end{array} \quad \text{is equivalent to} \quad \begin{array}{r} 0400 \\ +9993 \\ \hline (1)\ 0393 \end{array}$$

Thus to *subtract* the "increment" from the modifier, we need only place the ten's complement of the number to be subtracted in the increment part. (In machines where instead of an "increment" there is a "decrement" which normally *subtracts,* the same technique is used to make it add.)

Two instructions are available in DATAC for simplifying transfers between the indexer section of memory and other parts. Load index (operation code: LI) moves a word from the location specified by the address part of the instruction, and places it in the location specified by the indexer part of the instruction. Store index (operation code: SI) is just the reverse, storing a word from the indexer section of memory in any other part. The addresses of either of these instructions could themselves refer to the indexer section, since we assume in DATAC that memory locations 01–99 have exactly the same characteristics as any other part of memory—except that they can also be used in indexing or filtering. Load index and Store index can thus be used for memory-to-memory transfers having nothing to do with indexing or filtering, if desired.

The usefulness of indexers in reducing the bulk of loops may be illustrated by reprogramming the problems of the previous sections.

In the first example we were required to find the sum of the numbers in 1000, 1005, 1010, etc., up to 1245, and place it in 1250. The basic method is the same with indexers. The initialization is simpler since only the indexer need be set up, and the entire modification will consist of one instruction. The initial contents of the indexer can be reasoned out as follows. The counter must clearly be 50 to start, since the loop is to be repeated fifty times. The increment must obviously be 5, since the successive addresses differ by 5. The simplest way to set up the modifier is to make the modifier initially zero and the instruction address the location of the first number from the

LOOPS AND INDEX REGISTERS 149

list. The indexer, assumed to be in location 43, may then be initialized to

$$05000050000$$

The only other initialization required is to clear the R register. This is necessary because the sum will simply be accumulated in R; there is no need to store the partial sum back in memory each time, since the R register will not be needed for address modification or testing.

Constants:

        0107   05000050000
        0108   +0000000000

The entire routine now consists of five steps:

LOC.	S	O	ADDRESS	INDEXER	REMARKS
0350	L	I	0107	43	Load indexer with initial value
0351		B	0108		Bring zero to R
0352		A	1000	43	Add (indexed) number from list
0353	N	I	0352	43	Nonzero index jump
0354		S	1250		Store sum in 1250

Indexer 43 was chosen arbitrarily. Any one of them could have been used, since we assume nothing else is in the filter—indexer section of memory. In studying the function of the indexer in this example, recall that with Nonzero index jump the increment is added to the modifier and the jump executed if the counter is *not* zero after 1 is subtracted from it. Table 1 shows the contents of the indexer and the effective addresses of the indexed Add as the loop progresses:

TABLE 1

INDEXER CONTENTS	EFFECTIVE ADDRESS
05000050000	1000
04900050005	1005
04800050010	1010
04700050015	1015
04600050020	1020
.	.
.	.
.	.
00200050240	1240
00100050245	1245
00000050245	Jump not executed

Note the last entry in Table 1. When subtracting 1 from the counter reduces it to zero, the increment is not added to the modifier and the jump is not executed.

150   PROGRAMMING BUSINESS COMPUTERS

The tape reading and averaging program is similarly simplified. It shows the use of the Raise index instruction, in this case to count the number of records which have a 6 in the last character of the first word.

Constants:

700	00000010000	Initial value of record counter
701	02000070000	Initial value of indexer
702	ZZZZZZZZZZZ	Sentinel test
703	00000000006	
55		Record counter
58	00000000001	Last character filter
59	00000001111	Modifier filter
60	+0000000000	
600		Sum storage

LOC.	S	O	ADDRESS	INDEXER	FILTER OR TAPE #	MON.	REMARKS
200	S	I	0600	60			Store index in 600, to clear sum storage
201	L	I	0700	55			Initialize record counter
202	L	I	0701	56			Initialize indexer
203	R	T	0400		08		Read a block from tape handler 8 into 0400–0539
204	D	T			08		Delay until reading completed
205		B	0400	56			Bring first word of current record to R register, indexed
206		C	0702				Compare with Z's (sentinel)
207	E	J	0216				Equal jump to compute average
208		C	0703		58		Compare with 6 in last character, filtered
209	E	J	0211				Equal jump to add third word to sum
210	U	J	0214				Unconditional jump to test whether last word of block
211		B	0402	56			Bring third word of current record to R register, indexed
212	X	A	0600				Add to memory
213	R	I	0214	55			Add 1 to count of records which have 6 in last character of first word; jump to following instruction

(*Continued on next page*)

LOOPS AND INDEX REGISTERS 151

214	N	I	0205	56	Nonzero index jump to process next record
215	U	J	0202		Unconditional jump to read new block and reinitialize indexer
216		F	0060		Fetch zero to L register to set up division
217		B	0600		Bring sum to R
218		D	0055	59	Divide by modifier part of "counter" indexer, filtered
219	Store average and continue processing

At the instruction in 200 note the use of Store index to obtain the effect of a Bring-Store pair. This has nothing to do with indexing in the loop sense, but it is typical of the way an alert coder will take advantage of machine characteristics. Note also that one indexer was used to modify two addresses, which illustrates an advantage of indexing. One instruction each to initialize and modify the indexer replace eight instructions in the unindexed version. In the Raise index instruction, no advantage was taken of the ability to jump as part of the instruction; the address was made simply the location of the next instruction in sequence. The pair of instructions at 214 and 215 could have been

| 214 | Z | I | 0202 | 56 |
| 215 | U | J | 0205 | |

with no change in the results of the loop, but with a lengthening of the loop execution time. (The reader who satisfies himself of the accuracy of this statement will have demonstrated a thorough understanding of the operation of the Nonzero index jump and Zero index jump instructions.)

8.4 Another Loop Example

The following short routine shows how loops and indexers may be of use even though modification of addresses is not involved. Suppose there is in memory a number consisting as usual of a sign and ten digits. The number may have from zero to ten significant digits, i.e., there may be any number of zeros to the left of the first nonzero digits, or the number may consist of a sign and ten zeros. For reasons connected with applications which need not be elaborated here, it is desired to shift the number left until there is a nonzero digit in the leftmost character. If the word consists of all zeros, the routine should halt.* Table 2 may clarify the action to be taken. X stands (here) for any digit other than zero.

TABLE 2

ORIGINAL FORM	NUMBER OF LEFT SHIFTS	FINAL FORM
±X X X X X X X X X X	None	±X X X X X X X X X X
±0 X X X X X X X X X	1	±X X X X X X X X X 0
±0 0 X X X X X X X X	2	±X X X X X X X X 0 0
±0 0 0 X X X X X X X	3	±X X X X X X X 0 0 0
.	.	.
.	.	.
.	.	.
±0 0 0 0 0 0 0 0 0 X	9	±X 0 0 0 0 0 0 0 0 0
±0 0 0 0 0 0 0 0 0 0	Halt	

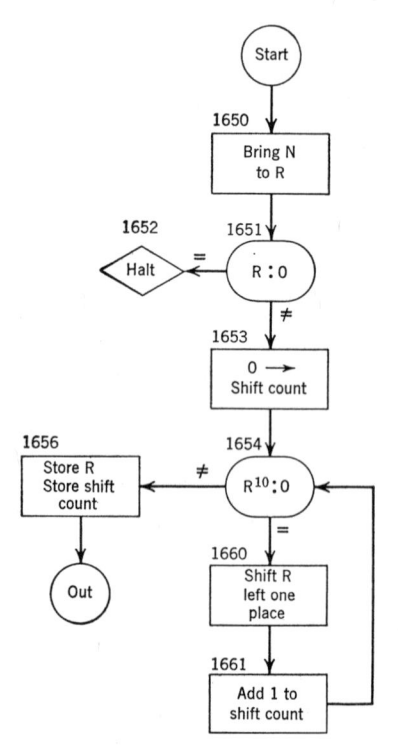

Figure 3. Flow chart of the normalizing loop discussed in the text.

*In a real situation the routine probably would not be designed to stop, but to take corrective action through a separate routine. We are concerned here with indexers, not system design, so we ignore this point.

LOOPS AND INDEX REGISTERS

Assume the original number, N, is in 0600 and the shifted number should be stored back in 0600 after the process is complete; the number of shifts required is to be stored as an integer in 0601. Incidentally, the process described here is usually called *normalization* of the number, which is necessary in some engineering and scientific calculations.

This routine will be our first contact with the Interrupted jump instruction (operation code: IJ). The function of this instruction is to stop the execution of instructions, either to indicate an error condition, to indicate the completion of the program, or to give the machine operator time to enter control data into the computer. The "jump" part means that when the operator presses the *start* button on the console, to be discussed later, the control circuits proceed as if an Unconditional jump had been encountered. Another way of saying this is that Interrupted jump is just like an Unconditional jump except that the machine stops in the middle of the execution and waits for the start button to be pushed.

In the flow chart of Figure 3, the comparison "$R^{10}:0$" means to compare character 10 (the leftmost excluding the sign) of R with zero.

Constants:

1400	+0000000000
1401	00000010000
90	01000000000
91	00000001111

LOC.	S	O	ADDRESS	INDEXER	FILTER	REMARKS
1650		B	0600			Bring N to R
1651	N	J	1653			Nonzero jump past halt
1652	I	J	(To error routine)			Stop if all zeros
1653	L	I	1401	12		Load indexer 12 with zero modifier (shift count) and increment of 1
1654		C	1400		90	Compare character 10 with zero. Filter to exclude other characters
1655	E	J	1660			Equal jump to shift and count
1656		S	0600			Store normalized number (if here, comparison showed leftmost digit not zero)
1657		B	0012			Bring indexer 12 to R (contains shift count in modifier portion)
1658		S	0601		91	Store shift count in 601; filter to include modifier only

(Continued on next page)

1659	U	J	1662		Unconditional jump to continue
1660	O	L	0001		Shift R one place left, excluding sign
1661	R	I	1654	12	Raise index and jump (counts one shift)
1662	Continuation

The address of the Interrupted jump instruction was left blank because we did not say what should be done about a number which consisted of all zeros. The Compare in 1654 takes advantage of DATAC filtering to effect in one instruction what might require several in most actual computers. This is defensible, however, as a general principle. Each computer has special features which may be used to advantage. The exact manner in which a particular function is coded always depends on the details of the computer being used. It might be said also that clever programmers frequently take advantage of machine characteristics in ways that the computer designers did not anticipate. On at least one major computer, programmers "discovered" a quite valuable instruction which the designers did not realize existed!

8.5 Indexers in DATAC Tape Functions

There are certain problems which must be faced in the original design of the characteristics of magnetic tapes. One problem, stated simply, is that the length of a tape block either must be fixed or there must be a way to specify to the machine the length of the block. This problem is dealt with in a variety of ways in real machines. In DATAC we assume that tape blocks are of completely variable length, and that the indexers are used to specify length where necessary.

One situation where indexing or something similar is necessary in real computers which have variable length tape records is in tape *writing*, or transferring a block of words from main memory to a tape. In DATAC the number of words to be written is specified by the increment part of an indexer. This is, of course, a completely different use of the indexer than is involved in loops, but such a special functioning is hardly rare in computer design. As we have seen previously, for instance, the "address" of a shift instruction does not refer to a memory location at all. Another special characteristic of DATAC indexers as applied to tapes is that the part which is used in loops as the *counter* is here employed to modify the tape handler number, if desired. The modifier part of an indexer may be used to change the effective address of the tape instruction. The built-in ability to modify the tape number is available on only a few real machines; it is quite valuable in multiple-reel file operations for ease in switching between tape handlers, as discussed in Chapter 13.

A complete description of a DATAC Write tape instruction (operation code: WT) is then as follows. The *modifier* part of the specified indexer is added to the *address* part of the Write tape instruction to get the effective address, which is the address of the *first* word of the block to be placed on tape. The *counter* part of the indexer is added to the *filter* part of the instruction to get the "effective tape number." The machine finally writes on tape the number of words specified in the increment part of the indexer. A few examples will help to clarify the definition.

        Write tape instruction   WT 1000 60 08 0
        Indexer 60   000 0080 0000

Since the modifier of the indexer is zero, the effective address is the same as the instruction address, and the block starts in 1000. The counter is also zero, so the tape handler number is 8. With an "increment" of 80, eighty words would be written; the memory block would thus consist of locations 1000–1079.

        Write tape instruction   WT 1000 65 04 0
        Indexer 65   002 0140 0200

The block in 1200–1339 would be written on tape 6.

        Write tape instruction   WT 1000 32 07 0
        Indexer 32   000 0010 9900

The block in 900–909 would be written on tape 7. (Note the complement subtraction.)

Now that we have discussed the function of indexers in tape operations, we may return to the Read tape instruction and describe its operation completely. It is actually a "dual" of Write tape. The tape handler number may be modified by the counter part of the specified indexer, if desired, and the address may be an effective address, i.e., it may be modified by the modifier part of the indexer. The one difference is that, instead of placing the number of words to be read in the increment of the indexer, the machine simply reads the entire record, counts the number of words read, and places this number in the increment. The difference between the two operations may be thought of as follows: on Write tape, the record is moved *from* memory to tape and the number of words to be read is taken *from* the indexer; on Read tape, the record is moved *to* memory from tape and the number of words read is sent *to* the indexer. On Write tape, an indexer *must* be specified; if on Read tape indexer 00 is specified, the number of words read is not stored anywhere, and the tape number and memory address are simply not modified. (This feature made it possible to discuss the Read tape instruction in Chapter 6, before indexers had been introduced.)

8.6 Indexing in a Tape Application

The example which will be presented here to illustrate the use of indexers in DATAC tape operations at the same time involves an important concept in sequential data processing. That is what is often called the *expanding file* technique, which was introduced in general terms in Chapter 2.

For our example of the method we shall consider a vastly simplified accounts receivable application. For the purpose here, the master file will consist of two-word records; the first word is the customer's account number and the second is his balance owed to the company. The transaction file consists of three-word records. The first is the account number which, as before, identifies the customer. The second is a dollar amount to be debited or credited to the customer's account. The third is a *transaction code* which identifies the transaction as a debit, a credit, an addition to the master file (a new account), or a deletion (a closed account). Both files are already in *ascending sequence on account number,* i.e., the first record on the master file is the one having the smallest account number, the next has the next larger account number, etc. (To get the transaction file into ascending sequence would require a previous *sorting* run since the transactions would not normally come into the system already sequenced. See Chapter 15 on sorting methods.)

Ordinarily the transaction file is much smaller than the master file, since in a given time period not all accounts have "activity." That is, not all customers make payments or purchases, and there are relatively few new or closed accounts.

The basic task is to produce a new *updated* master file which is the old master file as modified by the information on the transaction tape. The process is started by reading into memory the first transaction record and the first master record. The processing may be defined by the six possibilities which now exist; these possibilities also exist in later situations, i.e., on records after the first.

1. If the transaction is a credit (a customer payment is received), as identified by the transaction code, the corresponding master file

LOOPS AND INDEX REGISTERS

record must be found and the transaction amount subtracted from the amount receivable. Then the new master file record must be written on an output tape which will become the new master file.*

2. If the transaction is a debit (a purchase), the process is the same except that the transaction amount is *added* to the master amount.

3. If the transaction is a deletion, the corresponding master file record should simply not be written on the output tape. (This is a simplification which would certainly not work out in practice. At a minimum, there would have to be some consideration of what to do with close-outs when the balance was not zero.)

4. If the transaction is an addition, it must be placed on the output tape in correct account number sequence.

5. In any of the above, there will normally be many records read from the old master file tape which are *inactive*, i.e., unaffected by the transactions. These are simply written onto the output tape without altering the sequence.

6. Any transaction (except an addition) which does not correspond to *any* master file record indicates some type of error—often an incorrect transaction code or account number. In the program to follow we shall simply stop if this occurs.

The sample files below illustrate the required processing. We shall assume that credits, debits, deletions, and additions have the transaction codes 1, 2, 3, 4 respectively. (The fact that the illustration shows exactly one of each, and in order, means nothing in this case.)

TRANSACTION FILE	OLD MASTER FILE	NEW MASTER FILE
10065	10060	10060
$60.00	$65.00	$65.00
1		
	10065	10065
10083	$87.50	$27.50
$14.60		
2	10070	10070
	$400.00	$400.00
10099		
$0.00	10082	10082
3	$6.82	$6.82

(*Continued on next page*)

---

* We may note once again that with some computers it is possible to write the updated master record back onto the old master tape. The fact that we refer to this technique only in footnotes does not constitute a judgment of it: it simply reflects the fact that this book is an *introduction* to data processing, not an encyclopedia.

10111	10083	10083
$60.14	$67.10	$81.70
4		
	10084	10084
ZZZZZ	$99.60	$99.60
(sentinel)		
	10099	10105
	$16.78	$905.61
	10105	10108
	$905.61	$14.80
	10108	10111
	$14.80	$60.14
	10112	10112
	$62.03	$62.03
	10118	10118
	$40.00	$40.00
	ZZZZZ	ZZZZZ

Of course, the files shown in the example are very much shorter than a typical business file. It should be noted also that the fact that transactions in the example are in order of account number implies that the transaction file has already been sorted.

Figure 4 is a flow chart for the process, assuming that each record is contained in a separate tape block.

Note a few features of the logic of the problem. It is essential that the output tape be correctly ended *no matter which input tape runs out first*. That is, whether the transaction tape runs out of information first, or the master does (which means that the rest of the information on the transaction tape consists of additions with high account numbers*), both tapes must be read completely and a sentinel placed at the end of the new master.

It is possible that through some sort of error the master or transaction files could be out of sequence, or missorted. Since this almost always is a disabling error, it must be tested for. Analysis shows that (in this problem) when the method shown on the flow chart will catch the error, it will be signaled by a master record with an account number larger than the current transaction record, when the transaction

* Assuming, of course, that the transaction tape contains no errors such as wrong account numbers and that the master tape had no missing records. In practice, we would check for such errors as the remaining transaction records are transferred to the new master tape.

LOOPS AND INDEX REGISTERS   159

is not an addition. (A complete sequence check consists of testing successive records directly, to determine that they are in ascending order.)

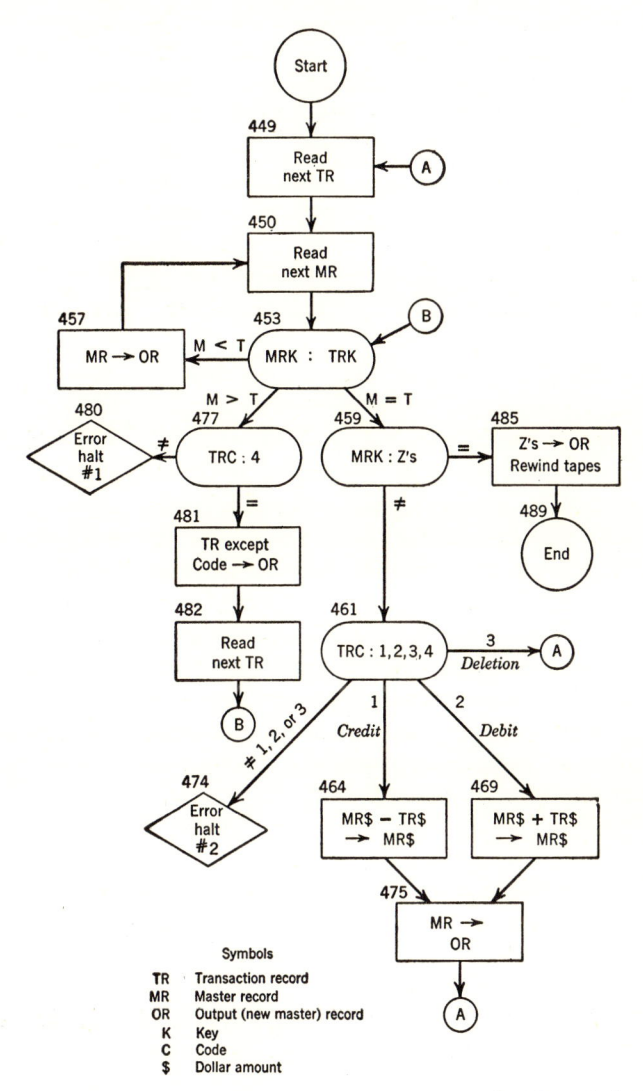

Figure 4. Flow chart of a simplified accounts receivable calculation.

Symbols
TR   Transaction record
MR   Master record
OR   Output (new master) record
K   Key
C   Code
$ Dollar amount

Observe that we have made another unrealistic assumption in order to simplify the problem: there is never more than one transaction per account. In actual practice, such an assumption would be totally impossible: an obvious case where it is not true is a situation where a customer makes two purchases in one day. This is not too hard to handle. One problem which must be considered in designing the system for multiple transactions is the priority of the different types of transactions. It is fairly obvious that the transactions should be sorted so that new account additions are processed before credits and debits; otherwise, a customer who makes a purchase shortly after opening his account would cause the system to give false error indications. Another example is bank check accounting, where deposits must be processed before withdrawals. Such problems must be considered in the system design.

Observe that this flow chart does not define coding methods, and in some cases is more indicative than definitive. The box

(TRC: 1, 2, 3, 4)

for instance says little about how to make the test—whether by Compare instructions, Zero jumps, address computation, or other techniques. This is characteristic of *useful* flow charts: we could draw a chart which literally defines every instruction, but this is too detailed to be of much use in getting the over-all picture.

In the following sample coding of this application, it is assumed that each word is in "normal" position, i.e., the quantity appears in memory to the far right of the memory cell or tape word. This is not realistic in practice either, but it simplifies the example so we may concentrate on other things. The sometimes unrealistic assumption of one-record tape blocks is similarly justified.

Assume the following locations:

Transaction record	200–202
Old master record	203–204
Indexer 22	000 0002 0000
300	ZZZZZZZZZZ
301	+0000000001
302	+0000000004

Assume that the transaction, old, and new master file tapes are on tape handlers 1, 2, and 3 respectively.

LOC.	S	O	ADDRESS	INDEXER	FILTER	REMARKS
449	R	T	200		01	Read next transaction record into 200–202
450	R	T	203		02	Read next master record into 203–204
451	D	T			01	Delay until reading complete

(*Continued on next page*)

LOOPS AND INDEX REGISTERS   161

452	D	T		02	Delay until reading complete
453		B	203		Bring master account number to R
454		C	200		Compare with transaction account number
455	E	J	459		Equal jump
456	H	J	477		High jump
457	W	T	203	22	03	If here, MR Key was less than TR Key. Old MR becomes new MR. Indexer 22 specifies two-word record
458	U	J	450			Unconditional jump to read next master record
459		C	300			Test for sentinel
460	E	J	485			Equal jump if sentinel, to write sentinel on new master and rewind tapes
461		B	202			Bring transaction code to R
462		M	301			Subtract 1
463	N	J	467			Nonzero jump
464		B	201			If here, code was 1 and transaction is credit
465	X	M	204			Subtract from memory to subtract payment from old balance
466	U	J	475			Unconditional jump to write tape
467		M	301			Subtract 1
468	N	J	472			Nonzero jump
469		B	201			If here, code was 2 and transaction is debit
470	X	A	204			Add to memory to add purchase to old balance
471	U	J	475			Unconditional jump to write tape
472		M	301			Subtract 1
473	Z	J	449			Zero jump if deletion, code 3
474	I	J				If here, code was 4 and an account number has been assigned improperly, or code was not 1, 2, 3 or 4, also indicating error
475	W	T	203	22	03	Write modified master on tape 3
476	U	J	449			Unconditional jump to process next transaction
477		B	202			Bring transaction record code to R
478		C	302			Compare with code 4
479	E	J	481			Equal jump means code was 4

(*Continued on next page*)

480	I	J				If here, code was not 4, indicating some type of error
481	W	T	200	22	03	Write record on tape 3 from first two words of transaction record
482	R	T	200		01	Read next transaction record
483	D	T			01	Delay tape until reading complete
484	U	J	453			Unconditional jump to process next transaction
485	W	T	300	22	03	Write sentinel on tape 3
486	A	T			01	Rewind tape 1
487	A	T			02	Rewind tape 2
488	A	T			03	Rewind tape 3
489	I	J				Stop at completion

This routine could be written in many different ways. The exact arrangement of the different parts, whether to use High jump or Low jump first, where to place the error stops, etc., is at the option of the coder. The routine shown is adequate, but not the only possible one; it is not even necessarily the shortest possible.

8.7 Summary

We have seen how loops take advantage of the distinguishing features of stored program computers, how they work, and how they are used. We have given a few examples of loop applications. It has been observed that loops can be set up to operate on a variable amount of data which need not be predetermined, as in the last example. We have observed that in essence a loop is a trade of instruction execution time for storage space, since it is often possible to conserve time—if that is the only objective—by not using a loop at all. It is sometimes advantageous to "unwind" loops, i.e., to "trade back" to save time; this can sometimes be done by the machine itself, as part of the operation of an automatic programming scheme, as discussed in Chapter 14.

All in all, loops are undoubtedly the single most important concept in coding, both from the standpoint of using the distinguishing features of a stored program computer and as a tool used in day-to-day work.

Exercises

Note: On many of the exercises below, DATAC indexing may be employed or not, as desired. This does not apply, of course, to certain tape operations where (in DATAC) indexing is required.

LOOPS AND INDEX REGISTERS

1. Flow-chart and code a loop to store +0000000000 in all memory location from 1000 to 1999 inclusive.

2. Two lists of numbers are already stored in 100–119 and 120–139. Flow-chart and code a loop to multiply the number in 100 by the number in 120 and place the product in 140, and similarly for all twenty pairs of numbers, storing the products in 140–159. Ignore decimal point location and overflow problems.

3. An employee is paid either a minimum weekly earnings or on a piece rate basis depending upon which amount is greater. Assume that the following master file and transaction file items are in memory, and assume that previous programming has established that there is equality between the items:

Master File Items

LOC	S	10	9	8	7	6	5	4	3	2	1
		Piece Rate						Emp. No.			
1500	+	X∧X	X	X	0	0	1	2	3	4
		Min. Wk. Earn.				YTD Earn.					
1501	+	X X∧X	X	X	X X	X∧X	X

Transaction Items

	S	10	9	8	7	6	5	4	3	2	1	
		Pieces						Emp. No.				
1600	+	X X X X∧	0	0	1	2	3	4	1st day
1601	+	X X X X∧	0	0	1	2	3	4	2nd day
1602	+	X X X X∧	0	0	1	2	3	4	3rd day
1603	+	X X X X∧	0	0	1	2	3	4	4th day
1604	+	X X X X∧	0	0	1	2	3	4	5th day

Flow-chart and code a loop that will accumulate the total number of pieces produced for the week. Determine the employee's pay on either the minimum rate or piece rate depending upon which results in the greater pay; place the answer in location 1750. Update YTD earnings. Show all constants used.

4. Extend Exercise 3 to include the master file and transaction file items for ten employees. Assume that all items are in memory.

5. Extend the example in Exercise 4 to include magnetic tape operations. Assume that the master file items are on tape handler #1, the transaction items on tape handler #2, and the updated master file items are to be written on tape handler #3. Test for Z sentinels on the input tapes, and write a Z sentinel following the last item on the output tape.

6. Starting in 0100 and continuing as far as required are a series of dollar amounts; there are at most 100 of these. After the last dollar amount, wherever the list may end, is a sentinel consisting of eleven Z's. Flow-chart and code a loop to compute the sum of the dollar amounts and find their average, but any dollar amount which is zero should not be used in computing the average. For instance, if the entire list consisted of the amounts $10.00, $0.00, $25.00, $40.00, $0.00, and then the Z sentinel, the correct average would be $25.00. Store the average in location 0210.

7. Write a loop to carry out the function of the DATAC Dollar edit instruction using other DATAC instructions. See Appendix 1 for a description of this instruction.

8. In locations 1200–1219 are twenty alpha-numeric words. Flow-chart and code a loop to do the following. Compare the first and second words; if the first one is smaller than or equal to the second (in the sense of the DATAC Compare instruction), do nothing, but if the first word is larger than the second, interchange the two words in memory. Now compare the first and third words and interchange them if the first is larger than the third (no consideration need be given to the fact that the first word may now be what used to be the second). Continue comparing and interchanging if necessary, operating successively on the first and fourth words, the first and fifth, etc., until the first and twentieth have to be compared and interchanged if necessary. (At the completion of such a loop it is certain that location 1200 contains the smallest number of the twenty.)

9. Extend the procedure of Exercise 8 as follows. Having gotten the smallest word in location 1200, get the next larger word in location 1201 by successive comparisons of the second and third words, the second and fourth, etc.; then get the next larger word in 1202 by operating on the fourth and fifth words, the fourth and sixth, etc. The last "pass" of the larger loop will consist of comparing the nineteenth and twentieth words and interchanging them if they are not in correct sequence. (This problem illustrates one method of arranging a series of words into a sequence, which is usually called *sorting*. The method illustrated here is sorting by *selection*.)

10. In locations 1200–1219 is a *string* of words which are in ascending sequence, i.e., the word in 1200 is the smallest, the word in 1201 is the next larger, etc. In locations 1220–1239 is another string of (different) words, also in sequence. Flow-chart and code a loop to *merge* the two strings into one string of forty words in 1240–1279, as follows. Compare the word in 1200 with the word in 1220. If the word in 1200 is smaller than or equal to the word in 1220, move the word in 1200 to 1240; otherwise, move the word in 1220 to 1240. Since the original two strings were already in sequence (by definition), this guarantees that the smallest word in both strings is now in 1240. The next larger word is found by a comparison between whichever word was *not* moved to 1240 and the word immediately following the word which *was* moved to 1240. Continue such a process until all words from both original strings have been merged into one string. Devise a suitable way of determining when all the words in one string have been moved, and a way of determining when the process is completed.

11. The words in locations 0523–0579 consist in each case of a three-letter "symbol" in the rightmost three characters, and a two-letter "value" in the leftmost two characters, i.e., the "sign" and "ten" characters. In location 0996 is a "test" word which contains a three-letter "symbol" in its rightmost three characters. Flow-chart and code a loop to determine if the "test symbol" is the same as any of the "symbols" in the list; if so, the "value" corresponding to that "symbol" should be placed in location 0997. If the "test symbol" does not correspond to any of the "symbols" in the list, place the "value" 00 in 0997.

12. The tape on handler #7 contains an unknown number of ten-word records. The LSD of the first word of each record contains what we will call the "code,"

which is guaranteed to be a digit between 1 and 9 inclusive. The second word of each record consists of a dollar amount in the rightmost characters; this amount is never over $10.00 (why is this fact needed?). The problem is to accumulate, in nine different memory locations, the dollar amounts corresponding to each of the nine codes, for all the records on the tape. The last record is followed by a Z sentinel. Flow-chart and code this problem, assuming whatever memory locations and constants may be needed.

13. The tape on handler #2 contains an unknown number of eight-word records, followed by a Z sentinel. The first word of each record is an eleven-character key, and the third word of each record is a dollar amount of not over $100.00 in the rightmost characters of the word. The records are all in sequence on the keys. There are ordinarily several records having the same key. The problem is to read the records successively, and prepare a summary tape on handler #4 on which the records are two words, consisting of the key and the total dollar amount for that key. The summary tape will thus be much shorter than the input tape; a Z sentinel should be written on the summary tape when the input tape has been completely read and summarized. Flow-chart and code.

14. Same as Exercise 13, except that the input consists of several reels of tape. The first tape of the file is initially mounted on handler #2, and has a sentinel consisting of ZZZZZZZZZZY. When this tape has been completely read, it should be rewound. Then input records should be read from the second tape, which is mounted on handler #3 (this is done so that processing of the second reel can proceed while the first is being rewound). The second tape, assuming it is not the last one, also has a sentinel consisting of ZZZZZZZZZZY. The third reel is mounted back on handler #2, etc. The reels of the input file are thus alternated between handlers #2 and #3. At the end of the file, whenever it occurs, is a sentinel consisting of ZZZZZZZZZZZ. It is assumed that the summary tape will not be over one reel. Flow-chart and code a loop to summarize the input file and write the summary tape, considering all the end-of-reel and end-of-file problems.

15. Same as Exercise 14, with the additional feature that each input tape has a *control total* in a one-word record immediately following the sentinel. This consists of the total of all the dollar amounts on the tape. As each record on a tape is read, the dollar amount should be accumulated in some location, without any consideration of key. As each record is written on the summary tape, the dollar amount should be accumulated in some other location. When the last input record has been read, the two control totals should be compared to see if they are equal—which, of course, they will be if there have been no processing errors. If they are equal, write the control total on the summary tape to allow for checking of further processing. If the two control totals are not equal, stop the processing.

16. What are the essential parts of a loop? What would be the consequence if some of the parts were missing?

17. Straight line coding generally requires more storage and less execution time than loops. Discuss.

18. Discuss the possibility of loops within loops.

19. What is meant by unwinding loops? What is a partially unwound loop?

166 PROGRAMMING BUSINESS COMPUTERS

20. Besides offering savings in storage space, loops offer some generality and flexibility that straight line coding cannot offer. For example, if a loop is entered via a different set of initialization instructions it can be made to perform different functions. Discuss.

21. Discuss infinite loops and their causes.

22. In the case of loops having more than one exit, is it preferable to initialize at the entry or reset at the exits?

23. Explain the following:
(a) Effective address.
(b) Modifier.
(c) Ten's complement.

24. What are the functions of indexers? Describe how indexers operate in DATAC.

25. List and discuss all the indexing instructions of DATAC. Do the same for two actual computers.

26. What is the estimated saving in operation time and storage for a computer having one index register compared to a computer without any, if both computers are performing typical business data processing applications?

27. What parts of a loop are affected by the use of indexers? Discuss each part affected separately.

28. The following are two methods used by actual computers to address more indexers than the indexer part of the instruction permits. Discuss.

(a) The indexer part of the instruction can specify eight different things. One through seven specifies indexers 1 through 7 directly. Zero means no index only if the contents of the *index address register* are zero; otherwise indexers 8–63 are specified by the contents of the *index address register*. This is sometimes called indirect index addressing.

(b) There is a 1 bit in the instruction which specifies whether the instruction is indexed or not. If the instruction *is not indexed*, the address part of the instruction can specify the full memory range. If the instruction *is indexed*, part of the address is given up to specify the 1–64 index registers. Now the actual address can no longer specify the full memory range, but the effective address (contents of index registers plus actual address) can still specify the full memory range.

9 SUBROUTINES

9.0 Introduction

It is frequently necessary in the writing of a large routine to use a basic group of instructions on several different occasions to perform a specific function. It is obviously wasteful of memory space to write the same group of steps many different places in the same routine. What we need is some way to write the steps only *once*, then arrange to jump there each time the operation is required and jump back to the correct place in the master program.

This is essentially a description of a *closed subroutine*. The "closed" means that the subroutine is not included in the main body of the routine, but is a self-contained section to which the main routine jumps, and which contains at its conclusion some mechanism for returning to the correct place in the main routine—regardless of where that may be. In somewhat less common use is the *open* subroutine, which is embodied *in* the main routine, without the need for a "return" mechanism. It, of course, saves no space, but once written can be simply incorporated into a routine and need not be rewritten each time; this is usually done by a *compiler*, to be discussed in Chapter 14. We shall be concerned here primarily with the closed subroutine.

9.1 Subroutine Linkage Methods

The primary conceptual problem in a closed subroutine is the method of "instructing" the subroutine where to return in the main routine. Observe that if the subroutine is to serve its purpose, it must be possible to jump to it from *any* point in memory and then return there, regardless of where the original jump to the subroutine was. In other words, it is necessary somehow to "tell" the subroutine how the routine got to it, so the subroutine will "know" where to go when it is finished. That is, along with the transfer of control we must transmit at least one piece of information, usually through an arith-

168 PROGRAMMING BUSINESS COMPUTERS

metic or control register. This idea of informing the subroutine how to get back has led to the name *linkage*.

There are many linkage methods, all of which depend to a certain extent on the characteristics of the particular computer being used. We shall investigate two methods which are fairly representative.

The subroutine example given here is a fairly realistic one, although as usual the exact methods depend on machine characteristics. The problem is that of preparing a dollars-and-cents quantity for printing, with a dollar sign and a decimal point. To simplify the task and to make the routine apply to any number of eight digits or fewer, we shall use the Dollar edit instruction (operation code: DE) of DATAC. The function of the instruction is to change all leading zeros or commas to blanks, and to place a dollar sign to the left of the first nonzero digit. The sign position is not considered. Thus

$$+0000012.34$$

would become

$$+bbbb\$12.34$$

where as usual the lower case b's stand for blanks. The decimal point must have been entered previously.

Suppose now that the convention has been established (for *this* subroutine) that a number to be edited is always placed in the L register before jumping to the editing subroutine, and that the subroutine leaves the edited quantity in L.

Aside from the linkage problems to be discussed shortly, the routine could be as follows. Assume that location 450 contains the constant 0.000000000.

LOC.	S	O	ADDRESS	REMARKS
402	E	R	0002	Shift number two places right into R (R gets sign of L)
403	O	R	0001	Shift R right one place
404		A	0450	Add period (decimal point)
405	E	R	0007	Shift L and R, now including period, seven places right
406	D	E		Dollar edit R
407	E	L	0010	Shift L and R left ten places to return edited amount to L

Although the workings of this routine are of course not the point of the current discussion, it might be well to amplify it so there will be no confusion as to what is being done. If the number in L at the start were +0000098267, then the contents of L and R after each instruction of the program is executed would be:

SUBROUTINES

INSTRUCTION LOCATION	L	R
Start	+0000098267	Immaterial
402	+0000000982	+67xxxxxxx
403	+0000000982	+067xxxxxx
404	+0000000982	+.67xxxxxx
405	+0000000000	+0000982.67
406	+0000000000	+bbb$982.67
407	+bbb$982.67	+0000000000

It is obvious that such a group of steps is often required in the course of most calculations which print dollar amounts. The central problem is how to set this up so that it may be used from *anywhere* in a larger routine. The first method for setting up the required linkage consists of leaving in the R register a record of where the routine jumped to the subroutine from. A simple way to do this is to execute a Bring instruction with an address which is the same as the location of the instruction. For instance, suppose that at 1382 in a main routine a number has just been placed in L and the subroutine is needed to edit it.

LOC.	S	O	ADDRESS	REMARKS
Previous calculations				
1382		B	1382	Bring instruction to R (linkage)
1383	U	J	0400	Jump to subroutine

The instruction at 1382 has the effect of bringing *itself* into the R register. Then when the jump to 0400 is executed, a number is left in R which identifies the location in the main program at which the subroutine was called. What does the subroutine do with the information? We must add three steps to the subroutine, two at the start and one at the end. Observe first that the subroutine should return, in this case, to 1384, i.e., two instructions beyond the address part of the instruction standing in R. All the subroutine need do, then, is add 2 to the address in R, and make that the address of a jump instruction at the end of the subroutine.

The memory addresses and constants:

	0451	+0000200000
	0450	0.000000000
	29	00111100000

LOC.	S	O	ADDRESS	FILTER	REMARKS
400		A	0451		Add 2 to the address
401		S	0408	29	Store address at jump, filtered
402	E	R	0002		Same as before

(Continued on next page)

170   PROGRAMMING BUSINESS COMPUTERS

403	O	R	0001	Same as before
404		A	0450	Same as before
405	E	R	0007	Same as before
406	D	E		Same as before
407	E	L	0010	Same as before
408	U	J	[bbbb]	Jump to computed address

0451 contains 2 in the address part, i.e., +0000200000; 29 has been set up as a filter which permits only the address part to be stored, i.e., 00111100000. This replaces, in most computers, an instruction of the "Store address" type which stores only the address part of an accumulator. The address of the jump instruction at 408 is shown bracketed to remind us that it is variable and is *computed* by the program. Following the execution of each instruction as the subroutine is *called*, the contents of the R register would be:

INSTRUCTION LOCATION	INSTRUCTION	FILTER	R REGISTER
1382	B 1382		0B138200000
1383	UJ 0400		0B138200000
0400	A 0451		0B138400000
0401	S 0408	29	0B138400000
0402–0407	As before		
0408	UJ 1384		
1384	Continuation		

Thus the subroutine automatically returns to the correct spot in the main routine. The linkage will work wherever it is called.

If another number is to be edited at 1407, the linkage would be

1407	B 1407
1408	UJ 0400
1409	Return

9.2 Indexed Linkages

In any computer with index registers and in many which do not have them, it is possible to set up linkages which require fewer instructions than the general type illustrated above. In most such machines this involves the use of a special instruction designed for the purpose. In DATAC the instruction is called Set index jump (operation code: SJ). Its function is to place the contents of the location counter in the modifier part of the specified indexer, and jump to the location specified by the address to obtain the next instruction. For instance, the instruction

1487   SJ 0402   42

SUBROUTINES

would result in the number 1487 being placed in the modifier part (the four rightmost digits) of the indexer 42, and an Unconditional jump to 0402 executed.

This simplifies the linkage problem greatly. A Set index jump is used to get to the subroutine, and an indexed Unconditional jump is placed at the end of the subroutine. The instruction

UJ 0001   42

placed at the end of a subroutine which was called by the Set index jump at 1487 above, would operate as follows. The effective address is the address as shown, plus the modifier part of the specified indexer. This is: $1 + 1487 = 1488$, so the effect is UJ 1488. Thus the pair

SJ 0402   42   (written anywhere in the main routine)
and UJ 0001   42   (at the end of subroutine)

will always result in the subroutine returning to one instruction past the Set index jump. It is usual in machines where this method can be employed to assign one of the indexers to this purpose. We shall use indexer 99 in this book.

It may be noted that, with indexing, neither arithmetic register is used for the linkage. It is therefore possible to leave quantities in both registers when jumping to a subroutine, in cases where there are two or more input quantities involved.

9.3 Calling Sequences

Often it is necessary to provide more information to a subroutine than can be put in the arithmetic registers. Suppose, for instance, that it is necessary in a payroll calculation to compute withholding tax at several different places in the program and it is desired to set up a subroutine without using indexing. Since the R register must thus be used with the linkage, and since there are two quantities (gross pay and number of dependents) involved, some system must be devised to get the necessary information to the subroutine.

The *calling sequence* technique is to write a linkage or a Set index jump, followed by a few words which contain the information necessary to define the problem to the subroutine. In the example mentioned above, the word following the linkage would contain the *address* of the number of dependents (the gross pay is assumed to *be* in the L register). The linkage will then appear, symbolically, as

n   B   n
n + 1   UJ   K
n + 2   D

172 PROGRAMMING BUSINESS COMPUTERS

where n is the location of the linkage, K is the starting address of the subroutine, and D is the *address* of the number of dependents. This calling sequence can be written any place in a routine, and D may be any address whatever. The subroutine must now "pick up" the address of the number of dependents, as well as determine the return address. We shall assume that the subroutine is required to leave the computed tax in the R register.

The situation may be made clearer by the following routine. Suppose the subroutine starts at 1200. Constants are:

1100	+0000200000		
1101	+0000100000		
1102	−00000013∧00		
1103	+00000000∧18		
1104	+0000000000		
0050	00111100000	Address filter	

LOC.	S	O	ADDRESS	FILTER	REMARKS
1200		A	1100		Add 2 to address part
1201		S	1204	50	Store address (filtered)
1202		A	1101		Add 1 to address part
1203		S	1215	50	Store return address (filtered)
1204		B	[bbbb]		Bring to R address of number of dependents
1205		S	1206	50	Store address of number of dependents (filtered)
1206		B	[bbbb]		Bring number of dependents to R
1207		U	1150		Unload L (gross pay) to temporary storage
1208		X	1102		Multiply by −$13.00
1209		A	1150		Add gross pay to exemption
1210	P	J	1213		Plus jump to 1213
1211		B	1104		Bring zero to R (if here, exemptions were greater than gross, and tax is zero)
1212	U	J	1215		Unconditional jump to end
1213		X	1103		Multiply by 18%
1214	R	R	0002		Shift right two places and round
1215	U	J	[bbbb]		Jump back to main routine

The crucial concept here is that the calling sequence contains the *address* of the number of dependents, not the number itself. And since the only information the subroutine has is the location of the linkage, it really has only the *address of the address* of the number of dependents. This explains the double set of address calculations at the start of the subroutine. The return address is, of course, now one location further beyond the linkage.

The actual calculation is fairly standard, except that the constant $13.00 (exemption per deduction) is stored with a minus sign to avoid

SUBROUTINES

writing a Store followed by a Subtract. It also differs from previous samples of the calculation in that a simple test is made to prevent calculating a negative tax in case gross pay is less than total exemption.

For a numerical example, suppose that the L register contains a gross pay of $63.90 and the employee has three dependents, which number is stored in 0432 this time. Suppose the calling sequence begins at 0750. It would be:

0750	B 0750
0751	UJ 1200
0752	0 0432
0753	Continuation

The "operation code" of zero in the "instruction" at 0752 means nothing, since this word is actually an instructional constant. It is usually necessary, however, to make such words "look like" instructions for reasons having to do with input routines and compiling or assembly routines (see later chapters). A zero is as handy as anything else. Sometimes the "operation code" can also be used to carry information to the subroutine.

The contents of L and R after the execution of each instruction are:

INSTRUCTION LOCATION	INSTRUCTION	FILTER	L	R
0750	B 0750		+00000063₌90	0B075000000
0751	UJ 1200		+00000063₌90	0B075000000
1200	A 1100		+00000063₌90	0B075200000
1201	S 1204	50	+00000063₌90	0B075200000
1202	A 1101		+00000063₌90	0B075300000
1203	S 1215	50	+00000063₌90	0B075300000
1204	B [0752]		+00000063₌90	00043200000
1205	S 1206	50	+00000063₌90	00043200000
1206	B [0432]		+00000063₌90	+0000000003
1207	U 1150		+00000063₌90	+0000000003
1208	X 1102		−0000000000	−00000039₌00
1209	A 1150		−0000000000	+00000024₌90
1210	PJ 1213		−0000000000	+00000024₌90
1213	X 1103		+0000000000	+000004₌4820
1214	RR 0002		+0000000000	+00000004₌48
1215	UJ [0753]		+0000000000	+00000004₌48
0753	Continuation			

The same routine can be written in somewhat shorter form if indexing is used. The advantage is that the calling sequence is easier to decode, and as usual the linkage is simpler.

The calling sequence is:

n	SJ	K	99
n + 1	0	D	

where the symbols are defined at the top of page 172.

LOC.	S	O	ADDRESS	INDEX	FILTER	REMARKS
1200		B	0001	99		Bring address of number of dependents to R
1201		S	1202		50	Store address (filtered)
1202		B	[bbbb]			Bring number of dependents to R
1203–1210	Similar to instructions 1207–1214 before					
1211	U	J	0002	99		Jump back to main routine, indexed

The calling sequence technique can be used effectively in many realistic situations. Some of the best examples, unfortunately, involve subroutines which are much too complex to present in their entirety here.

9.4 Subroutine Libraries

The subroutine examples presented in this chapter have necessarily been short and simple, and of the type that would normally be written by the same coder who writes the main routine which calls them. In practice, the subroutines are often written by persons who specialize in such techniques. The programmers who use such specially written routines then need only have a precise description of how the subroutines work, and a way of incorporating them into their programs with a minimum of difficulty.

The requirement of precise write-ups implies that for each subroutine there be on file and available for distribution to programmers a *complete* summary of all information needed by the programmer. The write-ups must give the exact function of the routine, its method of solution if pertinent, calling sequence, signals of error conditions, memory requirements, operating time, limitations, programmer's name, and any other information which may be pertinent. All such write-ups must be kept up-to-date, and in readily available form. This can be a full-time activity for one person in a large installation.

Easy incorporation into main programs usually involves having all the available subroutines on a master "library" tape. Where a subroutine is desired in a program, the programmer merely inserts a standardized symbol for the subroutine he wants. Then during the assembly or compiling step (Chapter 14) the actual subroutines are incorporated into the program from the master tape. Such subroutines must be written in what is sometimes called *relocatable* form, i.e., written so that their operation is not dependent on where they are

SUBROUTINES

located in memory. This topic will also be treated in Chapter 14 under relative address coding.

Properly used, a subroutine library becomes a very powerful tool which in effect multiplies the efficiency of each individual programmer. The libraries at some major installations include hundreds of subroutines—not only those written by the particular group, but also others supplied by the computer manufacturer, or obtained in an organized exchange with other installations.

9.5 Summary

Subroutines make possible the saving of much memory space and/or programming time, at the slight expense of the space and complexity of linkages and calling sequences. They are often used simply because they are already available in a library subroutine system. When this is so, programming convenience and programming time-saving are achieved, rather than a saving of memory space, plus the very important fact that a library subroutine may be assumed to be free of errors and to be efficiently coded.

In such use, the *open* subroutine would be just as good. That is, if the only reason for using a subroutine is that someone else has already written it, then it would be as satisfactory to put the routine in the main program right at the point where it is needed and simply eliminate the linkage and calling sequence. And, in a small way, the open subroutine is better, since getting rid of the red tape saves a little operating time and memory space. This, naturally, applies only if the subroutine is needed at only one place in the routine. If it is used many places, the sole advantage (although in some cases a considerable one) of the open subroutine is that it avoids the red tape of the calling sequence.

We are seeing here the beginning of a theme which will be developed further in later chapters: coding techniques to make coding simpler. Later topics in this development will be interpretive programming, subroutine compiling methods, relative programming and assembly methods, and compilers (Chapter 14).

Exercises

Note: in Exercises 1–4, any of the linkage methods discussed in the text may be used.

1. Suppose that the function defined in Exercise 1, page 163, is frequently required in a certain application. Set up a subroutine and the necessary linkage to carry out the operation from anywhere in memory.

2. Do the same for Exercise 6, page 163.

3. Do the same for Exercise 7, page 164, assuming that when the subroutine is called, the number to be edited has been placed in the L register, and that the edited amount is to be left in the L register when the subroutine exits to the main routine.

4. Set up a subroutine with a calling sequence, to carry out the function of Exercise 9, page 164, with the following generalization. Assume that the list of numbers to be sorted can start anywhere in memory, and be of any reasonable length. The calling sequence for the subroutine should be set up to define the starting address of the list and its length.

5. What are some of the possible motivations which led to the discovery of the subroutine concept?

6. Discuss the differences, advantages, and disadvantages of open and closed subroutines.

7. In many cases, it would be advantageous to provide alternatives of fast subroutines that require relatively large storage and slow subroutines that require relatively little storage. Discuss.

8. Discuss how indirect addressing may be used in a subroutine calling sequence. See Section 7.4 for an explanation of indirect addressing.

9. Discuss the several ways to keep a subroutine library tape:
(a) By type, function, and date.
(b) By date.
(c) By alphabetic order of code name.

10. It is possible to maintain a subroutine library tape according to a hierarchy. Every subroutine that uses another one within it is automatically assigned one level higher than the one which it uses. The subroutines are arranged according to hierarchy level and then by alphabetic order of code name. Discuss.

11. What is the minimum written information that should accompany a subroutine?

12. If a computer does not have the Set index jump instruction but has index registers, suggest a way to prepare the subroutine exit linkage.

13. If a computer does not have either the Set index jump instruction nor index registers, suggest a way to prepare the following:
(a) The subroutine exit linkage.
(b) Calling sequence requiring addresses of operands.

14. If the same name is accidentally assigned to two separate subroutines in a library tape, what are some of the likely consequences? How might errors of this type be detected?

15. If a computer is designed to be extremely flexible so that each computer produced is quite different from all the others, can we still have a subroutine exchange system between the different users?

16. Discuss how subroutines affect programming flexibility.

10 INPUT AND OUTPUT DEVICES

10.0 Introduction

In this chapter we shall explore the subject of physical devices which permit communication between the computer memory and the "outside world." There is a fairly wide variety of such devices, not all of which would ever appear in one system (excepting possibly the largest military computers). We shall be concerned here primarily with what the devices are; in the next chapter we shall discuss DATAC input/output devices and how to program them. We shall describe their principle of operation only sketchily; a good programmer needs to know more about the physical principles of operation of input/output devices than about other parts of the machine, perhaps, but still only the broad outline. The emphasis will be on magnetic tape, since it is the most important present input/output medium for business computers.

10.1 The Computer Console

The first part of a computer with which we have contact in running a problem is the console. It is not an input/output device in the same sense as the others to be discussed, in that it is not used for mass transfers of problem data, but it fits within the broad definition of an input/output device as a communication link between the computer and the outside. Besides its functions of allowing occasional manual entry of information into the machine and the displaying of the contents of registers and memory, it is always involved in getting the first few instructions of a routine into memory. The following list of functions is representative of those that are present on current computer consoles, or on the typewriters that are essentially part of the console on many machines.

1. *Register Display.* There must always be some method of displaying the contents of the arithmetic and control registers, and of

memory locations. These are necessary in order to provide information about the program when it stops, especially if it stops when it was not anticipated. We shall discuss the use of such information a little more fully in Chapter 12 on checkout techniques. Actual machines vary in the method of presentation. Some have a separate set of display lights for each of the arithmetic and control registers, plus a register which displays the contents of whatever memory location is set into certain keys on the console (see below). At the other extreme are the few computers which have no lights at all, but can be caused to type out the contents of specified registers on a typewriter which is a functional part of the console. Other machines fall somewhere between. In any case, the information is available. The actual method of displaying the registers in lights varies also. Most machines use some sort of binary coding of the decimal or alphabetic characters (see Appendix 2), usually but not always the same coding which is used in memory. It is therefore necessary to be able to "read" the binary coding for this reason if for no other. One unusual machine, not in wide use, presents the decimal information in ordinary Arabic numerals on the faces of small cathode-ray tubes, which are much easier to read, but this is not typical.

2. *Word Entry.* It is also necessary to be able to enter information into the arithmetic and control registers and memory. There is usually at least one set of keys or switches which can be set or turned to represent one computer word, and then entered into the machine. These keys or switches may require the characters to be in binary-coded form, or they may be in a form such as ten-position rotary switches which may be set to any decimal digit. Exactly what function is performed with a word so set up on the console is determined by the control buttons described next. In some machines it is possible to set up such switches, then by programming call for the word during the execution of the program, but this also is not typical. On machines having typewriters, characters can be entered directly via the keyboard.

3. *Control Buttons.* Most computers have a half dozen or more buttons which, when pressed, cause certain operations to take place. Usually many of them are under control of an *automatic-manual* switch, i.e., none of them have any effect unless this switch is set to *manual.* A *reset* button causes all arithmetic and control registers to be reset to zero. A *reset and clear* button, if there is one, resets the registers and clears all of memory to zero (or to blank, in some cases). This button is usually pushed before loading each new program, to ensure starting with a clear memory; if there is no such

INPUT AND OUTPUT DEVICES

button, a short routine can do the same thing. An *enter "x"* button causes the word set up on the manual entry keys or switches to be entered into register "x," where "x" is one of the arithmetic registers of the particular computer. A *display memory* button causes the display of a word from memory, the address to display being specified by some group of the console keys. If the particular machine has more index registers than can be economically displayed simultaneously, there may be separate *display indexer "x"* keys, one for each indexer. An *execute instruction* key causes the machine to execute the instruction set up in the manual entry keys taken as an instruction. This makes it possible to execute any machine instruction *from the console.* This feature is probably most useful in manually executing jumps when a program stops, in order to proceed to another part of the program during checkout or to initiate a corrective routine. A *start* button causes the program to begin execution at the address currently in the location counter, no matter how that address may have gotten there. The program might have stopped under the control of an Interrupted jump instruction; the program might have stopped because the automatic-manual switch was moved to manual and back to automatic, which stops the program execution; or a manual jump might have been executed from the console. Finally, there is sometimes a button named *load,* or *load cards,* or *load tape.* This has the same effect as the execution of about three instructions: an instruction which causes the card or tape reader to begin its mechanical operation, an instruction which brings the first few words or perhaps the first tape block into a predetermined location in memory, and finally a jump to that first word location. With such a button, all this is automatic. Obviously, such a feature greatly facilitates the loading of a program, because it is not very difficult to write a routine to appear in the first few words of a program, which will cause the rest of the program to be loaded into memory. We shall see in the next chapter how this can be done.

It is, of course, possible to get a program started without such a load button, and in many machines it is necessary to do so. Without it, it is necessary to manually load enough instructions into memory to call in the loading program from tape or cards.

4. *Condition Lights.* This term is used here, for lack of a better one, to indicate the lights on the console which show the existence or nonexistence of certain conditions in the machine: overflow, improper division (if different), certain errors in connection with tapes, arithmetic or memory errors on machines which have checking features, etc. These lights are turned on automatically, and are turned off either by

testing for the condition by programming (when this is possible) or by pressing the reset button. The exact number and function of such lights varies considerably from one machine to the next. They are ordinarily useful only when the machine stops, because things happen too fast to follow during high-speed operation.

5. *Single Step Key.* Almost all computers have some facility for executing a program one step at a time, slowly. That is, pressing the single step key once causes one instruction to be executed. It is also usually possible to execute a routine at a rate of perhaps ten instructions per second, either by pressing a separate key or holding down the single step key continuously. It is sometimes desirable, although rather infrequently, to "watch" a program being executed by this means.

6. *Branch Control Switches.* Most computers have some facility for controlling the execution of a program by means of switches on the console. These go by such names as *sense switches, alteration switches, conditioning switches, breakpoint switches, monitor switches,* etc. The devices vary markedly from one machine to the next; a few of them may be listed. One machine has six switches which may be either up or down; an instruction is available which will cause the following instruction to be *skipped* if the switch specified by the instruction is *down*. Another, mentioned previously, is able to "read in" the number set on the manual entry keys; the number can then be tested like any other, by conditional jumps. Another, under switch control, will *always* take one path or the other on a conditional jump. Since it is quite simple to set up a "conditional" jump which always goes one way (e.g., by placing zero in the pertinent arithmetic register and then executing a Zero jump), it is possible to control which path a program is to take at a given point. Several machines permit an auxiliary character to be added to some or all instructions; then if a correspondingly numbered switch in the console is set, the program will jump to some standard address with the contents of the location counter still available somewhere in the machine.

These techniques are useful, as we shall see, in checkout, where they permit certain things to be done only while a program is being tested, as well as in programs which contain alternatives as to method of solution, type of report, etc.

7. *Power and Maintenance.* There are usually a few lights and switches on the console which indicate or control certain electrical conditions. They are of no concern to the programmer, except that it may in some cases be desirable for him to be able to recognize conditions which would damage the equipment and know emergency

INPUT AND OUTPUT DEVICES

shutdown procedures. Such conditions are rare, however, and there are usually operators or engineers available who are qualified to cope with such situations.

10.2 Magnetic Tape

Magnetic tape for computer use is made either of a plastic base coated with a magnetic oxide or a bronze steel base plated with an iron alloy. Information is "recorded" or "written" on the tape by passing it over the cores of small windings called *heads* which magnetize small areas of the tape. Information is "read" from the tape by passing it over the same or different heads and sensing the voltage induced in them by the magnetized coating.

The information recorded on the tape must always be in binary form, i.e., represented by zeros and ones only (Appendix 2). This is done in the interest of gaining speed and reliability, since it is highly desirable to record only *two* physical conditions on tape, not ten or forty-seven. In many systems, a zero is recorded simply as *no change* in magnetization at a point; a one is recorded as a *reversal* of the magnetization. The table on page 59 showed a possible binary representation of the DATAC characters. As was pointed out there, the representations used in real machines vary—but are along similar lines. For use in tapes (and sometimes elsewhere) where the physical techniques are at present less reliable than we could wish, it is necessary to carry an extra binary digit to check the accuracy of recording and reading. This is usually called a *parity* bit, because it refers to an odd-even characteristic, or a *redundancy* bit, for it is not required to carry the information content and is therefore redundant. To illustrate the idea, Table 1 shows the appearance of the binary codes of page 59, assuming an *odd* parity bit. This bit is assigned in advance for each character, and is either zero or one—whichever is required to make the total number of ones in the representation an *odd* number.

Assuming that the character representation in high-speed memory does not have the parity bit, the tape control circuits compute it as the characters are written on tape. In either case (whether the parity bit already exists in memory and is simply written as is, or whether it is computed as the tape is written), the bits coming off the tape as it is read are checked for an odd number of ones in the representation of each character. If there are not an odd number of ones, some type of error has occurred and a signal of some sort is given. We shall discuss later the various types of error indications.

The possible errors include a failure of the recording system to place the correct information on tape, the presence of a flaw in the magnetic coating which makes correct recording impossible in a small section of the surface, and the presence of dirt or dust particles which momentarily lift the tape from the reading heads, which results

TABLE 1

CHARACTER	SIX-BIT CODE	PARITY BIT
0	000000	1
1	000001	0
2	000010	0
3	000011	1
4	000100	0
5	000101	1
6	000110	1
7	000111	0
8	001000	0
9	001001	1
A	010001	1
B	010010	1
C	010011	0
D	010100	1
E	010101	0
F	010110	0
G	010111	1
H	011000	1
I	011001	0
J	100001	1
K	100010	1
L	100011	0
Etc.		

in an unreadably small signal. The last of these is usually not a permanent error; backing up and rereading often eliminates the error since the first attempt dislodged the particle. The first two, however, represent potential loss of information. In order to detect such a failure as soon as possible after it happens, several of the newer machines have a separate read head placed a short distance behind the write head, rather than the more common combined read-write head. All writing is checked by automatically reading after writing (as part of the writing process—not requiring attention from the programmer). If the tape is written without failing any of the various tests which may be made, then it may safely be assumed that the information was satisfactorily recorded on tape.

INPUT AND OUTPUT DEVICES 183

The seven bits making up one character are recorded in a row across the tape, and we speak then of a seven-channel tape.* Figure 1 shows in schematic form the representation of the characters.

In present equipment there are about 200 characters per inch of tape. The tape typically moves at 100 inches per second, giving a character transfer rate of 20,000 per second. These figures of course vary from one machine to another; the maximum character transfer rate is about 90,000 per second at the present time. Some of the newer machines record several characters side by side across the tape to increase the effective character transfer rate.

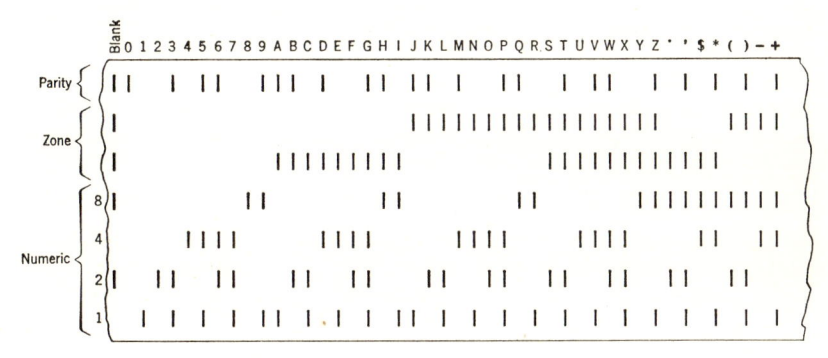

Figure 1. Schematic representation of the recording of information on magnetic tape. The character coding is that assumed for DATAC.

It is clear that with only approximately 1/200 inch between adjacent bits on the tape, and with speeds of 100 inches per second, it would be physically impossible to position the tape accurately enough to stop between specified pulses. For this reason, information is always recorded on the tape in discrete groups called *records*, also called *blocks*. These are most commonly separated by a gap of blank tape, but in some cases special marks designate the beginning and end of records and the tape is automatically repositioned after reading or writing a record, if necessary.

For some applications it is necessary to record on the tape a signal that there is no more information on the tape or at least not on that particular section of the tape. This signal is called either a *tape mark*

* In many machines the tape always has one extra channel which the programmer need have no knowledge of, which is involved in the hardware of tape reading and writing. It is usually called the *clock* channel, or (electronic) *sprocket* channel, for reasons which have to do with its function in the hardware.

or an *end-of-file* gap. It may be recorded and detected by programming. Most tapes have some means for detecting the physical end of the tape, to avoid attempting to write or read past the end of a reel.

It is always necessary somehow to be able to get the tape back to its starting point, either to reprocess the data or simply to take the reel of tape off the tape handler. This is called *rewinding* and, as we saw, is called for by a separate instruction. On some machines it is possible also to rewind a tape in such a manner that it cannot be read or written again until some action has been taken by the operator, which prevents accidental use of a tape which should have been removed. Most computers have some provision for a removable device (usually a ring) on the tape reel which will prevent writing on that reel, making impossible the accidental destruction of important information. On some machines it is possible, by using a separate order, to read a tape backwards. This is a very powerful feature in certain applications.

Magnetic tape is not usually addressable in the sense that a specific position on the tape corresponds to a specific address, as is true of most other forms of storage. Basically, it is necessary to know where each word is located on tape *with respect to other words and records on the same tape*. It is not enough to be aware that a, b, c, d, e, f, g, and h are present in a record; it is necessary to know also which quantity is first, which second, etc. It is similarly necessary to be cognizant of the relationship between records on a tape.

This statement should be qualified, however. Suppose it is known that the eight quantities above are always present in every record on a certain tape, and it is necessary to find the one record in which a is equal to 167. It would not be difficult to read each record from tape into memory, then immediately examine the first word of the record to determine whether this is the record in which a is equal to 167. If not, the next record would be read. Such a procedure can be programmed for any tape unit; in certain machines there are special instructions which make the search process nearly automatic. And in some equipment the search can proceed while the central part of the computer does something else. It is not usually necessary that the *key* for which the search is made (a in the example here) should be the first word of the record.

10.3 Punched Cards

Probably the most commonly used input medium is punched cards. They are familiar, allow integration of computer procedures with standard punched card devices, and their information content may be inspected visually. Cards are in wide use in many areas.

As almost everyone knows, a punched card is made of stiff paper (or lightweight cardboard, alternatively) and has many positions in which holes may be punched. Cards manufactured for use with equipment of the International Business Machines (IBM) Corporation most commonly have eighty *columns*, each of which contains twelve possible punching positions; the holes are rectangular. This is illustrated in Figure 2. (The IBM card is further described on page 201.) The card was prepared on a *keypunch*, which also printed the character corresponding to each column at the top of the column. Figure 2 thus shows the *combinations* of punches in a column that are used to represent letters and punctuation marks.

Cards for use with Remington Rand equipment employ round holes arranged in forty-five columns, but the characters are coded by combinations of punches in such a way that two characters can be punched in one column; Remington Rand cards are therefore often referred to as *ninety*-column cards. They are the same size as IBM cards, but of course cannot be processed by the same equipment.

The information on cards is usually read by small wire brushes which are allowed to contact a source of electricity wherever there is a hole. The card may be moving or stationary at the time it is read, depending on the equipment. An alternative reading method, not in wide use as yet, is based on a photoelectric scanning system. The latter promises to be much faster than the former.

On some computers, cards may be punched by equipment attached to the computer. On these and other computers, it is possible to punch cards from information on magnetic tape, using an optional *off-line* card punch which is not part of the computer proper. In any case, holes are punched in cards by placing the card over a die which has a hole for every possible punching position in each row; individually controlled punches are then activated electromagnetically to punch holes in the specified columns. In the usual punching system, this must be done for each row on the cards. Since the card, in this system, cannot be moving when it is punched, the card must move in jerks past the punch die. Present punches are therefore quite noisy and slow.

10.4 Printing Devices

Any computer must have some facility for communicating results to the outside world, which goes under the generic name of *output*. Almost all present computers include among their output devices

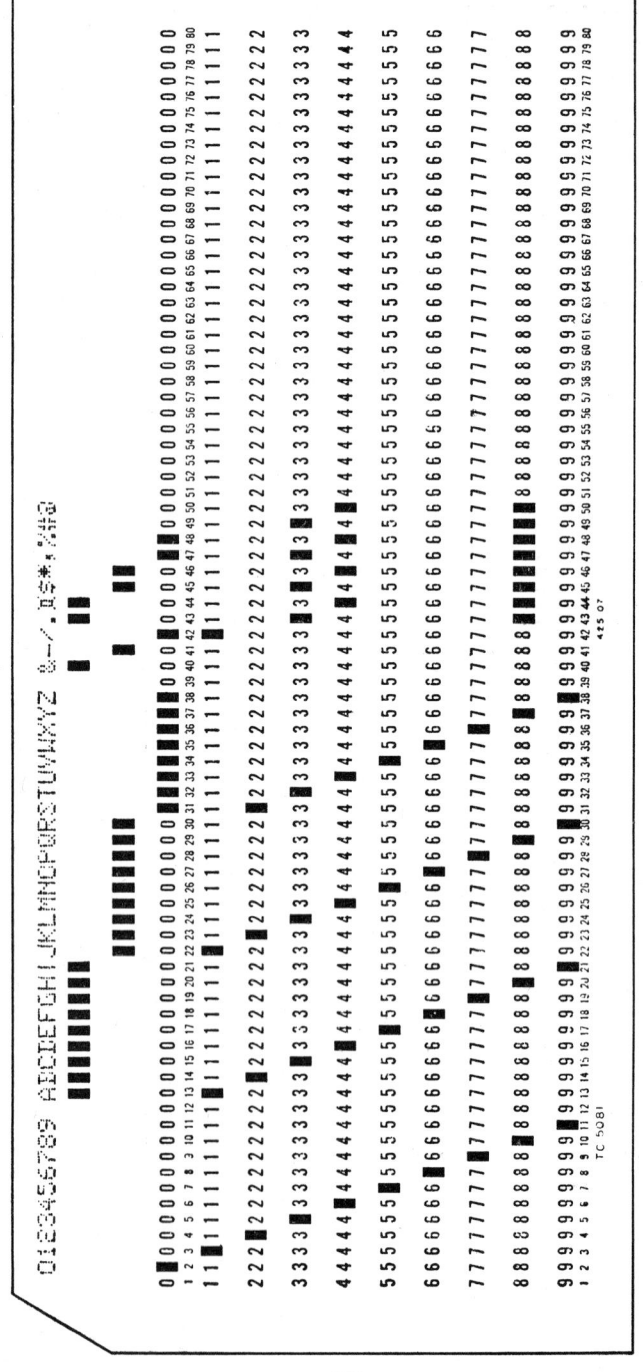

Figure 2. Sample of an eighty-column card. (Courtesy of International Business Machines Corporation.)

some means of producing printing. As we shall see more clearly in the discussion at the end of the next chapter, it is usually not economical to use such devices for the bulk of the output in business problems; indeed, some computers have rather limited facilities for printing directly out of memory, depending instead on the ability to "print" magnetic tapes, as we shall see. Still, most machines have at least some limited *direct-connected* printing capacity, i.e., the ability to produce printed results on paper by the execution of computer instructions.

The most commonly used printing device at the present time is the *line printer*. This is an electromechanical device that prints one complete line at a time, a line usually consisting of 120 character positions. Speeds vary between 150 and 1000 lines per minute, which, while fast by comparison with a typist, is excruciatingly slow compared with internal electronic speeds. The physical principles used vary, and are of relatively little significance to the programmer. For engineering reasons which do not concern us here, most of them revolve around some sort of wheel which has all the printable characters on its periphery; when the correct character is opposite the paper, either the wheel is moved against the paper which is supported by a platen, or a hammer strikes the paper from behind and moves it against the wheel. An important variant is called a matrix printer, because of the way the characters are formed by various combinations of dots.* This is illustrated in Figure 3.

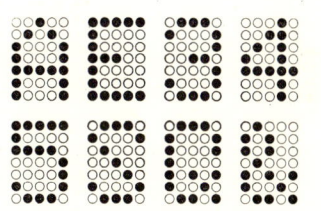

Figure 3. Samples of how characters are printed with a matrix printer. These are about four times normal size.

In order to print 120 characters at once, they must all be available in memory when the printing cycle is begun. In the next chapter we shall look briefly into the programming problems this imposes, as well as the computer instructions required to print a line once it has been prepared.

Many computers have a typewriter attached to them. In some cases it is used in combination with an optional direct-connected printer; in others it is the only printing device available. In the former case, it is used primarily for typing out stored comments or orders to the operator; for instance, instructions on changing tapes

* A good nontechnical description of these devices (and of many other features of computer hardware) may be found in *High Speed Data Processing*, by C. C. Gotlieb and J. N. P. Hume, McGraw-Hill Book Company, New York, 1958.

as discussed in Chapter 13. In the latter case, it may be used for reports of very small size, but the volume output would be written on tape and later printed off-line, i.e., with a separate printer which is not connected to the computer. These typewriters operate at a rate of about ten characters per second, which can be seen to be some hundred times slower than the average present line printer.

A second function of the typewriters is to provide a very limited amount of input, and sometimes to substitute for certain of the console functions. It is almost always possible with such typewriters to enter numbers directly into memory, after setting some type of switch which prepares the control and memory circuits to receive the information. Considering the time to set up the typewriter and to type in information, this is an extremely slow technique which can seldom be justified. It is occasionally used in the very earliest stages of checkout of a new machine, and for the operator to enter certain "control" information such as tape number, day's date, etc. The typewriter is never used to enter ordinary problem data, except perhaps rarely in checkout.

On a few computers, the typewriter replaces some of the functions of the console. For instance, it is possible for such functions as displaying memory to be initiated by typewriter operations: some preassigned letter, followed by a four-digit address, could cause the contents of that address to be typed. Other functions may also be carried out by a typewriter.

10.5 Paper Tape

Punched paper tape is used on a number of computers as the primary input/output medium, and on others as an important auxiliary. The latter is especially true when input to the system can conveniently be produced as an adjunct of other operations, e.g., cash register records, or telegraphic transmission of data.

The commonly used systems consist of five, six, seven, or eight channels along the strip of paper. Figure 4 shows a section of a six-channel tape and one commonly used character representation system. Since the various paper tape systems vary considerably from each other, we make no attempt here to explain the method of coding the characters. It may be noted, however, that the system shown in Figure 4 has provision for dealing with both upper and lower case letters; not all systems have this feature. The code used to represent characters on the tape need not be the same as that used inside the computer or on magnetic tape; indeed it could not be, in some cases.

INPUT AND OUTPUT DEVICES

It is a straightforward matter to translate from one code to another electronically.

Paper tape can be produced as a by-product of other operations, as mentioned above and in Chapter 1 in connection with integrated data processing, by a typing operation which also produces the usual

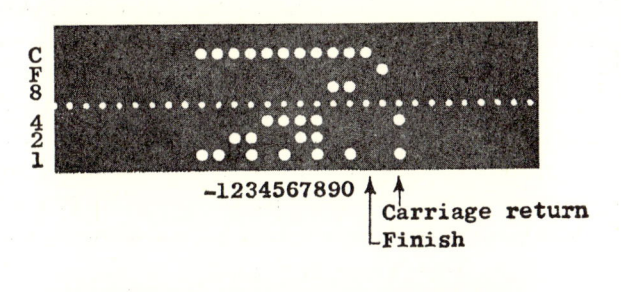

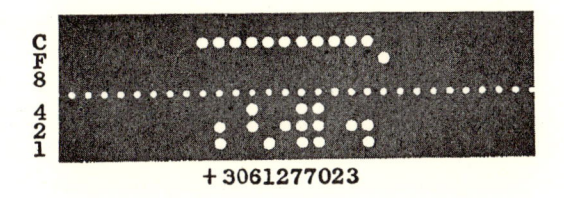

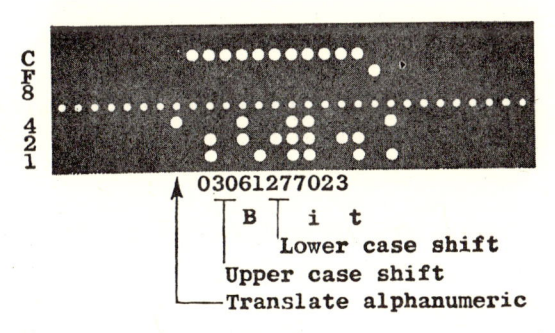

Figure 4. Samples of six-channel punched paper tape. The paper is normally white, of course; it is shown dark here to make punching clearer. (Courtesy DATATRON Division, Burroughs Corporation.)

typed "hard" copy. It can be read by brushes just as cards most commonly are, but it is fairly simple to read it photoelectrically. Reading speeds of over 1000 characters per second are possible. Computer output punching is necessarily slower, 60 characters per second being typical at the time of writing.

A paper tape reader and punch are built into the typewriter used with some machines.

10.6 Cathode-Ray Tube Output

A cathode-ray tube is a television-like device. One of the versions currently in use permits a line or point of light to be placed anywhere on the screen of the device. Several dots (the "points" do have width, after all) placed together merge together to *look* like a short line segment, and if placed properly, look like characters. This representation of characters by patterns of dots is very similar to the principle of operation of a matrix printer, except of course that the printer involves mechanical elements. Figure 3 shows a few characters represented by such a scheme.

The placement of the dots to make up characters can be done at a high enough rate to make it possible to display characters at the rate of perhaps 100 per second.

A second method allows the programmer to call out directly what character he wants and where on the screen he wants it. This more flexible method can display characters considerably faster.

The question immediately arises: so what? Who can read results this fast? The answer is that a camera can. Using either a temporarily darkened room and the same screen, or a separate precision screen for the camera, it is possible to get a very good picture. Memory contents can be displayed and photographed in a matter of a few seconds on some machines. The problem then becomes one of getting the film developed and printed. A Polaroid camera is good except that it produces a relatively small print which can be difficult to read if there are a thousand different numbers on it. Faster photographic techniques obviously are needed, and are said to be feasible within the foreseeable future. Actually, cathode-ray tube output is included here mainly for the sake of completeness, because it is not as yet widely used in business data processing. Engineering or scientific computation can make much better use of the device, especially in plotting results directly in the form of curves and graphs. Devices now under intensive development may change this picture, however.

10.7 Keyboard Entry and Inquiry Devices

There are, at the time of writing, a few instances of *real-time* business data processing, i.e., processing which keeps up-to-date with a business system in a scale of minutes instead of days or weeks.

For instance, a mail order concern with a very high volume at the Christmas period might need an up-to-the-minute (or at least hour) record of inventory levels. It would be totally inadequate for their purposes to have a weekly summary. They would therefore want a method of interrogating the computer system as each order comes in to determine if it can be filled, as well as immediate reduction of the inventory count for each stock item as orders are filled. Another example occurs in the life insurance field, where a policyholder may walk in off the street, unannounced, and ask for a policy loan. He may (or may not) be willing to wait a few days for a check, but he certainly does not expect to have to wait for a week, until the updating cycle on his policy rolls around, to find out what the cash value of the policy is and whether the loan can be granted. Perhaps the best-known example is the airline reservation problem, where prospective customers expect an immediate answer on the availability of space, and want the space to be reserved for them at once if available.

The solution to these and similar problems is the *keyboard entry and inquiry device*. This is a keyboard, or, said another way, a small console, which is connected to the computer. It is usually quite specialized, since it has only a few of the functions of the regular computer console. It has keys with which to enter such information as stock number, policy number, number of passengers in party, a key to indicate whether the entry is a request for information or a command to reserve stock, etc. In some cases it may be even more specialized, as in the case of the airline reservation system where a notched metal plate is inserted in the device to present the information on flight number, etc. Usually there are at least a few indicator lights, also commonly having quite specialized meanings. In a department store application a green light might mean that the customer has sufficient credit to justify the purchase he is making, a red light that he does not, etc.

So much for the appearance of the devices, of which there may be one or many attached to a system. Inside the computer, the problems are more interesting. Some systems are set up with no other purpose than to service the inquiries from these stations; here the only problem is that of priority, when two or more inquiries arise at about the same time. This problem is handled easily enough by arranging to deal with the inquiry stations in prearranged sequence. This may cause a given station to wait a few seconds, but this is sometimes not critical. The methods of queuing theory may be used to determine what delays may be expected.

In other systems, the expectation is that the inquiries will require a relatively small portion of the total operation time of the computer. Such systems are set up to proceed with some other task, perhaps unrelated to the inquiries, and interrupt the main program when an inquiry appears. This can be handled by a procedure as follows: checks are made, either by the control circuitry or by a special instruction, to determine if the program should be interrupted; if not, the main program proceeds. If so, then all registers are stored temporarily, again either by built-in control circuitry or by programming, and a jump is executed to a program which deals with the inquiry.

This interrupt technique of course implies that there is enough memory available for both the main program and the inquiry program. If the two are unrelated, or if the inquiry program requires large files, the problem becomes quite difficult or expensive. In any case, a large file requirement coupled with the necessity for an answer in seconds or less forces the use of some type of large random access storage (see Chapter 19).

Keyboard entry and inquiry devices are a powerful tool in the relatively few situations where their value outweighs their cost. As large random access storage becomes more common and less expensive, the use of these devices will probably grow.

10.8 Buffers

Although the reader may not have been struck with the fact, the speeds cited above for input/output devices are usually *very* much slower than internal arithmetic speeds. A direct-connected line printer operating at 600 lines per minute, for instance, uses 100 milliseconds to print one line; depending on details of program organization, this can be two to one hundred times too slow to keep up with internal operation. In this section and the next we shall look into two solutions to the problem made possible by additional equipment.

The first is *buffering*. The word is used here in the sense of the provision of an intermediate step by means of which the operations which precede and follow it are made relatively time-independent. The typical computer buffer between memory and either magnetic tape or a printer consists of a small temporary storage device which operates as follows. On input to memory, it accepts the words from tape as they become available from the tape reading circuits at the relatively slow reading speeds. When the tape block has been read or the buffer filled (depending on machine details), the entire contents of the buffer are read into main memory at the relatively fast electronic word-transfer speeds. All of this has to be set up, of course, by appropriate programming. The memory and arithmetic and control circuits are completely unaffected by the process of filling the buffer. On the output to tape (or, on a few machines, to the direct-connected printer) the procedure is just the reverse. The buffer is filled at high speed from memory; the main section of the machine is then free to go about other business while the buffer supplies words to the tape (or printer) as needed.

There are variations on the theme. Some machines have separate buffers for input and output, making it possible simultaneously to compute, read, and write. The problems where this can be utilized are perhaps slightly specialized, but where it is useful, it is *very* useful. A slightly different form of buffering, which is just about as powerful and considerably cheaper, may be called *direct memory buffering*. (Actually, the authors are not aware of an accepted term as yet and are here suggesting one.) In this technique, there is no separate storage device—with the exception of a one- or two-word register. Words coming from tape, to illustrate with the input case, are placed temporarily in a one-word register—which must be done whether the tape is buffered or not. Then the appropriate circuits begin waiting for a memory cycle which is not used by the arithmetic and control circuits, such as the execution phase of a shift or the bulk of a multiply or divide order. If such an unused cycle is available, the word is transferred to memory without having slowed down the arithmetic section at all. On the other hand, the tape circuits can wait only so long: the *next* word from tape must, after all, be placed in the one-word register. If necessary, then, the tape circuits override the control circuits, and interrupt the arithmetic section for one memory cycle in order to transfer the word to memory. A similar procedure is followed for writing. Considering that in the fastest tape system known at present words are transferred to or from tape only every 100 microseconds or so, and that typical memory access cycles are 10–20 microseconds, this technique at worst slows down arithmetic processing by only 20% (and much less if unused memory cycles are available).* Furthermore, the engineers tell us that direct memory buffering is considerably less expensive in equipment than the other type of buffering. The authors hazard the guess that, unless something better is invented, direct memory buffering will come to be the standard technique in new computers.

The time savings of buffering are appreciable. A typical tape

---

* It should be noted that the (presently) more common "block buffering" slows down computing, too, because processing must be temporarily interrupted to empty or fill the buffer.

buffer can be filled in perhaps 5–10% of the tape transport time; in an application which uses tapes heavily this can become quite significant. This assumes, however, that internal processing can be carried out in the time available between filling (or emptying) the buffer. If the internal processing time is ten times the tape time, say, then buffering is of little importance. In many business problems the latter is decidedly not the case and buffering really pays for itself. Observe that if a problem segment has exactly equal tape and internal processing time, and if buffer filling or emptying times are negligible, the total time savings due to buffering are 50% (which incidentally is a theoretical maximum saving and not actually attainable).*

10.9 Off-Line Tape Devices

Although buffering is quite significant in reducing the mismatch between internal and input/output speeds, there are many cases in which the input and output are so voluminous and the required processing so small that some other solution must be sought. The technique to be discussed is called variously *off-line, peripheral,* or *auxiliary tape* operation. In concept it is quite simple. On the input side, a magnetic tape is prepared on a tape unit which is not connected to the computer, by reading punched cards or punched paper tape and transferring the information to the magnetic tape, or by writing directly on the tape using a special device which is analogous to a keypunch. The reel of tape is then moved, when needed, to a tape unit which is connected to the computer.† The advantage, if it is not obvious, is that magnetic tape can be read much faster than cards or paper tape. For output, a magnetic tape reel which was prepared on-line is moved to an off-line tape unit from which the information is transcribed to paper tape, or cards, or printed. It is entirely possible—and often done—to have more than one of the various types of off-line tape devices, particularly printers. Equipment is now available to convert magnetically encoded documents to magnetic tape.

There are certain problems which must be faced in working with off-line tape equipment, having to do with format control. For instance, it is seldom desirable to prepare a tape such that each and

---

* Assuming there is only one buffer, and that only tapes are buffered; printers, card readers, and other input/output equipment can also be buffered.

† It is not always necessary to move the tape physically. It is possible to set up tape units so that they may be switched electrically from off-line to on-line operation and back.

every line to be printed is represented by one block on tape, including blocks of blanks for lines which are blank. Although it can be done, much of the advantage of off-line operation is lost through the programming effort required to get the tape into the necessary format. The amount of flexibility available to solve this problem varies considerably from one set of equipment to the next. One fairly new off-line printer is exceedingly fast, by present standards, but has no format control features whatsoever. Another system uses standard-speed printers, but allows a certain limited amount of format control by using the first character of each tape record to actuate relays in the printer, which in turn cause such actions as high-speed skipping to a new page or a new position on the same page. This latter makes use of a *carriage control tape*, a small loop of paper which permits flexibility in form control. Other systems have provision for extensive rearrangement of the characters, suppression of unwanted zeros, the printing of one tape record on several lines, the selective printing of a few characters originated from the printer itself, automatic page numbering, storage of headings, etc. All of these functions can be chosen at will by wiring a plugboard. Similar variations occur in card and paper tape punching and reading equipment.

At the time of writing a type of device was coming into use which might be characterized as a combination of off-line and on-line operation. It is a limited-purpose computer which is capable of editing input data and performing such operations as preparing control totals and perhaps sorting. Its output is a magnetic tape which is used as input to an ordinary computer, but now the computer can proceed immediately to processing. Actually, a small computer can be used in conjunction with a large one in such a manner also. In some cases this makes very good sense economically.

Depending on the nature of the application, off-line operation can save considerably more than the theoretical maximum that is made possible by buffers. Consider, for instance, an application which involves so little computation that 95% of the machine time is spent waiting on the card readers and the printer. In this case, all of the 95% can be saved except the tape reading time itself, which is much smaller than the times of the electromechanical elements. To put it another way, it is possible for off-line operation to double the total data processing capability of a computer system, at much less than double the cost. Unless and until very much faster input/output devices are invented and/or perfected, off-line operation is inevitably with us.

10.10 Summary

The significance of input/output operations in the time and cost economics of data processing is one of the major differences between the business or commercial computing which is the subject of this book and what is usually called scientific or engineering computing. The degree of this difference has occasionally been exaggerated but it is still real. In business data processing it is sheer folly to overlook the problems of time and cost and programming complexity imposed by the volume of input and output usually required. The devices and techniques presented in this chapter are fairly representative of those in use at the time of writing. Many new techniques are under intensive study and development, some of which seem to offer almost revolutionary advances. A suggestive, but surely not comprehensive, list of these might include the direct reading of printed or typed or even handwritten numbers and letters, printing by xerographic (dry photography) methods, printing on magnetically sensitized paper, and on-line and real-time input and output business recording devices.

Exercises

1. Classify input/output devices according to the following functions:
(a) To communicate between different computers or computer runs.
(b) To communicate between the computer and off-line peripheral equipment.
(c) To communicate between the computer and the outside world.

2. Discuss some of the suggested differences between the computer and the outside world as regards:
(a) Language.
(b) Speed.
(c) Representation of basic characters.

3. What is meant by input-limited, output-limited, and computer-limited?

4. Input/output devices may be used as auxiliary storage. Discuss the possibilities of using paper tape, punched cards, and magnetic tapes as auxiliary storage.

5. What are the basic items that should be on a computer console?

6. Magnetic tape handlers which read back what they write (2 heads) are better than those that do not (only 1 head). Why?

7. Discuss fixed record length versus variable record length recording on magnetic tape.

INPUT AND OUTPUT DEVICES

8. Discuss the pros and cons of entering the program through a direct-connected card reader versus magnetic tape (which may be prepared directly or through the off-line card-to-tape converter).

9. What are the advantages of a paper tape reader that can stop on a character (usually a special Stop character)?

10. Discuss how a magnetic tape reader which can read in both forward and backward directions may facilitate sorting operations.

11. How may a printer be used to plot curves? Suggest some special features or characters you would like to see incorporated in a standard high-speed printer to facilitate this function.

12. Suggest at least two systems of priority assignments and flow-chart the inquiry program (with the priority assignments) for a computer having 30 inquiry keyboards in the computer room and 100 inquiry keyboards located remotely.

13. In an unbuffered computer, the total processing time is input plus output plus internal processing. What is the approximate minimum total processing time of a computer with these features:
 (a) Read-while-write possible.
 (b) Read-while-write and tape-search-while-computing possible.
 (c) One buffer for input and output.
 (d) One input buffer and one output buffer.
 (e) Two buffers, each of which may serve as input *or* output buffers.

14. Direct memory buffering uses any part of the main memory as a buffer and borrows time in word transfer-time segments; the use of separate buffers merely utilizes special memories and borrows time in buffer transfer-time segments. Discuss the two systems.

15. Is buffering more valuable for a given computer with fast or with relatively slow tapes? How about buffering for punch card and paper tape equipment?

16. What kind of checking features would you want on:
 (a) Magnetic tape equipment?
 (b) A card reader?
 (c) A high-speed printer?

17. Suggest several analogies between buffers and things in everyday life.

11 INPUT AND OUTPUT PROGRAMMING

11.0 Introduction

In the previous chapter, we surveyed the electronic and mechanical devices which are commonly used to communicate with the memory of computers. Now we must look into the programming and procedures techniques which are utilized to make use of these devices. We shall discuss the planning aspects of input and output, some typical input/output instructions including a few for DATAC, some techniques used to signal and handle exceptional situations, and other related topics.

11.1 Planning for Input and Output

Assuming that the problem has been completely defined as regards sequence of major information flows, as to what information is entered into the over-all processing, and as to what reports are required of it, the next step is to obtain or define the exact *format* of the documents to be processed and the reports to be generated. Sometimes these formats are rigidly specified by factors outside the programmer's control. In that case he needs simply to represent the required format in a form suitable for his use, and proceed with the programming of input and output and editing instructions which will handle or generate the information in the sequence and spacing specified. If the formats are not so rigidly defined, the programmer and/or procedures analyst must first determine the answers to such questions as:

How are the source documents prepared originally? What is the best way to transcribe them to a machine-readable form if they are not so already?

Would there be any way to prepare them in a machine-readable form at the source and still retain visual readability if needed?

INPUT AND OUTPUT PROGRAMMING

What might be done to rearrange the input records to facilitate programming after the data enters the machine?

To what use will reports be put and what information from them is *really* needed?

Is there any possibility of printing only the exceptions to standard policy or conditions, leaving all the rest of the information on tape to be printed in full only occasionally?

What is the most readable arrangement and spacing of information on the output reports?

What must be done, after computer processing, to such output as cards and paper tape—and how can the arrangement be set up to facilitate such further processing?

How many copies must be printed and why are they needed?

These and similar questions *must* be answered, regardless of the time required. Failure to do so can only lead to ill-considered procedures, less-than-optimum usefulness of reports, and later reprogramming.

Some of these topics, however, are outside the scope of this chapter or book, and others are so inextricably bound up with the details and idiosyncrasies of particular input/output media and devices that we cannot treat the subject in detail here. We shall, therefore, discuss only one tool in format planning, the output format charts used to lay out printed reports.

This form, illustrated in Figure 1, has a box for each character position that can be printed on a page, i.e., as many characters as there are in a line and at least as many lines as there are on a page. Regardless of whether the output format is prescribed in advance or worked out by the programmer himself after an investigation, the chart should be drawn up for each report and report variation. The location of the headings, if any, the exact locations of any signs or credit symbols, etc., should all be shown. Each position where printing is expected should be filled in on the chart, either with a typical number or X's, and notes should be made showing what each item is. Needless to say, the *maximum* size of each field should be shown.

There are several benefits to be derived from a carefully prepared set of output format charts. They provide an over-all picture of the eventual appearance of the reports, making it possible to plan a balanced and uncrowded page. "Pretty" reports are not, of course, the primary goal of data processing, but if the general appearance can be improved by a little effort it is probably worth it. A second benefit

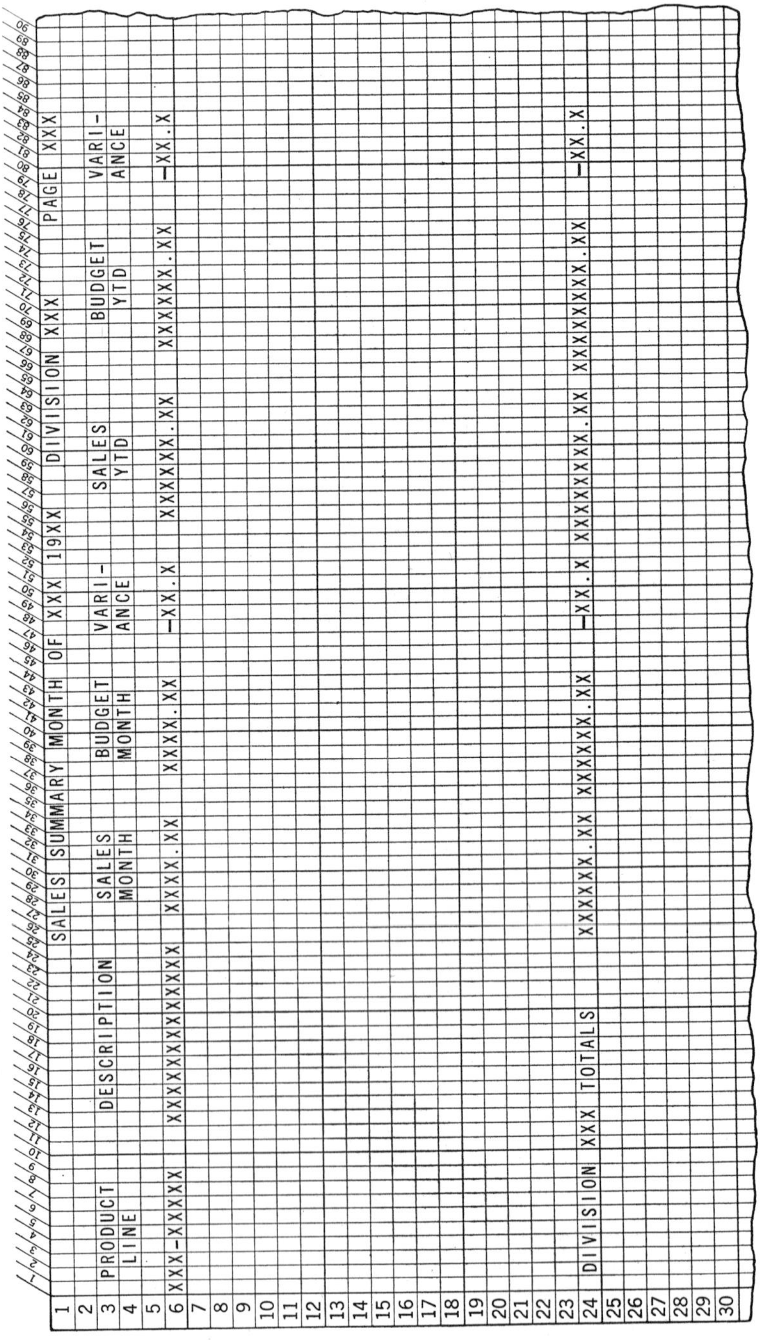

Figure 1. Sample of an output format chart. (Form courtesy Remington Rand Univac Division, Sperry Rand Corporation.)

is that all possible combinations of circumstances can better be anticipated. The situation here is not too different, although perhaps less crucial, than it is in the general procedures and programming case; i.e., the matter of foreseeing difficulties due to rare combinations. For instance, the format chart may show that if a certain alphabetic stock description ever reached fifteen characters and the preceding quantity were followed by a credit symbol, there would be no space between the "CR" and the next letter—leading possibly to considerable confusion. A third and obvious benefit of an output format chart is that it greatly simplifies the task of editing the information to be printed, or of wiring a printer plugboard. It is also often necessary to prepare a small paper tape loop to control the paper spacing of a printer; the format chart simplifies this minor task also.

This section is at best only indicative of the type of work which goes into preplanning of input/output functions. Other techniques are described by the equipment manufacturers for their particular media and devices. And, of course, a great deal depends on the application.

11.2 Input and Output Instructions and Programming*

In this section we shall outline briefly some typical input/output instructions and programming techniques. For the purpose, we shall use several DATAC instructions which have to do with the assumed DATAC input and output devices; these are a card reader and a line printer. We shall not discuss input/output aspects of magnetic tape since this has been done in previous chapters; in this section, however, we shall discuss certain assumed DATAC features having to do with the handling of unusual conditions which arise in the operation of input/output equipment.

The DATAC card reader reads eighty-column punched cards at a rate of 250 per minute. It reads the entire card as the result of one Read instruction, and reads each column as a DATAC character. That is, numbers, punched zero through nine, go into memory as numbers; letters, punched as a combination of two punches, go into memory as letters in the correct DATAC six-bit coding; special symbols, punched as one or a combination of two or three punches, go into memory in their six-bit codes. The six-bit codes are shown in the table on page 59; the standard IBM punching of letters and special characters is illustrated in Figure 2 of Chapter 10—although these special characters do not happen to correspond exactly to those assumed for DATAC.

* This section may be omitted without loss of continuity.

A card is read and the eighty characters entered in eight memory words by a Read instruction (operation code: R). Unless special measures are taken as described below, the sign positions of the memory words are not filled, but are set to zero. Eighty columns correspond to eight ten-character words; the address of the first of the eight consecutive words in memory to be filled from a card is specified in the address part of the instruction. The address may be modified as usual by an indexer. The filters have no function on this instruction. If any of the information on the card is numeric, some provision must of course be made for the signs. In the not too uncommon case where the numbers are always positive, it is possible to wire the plugboard on the reader so as to emit the plus signs sometimes needed to make DATAC arithmetic work properly. When the numbers can be negative, it is usual practice to signify the fact by an eleven-punch (first row above the zero row) over either the first or last digit of the number. If this were read directly, it would make that column look like a letter; it is possible, however, to "split off" this overpunch through plugboard wiring and enter it as a sign. The plugboard also permits flexibility of rearranging or regrouping the columns of a card before entering them into memory. For instance, in a case where fewer than eighty columns are used, it might be desirable to put fewer than ten digits in each word, in order to avoid the task of splitting up the numbers later. We shall return to the question of how best to handle the many variations of input format when we discuss input/output subroutines in Section 11.4.

The DATAC printer prints 120 characters per line at the rate of 600 lines per minute. Each character may be any of the DATAC characters, including a blank. A line is printed on execution of the instruction Print (operation code: P); its address specifies the first of twelve words of memory which will be printed. The address may be modified by an indexer as usual. The situation on signs is just the reverse of the reader; all the sign positions of the twelve words are "available" at the wired plugboard of the printer, to be printed or ignored as the situation requires. The printer plugboard also permits rearrangement of the characters, as does the reader plugboard. (It should be noted that not all printers have such a plugboard; in these cases the rearrangement must be programmed.)

To take a simple example of how the rearrangement might be done, suppose that the twelve words beginning at 1600 are to be printed; we shall consider only the first two of these. Suppose they contain

Character	S 10 9 8 7 6 5 4 3 2 1	S 10 9 8 7 6 5 4 3 2 1
	x 5 3 5 2 2 1 5 8 3 1	x 9 8 6 0 0 5 8 3 3 3

INPUT AND OUTPUT PROGRAMMING

which are actually to be printed as

Print
position   1 2 3 4 5 6 7 8 9 10 11 12 13 14 15 16 17 18 19 20 21 22 23 24 25 26 27 28 29
            5 3 5 - 2 2 - 1 5 8 3   1 9 8 6 0 $ 0 5 8 3 . 3 3

In short, those first two words actually contain three items packed into two: a social security number, a pay number, and a monthly salary rate. It would be a simple matter on some machines to wire the printer plugboard to space the three items and insert the dashes, dollar sign, and decimal point (assuming these last always went in the same column and were always printed). More elaborate examples could be given, but perhaps this illustration is suggestive of what can be done.

We must, at this point, anticipate some of the material in Section 11.4 on input/output subroutines, because a problem immediately arises. Since for DATAC we have assumed a printer as the only on-line output device, it will almost always be necessary to use several different output formats during a computer run. For instance, if the printer board were wired to properly space the memory words for a certain payroll register, the page headings and summary totals might be badly jumbled. And if it were necessary, in the middle of the run, to space to a new page and print instructions to the operator regarding a machine failure which required restarting the run, the instructions would almost certainly be badly jumbled.* Trying to solve this problem by requiring frequent plugboard changes is ineffective, because too much burden is placed on the operator and too much machine time is wasted. Furthermore, such a solution essentially wastes the power of the stored program concept. The best solution to this problem would be to wire one plugboard which prints all 120 characters in consecutive sequence across the page, and require the programmer to *edit* the material going into the twelve words to be printed, thus returning the spacing problem back to the stored program. This is not quite the onerous task it might appear to be, as we shall try to show in the section on input/output subroutines and in Chapter 14 on machine-aided coding.

---

* It should be noted that it is possible in many cases to have two formats wired into one board, with a signal from the computer choosing which is to be in effect for a given line. It often happens that two or even three formats are not enough, however, and the point is still valid. It may be noted, however, that when a computer has both a printer and a typewriter, operator instructions are usually typed out, not printed.

Several of the newer printers allow *selective printing,* i.e., it is possible to place several reports on the same magnetic tape and by means of an identifying key print only the appropriate records.

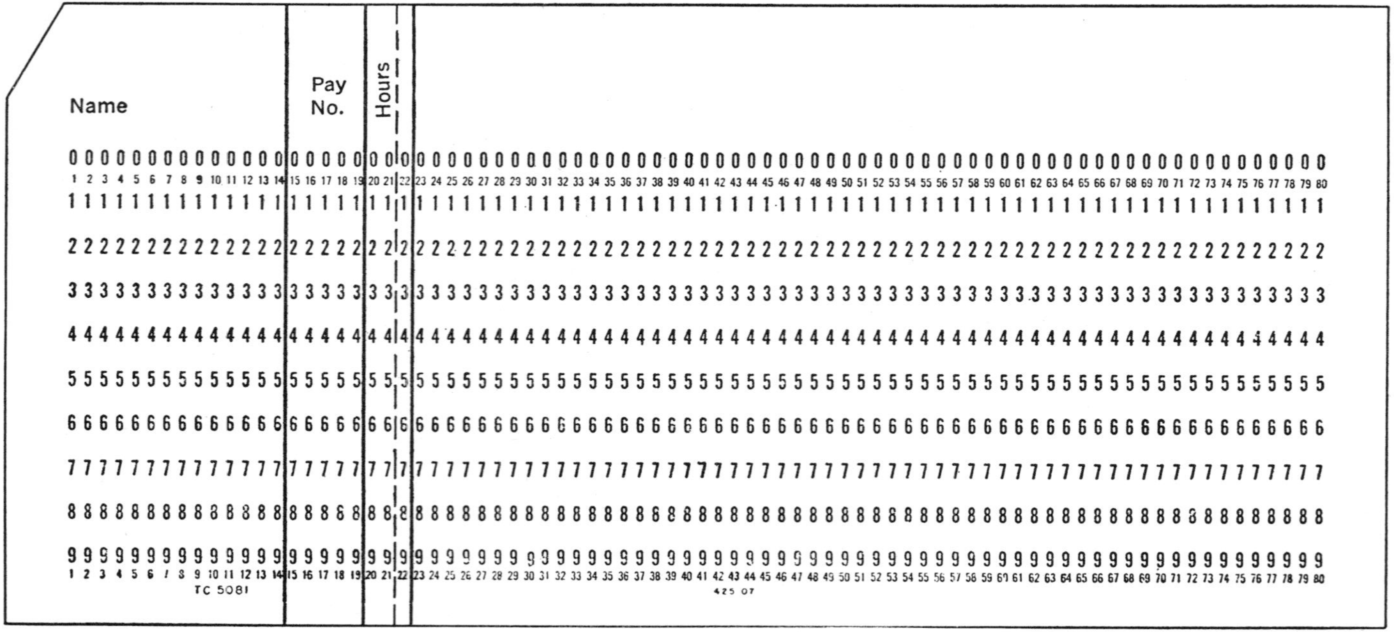

Figure 2. Format of input cards in text example.

INPUT AND OUTPUT PROGRAMMING

Finally, getting back to the DATAC input/output instructions, there is a variation of the Print instruction which calls for spacing the page, i.e., skipping over lines which are not to be printed. One line can easily enough be skipped by carrying out an ordinary Print instruction and giving the address of twelve words filled with the character *blank*. But to skip half a page, say, by this method would be too time-consuming. Instead, the printer carriage is equipped with a small paper tape which can control automatic skipping of lines. In essence, when the Space print instruction (operation code: SP) is

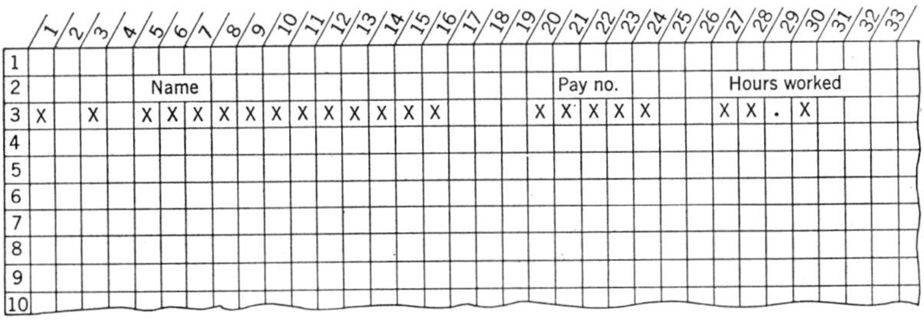

Figure 3. Printing format in text example.

executed, the paper is advanced until the next hole is sensed in the carriage tape. If this has been set up to correspond to the top of the next page, for instance, the rest of the current page would automatically be skipped.

In order to make these ideas more concrete, we may consider the following example. Suppose a deck of cards in the reader consists of labor vouchers—one or more (usually more) per man. The task is to read the cards, then compute and print the total hours worked for each man. (This is hardly a realistic example, since the task in practice would almost certainly be done as a part of other operations; furthermore, it would seldom be necessary to print the total in this manner. The reading and printing techniques are adequately illustrated, however, and that is all we are concerned with here.)

Suppose the card format is as shown in Figure 2.

    Columns   1–14   Name
                     15–19 Pay number
                     20–22 Hours worked, to tenths

Suppose the required printing format is as shown in the output format chart of Figure 3.

The flow chart of the program could be as illustrated in Figure 4. There are two minor complications in this example. When it is discovered that a new man's voucher has been read, that information must be saved while the information on the previous man is edited and printed. The other problem is to get the comparison started correctly when the *first* card is read. The method shown in Figure 4 involves the use of what are called *working storage* (WS) areas, one for input and one for output. Cards are ordinarily read into the input WS area and compared with the information in the output WS area—which is for the information on the previous card (or cards, if there was more than one). The hours worked are accumulated right in the output WS area. Then when it is discovered that the card just read is for a new man, the information in the output WS area is printed, and the card in the input WS area moved to the output WS area to prepare for reading the next card and comparing with it. The exception to this procedure is the first card, which is read directly into the output WS area. (We have completely ignored the problem of handling the *last* card, and, for that matter, knowing when the last card has been read. Exercise 1 at the end of the chapter considers this problem.)

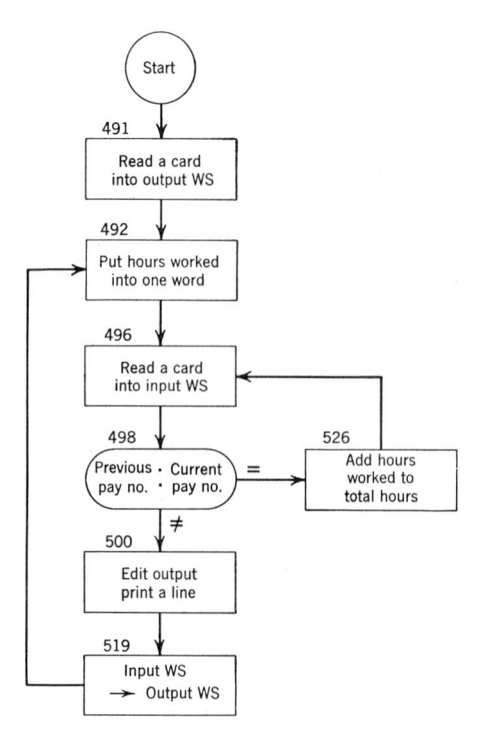

Figure 4. Flow chart of text problem on input/output programming.

Suppose that the reader board is such that columns 1–10 are read into characters 10–1 of the first word of the input area, columns 11–20 are read into characters 10–1 of the second word, etc.; i.e., signs are not wired to read into memory. Suppose the printer is wired similarly, except that there are, of course, 12 words and 120 positions instead of 8 and 80. Saying it another way, if we visualize the eight words of the input area as laid out in a row with the sign characters omitted, they will "look like" the card. For this reason, we sometimes speak of the memory words into which cards are read or from which lines are printed as the *card image* and *line image*, respectively.

INPUT AND OUTPUT PROGRAMMING

Assume the following memory assignments:

Input WS	800–807
Output WS	808–815
Line image (for printing)	816–827
00b0b000000	941
Blanks for editing name	
0000000bbb0	942
Blanks for editing name	
00000bb00.0	943
Blanks and decimal point for editing total hours worked	
00000111110	41
Filter for pay number comparison	
01111000000	42
Filter for name editing	
00000100000	43
Filter for editing pay number	
00000011110	44
Filter for editing pay number	
00000000110	45
Filter for editing hours worked	
00000000001	46
Filter for editing hours worked	

The routine could be as follows. An L and R register analysis of the routine may be found following the routine, along with a few notes which may be helpful. The routine makes heavy use of transfer shifting and filtering, which some readers may have elected to omit, so the routine may have to be skimmed.

LOC.	S	O	ADDRESS	FILTER	REMARKS
0491		R	0808		Read a card into output WS
0492		F	0809	46	Fetch first digit of hours worked to L, filtered (to get hours worked into one word)
0493		B	0810		Bring last two digits of hours worked to R
0494	E	R	0008		Shift characters of L and R right, except signs, eight places
0495		S	0810		Store hours worked
0496		R	0800		Read a card into input WS
0497		B	0801		Bring current pay number to R
0498		C	0809	41	Compare with previous pay number, filtered
0499	E	J	0526		Equal jump to add current hours to total hours worked

(*Continued on next page*)

208   PROGRAMMING BUSINESS COMPUTERS

0500		F	0808		Fetch first part of name to L
0501	E	R	0008		Shift characters of L and R right, except signs, eight places
0502	O	R	0001		Shift only R right, one place
0503	E	R	0001		Shift L and R right, except signs, one place
0504	O	R	0001		Shift only R right, one place
0505	E	R	0001		Shift L and R right, except signs, one place
0506		A	0941		Add blanks between initials
0507		S	0816		Store as first word in line image
0508	−8	B	0808		Bring ninth and tenth characters of name to R, shifted
0509	+2	A	0809	42	Add last four characters of name to R, filtered, shifted
0510		A	0942		Add blanks
0511	+5	A	0809	43	Add first digit of pay number, filtered, shifted
0512		S	0817		Store as second word of line image
0513	−5	B	0809	44	Bring last four digits of pay number, filtered, shifted
0514	−1	A	0810	45	Add first two digits of hours worked, filtered, shifted
0515		A	0810	46	Add last digit of hours worked, filtered
0516		A	0943		Add blanks and decimal point
0517		S	0818		Store as third word of line image
0518		P	0816		Print line
0519		B	0800		Move input WS information to output WS area
0520		S	0808		
0521		B	0801		
0522		S	0809		
0523		B	0802		
0524		S	0810		
0525	U	J	0492		Unconditional jump to 0492 to rearrange hours worked for next man, and read another card
0526		F	0801	46	Fetch first digit of hours worked to L, filtered (if here, voucher is for same man as previous voucher)
0527		B	0802		Bring last two digits of hours worked to R

(*Continued on next page*)

INPUT AND OUTPUT PROGRAMMING

0528	E	R	0008	Shift characters of L and R right, except signs, eight places
0529	X	A	0810	Add to memory, to get new total hours worked
0530	U	J	0496	Unconditional jump to read another card

Other instructions

Suppose the first three cards in the deck contain the following information.

```
H T W E I S S L E E V I S H 2 7 5 2 5 2 2 5
H T W E I S S L E E V I S H 2 7 5 2 5 1 8 5
D D M C C R A C K E N S K Y 4 7 5 0 0 3 2 3
```

The execution of the routine would proceed as follows, in reading these three cards, and printing the required line for the first two. Recall that we assumed signs are not wired so that the sign positions of the WS words contain zeros.

INST.	MEMORY REFERENCE	L REGISTER	R REGISTER
R 0808	0 H T W E I S S L E E	?	?
F 0809 46	0 V I S H 2 7 5 2 5 2	0 0 0 0 0 0 0 0 0 0 2	?
B 0810	0 2 5 0 0 0 0 0 0 0 0	0 0 0 0 0 0 0 0 0 0 2	0 2 5 0 0 0 0 0 0 0 0
E R 0008		0 0 0 0 0 0 0 0 0 0 0	0 0 0 0 0 0 0 0 2 2 5
S 0810	0 0 0 0 0 0 0 0 2 2 5	0 0 0 0 0 0 0 0 0 0 0	0 0 0 0 0 0 0 0 2 2 5
R 0800	0 H T W E I S S L E E	0 0 0 0 0 0 0 0 0 0 0	0 0 0 0 0 0 0 0 2 2 5
B 0801	0 V I S H 2 7 5 2 5 1	0 0 0 0 0 0 0 0 0 0 0	0 V I S H 2 7 5 2 5 1
C 0809 41	0 V I S H 2 7 5 2 5 2	0 0 0 0 0 0 0 0 0 0 0	0 V I S H 2 7 5 2 5 1
E J 0526		0 0 0 0 0 0 0 0 0 0 0	0 V I S H 2 7 5 2 5 1
F 0801 46	0 V I S H 2 7 5 2 5 1	0 0 0 0 0 0 0 0 0 0 1	0 V I S H 2 7 5 2 5 1
B 0802	0 8 5 0 0 0 0 0 0 0 0	0 0 0 0 0 0 0 0 0 0 1	0 8 5 0 0 0 0 0 0 0 0
E R 0008		0 0 0 0 0 0 0 0 0 0 0	0 0 0 0 0 0 0 0 1 8 5
X A 0810	0 0 0 0 0 0 0 0 4 1 0	0 0 0 0 0 0 0 0 0 0 0	0 0 0 0 0 0 0 0 1 8 5
U J 0496		0 0 0 0 0 0 0 0 0 0 0	0 0 0 0 0 0 0 0 1 8 5
R 0800	0 D D M C C R A C K E	0 0 0 0 0 0 0 0 0 0 0	0 0 0 0 0 0 0 0 1 8 5
B 0801	0 N S K Y 4 7 5 0 0 3	0 0 0 0 0 0 0 0 0 0 0	0 N S K Y 4 7 5 0 0 3
C 0809 41	0 V I S H 2 7 5 2 5 2	0 0 0 0 0 0 0 0 0 0 0	0 N S K Y 4 7 5 0 0 3
E J 0526		0 0 0 0 0 0 0 0 0 0 0	0 N S K Y 4 7 5 0 0 3
F 0808	0 H T W E I S S L E E	0 H T W E I S S L E E	0 N S K Y 4 7 5 0 0 3
E R 0008		0 0 0 0 0 0 0 0 0 H T	0 W E I S S L E E N S
O R 0001		0 0 0 0 0 0 0 0 0 H T	0 0 W E I S S L E E N
E R 0001		0 0 0 0 0 0 0 0 0 0 H	0 T 0 W E I S S L E E
O R 0001		0 0 0 0 0 0 0 0 0 0 H	0 0 T 0 W E I S S L E
E R 0001		0 0 0 0 0 0 0 0 0 0 0	0 H 0 T 0 W E I S S L
A 0941	0 0 b 0 b 0 0 0 0 0 0	0 0 0 0 0 0 0 0 0 0 0	0 H b T b W E I S S L
S 0816	0 H b T b W E I S S L	0 0 0 0 0 0 0 0 0 0 0	0 H b T b W E I S S L
−8 B 0808	0 H T W E I S S L E E	0 0 0 0 0 0 0 0 0 0 0	0 E E 0 0 0 0 0 0 0 0

(Continued on next page)

210 PROGRAMMING BUSINESS COMPUTERS

0509	+2 A 0809 42	0 V I S H 2 7 5 2 5 2	0 0 0 0 0 0 0 0 0 0	0 E E V I S H 0 0 0
0510	A 0942	0 0 0 0 0 0 b b b 0	0 0 0 0 0 0 0 0 0 0	0 E E V I S H b b b
0511	+5 A 0809 43	0 V I S H 2 7 5 2 5 2	0 0 0 0 0 0 0 0 0 0	0 E E V I S H b b b
0512	S 0817	0 E E V I S H b b b 2	0 0 0 0 0 0 0 0 0 0	0 E E V I S H b b b
0513	−5 B 0809 44	0 V I S H 2 7 5 2 5 2	0 0 0 0 0 0 0 0 0 0	0 7 5 2 5 0 0 0 0 0
0514	−1 A 0810 45	0 0 0 0 0 0 0 4 1 0	0 0 0 0 0 0 0 0 0 0	0 7 5 2 5 0 0 4 1 0
0515	A 0810 46	0 0 0 0 0 0 0 4 1 0	0 0 0 0 0 0 0 0 0 0	0 7 5 2 5 0 0 4 1 0
0516	A 0943	0 0 0 0 b b 0 0 . 0	0 0 0 0 0 0 0 0 0 0	0 7 5 2 5 b b 4 1 .
0517	S 0818	0 7 5 2 5 b b 4 1 . 0	0 0 0 0 0 0 0 0 0 0	0 7 5 2 5 b b 4 1 .
0518	P 0816	0 H b T b W E I S S L	0 0 0 0 0 0 0 0 0 0	0 7 5 2 5 b b 4 1 .
0519	B 0800	0 D D M C C R A C K E	0 0 0 0 0 0 0 0 0 0	0 D D M C C R A C K
0520	S 0808	0 D D M C C R A C K E	0 0 0 0 0 0 0 0 0 0	0 D D M C C R A C K
0521	B 0801	0 N S K Y 4 7 5 0 0 3	0 0 0 0 0 0 0 0 0 0	0 N S K Y 4 7 5 0 0
0522	S 0809	0 N S K Y 4 7 5 0 0 3	0 0 0 0 0 0 0 0 0 0	0 N S K Y 4 7 5 0 0
0523	B 0802	0 2 3 0 0 0 0 0 0 0	0 0 0 0 0 0 0 0 0 0	0 2 3 0 0 0 0 0 0 0
0524	S 0810	0 2 3 0 0 0 0 0 0 0	0 0 0 0 0 0 0 0 0 0	0 2 3 0 0 0 0 0 0 0
0525	U J 0492		0 0 0 0 0 0 0 0 0 0	0 2 3 0 0 0 0 0 0 0
0492	F 0809 46	0 N S K Y 4 7 5 8 0 3	0 0 0 0 0 0 0 0 0 3	0 2 3 0 0 0 0 0 0 0
0493	B 0810	0 2 3 0 0 0 0 0 0 0	0 0 0 0 0 0 0 0 0 3	0 2 3 0 0 0 0 0 0 0
0494	E R 0008		0 0 0 0 0 0 0 0 0 0	0 0 0 0 0 0 0 0 3
0495	S 0810	0 0 0 0 0 0 0 3 2 3	0 0 0 0 0 0 0 0 0 0	0 0 0 0 0 0 0 0 3
0496	Read next card and continue processing			

The line printed would appear as:

H T WEISSLEEVISH 27525 41.0

Note that all the additions are permissible within the rules laid down for DATAC even though no signs are provided. This is legal because all quantities involved are positive. It may be seen that over half of the instructions in this routine have no other function than rearrangement of data. For instance, the instructions at 0492–0495 are required to get the hours worked figure into one word, instead of being separated into two words, as they are when read. The instructions at 0519–0524 move the information in the input WS area to the output WS area.

This routine invites a comment. We have here a good example of the flexibility problem. Suppose that after this routine has been coded and is running, someone decides that fourteen characters are not enough for names. Since the original assumption of name length has been deeply imbedded in the coding, the routine would have to be almost completely recoded. To meet this problem, it has become common to separate the functions of input, processing, and output into distinct sections of the program. The input section, in this problem, would separate the name, payroll number, and hours worked into separate words (or groups of words). The processing would then be done as before, except that it would be simpler. The output section would rearrange the quantities as required for printing. The input and output routines would ordinarily be built around standard subroutines, to be discussed shortly, in which information is fed to the subroutines via calling sequences. Now, a change in format involves only changing a few parameters in the calling sequences. A little machine efficiency has perhaps been sacrificed, but it is very well worth it. The reader may also wish to bear this example in mind while reading the discussion of machine-aided coding in Chapter 14, comparing it in particular with the utter simplicity of doing the same thing with the report generator.

11.3 A Program for Loading Cards*

As we have noted before, memory is usually assumed to be empty when a problem is begun. It might be technically feasible, although it would be operationally undesirable, to leave a loading routine in memory at all times. This not being desirable, it is necessary somehow to get a few instructions into memory which can call in a loading routine, which then loads the actual routine from cards, paper tape, or magnetic tape. This type of loading routine is usually called *self-loading* (a term that is not completely accurate), which is intended to imply that it can get itself into memory with a minimum of manipulation by the operator. This involves the use of a load button described in the last chapter, if the machine has one, or the execution of a few instructions from the console if not. In this section we shall describe a self-loading routine to load cards.

It will be necessary first to define a card format and a reader board. Since in DATAC a *generalized* load program must accept eleven-character words, we shall set up the program and board accordingly. (This is of course a change from the assumption of the last example.) Furthermore, since we wish to be able to load cards into any part of memory, it will be necessary to require each card to have on it an *initial address* which specifies where the first word on the card is to be stored in memory, the others being stored sequentially after that. Since it may often be desirable to load a card containing fewer than the maximum number of words, we shall set up the load program and the card format to permit a *word count* which tells how many words there are on each card. The program is set up to load an indefinite number of cards. It will stop loading and jump into the program which has been loaded when a *transition card*† is discovered.

---
* This section may be omitted without loss of continuity.
† Also called a *transfer of control* card.

A transition card will be identified by the presence of *any* punch in column 6. When a transition card is encountered, the load program treats the initial address as a *transition address,* performing an Unconditional jump to that address, which is usually the starting location of the program which has just been loaded.

The card format is taken as:

COLUMNS	
1–4	Initial address
5	Word count
6	Transition signal
7–11	Blank
12–22	First word
23–33	Second word
34–44	Third word
45–55	Fourth word
56–66	Fifth word
67–77	Sixth word
78–80	Blank

The reader board is wired to send columns 1–11 to the first word of the card image, 12–22 to the second, etc., *including* the sign characters.

This is the format of the cards to be loaded. The loading program itself cannot be in this format, since the requirement of first getting itself into memory does not permit it. The sequence of cards in a normal program deck would then be:

Self-loading program	Five cards
Program cards	Variable
Transition card	One card
Data	Variable

The operation of the program below is based on the operation of the DATAC *load card* button (page 179). As pointed out previously, pressing this button causes a card to be loaded in locations 0–7 in memory and an Unconditional jump to location zero to be executed. In other words, it is equivalent to the automatic execution of the two-instruction sequence

Read	0000
Unconditional jump	0000

The first card of the self-loader is thus loaded "free," i.e., without the execution of any instructions from memory. This card can then call for the loading of the remaining cards of the self-loader. The program, once in memory, is then able to load the program which follows it and recognize the transition card.

The procedure is flow-charted in Figure 5. The routine follows.

INPUT AND OUTPUT PROGRAMMING

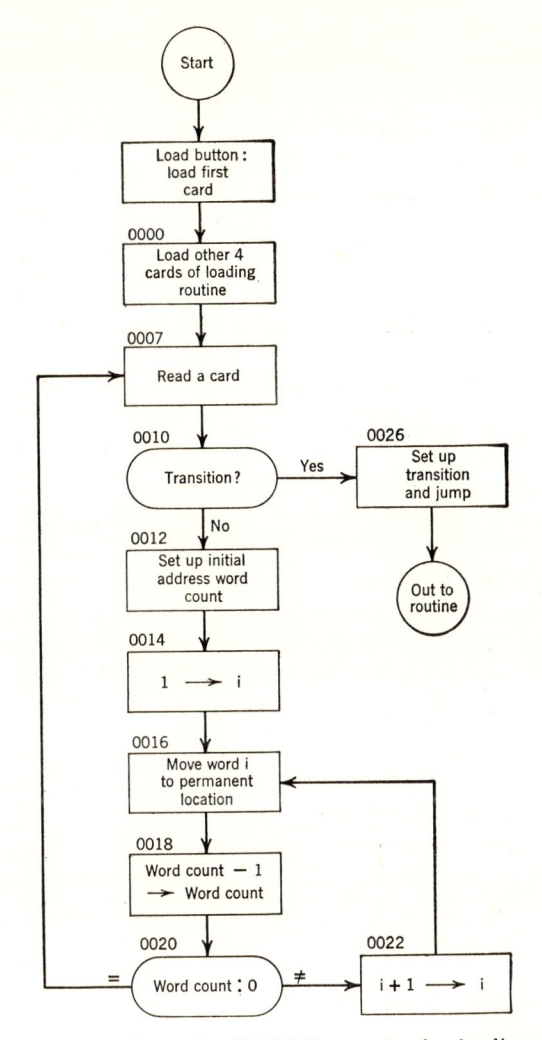

```
                    ┌─────────┐
                    │  Start  │
                    └────┬────┘
                         │
              ┌──────────────────────┐
              │  Load button:        │
              │  load first card     │
              └──────────┬───────────┘
                    0000 │
              ┌──────────────────────┐
              │  Load other 4        │
              │  cards of loading    │
              │  routine             │
              └──────────┬───────────┘
                    0007 │
              ┌──────────────────────┐
        ┌────▶│    Read a card       │
        │     └──────────┬───────────┘
        │           0010 │                0026
        │     ┌────────────────┐     ┌──────────────┐
        │     │  Transition?   │─Yes→│  Set up      │
        │     └──────────┬─────┘     │  transition  │
        │           0012 │ No        │  and jump    │
        │     ┌──────────────────┐   └──────┬───────┘
        │     │ Set up initial   │          │
        │     │ address word     │          ▼
        │     │ count            │       ( Out to
        │     └──────────┬───────┘        routine )
        │           0014 │
        │     ┌──────────────────┐
        │     │    1 ─→ i        │
        │     └──────────┬───────┘
        │           0016 │
        │     ┌──────────────────┐
        │     │  Move word i     │◀─────┐
        │     │  to permanent    │      │
        │     │  location        │      │
        │     └──────────┬───────┘      │
        │           0018 │              │
        │     ┌──────────────────┐      │
        │     │ Word count − 1   │      │
        │     │  ─→ Word count   │      │
        │     └──────────┬───────┘      │
        │           0020 │        0022  │
        │     ┌──────────────┐  ┌──────────────┐
        └──=──│ Word count:0 │─≠│ i + 1 ─→ i   │
              └──────────────┘  └──────────────┘
```

Figure 5. Flow chart of a DATAC program for loading cards.

LOC.	S	O	ADDRESS	INDEX	FILTER	MON.	REMARKS
0000		R	0007				Read second card
0001		R	0014				Read third card
0002		R	0021				Read fourth card
0003		R	0028				Read fifth card
0004	U	J	0007				Unconditional jump to 0007
0005							Unused
0006							Unused

(*Continued on next page*)

0007		R	0000		Read a program card into 0000–0006, which is now available
0008		F	0000		Fetch first word from card to L
0009	A	R	0013		Shift all characters of L & R right 13 places to put initial address in address part of R
0010		C	0030	33	Compare with blank in column 6 to check for transition card (filtered)
0011	E	J	0026		Equal jump to routine to store transition address
0012		S	0017	31	Store initial address in instruction at 0017, filtered
0013	−1	S	0028	29	Store word count at 0028, shifted, filtered
0014		B	0029		Bring constant 1 to R
0015		S	0016	31	Store as address of instruction at 0016 to initialize temporary storage location
0016		B	[ ]		Bring a word to R from card image
0017		S	[ ]		Store in permanent location
0018		B	0028		Bring word count to R
0019		M	0029		Subtract 1
0020	Z	J	0007		Zero jump to read next card; implies that all words from this card have been stored
0021		S	0028		Store modified word count
0022		B	0029		Bring constant 1 to R
0023	X	A	0016		Add to memory to increase address
0024	X	A	0017		Add to memory to increase address

(*Continued on next page*)

INPUT AND OUTPUT PROGRAMMING

0025	U	J	0016				Unconditional jump to move next word
0026		S	0027		31		Store transition address in 0027, filtered
0027	U	J	[ ]				Unconditional jump to start of routine which has now been loaded
0028	0	0	0000	00	00	0	Storage for word count
0029	0	0	0001	00	00	0	Constant 1 (written to look like an instruction)
0030	0	0	0000	0b	00	0	Constant: blank in column 6
0031	0	0	1111	00	00	0	Filter
0032	0	0	0000	10	00	0	Filter
0033	0	0	0000	01	00	0	Filter

A few notes may help to clarify the operation of this program. The first card is loaded automatically by the action of the load card button, but the four remaining cards must be loaded under control of the program which gets into memory on the first card. Such is the function of the four Read instructions. The following three locations could have been used for the program, but space has to be provided somewhere to hold each card temporarily until the load program interprets the initial address and stores the words permanently. Words 0–6 are as good as any. It may be noted that we have for the first time in the book used the lower section of memory to hold ordinary instructions instead of reserving that space for indexers and filters; this use of lower memory has been mentioned earlier, but not illustrated before. On the other hand, it would be simple enough to rewrite the program to operate from any part of memory that might be desired; load programs are often written to occupy the last few words of memory instead of the first few. It should be noted also that, although it is true that the cards which contain the load program do not have the same format as the cards they load, the only difference is the fact that the load program cards do not have an initial address and word count. The importance of this fact lies in the ability to use the same reader board to load all the cards in a deck.

The instructions at 0008 and 0009 may raise questions. The reason for using a Fetch-Shift all right pair rather than a Bring-Shift only R right is that with the assumed card format and reader board the sign characters contain numeric data, and there is no instruction "Shift only R right including sign." Various things could be done to shorten the program—at the expense of understandability, however. One obvious change would be to use indexing; the student may wish to rewrite the program using indexing, as an exercise. One word could be saved by storing the word count in 0000, because that location is no longer needed by the time the word count is stored. It should be pointed out that the last five words of the program are actually constants, written to "look like" instructions. It might have been possible to eliminate one of the filter constants by searching for a word elsewhere in the program which has the correct combination of bits in the characters. This, however, makes a program hard to follow, and, worse, treacherous to modify. Finally, observe that efforts to reduce the number of steps must, in this case, be made with the number of cards in the load program in mind. The program as it stands contains thirty-four words, and requires five cards. If this could be reduced to twenty-eight words, the program would fit on four cards. Having effected this savings, there would be little to gain by saving more steps unless the total could be reduced to twenty-one or less, because four cards would still be required. Unless, that is, time is important. We have not said enough about the timing of the card reader's operation to evaluate this question, but it might happen, for instance, that only by removing a few steps from the storing loop would it be possible to load cards at the full card reader speed.

It should be noted, in concluding this section, that techniques similar to those illustrated here are used in loading from any input medium, such as magnetic tape, paper tape, etc.

11.4 Input and Output Subroutines

The reader should by now have become painfully aware that programming related to input and output—as exemplified by the small illustrations of the previous two sections—is not something that every programmer should have to do each time he works on a new application. The task is too burdensome, it is subject to many errors because of its complex and detailed nature, and many of the common functions are needed in almost every program that is ever written. In this section we shall explore, in broad outline, some of the things that can be done to ease this burden. It may be pointed out that the type of programming we shall discuss here is often done either by the computer manufacturer and supplied "free," or by a small group of programmers in the installation who (normally) have no other duties. In other words, it is a type of work which is best done by specialists; common names for this work are *utility programming, programming research, techniques development,* etc. A complete set of the type of programs produced by such groups, whether provided by the manufacturer or done in the shop, represents a *large* investment which more than one new user has overlooked to his eventual sorrow.

For our purposes in this chapter, we shall classify these routines into three groups, although the classification is not intended to be all-inclusive or rigid. We shall discuss (1) *small input/output routines,* (2) *major input/output and editing subroutines,* and (3) *tape-executive programs.*

By small input/output routines is meant programs of the sort discussed in the preceding section. They usually perform some completely standard function such as loading in a program from cards or paper or magnetic tape, writing out in fixed format the contents of a specified section of memory, loading memory from a magnetic tape which was prepared off-line, etc. Generally, small input/output routines are not very long, are used on a high percentage of all the programs run in an installation, and are so completely familiar to the machine operators that they can use them almost without thinking. There are typically not very many of them, but they enjoy very high usage. These routines are usually available as a small deck of cards or a short piece of paper tape, and are widely distributed throughout the installation. They are usually set up to be executed from a fixed location in memory, in contrast to the major subroutines discussed next, which are set up so as to be usable from any place in memory which is convenient to the individual programmer.

The major input/output and editing subroutines are much longer and more complex than those in the previous category. They are generally set up so as to perform one major category of work, such as reading variable format cards, editing information in memory into a format desired for a particular report, reading and rearranging and checking for accuracy records from tape, etc. We shall look into the functions of a suggestive list of such subroutines next. The list is *only* suggestive. It is not to be inferred that the examples mentioned are exhaustive or even completely representative, since needs and customs vary widely from one machine to the next and from one installation to the next.

READING FIXED FORMAT CARDS

It seldom happens that the way a machine reads the information on cards into memory corresponds to an efficient and easy-to-use arrangement of data on the cards. That is to say, it is seldom practical to arrange the data on cards so that each quantity goes into a separate word in memory from which it can easily be used in internal processing. When, as usual, the card format is designed so as to be easy to keypunch, or so as to be easy to "read" visually, or so as to make efficient use of the card columns, it commonly turns out that the way the machine reads the card results in one memory word containing several pieces of card data or only part of a piece of data. (This particular problem is largely obviated on a variable word-length machine such as the IBM 705; it applies in slightly different form to machines which read paper or magnetic tape as input.)

The reconciliation of the diverse goals of a good card format and ease of internal processing is usually made with an input subroutine. The question we wish to discuss here is how to set up a general program which does not have to be altered to fit each new card to be read.

One way is through the use of a calling sequence as discussed in Section 9.3. The words following the linkage can be used to specify such things as the location of each *field* (piece of information, approximately), the location of decimal points if necessary, where the information from each field should be stored in memory, where to expect signs, which fields are alphabetic, etc. The calling sequence need not be of fixed length each time it is written, if provision for such flexibility is built into the subroutine. The subroutine, of course, extracts the controlling information from the calling sequence and proceeds accordingly. It will be recognized that planning and coding such a generalized subroutine are not the simplest of tasks. Not the least of the problems is deciding what flexibility to allow the programmer: it is not easy to strike a happy balance between length and complexity of the subroutine and a bulky and cumbersome calling sequence.

Such use of subroutines implies that the same subroutine can be used in different places in the same program to process cards of different format, which is often required. It also implies, unfortunately, that the subroutine must obtain and interpret the information from the calling sequence *each time a card is read*, which is quite wasteful of machine time. The *compiler* and *generator* concepts are attractive alternatives which achieve the same power and flexibility with a sizable reduction in machine time, at the expense of a preliminary machine run which sets up the input program. These ideas are discussed in Chapter 14. In the following examples we shall list the functions of programs without considering *how* they would be incorporated into the main program.

INPUT AND OUTPUT PROGRAMMING

READING VARIABLE FORMAT CARDS

A variation on the above is to set up a shorter fixed calling sequence, and then provide that each *group* of cards must be preceded by a *format control card* which contains all the information which before was in the calling sequence. This, of course, greatly reduces the length and complexity of the calling sequence, but requires that the format control cards be placed at the proper locations in the deck of input cards—which can be a bother.

Where it is advantageous to do so, it is completely feasible to punch a *format control code* on the data cards themselves, which instructs the program as to which of a set of prearranged formats is to be used.

EDITING SUBROUTINES

The reader will have observed that the relatively simple matter of printing a couple of numbers took a few dozen DATAC instructions. Although it is true that some computers have features which somewhat simplify the problem, it is still burdensome. It is very desirable to have a subroutine which accepts information from memory, along with information defining the desired output format, and then makes the transformation. The subroutine then proceeds to print the edited information or write it on tape as the case may be. In binary machines these subroutines also handle the conversion from binary to decimal and vice versa.

As an illustration of what such a subroutine might do, consider a calling sequence which specifies for each word to be printed:

Memory location
Printing position
Decimal point location
Comma signal
Dollar sign signal

Memory location is the place in memory where the word to be edited may be found. In some cases this would be omitted, the word always being placed in one of the arithmetic registers instead. *Printing position* refers to the place in the line where the last character of the word should be placed. *Decimal point location* tells the subroutine where to place a decimal point; a special symbol can designate that no decimal point is desired. The *comma signal* tells the subroutine whether to insert commas (as required) to the left of the decimal point or to the right of the rightmost character of the word. The *dollar sign signal* provides similar information; the subroutine could automatically place the dollar sign immediately to the left of the most significant character (leading zeros being dropped). If the word in memory contains any nonnumeric characters, the subroutine could recognize this and ignore, or not expect to find, any information about decimal points, etc.

Depending upon the machine characteristics and the preferences of the programmers, such a subroutine might be set up to be called once for each word, or to be of variable length and be called for the editing of many words.

What we have been discussing, actually, is a small part of a broad category of programs to assist the programmer, which he may incorporate into his programs without much effort. These include the input, output, and editing functions we have been discussing, plus programs for sorting, merging, evaluating mathematical functions (in engineering and scientific calculations), for calculating commonly used formulas in payrolls, etc. In fact, many programs begin to look as if the tail is wagging the dog—except that here it is good: the bulk of the instructions of the program are in borrowed subroutines, which the programmer "ties together" with a relatively few instructions of his own. This observation has led to more sophisticated ways of organizing the over-all program than the use of subroutines. These are the subjects of *relative programming, compilers* and *generators,* and, generally speaking, *nonmachine language coding.* These are discussed in Chapter 14 but the presentation here of one of the motivations for this type of work may serve to make the chapter more meaningful later. At a minimum, most of the subroutines would be used in connection with a system of relative or symbolic coding which permits the subroutines to be placed anywhere in memory, so that any combination of subroutines can be used without causing serious memory-allocation problems.

TAPE EXECUTIVE PROGRAMS

There are a great many "nonroutine" conditions which may arise in the use of magnetic tapes, whether for input/output or intermediate storage. Some typical examples: an error on reading, an error on writing, the approach of the end of the physical tape, a broken tape, need to rewind the tape, etc. Most computers have some type of signal to tell the programmer that some nonroutine condition has arisen and what it is, although the type and quantity of signals and the ease of using them are by no means the same in all machines. The question is, Why should the programmer have to write instructions to test the conditions of all the various signals and deal with the trouble? Many of the conditions are dealt with in completely standard ways, such as trying to reread several times on tape reading errors, then signaling tape failure if the error persists.

Depending somewhat on the machine, it is often a great saving of effort to provide a program to handle all the various nonroutine tape problems. These usually go under the name of tape-executive programs or routines. Their exact nature depends, as noted, upon machine characteristics, but also upon individual preference. Tape-executive routines are at this time in somewhat less wide use than the other techniques discussed in this section.

11.5 Summary

INPUT/OUTPUT ECONOMICS

We close this chapter with a few observations about costs. The first and obvious observation is that on-line input/output devices, at least to date, are vastly slower than the internal arithmetic speeds of computers. This has led to intensive efforts to develop faster devices, and to such measures as off-line tape printers and card readers. As a graphic illustration of the great speed disparity, the IBM 704 can very nicely carry out all the many arithmetic operations of converting a cardful of numbers from decimal to binary, while reading the cards at 250 per minute!

At a more fundamental level, the disparity has led to many forms of buffers, as discussed above and in Chapter 13. The essence of the buffer is to be able to match two different speeds: the internal operating speed and the transfer rate to the input/output device. Many types of buffers have been used; all have the goal of reducing the amount of time the main section of the computer is tied up with input/output functions. On some of the newer machines, there are several buffers—in some cases one for each input/output device. Of course, the increase in capacity does not come free—the buffer itself costs money. Some manufacturers have deliberately chosen not to provide buffers, apparently feeling that the additional power does not justify the cost.

Many similar decisions must be made by the users of computers. It is well to keep in mind, in considering such matters, that costs (as well as optimum coding techniques) cannot be analyzed in a vacuum. What is good on payroll may be mediocre for inventory control and completely impossible for engineering work. Before attempting to answer the question "Is this better than that?" we must know *for what*. Many fruitless arguments about equipment and techniques could be avoided if the combatants would first define their criteria.

These observations are, of course, not exactly original, but they seem appropriate here. It is in input/output equipment and techniques that some of the worst mistakes are made in estimating cost of computer applications. It is also here that some of the widest variations among different computers are found.

Exercises

1. In the programming example of Section 11.2, suppose that the end of the input deck is signaled by a dummy time card, the fact that it is a dummy being indicated by a payroll number of 99999. Revise the flow chart and the code to detect this end-of-deck signal, and properly process the time cards on the last man.

2. In the programming example of Section 11.2, suppose that the input could come into the computer either from cards or from magnetic tape. If it comes from tape, the tape records look exactly like the *card image* in memory described in the text. If the operator wants to read cards, he leaves monitor switch 1 up; if he wants to read tape, he puts monitor switch 1 in the down position. Look up the function of the monitor switch in Appendix 1 (page 431), and modify the routine to handle this added flexibility. Do the same for output, using another monitor switch.

3. Devise a loading routine which is loaded from magnetic tape, and which reads records from tape. Set up a suitable format for the tape records to be loaded.

4. What are some of the questions that a systems analyst must ask to plan input/output formats?

5. Discuss the DATAC instructions associated with input/output functions.

6. Discuss the input/output equipment and related instructions for at least two actual computers.

7. What are some of the conditions to test for in the following operations:
(a) Reading a card.
(b) Punching a card.
(c) Reading a tape record.
(d) Writing a tape record.

8. What are transition cards? Is there such a thing as transition tape record following a program on tape?

9. What console operations are replaced by the load card button?

INPUT AND OUTPUT PROGRAMMING 223

10. What are the three classes of input/output subroutines? Can you suggest others?

11. In some computers, it is possible to test the status of any selected input/output device. Discuss the pros and cons of this method versus the Delay type of operation in DATAC.

12. What are some of the safeguards that should be observed in the use of magnetic tape reels, tape transports, read-write circuitry, and programming, in order to prevent going off the physical limits of the tape reels?

13. Discuss the input/output problems associated with using binary computers for business data processing applications.

12 VERIFYING PROGRAM ACCURACY

12.0 Introduction

In earlier chapters we have primarily discussed techniques in programming: we assumed the existence of a clearly defined problem, and explored methods of communicating that problem to a computer in its language. Furthermore, we assumed that the problem was *properly* stated to the programmer, and that the programmer *correctly* translated it into the machine's terms. Here we begin by doubting both these assumptions, and investigating what can be done to detect and correct errors in the two areas. We do this not so much because of distrust of the people involved; it is not analogous to the way a teacher checks a student before allowing him to proceed, say, with a potentially dangerous chemistry experiment. It is more akin to the way a research director might ask for a review of a major project: he has confidence in the people, but he also has a mature awareness that failures in communication can develop in a large group and that complex tasks can lead to honest errors and oversights. (We are considering here only the errors *people* make; detecting the occasional machine malfunctions is discussed briefly in Chapter 21.)

A brief mention of some of the types of problems may help to indicate the scope of the task.

1. There is a great mass of detail in any sizable computer application. In writing a program which contains, say, 10,000 instructions, there are literally millions of ways to make crippling mistakes.

The consequences of small errors, furthermore, are out of all proportion to the ease of committing them. It is not at all like painting a picture, where a misplaced brush stroke or a slightly wrong color may detract only slightly from the total effect. It is more like a rat faced with a tremendously complex maze: one single wrong turn and he does not get the cheese. A mere slip of the pencil which changes one address from 1233 to 1234 can invalidate a complete application.

2. Any sizable application involves numbers of people, with the attendant communication problem. It is obviously essential that the person who defines the problem to the programmer, if as usual these are two different persons, should define the problem *correctly*. But often the originator is not aware of all the information the programmer needs, or he defines the problem in a form which is difficult to use.

3. It is probably a safe generalization that a good electronic data processing job involves a reconsideration of the basic objectives and approaches of the application, either in the light of the powers of the new tool or simply because it is a convenient point at which to take a new look anyway. This frequently leads to a redefinition of the problem and/or methods. Then when the new method is programmed, there is the double possibility of errors in the new procedure as well as in the program.

The preceding list indicated *what* can go wrong. The following attempts to bring the problem into sharper focus by mentioning some instances of *how* errors can be made.

1. Simple slips. Examples: writing a wrong address or operation code through fatigue or inattention, transcribing errors, misunderstanding of machine functioning, omission or reversal of cards in a deck, errors attributable to poor handwriting, marking an error for correction but forgetting to get it into the routine, etc. Disgusted programmers have come to call these *stupid* errors.

2. Errors in programming logic. A flow chart may be drawn incorrectly through misunderstanding of a correctly stated problem. The programmer may have considered a loop-testing method carefully, but still make an error which terminates it too soon, for instance.

3. Procedural errors. The problem may be incorrectly or incompletely defined. An infrequent exception may easily be overlooked. The procedures analysis preliminary to programming may fail to show the interrelationships between different parts of an application, or may contain contradictory or ambiguous statements. It is often possible to write a program which "correctly" carries out such a problem statement but which does not produce answers which are actually "correct."

The fundamental problem, then, is to write a routine which provides correct and usable information to the ultimate user. The general manager who originally requested a consolidated financial statement by the second working day after the end of each month is not concerned either with how wrong information is generated or how its generation is corrected. Our task, in reviewing the broad assignment of producing usable information, is to be certain that the problem is correctly defined, that the computer program follows the problem statements faithfully, and to learn techniques for detecting and correcting the almost inevitable errors.

It may seem at this point that the picture is almost black. However, this is only because this introduction has been written to emphasize the inevitability of trouble and the need for a systematic attack on it. And, of course, there *are* systematic ways to locate the difficulties. These make up the bulk of the chapter.

Unfortunately for the organization of the material, the techniques to be discussed do not seem to follow any of the classifications discussed above. A given checking method may help to detect almost any type of error. Therefore the material to follow is categorized according to the general work area in the total procedures and programming effort, rather than by types of errors.

12.1 Detecting Programming Errors Before Running the Program

There are a number of techniques which are often used to detect programming errors before the program is first run on the machine. They all take time—considerable time in some cases—but in view of the ratio of cost of computer time to personnel time for the larger machines, and the fairly universal experience that errors take a long time to find on the computer, it is usually wise to use some such approach. It might be added that considerable self-discipline is required; programmers have a tendency to feel that *this* time they have done it—the program is perfect! Why not just put the program on the machine and watch it pour out correct answers? Sad experience says they are wrong. It is the authors' experience that with the rare exception of a very few gifted individuals' work, *all* programs of any size contain errors when first written. And some programs are occasionally so bad, and so inadequately prechecked, that many months may go by before they actually run correctly.

It is therefore advisable to apply one or more of the following approaches before putting a program to the machine test.

INDEPENDENT CHECKING OF THE PROGRAM

One fairly commonly used approach is to have a second person check the programming. The checker must have a certain familiarity with the application, obtained if necessary by an orientation session with the original programmer, and he must have available all flow charts, output formats, problem statements, etc. Under this method, the independent checker simply reads over the program, determining to his satisfaction that it correctly accomplishes the purpose. He checks memory references, subroutine calling sequences, operation codes or abbreviations, loop logic, etc. There is, of course, nothing here that the original programmer could not have done, but the fact that a different person is doing it is quite important. The original programmer, in doing the same checking, would tend to "see" what he knows should be there, instead of what actually is. The problem is akin to proofreading a manuscript; the author will often overlook badly misspelled words, missing punctuation, or even the omission of whole words—simply because he already knows what the material says, and does not read for details.

On the other hand, the checker may do a little of the same thing, since he must become familiar with the problem and with what it should do. Furthermore, certain types of errors are simply hard to see unless a person actually studies the program character by character, in which case he may miss errors in the broad strategy. The following methods attempt to get around this problem.

PUNCHED CARD ASSISTANCE

In programming systems which involve the use of punched cards, such as for program input, there are certain things which may be done to make errors stand out a little more clearly. After the program has been punched on cards and the cards numbered sequentially so they can be put back in order, the deck of cards can be sorted in a variety of ways. It might be sorted on the operation code, listed on a tabulator, and the listing carefully checked to make sure all codes as punched at least exist. (Errors such as transposing SXJ to SJX, mispunching the letter O for zero or vice versa, etc., can be surprisingly difficult to see. In most programming systems they will be caught fairly quickly when the program is first tested, but again, machine time is usually expensive.) The deck might be sorted and listed by address field, to facilitate determining that constants are correctly referenced. This listing is often valuable later also, because it shows in effect all references to each address—which can be most valuable if addresses and constants are changed later. Other possibilities may suggest themselves in particular situations.

REDRAWING FLOW CHART FROM PROGRAM

This is a checking technique which at first blush may seem unduly difficult, but which has in certain limited cases been found useful.

Here, a second programmer is given only the completed code and a general description of the problem. He then produces a new flow chart based on the program as actually written. When he is finished, the new flow chart is compared with the old for discrepancies. It is difficult to see how very many errors in logic could slip by such a procedure. In problems where logical complexity is high, this approach can be quite helpful.

DESK CALCULATOR CHECKING WITH TEST CASES

Another technique which some people have found to be successful is to "simulate" the machine's operation on test data, using a desk calculator. In other words, actual data is obtained, and the execution of the program followed through step by step. It may facilitate the procedure to have a form made up which shows all the pertinent registers, and actually enter on the form the results of each instruction. To be thorough, it is necessary to test all branches of the program, which may involve several sets of data. Of course, one must be practical. It would be pointless to carry out *all* processing of data which was intended only to test rare exceptions; it might be excessively difficult to go through all the repetitions of a frequently used loop, etc. This approach has the virtue of checking both the details and the grand strategy. It is definitely time-consuming, but again, the time saved can be well worth the effort.

A digression on choosing test data is in order at this point. It applies equally to hand-checking and to later machine-checking. Good test data must test all branches, it must not allow masking of errors, and if at all possible it should be data for which the correct answers have been provided (independently calculated) by the problem originator.

It is perhaps obvious that a set of test data which does not bring into play all sections of a program does not test all sections. If in a payroll calculation, for a trite example, none of the test data causes YTD gross earnings to go just over $4800 this week, no test has been made as to whether the program correctly computes the social security contribution for such a case.

It is possible, usually inadvertently, to choose data which will cover up, or *mask*, errors. The following arbitrary formula illustrates the point in two different ways:

$$Z = (X - 2.407)(Y^2 - 6.983)^2$$

First, suppose that in a certain test X is chosen as 2.407. Then the first term is zero, and the correct answer is zero regardless of the value

VERIFYING PROGRAM ACCURACY

of the second term. A major error in the calculation of the second term could go undetected. Second, suppose that the constant 2.407 is actually incorrect, and should be 2.417. If X is large, say 100, this will represent a percentage error in the first term of only about 0.01%, which in many problems would go unnoticed and for that matter would be unimportant. But what happens if in the same problem X can be quite close to the value of the constant? If X is 2.427, the relative error in the first term is 100%. These two types of masking, in this case, are opposed, and to make a complete check it would be necessary to pick tests with both extreme values for X. In this particular problem one might not go to such effort, choosing instead to check carefully otherwise, but the point is clear that careless choices of test data can decrease the value of the test.

Whenever possible, the test data, along with correct answers, should be provided by the problem originator. There are at least two virtues to this approach: first, the programmer is relieved of the danger of making the same mistake twice and not realizing it; second, a double check is provided on the programmer's understanding of the problem and on the accuracy of the problem statement. It is unfortunately quite easy for the problem originator to overlook operations which are uncommon, or else so very familiar to him that he forgets he does them, or which have crept into the procedures in the course of time and which are not spelled out in the *written* procedures. These can often be caught by a test case which has been calculated according to the procedures actually in use.

When a test case has not been provided by the originator, there is always the temptation to make up a hasty, ill-conceived sample case on the rationalization that it is easier to track down the troubles in a simple test and that the thorough job can be done later. The unfortunate consequence is that often the thorough job does not get done, with the result that for months afterward errors still occur. After a period of time goes by, all concerned with the programming lose familiarity with it and errors become much more difficult to diagnose and remedy. All too frequently, the original programmer has left the installation, forcing someone else to try to unravel the threads.

The only really satisfactory approach is to regard the preparation of test data and results as an integral part of the programming task, a part which deserves its share of careful and logical effort. A parallel may be drawn with the quality control function in a manufacturing concern. No sane manufacturer would ship his product (at least not if it is even moderately complex) without testing it to make certain it operates as intended. Furthermore, no sane quality control manager would permit a testing procedure which consisted of an over-all test of the product with no plan for the course of action if the product does not meet requirements. Rather, he has elaborate statistical tools to tell him how much to test and how to interpret results, he has jigs and fixtures to facilitate testing, he has procedures for feeding the information back into the process to correct faulty processes, etc. The corresponding situation in complex programming is similar, the only failure in the analogy being that programming is not repetitive in quite the same way a manufacturing process is. This, however, argues for *more* careful planning of the programming test.

12.2 Using the Computer to Detect Programming Errors

PRELIMINARY PROGRAM ANALYSIS

Before launching into a discussion of the techniques commonly used to detect errors by actually running the program to see what happens, we may mention certain preliminary assistance which can be obtained. One fairly simple device is to set up a utility program to provide the type of information, mentioned above, which can also be obtained with punched card equipment: operation code checking, etc. This is of course *required* on those computers which do not use punched cards. As we shall see in Chapter 14, a considerable amount of such checking is often performed by assembly and compiler programs. A second preliminary analysis, which can often be most valuable, is what might be called a *cross-reference* listing. This listing summarizes for all addresses used anywhere in the program the locations of instructions which refer to them. One line of such a listing might appear as:

1050   1607, 1609, 1621, 1650, 1660

This would mean that 1050 was the address of the five instructions located in memory at 1607, 1609, 1621, 1650, and 1660. (For frequently used addresses, the listing would of course consist of several lines.) Certain niceties can be added to the cross-reference programs if desired, such as eliminating the address zero from consideration since it is usually only a "dummy" address which will later be computed by the program, and omitting from the listing addresses of such instructions as shifts which are not actually memory addresses. The cross-reference list is valuable in two ways. First, it can be used as another double check before trying the program on the machine, by determining whether all the memory references were intended; in this way it provides another breakdown of the program, or another way to look for errors. Second, it becomes very valuable during checkout when changes must be made. A frequent source of grief is to cause *two* errors in trying to correct *one*, by changing an incorrect constant without realizing that it was also used (correctly) elsewhere in the program. The cross reference makes it possible to determine quite simply what all the references to a given address are.

All preliminary testing completed, the programmer must next determine whether the program as executed by the computer actually does calculate correct answers. "Correct answers" implies that the machine results are compared with answers calculated by hand or by existing mechanized equipment. All of the remarks in the previous section regarding test cases apply with equal force here.

When a new program is first loaded into memory, there is always a chance that there actually are no errors and that correct answers will be calculated the first time. If as usual there *are* errors, the process of detecting and correcting them begins. We must now investigate some approaches to the problem of how to use the machine most effectively to track down programming errors. Most of these approaches, as we shall see, involve a separate program which must be in memory during and/or after the program being tested. These auxiliary programs which help to locate trouble are usually called *diagnostic routines.*[*] They are seldom prepared by the programmer himself, but by a separate group which specializes in preparing these and kindred tools for the use of other programmers. We may now turn to a consideration of some of the more common techniques.

CONSOLE OPERATIONS

An approach which is often used, but very seldom justified, is to sit at the computer console and look at the lights displaying the various arithmetic and control registers as the program is *stepped through,* i.e., as the appropriate button is pressed to cause individual instructions to be executed. The authors feel that the approach is used primarily by only two classes of programmers: very good ones and very inexperienced ones. Very good programmers will occasionally resort to the method to find errors in a small section of a program *after all else has failed,* or because other tools are not yet available such as when a machine is first delivered. The inexperienced programmers use it because they are not aware of how extremely inefficient it is compared with other techniques which should be available to them.

---

[*] This term is also applied to routines used by the maintenance engineers to locate machine malfunctions.

Watching the console lights has two drawbacks: it is usually *very* expensive, and it frequently fails in its purpose. The question of cost is most urgent on the larger computers, where lease and overhead costs may easily reach $10 per minute and in some cases even higher. In such a situation the simple sequence of looking up an address, setting the appropriate switches, and copying down the contents of an address may cost as much as $20! It is no answer to argue that the "costs" are not really that high because if the 2 or 3 minutes had not been used that way the machine would not have been used anyway, which implies that the machine is not yet loaded. This is either a temporary situation, in which case bad habits are being learned which will hurt later, or the computer is too big for the application.

The other problem with console analysis is that it usually leaves the programmer without the information he needs. A common experience after "getting off" the machine is to find that critical pieces of information about the state of the program are missing either because they were not recognized at the time as being important or because the programmer cannot decipher his hastily scribbled notes. This method is therefore either expensive or inefficient or both. It is justified only for rare cases of errors which have been "localized" but which for some reason are particularly elusive, or where the tool programs to be discussed next are not yet available—for instance, in the checking out of the tool programs themselves.

TRACING

The first tool program we shall discuss, although not the one with the most to recommend it, is commonly called *tracing*. It is necessary, with this technique, to have in memory, along with the "subject" program being tested, a "master" program which interprets it. (*Interpret* is used here in a specialized sense which is discussed in Chapter 14.) Without going into the method of operation in detail, we may simply state that the result of tracing is a line of printing for each executed instruction of the subject program. The line of printing gives all the pertinent information about each instruction: where it was located in memory, what the instruction was, the contents of the arithmetic registers after execution, the contents of the memory reference, the status of such flip-flops as overflow, and whatever else may be useful on a particular machine. The subject program is listed in the same sequence as it would actually be executed, i.e., jumps are correctly executed. On computers which have off-line printing facilities, the listing is often written on magnetic tape to increase speed.

Tracing gives greater detail about a program's progress than any other technique. It might be compared to a high-speed movie which can be slowed down to allow minute inspection of everything that happened. In some few cases, the amount of detail is the strength of the technique, but more often it is its weakness. When you are studying the opening of a rosebud, it is a great waste of film to take 200 frames a second. The analogy is not bad, really. It is relatively seldom that information is needed on *every* instruction in a program. Observe, for instance, that tracing a forty-word loop which is repeated one hundred times may produce a stack of paper nearly an inch thick and require nearly a half hour of printing time!

One way to alleviate the problem is to set up the tracing so that only certain crucial instructions are traced, by providing some extra information to the trace program in various ways which need not be discussed here. Now, perhaps, we trace only *one* instruction in each repetition of a loop, or only the jumps, or only the "store-type" instructions. The exorbitant printing time may easily be reduced by a factor of a hundred, and if the few instructions to be traced are chosen wisely, there may be almost no loss in useful information.

In some cases, however, it unfortunately happens that a certain crucial piece of information is not available from a trace. Then the programmer must change the situation slightly and return to the machine, thus wasting time. In any case tracing is slow, simply because the ratio of speeds between internal arithmetic and the present electromechanical input/output equipment is so very high. It is the authors' opinion that tracing is a "crutch" which is leaned upon heavily by many beginners, which they must outgrow. For most checkout problems, there are more effective tools which waste less machine time and often give *more* useful information.

MEMORY DUMPS

A common experience in using the methods discussed so far is for the programmer to discover, when he returns to his desk, that a few crucial pieces of information are not available. For instance, perhaps the last machine session made it possible to localize the error in a certain loop; if only there were some way of telling what a certain counter had contained at the stopping point, the trouble could probably be pinpointed! This type of trouble arises so frequently that it becomes very desirable to have a record of the contents of memory at certain points through the program, especially at the beginning and end of the problem and at machine error halts. Such a listing of memory contents is called a memory printout, or, more commonly, a *memory dump*.

The programming required to print out or write on tape the contents of memory is fairly straightforward in most computers. The dump program is either an auxiliary program which can be loaded and executed at the end of a checkout session, or a subroutine which is continually in memory and which may be used at several points through a run. The precise output form is an ordinary matter of computer characteristics and economy. Depending on the machine and the circumstances, memory dumps may be written on a direct-connected printer, magnetic or paper tape, or photographed from a cathode-ray tube device. In the interest of speed and economy, dump programs are usually set up so that only the desired section of memory is printed. For instance, if in a certain problem the first 700 words of memory are set aside for a standard input/output routine, there is generally no need to print that section. The programmer is usually able to specify the region or regions of memory he wants printed, by specifying the initial and final addresses of the part(s) he wants. This may be done by punching the addresses on a card, by entering the addresses through the console or the typewriter, or in the calling sequence of a subroutine—the latter being somewhat less common. By similar means he may often specify the form in which he wants the printing to appear: in octal (Appendix 2) in binary machines, in "floating decimal" in machines which have the feature, as instructions with the operation code printed out as an alphabetic abbreviation even though in memory the operation code is numeric, etc. As a final example of features which may be added to a dump routine, it is quite simple to program the dump not to print lines beginning with zeros. That is, in the fairly frequent situation where large sections of memory may be all zeros (or, in some machines, all blanks), the bulk of printing may be considerably reduced by skipping over such sections in the printout. Almost all memory dump programs produce a listing which has in the leftmost column the address of the first number on each line. Some dumps also print the contents of most of the arithmetic and control registers at the time the dump was called. With this information added, we have a complete "snapshot," or "cross section" of the progress of the program at the time of the dump.

So much for the mechanics. How can the information be employed effectively? Perhaps a few illustrations will make the usefulness clear.

A good test case provides adequate intermediate results, i.e., computed quantities which represent "milestones" in the calculation but which are not ordinarily a part of the computer output. The first step in checking out a program is usually to inspect the intermediate answers; the programmer is thus enabled to determine or localize trouble areas. Since the intermediate results are not usually printed, some way must be available for printing them during checkout. A dump of the pertinent region of memory places all the required data at the programmer's disposal.

It unfortunately happens occasionally that instructions, data, and constants are incorrectly entered into memory. The errors can occur in several ways: clerical errors on the programmer's part, errors in placing the program on cards or paper or magnetic tape prior to input, or malfunctions such as holes punched in wrong positions in cards. Because of the mass of detail and other effects discussed earlier, such errors are sometimes not discovered even though a fairly careful prechecking procedure may have been followed. Once the trouble has been localized to a particular section of the program, it becomes necessary to check a dump listing to discover what was actually in memory against original coding and/or data sheets.

As we observed in an earlier chapter, loops are at one and the same time a great source of power in the stored program computer and a disturbingly frequent source of errors. A memory dump can frequently assist in ferreting out flaws in loop programming. For instance, addresses are often computed as a part of a loop. The programmer knows what he *wanted* to accomplish and how he thought he set up the code to accomplish his purpose, but what did the program —*as executed*—actually do? A listing showing the instructions after execution tells the programmer what actually occurred and frequently enables him to spot an error with little difficulty (once he knows approximately where to look). Another frequent loop error is the incorrect specification of the number of repetitions. A listing can help in at least two ways here. One simple check is to see what the contents of a counter (page 137) were at the completion of a loop. Another is to inspect regions of memory which *should* contain results which were calculated by the loop; if the region has missing or extra results, the trouble is fairly well pinpointed.

These examples are intended to be illustrative rather than exhaustive. Many other uses arise in practice; the ingenious programmer will find a number of ways to make good use of memory dumps.

DIFFERENTIAL MEMORY LISTING

This relatively minor technique may occasionally be used to locate such errors as incorrectly computed addresses which result in destroying sections of memory far removed from the location of the error.

It consists of checking each position of memory (except that occupied by the differential print routine itself) against the original routine and data, and printing out the location and old and new contents wherever a *difference* is found. Hence the name. In the example mentioned, an address computation system might be incorrectly storing results throughout memory, in some pattern. Inspecting the differential print output might give a clue as to the pattern, and therefore, if the programmer is a good sleuth, lead back to the error. This example may seem a bit farfetched, but it is not unrepresentative of the type of occasional error which can require *days* to locate.

DYNAMIC ANALYSIS

Tracing provides a picture of the progress of a routine *as it is executed*, but it is either extremely expensive, or incomplete in the information provided, or both. Memory dumps (and occasionally differential listings) provide much more information, but at most the information is available at only a few points through the programs. An analogy would be that tracing is a poor-quality but still expensive moving picture, whereas a memory dump is a highly detailed photograph but which shows only one stage of a very complex process. We next investigate a compromise which might be compared to a high-quality movie taken by a special camera which exposes a frame of the film *only when something of interest in the scene moves*.

The technique goes by a variety of names, most of which have something to do with a special machine feature which makes the method simpler. Here, we shall simply call it *dynamic analysis* to imply that, first, it takes place as the program progresses, and, second, that it is to a certain extent an analysis and not just a listing as are traces and dumps.

The idea of dynamic analysis is actually quite simple, although some of the details of actual programs embodying it are less easy to follow. The essence of it, to continue the photographic analogy as before, is to provide the programmer with a "snapshot" of the current situation in his program's execution, *each time something of interest to him occurs*. However, he does not have complete freedom in how he defines his "interest" to the analysis program, and he must always define his interest in advance. In one widely used machine, it is possible, by programming, to cause all jumps *not* to be executed in their normal manner; instead, an Unconditional jump to location 0001 is executed, and the location of the jump instruction is placed at location zero. By means of a program which examines a table of jump locations previously supplied to the machine by the programmer, it is possible for the machine to determine whether the programmer is "interested" in the status of things at the time when this jump is about to be executed. For instance, the programmer might decide that he wishes certain information (of a type to be discussed shortly) whenever the jumps located at 1807, 2001, 2450, or 2678 are about to be executed. He would provide this fact to the machine via the usual input medium. Then the dynamic analysis program would check each jump to determine whether it is one of the four specified. If so, it would write out the desired information. In either case (whether this jump was one of the four or not), it would prepare to resume normal operations by (1) obtaining the location of the jump instruction from address zero, (2) getting the address from the jump instruction, and (3) executing a jump to the address it finds. (This machine is provided with a special jump instruction which *always* jumps, even though the program is in the operation mode whereby the address is placed in zero, etc. Otherwise, there would be no way of ever getting back to the program being analyzed!) Another computer, presently in somewhat less widespread use, has a feature which is slightly more general in that it is **not** limited to jumps. Here, the exit to the analysis program is under the control of a separate digit, provided in the instruction for the purpose, and a console switch, which in effect determines whether the programmer wants many, or only a few, or no instructions analyzed. In DATAC, there is a *monitor* digit, which, in conjunction with a console switch, causes the location of any instruction so designated to be placed in zero, and a jump executed to one of the locations one through nine. At these locations would have been placed jumps to various diagnostic routines. This would be then a combination of the features of the two computers above. Other actual computers have provisions of a more or less similar nature. And, finally, it is always possible to program such a system even on computers which have no built-in feature to facilitate it, by the interpretive programming methods discussed in Chapter 14. In this case, however, use of the technique can result in a very considerable reduction of the speed of execution of the program being tested.

So much for the method of telling the analysis program *when* to look. *What* should it tell us as the program progresses? The following listing is illustrative only; actual programs provide for more or less information, depending on the amount of memory space available and the ingenuity of the person writing the analysis program.

1. It is always essential to show where the program is, i.e., the contents of the location counter.

2. It is usually desirable to list the contents of all other control and arithmetic registers, along with the status of such things as overflow indicators.

3. It is frequently important to know the contents of certain memory locations. These might be specified as one or more regions of memory, and it may be helpful to be able to specify the format of printing, i.e., fixed or floating decimal instructions, etc., as mentioned above. The locations and format of regions to be listed must of course be specified in the input to the analysis program. It might be different for each point.

4. It is often informative to know how many times a condition has occurred. The analysis program could print a number which is the number of times the listing of the situation has been called for. In conjunction with this, it is possible to set up the analysis program so that, under control of further input information, it will list a given condition only a specified number of times, or *not until* a specified number of times.

5. With certain machines and under certain circumstances, it can be very desirable to know what the past few jumps were, whether listed by the program or not. In some cases this information can be requested.

It should be clear that some or all of such analyses of a program, *as it is executed*, can be a powerful tool, in that the amount and location of the listings requested can be altered as checkout proceeds, simply by changing the input to the analysis program. And, finally, the use of such a tool does not preclude the use of a more complete memory dump at the end. In conjunction with each other, the two attacks of dynamic analysis and memory dump provide a way of getting at almost any type of error.

12.3 Procedural Checks

There are certain things which can be done to avoid or to detect errors which are outside the scope of either programming in general or of machine-aided error detection. We may lump them under the heading of things a procedures analyst would normally be responsible for considering. Only a brief outline of the subject need be given here, since it is covered in more detail in Chapter 21.

One error-producing problem which must always be faced in a business computer system is the inaccuracy of input data. This consideration should be classified under two headings: file conversion and day-to-day input. File conversion means the changing of present files, whether punched card, tub files, file folders, or whatever, into the mass-storage medium of the particular computer, which usually means tape reels or some type of large random access storage. The whole subject of file conversion is an important one which is often underemphasized in preliminary planning; however, we are concerned here primarily with the *accuracy* of such conversion. This must be established by some technique such as batch totals on segments of the files before and after conversion, hand-checking of a sample of the records, etc. It is usually discovered during conversion that there are dozens or hundreds of errors in the files—errors which have been present for *years* without anyone knowing about them! This cleaning up of source files, incidentally, is one of the important side benefits of going to electronic data processing.

The day-to-day input can be wrong for a variety of reasons. It can be wrong at the source; input documents can be incorrectly filled out. The preparation of cards or tape from the source documents is prone to error, which is compounded if the forms are poorly designed. Various techniques are available for improving source data accuracy before it goes to the computer, and also for identifying and rejecting bad input after it enters the computer. Such *editing* of input data is essential; failure to do it almost always leads to eventual disaster.

The procedures analyst is a critical link in setting up a valid test case, because he is in the best position to know what combinations of input data will "prove out" the program.

It is almost mandatory, when an application is first put on a computer, to run for a while *in parallel* with the old system, i.e., preparing the reports, etc., by both systems concurrently. Results of the two computations are then checked for identity. The procedures analyst can be of assistance in knowing the crucial points to check for identity, in determining how long to continue the parallel operation, etc.

One of the most important general principles in business data processing, as indicated by experience, is not to try to program the treatment of all possible exceptions. Attempting to do so leads to extremely large programs, and worse, it is impossible to accomplish because there is really no way of anticipating *all* the things that could happen in the future. Rather, we try to set up routines which will handle almost all of the cases; then we try to formulate programmable rules which will *identify* the remainder and set them aside for manual handling, or correction and later re-entry into the computer. (Detection of some types of unanticipated exceptions often leads to reprogramming.)

Obviously the procedures analyst is essential in determining exactly what constitutes an exception and how it can be identified. (The observation regarding exception handling of course applies to any well-designed information processing procedure, whether done on a computer or not.)

There are other instances in checkout which could be cited, where the judgment required has to do with nonprogramming aspects of the total job. These are perhaps indicative.

12.4 Coding for Ease of Checkout

To consider the other side of the coin, there are a number of general rules the programmer or coder can follow in writing a program, which will tend to reduce the number of errors and make those that do occur easier to find. These approaches are relatively independent of procedures considerations. A few may be listed.

One rule, which some of the best programmers find difficult to follow, is easiest to express in the negative: do not program so ingeniously that no one else can understand what you have done. Some programmers find great delight in writing in *nine* steps what everyone else thought would take *ten*. The trouble is that they often do it by some fiendishly clever trick which cannot be understood without intensive study. Furthermore, such tricks can lead to considerable difficulty in checkout, because the errors caused by extreme cleverness usually result in the appropriate punishment of extremely misleading symptoms. And, of course, if any other programmer ever has to try to unravel the threads, much additional time can be wasted. (There are exceptions, of course. There are occasions on which it is necessary to boil the last digit and microsecond out of a program, with full knowledge of the consequences. Such occasions arise very infrequently, however, in the type of work we have discussed so far.)

Another general rule, which requires perseverance, is always to annotate a program carefully. That is, it is usually possible to make notes on the coding sheet as the instructions are written; one powerful technique is to note cross references to the flow chart. These become an invaluable tool during checkout; in a very large program it is surprisingly easy to forget what you had in mind at a certain point. And again, if anyone else ever has to take over a program, his task is at least ten times as easy if there are ample notes. However, one need not be quite so verbose as the authors have been in annotating the programs in this book, where the aims are, after all, somewhat different. A remark every few instructions, or where the purpose may not be clear, is sufficient. As an indication of the need for at least *some* notes, imagine trying to study the programs in this book if there were *no* notes!

It is almost always recommended, for similar reasons on a different level, to prepare a report describing the general nature of the problem which has been programmed, explaining the general attack, displaying all the flow charts, etc.

A final suggestion is to code in such a way that it will be fairly simple to make changes. As a perhaps trivial example, suppose that a state tax calculation contains, among other things, the constant factor 0.1. It is, of course, possible to program a multiplication by one-tenth as a shift of one place to the right—but what happens if the legislature changes the factor to 0.1089? The point is transparent. Other less obvious examples could be cited. A good general principle is to leave space in each run for corrections and additions, which are often called *patches*.

Incidentally, if this happened, it would ordinarily become necessary to insert a few instructions into the program at the point where the shift had been. But how is this to be done? There is obviously no way to drive in a wedge and make a little space in a program which has long since been placed on cards or tape. The answer is that it is usually not too difficult, even in a completed program, to add a few words at specific locations. The technique is to insert a jump instruction at the point of the error. The jump then causes the program to go to a previously empty section of memory, where now a few instructions are located which correct the error and finally jump back to the instruction following the jump which was inserted. This may sound sloppy, but it saves a fairly costly task of inserting extra instructions by other methods and is widely used. Some of the automatic coding techniques discussed in Chapter 14 make the insertion of instructions relatively simple.

12.5 Summary

The programmer who is adept at checking out programs relies on a combination of machine aids and good judgment. A few general observations may serve to summarize this chapter.

1. Programming errors do not necessarily imply a poor programmer. There is too much detail in programming and coding to expect perfection.

2. Nevertheless, some things can be done to minimize the error

rate. Considering the cost of machine time, one of the most effective of these is prechecking, *before* testing a new program on the computer.

3. Each time before going to the machine, *lay out a plan of what is to be done.* Nothing is quite so wasteful of extremely expensive computer time as the programmer who loads his routine into memory, pushes the buttons, then stands back in bewildered, disorganized confusion when his routine refuses to generate correct answers. It is necessary to know *in advance* what diagnostic tools are to be used, what regions of memory are to be dumped, etc.

4. Do not be a slave to one machine diagnostic tool. There is no one single approach which will efficiently assist the programmer in finding *all* types of errors.

5. When making a correction, do not generate more errors than you correct. It is all too often true that parts of a program are strongly interrelated, so that a change aimed at correcting one trouble causes two more.

6. When correcting an error, make sure that the correction accounts for *all* the symptoms. Often, more lies beneath the surface than is apparent at first glance. A little unhurried reflection on the symptoms of the error may uncover further errors that will have to be corrected later. More than one coder has had the experience of being delayed for an hour or two in getting on the machine, and discovering several more errors during the enforced wait.

7. Document *all* corrections. Experienced coders can tell sad stories of routines which contain corrections which no one but the original coder is aware of any more, and he has since left for another assignment.

In summary, never underestimate the magnitude of the checkout phase of a machine application. The job simply is not completed until it has been *demonstrated* to produce *correct* answers. Time must be allowed for the checkout phase in setting schedules.

Exercises

1. What is meant by program accuracy? Contrast it with at least two other types of accuracy involved in electronic data processing.

2. Debugging a program on the computer may be compared with the actual flight testing of an aircraft, and the person manually checking out a program prior to computer checkout may be compared with a flight-test simulator. Discuss.

3. Is it sufficient to plan a test case just to take the program through every exception or should the test case be planned to take in combinations of exceptions as well?

VERIFYING PROGRAM ACCURACY

4. Is it sufficient to plan a test case just to take the program through normal paths, or through error paths as well? Discuss how some of these errors can be introduced in a test case:
   (a) Tape read-write error.
   (b) Batch control total out of balance.
   (c) Nonexistence of master record called for by a change record.
   (d) Change records out of sequence.
   (e) Wrong labels.
   (f) Detecting a code that is not supposed to exist.
   (g) An unduly large bill calculated.
   (h) An unsigned input number.
   (i) Premature end of file.

5. The following are some of the worst enemies of systematic program accuracy. Discuss and name at least three more:
   (a) Sloppiness.
   (b) Taking short cuts.
   (c) A person checking the program carefully at the beginning and finding very few errors up to the halfway mark concludes that "all is well." The result is that the second half is largely unchecked.
   (d) "Machine time is cheap, let the machine do the debugging."
   (e) "Flow charts are for the birds, I've got it all in my head."

6. Discuss the various machine debugging aids.

7. Suggest another machine debugging aid besides those mentioned in the text.

8. What are some of the symptoms that can be revealed by memory printout?

9. What are the advantages and disadvantages of using the following methods to generate a test case:
   (a) Prepare the test case synthetically so that every branch in the program is covered.
   (b) Select the test case from the actual files and change records for a representative period of actual business operation.

10. List the possible stages between the stage when the code is first written and the final stage when the program is operative ("on the air").

11. Should only "actual" data be used for test data?

12. What advantages may accrue from running test data through a program in volume?

13 ADVANCED TECHNIQUES IN MAGNETIC TAPE PROGRAMMING

13.0 Introduction

This chapter is a collection of techniques which are related only to the extent that they all involve magnetic tapes. Some were developed in an attempt to make more efficient use of tapes, others to solve recurring problems in tape programming, and others to facilitate the efficient and error-free operation of a computer system after it has been checked out.

One word which occurs in several of these discussions must be clearly defined at the outset. A *run* may be described as one or more routines automatically linked so that they form an operating unit, during which manual interruptions are not normally required of the computer operator. A complete application usually consists of several runs; this is because with present main memory and auxiliary storage limitations it is not possible to carry out all phases of a data processing application in one uninterrupted sequence. A simplified illustration is a payroll application which consists of the following runs:

1. Read and edit time cards and labor vouchers.
2. Sort into payroll number sequence.
3. Merge with master payroll file, calculate gross **pay.**
4. Calculate net pay, update master file.
5. Write checks and earning statements.
6. Write tax and other deductions registers.
7. Sort into labor account number sequence.
8. Write labor distribution reports.

Most major applications for large computers have many more runs than this.

13.1 Interior Labels and Label Checking

An *interior label* (also called a *magnetic label*) is a group of characters recorded on magnetic tape to identify the contents of the reel. It is necessary to have positive identification of each tape reel since there is a strong possibility of a discrepancy between the external markings on a reel and the actual contents of the tape. There is also the possibility that the type of data is correct but that the file is an old one held for protective purposes. Then too, an external label may be lost, making it necessary to identify the tape by means of a printer or the central processor.

Every input and output data tape used in or prepared by production system runs should contain an interior label. This is usually put in the first record or block on the tape. A typical label might consist of digits representing month, day, and perhaps year, showing when the reel was produced; digits for data identification; and a digit or two for reel number, in the case of multiple-reel files. Sometimes codes are used in the label to indicate the application, pulse density of information on the tape (if this can be varied), and the type of material on the tape—master file, change items, etc.

Before doing any processing, a computer run should examine the recorded label of each input data tape to ascertain that the proper tape is present. If the input label check fails, a printout should be made on the control typewriter or printer showing the actual internal label and what the label was expected to be. The operator then has the option (programmed) to rewind the tape and replace it with the proper one, or, if circumstances require, to continue processing. An indication of the latter condition, which is called "forcing the label," should also be typed out. The label constant in memory should be replaced with the label from the forced tape to allow subsequent reels to pass checking automatically.

13.2 Sentinels

The programmer must have some way of knowing when he has reached the end of valid data on a tape reel, and when he has reached the last record of the entire file in the case of multireel files. He must know when to jump to a routine which will automatically alternate tape units and/or tell the operator to manually change reels. When the last record has been processed, the program must perform certain chores such as calculating totals, rewinding tapes, locating the next run in a series, etc. Since magnetic tapes can be reused many times, there is a danger that readable information may follow the last valid record on a reel, but which is really "hash" or "garbage" as far as the current run is concerned and should not be processed.

The most convenient way that this problem has been solved is by the use of *sentinels* or *fences*. Different machines require different handling of the problem, but the basic logic is the same. One type of machine has a special character which may be written after the last record of a reel or file. When sensed during a tape read instruction, an indicator is turned on. The programmer can test for this indication after each read instruction. When the indicator is on, a branch is effected to the end-of-reel or end-of-file program. On other machines the branch in the program when the special character is sensed may be automatic. Where a specific sentinel procedure is not built into the machine, a certain group of characters is chosen as a sentinel which cannot be confused with regular data codes. It is convenient to select the sentinel so that it will "sort high" on the particular machine's collation sequence, i.e., be larger than any other group of characters. On most machines this is a word of either all 9's or all Z's. On one machine ZZZZZZZZZZZY is frequently used as an end-of-tape sentinel and ZZZZZZZZZZZZ for end-of-file sentinel, twelve characters making up a word. The key of each record is then tested against ZZZZZZZZZZZY before other processing is performed. If the key is less than ZZZZZZZZZZZY, normal processing is followed. If not, a test is made for equality with ZZZZZZZZZZZY, which leads to the end-of-tape branch, or, if this fails, a test for equality with ZZZZZZZZZZZZ leads to the end-of-file procedure or possibly an error path. It is also possible to have many files on one tape reel if the conventions are set up to handle this.

When the input data has been exhausted and all processing is completed, the special character or word may be written on the output tape to show end-of-file as part of the windup procedure. If more than one reel is to be used, the programmer (with one type of machine) must count up to the number of allowable records that may be written on one reel and then place an end-of-reel mark, or sentinel word. Another machine has photosensed markers or reflective spots to warn of the approach of the physical end of tape. When this spot is sensed during writing, an indicator is turned on; the programmer after each tape write order tests for this indication. If on, he branches to his end-of-reel routine and writes the appropriate sentinel mark or word. If a record or block count is made on the written tape, it usually accompanies the sentinel.

MAGNETIC TAPE PROGRAMMING

For greater efficiency on machines without built-in end-of-file procedures, the sentinel may be placed in the key of the last record of a tape block or grouped record as well as in the key of the record following the last valid one on the tape. In this way the programmer on input need only check each block to see if it is a sentinel block. When this is detected, a switch is set so that the key of each record in that block only is examined for sentinels during processing.

13.3 Run Locators

The routines for operating computer systems are usually entered into the computer on magnetic tape, either because that is the normal input method or because it is faster to read magnetic tape than cards or paper tape where there is a choice. Each instruction tape normally has many runs on it, even though there may be a number of different master instruction tapes, one for each of the major applications. The problem arises of locating the correct run when a tape is mounted. It might be thought that an instruction tape could simply be mounted on a tape handler, the first run's instructions read into memory, and succeeding runs taken in sequence. This indeed may be done in some or even in the majority of cases. It fairly often happens, however, that the complete job is not planned to be done in one uninterrupted sequence, or that major machine troubles cause a break in the operation, or that high-priority jobs cause interruption, or that other unusual circumstances require a different sequence of runs to be carried out. In any such case, it is necessary to be able to locate the correct run on an instruction tape with as little manual intervention as possible.

A run locator is a routine which performs this function. In outline form, it might operate as follows:

1. The run locator routine is loaded into memory either from cards, a separate tape, or from the instruction tape which has been mounted on a tape unit.

2. If the machine has an on-line card reader, a *parameter card* is read which specifies the coded identification of the desired run. If there is no card reader, the routine types a "request" for this information and waits for the operator to type in the code. These codes must, of course, be assigned to all runs. They might consist of two or three letters to identify the application, and two or three for the run number. Example: PR 013 means the thirteenth run of the payroll system. If, as is often the case, a run consists of many blocks on tape, it is usual to identify only the first block with a run number.

3. The routine then reads successive blocks from tape, checking each to determine if there is a run code, and if so, if it is the same as that entered by the operator.

4. When the correct run is located, it is read into memory, and execution of the run begun.

5. If the run is not found on the tape, either the wrong instruction tape was mounted or the operator gave the wrong run identification. In either case the run locator rewinds the instruction tape and types or prints a message to the operator.

6. Somewhere before step 4 in this sequence (exactly where depends on machine characteristics and the way the instruction tape is set up) it is a good idea to fill memory with some special pattern of characters which will cause the machine to stop if the special characters are encountered. Then any sections of memory which are not used by the run will be "off limits," and if through error of any type the routine tries to execute an instruction in those areas, it will stop. If this is not done, and unused sections of memory contain routines from previous runs, *very* strange things can happen.

The only manual operation in the entire operation is entering the desired run number, and even that is done at card reading speed if there is a card reader. The use of an automatic run locator saves time and greatly reduces errors. It need not use memory space, if this is short, because it is usually possible to arrange things so that the routine which is loaded from the instruction tape, when the correct one is located, is loaded over the run locator.

Somewhat the same considerations apply to runs after the first. In the normal situation, one run follows another in a sequence defined in advance, and the correct routines can simply be read from tape in order. Frequently, however, circumstances require that runs be done in a sequence other than their order on tape.

A simple solution is as follows. Each run contains in its constants the code word of the next run in normal sequence. When the run is completed, the run locator is called into play again, by rereading it if it was not possible to leave it in memory. (It is also possible to put a run locator at the end of each run on tape.) Instead of simply proceeding to locate the next run as specified by the code word stored with the current run, however, the run locator types or prints a message to the operator that the current run is completed, gives the code of the run it is about to locate, and stops. If the operator wishes to proceed in normal sequence, he simply presses the start button. If he wishes to call for some other run next, he loads a card containing

MAGNETIC TAPE PROGRAMMING

the code of the desired run, or types it in. If he has to change tapes he does so, then presses the start button and the correct run is located as before.

13.4 Dating Routines

It is almost always necessary to print dates on the reports prepared by a computer. Since the dates obviously change each time the report is prepared, some method must be devised to get the correct dates into memory as needed. A number of alternative approaches are available.

It might seem possible to program the automatic computation of dates based on the fact, for instance, that the date of a weekly report advances by 7 days each time it is run. Such an approach is not feasible, however. It is quite possible to account for such things as the fact that the beginning of the week after January 28 is February 4, not January 35, although it is some trouble. What is not possible is to foresee all nonroutine conditions which can arise to destroy such a system. Suppose a run has to be restarted after it has been half completed. If no one thinks to modify the automatic dating routine, the printed dates will be wrong because the routine does not know that only half an hour has elapsed between repetitions—and not the normal week or month. A request for a special report could cause similar confusion. The existence of holidays and leap years further complicates the matter. All of these considerations presumably could be analyzed in advance and allowed for,* but it is not worth the trouble.

The straightforward approach is simply to load the appropriate dates into memory, where required, at the start of each run or series of runs. This can be done via the console typewriter, or, preferably, via cards or magnetic tape. This is relatively simple, but it can mount up to a considerable volume of card loading or typing, and can lead to errors if done hurriedly.

Probably the most sophisticated approach is to provide for each routine which must print a date or write a date on a magnetic tape a code which specifies whether the date is that of the current day, week, month, quarter, or whatever. The appropriate dates for each are loaded into memory at the beginning of the day's work (or whenever any of the dates change). A *dating routine*, which is somewhere on an instruction tape, places these dates wherever needed in any routine. Thus a dated master instruction tape is produced. This is,

* This is called the "you can do anything on a computer" school of thought.

of course, only a very brief outline of the technique; the details vary with the particular machine and other factors. Once set up, such a system operates with little attention and takes very little time per day.

13.5 Overlays

It fairly frequently happens that there is insufficient high-speed memory available to carry out all the functions required in a run. It would be possible, of course, to design runs so that they never exceeded memory requirements, by using many small runs. It turns out, however, to be more efficient to reuse sections of memory for different purposes at different points in a run. This is usually called the *overlay* technique. It may be noted that as new machines are introduced, memories tend to become larger, and this problem becomes less serious—although it will probably never be totally eliminated.

The overlay technique is made possible (and, for that matter, is made *necessary*) by the economic requirement of providing a computer with a hierarchy of storage devices. Ten million words of high-speed internal storage would be nice for the programmer, but is completely uneconomical with present techniques. Therefore, it is common practice to provide a computer with a relatively small high-speed memory, and one or more types of auxiliary storage devices which are much larger, slower, and cheaper per word stored.

Briefly, the overlay technique consists of setting up a run so that segments of the routine are brought into a section of high-speed memory from auxiliary storage *as the segments are required*, rather than having them available in high-speed memory at all times. For instance, certain functions need to be carried out only at the end of a run; these can be brought in from auxiliary storage only at the end of the run, leaving the high-speed memory required for those functions free for other purposes during the body of the run. A run can usually be divided into parts which are needed at only one point in a run, or which are needed infrequently. It is usually not economical to set up overlays which must be called in repeatedly during a run. For instance, it would not be practical in a payroll calculation to routinely call for several overlays *for every man*. It might be feasible, however, to use overlays for operations needed only at the beginning and end of a payroll run, or to handle special cases.

Overlays can be used with any combination of high speed and auxiliary storage. They are most commonly employed with magnetic tapes, but can be used very effectively on machines which have a magnetic drum as auxiliary storage. This latter is particularly desirable, because there is no sequential access problem with drums,* and drum reading speeds are generally at least a little faster than tape reading speeds. Using drums does mean, however, that the drum must be initially loaded by going from tape or cards through main memory; furthermore, the drum may be needed for other purposes. An economic balance must be achieved, as usual.

The mechanics of programming and coding an overlay system need only be outlined; for machines where it is used widely, the manufacturers can supply complete information. It is obvious that when an overlay is brought in from auxiliary storage, some area of high-speed memory must be available to receive it, i.e., must contain information which either is expendable or which can be reconstituted by a later overlay. It is sometimes desirable to set up a fixed area of memory which is reserved for the use of overlays. This makes some things simpler, but it is somewhat restrictive. It is clear that some identification scheme must be provided, in order to be sure of getting the correct overlay. A scheme similar to the run locator technique can be employed. It is also necessary to provide each overlay with some way of "knowing" what to do next, when it is finished, whether that means calling in another overlay, stopping, going back to the main body of the routine, or whatever.

The overlay technique is in some cases nearly an absolute necessity because an existing machine simply does not have enough high-speed memory. In other cases it may be an economical choice even though additional memory can be obtained, if the extra machine time is cheaper than the extra memory required to do the same things with fewer overlays. It must be used carefully, however, because if misused it can be very time-consuming.

13.6 Alternation of Tape Units

The use of electronic digital computers to solve business paperwork problems frequently results in the creation of large magnetic tape files. It becomes highly desirable to keep to a minimum the amount of time during which the computer waits while the operator is changing tape reels. Even with efficient handling this may add up to a considerable percentage of the total system running time.

There are really two problems: continuity of tapes between runs and continuity of tapes within each run. The first of these problems

* Not in this context, at least. In machines using magnetic drums as main memory there is, but here we mean no access problem *as compared to magnetic tapes*.

may readily be solved by proper planning on a system basis. Tape units may be allocated to facilitate the flow of data from run to run. Wherever possible, the output of one run becomes the input to the next run without manual intervention of the operator.

The problem of continuity of tapes within runs exists because, even with files of modest size, there rarely are enough tape units available to allow simultaneous mounting of all the required reels. It is therefore often necessary to physically alternate reels on tape units allocated for different input and output files. It is desirable to be able to switch from each reel to its successor without waiting for the prior reel to be rewound, removed, and replaced, since each such change may take several minutes. Techniques have been evolved which allow efficient alternation of tape reels within a run.

The basic requirement for a *tape swap,* as this technique is often called, is the allocation of two tape units to a particular type of data. Reels still have to be rewound and replaced by the operator; however, this can be done when a particular tape unit is inactive, processing being continued on the alternate unit. Since enough tape units may not be available to allow "automatic" alternation of each type of input and output for a particular run, the longest files should receive preference in the allocation of tape units. The instructions in the tape swap routines may remain in internal memory during regular run processing, if enough internal memory is available, or they may be brought in as an overlay from auxiliary storage. The amount of programming which has to be done to effect tape alternation varies with the particular machine. Each instruction referring to one tape unit for the data being alternated must be changed to refer to the alternate unit. On the next swap for this data the designated units must be reversed. If the computer has indexing facilities, tape instructions may be indexed, as discussed in Chapter 8. To change each instruction, only the number of the unit in the index register need be changed. This is done for each swap. In other machines the instruction modification is almost as simple even without indexing.

It is desirable, as part of the method of altering tape instructions, to allow for emergency changes. For example, if tape units 1 and 2 are alternated for certain data and unit 2 goes down for repair with no substitute available, it is desirable that a 1 be substituted for a 2 in all the tape instructions. This would require "alternation" on the same tape unit, but at least the program could continue. The operator should not have to type in changes to perhaps a dozen instructions from the console. With an indexed machine he need only change one instruction to accomplish this. "Editing" of tape orders allows this to be done on nonindexed machines. The numbers of the tape unit and alternate for each type of data are stored as constants in memory. The actual tape orders are written in general form, for example, "Read from tape unit n." At the start of a run, the computer executes a routine which picks the right constant for each tape order and substitutes it for the "n"-type designation. Therefore, on a swap, only the constants need to be switched before tape orders are re-edited, in order to accomplish alternation of tape units. Similarly, to change a tape unit allocation, the operator need only change the appropriate constant in memory before the editing process begins. An "extract"-type order is very useful for this editing function. Of course, this is all unnecessary on a machine which allows the numeric designation of a physical tape unit to be assigned simply by setting a switch.

The switching of the tape unit constants and the alternation of the tape instructions are only part of the tape swap routine. On input data being alternated, the completed tape is rewound, instructions are typed out to the operator, the internal label constant for this data has the reel number augmented by 1, a label check is performed on the new reel, and possibly other functions are accomplished. On an output swap, sentinels may be written on the completed reel, the block count written and the counter zeroed for the next reel (if required), the completed reel rewound, the reel number in the output label constant increased by 1, the label written on the new tape, etc.

13.7 Record Grouping

If records on magnetic tape are short, the time required to get the tape up to reading speed (acceleration time) can be considerably longer than the time required to transfer the information to high-speed memory. The same problem exists on writing tape. Furthermore, a number of machines have fixed length tape blocks, making it almost completely uneconomical to place only one record in a block. In either case it often becomes desirable to *group records* on tape, i.e., organize the tape information so that a number of records are read or written as a group. The problem then arises as to how to handle the records when they are in memory, because different records will be in various locations in memory. The techniques to handle this situation are often called *item advance* methods.

There are four general methods for handling the item advance problem. All of them in one way or another involve the use of loops, which has been treated earlier, so we only summarize the methods.

1. Repeat all instructions for each record in the group. That is, write a set of instructions to handle the first record, then another set with different addresses to handle the second, etc. This is probably the fastest method possible, but it is quite costly in memory space and is seldom used except in rather special circumstances.

2. After processing each record, alter all instructions which refer to the record location so that when reused the instructions refer to the next record. This requires fewer memory locations, in general, but in some situations becomes quite slow and cumbersome. It is fairly commonly used.

3. A variation of this method is to use index registers, if they are available. The difference is that with indexing it is only necessary to change the contents of the index register in order to change the *effective address* of all instructions which are indexed. This is both fast and concise, but of course not all computers have index registers.

4. Set up a *work area* the size of a record, and move each record to it before processing. All instructions which perform processing on the record can then have fixed addresses, and the only problem is moving the successive records to and from the work area. This latter is actually not hard to do, especially in machines which have facilities for *block transfers*, i.e., moving many words with one or two instructions. The work area method has the further slight advantage that checkout is facilitated, because when trouble develops the record which caused the trouble is in a known location.

13.8 Variable Length Records

Frequently, it is uneconomical to set up tape records to be of fixed length. Suppose, for instance, that every record in a bank checking account application must contain the customer's account number and his balance as of the end of the last processing period, but that almost everything else is variable. He may have written no checks or fifty; he may have issued stop payment orders; he may have written certified checks which require that part of his balance be "reserved"; there may have been special charges which have to be recorded, etc. It might theoretically be possible to set up the file records with enough space to hold all possible information and then use only as much as required, but the cost in wasted tape space and added tape processing time would be enormous. This is perhaps an extreme example, but it is not infrequent to come on situations which require some type of variable length record even though the motivation may not be quite so urgent as in this case.

The techniques for dealing with variable length records involve both machine characteristics and coding methods. The most significant machine characteristic is whether or not the length of a block of tape is fixed. If it is not, the use of variable length records is made somewhat simpler, but other problems arise, such as: how does the machine know how long the record to be read or written is? Reading is fairly simple, because some physical signal on the tape can signify the end of the record. On writing, either the number of words to be written must be specified as part of the tape writing instruction or some sort of marker must be placed in memory to signify the end of the information.

These are coding problems, however, and are not difficult to handle once one is familiar with the particular machine. More important is the question of how to deal with the variable amount of information once it is in memory. Since the amount of information *is* variable, it is obviously not possible to set up instructions to deal with it in an unvarying manner. Some type of code must be provided *in the record itself* which specifies, in one way or another, the amount and/or type of information. One common way to do this is to set up a minimum length record that contains the data which is always present, plus a code which specifies whether or not there is additional data. If there is, it is often necessary to set up the code so that it also identifies the type of additional information, if this is variable. The routine which processes each record then examines the code and branches to other routines accordingly, to handle any additional data that may be present. The additional data is usually called a *trailer*, since it follows the minimum amount which is always present, called a *header*.

Another technique, which applies if the trailer information is always of a fixed kind but of a highly variable amount, is to set up the tape file and the processing routine so that the routine normally expects to find trailers and keeps processing them until a code in the record signifies that there is no more data. The code would then be, in effect, an "end of record" sentinel, which could be a code identifying a new record. It may be either an actual coded sentinel written on the tape, or be set up using some convenient feature of the machine, depending on the circumstances.

All of these techniques naturally take computer time and require programming and coding time to set up. One must carefully analyze the economics of the situation to determine whether the tape time saved is worth the extra processing time.

13.9 Effective Use of Tape Buffers

We have discussed previously the usefulness and operation of tape buffers. In this section we consider some problems concerned with making the best use of them.

Suppose a tape processing job consists of updating a master tape with information contained on a transaction tape. Assume that the records are reasonably short and therefore have been grouped on tape. We then bring in a group of records from both tapes and proceed with the processing. Sooner or later we run out of records from one of the input areas; if nothing has been done to avoid it, the computer must then wait while another group of records is brought in from the tape. This would make no use at all of the buffering facilities. Obviously something should be done to provide for reading another group of records *while the previous one is being processed,* which is the whole point of buffering. The problem is, how can the central computer know which type of information (master or transaction) it will run out of first?

In the *standby block* technique, we simply ignore this question and provide an extra block from each tape. In other words, while one block of records from the master tape is being processed we bring another set into a standby block; when the processing of the first block is completed we switch to processing what *was* the standby block and bring another block into the other area, and similarly for the transaction tape.

Some means must obviously be provided to keep track of which block is currently being processed and which is currently the standby. Suppose we call the two areas A1 and A2. Figure 1 is a flow chart of a technique which keeps everything straight with a minimum of effort. The process would be initialized by filling the A1 block and entering the routine at the point corresponding to connector b. This would fill the A2 block from tape, set switch 1 to a, and proceed to process the A1 block. When it was exhausted the routine would go to switch 1, which is now set to a, resulting in A1 being filled, 1 set to b, and A2 being processed. The filling and processing of A1 and A2 would thus alternate in exactly the desired manner. Observe that "filling" the blocks consists merely of one or a few instructions which *start* the process of transferring the information to the block; processing of the other block then proceeds simultaneously. A similar system would be set up for each input tape (of which there could easily be more than two as in the discussion above).

MAGNETIC TAPE PROGRAMMING

In the situation where all incoming data is in sequence, it is possible to determine *in advance* which block will be used up first by comparing the keys of the last records in each block. In a machine which has a distinct buffer rather than what we previously called direct memory buffering, the buffer can simply be loaded in advance with a block

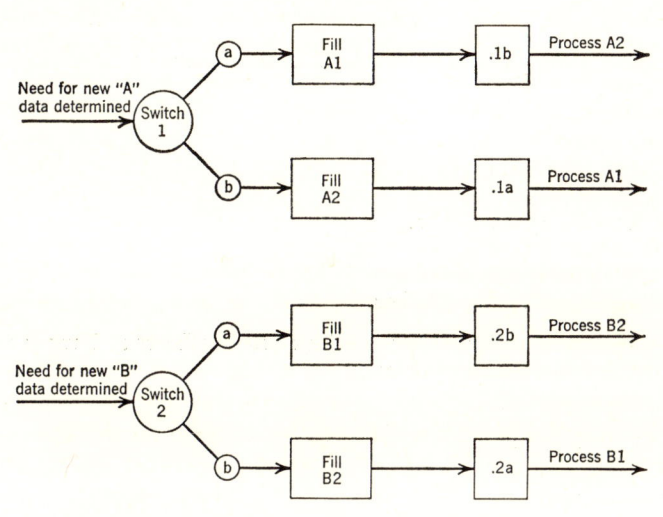

Figure 1. Flow chart of the standby block concept.

from the tape that will be needed next. Without such a buffer, the technique still can be used by establishing an input area for the purpose. This is usually called *preselection*, which involves a little more effort but saves memory space.

There are many variations of these two techniques which are useful in special circumstances. Since they are rather specialized and are adequately treated by the manufacturers of the equipment to which they apply, we shall not discuss the subject further.

13.10 Summary

This chapter has been an introduction to some of the advanced techniques for using magnetic tape. We have discussed them only briefly, because the details depend strongly on the characteristics of individual machines, and because they are rather specialized. A great deal of very good work has been done by the manufacturers of individual machines, most of which is available to all users.

Exercises

1. Many of the "chores" concerned with magnetic tape programming are not related to the problem to be solved at all and are hence referred to as "housekeeping chores." Discuss how these and other "housekeeping chores" affect programming costs, memory requirements, and program execution time.

2. Discuss the following advanced techniques for magnetic tape programming:
   (a) Labels.
   (b) Sentinels.
   (c) Run locators.
   (d) Dating routines.
   (e) Overlays.
   (f) Alternation of tape units.
   (g) Record grouping.
   (h) Variable length records.
   (i) Effective use of tape buffers.

3. Discuss if and how any of the subjects listed in Exercise 2 apply to any of the following types of magnetic tapes:
   (a) Program tape.
   (b) Input master tape.
   (c) Output master tape.
   (d) Input data tape.
   (e) Output data tape.

4. If a computer uses only punched cards for input/output (no magnetic tapes), how many of the subjects listed in Exercise 2 would still apply? If any of the subjects do apply, discuss the modifications, if any.

5. Of the techniques listed in Exercise 2, which are the essentials and which are luxuries or refinements? Discuss what would have to be done if these techniques were not programmed; what would be the penalties?

6. Can an overlay be regarded as a sort of super-subroutine? Outline the steps preliminary to calling in a subroutine and compare with the steps preliminary to calling in an overlay from drum or tape.

7. How can indirect addressing be used with alternation of tape units or record grouping? (See Section 7.4 for a discussion of indirect addressing.)

8. If information from a time clock is available to the computer in digital form, how could this information be used?

9. Discuss the advantages and disadvantages of the following systems of setting up trailers:
   (a) The trailers are packed. The total record is as long as the basic record plus the sums of all trailers that are present. Thus, if trailers 1, 3, 5, and 6 are present, the record in tape will look like:

| BASIC | 1 | 3 | 5 | 6 |

(b) The trailers are not packed. The total record is as long as the basic record plus all the trailers up to and including the highest trailer that is present. Thus if 1, 3, 5, and 6 are present, the record on tape will look like:

| BASIC | 1 | 2 (blank) | 3 | 4 (blank) | 5 | 6 |

10. Flow-chart and code a routine that will place dates where required in all the runs on an instruction tape. State all conventions used.

14 MACHINE-AIDED CODING

14.0 Introduction

Coding an electronic computer has been characterized as a problem in translating between two quite different languages: the language of the problem to be solved, and the language of the computer. In business data processing, the language of the problem consists of:

1. Description of data to be handled—how it originates, approvals required, when available, etc.
2. The calculation procedure to be applied to the data.
3. The form and frequency of reports to management, bills to customers, etc.
4. Checking procedures to be applied.

Such a statement of the problem gets changed into a flow chart fairly early in the game, but even the language of a flow chart is obviously quite different from that of coding, which is limited, elementary, and rigid.

It may be instructive to draw a parallel between the grammar of the English language and the grammar of coding. Each instruction corresponds to a sentence, containing one verb (the operation code) and, in a one-address machine such as DATAC and many actual computers, one noun (the contents of the address). The verb is usually active, present tense. In certain instructions, the noun is implied and the address is an adverb, such as in shift instructions; in others, the address may be thought of as an adjective, as in jump (transfer) instructions. We get the *effect* of a past tense verb only by storing results and inspecting them later in the sequence of instructions. We get the effect of adjectives modifying nouns with index registers, or by otherwise operating on addresses to change them. By any standard it is a very limited language. One is reminded of an Indian tribe in the U. S. Southwest whose language has only present tense verbs, and the great difficulty the children have when they start attending a

MACHINE-AIDED CODING

school where English is spoken. Those particular Indians are in a smallish minority and are forced to learn our language if they wish to communicate. With computers, however, things are different: we must either learn their language or hire (or train) a translator. If we may stretch this analogy just one step further, we might characterize machine-aided coding as a method of teaching the Indians to understand requests made in pidgin English, even though they will continue to talk among themselves in their own language.

There are other problems to machine-language coding than the difficulty of learning it and the fact that it is so different from the language of the problem. Once it is written, it is difficult to change. We have seen in earlier chapters that the problem of simply inserting one forgotten instruction leads either to changing one instruction and adding three more elsewhere or to the extremely burdensome and error-prone task of renumbering all following instructions and changing all addresses which refer to the renumbered instructions. As simple a change as adding one more deduction to a completed payroll program may involve literally weeks of work. Aside from the trouble involved in making changes, it is quite difficult to divide the coding of an application among several people. Either the different parts must be written almost as separate problems with the attendant duplications, or great effort must be put into the coordination of the parts.

The various types of machine-aided coding systems help to alleviate all of these problems to a greater or lesser extent. Some of them involve "talking" to the computer in a language which is quite close to its own, but which is nevertheless simpler for us than its actual language; others involve talking to it in a language which is greatly different from its own because it is much closer to ours.

Before launching into a description of the various ways of making the machine assist us in the clerical chores of the translation process, which is generically called *automatic coding* or *generalized programming*, we may note the existence of a spectrum of ways of coding, ranging from real machine language to ordinary English.

 1. Real machine language, also called absolute coding. Instructions are written exactly the way they will appear in memory (except, obviously, for the fact that we write them on paper whereas they will exist in memory as some physical phenomenon).

 2. Mnemonic operation codes. A computer can easily be programmed to accept letter abbreviations such as "ADD" for the operation codes instead of the machine's actual operation codes.

 3. Relative addressing. Addresses can be written relative to some starting location, which is assigned later.

4. *Symbolic addressing.* Addresses can be written as symbols which are more meaningful to the coder than numeric addresses are.

5. *Interpretive coding.* "Instructions" can be written which are not actually carried out by the machine as they stand, but which are rather condensed calling sequences to a set of subroutines, which are carried out *as the program is executed.*

6. *Compiling.* Rather than interpret the *pseudo instructions* as the program is carried out, the translation from pseudo instructions to real machine language can be carried out in a preliminary *compiling* pass done by the computer.

7. *Nonmachine language.* The distinguishing feature here is the fact that the pseudo instructions look nothing like the instructions in the machine, whereas in the previous types they do look more or less like actual instructions.

8. *The millennium.* Someday it may be possible to speak orders into a microphone and get problem answers as a result. The authors are not predicting the early arrival of such a golden age, but merely pointing out that it would be the ultimate. It may be noted, by contrast, that this always has been the only requirement in getting work started by human clerks.

We may now look into some of these techniques in detail.

14.1 Relative Address Coding

Let us first look a little more closely at the coding difficulties which make relative address coding desirable. Suppose the following loop has been coded in *absolute* (real machine addresses). Its function is the simple one of adding together one hundred numbers appearing in locations 1600–1699, shifting each number two places to the right before adding (to avoid possible overflow because the numbers are assumed to be very large), and storing the sum in 1700. 1700 initially contains zero, and the loop will be assumed to be properly initialized.

LOC.	S	O	ADDRESS	INDEX	FILTER	MON.	REMARKS
0400		B	[1600]				Bring next number to R register
0401	O	R	0002				Shift only R register two places right
0402	X	A	1700				Add to memory to accumulate partial sum
0403		B	0409				Bring address modifier to R register

(Continued on next page)

MACHINE-AIDED CODING 263

0404	X	A	0400				Add to memory to increase address
0405		B	0410				Bring instructional constant to R register for loop testing
0406		C	0400				Compare with modified instruction to test loop completion
0407	E	J	0411				Equal jump to continuation of program
0408	U	J	0400				Unconditional jump to repeat loop
0409	0	0	0001	00	00	0	Instructional constant: address modifier
0410		B	1700				Instructional constant: loop testing
0411	Continuation of program. Sum is in 1700.						

The operation of the routine is not particularly important; we wish simply to consider the effort required to *relocate* it, i.e., to change the location of the instructions. Also, we would like to investigate the trouble involved in making it apply to a different set of data. Suppose, first, that it becomes necessary to relocate the program so that the instructions are in 0600–0610 instead of in 0400–0410 as written. How do we go about systematically altering the addresses of the routine? We might profitably begin by classifying the addresses into several categories:

1. Addresses that depend on the location of data or results: viz., the instructions at 0400, 0402.
2. Addresses that depend on the location of the program: 0404, 0406, 0407, 0408.
3. Addresses that depend on the location of constants—which obviously need not have been written as instructional constants as was done here: 0403, 0405.
4. Address parts of instructional constants, which depend in this case on the location of the data: 0410.
5. Addresses which are invariant: 0401, 0409.

We see that relocating the program always affects the addresses of instructions which depend on the location of the program; i.e., category 2. This means that if the routine were relocated to start in 0600, only the addresses of the instructions at 0404, 0406, 0407, and 0408 would have to be changed. If, as shown here, the constants are written as instructions and stored in the instruction sequence, the addresses of instructions in category 3 would also need to be changed.

Altering the program to allow it to operate on different data would require changing the addresses in categories 1 and 4. Invariant addresses, by definition, never have to be changed—unless the problem specifications change.

Suppose we now rewrite the program, showing the category into which the address of each instruction falls.

ADDRESS CATEGORY	LOCATION	OPERATION CODE	ADDRESS
1	0400	B	1600
5	0401	OR	0002
1	0402	XA	1700
3	0403	B	0409
2	0404	XA	0400
3	0405	B	0410
2	0406	C	0400
2	0407	EJ	0411
2	0408	UJ	0400
5	0409	00	0001
4	0410	B	1700

The problem of relocating the program to start in 0600 is now much simpler. We can carry out the operation mechanically by simply adding 0200 to all instruction locations and to the addresses of all instructions in categories 2 and 3 (since 0400 + 0200 = 0600).

ADDRESS CATEGORY	LOCATION	OPERATION CODE	ADDRESS
1	0600	B	1600
5	0601	OR	0002
1	0602	XA	1700
3	0603	B	0609
2	0604	XA	0600
3	0605	B	0610
2	0606	C	0600
2	0607	EJ	0611
2	0608	UJ	0600
5	0609	00	0001
4	0610	B	1700

This purely mechanical way of relocating the program suggests a more general way of representing the addresses in the first place. Why not indicate initially that these addresses are *relative* to some starting point? We see that the addresses of instructions in categories 2 and 3, in this routine, are relative to the location of the first instruction of the routine. Similarly, in this routine, the addresses of the instructions in categories 1 and 4 could be indicated as being relative to the initial address of the data.

MACHINE-AIDED CODING

Suppose we symbolically indicate the initial address of the routine by "01A" and the initial address of the data by "01G," these symbols being chosen arbitrarily. Now the routine can be written as follows:

LOCATION (RELATIVE)	OPERATION CODE	ADDRESS (RELATIVE)
01A + 0000	B	01G + 0000
01A + 0001	OR	0002
01A + 0002	XA	01G + 0100
01A + 0003	B	01A + 0009
01A + 0004	XA	01A + 0000
01A + 0005	B	01A + 0010
01A + 0006	C	01A + 0000
01A + 0007	EJ	01A + 0011
01A + 0008	UJ	01A + 0000
01A + 0009	00	0001
01A + 0010	B	01G + 0100

Now we can change the location of the program and of the data at will, simply by substituting actual addresses for the symbols 01A and 01G and carrying out the indicated additions. It would be fairly simple to put the entire program into consistent form by setting up a dummy symbol for invariant addresses, which would be equivalent to using an initial address of zero. Let us call the dummy symbol 00I. Finally, we may observe that there is no real point to writing the plus signs, since they will always appear; they can just as well be understood as applying to all relative addresses. The program may now be written entirely in relative form.

RELATIVE LOCATION	OPERATION CODE	RELATIVE ADDRESS
0 1 A 0 0 0 0	B	0 1 G 0 0 0 0
0 1 A 0 0 0 1	OR	0 0 I 0 0 0 2
0 1 A 0 0 0 2	XA	0 1 G 0 1 0 0
0 1 A 0 0 0 3	B	0 1 A 0 0 0 9
0 1 A 0 0 0 4	XA	0 1 A 0 0 0 0
0 1 A 0 0 0 5	B	0 1 A 0 0 1 0
0 1 A 0 0 0 6	C	0 1 A 0 0 0 0
0 1 A 0 0 0 7	EJ	0 1 A 0 0 1 1
0 1 A 0 0 0 8	UJ	0 1 A 0 0 0 0
0 1 A 0 0 0 9	00	0 0 I 0 0 0 1
0 1 A 0 0 1 0	B	0 1 G 0 1 0 0

Observe what we have accomplished by writing the program in this form: it now makes no difference where either the instructions or the data is located. This may seem like a small gain for the effort, and indeed it would be in a routine as short as this one. However, in coding a large application such flexibility is very valuable. When coding is begun on a job which it is anticipated will almost completely fill memory, the problem of assigning actual addresses *in advance* becomes critical: the coder has no way of knowing how large the various sections of the routine will be, how much data can be brought into memory at one time, how many subroutines he will need and how long they will be, where to locate his constants so they will not get in the way of the other parts of the routine, etc. Furthermore, using relative coding, more than one person can work on the coding of an application with much less effort; as long as each person writes relative coding, the different parts can be fitted into the final program with much less cross checking required.

Of course, it is necessary sometime to translate back to absolute machine language. This can be done "by hand" if necessary, but it is much more desirable to set up a computer program to do it. The operation is usually called *assembly*, i.e., the translation from relative to absolute coding. Before proceeding, in the next section, to a description of a typical assembly program, we should point out a few characteristics of relative coding. First, the instructions that the coder writes are fairly close in format to the instructions that the computer executes. They still consist of an operation code, an address, and whatever other functions are pertinent to the computer at hand. Each instruction still carries out only an elementary part of the total application. We shall later investigate more powerful techniques, but relative coding is nevertheless a very sizable advance over absolute coding.

14.2 An Assembly System

For the assembly system which we shall illustrate with a detailed example, a few refinements should be added to the rudimentary system outlined in the preceding section. (However, a system similar to that one, elementary though it is, has been used fairly extensively.)

The first refinement is a way of inserting instructions more easily, in the fairly frequent situation where an omission is discovered before the program is assembled. This may be accomplished by relaxing the implicit restriction that all instruction locations be sequentially numbered, *with no numbers omitted*. Suppose we say that all addresses shall be written in the form

$$01A000.0$$

where the 01A, as before, symbolizes an address to which the instruc-

MACHINE-AIDED CODING

tions in that *region* (defined as any group of relative addresses having the same first three characters) are relative, the next three digits represent the sequence within the region, and the last digit is used only when making insertions. A period is indicated to remind us that the fourth digit has a slightly different function from the others. The region number, illustrated here by 01A, may be any combination of two digits and one letter, with the restriction that 00I is reserved for invariant addresses such as occur on shift instructions.

To illustrate these refinements, the routine has been rewritten, making the following assumptions:

1. The routine is written with the instructions in region 37G.
2. The (relative) starting address of the numbers to be added is 00K.
3. The sum is to be stored in (relative) address 01K.
4. The constants needed are stored starting in 02B (which does not now immediately follow the routine in memory).
5. The loop testing method has been changed to a counter.

LOCATION	OPERATION CODE	ADDRESS
3 7 G 0 0 0 . 0	B	0 0 K 0 0 0 . 0
0 0 1 . 0	XA	0 1 K 0 0 0 . 0
0 0 2 . 0	B	0 2 B 0 0 0 . 0
0 0 3 . 0	XA	3 7 G 0 0 0 . 0
0 0 4 . 0	B	0 2 B 0 0 1 . 0
0 0 5 . 0	M	0 2 B 0 0 0 . 0
0 0 6 . 0	S	0 2 B 0 0 1 . 0
0 0 7 . 0	NJ	3 7 G 0 0 0 . 0
⋮	⋮	⋮
0 2 B 0 0 0 . 0	00	0 0 I 0 0 1 . 0
0 0 1 . 0	00	0 0 I 1 0 0 . 0

We have here omitted the region number where it is the same as the preceding instruction. The 02B region would be somewhere outside the program area, so that the continuation of the routine would immediately follow 37G007.0. The constants have been shown here as instructional constants, but, as we shall see, this need not necessarily be so.

Suppose now that the routine is written, but before assembly it is discovered that an instruction has been omitted, namely the right shift which should have been the second instruction. If alternate lines were left blank on the coding paper, the shift could simply be written in; failing that, it would be an easy matter to recopy at most one page of coding. Either way, that net result would be:

```
        3 7 G 0 0 0.0          B           0 0 K 0 0 0.0
            0 0 0.1            OR          0 0 I 0 0 2.0
            0 0 1.0            XA          0 1 K 0 0 0.0
            0 0 2.0            B           0 2 B 0 0 0.0
```

As we shall see, the assembly program can with no difficulty handle the inserted instruction.

The second refinement we should like to add is the use of mnemonic operation codes. Mnemonic, of course, means aiding the human memory; mnemonic operation codes are thus supposed to be easier to remember than the machine's actual ones. This point is not so important in DATAC as in most real machines, because the DATAC codes were chosen to be indicative of the operation to begin with. In most actual computers, however, the operation codes either have no relation to the corresponding word-name, or are numeric and therefore obviously have no relationship to any word-names.* Mnemonic operation codes may be long or short, depending on the characteristics of the machine for which the assembly program must be written, and the preferences of the programmer. A possible list of three-letter mnemonic codes for some of the DATAC instructions might be:

NAME	DATAC CODE	MNEMONIC CODE
Bring	B	BRI
Store	S	STO
Add	A	ADD
Subtract	M	SUB
Add to memory	XA	ADM
Subtract from memory	XM	SBM
Multiply	X	MPY
Divide	D	DIV
Shift only R right	OR	SRR
Shift only R left	OL	SRL
Shift all right	AR	SAR
Edit	E	EDT
Dollar edit	DE	DED
Load index	LI	LIX
Store index	SI	SIX
Compare	C	COM
Zero jump	ZJ	ZEJ
Nonzero jump	NJ	NZJ
High jump	HJ	HIJ
Equal jump	EJ	EQJ
etc.		

The assembly program can quite easily translate these into real

* The equivalent of what we have called the "Bring" instruction in DATAC, in a sampling of real machines, has the operation codes 020, 00101000000 (binary), 01010 (binary), H, B, 64, 65.

operation codes. It is obvious that in a complex binary computer having a hundred distinct operations, mnemonic operation codes are much simpler to learn and remember than the actual operation codes.

The third refinement we should like to add is the ability to carry remarks along with each instruction, and to insert complete lines of remarks in the coding without disturbing the operation of the assembler. The value of such comments was discussed in Chapter 12. We shall, therefore, assume it to be possible to write a few words of remarks, if desired, to the right of each instruction, as has been done in this text. These remarks have no function in the assembly, but are simply printed out on the assembly listing exactly as they are entered into the machine at the start of the assembly. A complete line of remarks will be assumed to be permissible; the first character on such a line, however, must be some special character, to signal the assembly routine that the line is to be treated differently. We shall use an asterisk for the purpose. Such a line will also simply be printed out by the assembly program intact.

In order to assemble relative coding, the assembly program must know what the regions are relative *to;* i.e., the address at which each region begins. This address is sometimes called the *origin* of the region. In some assembly systems the origin of each region must be specified explicitly to the assembly program. In others, the assembly program will start assembling at some standard location and proceed sequentially unless instructed otherwise. We shall assume the latter. When it is desired to specify the starting point of a region, an instruction line is written which starts with a 1, contains the region number in the usual position, and contains the absolute origin of the region.

The example which has been chosen to illustrate this relative coding and assembly system is, as usual, simple because we wish to concentrate on these concepts rather than on the function of the routine. It consists of calculating, for each of 200 x's in memory, the function

$$y = a + bx$$

where a, b, and x are all integers. The x's are in locations 1000, 1002, 1004, . . . , 1398; the corresponding y's are to be stored in 1001, 1003, 1005, . . . , 1399. We shall assume that the x's have already been stored in these locations by a loading program or as the result of a previous calculation, and that the constants a and b have already been loaded. We shall use the following regional assignments:

Program	06A
First x	01F000.0
First y	02F000.0
a	10G000.0
b	10G001.0
Address modifier: 2	11G000.0
Counter: 200	11G001.0
Constant: 1	11G002.0

LOCATION	OPERATION CODE	ADDRESS	REMARKS

*COMPUTE FUNCTION OF XS AND STORE FOR PRINTING.

06A000.0	BRI	01F000.0	NEXT X TO R
001.0	MPY	10G001.0	
002.0	ADD	10G000.0	Y
003.0	STO	02F000.0	
004.0	BRI	11G000.0	MODIFY ADDRESSES
005.0	ADM	06A000.0	
006.0	ADM	06A003.0	
007.0	BRI	11G001.0	TEST LOOP
008.0	SUB	11G002.0	
009.0	STO	11G001.0	
010.0	NZJ	06A000.0	JUMP IF NOT FINISHED

*PRINTING ROUTINE FOLLOWS.

Assuming that we provide the assembly program with the necessary origin information, how does it go about producing absolute instructions? The assembly for this particular system would have to be done in two passes on the computer.

1. In the first pass the assembly program would read the relative program, and combine the origin information with the code to obtain an absolute equivalent to each relative instruction location. Thus, if in the example above the 06A region has an origin of 0400, the first pass produces a table showing the following equivalences:

06A000.0	0400
06A001.0	0401
06A002.0	0402
etc.	

(This operation would be much simpler if we had not allowed for the insertion of instructions between already written instructions. We shall see in the next section an answer to this objection.) Where origin information has not been provided, the assembly program simply assigns consecutive locations based on the order in which the relative program is loaded.

2. The second pass produces an actual machine-language program. Each relative address is looked up in the table produced on the first pass, in order to establish the absolute address. The mnemonic operation codes are looked up in a simple table. The complete instruction is "put together" the way it must appear in memory where it is later executed. Finally, the instructions are punched on cards or paper tape or written out on magnetic tape for later loading into the machine, and an assembly listing produced. This latter is a printed listing containing the instructions and remarks exactly as originally written, plus the absolute assembled instructions. The assembly listing becomes the working document for all later work; the original coding sheets could be discarded except that it is sometimes handy to be able to check for errors against the code as originally written. An assembly program is usually designed to check for certain errors and print a warning of them somewhere on the assembly listing. Typical errors which are discoverable by the assembly program include: nonexistent mnemonic operation codes, undefined regional symbols, out-of-sequence instructions, absolute addresses too large for the memory of the computer, etc.

It is most important to realize that when the assembly is completed, we do not have results of the problem; we have only an absolute program ready to be combined with data and a load program and *then* actually run on the machine. However, the assembly is only done *once*. (Assembly programs can, in fact, be set up to run the assembled program immediately after assembly. This is sometimes advantageous, but not often.) Once assembled, the absolute program can of course be used as many times as required, without reassembling.

Assume the following origins for the preceding example, some of which were given earlier.

06A	0400
01F	1000
02F	1001
10G	0050
11G	0052

The assembly listing which would be the output of assembling the routine with the assumed assembly system is shown in Figure 1. The printing and spacing are representative of an actual listing which could have been produced by a computer. The first lines are origin information in an arbitrarily assumed format, which might or might not actually appear on the listing, but in either case would not appear

```
1  06A                0400
1  01F                1000
1  02F                1001
1  10G                0050
1  11G                0052
*  COMPUTE FUNCTION OF XS AND STORE FOR PRINTING.
06A000.0  BRI  01F000.0    NEXT X TO R           0400  0B  1000  00  00  0
 001.0    MPY  10G001.0                          0401  CX  0051  00  00  0
 002.0    ADD  10G000.0  Y                       0402  0A  0050  00  00  0
 003.0    STO  02F000.0                          0403  0S  1001  00  00  0
 004.0    BRI  11G000.0                          0404  0B  0052  00  00  0
 005.0    ADM  06A000.0    MODIFY ADDRESSES      0405  XA  0400  00  00  0
 006.0    ADM  06A003.0                          0406  XA  0403  00  00  0
 007.0    BRI  11G001.0    TEST LOOP             0407  0B  0053  00  00  0
 008.0    SUB  11G002.0                          0408  0M  0054  00  00  0
 009.0    STO  11G001.0                          0409  0S  0053  00  00  0
 010.0    NZJ  06A000.0    JUMP IF NOT FINISHED  0410  NJ  0400  00  00  0
*  PRINTING ROUTINE FOLLOWS.
```

Figure 1. Output of the hypothetical assembly routine discussed in the text.

in the assembled program which would be loaded into the computer after assembly.

At first contact, relative coding must always appear to be a great deal more trouble than it is worth. A little experience with it, however, usually convinces most people that its advantages completely outweigh its disadvantages. The primary advantage, once again, is the freedom to proceed with the coding without having to determine *in advance* where the program and data are finally to be located in memory. The secondary advantages of easy insertion of corrections and the use of mnemonic operation codes are also valuable, but are not an essential part of the relative coding idea and are not present in all relative coding systems. In fact, it should be emphasized that the different techniques for simplifying coding can be combined in many different ways. The boundaries between relative, symbolic, and interpretive coding are never very distinct. What we actually have is a collection of simplifications which go under some more or less standardized names; the exact combination of them varies from one system to the next. In particular, many relative coding systems include simple techniques for incorporating standard subroutines, which we shall discuss next.

14.3 Symbolic Coding and Compiling

The term *symbolic coding* is used to designate a system not markedly different in concept from relative coding, but which usually has considerably greater flexibility than the type of system described in the previous section. In addition to relative addressing, a symbolic coding system usually has at least some of the following features.

1. There is much greater flexibility in the choice of symbols. These may usually be chosen at will, within a specified framework. Symbols can be chosen which suggest the name of the quantity stored in the location. Examples, assuming a limit of six characters per symbol:

NAME OF QUANTITY	POSSIBLE SYMBOL
Gross pay	GROPAY
Net pay	NETPAY
Commission	COMISN
Number of dependents	NODEP
Part number A16XF	A16XF
Address modifier 2	ADMOD2
Counter	CTR

In mathematical problems:

X	X
X_{10}	X10
Square root	SQRT
Greek letter δ	DELTA

Some restrictions must be observed, naturally. Usually, a symbol must contain at least one nonnumeric character so that all-numeric addresses can be recognized as absolute, as in shift instructions. Certain characters may be forbidden because other meanings are assigned to them, such as asterisk, comma, blank, and plus and minus signs. There is usually some maximum number of characters which may be used for symbols. A great deal of flexibility is still left to the needs and imagination of the coder. (One is still restricted to the characters available, however. For instance, no system at present allows question marks.)

2. It is usually not necessary to provide a symbol for each instruction location, except for instructions which are referred to by other instructions, such as with jumps or address modification. This makes the insertion or deletion of instructions (before assembly) about as simple as it could possibly be. Similarly, it is often not necessary to set up symbols for all data addresses, in situations where some of the data is grouped in sequential locations.

3. One feature of relative coding is retained, but in more flexible form: it is possible to refer to a location before or after the location corresponding to a symbol by the use of a minus or plus sign followed by an integer. For instance, if the symbol ABC corresponds to 0417, ABC + 10 would correspond to 0427 and ABC − 17 to 0400. This can reduce the number of symbols which need be invented, as can the use of a special symbol (such as an asterisk) to represent "the location of this instruction itself." For instance,

Jump   *− 7

would mean "jump to the instruction seven locations earlier than this one." If the assembled jump instruction eventually were located in 1720, say, its address would be 1713.

4. There is usually provision for much greater flexibility in assigning absolute values to symbols than in most relative coding systems. It is usually possible to *equate* symbols. Thus, if the symbol ABC is supposed to mean the same as the symbol XYZ which has been elsewhere defined, a line of coding which expresses the equivalence in the proper format would make the two symbols interchangeable. This is helpful when several people work on a program, allowing storage

assignments to be consolidated after most of the coding has been completed. It also permits a coder freedom to change his mind regarding symbols without having to make corrections.

5. Almost all symbolic coding systems have provisions for the easy incorporation of standard subroutines. In some systems, no effort need be made: the assembly program will recognize the calling sequence of a subroutine which is in its subroutine "library" and insert it in the assembled program at some appropriate point. In others, one *pseudo instruction* must be written, i.e., an instruction which does not result in the assembly of an actual computer instruction but is simply a control word to the assembly program. Such a feature goes under the fairly well accepted name of *compiling*, which is more properly used in this case than assembly, which strictly refers only to the translation from relative to absolute addresses. In short, compiling results in *many* instructions in the compiled program as the consequence of *one* pseudo instruction in the program as written. It obviously reduces the magnitude of coding effort by a significant amount, and greatly diminishes errors.

6. Entry of constants is facilitated by the availability of pseudo instructions which allow numbers to be written in everyday form, without the bother of having to disguise them as instructions. For use in connection with certain complex computers, a variety of such pseudo instructions may be provided for different purposes.

In summary, a symbolic address compiling system offers all the advantages of relative coding, plus much greater flexibility and the power of easy subroutine insertion. This is not to say that the compiling technique is restricted in applicability to symbolic coding systems; it is widely used for a variety of purposes. We shall return to compiling in the discussion of the problem-language coding system in Section 14.5.

It is important to remember that both assembly and compiling techniques always require a preliminary computer operation in which relative addresses, mnemonic operation codes, pseudo instructions, etc., are translated to real machine language. This, of course, takes time—more time than it saves, as a matter of fact, on very small problems. Furthermore, the result of this preliminary operation is a code which differs, more or less, from the code as written—which can lead to difficulties during the debugging of the program. This is not to say that assembly and compiling cause more trouble than they are worth, but simply that (1) they are not the final answer to the coder's every prayer, and (2) work remains to be done to make them more effective and simpler to use.

276 PROGRAMMING BUSINESS COMPUTERS

Rather than conjure up a DATAC example, we have chosen here to illustrate the symbolic coding ideas with a real system for a real machine. (See Figure 2.) The computer is the IBM 704, the system the SHARE Assembly Program (SAP), which despite its name also

```
                03720            ORG  2000 SUBROUTINE TO FIND SQ. ROOT OF FL. POINT NO. IN ACC.
03720  0 10000 4 00002     SQRT  TZE  2,4
03721  0 12000 0 03724           TPL  HERE
03722  0 76000 0 00003           SSP                  NEGATIVE ARGUMENT
03723  1 00001 4 03724           TXI  HERE,4,1
03724 -0 63400 4 03750     HERE  SXD  COMMON,4        STORE INDEX
03725  0 60100 0 03751           STO  COMMON+1        STORE ARGUMENT
03726 -0 32000 0 03746           ANA  EXPK
03727  0 76500 0 00001           LRS  1
03730  0 40000 0 03751           ADD  COMMON+1        X
03731  0 76500 0 00001           LRS  1
03732  0 40000 0 03747           ADD  CONST
03733  0 53400 4 03722           LXA  SQRT+2,4        3 TO INDEX C
03734  0 60100 0 03752     THERE STO  COMMON+2
03735  0 50000 0 03751           CLA  COMMON+1        X
03736  0 24000 0 03752           FDH  COMMON+2
03737 -0 60000 0 03753           STQ  COMMON+3
03740  0 50000 0 03753           CLA  COMMON+3
03741  0 30000 0 03752           FAD  COMMON+2
03742  0 40200 0 03746           SUB  EXPK            DIVIDE BY 2
03743  2 00001 4 03734           TIX  THERE,4,1
03744 -0 53400 4 03750           LXD  COMMON,4        RELOAD C
03745  0 02000 4 00002           TRA  2,4             SUBROUTINE EXIT
03746 +001000000000         EXPK OCT  001000000000
03747 +100400000000         CONST OCT 100400000000
                03750      COMMON BSS 4
                00000            END
```

Figure 2. SAP (SHARE Assembly Program) listing of a subroutine to take a square root.

includes compiling features. Neither the problem nor the listing will be explained; we hope only to communicate a little of the flavor of the subject. It should be noted, however, to avoid complete confusion, that the absolute instructions shown at the left appear in octal for convenience in debugging on the binary 704.

14.4 Interpretive Coding

Another approach to the problem of translating between the language of the application and the language of the machine is *interpretive* coding.

We may approach the concept of interpretive coding by observing that a calling sequence (page 171) is a rudimentary interpretive system, viewed in the following light. Each time the subroutine is executed, the subroutine must "go back" to the calling sequence to determine, or *interpret*, the information contained there as to what information it is to operate upon, where to place results, the limits of accuracy, or even what operation to perform. Two points should be emphasized: (1) this interpretation must be carried out *each time* the subroutine is executed, and (2) the calling sequence is written in a format which resembles that of instructions. The first point is central to the idea of an interpreter, and, as we shall discuss later, is its primary drawback; the second need not be true of interpreters in general.

Suppose that instead of a few subroutines, with their calling sequences scattered here and there through the program, we set up the entire program as a collection of calling sequences which refer to a complete set of subroutines. Suppose, further, that instead of writing a calling sequence each time we want a subroutine, we write a series of pseudo instructions which contain in condensed form the same type of information as the calling sequence normally would. These pseudo instructions may or may not have the same appearance as the computer's instructions, but they must be of such a length as to fit into memory words. Finally, suppose that associated with the set of subroutines is a routine which "interprets" the pseudo instructions by determining which subroutine is required and perhaps does a little other work, and also arranges to go on to the interpretation of the next pseudo instruction at the end of each subroutine.

Examples of complete interpretive coding systems of this type are easier to find in scientific and engineering computing; most commercial data processing, if it uses interpreting at all, uses it in combination with other techniques. We can illustrate the method, however, with an application which is an in-between category, namely, the simulation of one computer by another.

Simulation is required when it is desired to test programs for a machine which has been designed but not yet built, and in cases when it is desired to make use of existing programs from one machine on another machine rather than rewrite the programs. Since various computers are more or less different from each other, subroutines must be set up in the *subject* machine (the one doing the simulation) to simulate the operation of each of the instructions of the *object* machine (the one being simulated). Memory locations must be assigned in the subject machine to hold the contents of the various arithmetic and control registers. Instructions may now be written which look exactly like instructions for the machine being simulated, but which are actually pseudo instructions which control the operation of an interpretive simulation system. The simulator program inspects each pseudo instruction in turn. Through coding, it "decodes" or "interprets" the "operation code" of the pseudo instruction, determines what should be done with the address, and generally carries out the instruction of the object machine with the same result as if it had been carried out on the real machine, including jump (transfer) instructions and, where possible, input/output instructions. There must be a subroutine in the simulator corresponding to every instruction in the machine being simulated, and, of course, a "central interpreter" section which carries out such functions as keeping track of the simulated "location counter," etc. Provisions may be included in the simulator program for simplifying checkout. Naturally the simulator carries out a program a good deal more laboriously than the real machine would, since functions which would be executed in the object machine through electronics must be carried out with coding. Therefore, the simulation is considerably slower than the speed of the machine being simulated, unless the machine on which the simulation is done is much faster than the machine being simulated.

Actually, the idea of interpretive coding is not limited to complete, self-contained systems of this type. It is possible to set up systems which allow transition back and forth between pseudo instructions and real machine instructions (which led to names like DUAL and SEESAW). And as we saw, there are some interpretive elements to almost any program, including most compiled programs.

The one essential feature of the interpretive concept is that the interpretation of some "signal" to interpret—whether it is a pseudo instruction or a calling sequence or whatever—is done *every time the signal is encountered.* For instance, in the simulation example above, the "central interpreter" has to go through the work of decoding each instruction every time, ignoring the fact that it has gone through exactly the same effort many times before.

This inevitable waste of time in interpretive coding is, of course, a serious weakness of the method but it is the price paid for a corresponding strength: flexibility and the conservation of space. The alternative is compiling, or a variation of it. It would save considerable machine time, in the simulation example, to write out the instruction subroutines as they are required, rather than to use pseudo instructions and set up an interpreter. This could actually be done with a compiler which accepted pseudo instructions and compiled the subroutines into the correct sequence. But doing so would result in the need for a prohibitively large amount of memory and would mean rewriting the program and recompiling it every time it was necessary to make a change in the program being simulated. Thus it is necessary once again, as we have seen so many times before, to make a compromise: this time among the factors of memory space, total machine time, programming time, and flexibility.

We should like to emphasize once again, however, that interpretive coding is not an isolated technique which either is used in a given situation or is not; it is often employed in combination with other approaches. It is simply one more addition to the bag of tools which must be available to the good systems designer and programmer.

14.5 Nonmachine-Language Compiling

This name must obviously be qualified, since everything we have been discussing is in one way or another different from real machine language. However, all the previous techniques involve the writing of something which *resembles* the format of actual machine coding, if only vaguely. In nonmachine-language compiling systems we have in mind systems which involve writing something which has no resemblance whatever to the language of the machine. Instead, the program is defined in a language much closer to that of the problem being solved. It still is not possible to write "work out the payroll" on a piece of paper, push it into the machine, and get paychecks back. However, instead of writing 10,000 adds, stores, shifts, read tapes, etc., it may be possible to write statements such as

COMPUTE EXTENDED PRICE AND INSERT IN C ITEM.

or,

MOVE QUANTITY (W) TO QUANTITY (D).

and let a compiling program create from them a complete code.

In order to illustrate this important class of machine-aided coding, we shall turn to two actual machines and some of the *automatic coding* systems that have been developed for them.

The first is FLOW-MATIC, developed under the direction of Dr. Grace Murray Hopper for the Remington Rand Univac I and Univac II.* The name FLOW-MATIC is intended to imply that the emphasis in problem preparation using the system can be on the flow charting, rather than computer coding, i.e., on the problem to be solved instead of the computer. As we have said, this is just the goal of automatic coding. The first step in preparing a FLOW-MATIC code is to obtain (or already have) a perfectly clear understanding of the problem to be solved and the proposed method of solution—which is naturally the first step using any coding system. The second step is to prepare a flow chart of the procedure. Using machine-language coding we often prepare two flow charts: one

---

* FLOW-MATIC is not the only system which could be used to illustrate these ideas, but it is currently a representative one. Dr. Hopper has for many years been a leading proponent of improved automatic programming methods.

showing the over-all plan of attack, and the second showing in precise detail exactly how we propose to have the machine do the job. Using FLOW-MATIC, only the first is necessary, because from it one next prepares the "code." The word "code" is placed in quotes because the code in this case looks nothing like the actual computer code which will later come from the FLOW-MATIC compiler. Rather, it is ordinary English—almost. The coder's "English" must be restrained somewhat in the interest of keeping the compiler program within reasonable bounds. For instance, "Stop" and "Halt" might be interchangeable in ordinary English, but providing for the use of either one would add pointless complexity to the compiler. There are similar restrictions in sentence structure and punctuation.

The next step is to design the file layouts. It is here that a significant difference between FLOW-MATIC and ordinary coding appears. It is almost impossible, using any of the coding systems described previously, to code first and decide what the files look like afterwards, at least not if efficient use is to be made of magnetic tapes. (It is possible to design the files first using FLOW-MATIC if one wishes, but it is not necessary.) We shall try shortly to emphasize the flexibility that this independence of coding and file design allows in a practical situation.

Finally, the FLOW-MATIC "coding" and the file designs are read into the Univac along with the FLOW-MATIC compiler program, which then proceeds to prepare an actual machine-language code to carry out the defined procedure. As with almost any compiling system, the compiled program is then combined with the problem inputs to be run; i.e., the compiler does not run the problem itself.

A good example of the basic ideas of the FLOW-MATIC system appears in the manual published by The Remington Rand Univac Division of Sperry Rand Corporation. It is part of an inventory pricing application which is similar in concept, if not in detail, to illustrations used earlier in this text. Some of the details of the illustration naturally apply specifically to the Univac I and II, but this should be no obstacle to obtaining an idea of the general approach. The flow charting notation is only slightly different from that used in this text.

Figure 3 shows the initial version of the flow chart of the application. Figure 4 is the same flow chart with a few symbols added and with a few minor changes which bring the notation into correspondence with FLOW-MATIC conventions. Figure 5 is the actual FLOW-MATIC code. Figure 6 gives in over-all form the function and specifications of each file. Figure 7 shows in over-all form the *item layouts*

MACHINE-AIDED CODING 281

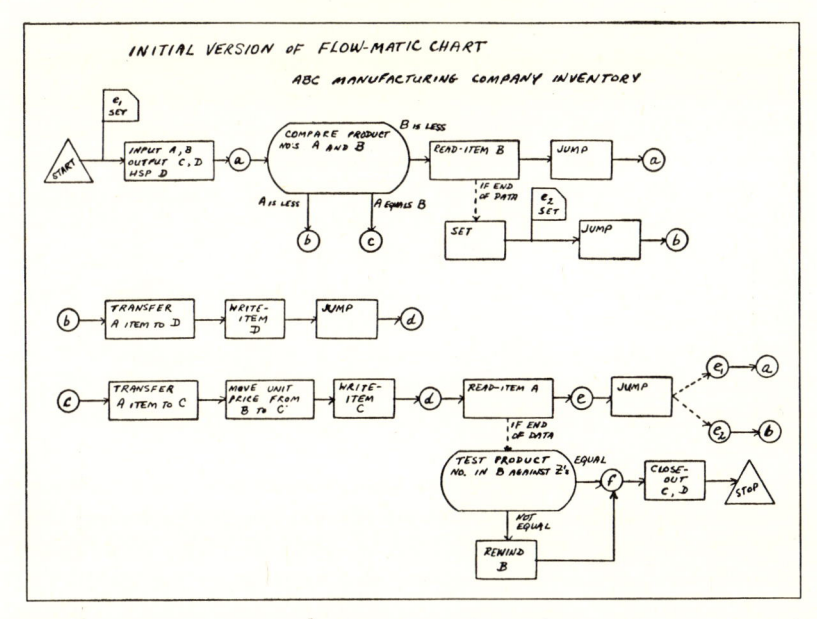

Figure 3. Initial version of the flow chart of a problem used to illustrate the FLOW-MATIC programming system.

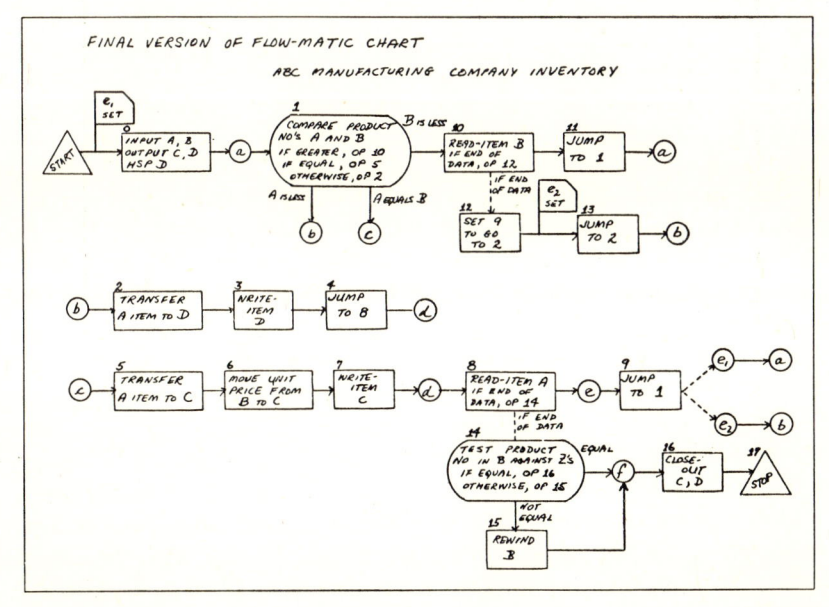

Figure 4. Final version of the flow chart of a problem used to illustrate the FLOW-MATIC system.

(Univac terminology) of the files. Figures 8, 9, and 10 show the complete definition of one of the files. It is worth noting that in order to take advantage of certain features of the Univac system, it is necessary to *pack* several inventory records into one tape record; this of course means that the machine coding must take account of

---

FLOW-MATIC CODE

(0) INPUT INVENTORY FILE-A PRICE FILE-B ; OUTPUT PRICED-INV FILE-C UNPRICED-INV FILE-D ; HSP D .

(1) COMPARE PRODUCT-NO (A) WITH PRODUCT-NO (B) ; IF GREATER GO TO OPERATION 10 ; IF EQUAL GO TO OPERATION 5 ; OTHERWISE GO TO OPERATION 2 .

(2) TRANSFER A TO D .

(3) WRITE-ITEM D .

(4) JUMP TO OPERATION 8 .

(5) TRANSFER A TO C .

(6) MOVE UNIT-PRICE (B) TO UNIT-PRICE (C) .

(7) WRITE-ITEM C .

(8) READ-ITEM A ; IF END OF DATA GO TO OPERATION 14 .

(9) JUMP TO OPERATION 1 .

(10) READ-ITEM B ; IF END OF DATA GO TO OPERATION 12 .

(11) JUMP TO OPERATION 1.

(12) SET OPERATION 9 TO GO TO OPERATION 2 .

(13) JUMP TO OPERATION 2 .

(14) TEST PRODUCT-NO (B) AGAINST ZZZZZZZZZZZZ ; IF EQUAL GO TO OPERATION 16 ; OTHERWISE GO TO OPERATION 15 .

(15) REWIND B .

(16) CLOSE-OUT FILES C , D .

(17) STOP . (END)

ABC MANUFACTURING COMPANY INVENTORY

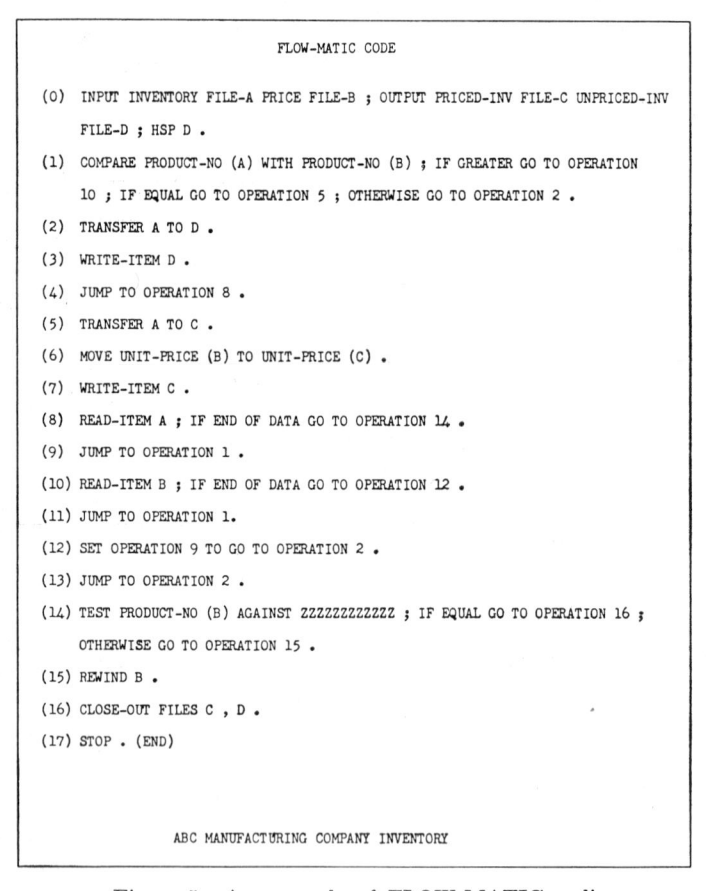

Figure 5. An example of FLOW-MATIC coding.

the fact that one tape record instruction will bring in several inventory items and must handle the tape record accordingly. This is taken care of automatically by the computer, as is the alternation of tape units (Chapter 13) on multireel files.

FLOW-MATIC, and other similar systems, have a number of important advantages. Some of these have been mentioned previously, but they are important enough to merit a summary.

MACHINE-AIDED CODING 283

1. The emphasis can now be on system design, rather than on the characteristics and idiosyncrasies of the machine at hand. This is precisely where the best effort should be placed: on the broad aspects of the job to be done, rather than on the details of how to do it.

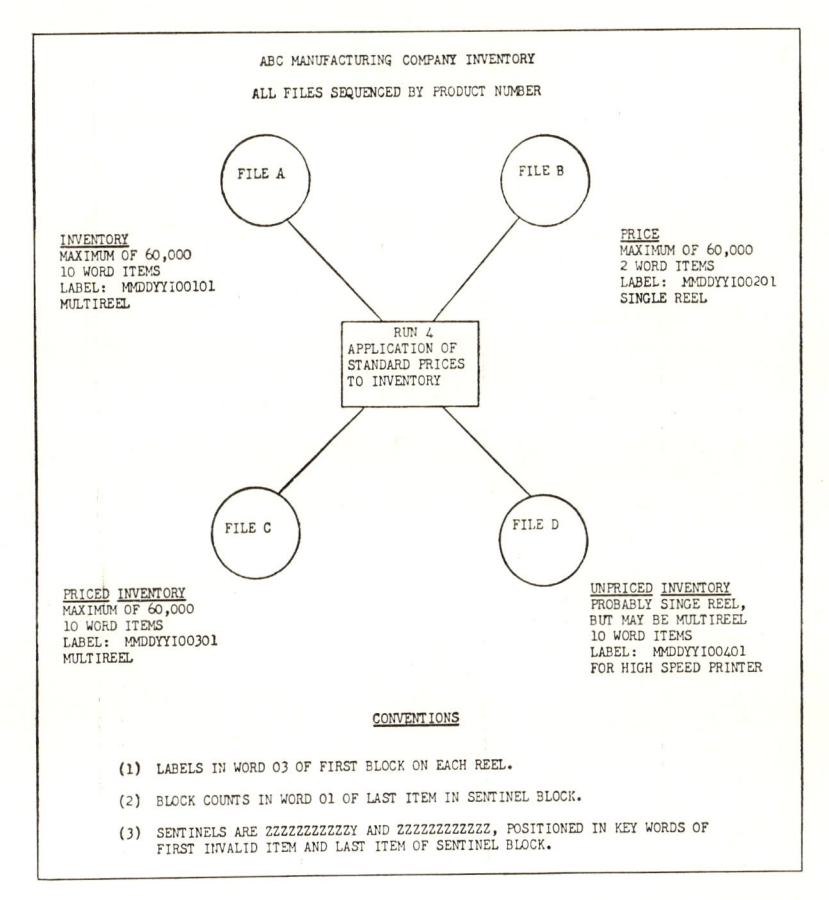

```
                ABC MANUFACTURING COMPANY INVENTORY
              ALL FILES SEQUENCED BY PRODUCT NUMBER

                  FILE A              FILE B

INVENTORY                                          PRICE
MAXIMUM OF 60,000                                  MAXIMUM OF 60,000
10 WORD ITEMS                                      2 WORD ITEMS
LABEL: MMDDYYI00101                                LABEL: MMDDYYI00201
MULTIREEL                                          SINGLE REEL

                         RUN 4
                    APPLICATION OF
                    STANDARD PRICES
                     TO INVENTORY


                  FILE C              FILE D

PRICED INVENTORY                                   UNPRICED INVENTORY
MAXIMUM OF 60,000                                  PROBABLY SINGE REEL,
10 WORD ITEMS                                      BUT MAY BE MULTIREEL
LABEL: MMDDYYI00301                                10 WORD ITEMS
MULTIREEL                                          LABEL: MMDDYYI00401
                                                   FOR HIGH SPEED PRINTER

                        CONVENTIONS

  (1) LABELS IN WORD 03 OF FIRST BLOCK ON EACH REEL.
  (2) BLOCK COUNTS IN WORD 01 OF LAST ITEM IN SENTINEL BLOCK.
  (3) SENTINELS ARE ZZZZZZZZZZZY AND ZZZZZZZZZZZZ, POSITIONED IN KEY WORDS OF
      FIRST INVALID ITEM AND LAST ITEM OF SENTINEL BLOCK.
```

Figure 6. Over-all function and specifications of each file in the illustrative FLOW-MATIC problem.

2. File design and coding are now two independent operations. This means that in the entirely typical situation where changes must be made in a program after it has been partially or completely finished, the task is not the almost overwhelming burden that it is when the two are inextricably intertwined. A change in file format to delete unneeded information, or, more commonly, to add information which

284 PROGRAMMING BUSINESS COMPUTERS

had been overlooked, does not mean a month's job of trying to find all the implications of the change to the program.

3. The separation of file design and coding, among other things, makes changes easy in general. What usually happens in setting up

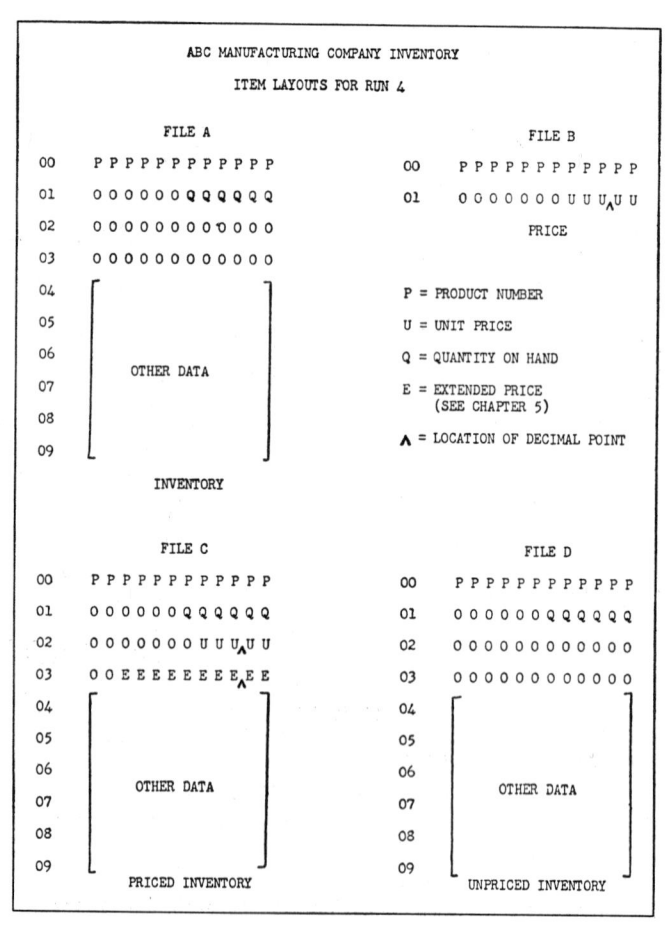

```
                    ABC MANUFACTURING COMPANY INVENTORY
                         ITEM LAYOUTS FOR RUN 4

                 FILE A                              FILE B
        00   P P P P P P P P P P P              00   P P P P P P P P P P P
        01   0 0 0 0 0 0 Q Q Q Q Q              01   0 0 0 0 0 0 0 U U U∧U U
        02   0 0 0 0 0 0 0 0 0 0 0                            PRICE
        03   0 0 0 0 0 0 0 0 0 0 0
        04   ⎡                 ⎤              P = PRODUCT NUMBER
        05   ⎢                 ⎥              U = UNIT PRICE
        06   ⎢                 ⎥              Q = QUANTITY ON HAND
        07   ⎢   OTHER DATA    ⎥              E = EXTENDED PRICE
        08   ⎢                 ⎥                    (SEE CHAPTER 5)
        09   ⎣                 ⎦              ∧ = LOCATION OF DECIMAL POINT
                  INVENTORY

                 FILE C                              FILE D
        00   P P P P P P P P P P P              00   P P P P P P P P P P P
        01   0 0 0 0 0 0 Q Q Q Q Q              01   0 0 0 0 0 0 Q Q Q Q Q
        02   0 0 0 0 0 0 0 U U U∧U U            02   0 0 0 0 0 0 0 0 0 0 0
        03   0 0 E E E E E E E E∧E E            03   0 0 0 0 0 0 0 0 0 0 0
        04   ⎡                 ⎤              04   ⎡                 ⎤
        05   ⎢                 ⎥              05   ⎢                 ⎥
        06   ⎢   OTHER DATA    ⎥              06   ⎢   OTHER DATA    ⎥
        07   ⎢                 ⎥              07   ⎢                 ⎥
        08   ⎢                 ⎥              08   ⎢                 ⎥
        09   ⎣                 ⎦              09   ⎣                 ⎦
              PRICED INVENTORY                      UNPRICED INVENTORY
```

Figure 7. The item design, in over-all form, of the files in the illustrative FLOW-MATIC problem.

a data processing application is that coding begins before all the details have been worked out in the systems design. This is done either because of pressure of time or, frequently, because the two are interrelated and it is not possible to know exactly what should be done in the systems design area until there is a little experience

MACHINE-AIDED CODING

N	A	M	E	Δ	O	F	Δ	F	I	L	E
I	N	V	E	N	T	O	R	Y	Δ	Δ	Δ	English name of file.
F	I	L	E	Δ	D	E	S	I	G	N	Δ
Δ	Δ	Δ	Δ	Δ	Δ	Δ	Δ	Δ	Δ	Δ	Δ
L	A	B	E	L	Δ	Δ	Δ	Δ	Δ	Δ	Δ
M	M	D	D	Y	Y	I	0	0	1	0	1	1.) Label (if constant), or date, with reel counter:- 2.) If no label, all Δ's (XXXXXX XXXXCC.)
L	O	C	Δ	O	F	Δ	L	A	B	E	L
0	0	0	0	0	0	0	0	0	0	0	3	Word location of label in label block.
M	U	L	T	I	Δ	R	E	E	L	Δ	Δ
0	0	0	0	0	C	0	0	0	0	0	1	1= Yes ; 0= No
B	L	K	Δ	C	T	Δ	I	N	D	Δ	Δ
0	0	0	0	0	0	0	0	0	0	0	1	1= Block count desired ; 0= No block count.
B	L	K	Δ	C	T	Δ	L	O	C	Δ	Δ
0	0	0	0	0	0	0	0	0	0	0	1	Word location of block count in last item of sentinel block.
E	N	D	Δ	R	E	E	L	Δ	S	E	N
Z	Z	Z	Z	Z	Z	Z	Z	Z	Z	Z	Y	End of reel sentinel.
E	N	D	Δ	F	I	L	E	Δ	S	E	N
Z	Z	Z	Z	Z	Z	Z	Z	Z	Z	Z	Z	End of file sentinel.
L	O	C	Δ	I	N	Δ	F	I	R	S	T
0	0	0	0	0	0	0	0	0	0	0	0	Word location of sentinel in first invalid item.
L	O	C	Δ	I	N	Δ	L	A	S	T	Δ
0	0	0	0	0	0	0	0	0	0	0	0	Word location of sentinel in last item of sentinel block.
												NOTE: Other entries may be added here, each
			go	on	to	next	page					consisting of a title and an information word.

INPUT AND OUTPUT DATA DESIGN—ABC MANUFACTURING COMPANY INVENTORY PROBLEM

Figure 8. Part of the file format definition of the illustrative FLOW-MATIC problem.

with a running program to go on. The way it works out is that reprogramming begins at approximately the moment an application starts to operate. The problem is nicely expressed by the lament, "If I had only known 4 months ago what I know now." The fact is that you cannot know what you want until you know how much trouble it is to get it and until you know how the alternatives would work out in practice. With ordinary machine-language coding methods

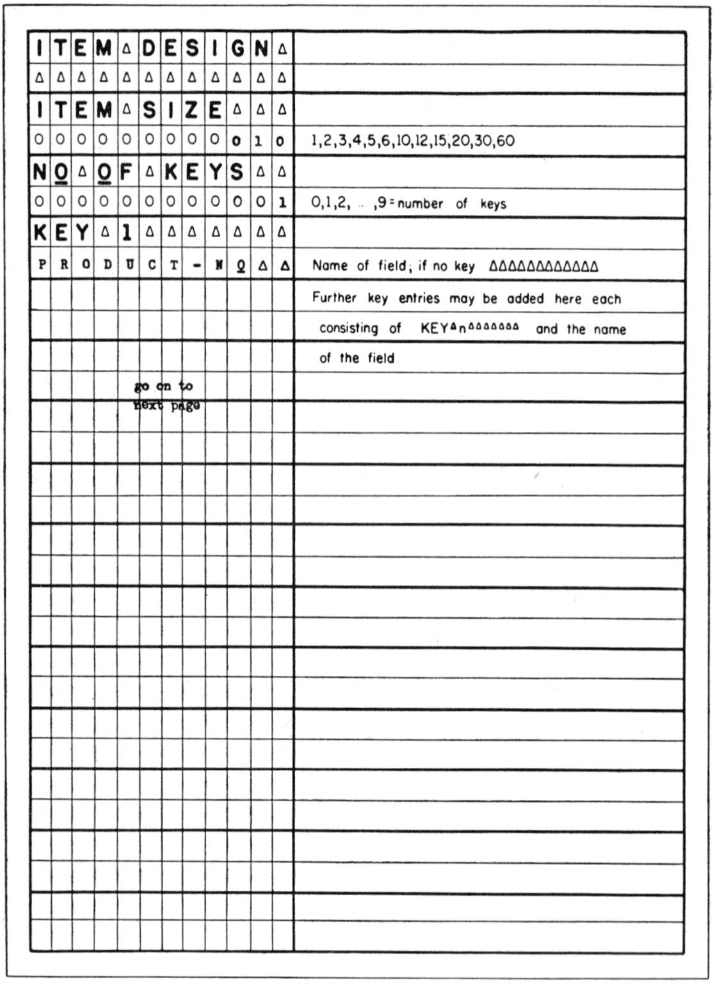

I	T	E	M	Δ	D	E	S	I	G	N	Δ
Δ	Δ	Δ	Δ	Δ	Δ	Δ	Δ	Δ	Δ	Δ	
I	T	E	M	Δ	S	I	Z	E	Δ	Δ	
0	0	0	0	0	0	0	0	0	0	1	0	1,2,3,4,5,6,10,12,15,20,30,60
N	O	Δ	O	F	Δ	K	E	Y	S	Δ	Δ
0	0	0	0	0	0	0	0	0	0	0	1	0,1,2, .. ,9 = number of keys
K	E	Y	Δ	1	Δ	Δ	Δ	Δ	Δ	Δ	Δ
P	R	O	D	U	C	T	-	N	O	Δ	Δ	Name of field, if no key ΔΔΔΔΔΔΔΔΔΔΔΔ

Further key entries may be added here each
consisting of KEY Δn ΔΔΔΔΔΔΔ and the name
of the field

go on to
next page

Figure 9. Part of the file format definition of the illustrative FLOW-MATIC problem.

it is very difficult to take advantage of the knowledge of experience, because recoding can be almost as much work as the original coding. With FLOW-MATIC and similar systems, the only effort required is to redefine the system, redraw the flow charts, make any necessary file format changes, and recompile. A good deal of what was done is probably still usable, and recompiling is not much trouble. It might seem that with ordinary coding methods much of the original work would still be usable, too, but it does not work out

MACHINE-AIDED CODING 287

F	I	E	L	D	△	D	E	S	I	G	N	
△	△	△	△	△	△	△	△	△	△	△	△	
P	R	O	D	U	C	T	-	N	O	△	△	Name of field.
0	0	0	0	0	0	0	0	0	0	0	0	Word location in item.
0	0	0	0	0	2	∅	∅	∅	1	C	0	Field descriptor of form OOOOOTPPSLNO
0	0	0	0	0	0	0	0	0	0	0	0	Extractor
Q	U	A	N	T	I	T	Y	△	△	△	△	Further field descriptions may be added here
0	0	0	0	0	1	0	0	0	0	0	0	each consisting of one or more four-word items.
0	0	0	0	0	3	∅	∅	∅	7	6	0	
0	0	0	0	0	0	1	1	1	1	1	1	
E	N	D	△	F	I	L	E	△	D	E	S	
0	0	0				0	0	0	0	0	0	
0	0	0	0	0								
		Space fill thru word 058										
0	0	0				0	0	0	0	0	0	
0	0	0	0	0								
0	0	0				0	0	0	0	0	0	
0	0	0	0	0								
0	0	0				0	0	0	0	0	0	
0	0	0	0	0								
0	0	0				0	0	0	0	0	0	
0	0	0	0	0	then type							
E	N	D	△	F	I	L	E	△	D	E	S	

Figure 10. Part of the file format definition of the illustrative FLOW-MATIC problem.

that way. In essence, then, we have here a coding technique which makes it possible for the systems designer to experiment, to good effect.

4. As we have said before, it is an advantage to be able, as we can here, to communicate with the computer in our language instead of its language. "Our language" is perhaps a little restricted, but it is certainly a different thing from writing individual machine-language instructions.

288 PROGRAMMING BUSINESS COMPUTERS

A second example of a nonmachine-language coding system, which uses a language much closer to the language of the problem than that of the machine, is FORTRAN, which is short for FORmula

Example: It is required to compute the following quantities

$$P_i = \sqrt{\sin^2(A_i B_i + C_i) + \cos^2(A_i B_i - C_i)}$$

$$Q_i = \sin^2(A_i + C_i) + \cos^2(A_i - C_i)$$

for i = 1, ..., 100. A possible FORTRAN program for this calculation follows.

STATEMENT NUMBER	FORTRAN STATEMENT
1	TRIGF(X, Y) = SINF (X+Y)**2+COSF(X-Y)**2
2	DIMENSION A(100), B(100), C(100), P(100), Q(100)
3	READ 8, A, B, C
4	DO 6 I = 1, 100
5	P(I) = SQRTF(TRIGF(A(I)*B(I), C(I)))
6	Q(I) = TRIGF(A(I), C(I))
7	PRINT 8, (A(I), B(I), C(I), P(I), Q(I), I = 1, 100)
8	FORMAT (5F 10.4)
9	STOP

Statement 1 defines the function TRIGF(X, Y) as equal to the expression $(\sin^2(X+Y) + \cos^2(X-Y))$. The DIMENSION statement indicates that the arrays A, B, C, P, and Q each have 100 elements. A, B, and C in the READ statement will cause all elements of A, then all elements of B, and then all elements of C to be read into the 704 from cards. Notice that the READ statement refers to a new type of statement (8), FORMAT. In this example, the FORMAT statement specifies the external arrangement for both input and output data. In this FORMAT statement, 5F10.4 means: "There are 5 Fixed point decimal fields per card or line, each field being 10 columns wide with 4 decimal places to the right of the decimal point." Hence, A, B, C, P, and Q will be read or printed in the form __±XX.XXXX, that is, two blanks, a sign, two digits, a decimal point, and four digits, a total of 10 columns. Statement 4 says: "DO the following statements through statement 6 for I=1, I=2, ..., I=100." Statements 5 and 6 compute P_i and Q_i. The PRINT statement says: "Print the arrays A, B, C, P, and Q for I=1, ..., 100 as specified by FORMAT statement 8." Statement 9 stops the computer.

Figure 11. Illustration of FORTRAN coding.

TRANslation. This is a system devised originally for the IBM 704, and later modified for use with other computers. It is intended for use with scientific or engineering problems, although with ingenuity

MACHINE-AIDED CODING

it could perhaps be applied to the type of work of interest to us in this text. It is mentioned briefly here because it is in wide use, and because it provides a good example of a different type of problem language which is far removed from that of the computer. Since it is directed toward a type of problem which is of less interest to us here, we present a smaller illustration. Figure 11 is a reproduction of a page from "Programmer's Primer for FORTRAN," published by the International Business Machines Corporation.

14.6 Generators and the Report Generator

The last type of nonmachine-language coding we shall describe deserves a separate heading because it embodies almost all of the previous concepts. A *generator* may be defined as a routine which produces a complete routine for a problem given only a few parameters which describe the desired routine. This definition may seem to define a compiler also; we imply in a generator, however, that the problem definition is in skeleton form, i.e., that a minimum amount of information is provided to the generator.

Some type of generation scheme is frequently used to create sorting routines, as will be considered briefly in the next chapter. This is often done even when the main routine is coded in a language similar to the machine's. The list of information which must be specified to a tape sort generator will give a better insight into the operation of a generator. The exact type and amount of information naturally depend to some extent on the computer involved, but the following list is representative.

1. Size of records.
2. Format and location of keys.
3. Nature of any record grouping.
4. Sentinel conventions.
5. Tape numbers.
6. Pulse density of input and output tapes, if variable.
7. Size of high-speed memory available, if variable.

Certain other information would have to be specified on particular computers. From only such a list of parameters, suitably entered on cards or tape, a sort generator routine would create a finished sorting routine to handle the conditions specified by the parameters. The finished result would, of course, vary greatly, depending on the type of situation it was supposed to handle. When it is considered that each individual sorting routine might easily require six man-months

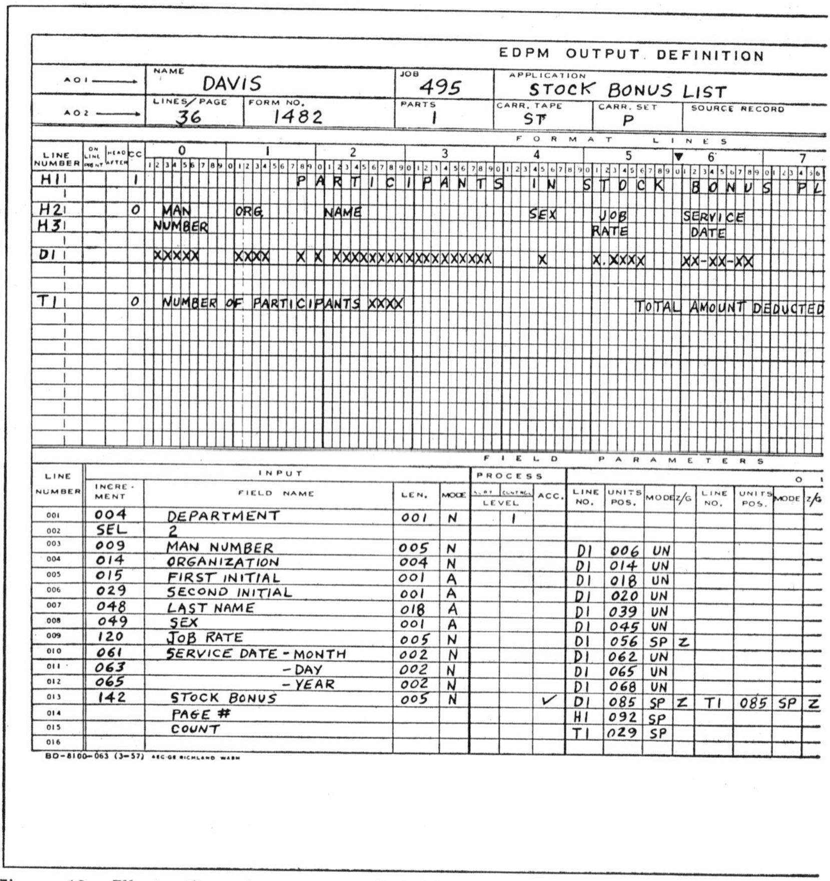

EDPM OUTPUT DEFINITION

	NAME	JOB	APPLICATION		
A01 →	DAVIS	495	STOCK BONUS LIST		
	LINES/PAGE / FORM NO.	PARTS	CARR. TAPE	CARR. SET	SOURCE RECORD
A02 →	36 / 1482	1	ST	P	

FORMAT LINES

LINE NUMBER	ON LINE INCREMENT	HEAD AFTER	CC	Format
H11			1	PARTICIPANTS IN STOCK BONUS PL
H21			0	MAN ORG. NAME SEX JOB SERVICE
H31				NUMBER RATE DATE
D11				XXXXX XXXX X X XXXXXXXXXXXXXXXXXX X X.XXXX XX-XX-XX
T11			0	NUMBER OF PARTICIPANTS XXXX TOTAL AMOUNT DEDUCTED

FIELD PARAMETERS

LINE NUMBER	INPUT INCREMENT	FIELD NAME	LEN.	MODE	PROCESS LEVEL	CONTROL LEVEL	ACC.	LINE NO.	UNITS POS.	MODE	Z/G	LINE NO.	UNITS POS.	MODE	Z/G
001	004	DEPARTMENT	001	N		1									
002	SEL	2													
003	009	MAN NUMBER	005	N				D1	006	UN					
004	014	ORGANIZATION	004	N				D1	014	UN					
005	015	FIRST INITIAL	001	A				D1	018	UN					
006	029	SECOND INITIAL	001	A				D1	020	UN					
007	048	LAST NAME	018	A				D1	039	UN					
008	049	SEX	001	A				D1	045	UN					
009	120	JOB RATE	005	N				D1	056	SP	Z				
010	061	SERVICE DATE - MONTH	002	N				D1	062	UN					
011	063	- DAY	002	N				D1	065	UN					
012	065	- YEAR	002	N				D1	068	UN					
013	142	STOCK BONUS	005	N			✓	D1	085	SP	Z	T1	085	SP	Z
014		PAGE #						H1	092	SP					
015		COUNT						T1	029	SP					
016															

BD-8100-063 (3-57) AEC-GE RICHLAND WASH

Figure 12. Illustration of an output definition form for the Report Generator.

if coded from scratch, it is clear that this technique represents a great saving of time.

The most advanced form of generator, and in many ways the most advanced form of nonmachine-language coding system in general, is the report generator. This is a technique which builds on all previous work and was contributed to by many workers, but which was apparently first developed in a fairly complete form at the Hanford Atomic Products Operation of the General Electric Company. A report* prepared by the data processing staff at Hanford explains the motivations that led to the work and outlines the characteristics of the

* "Generalization: Key to Successful Electronic Data Processing," General Electric Company, Hanford Atomic Products Operation, Richland, Wash. This work was done under contract for the U. S. Atomic Energy Commission. See also Chapter 14 listings in bibliography.

MACHINE-AIDED CODING

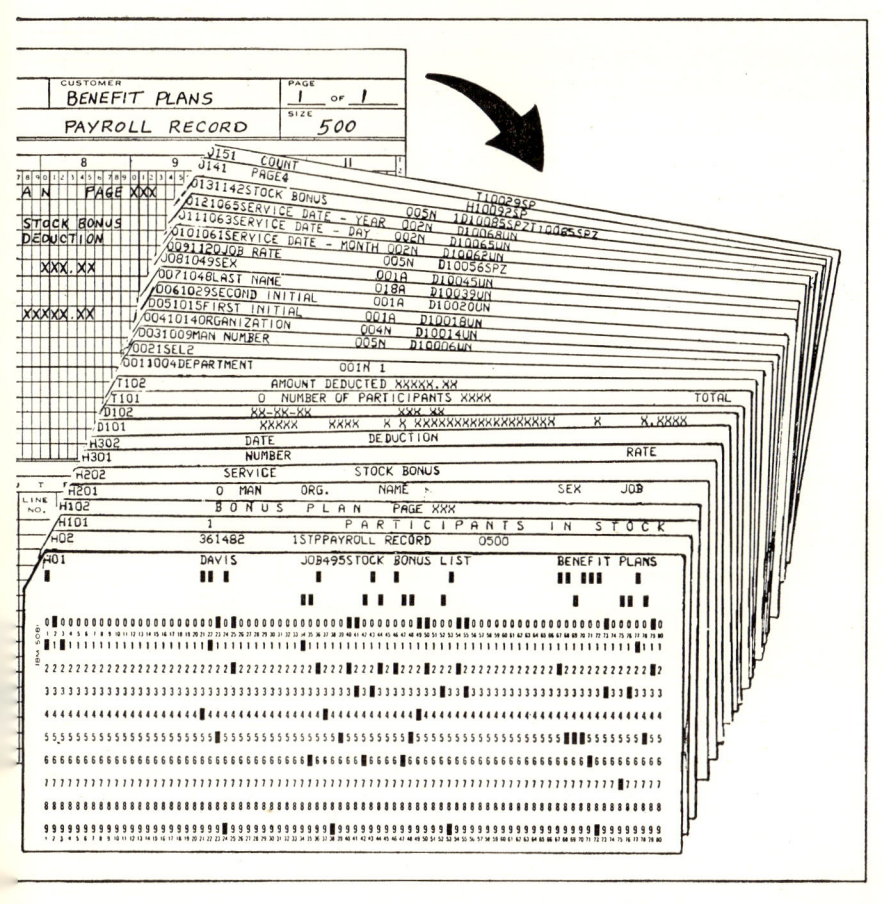

Figure 12 (*continued*)

first version of the Hanford system. Part of the following material is paraphrased from that publication.

A *report*, in this discussion, may be thought of as including just about any printed output that could be desired from a commercial data processing application: statistical summaries, checks and earnings statements, labor distribution details, etc., etc. In using the report generator, the report is first defined on an *output definition form*. (See Figure 12.) In the top part of the form, the report is laid out exactly as it is to appear in its final form. Report titles and columnar headings are shown here, and the positions in which the items are to appear on the report are designated by "X's" in the appropriate squares.

The lower part of the form is used to specify which fields in the record are to appear on the report. For each field, two kinds of information are needed: (1) where the field is to come from, i.e., its position in the file record; and (2) where the field is to go, i.e., its position in the report.

The completed output definition form is then keypunched directly into cards, and the cards are submitted, along with the file, for computer processing. As the first step in the processing, the report generation routine reads the output definition cards and *generates* the particular instruction patterns required to prepare the report. The

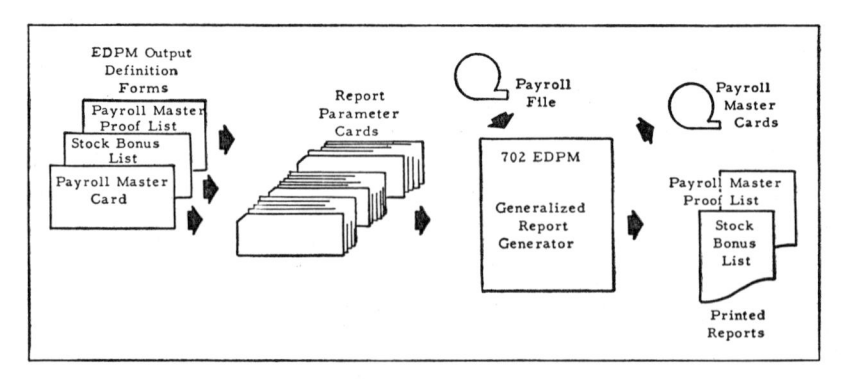

Figure 13. Schematic representation of the processing done by the Report Generator.

generated program then takes over, selecting out of each record in the file (which may be either on cards or on tape) those fields designated in the output definition and placing them in an auxiliary record in a form suitable for printing. When the file has been completely processed, the auxiliary records are printed on a line printer.

An important feature of the report generator is its ability to produce any reasonable number of independent reports from a given file on a single machine run. Output definition cards for each report desired are punched in the usual manner, and submitted for processing in "packets," one packet for each report to be generated. During processing, the report generation routine generates a separate, independent program for each packet submitted. As each record in the file is read, the generated programs are executed, one after another, so that the various reports are generated essentially simultaneously.

An example of generalized report generation is shown in the illustrations. Figure 12 shows a typical report defined on the output definition form, and the way in which this information is keypunched into cards. In Figure 13, a schematic representation of the computer processing is shown. Note that the report defined in Figure 12 is only one of several reports to be prepared simultaneously in this processing. Finally, Figure 14 shows the finished report resulting from the processing.

Certain additional features of the generalized report generator are worth noting. In the first place, instead of listing information out of every record in a file, it is possible to list information out of *selected* records only. In the illustration, for example, information is listed only for employees in department 2; the records for employees in other departments are ignored. Another important feature is the automatic formation and printing of *totals* of designated fields in different records. Provision is made for taking up to fifteen levels of totals, including final totals. Other features of the report generator include automatic page numbering, automatic record count, elimination of leading zeros, group indication (by means of which the printing of common line identifications may be suppressed), and the generation of records for use in subsequent processing.

This technique assumes that a master file being processed is on tape in what the Hanford workers call *generalized* form. Here, each file has as its first record a set of parameters which completely define the format of the rest of the records in the file. There are two important consequences of this *parametric description* of files. First, a field can be referred to on the output definition form simply by *field number*. From the field defining parameters, the report generator then creates the coding required to obtain the correct field when it is called for on the output definition form. The second major advantage is that almost complete flexibility of file design is possible. If a field must be added to the records, or a field deleted, or changed, it is only necessary to make a change in the parametric description of the file and run the file through what the Hanford workers call a *generalized file maintenance* run. This alters the file record formats as required; any subsequent processing by the report generator then operates automatically on the changed file. Thus both file design and details of processing may be changed with a minimum of effort.

Some aspects of data processing are difficult to generalize in the sense described above; these are the actual calculation phases, which we have seen before constitute a relatively small part of the total data processing task. The report generator system handles this problem by allowing for easy incorporation of what may be called "handwritten" coding, as distinguished from the coding which is automatically created.

An appreciation of the power of the report generator system may be

```
                    PARTICIPANTS   IN   STOCK   BONUS   PLAN        PAGE   1

  MAN                                          JOB       SERVICE          STOCK BONUS
  NUMBER    ORG.     NAME              SEX    RATE        DATE             DEDUCTION

  00001     2345    J R SMITH           M    1.9743     12-16-52              18.75
  00002     2111    M K DORAN           F    1.5796     07-14-56               5.00
  00003     2239    S S FINCH           M    2.3796     11-19-39               1.00
  04796     2119    M N DOE             M    2.1296     12-14-56               1.00
  12344     2179    A B JONES           M    3.0000     06-14-49
  12345     2431    J B DOE             F    2.9643     12-01-42              15.00
  12346     2117    R Y ABBOT           F    1.7963     12-17-54
  12348     2212    D D DODDS           M    2.0109     05-19-46              18.75
  23456     2793    S L DORE            F    1.3796     12-19-56

  NUMBER OF PARTICIPANTS     9                    TOTAL AMOUNT DEDUCTED       59.50
```

TYPEWRITER OUTPUT

```
TAPE UNIT REQUIREMENTS
INPUT FILE ON 0209
OUTPUT REPORTS AND/OR RECORDS 0200,0201,0202
0200  PAYROLL MASTER CARD
0201  STOCK BONUS LIST                   1 PART 1482      CC- P C.TAPE ST
0202  PAYROLL MASTER PROOF LIST          5 PART 1482      CC- P C.TAPE 18
IF LAST REEL HAS BEEN READ TURN 0911 ON
INPUT COUNT  7241
0200              SEL   6581     NON SEL   660
0201              SEL      9     NON SEL  7232
0202              SEL   7241     NON SEL
```

Figure 14. Illustration of Report Generator output and operator instructions.

This report was prepared simultaneously with two others - Payroll Master Cards (record generation) and Payroll Master Proof List (report generation). During processing each input record is counted. This count is checked against the select and non-select counts for each of the output reports.

gained by noting that in the report generator illustrated here, it is possible in some cases to call for the incorporation of a sorting routine wherever desired *by making one check mark.*

This particular report generator, as we have said, was built on the foundation of much other work, some of which was along somewhat similar lines although not as thoroughly developed. At the time of writing, much effort was being expended to convert the report generator from the machine on which it was first used, the IBM 702, to other equipment, while at the same time expanding the concepts.

14.7 The Place of Machine-Language Coding

The natural reaction to examples such as the last three is, "Why did I learn machine-language coding when these systems will do all the work for me?"

There are a number of facets to the answer to the question, none of which are intended to minimize the value or importance of automatic coding *where it is applicable.* For one thing, it is *not* always applicable. The designer of an automatic coding system is faced at the outset with a dilemma: if he tries to design a system which will handle everything he can think of which would be nice to have, he must expect that the system will be cumbersome, slow, and hard to learn, and that the system itself will be extremely difficult to design and program. On the other hand, if he makes it too simple, it will not do much. After the necessary compromise has been made, one is left with a system which is indeed useful, as we have seen, but which cannot be applied indiscriminately to every problem which ever arises. Where the automatic coding systems do not apply, obviously a machine-language program must be written, although some type of simpler assembly and/or compiling technique may still be very useful.

A second obvious reason for machine-language coding is that there is not a nonmachine-language coding system available for every computer, even though a great deal of effort is currently being put into their development. Furthermore, compilers and assemblers, so far at least, are usually not ready when the machine first becomes available.

A third reason is that certain tasks are too small to make automatic coding worthwhile. If a request comes in for a special listing of a master file which requires only a twenty- or thirty-instruction routine followed by an off-line listing, there is not too much point in going through a compiling phase to get it. This happens a good deal more often than might be imagined.

Finally, it seems to happen that even if a person intends to do his coding in a nonmachine-language system, he does a better job of it if he knows in fair detail how his computer actually operates. This is of little importance in "one-shot" jobs where the emphasis is on programming time rather than machine time, but obviously not all jobs are of this type. Furthermore, a compiled routine has to be debugged, because of errors in logic or in applying the compiler. Often, this debugging must still be done in machine language.

For a variety of reasons, then, we see that, important as automatic coding is, it will never completely replace absolute and relative coding. A fair analogy might be that most of us do not have to know how our automobiles operate, but we probably drive a little better if we do; we are certainly in better shape if, should the spark plug wires come off in the middle of the desert, we know how to put them back; finally, someone has to know how cars run so they can design, build, and repair them.

14.8 Summary

We have traced in this chapter a development of ideas starting with coding in the machine's preferred language and working up to coding in a language more satisfactory to human beings with a problem to solve. In the situations where they apply, the various systems are very useful and are widely employed throughout the computer industry. However, one must be practical and realize that they do not always apply, for a variety of reasons. A compromise must be made among programming time, computer running time, ease of learning, etc. Real machine-language coding and problem-language coding are both here to stay.

The future of this type of tool is a little hard to predict. Many improvements are currently being made in the type of tool described in this chapter, such as attempting to alleviate the annoying problem of debugging the machine-language routine produced by a compiler. One obvious question is whether it would be feasible to build a compiling system into the hardware of the computer itself, rather than requiring a program to do it. The answer is by no means clear at this time. Considering the amount of effort being expended and the rewards in less costly coding and wider computer applicability, we are sure to see great strides in nonmachine-language coding in years to come.

Exercises

1. What are some of the advantages of machine-aided coding techniques?

2. Name some of the functions performed by machine-aided coding systems.

3. Discuss how machine-aided coding systems affect the following phases of programming:
    (a) Estimating time and cost of programming.
    (b) Flow charting.
    (c) Clerical chores of coding.
    (d) Debugging: labor, machine time, elapsed time.
    (e) Making changes or corrections in the program.
    (f) Production running time (this will depend on the system used).

4. Discuss two available assembly systems for commercially available machines. Point out the strong and weak points, and the general pseudo-instruction format.

5. Macro-instructions can be built into the hardware or built into the machine-aided coding system. Discuss the relative advantages and disadvantages of each method.

6. Discuss the statement, "Computers should be designed with machine-aided coding systems in mind." Why? What effect will this have on the design?

7. As a new computer is brought into the market, an entirely new set of machine-aided coding systems has to be developed. How might it be possible to avoid some or most of this development work by a universal language with two-way translators to and from the universe of machines?

8. What can we do to prevent the awkward situation where the program is written in some meaningful pseudo language and the results of debugging and corrections are in unfamiliar computer language?

9. Name at least one machine-aided coding system that produces programs that will operate more efficiently than those produced by an "average" coder.

10. Design or describe a COUCH program that "psychoanalyzes" a program. For example, it may look for errors, estimate the timing, collect statistics on frequency of usage for different parts of programs, improve the program, etc.

11. Is it possible to have one computer prepare programs for a completely different computer?

12. With more prevalent use of machine-aided coding techniques, will computers of the future be inclined to be more complicated or more simple to program in machine language?

13. What are the relative merits of compilers and generators in scientific computation? In data processing?

14. What kind of service or utility routines would you like to come with your computer?

15 SORTING

15.0 Introduction

We saw in Chapter 2 on files and elsewhere that the most common method of processing information in files at present is based on sequential file organization. Furthermore, certain applications not having to do with file updating also require that the units of information be in sequence. It is frequently necessary to tabulate data according to various classifications; although this can sometimes be accomplished without having the information in sequence, it is usually essential. Other examples could be cited. Since it is so often necessary to arrange information into some type of sequence, it is obvious that systematic techniques must be available for carrying out the task, which is almost always called *sorting*.* This chapter presents several alternative approaches to the sorting problem, with numerical examples. Some indication is given of the conditions under which each method is applicable, but the techniques are not applied to any particular computer or to our hypothetical computer.

15.1 General Considerations

Before launching into a discussion of the various sorting techniques, we should review a few of the major file concepts, and establish a few matters of terminology.

We defined a file earlier as a collection of related information organized for some purpose. We noted that a file does not necessarily imply a sequence, but it does imply *identifiability*. In less general terms, a file is composed of *records*, each of which is identified by a *key* such as payroll number, part number, etc. To be perfectly precise, it is not essential that the keys be contained *in* the records, but we shall assume they are in this chapter. Sorting means to

*Other terms might be more desirable in some ways, such as *sequencing* or *ordering*, but the word sorting is fairly well entrenched at present.

arrange the records into ascending (or sometimes descending) sequence of the keys. It should be noted that the same file must often be sorted according to different keys contained in the records. For instance, a payroll file is most commonly arranged in payroll number sequence, but at other times it must be sorted into sequence according to name, organization code, location to which checks are sent, etc. The discussions and examples in this chapter assume a single key, but it should be understood that the key may be any desired field(s) in the file records. We shall not speak, in general, of the situation where the *physical media* on which the records are stored are sorted, such as is the case with the sorting of punched cards. Rather, we shall discuss the situation, more common in electronic data processing, where *information* is moved, such as the rearranging of the information content of high-speed memory or magnetic tapes.

In the examples in this chapter we shall show only the keys of the records. It is perhaps obvious that this is the easiest way to illustrate sorting methods, and also obvious that such movement of only the keys would be totally unrealistic.

In any sorting system, the sequence of the allowable characters must be determined. Clearly 6 is larger than 4, but is A more or less than 9? And what is the relationship between 7, K, and $? The prescribed sorting sequence of the characters varies from one machine to the next, particularly as regards whether the digits are greater or less than the letters of the alphabet. In DATAC we assumed that the Compare instruction would act according to the following ordering of the characters: blank, 0–9, A–Z, decimal point, comma, $, *, (,), —, +. This is roughly representative of some of the systems in common use. In the examples to follow we shall use only numeric keys.

We shall very often use the word *pass*, which refers to a reading of an entire file. Thus, one sorting scheme requires that we repeatedly exchange successive pairs of records if they are not already in sequence. Carrying out the comparing and (if necessary) exchanging for the entire file is called a pass; many such passes would in general be required to complete the sort.

It is nearly impossible to answer the question "which sorting method is best?" The obvious rejoinder must be "for what, on what machine?" We could not begin, in this book, to evaluate the various sorting methods against typical applications to show how they compare. Instead, we attempt to show the significance to each method of certain characteristics of the file to be sorted and of certain broad machine features. It should be noted, furthermore, that it is the usual practice in sorting large files to use a combination of *two* sorting methods to gain speed, to take advantage of special machine features, or to minimize the effects of various storage limitations. This point is discussed more fully in Section 15.6 on merge sorting, which is almost always one of the two methods.

We propose six characteristics of the file to be sorted which affect the choice of sorting method. Machine characteristics as applied to sorting methods are considered in Section 15.9.

1. Key length. For some methods, the difference between a two-digit numerical key and an eighteen-character alpha-numerical key is critical.

2. Key range. One file might have a key range of 0000001 to 9999999 although the total file contains only 300 records; another file, also containing 300 records, might have a key range of 9999700 to 9999999. If this fact is known in advance, there is no need to consider the first four digits at all. With some sorting systems this would make next to no difference; with others it might cut the sorting time in half.

3. Degree of original ordering. In some methods, the degree of original ordering in the file has a marked effect on the amount of data manipulation and/or the number of passes required. The problem is how to describe the degree of ordering. For some methods, the number of *strings* is the crucial factor. A string is an unbroken ascending sequence of keys. For instance, in the sequence 04, 09, 16, 14, 15, 41, 37, 34, 50, 91, the strings consist of (04, 09, 16), (14, 15, 41), (37), (34, 50, 91). We would then say that the original group had four strings. In other methods, the crucial factor may be how far down the list the smallest key occurs, or how far up the list the largest key occurs. In other cases it is, roughly speaking, where the ordering falls in a scale ranging from completely in sequence to completely out of sequence, i.e., in reverse order. This, unfortunately, is a difficult characteristic to describe precisely in simple terms.

4. File storage type.* Probably the overriding file characteristic in selecting a sorting method is type of file storage. As we have seen, there are two basic types: *sequential access* and *random access*. By sequential access is meant a storage system in which records may be processed *only* in sequence; magnetic tape is the common example. It is not practical to attempt to obtain information from magnetic

---

* As we shall see, there is always a need for some type of *working storage* in addition to the file storage, but this does not significantly affect the evaluation of different sorting methods.

SORTING

tape by any method except reading the records one after the other, either in the same sequence as they were recorded or the opposite sequence (in machines where it is possible to read tapes backwards). Random access simply means that it is possible to obtain any record in the file as quickly as any other. One must not split hairs, however, because most storage devices fall somewhere in the range between the two extremes. For our purposes in this chapter, the phrase "as quickly as any other" means *with respect to the essentially nonrandom access nature of magnetic tapes;* thus magnetic drum storage will be considered random access for this chapter, even though it is not as random as, say, magnetic core storage.

5. Number of records in file. This is obviously important, although it is not completely separable from the type of file storage since it will have a bearing on the type of storage which can be used.

6. Record length, or in some cases, the ratio of total record length to key length.

These file characteristics determine the primary sorting characteristics of each method, namely, the number of arithmetic and/or comparison operations per pass, the total number of passes (which is sometimes variable), and the amount of record movement required. In addition, we must give some consideration to the over-all complexity of the sorting procedure.

In practice it is always necessary to provide means for the computer to know when it has reached the end of a pass. This is usually accomplished either by knowing how many records there are in the file (or subfile, if less than the entire file is being sorted), or by providing a sentinel or fence after the last record. We shall generally ignore this question in the discussions to follow, since it applies equally to all sorting methods and furthermore is not particularly difficult to handle. The related problem of knowing when the sort has been completed does vary with the different sorting methods and will be described.

For clarity of explanation, the example used to illustrate the various sorting techniques was chosen with no duplicate keys. This is decidedly atypical for some applications, but represents no loss of generality since all the methods to be discussed will handle duplicate keys with no difficulty.

With these preliminaries out of the way, we are ready to examine some of the more common sorting techniques: *selection, exchanging, insertion, radix* (or *digit*), *straight merge,* and *probability merge.*

15.2 Sorting by Selection

Sorting by selection is probably the most obvious and easy to follow of all sorting methods. It consists of inspecting the file to find the record with the smallest key and placing that record at the beginning of the file, then searching for the next larger key, placing that record second, etc., until the entire file is sequenced. We have seen in earlier chapters, however, that digital computers cannot accept instructions like "find the smallest key in this file." The point is not that the statement is in English, but that it is not a sufficiently precise statement of *how* to locate the record having the smallest key.

There are several precise ways of formulating the procedure. One, which is also very easy to code for a computer, goes as follows: Compare the first and second records; if they are out of order, reverse them. Then compare the first and third, first and fourth, first and fifth, etc., reversing each time if necessary, until the first and last have been compared and reversed if necessary. This completes the first pass, which can be guaranteed to place the record with the smallest key in the first record storage position. The second pass operates in the same manner on the second and all following records, the third pass on the third and following records, etc. The process is continued until the last pass consists of one comparison between the next-to-the-last and the last records.

The example in Table 1 shows *only the keys* of sixteen sample records, and the rearrangement of the records during successive passes.

Several points bear observing. The first pass actually accomplished nothing but the interchanging of the first and second records. We might be tempted to ask why all the rest of the file need have been examined; obviously 06 is the smallest key in the list. The point is probably obvious: *we* knew it was the smallest by glancing at the whole list and seeing nothing smaller than 06, but a computer cannot do this without ploddingly examining every key. Of course, the file would not be recopied between passes as shown here. Since this technique is applicable only to random access file storage, the only data movement would occur in the interchanges; we have shown the file as it stands at the end of each pass to clarify the procedure. Actually, to be perfectly clear, we might have shown the file after each interchange. In Table 2, the keys of the records actually interchanged during the *second* pass are shown in italics. The first column shows the file at the start of the second pass, and the other three columns show the file after each of the three interchanges

SORTING

TABLE 1

PASS NUMBER

ORIGINAL FILE	1	2	3	4	5	6	7	8	9	10	11	12	13	14	15
34	06	06	06	06	06	06	06	06	06	06	06	06	06	06	06
06	34	12	12	12	12	12	12	12	12	12	12	12	12	12	12
91	91	91	14	14	14	14	14	14	14	14	14	14	14	14	14
70	70	70	91	17	17	17	17	17	17	17	17	17	17	17	17
17	17	34	70	91	18	18	18	18	18	18	18	18	18	18	18
27	27	27	34	70	91	27	27	27	27	27	27	27	27	27	27
58	58	58	58	58	70	91	29	29	29	29	29	29	29	29	29
14	14	17	27	34	58	70	91	34	34	34	34	34	34	34	34
35	35	35	35	35	35	58	70	91	35	35	35	35	35	35	35
36	36	36	36	36	36	36	58	70	91	36	36	36	36	36	36
18	18	18	18	27	34	35	36	58	70	91	46	46	46	46	46
12	12	14	17	18	27	34	35	36	58	70	91	58	58	58	58
68	68	68	68	68	68	68	68	68	68	68	70	91	60	60	60
46	46	46	46	46	46	46	46	46	46	58	68	70	91	68	68
29	29	29	29	29	29	29	34	35	36	46	58	68	70	91	70
60	60	60	60	60	60	60	60	60	60	60	60	60	68	70	91

required to bring the record with the second smallest key to the second position in the file storage area.

TABLE 2

START	FIRST INTERCHANGE	SECOND INTERCHANGE	THIRD INTERCHANGE
06	06	06	06
34	*17*	*14*	*12*
91	91	91	91
70	70	70	70
17	*34*	34	34
27	27	27	27
58	58	58	58
14	14	*17*	17
35	35	35	35
36	36	36	36
18	18	18	18
12	12	12	*14*
68	68	68	68
46	46	46	46
29	29	29	29
60	60	60	60

It is important to keep in mind that the numerical example used here and later shows only the keys of the records. Selection sorting, in common with most sorting methods, requires considerable record movement. If the records are quite long, as they often are, the bulk of the sorting time may be spent simply moving records between storage locations in memory. Some machines have facilities for simplifying this process, but it is a time-consuming effort in any case. This observation led to the development of what is called *address sorting* or *decapitation*.

The method assumes that the file (or, usually, the segment of the file) to be sorted is in main memory. The keys of the records are copied into another section of memory so that the full records need not be moved, and the address of the record corresponding to each key is "tagged onto" the key. The "records" to be sorted now consist only of the key and an address, which is much shorter than the actual record. These "pseudo records" may now be sorted just as though they were the actual records, but the sorting time will be appreciably shorter. When the "pseudo records" have been sorted, it is a simple matter to inspect their addresses to determine how the original records should be distributed to produce the correctly sorted file as desired. This may sound complicated, but the time savings which can be realized make it a fairly commonly used short cut. Its applicability is not limited to sorting by selection.

There is an interesting variation of selection sorting which involves address sorting in an unusual way. In it, a memory location is set up corresponding to each record. Then the keys are compared in exactly the same manner as described. Instead of moving the records at each comparison, however, a 1 is added to the location corresponding to the record having the *larger* key. When the process is completed at the comparison of the last and the next-to-last keys, the locations will contain numbers which show the ranking of the records. It is then a simple matter to compute from these numbers the sequence in which the records should be distributed to produce the sorted file.

As shown in Table 3, the first column consists of the keys of the unsorted file. The second column shows the number which is built up by adding a 1 to the location corresponding to the record having the larger key at each comparison. These numbers start at zero, and run to one less than the number of records in the file. In the illustration, the first record of the original file becomes record seven of the sorted file, the second record becomes record zero, etc. The third column shows the sorted file produced by carrying out the rearrangements dictated by the ranking numbers. (This almost must be tried to be believed!)

The technique may look complicated, but it is actually quite simple to program, and is a very good technique in certain applications. Observe that if it is known that the keys of a file to be sorted

TABLE 3

ORIGINAL FILE	RANKING NUMBER	SORTED FILE
34	7	06 (0)
06	0	12 (1)
91	15	14 (2)
70	14	17 (3)
17	3	18 (4)
27	5	27 (5)
58	11	29 (6)
14	2	34 (7)
35	8	35 (8)
36	9	36 (9)
18	4	46 (10)
12	1	58 (11)
68	13	60 (12)
46	10	68 (13)
29	6	70 (14)
60	12	91 (15)

form an unbroken sequence when sorted, such as 1, 2, 3, 4, 5, 6, 7, 8, etc., the same technique can be used with only one pass being needed and with no dependence of any kind on the original ordering of the file.

The six file characteristics listed above may be checked for their significance to sorting by selection.

1. Key length: little bearing except as it may be more or less difficult in different machines to operate on long keys.
2. Key range: no bearing.
3. Degree of ordering: fairly important. The only question is the number of record interchanges involved, since there appears to be no way to take advantage of any ordering in the original file in such a way as to reduce the number of passes. Thus, for a file of n records, $n-1$ passes must be made in any case. However, if the file is already in sequence, no interchanges are required; this is quite important if address sorting is not used, since the movement of records, if they are long, can be a very significant part of the total sorting time. A file of n records which is in reverse sequence to begin with will require $(n^2 - n)/2$ interchanges of records and $n-1$ passes.*

* This formula may be derived as follows. If the file contains n records and is in exact reverse sequence, then $n-1$ interchanges are required on the first pass, $n-2$ on the second, $n-3$ on the third, etc., until one interchange is required on the last pass. The total number of interchanges required is obviously the sum of these. The sum of the integers from 1 to $n-1$ is $(n^2-n)/2$, as may be verified by experimentation or by consulting a college algebra text, under arithmetic series.

4. File storage type: very important. The method is not practical using sequential storage, since it essentially requires that all the records be available at once, which is by definition impossible with sequential access storage.

5. Number of records in file: quite important. The expression $(n^2 - n)/2$ shows that the method becomes impractical for large files: in the case of reverse sequence, a file of 1000 records would require nearly half a million interchanges!

6. Record length: quite important, for same reason as (5), unless address sorting is used.

15.3 Sorting by Exchanging

Sorting by exchanging is a very simple technique to set up for a computer. Each pass consists simply of comparing each adjoining pair of records in the file successively and exchanging each pair that is out of sequence. That is, the keys of the first and second records are compared, then those of the second and third, the third and fourth, etc. It should be noted that if comparison of records one and two required an exchange, then when the second and third are compared the "second" record has become what was formerly the first. The process is continued until the file is in sequence, which is signaled by a pass that requires no exchanges. The technique is illustrated in Table 4.

TABLE 4

					PASS NUMBER						
ORIGINAL	1	2	3	4	5	6	7	8	9	10	11
34	06	06	06	06	06	06	06	06	06	06	06
06	34	34	17	17	17	14	14	14	14	12	12
91	70	17	27	27	14	17	17	17	12	14	14
70	17	27	34	14	27	27	18	12	17	17	17
17	27	58	14	34	34	18	12	18	18	18	18
27	58	14	35	35	18	12	27	27	27	27	27
58	14	35	36	18	12	34	34	29	29	29	29
14	35	36	18	12	35	35	29	34	34	34	34
35	36	18	12	36	36	29	35	35	35	35	35
36	18	12	58	46	29	36	36	36	36	36	36
18	12	68	46	29	46	46	46	46	46	46	46
12	68	46	29	58	58	58	58	58	58	58	58
68	46	29	60	60	60	60	60	60	69	60	60
46	29	60	68	68	68	68	68	68	68	68	68
29	60	70	70	70	70	70	70	70	70	70	70
60	91	91	91	91	91	91	91	91	91	91	91

SORTING

Observe that an extra pass is required to know that the file is sorted. It may be noted that this version of exchange sorting is particularly vulnerable to one type of original file sequencing: if the record with the lowest key is last, then the maximum number of passes will be required (one less than the number of records) regardless of the sequence of the rest of the file. (Although, of course, the number of record movements will still depend on the sequence of the rest of the file.) A modification of the technique immediately suggests itself: make alternate passes in the opposite direction. Table 5 shows the example reworked to include this improvement. We see

TABLE 5

	PASS NUMBER							
ORIGINAL	1	2	3	4	5	6	7	8
34	06	06	06	06	06	06	06	06
06	34	12	12	12	12	12	12	12
91	70	34	34	14	14	14	14	14
70	17	70	17	34	17	17	17	17
17	27	17	27	17	27	18	18	18
27	58	27	58	27	34	27	27	27
58	14	58	14	58	18	34	29	29
14	35	14	35	18	35	29	34	34
35	36	35	36	35	36	35	35	35
36	18	36	18	36	29	36	36	36
18	12	18	29	29	46	46	46	46
12	68	29	68	46	58	58	58	58
68	46	68	46	68	60	60	60	60
46	29	46	60	60	68	68	68	68
29	60	60	70	70	70	70	70	70
60	91	91	91	91	91	91	91	91

that three fewer passes were required, with only slight complexity added to the procedure.

One more refinement is suggested by a little reflection about the last example. We note that on the third pass, no interchange is required until we reach the third and fourth records. This means that the record which is at the "top" of the file can never be involved in later interchanges. Similarly, we note that as the sort proceeds, more and more records become "immune" to interchanges. The same thing happens at the "bottom." It is not too much trouble to keep track of this situation through appropriate coding, and avoid useless testing of records which cannot possibly require movement. Whether the savings are worth the trouble depends somewhat on the computer involved, as well as on the file being sorted.

The file characteristics:

1. Key length: little bearing, except as it may influence coding difficulty in dealing with long keys.
2. Key range: no bearing.
3. Degree of ordering: very important. If the file is completely sequenced to start, one pass and no record movements are required. In the worst case of reverse original sequence, the number of passes and record movements for a file of n records is $n-1$ and $(n^2-n)/2$, respectively, the same as for selection sorting. If alternate passes are made in the opposite direction, the number of passes and record movements is the same for the worst case, but for intermediate degrees of ordering the number of passes is reduced even though the number of exchanges is the same. By and large, the number of passes is more important than the number of record movements, so the slight modification required to make alternate passes in reverse order is well worth the trouble.
4. File storage type: variable importance, depending on other things. The technique can be used with either sequential or random access storage, especially if the sequential storage happens to be magnetic tape which can be read backwards, but the number of passes required becomes so prohibitive as the number of records increases that the method is not used by itself for large tape files. It may still be used in conjunction with some other method (such as merging) for sorting tape files, however, and is quite attractive for that purpose.
5. Number of records in file: very important, since in the worst case the number of exchanges is approximately proportional to the square of the number of records.
6. Record length: quite important, except that with random access storage the method is easily adaptable to address sorting.

15.4 Sorting by Insertion

Sorting by insertion is somewhat more complex than the previous two methods, but offers certain advantages, as we shall see. It consists of building up the final sequenced file one record at a time, by determining where in a partial file each record should be inserted, and moving all following records to make room for it. Several modifications of the basic scheme are possible; we shall first look at the example in terms of the straightforward approach, shown in Table 6.

Two features of the method stand out: the partial file must be searched each time to locate the correct place to insert the new record,

TABLE 6

INSERTION STEPS

ORIGI-NAL	1	2	3	4	5	6	7	8	9	10	11	12	13	14	15	16
34	34	06	06	06	06	06	06	06	06	06	06	06	06	06	06	06
06		34	34	34	17	17	17	14	14	14	14	12	12	12	12	12
91			91	70	34	27	27	17	17	17	17	14	14	14	14	14
70				91	70	34	34	27	27	27	18	17	17	17	17	17
17					91	70	58	34	34	34	27	18	18	18	18	18
27						91	70	58	35	35	34	27	27	27	27	27
58							91	70	58	36	35	34	34	34	29	29
14								91	70	58	36	35	35	35	34	34
35									91	70	58	36	36	36	35	35
36										91	70	58	58	46	36	36
18											91	70	68	58	46	46
12												91	70	68	58	58
68													91	70	68	60
46														91	70	68
29															91	70
60																91

so that as many insertion steps are required as there are records, and a great deal of record movement can be involved. The first characteristic suggests that a more sophisticated approach to locating the correct place in the partial file should be used. Since we know that at every stage the partial file is in sequence, it is possible to use a technique usually called *binary searching*. This technique consists of first inspecting the key of the record nearest the middle of the partial file. If this test shows that the correct location is in the first half of the partial file, the key of the record nearest the quarter point of the partial file is next inspected; if the first test showed the correct location to be in the upper half, the key of the record nearest the three-quarter point is next inspected, etc. The name "binary search" comes from the fact that each inspection eliminates one-half of the remaining records from consideration. The major advantage of the technique is that it greatly reduces the number of keys that must be inspected if the number of records is sizable. For instance, the correct location in a partial file of 500 records can be found with only nine inspections. The binary search is not difficult to program as a loop, despite the fact that it is necessary to take into account the variation in the file length as the process continues.

The second characteristic of insertion sorting—the large amount of record movement—can be avoided by using address sorting. In machines which are directed toward the type of application where this method is applicable, it may be desirable to build in a special instruction which facilitates the type of record movement required by the method; in the one machine which has such an instruction, it is appropriately called "tumble."

The effect of the six file characteristics:

1. Key length: little bearing except for any coding difficulty in dealing with long keys.
2. Key range: no bearing.
3. Degree of ordering: considerable importance. Although it is true that no direct advantage is taken of any ordering in the original file, that the number of insertion steps is always equal to the number of records in the file, and that the entire partial file must be inspected on each insertion step, the ordering is still of some importance because it affects the amount of record movement involved. An original file of n records in reverse sequence would require the movement of $(n^2 + n)/2$ records, which is expensive.
4. File storage type: quite important, since the method could not feasibly be used with sequential access storage by itself.
5. Number of records in file: very important because the number of record movements is roughly proportional to the square of the number of records in the file.
6. Record length: very important, unless address sorting is used, since so many record movements may be required.

15.5 Radix Sorting

Radix sorting, which is also called digit sorting, is a quite different method from those presented so far. It will be illustrated for a decimal number, but is applicable to any other number base and to alphabetic characters, although in the latter case special techniques are ordinarily employed. It is the basis of nearly all punched card sorting methods.

For a decimal key, eleven areas of storage must be available at each pass; to be safe, each must be able to store the entire file if necessary. On each pass, one storage area contains the file resulting from the previous pass. The other ten storage areas are numbered zero through nine. On the first pass, the unit's digit of each key is inspected; the record is placed in the correspondingly numbered storage area. After this has been done, the records are collected into one file in the original storage area, taking zeros first, then ones, then twos, etc. The file is now in sequence on the unit's digit; later operations will not

SORTING

destroy this particular sequence. The second pass consists of exactly the same operations, except that the ten's digit controls the distribution of the records to the ten storage areas. Observe that after this is done, the records in each area are still in correct sequence on the unit's digit. When the records are collected back into one file, they are in correct sequence on the last two digits. The procedure is continued until as many passes have been made as there are digits in the key. Table 7 shows the first pass of the sort, in terms of our example.

TABLE 7

PASS 1				STORAGE AREA						
ORIGINAL	0	1	2	3	4	5	6	7	8	9
34	70	91	12		34	35	06	17	58	29
06	60				14		36	27	18	
91							46		68	
70										
17										
27										
58										
14										
35										
36										
18										
12										
68										
46										
29										
60										

When the distributed records are collected back into one file, they become the input file to Pass 2. See Table 8. In this case, when the records are collected from the storage areas, the sort is complete.

A variation of the method is possible if twenty storage areas are available. In that case, the records need not be collected back into one file, except when the sort is complete. At each pass, ten storage areas constitute input; the records are distributed to the other ten. After each pass, the direction of information flow is reversed.

The name "radix sorting" is derived from the fact that as many storage areas must be provided as the radix (base) of the number system used. Incidentally, it is possible to get by with fewer storage areas than the number base, simply by converting to a smaller number base. This naturally is only possible when it is easy to carry out the number base conversion. In practice, the only place this stratagem

TABLE 8

PASS 2 INPUT	STORAGE AREA										
	0	1	2	3	4	5	6	7	8	9
70	06	12	27	34	46	58	60	70		91
60		14	29	35			68			
91		17		36						
12		18								
34										
14										
35										
06										
36										
46										
17										
27										
58										
18										
68										
29										

would be used would be in radix sorting on a computer when less than eleven tape units are available.

Radix sorting of alphabetics could be handled by setting up a "pocket" (in our case, a tape) for each character, but the number of pockets would be excessive. Instead, other approaches are taken. We may as well discuss these in punched card terms, since that is where radix sorting finds widest application. There are two rather different methods in use, both of which require more than one pass per character. The first method uses the first pass to distribute the records to five storage areas: one for the digits 0–9, one for the letters A–I, one for the letters J–R, one for the letters S–Z, and one for all the special characters. (This distribution is based on the punched card representation of the characters.) Each of these must be sorted separately and the five groups recombined, although it is possible to combine the sorting of each group with the recombination. Savings can be effected if the keys are known not to contain any numbers or special characters. The second method, which has been mechanized for a punched card sorter, takes all possible advantage of the fact that certain letters occur more frequently than others. We shall illustrate the method for a key containing only alphabetic characters. Twelve pockets are designated 0, 1, 2, 3, 4, 5, 6, 7, 8, 9, 11, and 12.

On the first pass the records are distributed to pockets as shown in Table 9.

SORTING

TABLE 9

POCKET	KEY CHARACTERS
0	A
1	C
2	E
3	G
4	I
5	L
6	O
7	R
8	U
9	X
11	B, D, F, H, J, M, P, S, V, Y
12	K, N, Q, T, W, Z

On the second pass, the records which were distributed to the 11 pocket are distributed to pockets 0–9, without removing the records already in these pockets. (Table 10.)

TABLE 10

POCKET	KEY CHARACTERS
0	A, B
1	C, D
2	E, F
3	G, H
4	I, J
5	L, M
6	O, P
7	R, S
8	U, V
9	X, Y

On the third pass the records from the 12 pocket are distributed to pockets 4–9. (Table 11.)

TABLE 11

POCKET	KEY CHARACTERS
0	A, B
1	C, D
2	E, F
3	G, H
4	I, J, K
5	L, M, N
6	O, P, Q
7	R, S, T
8	U, V, W
9	X, Y, Z

When the records are recombined, they are in alphabetic order. The primary advantage of this method is that only about half of the file, on the average, is distributed to the 11 and 12 pockets on the first pass because the occurrence of the letters is not uniform. The method can be extended to include numbers and special characters.

The six file characteristics:

1. Key length: very important. It is obvious that at least as many passes must be made as there are digits in the key, not counting collection passes.

2. Key range: possibly important. In the situation mentioned earlier, where the file consists of 300 records with keys between 9999700 to 9999999, the sort would need to be made only on the last three digits. Actual situations are seldom so simple, but fairly frequently it happens in radix sorting that some advantage can be taken of special characteristics of the keys.

3. Degree of ordering: no importance. No advantage can be taken of initial ordering unless it is realized in advance, because any ordering is lost as soon as the first pass is made. To take advantage of initial ordering requires individual human attention to the file, which is possible only in punched card sorting.

4. File storage type: quite important. For use with random access storage, better methods are available. One serious limitation of the method for random access storage is the fact that each temporary storage area must be as long as the original file, to allow for the possibility that some digit of the key will be the same for all keys of the file. For example, it might happen that all keys start with zero. This would be unlikely, and if one knew it in advance the pass for that character could be skipped, but it could be *nearly* true. It is decidedly not possible to set up the temporary storage areas only a little larger than one-tenth the length of the initial file, which is what would be needed if all digits of the keys were evenly distributed.

5. Number of records in file: fairly important. The number of records which must be moved is proportional to the product of the number of records in the file and the number of digits in the keys.

6. Record length: quite important, usually. Since each record must be moved many times, much of the processing activity is proportional in time to the record length. This is often not true in punched card sorting, however, since any number of characters, up to the number of columns on the card, may be moved with no additional time penalty. This leads to the not uncommon practice of sorting

the input to an electronic computer on punched card equipment, since it can be considerably cheaper in many cases.*

15.6 Straight Merge Sorting

Sorting by selection, exchanging, and insertion are suitable for short files and for random access storage, which means in electronic computing that they are suitable for sorting in high-speed memory. Radix sorting is suitable for tape sorting if the keys are short and numeric, but useless otherwise. We come then to merge sorting, which is about the only feasible approach to sorting large tape files with the type of keys usually encountered. As we shall see, there are many

TABLE 12

PASS 1 ORIGINAL	OUTPUT TAPES A	B
34	34	06
06	91	70
91	17	27
70	58	14
17	35	36
27	18	12
58	68	46
14	29	60
35		
36		
18		
12		
68		
46		
29		
60		

variations of merge sorts, and they are almost always used in conjunction with other methods which reduce the number of passes required.

The simplest variety of merge sort is a two-way merge with fixed-length strings. The essence of the method is to begin with strings one record long, then build up strings of two records, then four, then

* Except that it is possible to make a great many mistakes in punched card sorting, especially of large files. Estimates of sorting costs must take into account the expense of recovering from the effects of such mistakes. Also, punched card sorting takes considerably longer than electronic sorting, in most cases, which may affect scheduling of machine operations.

eight, etc., doubling the length of the strings at each pass, until finally there is only one string the length of the file. To be more specific, we start with the unsorted file on one tape, and distribute the records to two other tapes, alternate records going to alternate tapes, which we shall call tapes A and B. Table 12 shows the first pass of sorting our sample records.

We now have two tapes, each with eight records. If we now take one record from tape A and one from B, we can write the two of them in correct sequence onto another tape, which we shall call C. Taking the next two records from A and B, we write them in correct sequence onto a tape D. This process is continued, taking one record each from A and B, and writing them in correct sequence alternately on C and D. This is shown in Table 13.

TABLE 13

PASS 2

A	B	C	D
(from pass 1)			
34	06	06	70
91	70	34	91
17	27	17	14
58	14	27	58
35	36	35	12
18	12	36	18
68	46	46	29
29	60	68	60

We are now guaranteed of having four strings of two records each on each tape. Observe that one of the tapes C or D could have been the tape which contained the original file. Besides being easier to explain without doing this, it is fairly common practice to save the input file for purposes of safety. That is, if something should happen in the middle of the sort to destroy one of the tapes or otherwise make it impossible to continue sorting, it would be possible to start over at the beginning if the original file had been saved by not writing on that tape in the merging process.

We now have a total of eight two-record strings on the tapes. Actually there may be fewer strings than that, as it happens, but the fixed-string method will not take advantage of the fact. We would now like to produce a total of four strings of four records each. To do so, we first read a record from C and one from D and write the one having the smaller key on tape A. We then read another record from whichever tape supplied the record which was written onto A.

SORTING

We next write the record having the smaller of the two keys now under consideration onto tape A, and read the last of the four records from the appropriate tape. These last two records are finally written in correct sequence on tape A. The process is repeated, this time writing onto tape B. It is continued until tapes C and D have been completely read. (Table 14.)

TABLE 14

PASS 3

C	D	A	B
(from pass 2)			
06	70	06	14
34	91	34	17
17	14	70	27
27	58	91	58
35	12	12	29
36	18	18	46
46	29	35	60
68	60	36	68

The next pass follows exactly the same scheme, except that strings read and produced are now four and eight records long, respectively. (Table 15.)

TABLE 15

PASS 4

A	B	C	D
(from pass 3)			
06	14	06	12
34	17	14	18
70	27	17	29
91	58	27	35
12	29	34	36
18	46	58	46
35	60	70	60
36	68	91	68

The final pass (in this case) consists simply of merging the two eight-record strings onto one tape to produce one sixteen-record string which is the final sorted file. (Table 16.)

It will be observed that the problem has been simplified by starting with a number of records which is a power of two. This is not in any sense a limitation of the method; it was done only to simplify the explanation. With proper consideration of sentinels or tape marks to

TABLE 16

PASS 5

C (from pass 4)	D	SORTED FILE A
06	12	06
14	18	12
17	29	14
27	35	17
34	36	18
58	46	27
70	60	29
91	68	34
		35
		36
		46
		58
		60
		68
		70
		91

signal the ends of the files, which we have neglected throughout, a file of any size can be handled.

The procedure shown above is the simplest possible version of merge sorting. One improvement, which would surely be made in practice, would be to eliminate one pass by forming two-record strings when the input file is distributed to tapes A and B. This leads to the observation that anything which can be done in the first pass to lengthen the strings will materially reduce the total number of passes. At any point in a two-way fixed-string merge, the number of remaining passes is given by

$$N = [\log_2 S]$$

where N is the number of passes remaining, and S is the total number of strings on all tapes. The brackets mean that we take the *next larger integer* if $\log_2 S$ is not an integer.* Notice that this formula does not count what we called the "original" pass, which in the example may be seen to perform no merging.

Let us now investigate what the formula implies about the value of

* $N = [\log_2 S]$ is simply mathematical shorthand for "N is the power to which 2 must be raised to equal or exceed S." Thus if $S = 16$, $[\log_2 16] = 4$, which is exactly the same as saying that $2^4 = 16$. If $S = 200$, $[\log_2 200] = 8$, since the smallest power to which 2 can be raised and get a number greater than 200 is 8 ($2^8 = 256$).

SORTING

reducing the number of strings by an initial *string-building* pass. Suppose we have a file of 50,000 records to be sorted. If we start by simply distributing the records to two tapes as in the example, producing two tapes with 25,000 records each, the number of passes will be

$$N = [\log_2 50{,}000] = 16$$

which with the initial distributing pass totals seventeen passes. However, if on the first pass we use one of the earlier methods to build strings of 100 records and distribute them to two tapes, we will have 250 strings of 100 records each on the two tapes, requiring

$$N = [\log_2 500] = 9$$

passes to merge, which with the initial string-building and distributing pass totals ten passes. The first pass will, of course, be longer than it was before, and complexity has unquestionably been added to the routine, but the saving of seven passes over the file of 50,000 records would be well worth the trouble. This is because, in general, the tape reading and writing times saved would considerably exceed the extra internal processing time. With twelve-word records and assuming typical current tape characteristics, this would save half an hour of computer time at an absolute minimum.

There is a break-even point principle here, however. One cannot blindly assume that *anything* which reduces the number of passes is worthwhile. We must compare the time saved by reducing the number of passes with the time and effort added to the program by doing so. In sorting, as elsewhere, ideas which look good in theory may fall apart in practice.

We have so far spoken of a two-way merge, which is often called a four-tape merge for obvious reasons. It is perfectly possible, and not uncommon, to use three- or even four-way merges. With a three-way merge, the input file is first distributed to *three* tapes, then built into strings using a total of six tapes. The general formula for the number of passes in an n-way merge (as usual not counting the initial distributing pass) is

$$N = [\log_n S]$$

where the symbols N and S are defined as before. Applying a three-way merge to the sort of 50,000 records, we would initially produce two tapes with 16,667 records each and one with 16,666; the number of passes after this would be

$$N = [\log_3 50{,}000] = 10$$

which totals eleven passes with the initial pass. Compared to the seventeen passes required by the two-way merge, we have a significant reduction in the number of passes, if the extra tapes are available. Building strings of 100 records and distributing to three tapes on the first pass, we require only a total of seven passes to sort the file. The corresponding figures for a four-way merge are nine and six. Thus the four-way merge does not make nearly as much improvement over the three-way as the three-way makes over the two-way, which is true in general. Furthermore, the four-way merge requires eight tapes, which may be more than are available, and the internal processing is more complex and therefore slower. It is entirely possible to use what might be called "mixed-way" merges, e.g., merging from three tapes to two, then from two to three, etc. The saving is usually not worth the extra trouble, however.

Checking a two-way fixed-string merge sort against the six file characteristics:

1. Key length: little bearing, except as usual for any coding difficulty in dealing with long keys.
2. Key range: no bearing.
3. Degree of ordering: no bearing.
4. File storage type: important. The method actually *may* be used with random access storage, but it offers no particular advantage over other methods unless the file is long, which at present implies the use of magnetic tapes. Very powerful for sequential files.
5. Number of records in file: important in one sense. The method is not economical for short files, so we might say that the files must be long for the method to be applicable. However, the difference between, say, 10,000 records and 30,000 records does not affect total sort time in any such disastrous manner as it does with some of the other methods where the total record movement is proportional to the square of the number of records, in the worst case.
6. Record length: little bearing. The longer the record, the more tape time is required, but total time is not directly proportional to record length because usually not all the sort time is spent in moving tape.

15.7 Probability Merge Sorting

In essence, a probability merge sort is quite similar to an ordinary merge sort except that full advantage is taken of any and all ordering of the original file. The strings are not restricted to fixed lengths,

SORTING

and the number of passes will depend on the number of strings in the original file. For a file which is in correct sequence, only one pass is required: that needed to discover that the file is in sequence. If the number of strings is more than half of the number of records in the file, the probability merge saves no passes over a straight merge.

The heart of a two-way probability merge can be briefly stated as follows. As long as a record can be found which has a key larger than or equal to the key of the record most recently written on an output tape, we continue to build the string. If two records are available, *both* of which satisfy this criterion, we write out the one having the smaller key. Each time a record is written, we get a new record from the tape that supplied that record. When both of the records in memory have keys which are less than the key of the record most recently written, we switch to the other output tape and start building another string, using the same procedure. As usual, the first pass reads only one tape. The end of the pass is easily determined, if sentinels are used which "sort high," i.e., are larger than any key in the file. Incidentally, if this is done, no thought whatsoever need be given to the number of records in the file, as must be done with a straight merge.

As soon as the input tapes have been completely read, the "input" and "output" tapes are "switched" and the process repeated. When a pass is made which results in the entire file being written on only one output tape, the sort is complete. The procedure may be illustrated with an example, shown in Table 17. Here, the passes are shown across the page, the two output tapes of one pass becoming the input of the next pass. The beginnings of strings are marked with asterisks.

In this case the probability merge saved nothing over a straight two-way merge in which two-record strings are built on the first pass. Suppose, however, that the file had been slightly different, namely, that the records with the keys of 29 and 60 had been the third and fourth records instead of the last two. This rather slight change in the file results in one less pass, illustrating the dependence of the number of passes on original ordering. (Table 18.)

Determination of where a merge sort lies between these two extremes of only one pass and the same number of passes as a straight merge is a matter requiring considerable knowledge of the file in question, together with advanced statistical analysis. It is doubtful, however, whether many business files are processed where the initial ordering is so good that there would be no need to use some type of string-building procedure on the first pass.

TABLE 17

	PASS 1		PASS 2		PASS 3		PASS 4	
ORIGINAL	A	B	C	D	A	B	C	D
*34	*06	*17	*06	*12	*06	*29	*06	
*06	34	27	17	14	12	60	12	
91	70	58	27	18	14		14	
*70	91	*12	34	35	17		17	
17	*14	18	58	36	18		18	
*27	35	46	70	46	27		27	
58	36	68	91	68	34		29	
*14	*29		*29		35		34	
35	60		60		36		35	
36					46		36	
*18					58		46	
*12					68		58	
68					70		60	
*46					91		68	
*29							70	
60							91	

Checking the six file characteristics as applied to the method:

1. Key length: little bearing except, as usual, that long keys may cause coding difficulty in some machines.
2. Key range: no bearing.

TABLE 18

	PASS 1		PASS 2		PASS 3	
ORIGINAL	A	B	C	D	A	B
*34	*06	*17	*06	*12	*06	
*06	29	27	17	14	12	
29	34	58	27	18	14	
60	60	*12	29	35	17	
91	70	18	34	36	18	
*70	91	46	58	46	27	
*17	*14	68	60	68	29	
27	35		70		34	
58	36		91		35	
*14					36	
35					46	
36					58	
*18					60	
*12					68	
68					70	
*46					91	

3. Degree of ordering: important. See discussion above.
4. File storage type: see discussion under point 4 on page 320.
5. Number of records in file: see discussion under point 5 on page 320.
6. Record length: see discussion under point 6 on page 320.

15.8 A Flow-Charted Example

All of the discussions so far have been greatly simplified by the omission of detailed procedures for starting the sort, for determining when the ends of the various storage areas have been reached, and for determining when the sort is completed. To give the reader a little of the flavor of the preciseness with which such matters must be specified, a detailed flow chart for the probability merge method is shown in Figure 1. Inevitably, such a flow chart uses some arbitrary symbols and conventions, which must be explained.

The first convention appears in the first box of the flow chart, which shows part of the initializing section. Some notation must be invented to represent the fact that the functions of the four tape units change as the program progresses. On the first pass, there is only one input tape and two outputs. On the second pass, the two "output" tapes become "input" as the files are merged back onto the tape which contained the original file, plus another tape. Furthermore, the merging always involves only one output tape at any moment; when a string is ended, the other output tape must be designated as the tape to be written on next. Thus, while there are always two input tapes (except on the first pass) and two outputs (except on the last pass), the function of each actual physical tape unit is continually changing. In coding, this means changing the tape designations in the tape reading and writing instructions. On the flow chart, the situation is handled by designating the *physical* tapes as 1, 2, 3, and 4; the *functions* of the tapes are designated by the letters A, B, C, and D. Tape A contains the input file; tapes A and (except on first pass) B are always input tapes; tape C is always the current output tape. Thus, the symbolism C ↔ D means to change the appropriate tape writing instructions so that the *other* output tape, whichever one it may *actually* be, becomes the current output tape. (It does not imply physically changing the tape reels.) The first box shows the initial correspondence between the actual and functional designations of the four tapes. (It should be pointed out that this procedure means that the input file is destroyed by the sort. This is often not wise; modification of the flow chart to show the use of four tapes *in addition*

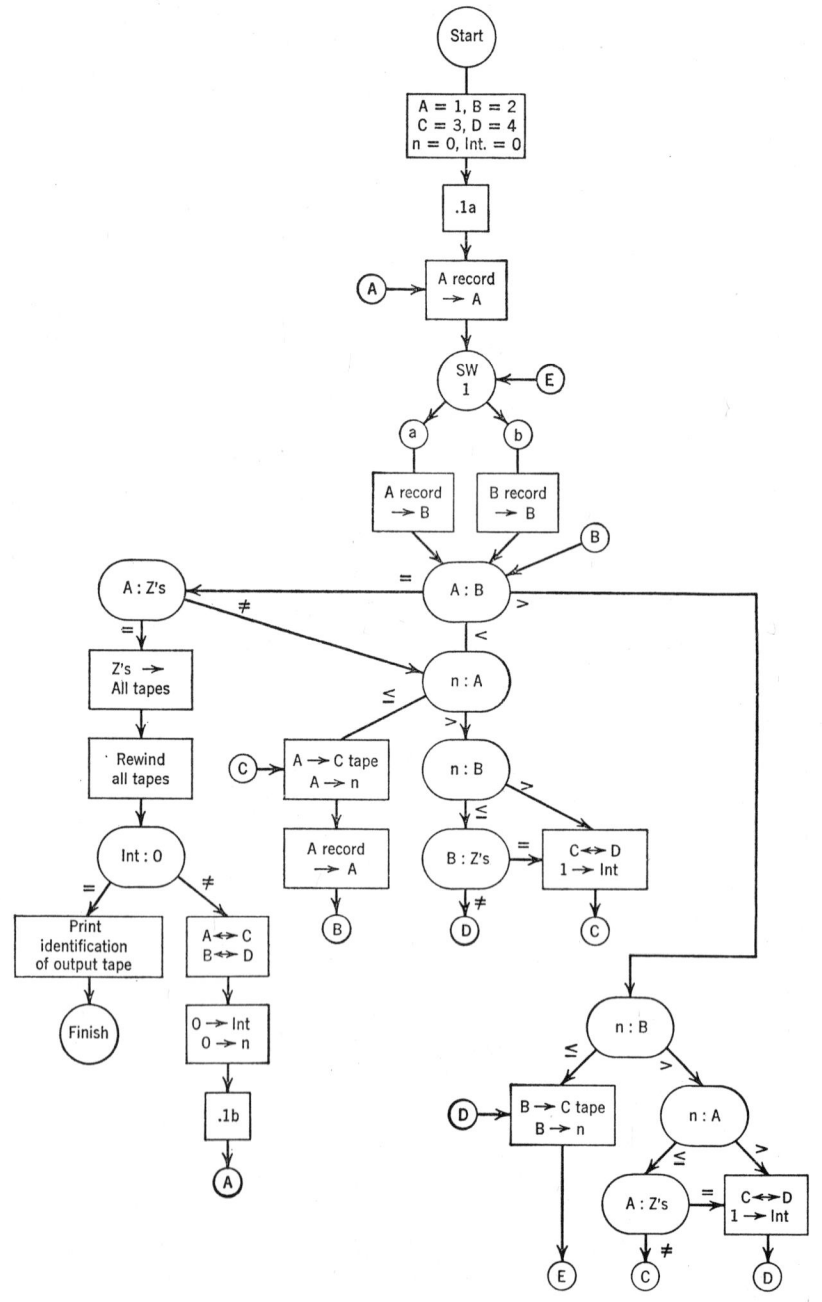

Figure 1. Flow chart of a probability merge sort. The assumptions made and the symbols are explained in the text.

SORTING

to the input tape would not be difficult. Alternatively, the input file tape could be removed after the first pass and another reel substituted.)

The letter n is used to indicate the key of the record most recently written on an output tape. This must always be known so that strings can be made as long as possible. n is initially set to zero (or to whatever is the smallest character in the Compare instruction's collation sequence) so that the program will not be "confused" as to the status of the first record on each pass. The symbol "Int" is used to indicate what will be called here the *interchange indicator*. The way the program knows it is finished with the sort, as set up here, is by keeping a record of whether it was ever necessary to interchange output tapes; if not, then the entire file must have been one long string on one tape and the sort is completed. Int is set to zero initially, and each time the output tapes are interchanged, a 1 is stored in the location assigned to the indicator. Then when each pass is completed, this location can be inspected by the program to determine if more passes are needed.

Switch 1 is used to control the reading of the input tapes; on the first pass we wish to read from tape A exclusively, but on following passes from both A and B. Switch 1 is set to the a path at the start of the program, and set to the b path at the end of the first pass (and of all following passes, as it happens here).

Two working storage areas are assumed in memory, designated A and B to signify that they correspond to functional tapes A and B. On the first pass, however, both of them are loaded from tape A as shown by the action of switch 1.

At all times we wish to write onto tape C whichever of the two records in working storage has the smaller key; the comparison A:B sets up this choice. Before going into the operation of the "greater than" and "lesser than" paths out of this comparison, however, we must observe that at this point we have a simple way of detecting the end of a pass. Assume that *sentinels* (see page 245) are written at the end of each input tape to signify the end of information. We shall assume that a sentinel record contains a key made up of Z's, since Z compares higher than any other letter or number in DATAC. Then if at any comparison we find that both keys are equal and consist of Z sentinels, we know that all the records on both input tapes have been read, and written on the output tape(s). Accordingly, the "equal" path out of the A:B key comparison goes to a comparison which determines whether one of the keys was a sentinel; if one was, both were. If so, the end-of-pass routine is entered; if not, i.e., if we simply have two records with the same key, we wish to return to the main stream with the net effect of a "less than or equal" path. We shall examine the end-of-pass and end-of-sort procedures shortly. (This particular set of assumptions forces us to record *two* consecutive sentinels on the original file. This is not realistic, perhaps, but the added complexity required in the flow chart to handle a single sentinel is more trouble than it is worth for our purposes here.)

Suppose that the key of the A record is less than or equal to the key of the B record. We now want to know if n, the key of the last record written, is less than or equal to the key of A, because if so, the A record continues a string and may simply be written on tape. The n:A comparison sets up this choice. If A does fit in the string, it is simply written on the C tape, the A key is recorded as n, a new record is read from the A tape into the A working storage area, and the program returns to the A:B comparison.

If n is greater than the A key, then the A record is out of sequence, but perhaps the B record is still in sequence. Accordingly, a comparison between n and B is made. If n is less than or equal to the B key, it means that the B record will fit into the string, *unless the B key is a sentinel*. A test for this possibility is made, and if the B key is not a sentinel, connector D takes us to the box which calls for writing the B record on the C tape, etc. If n is greater than the B key or if the B key is a sentinel, then functional tapes C and D are interchanged, a 1 stored in the interchange indicator, and connector C takes us to the box which calls for the A record (which was the smaller of the two) to be written out on tape C—which is now a different physical tape.

The path out of the A:B comparison when the A key is greater than the B key is very similar to the above, except that the B record is now the one with the smaller key and the various operations are arranged accordingly. At the point where a new record is to be read from the B tape we find connector E which returns to switch 1 to decide, in effect, whether this is the first pass or not.

Now we may return to the question of what happens if the A:B comparison shows equal and the subsequent comparison shows that the keys are sentinels. This means, as we discussed, that the pass is complete. In any case we then wish to write sentinels on the output tapes and rewind all the tapes. It may happen, however, that because of coding problems it is easier to write sentinels on all the tapes, as shown here. Next we must determine by inspecting the interchange indicator whether the sort is complete. If it is, we print on the console typewriter or on-line printer an indication to the operator as to which tape contains the sorted file, since it could be any

SORTING 327

one of the four physical tapes. This may be done simply by inspecting, through coding, the tape unit specified by any of the instructions which call for writing on tape C.

If the sort is not finished, we interchange tapes A and C, and B and D; reset the interchange indicator and n to zero; set switch 1 to the b path, and return through connector A to start the following pass.

15.9 Computer Considerations in Sorting

The characteristics of the computer at hand can have an important effect on the way the sorting problem is attacked. A few of these may be mentioned briefly.

All tape units in current use require an appreciable amount of time to get up to full speed before the first record can be written or read. This is called either *acceleration time* or *start/stop time*. With fairly short records, the acceleration time is considerably longer than the time required to read the entire record. This leads, as we have seen, to grouping records into blocks on tape. In any situation except the fairly uncommon one of extremely long records, the sort program would have to take into account this grouping of records into tape blocks. This naturally adds complexity to the programming but does not change any of the sorting concepts we have discussed.

The problem of long keys can result in considerable expenditure of time in making the many comparisons required in any sorting procedure. In a variable word length computer, this is not particularly difficult to code but even in this case it may involve a considerable cost in machine time. One technique for getting around this time expenditure is to observe that if the high-order character or word of the key is sufficient to establish the comparison, then the rest of the key need not be compared. If it is not, then of course the rest of the key must be examined. For instance, by looking at only the first digit it can be established that the key 5329 is greater than 3278. With four digit keys one would probably not bother to take advantage of this fact, but with forty digit keys (which can happen) it may be well worth it to go to the trouble. It is probably not worthwhile to make this comparison on a character-by-character basis, but rather in small groups of characters. In fixed word length computers this breakup of long keys occurs automatically. With variable word length machines special action may be required to conserve time.

Certain types of applications involve sorting files which contain a large number of records with identical keys. For instance, in a check accounting application a certain branch bank may receive

10,000 payroll checks weekly from some large industrial firm in the area it serves. All these checks have the same account number. Depending on the circumstances and the computer, it may save considerable time to make a preliminary pass which writes these high-frequency items onto a separate tape, and then handle them separately later.

It is entirely possible to build equipment which mechanizes some sorting method rather than program a general-purpose computer to do it. This has been done in a few cases, with the probability merge method typically being used.

A number of general computer characteristics will influence the choice of sorting methods for a given application.

1. The characteristics of the large sequential access storage available, if any, which in practice comes down to the number of magnetic tape units available.

2. The size of the internal high-speed memory, which must do the entire job if tapes or magnetic disks are not available, and which is used in any case to build strings on the first pass.

3. The structure of the operation code list of the machine. Of particular importance in this connection are: any indexing facility which may be available which simplifies the *item advance* operations, i.e., moving through the group of records from a tape block; indexing facilities which simplify tape alternation; the facilities for making comparisons on alpha-numeric keys of varying lengths; the facilities for making memory-to-memory transfers of records.

4. The characteristics of input/output equipment, such as the availability of buffers, the maximum and minimum lengths of tape records, the tape rewind time, and the ability of the machine to read tape backwards—which makes it unnecessary to rewind tapes between passes on several of the sorting methods.

15.10 Sort Generators

In the early days of the application of computers to sorting, a different program was typically written for every different application. For example, several thousand instructions might be written for a three-way merge to sort 50,000 records, 30 digits long with 12 character keys; and on a different application several thousand more instructions would be written for a three-way merge to sort 10,000 records, 80 digits long with 24 character keys. A comparison of the two programs showed that large sections of the two programs were essentially the same. Other sections differed only because of the different file characteristics involved. Realizing this, effort was then put into writing a general sort program which left many instructions as variables that could be set up in an initial phase of each sort run. Naturally the setup phase of the program required memory space and execution time. This space and time was wasted every time the program was used.

The final refinement of sorting programs, at present at least, is to separate the setup phase from the actual running of the program. A *sort generator* program accepts the specifications of the file to be sorted and the way to go about it (such as two-way or three-way merge) and *generates*, or produces, a complete sort program. During this generation phase no sorting is performed; thus it is analogous to assembly or compiling phases in automatic programming. After the sort program has been generated it may be used over and over without wasting the setup time or memory space every time it is used.

Sort generators may become extremely complex if one attempts to include a wide variety of file conditions or to produce a highly efficient program under widely varying conditions. As we have seen in so many other cases, some type of compromise must be made between what is desirable and what is practical. It is often necessary to provide a number of different sort generators for widely varying purposes, and it is often possible to incorporate small sections of "handwritten" coding.

15.11 Systems Considerations in Sorting

It is usually not efficient to sort a tape file consisting of many reels of tape in one sort run. Rather, each reel of the file is sorted separately and then the sorted reels are merged. There are many different ways to merge a number of reels of tape into one or more reels. If the number of reels to be merged is greater than the number of available tape units, which very frequently happens, several merge passes may be required. We may state in general that the optimum method of setting up the merging is the one that requires the least number of "reel passes." Unfortunately, it is not possible to state any general rules of how to accomplish the minimization.

The sorting operation is seldom isolated from other operations in a data processing application. A file to be sorted is often an output file from some other run; the sorted file usually becomes the input file to a following run. Furthermore, there are many tasks which are closely related to sorting or which may be done as part of a sorting run, such as editing, batch balancing, creating new control totals, etc. In general, sorting should be planned as an integral part of the overall application and the selection of the sorting method should be made in the light of any associated tasks which may be lumped with the sort run. For example, suppose it is required to edit, batch-balance, sort, sequence-check, and create new control totals for 50,000 cash payment records, then merge the sorted file with another file. One approach would be to precede the sort with a run which edits and batch-balances and follow it with a run which sequence-checks, creates new control totals, and merges the file with another file. However, this would add two extra passes of the file to be sorted. A much more satisfactory approach would be to combine the editing and batch-balancing operations with the first sort pass and combine the functions of sequence checking, creation of new control totals, and merging with the other file with the last sort pass.

It may be possible in some cases to avoid completely the need to sort, by means of system design—especially as larger memories and random access devices become available. Transaction information can sometimes be arranged to arrive at the data processing center in sequence, either by prior punched card sorting or by other means. A sequence check can then be made, as a double-check on the ordering of the input, to determine if sorting is required.

As a final indication of the type of systems consideration which should be given to sorting, suppose that we are faced with the choice between a four-way merge and a three-way merge at a given point in an application. The four-way merge of course takes less time, but on the other hand it ties up eight tape units. If only ten tape units are available altogether, the speed gained by using a four-way merge may be completely lost because of considerations having to do with preceding or following runs. If, for instance, four tape reels from the preceding run have to be removed before the sorting can begin, and if four other tape reels have to be mounted before the following run can begin, tying up eight tape units in the four-way merge will mean that the machine has to stand idle while the tapes are changed. However, with a three-way merge all of the tape changing can be done during the sort run. This type of thing is easily overlooked and can make the difference between a mediocre job and a good one.

We have seen that with all of the sorting methods, characteristics of the key have some influence on the ease or speed with which sorting may be done. In some of the methods, it is a critical influence. Wherever it is possible the systems designer should attempt to set up the keys in such a way as to simplify the operations involving them. It is unfortunately true, however, that for historic reasons this is often completely impossible. For instance, a certain electric utility company has 1½ million customers, which would require in theory only seven numerical digits in the key; in fact, fourteen alpha-numeric characters are used so that the entire file can be kept in geographical location sequence. This sort of thing is frequently encountered. The systems designer can in some cases revise the keys entirely; in others, he may be able to make slight modifications; in other cases, the historic precedent may be so strong or the cost of key changes so great that the original key structure must be accepted as it stands even though expensive in terms of computer time.

15.12 Summary

On most, although not all, computer applications sorting is an integral part of the data processing. We have attempted to present a number of different sorting methods which can be used and to show in broad outline how they compare with each other. The final choice, however, must always be made in the light of the particular machine at hand, the characteristics of the files to be sorted, and the programming time available.

Exercises

1. Sort these keys

    391, 638, 126, 268, 748, 227, 469, 073, 536, 845, 521, 109, 917, 360

into ascending sequence by the following methods:
   (a) Selection.
   (b) Exchanging.
   (c) Insertion.
   (d) Radix.
   (e) Straight merge (2-way).
   (f) Probability merge (2-way).

2. Sort these keys

    89, 47, 38, 28, 55, 42, 07, 19, 13, 62, 49, 35, 30, 24, 13, 19, 45, 81, 64, 52, 95, 77, 84, 47, 70, 01, 19

into descending sequence by the following methods:
   (a) Straight merge (2-way).
   (b) Probability merge (2-way).
   (c) Straight merge (3-way).

3. Sort these keys

    bear, dogs, cats, rats, deer, wolf, lion, rams, fawn, bull, goat, mule, hare, lamb, swan, boar

into ascending sequence by the following methods:
   (a) Selection.
   (b) Exchanging.
   (c) Insertion.
   (d) Straight merge (2-way).
   (e) Probability merge (2-way).

4. Why is sorting important in electronic data processing? Is it important in manual or punched card data processing?

5. In electronic data processing, what other functions besides sequencing of records require sorting? Name and discuss at least two such functions.

6. Discuss the salient characteristics of the computer which affect sorting in general, and for each sorting method.

7. Discuss the salient characteristics of the file which affect sorting in general, and for each sorting method.

8. Discuss the relative advantages and disadvantages of the probability merge and the straight merge. Suggest a situation where the probability merge would have a distinct advantage over the straight merge.

9. Assuming that we are not limited as to the number of tape units, is it true that a 3-way merge is always more efficient than a 2-way; 4-way more efficient than 3-way; 5-way more efficient than 4-way? Discuss.

10. What other piece of standard equipment besides the sorter may be used for sorting in a punched card installation? How? (*Hint:* One possible method would involve a probability merge.)

11. A sort program for a computer is usually divided into three parts: the *first pass, the second and subsequent but not last,* and the *last pass.* What are some of the data processing functions that may be added to each of the three parts (e.g., balancing batch totals)?

12. The number of passes in a merge sort depends on the number of strings. Suggest a way of determining, at the end of each pass, whether the *next* pass will be the last one.

13. The probability merge sort is flow-charted in the text. Flow-chart the other methods, taking into consideration any differences between the first and subsequent passes, and including end-of-pass and end-of-sort tests.

14. In exchange sorting, we know the sort is complete when a pass is made which requires no exchanges. Can we say anything analogous for selection sorting?

15. How could the availability of a large random access auxiliary storage device (Chapter 19) eliminate completely the need for sorting in some applications? How about increasing the size of high-speed memory?

16 ECONOMIZING AND ESTIMATING COMPUTER TIME

16.0 Introduction

It is an established historic fact that many of the early business electronic data processing installations nearly "went on the rocks"— in fact, a few actually did so. Naturally, the factors causing such a fiasco are many and varied, but one of the most important was the failure to estimate the realistic time requirements of an application. There are cases where the actual time required exceeded the estimated time by a factor of three or four, leading to an impossible situation for both the user and the manufacturer of the equipment. Time estimates must be considered in the selection of the best computer for a given application, whether the choice is between competitive equipment or between different sizes or types of equipment from one manufacturer. Furthermore, the claims and counterclaims of various systems of processing, such as sequential versus random access processing, have no meaning apart from a careful consideration of the time and cost *for a particular application.*

After the application and computer have been selected, skillfully carried-out time estimates should serve as a guide in planning an efficient and realistic approach. During the months usually required for programming and coding, it should be expected that there will be many changes made both in the statement of the problem and in the general scheme of programming approach. Every change will affect the time required. It is wise to re-estimate time and cost periodically, and especially before committing the programming staff to a major change. For example, suppose the original time estimate for a particular application was 10 hours per day based on a 5-day file maintenance cycle (processing one-fifth of the master file each day so the complete file will be processed in a 5-day cycle). If it should later be required to change the file maintenance cycle from 5 to 4 days, a superficial estimate of the new time required would be 10 × 5/4 = 12.5 hours per day; more careful analysis, however, would more likely show this estimate to be significantly in error. The trap in this case is that total computer time required for an application is not directly proportional to the amount of data involved: such things as tape reel changing, sorting times, etc., make the proportionality assumption invalid. One must be constantly alert to such traps.

In the body of this chapter, we shall examine the time and cost considerations involved at three different levels of the preparation of a data processing application:

1. *Systems design,* where top level flow charts of the entire application (page 27) are drawn, and the contents (but not the detailed layout) of the various files decided upon, and, sometimes, the processing allotted to the various computer runs.

2. *Programming,* where over-all flow charts for each computer run are drawn and the formats or detailed layouts of the files and memory are designed. This level begins with the "output" of the systems design level and plans the structure of each computer program, within the framework of the over-all problem approach decided upon in systems design.

3. *Coding,* where the results of the previous levels are translated into actual computer language (often, of course, with the assistance of assembly and compiling programs). This is the level where all the detailed work is done and where the final program used by the computer is produced.

Before proceeding to the time implications of each level, it should be pointed out that a system of information feedback between the three levels is essential. For instance, it is quite common to discover, as programming proceeds, ways to improve the systems design. A typical case of this type is the division of the application into runs; it is often discovered that a particular run exceeds memory capacity and must be split into two separate runs, or that it is possible to combine several runs into one run. Another example is the detailed layout of the various files. It is very difficult to determine before some of the flow charting and coding is done what the effect will be of changes in file contents and layout.

It should always be kept in mind that the primary objective of the planning of an application is to minimize the *over-all* cost. We have in mind here the too frequent tendency to evaluate alternative approaches solely on the basis of machine time per day required,

ECONOMIZING AND ESTIMATING COMPUTER TIME

without proper weight being given to the cost of such things as programming and coding, file conversion, and cost of extra equipment which may be required. In this chapter we shall discuss primarily the time and cost of the final computer program, but the other considerations should be kept in mind constantly.

16.1 Timing Considerations in Systems Design

Systems design is probably the most important of the three levels mentioned above. It is the level where the basic decisions are made which determine the general course and organization of the entire application. The following are some of the basic decisions required:

1. Should this application be done at all?
2. What is the best computer system for the application?
3. Should the entire application be put on the computer or are there some phases of it that can more economically or efficiently be done by other methods?
4. What is the estimated daily computer time for carrying out each of the alternative approaches?
5. What is the over-all cost of each alternative?

It is clear that a wrong decision at the systems design level may mean the difference between success and failure in a data processing application. It is also clear that the most important decisions which are made at this level depend on estimates of computer time. Thus it is obvious that a careful examination of the factors affecting time requirements at the systems design level must be made.

One of the important examples of this concept is the planning of the various files used in the system, which affects the total time required to carry out an application. The size (both record size and number of records) and over-all design of a master file determine to a large extent the time required to process it. A larger master file requires more updating and takes longer to read. If one master file is broken up into several smaller files, the processing will also be longer because of the duplication of information; for instance, the same key must be carried in each and some means of cross reference must be included if the files are not in the same sequence. However, in the many cases where it is uneconomical to use only one master file, the contents of the various files should be planned very carefully to avoid all *unnecessary* duplication.

The design of keys used in files can have a very significant effect on total time. For instance, a long key usually takes longer to test than a short one. Perhaps more fundamentally, choice of the type of key implies the selection of the sequence of processing the records. From the standpoint of computer time it is unfortunate that the systems designer often has little control over the design of keys; there are many cases where it is not practical to change such things as part numbers or customer account numbers which are in very wide use, even though the existing keys are extremely cumbersome and a redesign could result in appreciable cost savings in data processing. Furthermore, it is true here, as in many other instances, that a realistic compromise must be made between what is best for the computer and what is best for the user of the computer. (As a trivial example of this point from a different field, we may note that telephone numbers could just as well be entirely numerical from the standpoint of the telephone, but they would be much harder to remember from the standpoint of the user.)

It is often necessary to make compromises in the manner in which records are stored in a master file. It is a paradox that in general a tape with an "efficient" arrangement of the information takes more processing time than a slightly less "efficiently" arranged file. For instance, less total tape time is required in certain types of machines if several pieces of information are "packed" into one word—but of course the packing and unpacking of this information inside the computer takes time, too. It should be pointed out immediately, however, and this is a crucial point, that in tape processing the limiting factor is often the time required to *read* the tape, *not* the time required to process the information once it has been read from tape. Many very serious blunders in computer time estimating have been made on this point.

A similar compromise (with a similar caveat) must sometimes be made in determining the size of file records. In certain types of machines it is desirable that the records should all be of the same length. Frequently, however, this is unrealistic because the amount of information contained in each record is variable. A compromise solution is to carry infrequently occurring information in a *trailer* record (Chapter 13). Doing so reduces tape reading and writing time but requires many tests to determine if each record has a trailer record and if so what type, where, etc. Once again the compromise between tape reading time and internal processing time must achieve a proper balance between the two.

Another phase of systems design is the division of an application into various computer runs. Theoretically, a computer with a large enough memory and sufficient tapes should be able to do an entire

ECONOMIZING AND ESTIMATING COMPUTER TIME

application in one run. However, this is usually not economical because of the prohibitive cost of large internal memories and many tapes. In general, the fewer runs there are the better because of what may be termed the "fixed costs" that accompany each run, e.g., loading the program, changing tape reels, computing control totals, and various other housekeeping functions. Furthermore, there is often the possibility that combining several runs into one run may completely eliminate certain master files or may reduce the number of times a master file must be read.

As we shall see in Chapter 21, checking and auditing techniques are usually required in any data processing application, but the cost of providing this information must be carefully balanced against its value. Unfortunately, this is a rather difficult balance to achieve, since the value often involves intangibles to which it is sometimes hard to assign numeric measures. Perhaps the tendency to set up excessive checking is a carry-over from punched card practice where such checking may often be done at very little extra expense of equipment time.

One of the most crucial decisions in systems design is the extent to which the machine should be expected to handle exceptions in procedures. It is true that a computer can be programmed to handle any condition which can be defined in quantitive terms, but it is very often not practical to do so. Furthermore, it may be stated categorically that it is impossible to anticipate all possible future exceptions to a standardized procedure. One must strike a balance beween the desire to let the computer do all the work and the practical realization that trying to do so increases computer costs out of all proportion to value received, and that, in any case, one can never foresee all possible difficulties. It is not easy to make generalizations as to what percentage of the exceptions one should attempt to handle automatically; this varies for each different application. Whatever level of exception handling is established, however, it may be stated that in general it is most desirable that the computer not stop when an exception is discovered. Rather, the exception should either be printed or written out on an exception tape and correction made manually. The corrected data may then be re-entered later, if necessary. In this sense "exceptions" include both conditions which were not anticipated in systems design and incorrect data which must be reworked before the computer can handle it. To summarize, the systems designer must search his soul and decide how much of the processing he thinks the computer can efficiently handle. He then tries to define to the computer through rules and tests what *con-*

stitutes an exception, even though he may not then tell the computer what to do about it. Instead, he simply sets up the computer program so that these exceptions will be "kicked out" and either handled manually or re-entered in the computer at a later run.* (It may be of historic interest to note that some of the earliest major data processing installations made complete fiascos of their early applications by attempting to do everything in the computer. Unfortunately, however, even though these fiascos have been fairly well publicized, some later users seem not to have learned the lesson.)

Planning for the retrieval of information from a master file for random interrogation purposes has an effect on the total computer time required for an application. There is often a great temptation to attempt to set up the system so that immediate random access to any part of a master file is possible—preferably while the customer or shop foreman is still on the telephone! The extremes of this approach are usually prohibitively expensive. Even with random access file organization and media, one must remember that such immediate interrogation does not come free. For instance, in order to be able to handle the *peak* interrogation rates without excessive delay, it becomes necessary to install more inquiry stations (and perhaps more computing equipment) than is required by the *average* interrogation rate—which costs money. Once again one must make compromises. It is often possible to classify the information in master files according to the relative frequency with which it is needed. It may be necessary to produce printed reports of certain parts of the information in a master file only monthly, whereas other parts of the same file may be needed daily.

All of these considerations, and others which might be listed, show that systems design cannot be divorced from time considerations. All alternatives and all proposed changes must be evaluated in the light of the question "What is the difference and is it worth it?" As mentioned above, one must always keep in mind both *total computer time* and *total cost*, which involves (in addition to computer time) procedures analysis and programming time and differences in machine cost.

---

*A prime example of an overconscientious attempt to include everything in the computer program occurred at an early data processing center. The company had been in business a long time and found itself with a variety of different pension plan calculations, some of which had originated decades previously. One of these old plans applied to *only one man,* but an involved calculation was set up for this one man and every record tested to see if it was his!

16.2 Timing Considerations in Programming

If systems design is considered to be analogous to the division of a book into chapters, programming is analogous to making a detailed outline of each chapter. The detailed design of a file, the final division of the application into runs, and the over-all flow charting of the different runs are some of the larger programming activities. In this level of planning, one becomes more conscious of the characteristics of the particular computer involved and tries to find the best way to fit the job into its peculiar limitations and capabilities.

The *contents* of the various files are determined at the systems design level; the detailed *formats* (layout) of the various files are determined at the programming level. Variations in file layout can have an important effect on processing time. For instance, if several different trailer records are used, the fields that are likely to be used together should be grouped into the same trailer record. It is sometimes more efficient to duplicate certain fields in order to save processing time, particularly if additional sorting can be avoided thereby. It is sometimes possible to provide in the records extra information which has no real function except to provide a quick method of determining whether a given record is pertinent to a certain part of the processing. If attention is given to the allocation of files to tape handlers from run to run, the amount of costly tape mounting and dismounting time may be held to a minimum.

The choice between using existing generalized subroutines or preparing special subroutines has an effect on over-all time and cost requirements. Generalized subroutines are by definition intended to cover a *general* class of conditions, with the frequent result that they are not the most efficient for any *particular* function. Thus it is often possible to save computer time by preparing special subroutines which are tailored to the particular job. However, computer time is not the only component of over-all cost: the cost of programming a special subroutine must be considered also. For example, suppose it is required to produce a program to sort 40,000 records of 30 digits each with a 15-character key. Suppose an existing sort generator can produce a program that can sort these records in 30 minutes, with negligible programming costs to the user. A specially tailored sort program might be produced at a cost of 6 man-months of programming and 20 machine hours for debugging which would sort the same records in 25 minutes instead of 30. The obvious question is, are the 5 minutes per day of machine time worth the programming and debugging costs and the 6 months' delay? In some cases it might be and in others it clearly would not.

Another example of this type of choice revolves around the selection of a nonmachine-language coding system. Generally speaking, there is a choice between a language which is similar to the machine language but far removed from the users' language, and vice versa. Usually, the farther the language is from the machine's natural language, the less efficient is the program it produces (although there are notable exceptions). On the other hand, the closer the language is to the language of the user, the smaller the programming effort and cost. As always, a balance must be struck.

Most programs have many alternate branches; which branch or path to follow for a particular situation is usually determined by the codes and data in the records to be processed. It is perhaps unnecessary to observe that different branches have different relative frequencies. For instance, in a payroll application union dues are much more common than garnishments. This leads to two observations. The first is that the most effort should be put on economizing time in the most frequently used branches. The second is that the planning of the file layout and the flow charting of the decisions among the various branches should be made in such a way as to make the most frequently used decision paths the shortest. For instance, in the case where branches A, B, and C come out of a single decision, suppose branch A is typically used 150,000 times per week, B is used 10,000 times per week, and C only 50. It is clear that the most effort should be put into minimizing computer time within branch A and that the computer decision operations should be planned so that the test for A is made first, then the test for B, and then the test for C. Such relatively minor considerations can add up to the difference between an efficient application and a mediocre one.

Determining the relative frequencies of branches is sometimes difficult to do. It can be facilitated by obtaining and analyzing samples of the data to be processed. It is sometimes possible to add a few steps to a completed program so that it can print out relative frequency data which may then be used to produce an improved program.

It is always necessary at the programming level (and also during coding) to take best advantage of the capabilities and limitations of the particular computer at hand. Many examples could be cited. A decision must often be made as to whether it may not be more efficient to carry out certain initial processing of the data on punched card equipment, rather than do the whole job on the computer. Sometimes there is a choice between high and low density of recording on magnetic tapes, where the low density recording must be used if the tape is to be printed off-line. In such situations one has the choice between carrying the entire master file in low density form so that it may be printed when occasionally necessary, or carrying the master file in high density form to save processing time and then rewriting the file in low density form when it must be printed. Many other such examples could be cited; most of them seem to involve questions of input and output.

16.3 Timing Considerations in Coding

Coding is the final step in preparing an application for the computer. As we have seen, it is a step that involves much detailed work and usually requires intimate knowledge of the particular computer's characteristics in order to prepare an efficient program (even when nonmachine-language coding is used). Since each computer has its own characteristics, we can only make some rather broad generalizations about factors affecting time requirements. "Efficient coding" must be defined within the framework of the systems design which has been laid down. For instance, it is obvious that straight line coding (no loops) requires much less computer time than coding with loops, but needs much more storage. Thus if one run becomes two runs because of the excessive use of straight line coding, the over-all time required might increase instead of decrease.

It is difficult for the programmer or coder to properly appreciate the capability of a machine with which he is unfamiliar. It is good practice to familiarize oneself with a new computer by trying several different coding methods at first. The earlier remarks regarding the optimization of the various branches in an application apply with equal force at the coding level. Situations can easily arise in which it is best to make one branch less efficient in order to make a very frequently used branch more efficient. It is perhaps obvious, as has been mentioned in earlier chapters, that in writing loops one should put the most emphasis on the instructions that are actually repeated. If the repeated section of a loop can be made four instructions shorter by adding ten instructions to the initialization, it would probably be wise to do so. Similar considerations apply to frequently used subroutines; is it better to set up one completely general subroutine to handle a certain type of processing, or several specialized subroutines? In both the previous examples we see once again the old choice between time and space. It is often difficult to know, when coding is first started, exactly how this balance should be made. Often it is necessary to do the coding with some arbitrary approach to the balance between time and space, then recode a segment if it appears that extra memory space is available—in which case time can be reduced—or that not enough memory space is available—in which case the recoding must be done at the expense of time.

There are three observations which should be made about the coding level in connection with the statement above that our objective is to minimize total cost. The first is that coding should be done in such a way as to simplify debugging. Occasionally, extra instructions must be written in order to produce intermediate results which will assist in locating errors in the code. The ideal situation would of course be to produce these debugging additions without lengthening the running time of the program after it has been debugged. This can sometimes actually be achieved, by judicious use of computer console features, special branch instructions, etc. The second observation is that coding should be done with future changes in mind, especially since experience shows that in data processing applications a *status quo* is never reached. The third observation is that it is possible to go too far in attempting to minimize time or memory requirements. We have in mind here the subject of "clever coding" which has been previously denounced.

16.4 Estimating Computer Time

Actually making an estimate of the time that will be required for a computer to carry out an application is not too difficult, but one must always keep in mind that there are pitfalls awaiting the unwary. The outline below is perhaps a little simplified, but it may help to give an idea of how to go about the job. The various headings cover the major aspects of computer processing time.

1. Input/output. When the contents of the various files have been specified, formats roughed out, and volumes estimated, the calculation of input/output time is relatively simple and accurate, given specifications on the speed of input/output equipment. A special problem exists with magnetic tapes, since the time to accelerate and decelerate tapes is frequently a significant fraction of the total tape reading and writing time.

2. Sorting. The manufacturer usually provides sorting tables which allow rapid determination of the time required to sort a file, given such parameters as record length, number of records, nature and size of keys, etc.

3. Calculation. It is essential to flow-chart and, if at all possible,

ECONOMIZING AND ESTIMATING COMPUTER TIME

code the main paths and loops which get heavy usage. The instructions written can be counted according to the number of executions and multiplied by the time required for the execution of each type of instruction. The branches having low usage can be estimated more roughly. The degree of overlap between calculation and input/output, if buffering is used, must of course be considered extremely carefully.

4. Input/output editing. The situation here is similar to calculation; we mention it because it is a matter which the beginner often tends to overlook. The availability and characteristics of plugboards must be considered since they may significantly affect central processor time.

5. Off-line equipment. From card volumes, output lines to be printed, and other requirements of the job, the need for and loading of off-line equipment can be calculated.

6. Red tape. It is essential to consider many time-consuming activities which are frequently overlooked in time estimating. Examples: sentinel checking (if not provided for in the hardware), item advance (costly if records are short and indexing features are inadequate), tape mounting and dismounting between runs, rewind time (how much overlapping is possible when several tapes have to be rewound?), the effect of items like headings and form spacing on printing times, etc.

16.5 Summary

The most frustrating phase of the installation of a data processing system is usually the preliminary estimates of the time which will be required for each application. This estimating must often be done under severe time pressure and on the basis of incomplete facts. This is most unfortunate, since so much hangs in the balance: the decision of whether to get a computer, the decision of which computer to get, cost saving estimates, staffing requirements, etc. The only really satisfactory way to estimate computer time is to take a representative part of the application and actually code it. Based on time required for each operation, time required for input/output functions, etc., a reasonably accurate time estimate can then be made. This ideally would be done for each different computer system being considered and each different approach to the solution of the data processing problem. Users who have invested this effort in their planning work rather than accepting ready-made answers from other users or from the manufacturers have been well repaid for their trouble.

There are a few general considerations which have been so frequently overlooked in the past that it may be well to underline them by a summary listing:

1. In making comparisons of alternative equipment or approaches by coding representative sections of the application, be extremely careful of two points. First, be completely certain that the "representative" section really is representative; do not assume that the time required for such things as data auditing, exception handling, etc., can safely be guessed. Second, make certain that the different sample codes are written by equally competent people and with equally thorough knowledge of the different equipment and approaches. It does little good to have your best coder try one method and an inexperienced coder try another, and then compare the results.

2. Be extremely cautious of careless generalizations regarding the ratio of input/output speed to internal processing speed. In many important applications internal processing speed is almost completely unimportant since the great bulk of the time is taken up with tape reading during which the central computer does *absolutely nothing*. Similarly, bad estimates can be caused by careless assumptions regarding the amount of time to be saved by buffering in a particular application.

3. In a machine with nonimmediate-access main memory, general statements about the time savings to be realized by minimum access coding should be taken with a grain of salt. What is perfectly true in general may be completely false in particular. Or in a situation where the calculation is input/output-limited, optimum programming may make no difference anyway.

4. It is questionable whether a program has ever been written which was as good as it ever could be when it was first written. It has been a not uncommon experience to find that computer time can be reduced by 10–80% by system redesign and reprogramming in the light of experience.

5. The chronology of data processing functions can introduce complications which are not apparent in a superficial study. When does the bulk of the input data arrive at the data processing center? How late can it be and still be included? Are certain applications interrelated in such a way that if one is late getting started because of missing data, the others are all delayed too? When are reports required, and how late can they be without serious difficulties arising? What is the ratio of peak load to average load? Such questions can have profound implications on timing and equipment requirements.

6. Always allow a safety factor. If cost considerations are crucial

ECONOMIZING AND ESTIMATING COMPUTER TIME 345

in determining whether an application should be done or not or which machine to select, it is unwise to assign high accuracy to any type of estimate no matter how carefully done or how experienced the people who do it.

Exercises

1. What are the common factors that relate economizing computer time and estimating computer time?

2. Why is it important in the early planning stages to have a reasonably accurate estimate of the computer time required to do the job?

3. If the actual computer time should drastically exceed the original estimate, some of the following remedies may be applied. Discuss each of these and suggest at least three more possible remedies.
   (a) Cancel the computer and order a faster one.
   (b) Order a larger memory.
   (c) Order tape buffers if the original equipment does not have buffers.
   (d) Order more off-line equipment, such as card-to-tape, high-speed printer, tape-to-card.
   (e) Redesign the system.
   (f) Redesign the program.
   (g) Redesign the code.
   (h) Negotiate with the "customer" to cut down requirements for the application.
   (i) Put sorting on punched cards instead.
   (j) Order faster tapes.

4. What are some of the factors in systems design that affect time requirements?

5. What are some of the factors in programming that affect time requirements?

6. What are some of the factors in coding that affect time requirements?

7. What are some of the factors in actual machine operation that affect time requirements?

8. "Suboptimization," the process of optimizing a small part to the possible detriment of the whole, is often the cause of inefficiency in an electronic data processing installation. Name some of the possible areas where suboptimization can occur.

9. If we accept the fact that changes in a program are inevitable, what are some of the provisions that must be made in programming to make changes easy?

10. A flexible modular computer system offers more safety (with regard to time estimates) than a rigid computer system, because the size of memory, the type, number, and speed of input/output equipment can all be increased or decreased. Comment.

11. In view of the interaction between systems design, programming, and coding, is it desirable to have specialists in each of the phases or programmers experienced in all three phases to estimate computer time requirements?

12. Discuss the advisability of monitoring computer time estimates once the programming task is under way, i.e., continually comparing against the previous estimates.

17 RERUN TECHNIQUES

17.0 Introduction

There are a number of important considerations in electronic data processing which seldom occur to the uninitiated. One of the most important of these is the question of how to "recover" from an error or machine failure which occurs during computer operation. We are speaking now of errors which happen in spite of thorough debugging; i.e., other than programming errors. Examples are machine failures, errors in input data, loss of files, and the errors which will occasionally be made by machine operators—even experienced ones. Machine failures are due to power supply failure, complete failure of some component, or *transient* errors which occur only occasionally. Errors in input data result from simple transcription errors, missing data, damaged cards which will not read properly, etc. Operator errors include such things as mounting wrong tapes and a variety of possible mistakes in operating the machine console. These errors may or may not give an obvious indication that they have happened.

One solution to these problems, of course, is simply to stop the machine when the errors arise and rely on manual corrections. This usually implies starting a program over from the beginning when a disabling error happens. Many of the important applications of computers to commercial data processing problems, however, involve many *hours* of computer time and it is simply impractical to rely on starting over from the beginning. Worse, depending on how the application is set up, it may be almost impossible to do so, because, for instance, input tapes may have been destroyed by using the same reels as working tapes later in the application. Furthermore, manual corrections made under the pressure of meeting, say, a payroll deadline, are notorious for their inaccuracy.

What we need, clearly, is a carefully planned method of returning to the last point where all results were correct before the error occurred. The essence of the *rerun technique* (also called *restart procedure*) is to make periodic checks on the accuracy of results; if everything is all right at a given point, we make a provision so that if an error is discovered later in the processing it is relatively simple to return to the rerun point and start over from there—not the beginning. Whenever practical, we attempt to let the computer do the checking and make the provisions for easy return to the last point of good results. This technique, as we shall see, is applicable in a general way to several types of failure. It is suitable for transient machine failures such as tape reading errors, where it may be possible simply to repeat the operation in the hope that the error will disappear the second or third time around. It applies to what can otherwise be a catastrophic machine failure in the middle of a long run. It also allows for relatively simple restart procedures if the operators have made mistakes.

17.1 The Rerun Principle

The rerun principle finds application in a wide variety of situations ranging from rereading a tape record in the hope it will read correctly the second time to providing methods for restarting a 20-hour application in the 19th hour. Regardless of the scope of the situation, however, there is an underlying concept which applies to all rerun situations.

We begin by defining an *operation* in general as a convenient unit of work bounded by two *rerun points*. An operation in this sense might consist of all of the processing concerned with one reel of a multiple-reel input file, or it might consist of all of the processing having to do with one employee's pay calculation, or the reading of one tape record, or one run of an application which requires a total of twenty runs. At the end of each operation some type of check is normally made to determine that the calculation to that point is ostensibly *error-free*. Then if an error is detected anywhere in the next operation, we wish to return (after correcting the error-producing condition) to the end of the preceding operation which we believe to be error-free and which is called a rerun point. Obviously, it is essential that enough information be retained at each rerun point so that the program can automatically restart from that point if it is necessary to return to it. This is sometimes a rather involved process about which we shall have more to say later. The provision of this rerun information must be done at the end of each error-free operation, which is called *advancing the rerun point*. Some provision must be made, however, for the possibility that a permanent error would cause an automatic procedure to go around in circles. For instance, it is not uncommon to program a tape reading routine so that if a reading error

RERUN TECHNIQUES

is detected, the tape is automatically backspaced and reread. If the cause of the error is (as usual) a speck of dust, the tape may reread

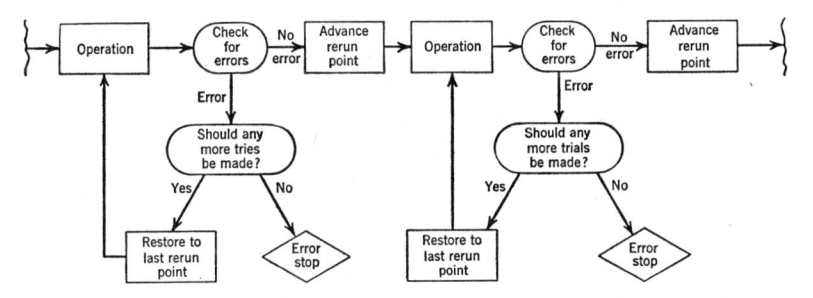

Figure 1. Flow chart of the rerun process for two successive operations.

correctly the second time. If, however, the cause of the error is a permanent flaw in the tape or incorrect writing at an earlier stage, the reading can never be correct; in this case an automatic reread pro-

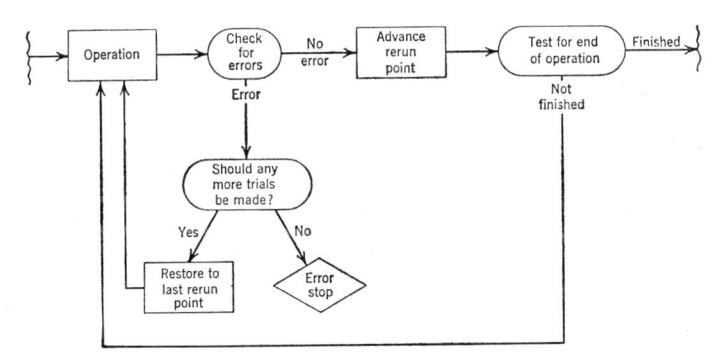

Figure 2. Flow chart of the rerun process applied to a loop situation.

cedure could literally tear up the tape if the operator did not notice what was happening. For this reason, it is sometimes necessary to design into the rerun procedure a *limit* to the number of times an operation should be repeated if an error is detected. Figure 1 is a flow chart of the complete rerun procedure for two successive operations. Figure 2 shows the corresponding situation for successive operations which are the same; i.e., a loop situation.

17.2 Rerun Procedures for Small Program Segments

There are at least two types of situations in which it is desirable to build rerun procedures around relatively small segments of a program: "weak" operations, and calculations which if in error would propagate widely to the other parts of the program. The best example of a "weak" operation is magnetic tape reading. It is well known that the reading and writing of magnetic tapes are much more susceptible to error than the internal electronic processing of data. (We should perhaps say *relatively* more unreliable. Present magnetic tapes are probably still more reliable than punched card operations, all things considered, but not as reliable as internal electronic hardware.) It is common practice to code a specialized rerun procedure for every tape reading operation and in many cases for tape writing also.

In the case of tape reading the procedure is simply to check for an error at the completion of reading each record (using whatever method is built into the machine); if an error is detected the tape is backspaced and reread. As we have discussed, it is necessary either to program a limit to the number of times this should be done or else cause the machine to stop each time it occurs and put the number of rerun attempts under operator control. This latter may seem like a contradiction of the point made above regarding stopping the machine in case of error. It must be remembered, however, that the operator and maintenance engineers need some indication of any machine malfunction.

In the case of tape writing, the procedure depends somewhat on the characteristics of the machine used. In some of the more recent machines, tape writing is automatically checked by a second set of heads; an error indication is available for writing just as for reading. In this case, the procedure is simply to test for the presence of an error and if one is found, backspace the tape and rewrite. If such write checking is not available, there are two alternatives. One is to take the point of view that an absence of parity checking errors on reading the information just written is satisfactory proof of correct writing. If this point of view is taken, it is simply necessary to backspace the tape and read it into a dummy storage area to test for a reading error. On certain machines on which it is possible to read tape backwards, it is common practice simply to read each tape backwards after it has been completely written rather than use the rewind operation. A major disadvantage of this latter procedure, however, is that if an error is detected on rereading the completed tape, much time is wasted in regenerating the correct information. The other alternative on machines which do not have built-in write checking is to backspace each record after it is written, read the same record back into memory, and check what is read against the memory information from which the record was written. On some machines there is a separate operation which makes this procedure very simple. In any case, however, programmed write checking is very expensive in time. This time penalty, combined with the fact that writing is generally more reliable than reading, results in the fact that tape writing is generally checked only on the most important files where it would be very difficult and expensive to correct an error at a later time.* There may be other situations also where the motiva-

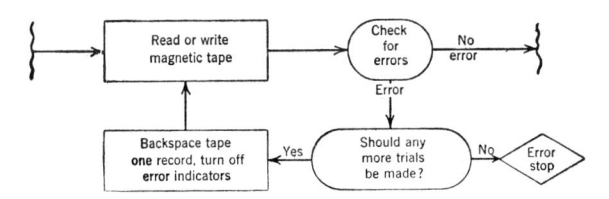

Figure 3. Flow chart of a rerun procedure for reading or writing magnetic tape.

tion for building a rerun procedure around a small part of a program is based on the inherent unreliability of some operation. Figure 3 is a flow chart of a rerun procedure for reading or writing magnetic tape.

The other situation where such specialized rerun procedures are desirable is the case where an error—even though it may be very minor—would propagate itself widely throughout the rest of the application. A good example of this situation is the case of electric utility billing calculations. The results of a billing calculation (i.e., the amount which the customer owes the company) eventually turn up in almost every branch of the application, e.g., accounts receivable, credit and collection notices, billing statement and registers, reports for management and tax purposes, and the various control and audit totals. If an error is made in the original calculation, a great deal of effort might be necessary later to correct all of the places affected by the error. In view of the critical nature of this one part of the

* It should be noted that it is possible to carry sufficient information along with a tape record to be able to *correct* most errors, as well as *detect* them. (We say "most" here only to re-emphasize the point that no error detecting or correcting system is *absolutely* foolproof; in practice, however, the systems in use catch an extremely high percentage of the errors.) With built-in error correction, there is no need to read the tape immediately after writing it, because if an error is detected later it can be corrected using information still on the tape. Of course, this assumes that the extra error correcting information is itself correct, but this is also checked. At least one recent computer has such a tape system.

For a general discussion of error detecting and correcting codes, see the article by Hamming listed under Chapter 21 in the bibliography.

calculation, it would be quite reasonable to program a check on the calculation or perhaps even two dissimilar checks. One possible check would be to recalculate the bill using different memory locations, different sequences of calculations, if possible, different arithmetic registers and perhaps mathematical identities which give the same result, but which use different computer operations. An example of the latter is the fact that

$$a \times b = \frac{a}{1/b}$$

This type of procedure gives a fairly reliable check on machine functioning but it provides no assurance that the *data* is correct. One method of checking the latter is to apply a *reasonableness* test.

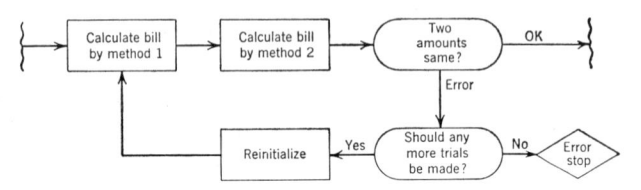

Figure 4. Flow chart of the rerun procedure as applied to a utility billing calculation.

Offhand examples of this might be the fact that a residential electricity user rarely triples his consumption from one month to the next or perhaps that the bill for a single month's residential electricity consumption is almost never over $200, say. If unreasonable results of this sort are detected, it may be worthwhile to rerun the calculation, but very likely the cause of the trouble is incorrect data, in which case the transaction must be written out onto an error tape for inspection, corrected if necessary, and re-entered for processing. Figure 4 is a flow chart of the rerun procedure for this example based on recalculating the billing amount by different calculation methods.*

17.3 Program Reruns

The discussion of the previous section had to do with small segments of programs. We wish to consider now much larger segments of a total application, for instance, a segment bounded by the complete processing of one reel of a master tape. The point of reruns here is not so much to automatically check for occasional machine mal-

* The subject of systems checks is discussed more fully in Chapter 21.

functions as to provide some technique for getting started again in the event of errors which are of a somewhat more catastrophic nature. Examples are power supply failure, machine failures which totally incapacitate the system, tape breakage, and operator errors such as mounting a wrong tape which results in incorrect writing of part of the new master file. The situation here is considerably more complex than in the previous section because there are many more features to consider.

The essence of the problem is the technique for advancing the rerun point so that if a rerun becomes necessary the machine or the operator can know exactly the condition of memory and the positioning of the various tapes involved, as of the last rerun point. In general, one must obtain a complete "photograph" of the computer memory and arithmetic and control registers for each point where a rerun might later be started. This can be obtained by dumping the entire memory into tape. The tape used for the purpose may be either a separate rerun tape or a miscellaneous tape, or memory may be routinely dumped onto the end of each output master file reel. The arithmetic and control registers, if they are essential to the rerun procedure, can be dumped simply by storing them in memory before memory is dumped.

If internal label checking is used, as discussed in Chapter 13, then there will always be enough information in memory at the time the rerun point is advanced to identify which tapes were on the machine. The determination of the position of each of the tapes is somewhat more complex, however. Two different situations may arise: it may be necessary to move a given tape either forward or backward if a rerun becomes necessary. In the case of a tape which is still on the machine when a rerun becomes necessary, the tape can be backspaced a number of times equal to the number of records which have been written since a rerun point. This number must be generated and stored in memory. In the case of a tape which has been removed from the tape unit since the rerun point or in the case of a complete disaster where all the tapes may have to be removed from the machine for an extended period of time, it is necessary to know how many records to skip over before the correct location on a tape is reached. Part of the information necessary at each rerun point is therefore the number of records between the beginning of the tape and the point where the tape now is. These two numbers—the number of records between the front of the tape and the rerun point, and the number of records between the present position of the tape and the last rerun point—must both be initialized and updated in the program. These two counters for each tape unit, since they are actually stored in memory, would be available on the rerun memory dump tape. To restore the program to the last rerun point manually, one would rewind (or remount) all tapes, read the rerun dump tape into memory, use a small program to position all tapes according to the appropriate counters, and execute a manual jump to the first instruction of the next operation, the location of which should be contained on the memory dump tape. It is probably wise to store the keys of the various records being processed at the rerun point, to allow verification of tape positioning.

This procedure is fairly complex and takes a certain amount of time; the effort required to advance the rerun point is a penalty we pay for the ability to restart the program simply in case an error occurs. An obvious question is, how often is it economical to do this? The selection of the most economical interval between rerun points depends on three factors: the expected frequency of errors, the time required to check for errors and to advance the rerun point at the end of each operation, and the time required to restore the program to the previous rerun point in case of error. When these times are known, it is possible to select the optimum interval between rerun points so that a balance is achieved between the time wasted by the rerun procedure if it *is not* needed and the time saved by the rerun procedure if it *is* needed. Intuitively we know that if the interval between rerun points is too long, then each time an error occurs the computer will have to repeat a long operation to correct the error. The extreme case is when no rerun procedure is provided. In effect, then, the beginning of the program becomes the only rerun point. On the other hand, if the rerun points are too close together, the computer will be spending too much of its time in checking for errors and advancing the rerun points. The optimum rerun interval may be computed mathematically if sufficiently accurate data is available on the three factors mentioned at the beginning of the paragraph.

There are other factors to consider in the selection of rerun points besides timing considerations of this sort. There are points of "no return" or "almost no return" in the program where it is very difficult for the program to return to a rerun point *automatically*. For example, in processing a file that is contained on more than one reel of tape, the point in the program which finishes one reel and begins processing the next is such a point of "no return" (as regards an automatic rerun not requiring manual intervention). This applies equally to input/output and master tapes. Another example might be the situa-

RERUN TECHNIQUES 355

tion where several files are contained on the same reel of tape. It is desirable that a rerun point be provided wherever a change of tape reels is involved. Figure 5 is a flow chart of an over-all program rerun procedure incorporating some of these points.

The method used for checking for errors in program rerun depends largely on the type of machine and the amount of checking which appears to be economical. On some machines errors do not necessarily stop the machine but may merely set corresponding error triggers.

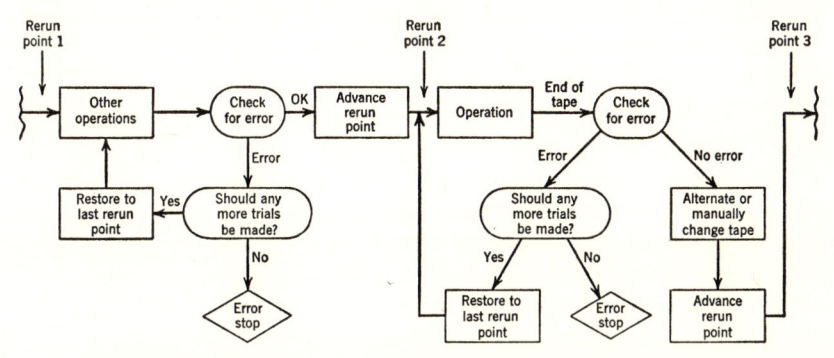

Figure 5. Flow chart of an over-all program rerun procedure.

These triggers may be interrogated to determine if any errors have occurred since the last time they were checked. If this is not considered sufficient evidence that the machine has operated without errors, one may also provide other checks such as balancing control totals or hash totals or, in the extreme case, even repeat the entire program from the last rerun point and compare the results with those obtained the first time. The degree and extent of the checking should be consistent with the nature of the application and with consideration of over-all economics.

17.4 System Reruns

The system rerun approach considers one computer run to be an operation. Thus the rerun points can coincide with the divisions between computer runs. The concepts and necessity of system rerun techniques are simple, although not necessarily obvious.

Computer runs normally communicate with one another by means of magnetic tapes. These tapes include master tapes, working tapes, and input/output tapes. Master tapes are usually well protected by such procedures as saving the tapes from one or two "generations" back. (See Chapters 13, 21.) The input/output and working tapes are usually not so well protected since they are considered to store data only "temporarily." In fact, each working tape is often used for several different computer runs in a typical day. Actually, some of these "temporary" working tapes may require temporary protection just as master tapes do. Consider the situation shown in Figure 6, where the circle labeled tape 1 represents an input tape to run A; the tape labeled 2 may be thought of as either the output of run A or the input to run B, etc. Tape reels represent only temporary storage. It should be theoretically possible to reuse them for other purposes

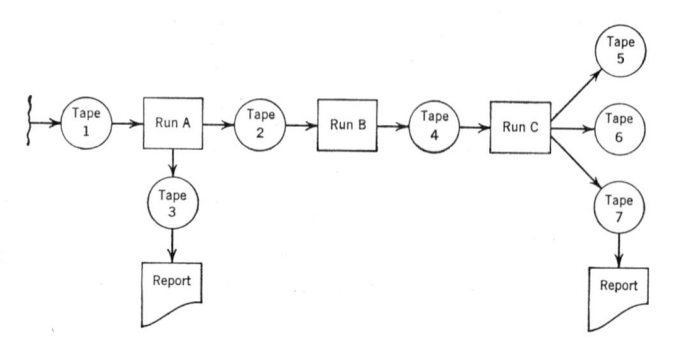

Figure 6. Flow chart of a system rerun situation.

as soon as they have been read by the succeeding program. Thus the physical tape reel called 2, which is used in run B, might be used in run C as one of the output tapes. This approach has considerable appeal because it is then not necessary to dismount the physical tape reels between runs. However, if this is done, it inevitably enforces some limitations on the way rerun points can be set up. If the information on tape 2 is destroyed by using the same physical tape reel for an output file on run C, then the rerun point for run C may be prior to run A. In the extreme case it might be necessary to go all the way back to the beginning of the application, perhaps even to the reading of input cards onto magnetic tape. The situation is not as hopeless as it sounds, however; it should not be implied that it is necessary never to reuse working tapes. Suppose, for instance, that tape reel 1 is the input tape for the entire application. It is clear that the physical tape reel should not be reused any time during run A or run B since a restart procedure made necessary by an error in either of these runs might require the use of reel 1. However, once a rerun point has been established at the dividing line between run B

RERUN TECHNIQUES

and run C, reel 1 is not likely to be needed again if rerun points have been set up between A and B, and B and C. Thus it is possible to strike a realistic balance in system rerun considerations between one extreme of providing no rerun procedures and the other extreme of wasting a great deal of time in providing for rerun points that may not be needed.

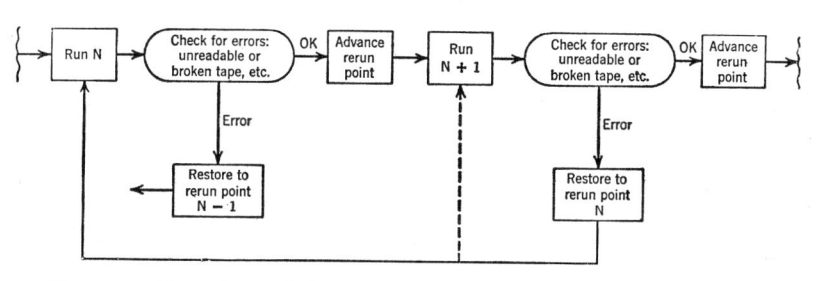

```
Run N → Check for errors: unreadable or broken tape, etc. →OK→ Advance rerun point → Run N+1 → Check for errors: unreadable or broken tape, etc. →OK→ Advance rerun point →
         ↓Error                                                                              ↓Error
         Restore to rerun point N−1                                                          Restore to rerun point N
```

Figure 7. Flow chart of the rerun procedure for an over-all application.

In practice, key tapes are often saved longer than theoretically required, because the checking done before the rerun point is advanced does not usually insure *100%* accuracy in processing. Frequently, the checking of a report is a prerequisite to the reuse of such tapes.

Figure 7 shows a flow chart of the rerun procedure for an over-all application. The flow diagram for the system rerun differs from the others only in the error return. Normally, in the case of error, we return to the previous rerun point; however, in system rerun the nature of the error determines how far back we must go to initiate rerun.

17.5 Summary

Experience has taught systems analysts and programmers to give careful thought to questions of how to get started again when errors occur and to do this planning *early* in the game. This does not imply that computers are basically unreliable (in fact, they are much more reliable *per operation* than other means of data processing), but that when an error does occur it can be very expensive to correct. As we have seen, it is possible to provide means by which the program can either automatically attempt to correct error conditions without manual intervention or greatly simplify the task if manual intervention is required. It may seem that these procedures are extremely complex. They are indeed somewhat complex, but experience has shown that in certain situations they are well worth the effort. Furthermore, this complexity does not add materially to the processing time once the planning and coding effort has been expended.

Exercises

1. Why is it necessary to have rerun procedures in electronic data processing? Why not in manual systems?

2. Discuss the three levels of rerun procedures.

3. Should planning for rerun procedures be done along with the programming or added later? Discuss.

4. Would a computer which has extensive built-in internal checking require the same rerun procedures as a computer without internal checking? Discuss.

5. In some cases, program rerun is not planned for, i.e., the program is permitted to run to its conclusion and then checked to see if everything is all right. Show how this fits into the basic rerun principle and the penalties paid for lack of an automatic rerun procedure.

6. Show how the grandfather-father-son principle of sequential file maintenance fits into the basic rerun principle.

18 NONRANDOM ACCESS MAIN MEMORIES

18.0 Introduction

We have implicitly assumed throughout the text so far that main memory is of the *random access* type. By definition this means that the same amount of time is required to obtain a word from memory, regardless of what the address is. Magnetic core memory is the most important type of random access main memory now in use; earlier types (considerable numbers of which are still employed) include electrostatic and (less importantly) relay and vacuum-tube storage. The important main memories which are not random access are magnetic drums and delay-line storage.

With a magnetic drum, information is recorded on the magnetic surface of the rotating cylinder by *heads*, which are coils of wire with associated *pole pieces* to concentrate the magnetic flux. Each head records in a *track* as the drum rotates, and later the same head is capable of reading the information in that track. Each track can typically hold 10 to 100 words. The problem is that at the instant a given word is needed, the drum most likely will not be in the proper position to allow reading of the word. The delay is quite significant. In one very commonly used drum computer, the maximum delay—which is the time required for a complete drum revolution—is just under 5 milliseconds (ms), compared to the less than 1 ms required to carry out the ordinary arithmetic instructions.

The problem of this chapter, then, is to indicate techniques which can be used to minimize the delay associated with drum and delay-line type storage. This is an important problem which will, in all probability, be with us for many years. Although the delay-line memory is being superseded, drum memory is so economical and reliable that its complete replacement in medium size computers will probably wait for a major invention in storage techniques.

18.1 Optimum Placement of Data and Instructions

One solution to the problem will have already occurred to many readers. Wherever possible, why not *plan* the location of data so that each word *is* in the correct position to be read just when it is needed? Figure 1 is a schematic diagram of the placement of information on a simplified magnetic drum. For instance, suppose that we

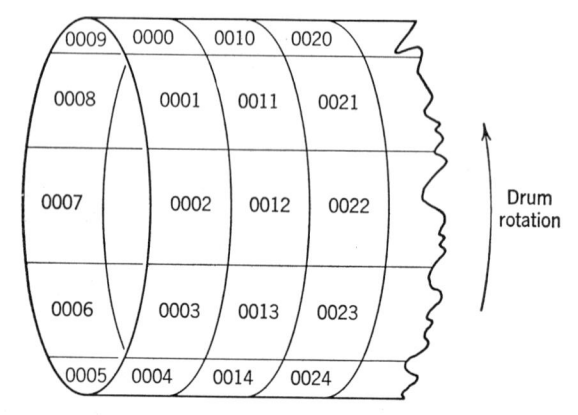

Figure 1. Schematic representation of the placement of information on a simplified magnetic drum.

know how long it takes for a word to pass by a head, that we also know how long each instruction takes, and finally, that we know that certain groups of addresses are all available at the same time. To give an example, suppose that one word goes past its head in 0.1 ms; that the time from the start of reading an instruction from the drum until the time the control circuits are ready to obtain the word specified by the address is 0.2 ms; that all add-subtract types of instructions take 0.3 ms; and that all addresses with the same last digit are equivalent in time, i.e., there are ten words in each track. For instance, at the time address 167 is under its head, 177, 187, 197, etc., are also under their heads. Suppose now that we wish to calculate $X = A + B + C$, selecting the addresses for A, B, C, and X in such a manner that the total delay is a minimum. If the first instruction is located at 560, the analysis could proceed as follows:

1. 0.2 ms must elapse (we assumed) before the control circuits are ready to accept the data word. Since each word requires 0.1 ms to

NONRANDOM ACCESS MAIN MEMORIES

pass the head, we must choose a data address with a last digit of 2 or greater; otherwise the word may have just passed the heads when we are ready for it.

2. 0.3 ms will elapse while the arithmetic is carried out (presumably a Bring type of instruction). However, the next instruction will not be read until some time later anyway, since it is located at 561. Actually, then, we could have chosen any data address with a last digit between 2 and 8.

3. Similarly, the second data address could be anything between 3 and 9, etc.

Let us arbitrarily choose addresses 682, 685, 695, and 718 for A, B, C, and X, respectively, and analyze the delays. The four times of interest are abbreviated as follows:

Control: the time between starting to read the instruction and the time when the circuits are ready to accept the contents of the address, assumed to be 0.2 ms.

Address-delay: the time between when the circuits are *ready* to read the addressed word and when it actually appears under the head.

Arithmetic: the time required to read the addressed word and carry out the "arithmetic," assumed to be 0.3 ms for these operations. "Arithmetic" is used in a very broad sense here, to cover all the machine functions which go on between the time the data word (if any) has been brought from memory and the time the machine is ready to execute the next instruction.

Instruction delay: the time between completion of arithmetic and the arrival of the next instruction under the heads.

			CONTROL	ADDRESS DELAY	ARITHMETIC	INSTRUCTION DELAY
560	Bring	682	0.2	0.0	0.3	0.6
561	Add	685	0.2	0.2	0.3	0.4
562	Add	695	0.2	0.1	0.3	0.5
563	Store	718	0.2	0.3	0.3	0.3

The total time required is thus 4.4 ms.

To show what can happen if the addresses are not properly chosen, suppose the addresses had been 681, 682, 701, 903:

			CONTROL	ADDRESS DELAY	ARITHMETIC	INSTRUCTION DELAY
560	Bring	681	0.2	0.9	0.3	0.7
561	Add	682	0.2	0.9	0.3	0.7
562	Add	701	0.2	0.7	0.3	0.9
563	Store	903	0.2	0.8	0.3	0.8

The total time required is 8.4 ms, almost twice as long as the other. (The inquiring reader may wish to investigate why the total time to execute an instruction is always either 1.1 or 2.1 ms.)

This has been a quick sketch of what usually goes under the name of *optimum*, or *minimum access*, or *minimum latency programming*. Actually the problem is considerably more complex than indicated here, as the following considerations show.

The time called "arithmetic" delay here (which is not a universally accepted terminology) is naturally not a constant for all operations. Certain classes of instructions take longer than others. Worse, the times for certain operations are variable (in many machines), depending on the data involved; multiplication and division are the prime examples, depending in most computers on the digits involved. Another problem is subroutines: if a subroutine is to be entered from several places in a program, as it usually will be, it is virtually impossible to avoid delay with some of the entries. A final problem which may be mentioned is that of frequently used constants. Numbers like one-half, the small integers, zero, etc., tend to be used in many places throughout a program, and it is impractical to try to juggle the needs for these constants to avoid delays. A partial solution is to store the most important ones in several places in memory, "spaced" from each other in the timing sense. Common sense must be applied, however, to arrive at an economic balance between the time to be saved and the extra memory and programming effort required. All these problems are compounded, in the case of one important machine which uses a form of minimum latency coding similar to that outlined above, by having two instructions in each word in memory.

All of these complications, however, do not change the fact that in certain situations there is much to be gained by going to the trouble of *optimizing* the program, as this is usually called. In some cases it is possible and feasible to set up a program which lets the computer itself take over part of the routine clerical work of program optimization. The techniques used, although interesting, are not of sufficient generality to be worth the space here; the manufacturers involved provide adequate literature on the subject.

The discussion so far has assumed a computer which executes instructions from sequential addresses. Although the majority of present machines are of this type, by no means all are. An important group of machines has an extra address, called the *instruction address*, which specifies the location in memory of the next instruction to be executed. The IBM 650 is the most important machine in this category. This is done primarily to help solve the delay problem in a computer with a drum memory, with its relative slowness.

The instruction address provides another degree of freedom in reducing the delays. It is now possible to choose the locations of instructions so that as soon as the arithmetic part of one instruction is completed, the next instruction is immediately ready to be read with no delay. It should be pointed out that the potential time savings which may be effected by optimum programming of a drum machine are considerably greater than implied by the example above, because the number of words in one band is usually much greater than ten words. In the IBM 650 it is theoretically possible to improve a *sequential address* program—one coded with no attempt to optimize—by a factor of four or five, depending on the exact mixture of instructions involved. Savings of a factor of two can actually be realized without excessive effort. In extensive problems, a factor of two in total time is obviously significant. Observe, however, that if the application is such that all the internal processing can be done faster than the input/output devices can handle the flow of information (in a buffered machine), there is absolutely nothing to be gained by speeding up the operation of the program. Here, as in everything else we have discussed, an economic decision must be made as to whether a given course of action is worthwhile. It may happen that it is worthwhile to optimize some sections of a routine but not others.

18.2 Rapid-Access Loops

Another solution to the delay problem, used in several current drum computers, is to provide a small section of memory which has significantly lower access time than the main memory. This is frequently accomplished with *recirculating loops*,[*] shown schematically in Figure 2. These are based on the idea of placing a read head and a write head fairly close together around a drum so that the read head "sees" what the write head has just written. When new information is being placed in the loop, the write head is used in the ordinary way to record the information on the surface of the drum. At all other times, the information read by the read head is immediately returned to the *write* head and *rewritten*. Thus the information in the loop "circulates" between the two heads. The average access time of the main drum is reduced by the ratio of the distance between the two heads to the circumference of the drum. There may be one or several such loops.

[*] Also called *revolvers*.

A computer which has recirculating or fast-access loops usually also has special instructions which load the loops quickly. They are used for two purposes: executing instructions from them, and placing much used data or constants in them. For the first purpose, a block of instructions (twenty is a typical number) would be moved to a fast-access loop and a jump to the loop executed; sometimes these two functions are combined in a single instruction. The program

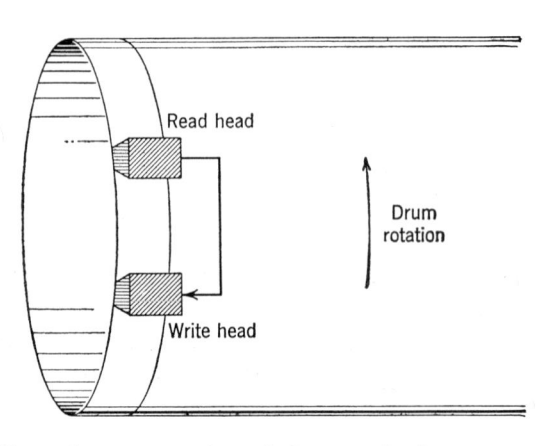

Figure 2. Schematic representation of the way heads are arranged to make circulating loops.

thus proceeds in the normal way, except that what we called "instruction delay" is now greatly reduced. When the first twenty instructions have been executed (including loops if any), another block must be entered. This adds instructions, of course, but the time advantage makes it well worthwhile.

Perhaps it is obvious that any instruction modification must be done after deciding whether the instruction needs to be modified as it appears in the fast-access area, or as it appears in main memory. The problem is both a burden and a blessing; it may well be an advantage to be able to modify instructions in the fast-access area only, because initialization may become unnecessary.

Speeding up program execution by storing constants and data in rapid-access loops might be divided into two subclassifications. In the first we have the semipermanent storage of very frequently used constants in a recirculating loop. In the second we have the situation where it is desirable to move small blocks of data to a loop before performing calculations involving them.

18.3 Summary

This short chapter has discussed two solutions to the time problems created by the use of memory systems having nonrandom access. Considering the attractive cost and reliability of magnetic drum memories, these problems will exist for some time, aside from the fact that there are already a very large number of drum machines in operation. The examples here have been intended only as samples of what can be done, and to show in general terms what is to be gained. There are a few other techniques for reducing delays, but those presented here are by far the most commonly used.

Exercises

1. Define the *efficiency of optimization* as the ratio between the time that would be required to execute a routine if there were no access delays, and the time actually required to execute the routine. Thus, a perfectly optimized routine would have no delays and an efficiency of optimization of 1; a routine which is not optimized at all would have an efficiency of perhaps 0.1 or 0.2, depending on the machine characteristics; the better the optimization, the closer the efficiency approaches the ideal of 1.

(a) Suppose we have a drum computer which has fifty words in a track, has single-address logic, and performs an operation in five word-times (i.e., the time required for five words to pass the drum heads). Assuming average access (twenty-five word-times) for both instructions and data, what is the efficiency of optimization?

(b) For the same computer as in (a), analysis of a certain routine shows that out of every ten data words, five can be obtained with zero delay, three with five word-times delay, one with ten word-times delay, and one with twenty-five word-times delay. Assuming average access for instructions, what is the efficiency of optimization?

(c) Suppose we are dealing with the same computer as in (a), except that it has a one-plus-one instruction, i.e., each instruction specifies where the next instruction is located. Suppose now that for a certain routine it has been established that both instructions and data have the following distribution of delays:

four words out of ten	0
two words out of ten	3
one word out of ten	5
one word out of ten	10
one word out of ten	25
one word out of ten	45

What is the efficiency of optimization?

(d) What is the efficiency of optimization if the distribution in (c) is changed by an improvement which makes the "one word out of ten" with forty-five word-times delay into zero word-time delay?

2. What are some of the conditions which will prevent full efficiency of optimization?

3. If there is a conflict in assigning optimum storage locations between data and instructions, what are some of the deciding factors in resolving the conflict?

4. If the computer is used to assign optimum storage locations for data or instructions, a priority may be used to indicate the relative importance of each data word or instruction. Suggest how such a priority might be assigned.

5. In single address magnetic drum computers, a technique of *interlacing* is sometimes used to assign addresses on the drum. Thus, for an n-word interlace, words 001-002, 002-003, etc., are actually n words apart. A four- or eight-word interlace is commonly used. In these cases, consecutive instructions are located four or eight words apart. Discuss how this might increase efficiency of optimization.

6. Assume a single address computer which takes five word-times for an operation with minimum access and which has fifty words in a track. Suppose a ten-word interlace is used. Analysis shows that, for a given program, nine times out of ten we can locate the data somewhere in the ten-word spacing between consecutive instructions; one time out of ten this requirement cannot be met and an entire drum revolution is used for an operation. What is the efficiency of optimization? Compare with results of Exercise 1(*b*).

7. How does an index register speed up a computer with nonrandom access main memory?

8. If you were given a choice of eighty words of fast-access storage loops in the following make-up, what would you choose to speed up operation time? Why?

        four rapid-access loops of twenty words each
        eight rapid-access loops of ten words each

9. A very simple way to "semi-optimum code" with a one-plus-one address computer is to locate the consecutive instructions n words apart, i.e., a programmed interlace scheme. The cost of programming is drastically reduced because of its ease and simplicity. Discuss.

10. A nearly perfect optimum program, i.e., one with high efficiency of optimization, is generally more difficult to change than a less efficient one. Discuss.

11. A more efficiently optimized program generally uses up more memory than a less efficient one. Discuss.

12. Name some simple operations which might be completely optimized, e.g., looking through a table, adding two numbers, etc.

13. What are the advantages and disadvantages of recirculating loops?

19 LARGE RANDOM ACCESS FILE STORAGE

19.0 Introduction

As we have seen, the data processing problem can frequently be reduced to a problem in the processing of files. We have also noted that files which must ordinarily be processed are much too large to be stored in the internal memories of computers which are available now or will be in the foreseeable future. In this book we have concentrated on techniques involving magnetic tape as the file storage medium, because it is currently in widest use and because of its present cost advantage over other forms of bulk storage in most situations.

However, there are problems associated with tapes. The most important of these is the unavoidable restriction that the records in the file be processed *sequentially*. This is not always a serious limitation, and many techniques have been developed to work within the restriction—but in some cases it is a serious problem. To summarize the essential characteristics of sequential file processing as presented in Chapter 2 and illustrated elsewhere:

1. All files being processed in a particular run must be in the same sequence on the keys of the records. If some of the information is not already in such a sequence, it must be sorted.

2. *All* the information in the master file must be inspected, or at least passed over, regardless of the activity ratio.

3. If information must later be used in a different sequence than that in which it was processed, it must be resorted.

4. In most tape systems, the tape records have no addresses in the usual sense, i.e., there is no correspondence between location on tape and an identifying label. The routine (or the processor hardware, in some cases) must therefore inspect *every* record in order to identify it.

5. Since an appreciable amount of time is required to process the entire master file, the transactions to be processed against it must

ordinarily be batched, i.e., accumulated until a reasonable number may be processed at one time.

As we have said, these factors may or may not be serious restrictions in a given case. When they are a problem, a random access storage system may be indicated, because, if the processing is properly organized in a random access system, all five of these characteristics may be avoided.

19.1 Large Random Access Storage Devices

A large random access storage device may be defined for our purposes as a device in which a large number of file records may be stored, where the time of access to a record is not prohibitive regardless of which record was processed most recently.* It is a compromise between magnetic tapes and high-speed storage devices such as magnetic cores, in both average access time and cost, in keeping with the generalization that for the same capacity faster access time costs more money.

Several different forms of storage are in use at the present time, ranging in capacity from 2,000,000 to 20,000,000 digits and in access time from $\frac{1}{50}$ second to $\frac{1}{2}$ minute. The devices used include very large magnetic drums, a system of many relatively short strips of magnetic tape, and a system involving a stack of rotating magnetic disks often called *jukebox* storage. For this discussion, since it does not involve a cost or speed evaluation, we may regard these as all conceptually equivalent as regards record size, access time, the machine's method of addressing, and total capacity. We must consider, however, three other factors having to do with how such a storage system fits into the rest of the computer: availability of buffers, variable versus fixed record length, and availability of a table look-up feature.

There may be no buffers, one buffer, or more than one buffer between the random access storage and fast memory. If there is no buffer, there can be no overlapping of processing in fast memory with search-

---

*This definition is deliberately a little vague. It is more common to define random access storage as one for which the access time to a record (or word, in the case of internal memories) is *the same* regardless of which record (or word) was addressed most recently. This happens not to be the case for the large random access file storage devices currently available, which might better be called quasi-random access. That is, the time to locate a given record is dependent on the location of the record last processed, but not nearly so strongly as in the case of sequential access media, e.g., magnetic tapes.

LARGE RANDOM ACCESS FILE STORAGE 369

ing or reading or writing in random access storage. In this case, programming is more straightforward than when there are buffers, but processing times are naturally longer. It is necessary to reduce searching and information transfers to an absolute minimum in this case. With one buffer there can be some overlapping, such as processing one record while obtaining the next. By proper organization it is possible in some cases to hold total processing time almost to average read plus write time. The techniques for doing this are not greatly different from those discussed in Chapter 13 in connection with tape buffers. With more than one buffer, even greater time savings are possible, but the programming becomes considerably more complex.

The second consideration regarding how a large random access storage system fits into the rest of the picture is whether records to be transferred can be of variable size or are restricted to one fixed length. If variable length records are permitted in transfers, some input/output time can be saved since only necessary characters need be transferred. Also, packing several records into one group becomes much more manageable if variable size is allowable.

The third consideration is the availability of a table look-up feature, i.e., a semiautomatic technique for locating the record corresponding to a specified key. If no table look-up is available, it is necessary to know the exact location of a record before trying to read it, or else to code a search similar to the techniques used with magnetic tapes. The simplest table look-up system signals when it finds a key *equal* to that for which it is searching. If, in addition, a signal is given for *greater than* and/or *less than,* more sophisticated attacks on some problems are possible. For instance, it would be possible to select (or simply count) all records having sales of over $10,000 without sorting into a sequence of sales amount and without explicitly coding a test of the amounts.

19.2 Addressing of Records

Records are identified in large random access memory just as words are identified in high-speed storage, i.e., by a group of digits which is associated with each possible record storage location. Even though the number of characters per record in random access storage is ordinarily greater than the number of characters per word in high-speed storage, the number of records is also greater than the number of words. Thus five or six digits may be required to identify each record uniquely.

If it is possible to use the key of each record as its address in storage, programming is greatly simplified. Unfortunately, this does not happen very frequently, either because the addressing system is simply not compatible with the keys no matter how the keys might be set up, or because the keys have been established by other considerations and cannot be changed. In this case it is necessary somehow to establish a correspondence between keys and the addresses of the records.

A deceptively obvious solution to this problem is to make up a table of the keys versus addresses. This will insure a unique address for each record. However, there are many difficulties in using this method. One difficulty is the constant updating which the table requires. Every time a record is deleted, that particular address must be noted as being available for future use to store other records. Every time a record is added, a search must be made for available space, and after the assignment is made, that particular address must be noted as being in use. Another difficulty is: where should such a table be stored? If it is stored in random access storage itself, then a search has to be made in the table prior to reading a record out of storage. This search may take up considerable processing time. The table might be stored in the records of the transaction file along with the key, as an extension of the actual key. This would present tremendous problems, however, especially if the transaction records are manually prepared, because both the key and the address must be manually transcribed. The possibility of introducing errors by this method is quite high, and more space is required.

An alternate method of assigning addresses is based on not requiring the addresses to be unique (i.e., one and only one record assigned to each address). Thus, some of the records may be assigned identical addresses. Obviously, unless something is done about these nonunique assignments, errors will result. One way to handle the problem is to "tag" the duplicate records and list in a small table the actual locations of the duplicates. Various other ways are possible to locate the correct record in these situations.

This *probability method* of assigning addresses, where some of the addresses may be nonunique, involves the generation of what may be called a *functional key* which can be used as the random access storage address. The functional key can be generated by performing arithmetic operations on the actual key. There are many ways to do this; some of the articles in the bibliography discuss this. The criterion of choosing the best method for generating the functional key is to minimize the probability of assigning more than one actual record

LARGE RANDOM ACCESS FILE STORAGE 371

to any functional key. Another way to state the criterion is to minimize the number of addresses which are not unique. The number of addresses which are nonunique depends on the number of distinct addresses, the number of records in the file, and the distribution of the functional key. The probability method has been successfully used because it takes advantage of the principle that it may be possible to save some over-all time by processing the majority of the records (those with unique addresses) rapidly, but processing the minority of them (those with nonunique addresses) more slowly. Careful study should be made to select the most economical method. It is important to realize that many techniques exist for generating a functional key, and one need not be concerned about the small percentage of nonunique memory assignments, because they can be detected and corrective measures taken readily.

It must be recognized that there are problems here, as with anything else. Briefly, these are as follows. First, the generation of the functional key requires time—not much, perhaps, but it may be significant in some cases. Second, some method must be devised to identify and locate the duplicates for the nonunique addresses; even though there are relatively few of them, this can add complexity even if it does not add much time. Third, and most important, a procedure must be set up to handle new records correctly as they are created. After the functional key of a new record has been generated, it must be tested to determine whether or not it is unique. If it is unique, i.e., if it does not duplicate any of the functional keys already in the file, then the processing may proceed normally. If it is not unique, then the table of duplicate keys must be revised, and we must tag the new record [as well as the record(s) it duplicates] as being nonunique. Similarly, as records are deleted from the file, a check must be made to determine whether the record deleted was nonunique; if it was, and if it duplicated only one other record, then that other record is now unique and appropriate action must be taken to indicate this fact.

19.3 Uses of Large Random Access Storage

The introduction of random access storage into the available line of computer hardware makes it possible to consider many small and medium sized data processing applications previously thought uneconomical or impractical. One should bear in mind that there will always be data applications which will require magnetic tape sequential processing, because of the tremendous size of the files—say 500,000,000 digits of storage. Perhaps the random access storage devices of the future may make it feasible to store these large files, but presently available sizes, speeds, and costs generally confine their attractiveness to small and medium sized data processing applications. It is the purpose of this section to point out some of the ways in which random access storage may be used, and some of the associated problems.

RANDOM ACCESS STORAGE OF THE MASTER FILE

This is probably the most common use of random access storage. Ordinarily, the file is left in storage permanently, which implies that it can be used for only one application unless the applications are quite small. This is so because of the prohibitively long times required to load and unload a large storage system. There are exceptions, of course, but this is the most common situation. This is not to say that the file is never read out of the random access storage; it is necessary to do this occasionally to provide some measure of data protection, so that if a catastrophe occurs it is possible to reconstruct the file from the last "dump" of it. This is somewhat analogous to the situation with magnetic tapes, where tapes are saved for a certain period of time for exactly the same purpose.

With the file storage in random access form, transactions may be processed in any order, with no need for sorting or classifying. If it is advantageous, there need be no batching: transactions can be processed as they occur or with only a short delay. A random access storage system can be set up with keyboard entry and inquiry stations (page 190) so that transactions actually may be processed on a "real time" basis. A good example is the system of reservation accounting used by the airlines.

TABULATION OF STATISTICS

Tabulation of business statistics is a very common data processing application. In many cases, the tabulation may be associated with a major data processing application; in other cases, it may be an entirely independent operation. When the tabulation of statistics is associated with a major data processing application, it is generally called *report preparation* or *analysis*. In any case, it is a valuable tool with which to reduce masses of data into more compact and meaningful form.

If statistics tabulation is an integral part of a data processing application, one pass of the file is usually sufficient to do both file updating and statistics tabulation. In fact, should more than one tabulation be required, all these may be done simultaneously, provided there is sufficient storage to perform the various statistics accumulations. For example, in a finished goods inventory application, it may be required to gather statistics for both the sales and production departments. The sales department might be interested in sales volume by salesman, branch office, and sales region; the production department might be interested in inventory on hand classified into various other categories. As the sales orders are processed against the master file stored in random access storage, statistics for the period and year to date can be produced to satisfy both the sales and production departments.

If the statistics tabulation is a distinct data processing application, there is considerably more flexibility in planning the program since it no longer is tied to a file updating application. Since larger storage is available also, larger tables can be compiled or more tables compiled in the same pass.

It is quite evident that one of the advantages of using random access storage for statistics tabulation is the large storage available for *accumulation* of the statistics. It is rarely necessary to sort the input records and tabulate in parts. Furthermore, many different tables of statistics may be accumulated simultaneously. Whether the system is used to perform independent statistics tabulations or perform statistics tabulation as part of a larger data processing application, it is possible to prepare large statistics tables (or many tables) all in one pass, without any sorting, and make them available on an up-to-the-minute basis.

RANDOM ACCESS STORAGE AS AN AUXILIARY TO MAGNETIC TAPES

The characteristics of random access storage are generally in contrast to the characteristics of a processor using magnetic tapes in sequential processing. Thus an application may be suitable for one but not for the other. However, there are certain applications where some parts are suited to random access storage, other parts to sequential processing. In these cases, using random access storage to supplement the magnetic tapes may effect significant economies that would be impossible if only one or the other were used. For example, some of the functions that are common to many data processing applications include on-line interrogation, updating auxiliary files, performing statistics tabulation. Random access storage is well suited for these functions, whereas sequentially processed magnetic tapes are definitely not efficient. In order to use random access storage as auxiliary equipment to magnetic tapes, the two types of equipment must be able to communicate in a common language. The common language is most likely to be magnetic tapes. Since it is also quite likely that the computer will have other slower forms of input/output equipment, such as cards, paper tape, etc., the random access storage can sometimes be used as the off-line conversion equipment instead of the conventional card-to-tape and tape-to-card equipment.

19.4 Summary

The introduction of large random access storage devices has widened the range of techniques which may be used to attack data processing problems, and has expanded the list of problems which are amenable to solution with electronic data processing. The programming is no longer restricted by the rigid requirement to process a master file sequentially. Real time processing of transactions is possible.

Still, there are problems. The freedom to use any record at any time is paid for by the difficulty of locating the record corresponding to a known key. Present "random access" devices are not *really* random; the time to locate a particular record *does* depend on which record was processed last. Data protection is a more serious problem than with magnetic tapes, precisely because it is not necessary to create a new master file each time it is processed; if the file has not been protected by reading it out onto tape or cards, or by other time-consuming processes, damage to the file information can be almost irreparable. At present, random access storage is considerably more expensive per character than magnetic tape storage.

In spite of these serious problems, which are often carelessly minimized, random access storage has its place. It will in all probability become increasingly important as experience in its use is gained and new techniques and cheaper and better devices are developed.

Exercises

1. What are the characteristics of applications that can make good use of large random access file storage?

2. What are the advantages and disadvantages of sequential file processing versus large random access file processing?

3. If batch processing is not used with large random access file processing, how should controls be set up?

4. How can we positively protect against accidental erasure of records stored in the large random access file?

LARGE RANDOM ACCESS FILE STORAGE

5. Name several functions served by a large random acess file storage.

6. Discuss the various ways to address the large random access file storage.

7. A common way to generate the functional key is to take part of the actual key, perform arithmetic operations with it (e.g., multiply the part by itself), and then select a certain part of the result. Discuss how we should exercise care in selecting the proper parts of the actual key to avoid excessive nonunique assignments.

8. The actual key used in a certain payroll application is entirely numeric and is made up of department (2 digits), cost center (3 digits), and serial number (6 digits). A new serial number is assigned to every new employee added to the company payroll. Suggest a method of obtaining a functional key to address a large random access file with a capacity of 1,000,000 records.

9. A large random access file storage application used the probability method of addressing the file. It was beset with an intolerable percentage of nonunique addresses. Analysis showed that it was using the parts of the actual key which hardly changed from record to record to generate the functional key. Also, the random access memory was 95% filled. Discuss how we might decrease the percentage of nonunique address assignments.

10. Keyboard inquiry stations are a means for providing typewriter or other types of keyboard input/output directly connected to the computer. They are, in a certain sense, auxiliary consoles. Plan a program to control and operate ten inquiry stations, with stations 1 and 2 having high priority and the other eight having low priority.

11. Name several data processing applications where "real time control," i.e., almost immediate access to information in the file, is required.

20 STEPS IN PLANNING AND PROGRAMMING COMPUTER APPLICATIONS

20.0 Introduction

The techniques so far presented in this book should have provided the conscientious reader with enough background to allow him to work effectively in many of the individual areas of electronic data processing. However, many readers may feel at this point that their knowledge consists of isolated fragments which do not seem to fit together. In this chapter we propose to discuss in outline form the sequence of steps which must typically be gone through from the inception of an application until the time when it is successfully operating. Most of these steps have been covered in detail elsewhere in the book, and others are outside the scope of the book. It should be clear, therefore, that we are not attempting here to present new material but rather are trying to help the reader organize his knowledge.

20.1 The Systems Study

We shall assume in this discussion that all of what may be called the installation phase has been completed. That is, we shall not consider the work that goes into studying the feasibility of getting a computer, nor of which computer to get, nor of which applications to put on the computer first. We do not wish to minimize the importance of this preliminary work; it is crucial that it be well done, and it is something that often requires several man-years to carry out. However, these functions, important as they are, are outside the scope of a book on programming. The reader who is faced with these problems will find much helpful guidance in the material listed in the bibliography. It should be noted also that the following discussion of the systems study is only a sketchy outline, not a complete treatment.

The first thing that must be done to get any data processing applica-

STEPS IN PLANNING

tion running on a computer is to obtain a complete and detailed definition of the job to be done. This, of course, is necessary no matter what method of data processing is to be used, whether manual, mechanical, or electronic. This is usually termed systems and procedures work. For our purposes here, we may define a *procedure* as a sequence of operations usually involving several people in one or more areas, established to insure uniform handling of a recurring transaction of the business, and a *system* as a network of related procedures developed according to an integrated scheme for performing a major activity of the business. A person who works in this area of obtaining or developing a problem definition is usually called a *systems analyst*.

We shall assume that the systems analyst begins his activities after the general area of data processing has been specified, although in practice the same individual may have been involved in determining the sequence in which different applications are to be put on the computer. If he does not already have it, a systems analyst must quickly acquire fundamental information on the nature of the business and its organization. It is essential to know the goals of the business, its products, status, and its special problems (such as seasonal variations). An organization chart is usually desirable because of the light it sheds on the way the business is set up and because it provides the names of people who may have to be contacted during the study.

The effort required to develop a complete definition of the problem to be done is very often underestimated. A great many different facts must be very precisely established without which succeeding phases will inevitably founder. A detailed description of the information to be processed must be obtained along with estimates of the quantity of information and when each type is available during the processing period. The calculations to be performed on the data must be precisely defined, which usually implies the sizable task of specifying how the many exceptions are to be handled. The nature of the accounting controls must be established. All of the reports to be produced must be defined along with time schedules telling when they must be completed during the processing period. Procedures must be established for dealing with exceptions which cannot be handled by the computer. There are many other things of this nature which must be defined also, but perhaps these are indicative.

In some exceptional cases, all of this information may already be available. If so, however, it is usually because the application being set up for the computer is a replica of a system which is already in operation; this course of action seldom leads to either an efficient computer operation or to one which is well integrated with the rest of the work being done on the computer. Lacking the crutch of simply copying the existing system, the analyst must set out to get the information he needs. One common way to begin getting this information is to conduct interviews with the people now doing the work, if it is now being done, or perhaps with their immediate supervisors. Special care must be taken to insure that all exceptions to the regular procedures are uncovered. These are often not specified in existing written procedures manuals. Through a series of such interviews, the analyst can begin to get a grasp of the over-all situation. At frequent intervals during the systems study, the information gathered so far, along with the questions raised by it, should be reviewed with the supervisors and managers in the areas affected. (It is, of course, essential that all of this be in written form.) It is not uncommon for these review sessions to turn into discussions of goals: "Why do we make *eleven* copies of this report?" "Does anybody really read this weekly stock status report?" "Do you think it is smart to allow these changes to be made without the approval of a little higher level authority?" "Do you think it is better to send these bills out on prepunched cards or in envelopes? You can put advertising in the envelopes." Questions and comments like these are typical, and are necessary to the proper definition of the job. If they are not asked someone is taking too much for granted.

It is a very foolish and unwise systems analyst who gives no thought to human relations problems during this study. Anyone resists change to a certain extent; everyone is understandably apprehensive about something which has even the slightest possibility of threatening his job security. It is well known that rumors spread very quickly in an office or factory. The systems analyst is simply insuring his own success if he takes some pains to be sure that there is complete managerial support for his project, that it has been explained by management to the people involved, that anyone even remotely affected is assured that no one will be laid off as a result of the computer work (if this is true), and that the people involved understand in at least general terms what can and cannot be done with a computer. Every situation is different and no hard and fast rules can be given. It is fairly safe to state, however, that if this aspect of the systems study is ignored, the job will be a great deal more difficult, if not a complete failure.

After an initial problem definition has been developed, the next step is to prepare the over-all plan of action to accomplish the objectives within the specified scope and time. The analyst should present a written report of his study which summarizes his recommendations, gives a brief history of the study including a review of its objectives, and compares in summary form the old and new systems. The summary should be backed up by detailed reports which include at least top level flow charts of the proposed solution. The cost and efficiency of the old system should be compared with those of the new even if the major goals of the new system are not clerical cost savings. Unfortunately, some of the data required for such a comparison is often difficult to obtain. Some of the costs which must be considered in a computer solution are rental or amortized purchase price of the computer and associated equipment, installation costs, conversion costs, salaries of computer personnel, maintenance costs if not part of a rental contract, cost of space, and tax considerations.* The report should present an estimated time schedule for implementing the proposal.

A thorough review of this report with management will ordinarily result in minor (or major) revisions in the plan of attack. This is to be expected since a project of the scope and importance of a sizable data processing application generally goes through several stages of revision. It is usually unwise to attempt to do a systems study on a "crash" basis. If management does not feel there is sufficient time to do a careful systems study, then it is probably not wise to attempt anything but minor modifications in an existing system. A balance must be struck, however; the systems analyst and the management involved must both realize that a significant problem can rarely be so *completely* defined that no changes will ever have to be made in the system proposed to handle it. This applies even after a system is successfully in operation.

20.2 Preparation of Top-Level Flow Charts

The systems and procedures analyst in his systems study will generally have prepared top-level flow charts. These may be comprehensive in nature or may only indicate the gross strategy of the proposed computer solution. As a result of the review by management of the study report, it is quite possible that changes will be required in the plans for mechanization; these may be reflected in a need for new top-level flow charts. As implementation of the solution proceeds, new problems and new insights develop, which may also require changes in the top-level flow charts.

* A commonly used and fairly reliable rule of thumb is that equipment costs are usually about equal to personnel costs.

If the top-level flow charts in the study are confined to an outline of the gross strategy of the proposed system, additional top-level charts will ordinarily be drawn as the first phase of the actual programming. If, as usual, a series of computer runs is required, drawing top-level flow charts for all runs in the series before proceeding with any detailed charts will aid in working out a better distribution of work between runs. The size of memory, number of tape handlers available, and other such considerations will also be brought to bear here.

20.3 Design of Input and Output Forms and Records

A *form* may be defined for our purposes as a printed document with blank spaces for the insertion of information. The major considerations in the design of forms are the productive efficiencies of their use, minimization of opportunity for clerical errors, and the cost and esthetics of the forms. If a form is to be used in keypunching a card, an attempt should be made to maximize the ratio of productive key strokes to wasteful positioning operations. A form should be designed so that a person using it is not required to skip around over the card or paper in order to get the information in the sequence needed. Consideration must be given to ease of working with the information on a form when it is entered into the computer, although this factor should not override ease of readability.

The subject of forms design is a very specialized field and no attempt will be made here to discuss it comprehensively. In addition to the general principles mentioned above, consideration must be given to size, number of copies, weight of paper, usage and economical order size, bursting (separation of continuous forms), margins, form numbers, mailing requirements, etc. Fortunately, specialists are available to do this work or to give advice to others doing it. The forms manufacturers will always provide competent advice in this area.

Every computer run in general involves the design of certain tape or card records. There are no hard and fast rules which determine how a file record should be designed, but a few general considerations should be kept in mind. One obvious requirement is that if output records from one run become input records to another the two must be compatible, and if changes are made in either record the person responsible for the other should be informed. This may seem obvious, but minor fiascos resulting from such a communication failure are not as uncommon as they should be. Another important consideration is that the keys of records must be compatible with any generalized routines which are to be used, such as sorting. Finally, it is always necessary to arrive at a compromise between the savings in tape time achieved by packing information into a record very tightly and the processing time which is saved if this is not done.

20.4 Tentative Layout of Memory and Allocation of Tape Units

A layout of the memory of the computer gives the programmer an indication of the memory problems which he may expect to encounter. This may or may not be critical depending on the amount of memory available and the nature of the application. At this point it may become necessary to reallocate the work among the various runs. Plans may be made for the use of auxiliary storage. It may be desirable to set up standard conventions for the use of memory, certain locations for tape handling routines, input and output working storage areas, temporary storage, etc. This will tend to simplify the work of the machine operators later as well as facilitate communication between programmers if, as usual, more than one is working on an application. The memory allocation problem is somewhat simplified by the use of relative or symbolic coding systems which do some of this work semiautomatically, but it is still necessary to estimate the amount of memory required in order to foresee space problems. Memory layouts on specially designed forms should become part of each run book.

The allocation of tape units on a systems basis promotes the smooth flow of data from run to run. Switching reels between different tape units as processing proceeds can prove costly in time and lead to errors in handling. Again, good communication is required to keep members of a team advised of any changes in allocations which affect them. It may be desirable to indicate tape assignments on the top level flow charts of the system.

20.5 Preparation of Detailed Flow Charts

The techniques of flow charting were discussed in Chapter 3, and small samples of detailed flow charts have appeared throughout the book. We mention them here only to emphasize once again the necessity for doing a thorough job of preparing them before coding is begun. To summarize the reasons for doing so:

1. Coding is *much* easier if the work has been carefully flow-charted.
2. The coding will have fewer errors.
3. Flow charting in advance helps the programmer to recognize

which tasks have to be done many times, thus making it simpler to organize the work into subroutines—which is almost always desirable.

4. Flow charts can be reviewed by others a great deal more easily than coding, making for the early detection of errors in logic and in problem definition.

20.6 Coding

Coding from detailed flow charts is a relatively rapid process. A considerable part of this book has been devoted to it, so once again we shall only mention a few suggestions of general procedure here.

1. It is desirable, where possible, for the systems analyst to do his own coding. This saves considerable time, because the problem does not have to be explained to another person, with the attendant possibility of misunderstandings. Furthermore, as pointed out elsewhere, systems design, programming, and coding are not independent activities. During coding, the systems analyst may discover inconsistencies in the systems design, or recognize improvements that can be made.

2. It is highly desirable to leave some free memory space in every run, even if doing so requires some reassignment of the work among runs. Changes are inevitable, and there is nothing quite so frustrating as trying to make a twenty-word addition when only fifteen words are free.

3. We have recommended elsewhere that extensive use be made of the "remarks" column on the coding paper. Trying to understand someone else's code (or even your own) given only a listing of the instructions, is an exercise in mental gymnastics to tax the ability of a cryptographer.

4. It is wise to cross-reference the coding with the corresponding detailed flow chart, to simplify the checking of the coding.

5. Some method should be devised to cross-reference the coding itself, to show the points at which jumps enter. Many coding errors are caused by forgetting that a section of the code is entered from other places.

6. It is necessary at some point to stop trying to improve a code. The problem is much the same as that faced by an engineer in designing a new product: he can always think of some way of improving the design, but if it is ever to get manufactured and sold to the customer, he has to decide sometime that what he has is good enough. Probably no code has ever been written, with the exception of some small subroutines, that could not have been shortened or speeded up

STEPS IN PLANNING

a little. The question to ask is, is it worth it? Is a saving of 2 minutes in a 1-hour run worth 3 weeks' recoding and debugging? This is not to say that revisions should never be made, but that a line has to be drawn somewhere.

7. Every page of coding should be identified, dated, numbered, and signed. There is no need to go overboard here, but some systematic identification should be used.

8. As we have already stated several times, it is important to reach some type of compromise between the wish of most coders to be clever and the desirable goal of producing codes which are easy to debug, understand, and modify. Excessive cleverness is seldom a good investment.

At some stage in this process it is necessary to wire the plugboards which are required on many computers in connection with input, output, and off-line input and output. We are completely omitting a discussion of this subject, because it is very highly specialized and because it is adequately described in the manufacturers' literature.

20.7 Checking and Review

The amount of review is the largest variable in the development of a computer program. Review steps may be inserted at several stages of the system development depending upon the nature of the application, the time and manpower available, the policies and experience of the installation, and the working habits of the individuals concerned. The subject is inserted at this stage of the development because desk checking of coding is one of the most common review steps. The objective of reviewing coding is to determine that the coding does what the flow chart prescribes. A review of coding does not embrace a review of flow chart logic, though often errors in the logic are turned up. Independent review of coding is more effective than desk checking by the programmer who did the coding, but frequently the latter must suffice. Desk checking of coding is an excellent assignment for a programming trainee. Not only is the coding checked, but the trainee is exposed to sophisticated efforts.

The reviewer should pay particular attention to positioning of tapes, bringing up successive records for processing, disposing of processed records, the number of times through a loop, etc. Errors of these types are difficult to find in debugging and it is essential that they be caught. It is not necessary to waste time checking matters which the computer will find without causing delays in the debugging.

Examples of this are type-outs and details of intricate computations which will be checked when results are compared to predetermined solutions. The conditions under which subroutines are entered and the details of switch settings are frequent trouble spots. The reviewer should also look for characters which are frequently confused, such as 1 and I, and see that recommended conventions are followed.

Techniques of desk checking vary considerably with the temperament and experience of the programmer. At one extreme there are individuals who cannot stand the required attention to detail or who feel that a few minutes on the computer will give results equivalent to days of desk checking. This approach in many cases will actually speed up the job; however, the danger is that if many errors exist in the program, the programmer will not know where to start in his debugging but will flounder around using up valuable machine time. At the other extreme is the individual who can mimic the computer, meticulously follow through all the details of processing, and produce an almost perfect program. The danger of this approach is that too much time may be spent in desk checking without adequate use being made of the power of the computer. It would seem that a happy medium should be adopted. One essential thing is that the reviewer have a critical approach and take little for granted. This is where independent review is so valuable, for the original coder may fall into the same error patterns when he reviews his own coding.

20.8 Getting the Coding into Machine Language

Since current machines cannot scan the programmer's handwritten sheets (although active research is being carried on in this area), some means is required to put the written coding into machine-sensible language. The method used will represent a choice among the different input alternatives of the specific computer. Clerical help should be available to keypunch cards, type directly on magnetic tape, prepare punched paper tape, or prepare input in other media from the programmer's coding.

The input rates of information transfer may vary considerably among the different alternatives, but so may the convenience of working with the coding during the debugging phase. If the undebugged instructions are placed on magnetic tape initially, computer time, which may be expensive and hard to come by, may be required each time a change has to be made. It is extremely rare to find a program of any significant length to be completely error-free the first time that it is run. If the program is put on punched cards, the programmer

STEPS IN PLANNING 385

may easily delete incorrect cards, punch a few new ones, and insert them into the program deck without using computer time for the correcting process. Debugging must, of course, still be done on the computer. When the program is considered to be error-free, it may then be converted to a more efficient input medium such as magnetic tape, if this is available. On several important machines, however, it is more trouble to work with cards than tape; routines have been devised for these machines which make the insertion of corrections relatively painless.

The clerical process of transferring the coding into machine-sensible language may generate a significant number of errors. As described in Chapter 3, handwritten numbers and letters are very frequently confused, or the operators may simply strike the wrong keys. The clerical personnel usually do not understand the coding. It has been found imperative to have such punched or typed coding verified. This may be done by another clerk on a special machine for the purpose, by the use of a printout of the coding and a check by the programmer or an assistant against the original hand coding sheets, or by a combination of methods. Time spent this way is usually well worthwhile. Obviously, the more expensive computer time will be saved when routine clerical errors are detected by such checking.

Even if verification has been performed on special machine verifiers, a printout should be made for the programmer's reference during the debugging phase. As another preliminary to debugging, certain analyses may be made of the coding. For example, all references to each memory cell may be indicated. Such analyses may be made on the computer or on peripheral equipment. These analyses may show up coding or clerical errors before formal debugging actually starts.

20.9 Preparation of Test Data and Accuracy Checking

It is necessary to devise a set of test data to use in determining the correctness of the system. Sometimes actual data may be available for the purpose, but often it is necessary to make it up. Actually, the latter course has advantages, because one of the critical aspects of debugging is the determination that all branches and exception-handling routines operate correctly. Actual data may not provide for such a test. Often people in the application area or the auditor may be able to provide advice on test data design. When a system utilizes a basic data file, such as an employee earnings file in a payroll system, a single comprehensive test file should be prepared for the use of all programmers who require the basic file in their runs. Test data must be converted to machine language and carefully checked for format and other significant details. The actual numbers used often are not significant. There will inevitably be significant errors in the test data, but these, if not excessive, can serve a useful purpose by testing different error paths in the system. Thought should be given to the use of the computer to generate random numbers, calculate check digits, etc. This subject of verifying program accuracy has been discussed extensively in Chapter 12.

20.10 Volume Test and Conversion

Before a run is considered debugged, it is advisable to subject it to a *volume test*, which is the use of considerable amounts of data run again and again. This will invariably show up additional bugs. It may be feasible to code a simple routine to generate volume data. However, it is preferable to use actual data. This may be tied in to the *conversion* process, which is the change-over from the previous data processing methods to the computer system.

The job of conversion may be a staggering task and in almost every case merits careful attention by the system planners, starting early in the system development. Unfortunately, with many pressing tasks competing for attention, the problem of conversion may be shunted aside until it is almost too late. This is not realistic when one considers that more man-hours may in some cases be expended on the conversion process than on the rest of the system combined. There are several reasons for the scope of this problem. Many one-time runs may have to be programmed to accomplish conversion. Depending on the application, of course, vast files may have to be converted from a manual basis to machine language, perhaps by punching cards or paper tape. Not only are new errors generated in such file production (even though the most skilled keypunchers or typists are used), which errors must be laboriously corrected, but all the inadequacies of the prior system are subjected to cold, methodical, and precise scrutiny by the computer. This machine does only what it has been told in advance to do, which cannot include insight into all the mistakes and deficiencies of the past.

It may seem obvious that a period of parallel operation of the old and new systems would be desirable. This would provide a safe volume test in its most precise form, for there could be a side-by-side comparison of results. For a variety of reasons, this was not done on several of the early computer applications. In some cases time was a problem, in others the lack of physical facilities and manpower to undertake parallel operations, in some false economy or just plain ignorance of what problems were presented in the conversion process. The attitude also existed in some cases, especially when business computers had not yet proved themselves, that the bridges had to be burned behind the people in the organization. This not only spurred on the computer group, but forced cooperation of people in the application area. If a parallel operation is undertaken, it should be as short as feasible because of its costliness.

Where the conversion process is a lengthy one, it is preferable or even necessary to do it on a cyclic basis. Branches, departments, billing groups, or other logical subdivisions of the business may be converted one by one. Temporary workers may be required on large jobs even with a cyclic approach. The first conversion is the most difficult and it is desirable that at least a short period of parallel operation be provided as a means of final debugging. On smaller jobs a crash program over a weekend may be adequate to accomplish conversion. It may be possible to get a jump on some phases of the job, such as by making up a skeleton master file in advance containing all required information except the current operating figures. A danger exists (with or without parallel operation) that once the files have been converted, so much computer time will have to be spent on cleaning them up that transactions will pile up at an excessive rate. This will seriously interfere with the operating efficiency of the business. Often, to keep up with transactions, errors are allowed to remain in the files for considerable periods of time. When erroneous reports keep appearing, serious damage to morale occurs. Debugging in production brings the dirty linen out in public on a large scale. The authors have seen cases of so much lack of confidence in the computer system that surreptitious parallel manual operations by clerks continued in the application areas for a year and more after thorough debugging of the computer system had occurred.

20.11 System Write-up

A system is next to worthless if it is not adequately documented. This has happened to so many different organizations on such a wide variety of jobs as to constitute an axiom. Several common types of write-ups are necessary.

PROGRESS REPORTS

During the course of the study and system development, periodic progress reports should be prepared for the "client," the management personnel for whom the job is being done. The reports should be reviewed by a supervisor on the computing staff before release. They should either be scheduled to cover fixed periods of time during which progress can be expected, or released whenever significant new developments can be reported. The scope of the project and the number of people active on it determine whether reports should be issued every few weeks or months. If issued too often, too much time will be wasted and there will be little interest developed in them. If too infrequent, their valid functions may be negated. Some suggested contents of a progress report are:

1. The current status of the project, and progress since the last report.
2. Flow charts, documents, and other materials developed.
3. The definition of specific problems and proposed solutions.
4. Schedule revisions, if necessary.

The progress report allows step-by-step review of the work by people who will be served by the system, safeguards the procedures analysts and programmers from unjustified criticism by serving as a history of the project, expedites subsequent work including procedures manuals, and provides an excellent channel of communication between the computer people and their clients. Where possible, oral presentations should accompany the written reports.

OPERATING INSTRUCTIONS

The programmer should prepare instructions to the computer operator for each run and also instructions on the handling of peripheral equipment required by the system.* For example, there may be different levels of paper tape allowable in the system, or certain plugboards and paper control tapes may have to be used on the high-speed printer. The operator must know which magnetic tapes to mount as inputs and what to do with output tapes. An essential part of the operating instructions are the error correction procedures, whether directed to the computer operator or an assisting clerk. There must be written procedures for handling every error which the program has been designed to detect.

RUN BOOK

This might be called the program procedures manual. This book should be prepared for every run, whether generated or entirely hand-

---

* In many installations he also includes his home phone number!

coded. Its purpose is to provide a written record of everything pertinent to the run. By means of the run book, an experienced programmer who had nothing to do with programming the run should, in a reasonable amount of time, be able to become sufficiently familiar with the run to determine the causes of any troubles which may arise and make necessary changes. He should also be able to go into a strange run when system requirements change and be able to make necessary changes in an emergency.

By the time the programmer has reached the debugging stage, he will have assembled a folder of working papers. He needs only to put in last-minute changes and perhaps redo flow charts and other papers in cleaner form. The run book may include the following items:

1. A run number and title.
2. The name of the programmer.
3. The date of completion of the run.
4. A sheet summarizing the computer operating instructions for ready reference, including labels and descriptions of tapes and their disposition, error or special procedures, rerun instructions, average run time, and switch settings.
5. A one- or two-paragraph description of the purpose of the run.
6. A complete set of flow charts. These should include the top level flow charts which show how the run fits into the system, and detailed flow charts cross-referenced to the coding (showing for each symbol the starting line of the coding which performs that operation). For some generated runs this last may not be feasible.
7. Completed forms, when applicable, for:
   Memory allocation
   Record designs
   Operating instructions for high-speed printer, converter, or other peripheral equipment
   Plugboard layouts
8. A printed list of the coding including computer or other machine analysis of it, comparisons of assembly language coding and machine-produced coding, etc. Changes to the coding after the run has been debugged should be entered in red pencil, initialed, and dated.
9. A layout of the run on the instruction tape, if feasible and applicable.
10. A sample of each report produced by the run.
11. Suggestions for future changes and special warnings about making changes.
12. Generating specifications for the run, if relevant.

PROCEDURES MANUAL

This might be called the client's procedures manual. It governs the relationship between people in the application areas affected by a computer system and the data processing installation. As the name indicates, the manual states the procedures which the client's personnel must use to utilize the computer system effectively. Typical contents of such a manual are:

1. Exhibits of input documents to the data processing installation with instructions for their preparation and transmittal procedures.
2. Exhibits of output forms and reports with an explanation of their contents, discussion of the frequency of their preparation, etc.
3. Flow charts in sufficient detail to give a clear picture of the system. (Not as common as items 1 and 2.)

20.12 Program Maintenance

One of the most frequently overlooked costs of electronic data processing is the maintenance of a program, i.e., the changes required *after* it has supposedly been completely debugged. Program maintenance can be classified into two major types: those changes required because flaws are discovered and because ways are found to improve efficiency, and those made necessary by changes in the system.

It is not at all uncommon to discover errors in a program after it has been running satisfactorily for months or even years. This can happen because of errors in rarely used sections of routines that were never completely checked out but have never been called on before, and because of unlikely combinations of circumstances. It is impossible to predict all possible combinations of, say, deductions in a payroll system. It may turn out that a man who claims eleven dependents, who is a union member but does not belong to the credit union, who has been sick a great deal, and whose pay is being garnisheed, will cause some part of the gross-to-net section to run amok. This particular example is obviously contrived—but such things have happened. These types of things, plus many others which may not be quite so unlikely, must be cleaned up when they occur. It may be discovered, for instance, that input data is coming in with many more errors than had been anticipated, requiring, perhaps, a revision in the input editing routine.

It almost always happens that after a system has been running for a while ways are seen to improve running times, operator convenience, accuracy, etc. Sometimes it is worthwhile to make such changes as they come along; in other cases it is wiser to wait until there is time to reprogram the whole application (which is sometimes a rather long wait).

Under systems changes we consider changes in what a program is expected to do. Examples: changes in tax laws, union dues, blanket wage adjustments, and changes in company or governmental reporting requirements, to name a few in the payroll area. These changes often come with little warning and carry great urgency—or so it seems, at least. It should be emphasized that such changes arise much more frequently than most people imagine. When they do happen, someone must be available—without delay, usually—who knows the system intimately and can make the required changes quickly and correctly. It is not uncommon with the major computer applications to find one or more persons who have no other duties than the maintenance of one system.

20.13 Training Activities

A certain amount of training will be required in installing any new system. The timing, nature, and magnitude of training activities depend upon the particular situation encountered. If the system being developed is a first computer application, the manufacturer, a consultant, or a senior programmer who has been hired by the business will have to give a programming course fairly early in the effort to develop additional programming support. Without the support of top management a computer installation stands small chance of success. "Executive" courses, such as management seminars, progress reports for key personnel, and the like, may be necessary to develop high level support and the comprehension of computer capabilities essential for full exploitation of the new tool. Operating personnel in the data processing area have to learn how to run the new job. People in the application areas will have to learn new procedures. This frequently takes a considerable amount of time and effort. The books and manuals described in Section 20.11 will be of use here. Less obvious is the frequent need for the senior man developing the system to train a replacement for himself, even if the project leader is a permanent company employee. He will probably go on to a new assignment, leaving a less experienced man to follow the system through its last phases and into regular production. Such training may continue through a major part of the system development as a personnel development program and to provide a measure of insurance should the project leader have to leave the assignment for any reason.

20.14 Evaluation

Evaluation is a continuing process in the development of a computer system. Contact with the client's personnel feeds back information against which the work to date is reviewed. Frequently changes are requested, but previous decisions may be adhered to in the interest of getting the job done within a reasonable time. Notes of desirable changes, however, may be made for future reference. The project team will generate ideas on their own for improved approaches to their task. One of the difficulties of business applications of computers is the lack of complete and accurate formulation of problems. The debugging, conversion, and production phases are most illuminating in exposing system deficiencies.

It often becomes apparent that significant increases in efficiency can be achieved by redesigning the system or recoding those sections most heavily used or where the deficiencies are greatest. The authors have seen systems where five-to-one savings in computer running time were achieved by system redesign and recoding. Most savings occur by reworking the first systems put in at an installation; subsequent systems tend to be more efficient as the technical proficiency of the staff increases. Increased use of automatic techniques reduces coding inefficiencies but still leaves the problem of good system design. It is the rare computer system that does not merit some redesign within a year of initially going into production.

It might be pointed out here that evaluation of a computer system is a double-edged sword. The personnel in the application areas served by the machine generally have doubts and skepticism which must be overcome. At a company computer orientation seminar, Mr. L. E. Mackey, a General Electric departmental Manager of Office Procedures at Appliance Park, Louisville, Ky., listed ten stages of "Univac in Transition" as follows:*

Stage 1. BEHOLD THE STAR—Computers will revolutionize our office work.

Stage 2. HAPPINESS AND OPTIMISM—Computer is installed and there is nothing to stop us now—April, 1954.

Stage 3. MAÑANA—Takes just a little longer to get ready than we anticipated, particularly when people keep changing their minds about the reports we are supposed to produce.

Stage 4. IMMINENT RESULTS—All initial projects are 99% complete.

*Automatic Coding at G.E., R. M. Petersen. Reprinted with the permission of the editors of the *Journal of the Franklin Institute,* Monograph 3, April, 1957, page 4.

Stage 5. FIRST RESULTS—People are actually being paid untouched by human hands—October, 1954.
Stage 6. TO HECK WITH THE STAR—Takes so long to get ready and the processing time is longer than predicted. Is it really worth it?
Stage 7. GRADUAL ACCEPTANCE—Revisions are made capitalizing on experience gained. We begin to show improvements.
Stage 8. DEPENDENCE—More and more processing responsibility is assumed and managers come to rely upon the reports produced.
Stage 9. MORE MAYBE?—Surely there are additional things we could be be doing with our computer.
Stage 10. MORE RIGHT AWAY!—Let's integrate the systems we have and continue on full steam ahead.

20.15 Summary

We have described in step-by-step fashion a procedure which may be followed in a computer application from the origination of the problem until the debugged and documented system is turned over to operating personnel. We have concerned ourselves primarily with those aspects of an application which affect the systems analyst or programmer. The physical installation of equipment has not been discussed because of its engineering aspects and the one-time nature of this problem. Computer manufacturers are prepared to consult on the installation of their equipment. We have not attempted to provide a rigid check list which must be followed in all cases, because individual problems vary so greatly. Rather, we have given a general guide to the programming of computer runs, a logical sequence of the work steps which may be required.

The largest variable in the steps in programming a computer application is the amount of review, both that done independently and that done by the programmer himself. Only a minimum has been indicated in these pages. Experience and the nature of the problem and personnel will determine the optimum amount of checking. At some stages of the procedure time estimating will be desirable, both to determine remaining work schedules and equipment operating time. The further along in the work, the more accurate will such time estimates be. Several such appraisals may be necessary during the course of a project.

Exercises

1. Name the steps in planning and programming computer applications. Discuss.

2. Suggest a very abbreviated and a very elaborate *sequence* of steps in

planning and programming computer applications. In the abbreviated sequences, discuss why certain steps may be omitted, and in the elaborate sequence, discuss why certain additional steps are needed.

3. In the evaluation of a computer system, it is the total cost to do the job that is important. Name and discuss some of the costs in installing an electronic data processing installation.

4. What are some of the considerations that should go into form design for electronic data processing?

5. Are there any major differences between procedures work for manual systems, punched card systems, and electronic data processing systems? Discuss.

6. Discuss the alternatives of using manual methods, punched cards, and the electronic computer itself to perform the clerical work of conversion.

7. Assuming that it is required to "freeze" the conversion of records for a short period for manual work (say 5 days) before the changes are reflected in the new master tape, how should the changes which refer to these frozen records be processed?

8. If the entire master file is to be converted over a period of 6 months, selecting a few ledgers (convenient group of accounts) each month, then some means must be provided to distinguish and separate the changes, inquiries, and normal inputs to the following categories:
(a) Master record in old system.
(b) Master record frozen.
(c) Master record in new system.
Describe a system to perform this function.

9. Discuss some of the problems involved in conversion if the account numbers (or payroll numbers, etc.) are changed in the process.

10. Discuss the human relations problems frequently encountered in developing computer systems, and show what may be done to ease them.

11. Plugging a computer into an existing punched card or manual system has been compared to hooking a gasoline engine to a wagon to make an automobile. Discuss the need for new systems analysis when a computer is to be installed.

12. What is the significance of documentation in computer applications?

21 ACCOUNTING, AUDITING, AND DATA PROTECTION

21.0 Introduction

It is not to be expected that a major step forward in the mechanization of record keeping would not pose some new problems while solving old ones. We shall discuss in this chapter questions such as the following. How can an auditor inspect records which are stored invisibly on magnetic tape? How can *anyone* know that the processing is being done correctly? What is left for the accountant to do? What happens when a computer "fails" and cannot be restored to operation for 3 days? What can be done to prevent a machine operator from doubling his pay rate by altering his master payroll record during a slack night shift?

Fortunately, there are some answers to these questions. In this chapter we explore some of the problems, and try to indicate what the solutions are. Some of the solutions are only partial solutions as yet, but we shall try to show that there is no cause for panic.

21.1 Some Characteristics of Accounting by Computer

To begin this discussion, we shall summarize some of the characteristics of computer accounting which distinguish it from other accounting methods.

CENTRALIZATION OF CONTROL FACILITATED

Data processing naturally tends to become centralized in one location, because of the fact that a large computer is cheaper *per operation* than a smaller one (if it can be kept busy). This has a number of implications. It may be significant to the auditor that the data processing is being carried out at a location physically isolated from the origination of the information and the use of the results. The centralization of data processing seems to run counter to the current trend toward decentralization of authority in many large concerns, although it is possible that decentralization of authority is not incompatible with centralization of information. It is undoubtedly true that centralization of data processing puts all the eggs in one basket. If no duplicate files are kept, for instance, all of a company's accounting records might be located in one cabinet of magnetic tapes. A fire could cause complete loss of irreplaceable records. Actually, this is not as serious a problem as might appear at first glance: it is a great deal easier to duplicate magnetic tape files than files kept on paper. We shall discuss precautions against catastrophe more fully later.

STANDARDIZATION OF PROCESSING

The instructions which control a computer are fixed; similar transactions *must* be processed similarly. This is in contrast to human processing, where different individuals may handle like situations differently, or where fatigue or carelessness may produce variations. Furthermore, it is possible, since all processing is done at one location, to achieve standardization of forms, reports, calendars, etc., among different groups in a company. The benefits are the same as in factory automation, where we have seen fewer standard parts used in larger volume.

DATA DISCIPLINE

Closely allied to standardization is data discipline, by which is meant that data must be presented to the computer in standard form, and must be correct. Data must arrive at the computer on time. Much can be done to detect bad data, both by punched card procedures and by input editing after the data is entered into the computer, but too large a volume of exceptions can lead only to incomplete reports and missed deadlines.

FLEXIBILITY

The pencil with an eraser on one end is undoubtedly the most flexible data processing tool yet invented. The recent increase in mechanization of clerical operations has unfortunately seen the eraser thrown out along with the pencil, in many cases. Basically, a computer should allow significant flexibility in business accounting because of its intrinsic power. The many rigid data processing systems which are encountered are more a reflection on the systems analysts and programmers than on the machines, which after all are passive tools

ACCOUNTING, AUDITING, DATA PROTECTION

in the hands of their users. The accountant who needs a one-time report and finds the cost prohibitive or the time delay intolerable in getting it from the data processing center has a legitimate complaint. When he learns what is required to make a change to a system in production on a computer, he begins to yearn for the "good old days." There is developing, however, a set of automatic coding tools, described in Chapter 14, which can help the programmer meet such needs of the application areas.

The good computer systems designer must anticipate trouble and plan ahead. One question which should be asked is whether the system will be able to handle business conditions in the future. Perhaps an extra digit should be allowed for a part number code or room provided for a larger number of models in designing a table look-up preparatory to a large posting operation. It may be worthwhile to build an option into the system to process partial files. Therefore, in an emergency, the accountant from Department X can get his journal entries on schedule even if Department Y is late with data. The areas of file maintenance, exceptions, and error conditions are rich in opportunities to develop flexibility. The major consideration is that flexibility is no accident but is a philosophy of systems design. It may be noted that computer procedures are in one sense easier to change than manual: there are fewer people to retrain. Recent developments in automatic coding are also making it easier than formerly to change computer programs.

SPEED OF PROCESSING AND TIMELINESS OF REPORTS

It has been shown earlier that basic arithmetic and logical operations of computers may be measured in microseconds (millionths of a second). Some of the earlier business computers, having developed out of scientific prototypes, were unbalanced. Input/output speeds could not match the computational speeds. Recent technological developments, however, have produced more balanced machines for business needs. As an example of the speed of computers, consider profit and loss forecasting for alternative product "mixes." When manually prepared, these may take months each. The implications of each product mix are calculated in myriad detail to determine their effect on the operations of the business. A large computer, however, can produce a top level and detailed profit and loss statement at the rate of one every 15 minutes. The executive making a request in the morning may compare half a dozen plans the same afternoon. Of course, several man-years may have been required to do the initial planning and programming to make this possible.

It is now possible with the random access type of machines to have records follow transactions with negligible time lag, much as they are kept in a very small business. In general, with computerized accounting, the goal of current rather than historical reports is approached. As one example, journal entries and a general ledger can readily be produced a few hours or days after the end of an accounting period, rather than weeks after closing.

FEASIBILITY OF NEW KINDS OF REPORTS

The profit and loss forecasting application which we have been discussing illustrates the type of report which becomes feasible with electronic computers. These machines make possible much better managerial control and allow greater use of scientific methods of decision making.

ECONOMICS

Every computer has to be justified on some type of economic basis. Even though many managements concede that the greatest potential value of computers may lie in improved management control or in peripheral areas such as occasional engineering work, the benefits are so hard to evaluate that the initial justification must be made on the basis of clerical cost savings. The purpose of a computer feasibility study is normally to determine whether a machine is warranted on such a basis.

There are at least two benefits of electronic data processing that fall in between clerical cost reduction and the potentially important but rather uncertain management control improvement. It is often possible to consolidate many files which, although not complete duplicates, do contain some of the same information.* Another important side benefit is that the process of defining the job during a systems study almost always uncovers inconsistencies, duplications, unused copies of reports, etc. Thus there is a great deal to gain by the systems study alone.† This may be deceptive, however. The process of uncovering such wasted effort costs money; the long systems study which is a prerequisite to a good computer operation represents

---

* One large plant discovered that on the average each employee's name was written down in *fifty-two* different places!

† The comptroller of a major corporation once made the statement that the way to get the most out of a computer project is to place a computer order for delivery about 2 years in the future, do all the work necessary to get ready for a successful operation, then cancel the order. He was not speaking seriously, as evidenced by his company's heavy use of computers, but there is a large element of truth in the statement.

a large investment, all the benefits of which are not apparent for years.

A few cautions concerning clerical cost reduction are in order. Getting a computer going is considerably more expensive than was thought a few years ago. Man-years must be spent getting ready before the machine is delivered. The computer is expensive. The speeds ("this machine can do 40,000 additions *in just 1 second!*") are deceptive, because a great deal of "housekeeping" must be done along with each arithmetic operation which actually operates on data. An important warning concerns the frequent use of payroll as a starting application because it is a well-defined, high-volume operation. A number of computer installations have discovered that unless some attempt is made to achieve integration of payroll with other data processing functions, a computer payroll is just barely competitive in cost with a good punched card system. And of course the old joke about losing money on each sale but making it up on volume is just as wrong applied to a million-dollar computer as to a corner fruit stand. Only if a small loss on an application (considered by itself) is made up by gains in integration and management control is such a policy valid.

It should be pointed out that some of these problems are becoming less pressing. Some of the time spent in early systems studies was attributable to the inexperience of the personnel. With the improving availability of experienced personnel and assistance from the manufacturers and consultants, this training cost may be smaller in the future. The automatic coding tools being developed apace promise to reduce the cost of coding as well as greatly improve flexibility.

HANDLING OF EXCEPTIONS AND ERRORS

In general, exceptions and errors are more of a problem with computers than formerly, because they must be anticipated before they arise and because lost computer time is much more expensive than lost time of clerks or punched card machines. As we have suggested elsewhere, this rigidity in handling transactions is not all bad, in that it may help to "clean up" procedures. Two important considerations should be noted. First, it is unwise, expensive, and nearly impossible to try to anticipate *all* exceptions and program them. Second, it is usually possible, failing this, to program a computer to *recognize* an exception or error, even though it is not economical to try to tell the computer what to do about it. Thus, although we cannot hope ever to endow a computer with human judgment, we can at least give it the ability (possessed by any clerk) to say, "I've never seen this kind of thing before. Let somebody else handle it."

MANAGEMENT BY EXCEPTION

The use of computers makes feasible and even necessary the concept of "management by exception." Since the computer can make certain logical decisions, it can be made, for example, to decide whether a stock level has fallen below a reorder point. This requires only a comparison of two* amounts. If reorder is indicated, this fact can be printed out for the attention of the person who needs to take action. Since computers can produce rapidly such vast amounts of information, techniques like management by exception are required to keep the accountants, managers, and other personnel from being overwhelmed with details.

ACCURACY AND RELIABILITY

Computers can set new high standards for freedom from error in data processing. Since this topic is of such significance to people designing, using, auditing, or even contemplating electronic data processing systems, it will be the subject of a separate section.

21.2 Reliability of Computers

Reliability of computer operation is obviously very important in business problems. A series of errors in payroll calculations could lead to serious labor relations problems.† An error in a production control system could lead to idle workers and lost sales. To add to the concern over reliability is the fact that besides making calculations at a tremendous rate, computers can also make mistakes fairly rapidly.

Because of these potential consequences of mistakes, a great deal of effort has been put into designing computers so that they are reliable, into extra equipment and programs to detect errors and give a signal if they are made, and into techniques for correcting nonrecurring errors as automatically as possible. Fundamental to all discussions of reliability is the fact that checking costs something. The cost may be extra computer hardware, longer running times, or extra systems design, programming, and coding time to set up error detection and correction procedures. The word "extra" is a capsule definition of the technical term used to describe checking—*redundancy*. When

---

* In principle, at least. We realize that in fact it is necessary to consider the amount on order and the amount committed for future use, for instance.

† In a slightly different vein is the true story of a new computer payroll program which produced incorrect salary checks *3 months in succession* for the manager of finance who controlled the machine.

extra information is carried to check accuracy, it is called redundant information. In a nutshell, the problem in checking reliability is achieving an economic balance between the cost of checking and the cost of the type of error being checked against. Except for redundancy which is built into the hardware of the computer, this balance must be determined for each application. In a payroll, where large amounts of money are involved, employee relations problems are critical, and there are rigid contractual and governmental obligations present, it is worthwhile to spend considerable effort and money on checks and controls. On the other hand, in a sales analysis application where the data may be of only statistical reliability* anyway, checking requirements are much less stringent.

To return to our discussion of the reliability of computers, a first step by the manufacturers in achieving reliability is the *investigation of components* from different suppliers. These are subjected to stringent life tests under different environments. If necessary, new components with the desired characteristics are developed. The last few years have seen the appearance of much more reliable devices such as ferrite cores, transistors, and magnetic amplifiers, many of which may have indefinitely long life. They replace less reliable relays, vacuum tubes, electrostatic storage tubes, etc. Statistical quality control is established to insure that minimum standards are met on a continuing basis.

The design of circuits is complicated by the need to combine literally hundreds of thousands of components into a system. As a result, an extremely *conservative design* is used so that many circuits continue to operate even though component values, voltages, frequencies, temperatures, and other factors which make up the electrical environment may change in an unpredictable manner. Design tolerances are established so that the probability of failure of each individual component is kept to a very low value. It is manifestly outside the bounds of economic as well as physical possibility, however, to design circuits that *never* fail. We are more concerned with *undetected* errors than errors *per se*. We want the machines to detect their own occasional error, and to go automatically to a routine that corrects the error, if possible, without wasting time with human intervention. If the error cannot be corrected, this condition should be signaled. The maintenance man wants an indication of where the error occurred so that repair or replacement may be rapid. If this is not done his task may

* We realize, of course, that we can only say of *any* data that it is *probably* correct. If a difference in *degree* is large enough, however, it becomes a difference in *kind*.

be nearly hopeless in the face of the machine's complexity. There are various means of accomplishing this.

Preventive maintenance is a universal means of attempting to prevent unscheduled machine down time. It is equivalent to having a car checked regularly and replacing doubtful parts rather than risking a breakdown on the road. Most computer installations directly or indirectly are served by trained maintenance engineers equipped with test equipment and a spare parts inventory.

Diagnostic routines are used during maintenance. They are elaborate programmed test problems which execute every order the machine is capable of many times, with self-monitoring to see that execution is correct. If wrong answers are produced, other routines are utilized which tend to point out the trouble area as specifically as possible. Since machines are generally constructed in modular fashion—small groupings of components in standard packages—usually all that has to be done is to replace one plug-in board with another. The defective part or parts may then be repaired at leisure.

Another technique called *marginal checking* assumes that component failures are preceded by a gradual deterioration. This is sufficiently valid to afford a highly useful technique. Test problems are run which use different parts of the circuitry, generally with certain voltages raised or lowered to marginal levels. This causes errors and allows poor components to be pinpointed and replaced before they can fail in normal operation. (Certain intermittent or catastrophic failures, however, may not be detectable in advance.)

The maintenance checks which have been described, and others, are performed at regular intervals. On large machines maintenance tests are usually performed daily during scheduled periods. Most checking is done after the regular machine shift or shifts, generally at night, and some warm-up tests are performed before the main shift each day. The maintenance engineers also install a steady stream of *engineering changes* from the manufacturer. Their purpose is to clean up trouble spots which have become apparent or to utilize superior designs which have been developed to improve performance. A computer, from several angles, may be said to improve with age.

We next turn to the subject of *internal checking*. The degree of internal checking which is built into computers varies considerably and should be determined for the specific computer which the programmer will use. The most common machine check encountered is probably the *parity check*. This is a true redundancy check, using the term to denote the carrying of extra information for checking purposes, not necessary to the message. An extra binary *one* is either

ACCOUNTING, AUDITING, DATA PROTECTION 403

added to or omitted from each character to make the total number of ones for each character either all odd or all even, depending upon the manufacturer's convention. When a character is transferred to or from magnetic tape or (less frequently) upon internal transfers within the computer, the number of ones may be counted and a new parity bit generated. This is compared to the bit transmitted with the character, which allows the determination of whether an error exists. The generation and checking of parity bits are performed automatically by the computer. See page 181 for a further discussion of parity checking.

Many other techniques along this line are in use. One example is the *bi-quinary* number system described in Appendix 2. Another checking feature which is very useful during the testing of a routine before it is in productive operation, and which occasionally detects errors during regular runs, is the detection of impossible operations. Some machines stop if an attempt is made to add alphabetic information; almost all stop or at least signal an error if division by zero is attempted, etc.

A very powerful but controversial checking feature is the use of *duplicated circuits* in the control and arithmetic units. Operations are performed twice, independently and at the same time, and the results compared. Although there is more circuitry to go bad, machines utilizing this feature have performed with practically complete freedom from undetected machine errors. Theoretically, each circuit built on the same plan could make the same type of error under certain circumstances, but this has not been a serious consideration. There are several advantages of simultaneous duplicated arithmetic over programmed checks which will be discussed later in this chapter. The latter require a programmer's time and judgment, computer time, and some memory to store the instructions. Even if a programmed calculation is performed another way so as to use some different components, there is no assurance that a permanent failure will be detected, although intermittent ones probably will be. The trend is away from this type of computer construction because of its high manufacturing cost.

Repeated arithmetic is another internal checking method. It is very similar to the programmed recalculation and comparison mentioned in the last paragraph, but it is built into the hardware so that it occurs automatically. The same unduplicated circuitry is used, but preferably a different method of calculation, such as the use of complements. An example of one alternative is: if $a + b = c$, then $c - b$ should equal a. On at least one machine using repeated arithmetic, the programmer's discretion regarding the need for this checking in a given application is retained.

Since it has been estimated that with most computing systems well over half the down time is caused by input/output failures, it is worth considering some of the checking techniques that have been developed for peripheral equipment. Magnetic tape and tape handling units have improved significantly in quality and performance in recent years. Parity bits are almost universally used to check the accuracy of information transfer to and from magnetic tape. Parity checks are frequently used on paper tape equipment also.

The only really positive way to check output is to reread what was actually produced, whether magnetized spots on tape, holes in cards, etc. It is desirable to do this immediately after producing the output, because the correct information is readily available for checking purposes, and can be used to produce a new output upon detection of an error. The use of a reading head following a writing head, for example, allows verification of magnetic tape recording. Upon detection of error, the tape may automatically be backed up, rerecorded, and rechecked a certain number of times before the computer will halt with an error condition. Checking may consist of verifying parity bits or characters, character counts, etc.

Card reading equipment may detect undesired blank columns or excessive punches, and card counts may be made. By means of two reading stations, comparison may be made to see that results agree before the information goes to the computer or to magnetic tape in a converter.* The number of holes in each horizontal row of a card may be determined to be odd or even. Upon entry into the computer or upon conversion to tape, the information may be reconverted to card code and another odd-even count made of each row. This is compared to the original count and, if not identical, an error condition is signaled. On card punching, holes may be read back after punching for checking, odd-even row counts may be made, double punch and blank column detection made, etc. *Echo checking* is used to verify the accuracy of printing by "reading back" the information

* In a number of important instances, what really happens is that the information read at the first reading station goes into the computer or onto tape, and is then read back and compared with what is read at the second reading station. This is much more powerful than merely reading the information twice and determining that the same thing is read both times. In the case of off-line card-to-tape conversion, for instance, we know not only that the cards were read correctly, but that the information was correctly written on tape, and was readable.

printed by the printer, and comparing with the original information in memory.

This discussion by no means exhausts the subject of machine reliability checking, but perhaps it gives an idea of what can be done. The interested reader will find further discussion of the subject in some of the works listed in the bibliography.

21.3 System Checks

Much as the equipment manufacturers may do to insure reliability, the ultimate responsibility must rest on the user. Speaking broadly, we mean by system checks all checks which are not built into the hardware, but are programmed. Much of this type of checking has been discussed elsewhere in the book, so we shall only summarize the subject here, and introduce a few new topics.

It is perhaps obvious that results cannot be accurate if the source data is wrong. One technique which has been in use for many years in manual systems and should not be discarded with the advent of computers is review of the source documents. This may consist of a quick visual inspection to determine that all needed information is entered on the form and "looks reasonable." In other cases the review may consist of such checks as determining that the part number on an invoice actually exists; this type of thing may be done by a computer routine.

The most common method at present of insuring proper entry of data into machine language, directly or via converters, is verification by repetition. One operator enters the information originally into punched card, paper tape, or magnetic tape, and another repeats the process on a verifier, a machine which compares the two operations and allows correction of any errors detected. Verification does not provide 100% accuracy under any circumstances. Although computers impose more stringent requirements for accuracy than do other data processing methods, there is still a tendency toward overprotection in the matter of data verification. It is often a case of being penny wise and pound foolish when an inordinate amount of key verification costs more than the risk taken in allowing some possibility of error.

One approach to this problem is to study such situations and either directly eliminate verification of any data not worth such protection or to "quality-control" this data. A systematic selection of random samples will indicate error content and allow corrective action in many cases. Mark sensing of cards is an example of a technique which lends itself well to quality control and policing. A second approach is to use more automatic methods of verification such as self-checking number devices on card punches (see "check digits" later in this section), double punch and blank column detection on various card machines, balancing certain fields against control totals, collator comparison of codes against master cards for validity, etc. A third approach to reducing the amount of expensive key verification is now coming into popularity with the development of integrated data processing equipment. This involves the creation of data in some machine-sensible language as a by-product of the origination of a form which is visually checked during preparation. Because cards or tape are produced automatically, no key verification is required if the original document is correct. Since integrated data processing tends to reduce the repeated entry of the same basic information into machine language, accuracy is further increased.

An inefficient approach to verification is to put the information into machine language twice and let the computer compare both versions for identity. As character-reading devices become available which can read information on documents such as bank checks directly into machine language, the opportunity to introduce erroneous data into the system through human mistakes will be sharply reduced.

It is essential to insure that the data processing system processes all the approved data and that it does not accept any unapproved, incorrect, or dishonest data. Techniques which have been developed for other types of systems may be adapted to computer systems— batch control totals, consecutive transaction numbers, etc. There is also a great danger in computer systems that erroneous files may be used inadvertently, e.g., an obsolete master payroll file on magnetic tape kept for protective purposes. Protective measures may take the form of an elaborate control system, physical labeling on the exterior of files, interior labels in the file by means of which the computer may verify the proper file, dating routines for the same purpose, type-outs at the start of processing for the operator to check, etc.

The computer may be programmed to perform several other useful input checks on data. Very frequently the input sequence of the data is verified. The validity of change sources may be checked by the machine. The machine may check for alphabetics, blanks, or double punches in fields where they do not belong, or external equipment may perform this function.

There are various systems which use some formula to compute one or more additional digits, called check digits, to attach to the original number. These become part of the number and go along with it during further processing. At any point the same calculation may be made and compared to the check digit(s) carried by the number, thus the term *self-checking number*. The major use of this technique is to verify certain key numerical information, such as employee pay numbers, part numbers, bank account numbers, etc. They generally allow the detection of a change of a single digit (such as changing a 1 to a 3) or the transposition of adjacent digits. No checking system can ever eliminate all errors, however; compensating errors can occur. All we can hope to do is greatly reduce the probability of such compensating errors. Errors made in the original coding of a source document as well as its transcription may be detected. This is a redundancy check technique and may be made inside or outside the computer. Two methods of creating the check digit are called "weighted counts" and "casting out nines."*

One commonly used system check involves what are called *batch totals* and *control totals*. With random access types of computers, transactions may be entered as they occur. Most machine accounting, however, has tended toward batch processing. Groups of transactions are accumulated, generally at some application area, until a convenient lot size has been reached or until some time period has elapsed, such as a day, week, or month. Totals of some significant piece of information are accumulated for this lot (usually by an adding machine), e.g., total invoice dollars or employee hours. The batch along with the control total is sent to the data processing center. The control total is recorded as the last record, in the same format but with a different coded designation to indicate its function. One of the first runs of a computer system usually performs various checking and input editing procedures, including that of balancing. As each record comes into the machine, totals of the significant field are accumulated. These are then checked for equality with the predetermined control total. This checking may be done for many control groups in a file or by means of one grand total. Corrective action, however, is simpler with small groups. Being out of balance may cause the typing out on the control console of a notification of the trouble condition. There would then be an error halt, the machine could go on to some error routine, or continue processing. Assuming the in-balance condition exists, control totals may be carried through several runs to make certain that none of the data is lost or changed during processing. Even if an accounting machine is used to balance

* *Electronic Data Processing for Business and Industry*, Richard G. Canning, John Wiley & Sons, 1956, pp. 189–191, 322–323.

batches upon receipt by the data processing center, it is wise to balance on the computer also. This is because physical transportation of data may be required even if distances within the center are small, or time delays before processing the data may be significant and therefore some of the records might be displaced or tampered with. The balancing procedure usually adds only seconds to the total processing time.

Another useful technique is the *record count,* which is a tally of the number of records in a file. The count is normally taken when the file is first assembled. The total quantity of records is then carried as a control total at the end of the file and is adjusted whenever records are added or deleted. Each time the file is processed, the records are recounted and the quantity is balanced against the original or adjusted total. If the recount agrees with the control total, it is accepted as a tentative indication that all records have been run. If there is lack of agreement, this is indicated to the operator. Record counts may also be established by batches. This is desirable when original records are to be put into the procedure for the first time. The number of records on each reel of tape is often totaled to prove processing.

The record count says nothing about the accuracy of information on the tape. It merely confirms that probably no records have been lost in processing the tape or processed more than once. Failure to balance does not indicate precisely which records are involved. Since records once placed on a tape are ordinarily not misplaced by a valid program, an incorrect record count often indicates a machine failure. The doubtful portion of the file is usually rerun for correction, or checks made against a duplicate file or listing. Since the type of malfunction detected by record counts is one of the more common ones, this is a useful precaution, especially with critical files. It is easy to program and usually adds relatively little to processing time. Some computers organize information into blocks containing a fixed number of characters, which may contain several records, one record, or a part of a record. It is frequently more convenient here to count blocks instead of individual records, hence the term "block count." The logic, however, is the same.

Hash totals are very similar to control totals except that the fields accumulated give sums which are not meaningful except for control purposes. An example is the summation of model or stock numbers. This accomplishes the same basic goal as a record count but also insures that the contents of the summed field have been read correctly into memory.

ACCOUNTING, AUDITING, DATA PROTECTION

For machines which do not have automatic checks on the accuracy of arithmetic, various repeated arithmetic checks may be programmed. This is needed in critical applications because very infrequently malfunctions do occur in these circuits.* Some of the approaches are similar to those used internally for checking machine arithmetic. A straightforward approach would be to make a calculation, store the result, make the same calculation again, and compare results. If they do not agree, the program can signal an error. The danger in this method is that if the trouble is not cleared up by the time the second calculation is made, the results can very well agree. A better method would involve manipulating the checking calculation so that other circuits than the original are used as much as possible. Reciprocals of quantities may be used or, in an addition for example, one can reverse the sign of one operand and subtract it from the result to see if it equals the other operand. A reassuring point is that in general the arithmetic circuits are among the most reliable in a computer.

Proof figures are sometimes used to check an important multiplication in a program. We quote a description of its use taken from the IBM Type 705 Manual of Operation:

An example of this is the multiplication of quantity by cost required in grocery billing. The check is based on a relationship between cost and a so-called proof cost. An arbitrary fixed figure Z, larger than any normal cost, is set up. For example, if the cost range for all products is from $.05 to $10.95, Z might equal $11.00. The proof cost is expressed by the formula: Cost + proof cost = Z, or proof cost = Z − cost. When quantity is multiplied by cost, it is also multiplied by proof cost (a figure having no other significance, which is carried in the record. Z is a constant which can be stored in memory). Normally, two of the totals needed for the check, quantity and quantity times cost, are accumulated during the program. The other factor needed for the check (quantity times proof cost) is also accumulated in the program. Now it is possible at any point to check as follows:

Total (Qty. × cost) + Total (Qty. × Proof Cost) = Total (Qty. × Z)

* A horrible example of what can happen occurred during a payroll run of a major manufacturing concern. A payroll clerk scanning over the payroll register noticed that a certain employee whose hourly rate was several dollars an hour and who had worked all week was getting a check for about $30. He checked further; it soon became apparent that many of the 30,000 checks produced that week were in error. The situation that resulted can best be described as panic. The local maintenance engineers, plus some flown in by the manufacturer, worked desperately to locate the trouble, which was in the multiplication circuits. The tapes were flown to another installation in an effort to get out corrected checks before the payroll deadline. There was not time to recompute all of them, and about a fourth of them had to be distributed in error and followed by corrections. Needless to say, the installation now has much more extensive checking in their routines.

The left side of the equation can be calculated by a single addition of the two progressive totals accumulated during the program. The right side of the equation can be calculated by a multiplication of the accumulated quantity and the factor Z. This check insures that each particular multiplication was performed correctly. This type of check applies to other applications by the same general approach, that of adding check information.

There are many ways of checking on the *reasonableness* of information. Utilities, for example, may compute the average of several previous bills, multiply by a factor to allow for seasonal and other potential changes, and then compare this to the current bill. If the latter is out of line, the situation may be flagged for review before issuing the bill. This type of check prevents the bad publicity which has occurred in computer-calculated bills, where a small householder gets a utility bill for 1 month's service of $2312.00. A *limit check* may be built into a payroll calculation program to prevent certain predetermined limits from being exceeded, say $200 for a weekly paycheck. One company getting stock market information found it necessary to test for reasonable variation from the last price before further processing with its computer. This type of check can be very effective in helping to prevent fraud or error, human or machine.

The machine may be made to perform a *cross-footing check* which is similar to one used by accountants on work sheets. For example, in computing a payroll, the sum of net pay for all employees, plus the sum of all deductions, should equal the sum of all the gross pay. These totals may be checked at any point in the program as well as at the end.

There are no hard and fast rules which define all possible trouble spots. The systems analyst, programmer, and coder must simply be alert for trouble, just as one of the characteristics of a good driver is the assumption that everybody else on the road may do something foolish at any time.

As another example of anticipating trouble and building checks into the routines, suppose five different types of transaction codes exist in a system. One could test for the first four codes (in order of most frequent occurrence for the sake of efficiency) and then go down the fifth path if the first four tests fail. This saves time, but will obviously lead to trouble since inevitably a wrong code will occasionally occur. Good procedure would be to make a fifth test for equality and, if this fails, then to take an error path.

With the development of random access devices, a serious control problem arises because of the possible insertion of data from remote stations. One solution is to limit a remote unit to inquiry only and not permit data insertion into the files from it. This is not too feasible for many applications and does not prevent unauthorized inquiries. Another method is to channel all inquiries by telephone or other means to one inquiry operator who actually communicates with the machine. This, however, may create bottlenecks. By means of programming and the use of program tapes or mechanical devices at inquiry stations, each station can be limited to a certain type of contact with the files stored in the computer memory. This can significantly reduce the scope of the problem. A transaction record may also be produced to show what has occurred, for purposes of control. No doubt other techniques will be developed as this equipment comes into heavier usage.

21.4 Data Protection

Some provision must be made in any computer system for insuring that valuable files are not lost or damaged, either by environmental conditions or by being processed incorrectly. A number of techniques have been developed for this purpose, some of which are summarized below.

Exterior labels are a visual means of identifying files. This may be done with pencil or crayon on a box of punched cards, by writing on pressure-sensitive tape stuck on magnetic tape reels, or by other means. Usually some identification of the data is given: the date produced, the computer run number producing the data, the tape unit used, the disposition of the reel, the printer plugboard number if any, the expiration date, the number of blocks or records on the tape, or other useful information. During debugging or conversion operations, the initials of the programmer to whom reference may be made for information on the file are often useful. Too much information can be confusing, so the exterior label should contain only the minimum amount of information deemed necessary for normal use and to protect the file. One large installation, with 600 reels of magnetic tape, prints colored tape labels with an accounting machine from a card file. By this means the job of tape librarian was eliminated. Another installation has a label program on tape which in less than 3 minutes of computer time produces a week's supply of labels (1600) which are printed on special forms on the high-speed printer.

By the use of an *interior label,* recorded at the beginning of each reel of tape, the computer may be programmed to check that the correct tape is actually being used for a run. This subject was covered in detail in Chapter 13. In conjunction with the interior labels, the computer may be caused to type or print out a brief message. This allows the operator to visually check the situation when the labels have not passed checking, for valid or invalid reasons. Typeouts may also be used to show that processing is proceeding normally.

Most tape handling equipment has some device to help prevent undesired erasure of a file. Some tape units can only read and not write on a tape reel which has a ring inserted in its interior diameter. As soon as a key tape is produced, the operator places the ring in the reel. In subsequent usage of this reel, the computer cannot write on it until the ring is removed, even if the reel is inadvertently placed on an output tape unit. This is not a foolproof system, but strict rules regarding who may remove rings and requirements for scrutiny of the exterior label before removal of a ring can help to prevent a catastrophe. On other tape units in existence, the convention is reversed and removal of the ring allows only the nondestructive reading of the reel. One large tape file utilizes many individual strips of magnetic tape. Each tape position is provided with a lever which, when thrown, operates a switch preventing the information on that tape from being altered inadvertently. Many computers have two types of rewind orders for their tape units. One allows full and immediate reuse of the reel after rewinding, which is desirable in sorting, for example. The other command provides for a special rewind which locks the tape unit upon completion of the rewinding process. The operator must then remove the protected reel and replace it with a blank or spare reel or throw a switch to allow reuse of the protected reel if the situation requires it. This is a protection which the programmer can specify in his coding. There are other protective devices which may be incorporated into the data processing equipment by the manufacturer.

Some organized system for the storage of files must be used. At large installations there may be hundreds or even thousands of tape reels, hundreds of thousands of punched cards, and many reels of paper tape. If a systematic approach is not used, chaos results with the inevitable destruction or misplacement of essential data. Equipment is now available to help the physical filing problem, for transportation of data, and for temporary storage of files in actual use. The responsibility for file storage should be delegated to one individual, whether as a part-time duty or as a full-time file librarian. Valid tapes should be placed in labeled file racks and only certain authorized personnel should be permitted to have access to these racks.

Files must be physically protected through the control of environmental conditions. Punched cards warp if exposed to high humidity.

Some types of magnetic tape shrink or expand if exposed to low or high humidity or high temperatures, and all tapes must be protected against dust and strong magnetic fields caused by nearby high-current wiring. At the time of writing there have been no major fires in a data processing installation, but in the case of certain types of crucial files, storage in fireproof vaults may be wise.

Because the penalty for releasing a tape too soon may be very severe, there is a tendency to save tapes longer than may actually be necessary. What is required is a system which will prevent unnecessarily large accumulations of tapes but which, at the same time, will provide adequate protection against lost, broken, or otherwise unreadable tapes. The *expiration plan* is such a system. The purpose of this plan is to preserve the tape which would be needed to replace a tape which is an input to a current production run. For example, consider a situation where Monday's tape is used to make Tuesday's, and Tuesday's to make Wednesday's. If in making Wednesday's tape, the Tuesday tape is broken, the Monday tape should still be available to remake the Tuesday tape. No tape prior to the Monday tape would be needed. Of course, in remaking Tuesday's tape, Monday's tape may break and in remaking Monday's, Friday's may break, etc. However, the chances of such compound accidents occurring are small and the expiration plan does not attempt to guard against them.

The basic rule for determining when a tape expires under the expiration plan is simple and may be stated as follows: No data tape will expire until two successive tapes based on the original have been prepared. In other words, when a data tape becomes a "grandfather," it is allowed to expire and be reused. The application of the basic rule depends on the type of data tape and the conditions under which it is prepared. The situation may get a little involved when daily output tapes must be saved for weekly runs, weekly for monthly runs, etc. Figure 1 provides some illustrations of the rule. (Note the fairly standard abbreviation "A/C" for "account.") Tape A expires when Tape C is produced. Tape D is produced weekly and expires after K is produced, not J. This is because both H and I are prepared from D. Once these are produced all the C tapes for 1 week expire. Basic file tape G is created by processing its predecessor (tape E), together with a tape of changes required, in a weekly run. Tape G will be used in the following week to produce a new basic file tape. At this time, tape E together with the tape of file changes (F) will expire. Tape G, in turn, will expire 2 weeks after it is made. In practice, some tapes may be held somewhat longer than theoretically

414 PROGRAMMING BUSINESS COMPUTERS

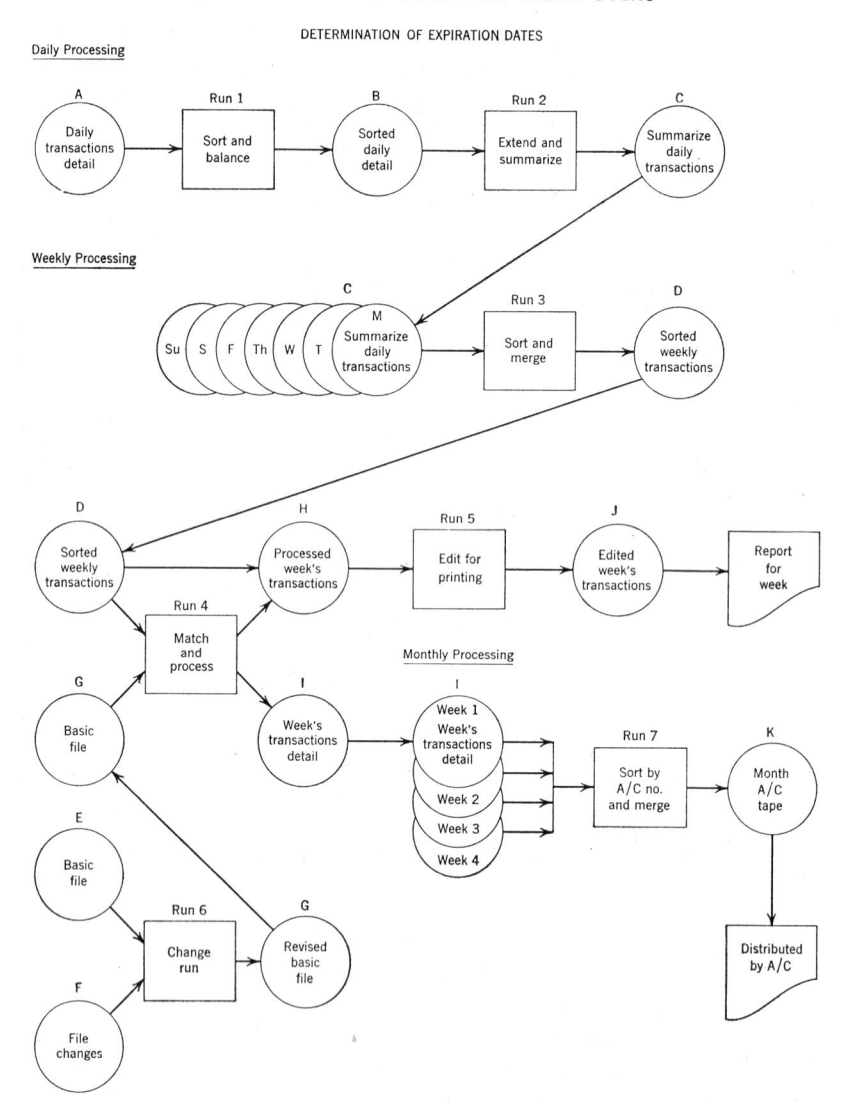

Figure 1. A flow chart to illustrate the expiration date system, involving an application where daily summaries are used to produce weekly and monthly summaries.

required under the expiration plan, until a convenient determination of the accuracy of processing may be made, such as the printing of a report following a long chain of processing.

Report tapes and their predecessors may require different rules. They should not be allowed to expire until it can be reasonably

ACCOUNTING, AUDITING, DATA PROTECTION

expected that no additional copies of the reports will have to be printed. Therefore the number of copies originally prepared, the use of the report, the frequency of preparation, and similar factors will have to be considered in fixing the time limit for expiration of each tape of this type.

In addition to saving the tapes as determined by the expiration plan, it may be desirable to save a certain few key tapes for longer periods. It would then be possible to recreate lost data from these tapes, although it may require considerable time to do so. The determination of which tapes to save in order to facilitate rerunning under these circumstances is more or less arbitrary and will depend upon the special conditions involved in a particular installation.

To the extent that it is possible to translate expiration conditions into time periods, *expiration dates* may be used. When expiration dates are used, the normal procedure is for every tape to carry its expiration date as part of its internal label. This may be calculated by the computer for an output tape from the input date by adding a constant. The desired goal is automatic protection of valid data tapes by having the computer check the expiration date on prospective output tapes before they are written on and thus erased. Therefore output as well as input tapes would have labels inspected by the computer.

While theoretically sound, the expiration date system has several practical limitations which tend to make its use burdensome. First, it is extremely difficult to translate conditions into time. Various delays can upset the regular processing schedule. Many tapes expire on the same day that they are made. Some tapes must be used in nonproduction work which does not test dates. Debugging and other tapes may not be able to pass the expiration test. As a result, the expiration date test begins to be forced frequently, and once the door has been opened in this fashion, the value of the entire system becomes very questionable. Other techniques, such as the use of reel rings and exterior labels, can provide adequate protection.

21.5 Planning for Emergencies

It is always necessary to give some thought to what could be done in the event of a major catastrophe such as loss of essential data or protracted periods of computer malfunction. These are relatively rare, but when they do occur something has to be done and quickly.

When essential data is destroyed or missing, the first thing to check is to see if the material has been duplicated, although the use of duplicated files is a costly protection and should be kept to a minimum. Frequently, certain key tapes (or cards) are duplicated, such as the master program tapes. The next simplest alternative would probably be to recreate the missing information by means of the computer. If the expiration plan has been followed correctly, a few minutes or at most a few hours of processing should be required. It may be necessary to reconvert cards or perhaps repunch source documents. The more hand labor required, the more painful the solution. Probably the costliest is to take the printout of a file, if one exists, and keypunch it. There have been catastrophes where data processing groups considered themselves extremely fortunate to have a printout of a file. Teams of keypunchers have worked for days in such emergencies. Such catastrophes, it must be noted, are products of poor organization of the data processing center.

Another type of emergency is the late or partial arrival of data. Even though data processing centers must adhere to strict scheduling, some attempt is usually made to revise schedules to meet this emergency. Frequently, overtime operation is scheduled, if this is available. It is often helpful to arrange the program so as to be able to process partial files, for example, when one department out of many is late. Emergency communication may bring in missing information for manual recording and entry into machine language at the data processing center, especially when outlying areas are involved. If the precision of data is not extremely critical, useful reports may still be produced by running the previous period's data in place of certain missing current information. Thus for sales statistics, if a few distributors out of many have not reported weekly sales by the deadline, their previous week's sales may be picked up. In the subsequent week, file maintenance procedures may be used to correct the errors. Meanwhile, regional and other statistics are more valid than had no sales at all been recorded for the erring distributors.

Occasionally, protracted machine failures do occur. If the local maintenance personnel cannot get the computer back into operation within a few hours, regional or national maintenance experts may be flown in by the manufacturer, as are special parts. Depending on the nature of the business, the loss of a shift or a day or two may not be very serious. Overtime operation can often replace the lost time. If the down time is excessive, tapes and personnel may be sent to an alternate facility, as close geographically as possible. Usually a reciprocal arrangement is made in advance with other processing centers having the same equipment. This is sometimes complicated by programs requiring larger than usual memories, special features such as index registers or extra magnetic drums, and the like, even when the same brand and model of computer is available. Manufacturers of computers usually have one or more service bureaus established where their equipment is available to handle such emergencies, among other functions. With the growing use of electronic data processing, the problem of finding alternate facilities is eased. It is rare that stand-by manual or tabulating equipment procedures can be used in the event of protracted computer failure. In general, adequate manpower, equipment, and the know-how to accomplish this are no longer available.

21.6 Auditing Problems

Many conflicting views have appeared in the literature, since the advent of electronic data processing, about the effect of electronic systems on internal control procedures and the auditability of the records. Some writers predict revolutionary changes in accounting and auditing. Others say that the impact of such machines will be negligible. There are several reasons for the latter attitude. One is that most of the first several thousand computers put to use on business applications have been punched card machines whose required departures from conventional tabulating techniques have not been great. Another reason is that several of the trends are only in their incipient stages, such as the elimination of source documents, the elimination of journal entries, and the use of various scientific techniques for the control of a business.

Many of the basic tenets of auditing should continue to be valid, though electronic data processing will no doubt have a far-reaching effect on their implementation. The trend will probably be evolutionary over the next decade or so, allowing development of auditing techniques to meet new situations, but the end result most certainly will be a revolution in clerical work. Some of the problems and trends will be explored in this section. Let us first review some of the basic auditing principles.

Auditing, as we shall be concerned with it, may be defined as the systematic verification of the financial and legal records of a business in order to determine the accuracy and integrity of the accounting, thereby to show the true results of operations and establish the actual financial condition of an organization. Whether performed externally or internally, the results of the auditing should be the same. It is not possible to set down a precise set of rules by which auditing should be accomplished or its efficiency measured and evaluated. Certain principles, however, may be established.

It is manifestly unfeasible, from the practical viewpoint, to completely check and verify every transaction of a large and complicated business. Except in special cases of known or suspected fraud, the auditor utilizes test checks in examining supporting documents such as canceled checks, physically counting inventory, footing books of original entry, and the like. He reviews the degree of internal control in the company in determining the scope of the audit needed to satisfy himself as to the fairness of the business' financial statements, themselves a product of judgment and slowly evolving concepts of good procedure. By internal control is meant a system of checks and balances to safeguard the assets and income of the business by preventing honest errors, as well as fraud. Duties may be divided among employees so that one checks another in critical areas and so that no clerical employee has complete control of important transactions. Certain documents and transactions may require approval, for example. Any practical system of internal control, as well as the auditing of it, must run a calculated risk to balance the protection given against the cost.

At one meeting of auditors concerned with electronic data processing it was proposed that all that is necessary for checking such systems is for the auditor to build his own balances from basic documents and to check these against machine balances. Supposedly he need not worry too much about how the results are accomplished if the results check out. This is fine, except that how things are done determines to a certain extent how much checking the auditor must do to convince himself of the accuracy of processing. Therefore we come finally to the basic evaluation of the control system by the auditor. Earlier in this chapter we discussed checks or controls built into the machine by the manufacturer, some controlling data coming into the center, some incorporated into the computer programs, and some established inside the data processing center. The auditor will want to establish the adequacy of these controls, as well as to review conventional safeguards such as the division of duties among employees, the approvals required for certain transactions, etc. He must also evaluate the controls established over the employees of the center to insure accurate handling of the data and to preclude fraudulent alteration of this information. Controls over the center are usually placed in the hands of a group specially organized for this purpose. This is desirable for the business organization as well as the auditor. The function of the control group has been very comprehensively described

ACCOUNTING, AUDITING, DATA PROTECTION

in a report* which should be in the library of every auditor. This example will serve to illustrate some of the ideas:

One company processing payrolls has established procedures whereby all changes in rates, payroll deductions, and number of employees are routed through the payroll department. This department maintains memorandum control records of the totals of each of the categories listed below:

1. Aggregate hourly rates by convenient employee groups.
2. Withholding tax exemptions, i.e., the aggregate number of persons for whom exemptions were claimed.
3. Retirement annuity participation code totals, i.e., the number of people who participate in the retirement annuity programs.
4. The gross dollar amount of all types of deductions.
5. Man count.

Changes in each category are posted in the payroll department in total to memorandum control books, and the authorization documents are then forwarded to the data processing department. The first operation in that department consists of updating the master file of rates and deductions. As a part of this updating, written reports of the changes in the master file are produced. These reports are returned to the payroll department by the data processing section, and each total is checked against the control books.

When employment is terminated it is necessary not only to remove the name of the employee and his base rate from the records, but also the details of his various deductions. Where employee turnover is not great, these details should be determined by the payroll department from listings prepared for reference purposes. In this particular installation, however, the volume of terminations is currently so great that the termination information is extracted from the master file by the data processing machine and the details are reported back to the payroll department, where the appropriate adjustments are made in the memorandum control books. In order, however, to insure that the data processing section removes information pertaining to all terminated employees from the records, a man count control is maintained over termination information.

This particular company pays its employees by check, the payroll department controlling the number of checks by taking custody of blank checks and issuing them to the data processing section as requested. The payroll department accounts for all checks including those which have been voided.

The payroll department also establishes the over-all arithmetical accuracy of the entire payroll by checking the footing of gross to net pay for each group of one thousand clock numbers. The advantage of this check seems to be one of timing, since an error in cross casting payroll totals should come to light eventually in any system of double entry bookkeeping. Accumulated year-to-date figures are also proved by the payroll department by adding the total of the current week's payroll to the current week's accumulated to-date figures. In addition, the calculation of the withholding tax deduction is spot-checked by applying a formula on an over-all basis for certain groups of employees. The amounts of total payroll, total hours and man count must also agree with

* Price Waterhouse & Co., "The Auditor Encounters Electronic Data Processing," IBM Form **32-7489.**

the payroll department's control totals. In this particular installation, control over pay checks to see that a check is received for distribution to each employee listed on the pay register is established through a separate paymaster's department, thus recognizing the fact that to allow the payroll department to perform the paying function would destroy effective control over the operations of that department.

In discussing the actual audit procedures, the same source describes the questionnaire method of evaluating the safeguards surrounding the payroll as part of the test of the adequacy of the system of internal control. The second major purpose of the auditing procedures, the establishment of the integrity of specific items appearing on the financial statements, brings these comments:

In examining a payroll the auditor selects, as a rule, the names of a number of employees appearing on the payroll and checks the files of the employees for authorization of employment and wage rates. He may call for time cards or other time or piece-work records in support of the hours worked or quantities produced upon which the employees' wages are computed. He will want to examine approvals of overtime hours, check the calculation of gross salaries and the deductions for withholding taxes, payroll taxes, union dues, etc. He would check the arithmetical accuracy of the payroll totals and the amount of net pay for each selected employee. With a payroll register all of these steps can be carried out regardless of the type of system, electronic or otherwise, in use.

An audit step that, upon first thought, appears to the uninitiated to be of minor significance is the checking of the addition of the payroll. To the auditor, however, adding a payroll has really two purposes. The first, of course, is to satisfy himself that the payroll totals have been properly compiled. The more important reason for footing the payroll, however, is to satisfy himself that the listing of the individual employees constitutes the complete payroll for the period he is reviewing. In order for any sample to be proper, it must be drawn from the entire group being audited. The manner in which the auditor assures himself that he has the entire group is to see that the details add up to the group total.

But it is not necessary for him to check the additions to the entire payroll. There are methods of test-checking footings, just as there are methods of test-checking individual pay calculations. In one of the payroll installations the processing routine produces the totals for each column in the payroll register at the end of each 20th part of the payroll. These totals are printed on the typewriter of the console. As explained elsewhere, this is done as an interim check on the proper functioning of the processing routine. These group totals are useful to the auditor, since he can check the footings of one or more groups in detail and then add the group totals to arrive at the grand total of the payroll. For another installation, no interim register totals are completed during processing, but at the end of each one thousand pay numbers, block totals are computed and typed out on the console typewriter. Under this procedure the auditor can select any group of one thousand pay numbers, check the footings of the detail and compare the totals with the block totals. The block totals can be added to arrive at the grand total which is easily traced to the general books of account.

In addition to the above, the auditor will want to examine pay checks and pay receipts, reconcile payroll bank accounts, and perhaps personally observe the delivery of pay checks and pay envelopes to the employees by the paymaster or another delegated employee. These operations are not affected by the system, electronic or otherwise.

Many sources in the literature mention that one of the auditor's prime concerns in an electronic installation is whether the programs will do the jobs for which they are designed. This is certainly true, but the key problem here is what method to use. We feel that this should be determined by making certain that a diversified number of actual calculations are handled correctly, in other words that the *results* of machine calculations are correct. However, one occasionally encounters statements like this one: "By checking out all programming in detail, using a presolved problem, the correctness of the program can be established with relative ease." This is utterly absurd, more often well-nigh *impossible* to do than to do with "relative ease."

There are several reasons for the difficulty of checking out programs in detail. First, how many different machines can an auditor know in complete detail? If he requests the card or tape program file to check, how does he know the one he gets was actually used, since copies are kept at the data processing installation? Since programs are easily copied with changes, how does he know that unauthorized versions of the program do not exist? If the auditor keeps a personal copy of the programs, they will soon be obsolete, for in some large systems changes are a daily or weekly occurrence. Large programs have so many alternate paths that writing a problem to explore them all is something like trying to write down all the possible combinations in a chess game. Assuming that this could be done, what is to prevent the operator from having branches in an otherwise perfect program controlled by certain input data or by switches on the console? With a perfect program the operator can still quickly interrupt processing from the console and change information in the internal memory, for which there may be no other evidence than the fraudulent result. If the auditor attempts to desk-check the written program, besides some of the problems mentioned above, he may find this extremely time-consuming and laborious, if at all possible for someone who has not been in on the development of the program. Write-ups are often incomplete and may be obsolete.

This argument can be continued further, but it should be evident that the auditor is on safe ground when he sticks to what should have gone into the data processing center and what should have come out. He no more needs to check actual machine instructions than he needs to check the wiring boards on conventional punched card equipment or the programming bars on bookkeeping machines. There is, however, considerable justification for his knowing the basic ideas of electronic data processing; this will be discussed later.

Related to the subject of machine knowledge is the possible use of the computer as an auditing tool. This will require detailed machine knowledge, programming time, and computer running time which may be scarce at some installations. The new automatic coding techniques can be used to reduce the programming burden. The advantage, of course, is the harnessing of the tremendous speed and power of the computer for many of the laborious details of auditing work. Detail records may be footed, records may be excerpted from files for testing, clerical work on the physical inventory may be performed, aged listings of accounts receivable prepared, etc. Records which do not have regular printouts may have to be edited by the machine before printing. In any auditing operations using the machine, control over the operator's actions must be exercised so that no improper influence is exerted.

The way this discussion of auditing problems has been presented, an impression may have been created that the external auditor will come in and evaluate an established electronic accounting system. Unfortunately, this has been exactly the case in many of the early data processing installations with which the authors are familiar. Except for those requirements imposed by accountants in some of the application areas and the influence of occasional accountants on the programming staff, little attention was paid to auditing needs. On one job, as a matter of fact, one of the authors requested that the internal auditor of the company concerned participate in the development of the electronic system. He was overruled by the highest financial officer in the company, who felt that this would be a waste of the auditor's time! It is manifestly desirable that the auditors, internal and external, should assist in the planning of the electronic data processing system in order to recommend the adoption of necessary controls before the procedures are too far advanced for their incorporation into the system to be simple and inexpensive. This does not mean that their recommendations should be blindly accepted, for if they are conservative people they may tend to impose too onerous requirements. These questions must be argued out and compromised. Probably the internal auditor, or someone else within the company

ACCOUNTING, AUDITING, DATA PROTECTION 423

who can assume this responsibility, should participate in the development of the system very actively. The external auditor can follow the planning and review the system from time to time. He must wait long enough for scrutiny in detail so that he is not wasting his time on what will prove to be discarded plans, yet not too late for suggestions to be effective.

One of the problems the auditor should consider is the actual conversion period from one system to another. This phase of the installation of an electronic system can present extremely serious problems and prove very costly, yet it is frequently glossed over and left to a very late stage of planning. Often the inadequacies of the previous system must be cleaned up in the preparation of the new master data files. Many exception situations may be realized for the first time at this stage. The auditor should be very much interested in avoiding a fiasco during the period of parallel operation, whether in the loss of records, accidental or fraudulent changes in records, etc., and in insuring an audit trail for the activities of this period. The auditor may also be familiar enough with problems in the client's business to offer valuable advice for the debugging phase of the system.

The use of invisible records, such as those on magnetic tape, tends to cause concern to many on first exposure to electronic data processing. With proper controls, such as those discussed under data protection, no severe problems have been experienced in practice despite increasingly heavy usage during the last few years. One of the legal problems is that magnetically recorded records can be erased easily, with no evidence of the erasure. It must be remembered that punched cards ran into much opposition, too. A former comptroller of one of our largest manufacturing companies once rejected certain proposed punched card procedures, saying, "We shall not pay out our good money over holes in punched cards." A government agency has already accepted tax reports filed on magnetic tape by this company!

The problem of the capacity of the operator for mischief has not been seriously tackled by most computer installations. The major deterrent should be the monitoring of results by the internal control group and the auditors. Before hiring an operator, his background should be extensively checked, and it is also perhaps desirable to bond him. Alternatively, qualified and proven employees from the business may be trained as operators. Denying the operator access to input data preparation devices may not be feasible. Strict safeguards surrounding the use of the control console seem to be in order, such as forced printing of all control actions by the operator via the console typewriter if there is one. On one machine, controls which do not print (such as for maintenance) are locked by key. There should be restricted access to the machine, especially in off hours, because the possibility of machine sabotage may be catastrophic.

We may observe in passing that these problems of operator honesty (and, for that matter, of the honesty of everyone concerned with the data processing function) are not unique with electronic data processing. Of course we worry that an operator might sneak in at night and double his pay rate on the payroll master tape; but we worry about the same thing with manual methods. Actually, some of the controls that are built into an automatic data processing system to prove system reliability, such as batch control totals, can make it fairly difficult to do this sort of thing without intimate knowledge of the system. At some point, however, we must stop worrying about "Who guards the guards?" In every business we eventually have to trust someone, or some combination of people. We of course build in checks, but collusion among enough people will defeat any checking system, and we still hear occasionally of a treasurer who had been with a company for 30 years absconding with funds. There are problems, but they are not new, and are not so much different just because the ledgers are now on magnetic tape instead of paper.

We have tried to show in this section that the advent of electronics in record keeping does not pose insurmountable problems for the auditor, but that if he sticks to basic principles and adjusts his procedures to meet evolving requirements, he will learn to live with the new systems. He needs an auditable record which can show the details of movement in the account and he must be able to move back to the source of the entry.* This dictates at least a minimum amount of printing for audit purposes. The auditor may be forced to check transactions closer to the time when they originated rather than attempt to reconstruct them later when tapes have been reused, for example. The auditing procedure must not become too costly, for the cost of controls must be weighed against the risks taken in keeping the controls to a minimum. Therefore, such techniques as "control by exception" should be investigated, as part of the general philosophy of "management by exception." Fortunately, the regular needs of the business for printouts and reports are of great help to the auditor. Many of the functions of a control group may be tied in to regular duties of different application areas.

* See Canning, op. cit., pp. 193–195, for a (costly) approach to this problem.

21.7 The Role of the Accountant

An interesting question that may be asked about the installation of an electronic data processing machine is, "What happens to the accountant?" After reading the previous section, it ought to be apparent that we should find him very much in the picture. The computer will take over the routine aspects of the accountant's tasks, the clerical drudgery. This will free the accountant for the more creative elements of his work, the ones whereby he may make a greater contribution to his organization. In effect, he is given more powerful tools to work with.

The electronic age accountant need not be an electronic or mechanical expert to use the computer as a tool for better control of the business, any more than he need know the internal gear arrangements to use an adding machine. It is recommended that he try to learn the basic logic of data processing by machines. The best way for an accountant to learn computers is to learn to program at least one machine. There is no better way of learning this field than by doing. Some of the benefits of a knowledge of programming will be apparent in the following listing of opportunities available to the accountant in an electronic era:

1. Advising management in the selection of electronic data processing equipment.
2. Analyzing procedures and developing computer systems.
3. Programming computer systems, especially in the financial area.
4. Designing system controls and setting audit requirements for the computer installation.
5. Evaluating reports and statements.

The last point is potentially the most significant. Insight into the logic of computer techniques will develop confidence in the accountant as a user of computer output and lead to his recommendation of new applications, for further harnessing of the computer's power. Instead of burning the midnight oil for weeks after the monthly closing to get out the statements, he will get them from the computer in a matter of a few hours or days. He will spend his time analyzing the significance of the figures, investigating problems which they reveal, recommending methods for increased productivity, better controls, increased sales, and reduced costs. He will further develop useful accounting concepts such as standard costs, budgetary controls, measurements of job performance in new areas, management by exception, and responsibility accounting which would otherwise be bogged down by vast expenditures of clerical effort. The accountant's figures will be current, not historical.

The introduction of punched card equipment in its day produced dire predictions of the displacement of accountants and auditors. There are now more people in these professions than ever. The new techniques will, however, require a certain amount of effort and adaptability from many of these people. This in the long run should help the accountant, for he will be forced to think about new approaches to his goal of effective control of a business rather than stressing the importance of figures in themselves.

21.8 Summary

In this chapter we have attempted to show some of the power and some of the problems which accompany the use of electronic computers for business data processing. It has been estimated that an electronic computer will not make more than one error to every 10,000 or more human errors. This factor, plus the ability of the computer to make calculations and manipulate data in a small fraction of a second, cannot but help to affect the accountant and auditor significantly.

Accuracy in data processing systems is no accident. Reports are only as good as the source information, which must be controlled. Despite the basic accuracy of some of the new machines, and despite some deceptive claims for error-free operation, all system components may eventually be expected to make errors. Therefore, system controls and program checks are necessary. Considerable care must be exercised in their choice so as to provide the necessary protection without at the same time imposing excessive burdens on the operation. Adequate physical protection of data can be a severe problem and some thought must be given to the event of the occurrence of an emergency. The auditors of the business should be in on at least a minimum of the system planning to make certain that effective controls will be incorporated into the system. The "crash" nature of the development of many computer systems may cause this concern to be regarded as a luxury, if care is not taken to prevent this attitude.

In many respects the art of electronic data processing is in its infancy. New technological developments which may allow elimination of source documents, for example, will probably produce evolutionary rather than revolutionary changes in accounting and auditing procedures because of the basic conservatism of financial people. However, the rewards in less costly, more useful, and more timely

ACCOUNTING, AUDITING, DATA PROTECTION 427

accounting and cost information may give a great competitive advantage to the bold pioneers in this relatively uncharted area.

Exercises

1. What are the roles played by the auditor, accountant, systems analyst, and programmer in an electronic data processing installation?

2. How do accounting methods for electronic data processing differ from punched card and manual methods?

3. In systems planning, flexibility usually costs something extra. Point out some examples of systems planning where flexibility is achieved at the expense of:
(a) Increased computer operating time.
(b) Increased programming cost.
(c) Increased computer operating time and programming time.
(d) Nothing except the ingenuity of the programmer.

4. Distinguish between computer reliability and systems reliability.

5. If a magnetic tape unit does not have a read head to read back what is written on the magnetic tape:
(a) What does a tape write-check error mean?
(b) What are the consequences of letting subsequent computer runs or peripheral equipment operation detect that the tape might be unreadable?
(c) What are two possible ways to check tape readability in the same run?

6. Discuss the pros and cons of built-in computer checking versus programmed checking. Are these two systems of checking mutually exclusive?

7. What is the difference between the functions of computer checking and diagnostic analysis?

8. Discuss the following statements:
(a) The computer can repair itself.
(b) The computer was thoroughly checked for an hour this morning and given a clean bill of health; thus we may expect error-free operation for the next shift.
(c) A computer with dual arithmetic and control circuits is more reliable than one with a single set of circuits where one must rely on programmed checking.
(d) Repeated arithmetic is absolutely fail-safe.

9. List and discuss the items that fall under the classification of system checks.

10. In an actual customer billing operation, the write tape operation was not executed owing to a computer malfunction and several hundred customers were thus "lost" for a week. Discuss the type of checks that might have prevented or detected this type of error.

11. Devise a system of checking to insure that only authorized personnel may

make inquiries using the directly connected inquiry stations (some of which may be remotely located).

12. Suggest the difference in auditing problems in keeping the master tapes in printable mode versus unprintable mode. In the printable mode, the master file tape reels can be processed directly either by the computer or the off-line printer; in the unprintable mode, the master file tape reels must first be processed by the computer into the printable mode before the contents can be printed.

13. What are the auditing implications when a change record or a master record is flushed out of the system for manual attention and re-entered into the system at a later date?

14. If the computer is for business or military simulation, how may we check that the simulation is a reasonably faithful reproduction of the true life situation? Can the basic principle of auditing be applied?

15. Discuss the computer as an auditing tool.

16. Devise a self-checking number system. Which classes of errors will it detect and which will it not detect?

17. What is meant by an expiration plan? In the diagram on page 414, when do tapes D and J expire?

18. What is meant by a control group? Give several examples of what one might do.

19. Explain what is meant by management by exception, and give an example of a computer application of it.

20. Define the term "audit trail," and discuss the problem it poses in computer systems.

21. What are the implications of the elimination of source documents in data processing systems?

Appendix

1 DATAC

A1.0 General

DATAC is the name given to the mythical computer used for instructional purposes in this text. Its characteristics are intended to be representative of the principal features of all modern computers, including some which were not yet on the market at the time of writing. It is intended that most of the individual DATAC features may be omitted, if the actual machine being studied does not have equivalent features.

A1.1 Machine Characteristics

DATAC is a stored program computer, having 2000 words of high-speed, immediate-access storage which may be used to store data, instructions to the computer, or constants. Each word consists of eleven alpha-numeric characters of six bits each; if the word is numeric, the first character holds the sign. The bit patterns for each character are shown in Figure 1. Ten buffered magnetic tapes are also available as auxiliary memory, or for data input and output when used with off-line converters; records may be of variable length. Operation times for most instructions are taken as 100 μs, with the primary exceptions of multiplication and division which average 1000 μs; actual time varies, depending on the digits of the multiplier and divisor. Twenty μs each are added for indexing, filtering, transfer shifting, and monitoring—described below—if they are active on an instruction. Locations 0001–0099* in high-speed memory may be used as indexers or filters (or for any other purpose).

The indexers—also called index registers, base registers, and B-boxes

---

* Locations 00–09 are ordinarily reserved for use with the monitor character function, so the text examples use only locations 10–99 for indexers and filters.

—are most commonly used for modifying instruction addresses and for counting loop repetitions. An indexer may be specified as any address from 01 to 99 inclusive. An indexer location consists of three

Numeric \ Zone	00	01	10	11
0000	0			
0001	1	A	J	
0010	2	B	K	S
0011	3	C	L	T
0100	4	D	M	U
0101	5	E	N	V
0110	6	F	O	W
0111	7	G	P	X
1000	8	H	Q	Y
1001	9	I	R	Z
1010		.	(	Blank
1011		,	)	
1100		$	—	
1101		*	+	

Figure 1. Bit patterns of the DATAC characters.

parts, called the *counter*, the *increment*, and the *modifier*, laid out as follows:

```
  S  10  9  8 | 7  6  5 | 4  3  2  1
  |  Counter  | Increment |  Modifier  |
```

When an indexer is specified by an instruction, the modifier is added to the address part of that instruction *before the instruction is executed*, giving what is called the *effective address*. Certain instructions are provided to change the contents of indexers; the increment is then added to the modifier, the counter diminished by one, and a conditional jump executed based on the new value of the counter.

A filter causes certain parts of a word to be deleted in transfers between memory and the arithmetic registers. Each character of a filter which is a *one* specifies that the corresponding character of the word being transferred is to "filter through." Characters corresponding to zeros in the filter are replaced by zeros on a memory to arithmetic transfer, and simply not stored on an arithmetic to memory transfer. This function under slightly different conditions goes under the more common names of extraction, insertion, or masking.

Most operations involving arithmetic registers may specify that the transfer be executed *after* a shift to the right or left, of up to nine places. The operation of indexing, filtering, and shifting may be used in any combination. If filtering and shifting occur on the same instruction, filtering takes place first on a transfer from memory to the arithmetic section; shifting takes place first on a transfer in the other direction.

Any instruction may be "monitored." A monitor character in the instruction word may be any digit zero through nine. There are nine switches numbered one through nine on the machine console. If an instruction contains the same monitor digit as the number of a switch on the console which is depressed, then after the execution of that instruction control is transferred to the corresponding location in memory, i.e., one through nine, and the location of that instruction is placed in location zero. If monitor switch nine is depressed, then the presence of *any* monitor digit one through nine causes control to be transferred to location nine; nine thus provides an overriding monitor.

Input and output equipment includes a 250-card-per-minute punched card reader and a printer which prints lines of up to 120 characters at 600 lines per minute. When used with auxiliary equipment, the magnetic tapes become input/output devices.

A1.2 Instruction Format

An instruction word consists of six parts, not all of which are always required. These are, in the order they appear in the instruction: the suboperation code (which is part of the operation code on some instructions, and in other cases specifies the number of shifts before arithmetic and transfer operations), the operation code, the address, the indexer number, the filter number, and the monitor number.

S	10	9 8 7 6	5 4	3 2	1
Suboperation	Operation	Address	Indexer	Filter	Monitor

This diagram also shows the character numbering convention adopted for the mythical machine. The suboperation (if required) and the operation codes may be alphabetic; all other characters are always numeric. This would, of course, be a waste of instruction bits in a real machine—perhaps an intolerable one—but a major "design" criterion in this computer is teachability, which is enhanced by an uncomplicated instruction format. On most instructions the only essential parts are the operation code and, if required, the suboperation code, and usually an address.

A1.3 Arithmetic and Control Registers

There are two arithmetic registers, designated L and R for left and right. L and R combined contain a full-length product or dividend, with L being more significant. R contains the multiplier before multiplication; L contains the remainder and R the quotient after division. Only R may be used in other arithmetic and decision operations, although a carry is propagated from R to L if required. These two registers for many purposes may be thought of as forming one long twenty-two-character register. The signs of the two are their respective leftmost characters. For many purposes the sign characters are not really signs, as in manipulation of alpha-numeric data. When the signs actually are signs, the sign characters behave as signs only, as in all arithmetic operations. Two modes of shifting are provided, to include or exclude the sign character positions.

A four-digit *location counter* contains the address of the instruction currently being executed. An eleven-character *instruction register* holds the current instruction itself. An eleven-character *index register* holds the current indexer, if any. An eleven-character *filter register* holds the eleven filter characters, if any. An eleven-character *memory register* acts as a buffer between storage and the arithmetic and control sections; it also temporarily holds the multiplicand and divisor during multiplication and division.

The shifting which may optionally be done on information transfers between memory and the arithmetic registers or vice versa is called for by the suboperation code of instructions on which it is allowable. A one in the most significant bit of the suboperation code (the left zone bit) calls for a left shift; a one in the next less significant bit (the second zone bit) calls for a right shift. The numeric portion of the suboperation code specifies the number of shifts. Analysis of the bit codes shown in Figure 1 shows that these combinations work out as follows:

DATAC

SUBOPERATION CHARACTER	SHIFT
Zero	No shift
A	Shift 1 place right
B	" 2 " "
C	" 3 " "
D	" 4 " "
E	" 5 " "
F	" 6 " "
G	" 7 " "
H	" 8 " "
I	" 9 " "
J	Shift 1 place left
K	" 2 " "
L	" 3 " "
M	" 4 " "
N	" 5 " "
O	" 6 " "
P	" 7 " "
Q	" 8 " "
R	" 9 " "

The relationships among the arithmetic and control registers are shown in Figure 2 of Chapter 4.

On instructions which require a memory address reference, an indexer, a filter, shifting, and a monitor, the execution sequence is: a memory reference is required to obtain the instruction itself; a second reference obtains the indexer; a third obtains the filter; the contents of the effective address (address as written plus the indexer) are obtained from memory, filtered, shifted, and the operation performed; a jump to the memory address corresponding to the monitor digit is executed and the location of the instruction is placed in location zero.

A1.4 Instruction Details

The following descriptions of the instructions of DATAC give the operation code, the operation name, a symbolic description of the operation, and a word description of the operation. The notation "(X)" is used to signify "the contents of X" where X may be a location in memory (M), or an arithmetic register, (L) or (R). Permissible use of transfer shifting, indexing, and filtering is noted for each instruction. Monitoring is always permitted. When indexing is involved, the address, (M), is the effective address.

ARITHMETIC INSTRUCTIONS

    B   Bring to R   (M) → (R)

The contents of the memory location specified by the effective address replace the previous contents of the R register. The memory location contents are unchanged. Transfer shifting, indexing, and filtering are allowed.

F   Fetch to L   (M) → (L)

The contents of the memory location specified by the effective address replace the previous contents of the L register. The memory location contents are unchanged. Transfer shifting, indexing, and filtering are allowed.

S   Store R in M   (R) → (M)

The contents of the R register replace the previous contents of the memory location specified by the effective address. The R register contents are unchanged. Transfer shifting, indexing, and filtering are allowed.

U   Unload L to M   (L) → (M)

The contents of the L register replace the previous contents of the memory location specified by the effective address. The L register contents are unchanged. Transfer shifting, indexing, and filtering are allowed.

A   Add to R   (R) + (M) → (R)

Case 1. All characters of (R) and (M) are numeric, except the sign positions which contain signs.

The contents of the memory location specified by the effective address are added algebraically to the contents of the R register, and the sum is placed in the R register. If the sum exceeds ten digits, the overflow digit is added algebraically to the contents of the L register and the overflow indicator is turned on.

Case 2. Any character of (R) or (M) is nonnumeric or the sign positions contain anything but signs.

The contents of the memory location specified by the effective address are added to the contents of the R register and the sum is placed in the R register. The sign position of (M) is ignored completely and the sign position of (R) is unchanged in any case. Nonnumeric characters must be added only to zeros, and a carry must never be propagated into a nonnumeric character or into the L register. If these rules are violated, the addition is not completed and the *adder-alphabetic error* indicator is turned on.

In either case 1 or case 2, transfer shifting, indexing, and filtering are allowed.

M   R minus M   (R) — (M) → (R)

Same as Add, except the contents of the memory location specified by the effective address are *subtracted* from the contents of R.

XA   Add R to memory   (M) + (R) → (M), (R) unchanged

The contents of the R register are added to the contents of the location specified by the effective address. The contents of the R register are unchanged. If the sum exceeds ten digits, the overflow character is not stored in memory and the overflow indicator is turned on. Transfer shifting is not permitted, but indexing and filtering are permitted. Nonnumeric characters are treated as in the Add instruction, with the sign of the word in memory dominating.

XM   Subtract R from memory   (M) — (R) → (M), (R) unchanged

Same as Add to memory, except the contents of the R register are *subtracted* from the contents of the memory location specified by the effective address.

X   R times M   (R) × (M) → (L, R)

The L register is cleared to zero, destroying any previous contents. Then the contents of the memory location specified by the effective address are multiplied by the contents of the R register. The product is developed in the L and R registers combined, with the more significant digits being in the L register. If the signs of (M) and (R) before multiplication were the same, the signs of the L and R registers after will both be plus; otherwise they will both be minus. If either (M) or (R) contains any nonnumeric characters in positions 10–1 or any other character than plus or minus in the sign position, the multiplication is not carried out, and the *adder-alphabetic error* indicator is turned on. The multiplier in R is lost during the process of multiplication; the contents of the memory location are unchanged. Transfer shifting, indexing, and filtering are allowed.

D   Divide   (L, R) ÷ (M) → (R)

remainder → (L)

The number in the L and R registers combined (the number in L being more significant) is taken as the dividend; the contents of the memory location specified by the effective address are taken as the divisor, the quotient is developed in the R register and the remainder in the L register. If the signs of (R) and (M) are the same before division, the sign of the quotient in R is plus; otherwise minus. The remainder in L always has the sign of the dividend. Only the sign of R is considered in determining the sign of the dividend, i.e., if the L and R signs are different, the R sign is taken as sign of the dividend. If (L), (R), or (M) contains any nonnumeric character in positions 10–1, or if the sign positions contain any character other than plus or minus, the division is not completed and the *adder-alphabetic error* indicator is turned on. The dividend in L and R is lost during the division process, but the divisor in memory is unchanged. If the number in the L register is not smaller than the divisor (not considering sign and with the same decimal point assumed for the number in L and the divisor), the division is not performed and the *overflow* trigger is turned on. This is called the *divide overflow* condition. Transfer shifting, indexing, and filtering are allowed.

JUMP INSTRUCTIONS

UJ   Unconditional jump

The next instruction is taken from the memory location specified by the effective address. Indexing is permitted, but transfer shifting and filtering are not permitted.

PJ   Plus jump

If the sign position of the R register contains a plus sign, the next instruction is taken from the memory location specified by the effective address. If the sign position contains any character other than a plus sign, the next instruction is taken in sequence, as usual. Indexing is permitted but transfer shifting and filtering are not permitted.

MJ   Minus jump

If the sign position of the R register contains a minus sign, the next instruction is taken from the memory location specified by the effective address. If the sign position contains any character other than a minus sign, the next instruction is taken in sequence, as usual. Indexing is permitted but transfer shifting and filtering are not permitted.

ZJ   Zero jump

If positions 10–1 of the R register contain zeros, the next instruction is taken from the memory location specified by the effective address; otherwise, the next instruction is taken in sequence, as usual. The sign position is not considered. Indexing is permitted, but transfer shifting and filtering are not permitted.

NJ Nonzero jump

If any of the positions 10–1 of the R register contain a character other than zero, the next instruction is taken from the memory location specified by the effective address; otherwise, the next instruction is taken in sequence, as usual. Indexing is permitted, but transfer shifting and filtering are not permitted.

C Compare (R) and (M)

The contents of the R register are compared with the contents of the memory location specified by the effective address. All eleven characters are taken together, with the sign character as the highest order character, and the comparison is made on the basis of the following ascending collation sequence: blank, zero through nine, A through Z, decimal point (a period), comma, dollar sign, asterisk, left parenthesis, right parenthesis, minus sign, plus sign. Note that since a plus sign is greater than a minus sign, comparison of two signed numeric quantities is algebraic. If (R) is greater than (M), the *High* indicator is turned on; if equal, the *Equal* indicator is turned on; if (R) is less than (M), the *Low* indicator is turned on. In any case, only one of the three indicators can be turned on; the other two are always left turned off. Neither (R) nor (M) is changed by the comparison. Indexing and filtering are permitted; characters filtered out of the comparison are ignored in both (R) and (M). Transfer shifting is also permitted.

HJ High jump

If the High indicator is on, the next instruction is taken from the memory location specified by the effective address; otherwise, the next instruction is taken in sequence, as usual. Indexing is permitted, but transfer shifting and filtering are not permitted. The High indicator is left on.

EJ Equal jump

Same as High jump, except the Equal indicator is tested.

LJ Low jump

Same as High jump, except the Low indicator is tested.

IJ Interrupted jump

The execution of the routine is interrupted. When the start button on the console is pressed, the next instruction is taken from the location specified by the effective address. Indexing is permitted, but transfer shifting and filtering are not.

AJ   Alphabetic error jump

If the *adder-alphabetic error* indicator is on, the next instruction is taken from the location specified by the effective address and the indicator is turned off. If the indicator is already off, it is left off and the next instruction taken in normal sequence. Indexing is permitted, but transfer shifting and filtering are not.

OJ   Overflow jump

If the *overflow* indicator is on, the next instruction is taken from the location specified by the effective address and the indicator is turned off. If the indicator is already off, it is left off and the next instruction taken in normal sequence. Indexing is permitted, but transfer shifting and filtering are not.

TJ   Tape error jump

If the *tape-error* indicator is on, the next instruction is taken from the location specified by the effective address and the indicator is turned off. If the indicator is already off, it is left off and the next instruction taken in normal sequence. Indexing is permitted, but transfer shifting and filtering are not.

SHIFT INSTRUCTIONS

AR   Shift all right

All characters in the L and R registers are shifted right the number of places specified by the right two digits of the effective address. Zeros are entered into the sign position of L; characters shifted out of the sign position of L enter position 10 of L; characters shifted out of position 1 of L enter the sign position of R; characters shifted out of the sign position of R enter position 10 of R; characters shifted out of position 1 of R are lost. Indexing is permitted, but transfer shifting and filtering are not permitted. The memory location corresponding to the effective address has no function and is unaffected by the shifting.

ER   Shift right, except signs

All characters in the L and R registers, except the sign characters, are shifted right the number of places specified by the right two digits of the effective address. The sign of the R register is made the same as that of the L register; the signs do not shift. Zeros are entered into position 10 of the L register; characters shifted out of position 1 of the L register are entered into position 10 of the R register; characters shifted out of position 1 of the R register are lost. Indexing is permitted, but transfer shifting and filtering are not permitted. The memory location corresponding to the effective address has no function and is unaffected by the shifting.

AL   Shift all left

Similar to Shift all right, except the characters are shifted left.

EL   Shift left, except signs

Similar to Shift right, except signs, except the characters are shifted left and the sign of the L register is made the same as that of the R register.

OR   Shift only R right

The characters of R, excluding the sign character, are shifted right the number of places specified by the right two digits of the effective address. Zeros are entered into position 10 of the R register, and characters shifted out of the right end of the R register are lost. The sign character of the R register, and all characters in the L register, are unaffected. Indexing is permitted, but transfer shifting and filtering are not permitted. The memory location corresponding to the effective address has no function and is unaffected by the shifting.

OL   Shift only R left

Similar to Shift only R right, except the characters in the R register are shifted left.

RR   Shift R right and round

The characters in the R register, excluding the sign character, are shifted right the number of places specified by the right two digits of the effective address. After the shifting is completed, the last character shifted out of the R register (which is retained in a special one-character register) is examined. If it is five or greater, or if it is any nonnumeric character, a one is added to position 1 of the R register if the R register is positive, or subtracted if the R register is negative. If the last character shifted out of the R register is four or less, nothing else is done. If the rounding causes violation of any of the rules for

440 APPENDIX

addition with nonnumeric characters (see page 434), the *adder-alphabetic error* indicator is turned on. Indexing is permitted, but transfer shifting and filtering are not permitted. The memory location corresponding to the effective address has no function and is unaffected by the shifting.

EDITING INSTRUCTIONS

    E   Edit R

Zeros and commas to the left of the first significant digit in the R register are replaced by *blank* symbols. A decimal point is considered to be a significant digit, if it is the leftmost character. The sign position of the R register is not considered. Transfer shifting, indexing, and filtering have no meaning, nor does the address part of the instruction.

    DE   Dollar edit

Same as Edit, except that a dollar sign symbol is placed in the position just left of the leftmost significant character. If position 10 of the R register is the leftmost significant character, the instruction has no effect.

INDEXER INSTRUCTIONS

    RI   Raise index and jump

The increment part of the specified indexer is added to the modifier part of the specified indexer, and a jump is executed to the memory location specified by the address. Note that the address of this instruction is *not* an effective address: the modifier part of the indexer is not added to the address of the instruction before executing the jump. The addition of the increment to the modifier retains only four digits, i.e., any carry digit is lost. Transfer shifting, indexing (in the usual sense), and filtering have no meaning.

    ZI   Zero index jump

One is first subtracted from the counter part of the specified indexer. If the counter is now zero, the next instruction is taken from the memory location specified by the address of the instruction. If the counter is not zero after one is subtracted from it, the increment part is added to the modifier part of the specified indexer, and the next instruction is taken in sequence, as usual. Note that the address of this instruction is *not* an effective address: the modifier part of the indexer is not added to the address of the instruction before executing the jump. The addition of the increment to the modifier, if it occurs, retains only four digits, i.e., any carry digit is lost. Transfer shifting, indexing (in the usual sense), and filtering have no meaning.

NI   Nonzero index jump

One is first subtracted from the counter part of the specified indexer. If the counter is now zero, the next instruction in sequence is executed, as usual, and nothing else happens. If the counter is not zero after one is subtracted from the counter, the increment part is added to the modifier part of the specified indexer; the next instruction is taken from the memory location specified by the address of the instruction. Note that the address of this instruction is *not* an effective address: the modifier is not added to the address before executing the jump. The addition of the increment to the modifier part, if it occurs, retains only four digits, i.e., any carry digit is lost. Transfer shifting, indexing (in the usual sense), and filtering have no meaning.

LI   Load index

The contents of the memory location specified by the address replace the contents of the specified indexer. Note that the address of this instruction is not an effective address: the modifier is not added to the address before the memory word is obtained. Transfer shifting, indexing (in the usual sense), and filtering have no meaning.

SI   Store index

The contents of the specified indexer replace the contents of the memory location specified by the address. Note that the address of this instruction is not an effective address: the modifier is not added to the address before the word is stored in memory. Transfer shifting, indexing (in the usual sense), and filtering all have no meaning.

SJ   Set index jump

The contents of the location counter are placed in the modifier part of the specified indexer, and the next instruction is taken from the memory location specified by the address of the instruction. Note that the address of this instruction is *not* an effective address: the modifier part of the indexer is not added to the address of the instruction before executing the jump. Transfer shifting, indexing (in the usual sense) and filtering have no meaning.

INPUT/OUTPUT INSTRUCTIONS

    RT   Read tape

A record is read into memory from the tape reel on the tape handler specified by the *filter* digits of the instruction, as modified by adding to the filter digits the contents of the *counter* part of the specified indexer, if any. The first word of the record is stored in memory in the location specified by the effective address, and the following words are stored in sequentially higher-numbered locations. The number of words in the record is placed in the *increment* part of the indexer, if one is specified; if none is specified, the number of words is not stored anywhere. If a tape parity error is detected in reading, the *tape-error* indicator is turned on. Indexing is permitted; transfer shifting and filtering are not.

    WT   Write tape

A record is written from memory onto the tape reel on the tape handler specified by the *filter* digits of the instruction, as modified by adding to the filter digits the contents of the *counter* part of the specified indexer. The first word of the record is taken from the memory location specified by the effective address, and the following words from sequentially higher-numbered locations. The number of words to be written is specified by the contents of the increment part of the indexer. If indexer 00 is specified, the instruction will not be executed. Indexing is permitted, but transfer shifting and filtering are not.

    AT   Rewind tape

The tape reel on the tape handler specified by the *filter* digits of the instruction, as modified by the *counter* part of the specified indexer, if any, is rewound so that it is *at* the beginning of the reel ready to be removed, reread, or rewritten.

    IT   Interlock rewind

Same as Rewind tape, except that after rewinding the tape handler is *interlocked* so that it cannot be rewritten or reread until a button on the tape handler is pressed.

    DT   Delay tape

The tape handler is specified by the *filter* digits of the instruction, as modified by the *counter* part of the specified indexer, if any. If this tape handler is still in use from a previous tape instruction, the execution of the routine is delayed until the tape handler has completed its operation. If the tape handler is not in use, the Delay tape instruction has no effect. Indexing, filtering, and transfer shifting are not permitted.

R   Read

An eighty-column card is moved through the card reader and the information on it read into memory. The columns of the card are read into eight consecutive words in memory, the first of which is specified by the effective address of the instruction. The assignment and arrangement of columns into the eight words is under the control of a plugboard on the card reader. Any numeric words must usually be supplied with signs. Plus signs can be "emitted" from the card reader, through the plugboard, and signs which are overpunched in columns containing digits may be "split off" into the sign positions of words going into memory. Transfer shifting and filtering are not permitted. Indexing is permitted.

P   Print

One line consisting of 120 or fewer characters is printed. The location of the first of the twelve consecutive words in memory from which the 120 characters are taken is specified by the effective address of the Print instruction. The exact correspondence between the characters of the words in memory and the print positions is under the control of the plugboard on the printer. Transfer shifting and filtering are not permitted. Indexing is permitted.

SP   Space print

The paper in the printer is advanced at high speed to the position specified by the next hole in a paper tape loop which controls paper positioning. This is usually used to advance paper to the top of the next page. The address has no meaning. Transfer shifting, indexing, and filtering are not permitted.

Appendix

2 NUMBER REPRESENTATION

A2.0 Binary Numbers

The binary number system, which is at the heart of all digital computers, uses only two (hence, *binary*) digits, zero and one. This is so because binary numbers are so easy to represent and operate upon with physical devices. Common examples of binary storage devices are: an electric switch which is either on or off; a specific location (the intersection of a row and a column) of a punched card which either has a hole punched or does not; an electron tube or a transistor which is either conducting current or is not; a track on a magnetic tape which either has a change in magnetization at a given point or does not; a magnetic core which is magnetized in one direction or the other. In each case, the device or state has just two stable, mutually exclusive conditions. The digit zero is assigned to one of these conditions and the digit one to the other; the circuits of the computer are built to act according to the rules of binary arithmetic on combinations of the two states.

Some present computers operate explicitly in the binary number system, i.e., numbers and instructions must be *entered into* the machine in binary form, and output accepted likewise. In practice, such machines almost always are *programmed* to accept and write out decimal and alphabetic information, but this effort must be made; internal operations on nonbinary information—although entirely feasible—are matters of rather arduous programming.

Most machines intended for the type of work of primary interest to readers of this book are built to work with decimal and often alphabetic information directly. The word "directly" must be qualified, however. To the programmer, the statement is true as it stands; it is still necessary for the designer to deal with binary variables, because in such machines each character is represented by combinations of binary digits. Thus we see that *all* digital computers are binary "on the inside." Those that use small groups of binary digits to represent individual characters pay a penalty by the fact that the equipment is used less efficiently, but gain the considerable reduction of programming effort and the increased sales appeal that accompanies direct decimal and alphabetic representation.

In this appendix we shall examine the idea behind binary numbers, arithmetic operations in binary, methods of conversion between binary and decimal, and some of the more common methods of representing decimal digits in binary notation.

A2.1 Number Representation

The central feature of the Arabic number system is the fact that a given digit can have more or less value depending on where it appears in the number. For instance, the digit 3 may be worth ten times 3 in 30, or 1,000,000 times 3 in 3,000,000, or one-hundredth of 3 in 0.03. (Recall that there is no such general place value in the Roman number system, since there is no zero.) This fact is so familiar to us in everyday life as to be overlooked. What we really mean by a number like 744.819 is

$$744.819 = 700 + 40 + 4 + 0.8 + 0.01 + 0.009$$

or, what is the same thing written in exponential notation,

$$744.819 = 7 \cdot 10^2 + 4 \cdot 10^1 + 4 \cdot 10^0 + 8 \cdot 10^{-1} + 1 \cdot 10^{-2} + 9 \cdot 10^{-3}$$

since any number to the zero power is one, and since $10^{-n} = 1/10^n$, where n is any number. Another way of stating the place value idea, in terms of this example, is that the first 4 is worth ten times as much for being written where it is as is the second 4.

The question we must ask is, why this number ten, or why just ten digits? Why not six, or twenty—or two? The answer, in all probability, arose from our having ten fingers. If we use some other place value, we will of course need the same number of digits as the number base, which will require invention of some new ones if there are to be more than ten.

In the case of binary numbers we need only two—zero and one—and the place value between adjacent digits is just two. For instance, in binary the number 1101 means:

$$1101 = 1 \cdot 2^3 + 1 \cdot 2^2 + 0 \cdot 2^1 + 1 \cdot 2^0$$

In this case, the first 1 is worth twice as much as the second 1, and eight times as much as the last. The basic idea of place value is unchanged: the amount of the place values is now simply *two* instead of the familiar ten.

Since a number involving only zeros and ones could in some cases be taken as either binary or decimal, we must be careful to specify the place value (more precisely called the *base* or *radix*) wherever there could be confusion. This is usually indicated by enclosing the number in parentheses and writing the base as a subscript, in decimal. Thus:

$$(1101)_2, \quad (1101)_{10}$$

As an exercise in interpreting the meaning of binary numbers, we may take a direct method of conversion from binary to decimal. The number $(11101.101)_2$ means:

$$\begin{aligned}
(11101.101)_2 = \quad & 1\cdot 2^4 & = & \quad (16)_{10} \\
+ & 1\cdot 2^3 & = & \quad (8)_{10} \\
+ & 1\cdot 2^2 & = & \quad (4)_{10} \\
+ & 0\cdot 2^1 & = & \quad (0)_{10} \\
+ & 1\cdot 2^0 & = & \quad (1)_{10} \\
+ & 1\cdot 2^{-1} & = & \quad (0.5)_{10} \\
+ & 0\cdot 2^{-2} & = & \quad (0.0)_{10} \\
+ & 1\cdot 2^{-3} & = & \quad \underline{(0.125)_{10}} \\
& & & \quad (29.625)_{10}
\end{aligned}$$

or $(11101.101)_2 = (29.625)_{10}$. Binary fractions may be confusing at first. It may help to observe that:

$$(0.1)_2 = 1\cdot 2^{-1} = \tfrac{1}{2} = \tfrac{5}{10} = (0.5)_{10}$$

Octal numbers fit into the same pattern; here the base is eight, and only eight digits, zero through seven, are needed. For example:

$$\begin{aligned}
(327.41)_8 = \quad & 3\cdot 8^2 & = & \quad (192)_{10} \\
+ & 2\cdot 8^1 & = & \quad (16)_{10} \\
+ & 7\cdot 8^0 & = & \quad (7)_{10} \\
+ & 4\cdot 8^{-1} & = & \quad (0.5)_{10} \\
+ & 1\cdot 8^{-2} & = & \quad \underline{(0.015625)_{10}} \\
& & & \quad (215.515625)_{10}
\end{aligned}$$

The simple reason for the use of octal (also sometimes called octonary) numbers is that the conversion from binary to octal can be carried out mentally, and only a third as many digits are required to carry the same information. All that is necessary to convert from binary to octal is to group the binary digits in groups of three's

NUMBER REPRESENTATION

from the binary point, and write down the decimal value of each group taken as an integer. Thus:

$$(11/011/010/110.110/001/110)_2 = (3326.616)_8$$

The basis for this may be seen readily from an example:

$$(101011)_2 = \left.\begin{array}{r}1\cdot 2^5 \\ +\ 0\cdot 2^4 \\ +\ 1\cdot 2^3\end{array}\right\} = \begin{array}{r}4\cdot 2^3 \\ +\ 0\cdot 2^3 \\ +\ 1\cdot 2^3\end{array} = 5\cdot 2^3 = 5\cdot 8^1$$

$$\left.\begin{array}{r}+\ 0\cdot 2^2 \\ +\ 1\cdot 2^1 \\ +\ 1\cdot 2^0\end{array}\right\} = \begin{array}{r}+\ 0\cdot 2^0 \\ +\ 2\cdot 2^0 \\ +\ 1\cdot 2^0\end{array} = 3\cdot 2^0 = 3\cdot 8^0$$

or $\quad (101011)_2 = 5\cdot 8^1 + 3\cdot 8^0 = (53)_8$

The same simplicity of conversion could be accomplished using any base which is a power of two. Four would be the quaternary system, which would have no particular advantage over octal and would indeed require more digits to represent the same number. Bases 16 and 32 are both in use by at least one computing installation. They accomplish a further reduction in number of digits at the expense of requiring new symbols for the extra six or twenty-two digits. In the balance, the disadvantages of these latter outweigh the gains unless there are overriding factors such as the characteristics of input/output equipment.

Octal numbers find little use in machines which use binary coding of individual decimal digits and alphabetic characters so we shall not discuss them further.

A2.2 Binary Arithmetic

Before plunging into the subject of arithmetic in the binary system, it might be helpful to mention briefly the mechanics of counting in binary. When counting in decimal, we first write the ten digits in order. Then we continue by writing 1 to the left, giving it a place value of ten—the base of the number system. The process is similar for counting in any other number system: we write the digit symbols until we run out, then start writing a 1 to the left, giving it the place value of the system. As soon as we run out using two digits, we write another 1, giving it the value of the number base squared. This, of course, is nothing more than we have already discussed, but the difference in viewpoint may make the scheme clearer. Counting in decimal and binary, we have:

APPENDIX

DECIMAL	BINARY
0	0
1	1
2	10
3	11
4	100
5	101
6	110
7	111
8	1000
9	1001
10	1010
11	1011
12	1100
13	1101
14	1110
15	1111
16	10000
17	10001
18	10010
19	10011
20	10100
Etc.	Etc.

Binary addition is really quite simple once the rules are learned, because there are so few possibilities. The complete binary addition table is:

$$0 + 0 = 0$$
$$0 + 1 = 1$$
$$1 + 0 = 1$$
$$1 + 1 = 0 \text{ with 1 carried}$$

The last line of the table is the only one which is not completely obvious. It corresponds in decimal, roughly, to an equation such as:

$$1 + 9 = 0 \text{ with 1 carried}$$

It may also help to notice that going one place past 001 in the table of binary integers (which corresponds to the addition of 1 and 1) gives 010.

We may now carry out some addition examples, after noting that $1 + 1 + 1 = 1$ with 1 carried—which will sometimes occur with carries.

BINARY ADDITION EXAMPLES

Carries

```
    1                 111              1111111
  101010           10111000           11111111
 +001001          +  101011          +        1
  ——————           ————————           —————————
  110011           11100011          100000000
```

NUMBER REPRESENTATION

The table for binary subtraction is not much more complicated than that for addition:

$$0 - 0 = 0$$
$$1 - 1 = 0$$
$$1 - 0 = 1$$
$$0 - 1 = 1 \text{ with 1 borrowed from next digit}$$

Binary subtraction is often confusing. It may help to note that the borrowing may be thought of in two different ways. One is to think of a one being subtracted from the digit to the left in the minuend (the number "on top"). Another is to think of a one being added to the digit to the left in the subtrahend. Either system works; the choice is a matter of preference.

BINARY SUBTRACTION EXAMPLES

```
Borrows        0              0 001
             X01101          X0XX0010
           − 11001         − 10101010
           ───────         ──────────
             10100           10111000
```

Subtractions which give negative answers can be handled as usual by subtracting in reverse order and attaching a minus sign to the difference.

Subtractions are actually carried out in computer electronics by the addition of complements. This method is based on the following, illustrated with a six-digit decimal number:

$$493{,}201 - 126{,}944 = 493201 + (1{,}000{,}000 - 126{,}944) - 1{,}000{,}000$$

The subtraction 1,000,000 − 126,944 can be very simply performed by subtracting each digit from 9 except the last, which is subtracted from 10 (if the last digit is 0, the next to the last is subtracted from 10, etc.). This is then called the ten's complement. Thus

$$1{,}000{,}000 - 126{,}944 = 873{,}056$$

Now adding:

```
        493,201
        873,056
      ─────────
      1,366,257
```

The 1,000,000 is subtracted off again simply by deleting the 1 at the beginning.

An alternative method uses the nine's complement, which is formed by subtracting each digit from 9, including the last. After the addition of the complement, the leading 1 is deleted and a 1 is added to the units position. This is sometimes called "end-around-carry." In either method, a negative difference will be in complement form, and must be reconverted. Also, no end-around-carry is required. A negative difference may be recognized by complementing one more digit than necessary, i.e., adding a 0 at the front; a negative difference will be signaled by a 9 in the first position, instead of a 0.

Examples

0456789	becomes	0456789	
−0123456		9876543	nine's complement
		①0333332	
		↳1	
		0333333	
0123456	becomes	0123456	
−0456789		9543210	
		9666666	which becomes
		−333333	on reconversion

This may seem to be an exceedingly difficult way of subtracting two numbers. It is used (or the equivalent thing in binary) because it is far simpler to form a digit-by-digit complement than to build circuits or devices to "borrow." This is especially true in binary, where the one's complement is formed simply by changing ones to zeros and zeros to ones, which can be done with great ease electronically.

In fact, in some machines negative numbers are represented entirely by complements rather than by the use of minus signs. Again circuit simplicity makes for programming difficulty. This is the reverse of the current trend.

MULTIPLICATION

Multiplication is simply a process of repeated addition. We can multiply in binary simply by developing an appropriate multiplication table and following a process similar to decimal multiplication.

In binary we have:

$$0 \cdot 0 = 0$$
$$0 \cdot 1 = 0$$
$$1 \cdot 0 = 0$$
$$1 \cdot 1 = 1$$

Example

```
  1011011
     1101
  1011011
  0000000
 1011011
1011011
10010011111
```

In a binary computer, no multiplication table need actually be stored since the table is so simple. Each digit of the multiplier is examined in turn: if it is a 1, the multiplicand is added; if it is a 0, no addition takes place. This is all done quite simply electronically, and is another reason the binary number system is so attractive to computer designers.

In most decimal machines, no table is stored, but multiplication is carried out by adding the multiplicand as many times as the digit value of the multiplier.

Example

```
12345 × 123 =   1234500
             +   123450
             +   123450
             +    12345
             +    12345
             +    12345
                1518435
```

Advanced machines do, however, have multiplication tables "built into" the electronic circuity, gaining speed at the expense of circuit complexity.

DIVISION

Division can be carried out in binary by the same process as in decimal: repeated subtraction.

Binary

```
          1001
    1011|1101101
         1011
         0010101
           1011
           1010  remainder
```

For most work in computer programming it is not necessary to be *expert* at nondecimal arithmetic, but it is often useful to *know how* it is done.

A2.3 Number Base Conversion

It is often necessary to know what is the equivalent, in one number base, of a number expressed in a different base. For instance, it may be desired to enter a decimal number into the memory of a binary machine directly, without using the conversion system programmed for usual data loading. Although it is possible to use methods based on experimentation, with the principles presented so far, or to use prepared tables, systematic methods are available.

CONVERSION OF DECIMAL INTEGERS TO BINARY

The basis of the method may be presented as a series of algebraic manipulations with an example. All arithmetic will be carried out in decimal.

Example. $(27)_{10}$ to *binary.*

$$27 = \frac{27}{2} \cdot 2 = (13 + \tfrac{1}{2})2 = 13 \cdot 2^1 + 1 \cdot 2^0$$

But $\quad 13 = \dfrac{13}{2} \cdot 2 = (6 + \tfrac{1}{2})2 = 6 \cdot 2^1 + 1 \cdot 2^0$

So $\quad 27 = (6 \cdot 2^1 + 1 \cdot 2^0)2^1 + 1 \cdot 2^0 = 6 \cdot 2^2 + 1 \cdot 2^1 + 1 \cdot 2^0$

Again $\quad 6 = \dfrac{6}{2} \cdot 2 = (3 + 0)2 = 3 \cdot 2^1 + 0 \cdot 2^0$

So $\quad 27 = (3 \cdot 2^1 + 0 \cdot 2^0) \cdot 2^2 + 1 \cdot 2^1 + 1 \cdot 2^0$
$\qquad\quad = 3 \cdot 2^3 + 0 \cdot 2^2 + 1 \cdot 2^1 + 1 \cdot 2^0$

Finally $\quad 3 = \dfrac{3}{2} \cdot 2 = (1 + \tfrac{1}{2})2 = 1 \cdot 2^1 + 1 \cdot 2^0$

So $\quad 27 = (1 \cdot 2^1 + 1 \cdot 2^0)2^3 + 0 \cdot 2^2 + 1 \cdot 2^1 + 1 \cdot 2^0$
$\qquad\quad = 1 \cdot 2^4 + 1 \cdot 2^3 + 0 \cdot 2^2 + 1 \cdot 2^1 + 1 \cdot 2^0$

This last is precisely the meaning of the binary number **11011**, so we have effected the conversion.

The procedure may be summarized in the following rule:

To convert a decimal integer to binary, divide repeatedly by 2. Each time write down the remainder, starting from the right, and divide the quotient by two to get the next digit. The sequence of remainders will be the binary number.

It may be noted that this process is inherent in the definition of the binary form. If an integer N is to be converted to the form

$$N = a_n 2^n + a_{n-1} 2^{n-1} + \cdots + a_1 2^1 + a_0 2^0$$

NUMBER REPRESENTATION

then a_0 is the remainder on division of N by 2, a_1 is the remainder on division of this quotient by 2, etc.

Example. $(27)_{10}$ to *binary*.

$$
\begin{array}{r}
13 \\
2\overline{)27} \\
\underline{26} \\
1
\end{array}
\qquad \text{1 (First remainder)}
$$

$$
\begin{array}{r}
6 \\
2\overline{)13} \\
\underline{12} \\
1
\end{array}
\qquad \text{11 (First two remainders)}
$$

$$
\begin{array}{r}
3 \\
2\overline{)6} \\
\underline{6} \\
0
\end{array}
\qquad \text{011 (First three remainders)}
$$

$$
\begin{array}{r}
1 \\
2\overline{)3} \\
\underline{2} \\
1
\end{array}
\qquad \text{1011 (First four remainders)}
$$

$$
\begin{array}{r}
0 \\
2\overline{)1} \\
\underline{0} \\
1
\end{array}
\qquad \text{11011 (All remainders)}
$$

and as before, $(27)_{10} = (11011)_2$

Since division by 2 can be done mentally, the process can be condensed:

27	1
13	11
6	011
3	1011
1	11011

CONVERSION OF DECIMAL FRACTIONS TO BINARY

A somewhat similar process is used for conversion of fractions.

Example. $(0.62)_{10}$ to *binary*.

$$0.62 = \frac{0.62}{2} \cdot 2 = \frac{1.24}{2} = 1 \cdot 2^{-1} + (0.24)2^{-1}$$

$$0.24 = \frac{0.24}{2} \cdot 2 = \frac{0.48}{2} = 0 \cdot 2^{-1} + (0.48)2^{-1}$$

So $\quad 0.62 = 1 \cdot 2^{-1} + (0 \cdot 2^{-1} + 0.48 \cdot 2^{-1})2^{-1}$
$\quad\quad\quad = 1 \cdot 2^{-1} + 0 \cdot 2^{-2} + (0.48)2^{-2}$

$0.48 = \dfrac{0.48}{2} \cdot 2 = \dfrac{0.96}{2} = 0 \cdot 2^{-1} + 0.96 \cdot 2^{-1}$

So $\quad 0.62 = 1 \cdot 2^{-1} + 0 \cdot 2^{-2} + (0 \cdot 2^{-1} + 0.96 \cdot 2^{-1})2^{-2}$
$\quad\quad\quad = 1 \cdot 2^{-1} + 0 \cdot 2^{-2} + 0 \cdot 2^{-3} + 0.96 \cdot 2^{-3}$

$0.96 = \dfrac{0.96}{2} \cdot 2 = \dfrac{1.92}{2} = 1 \cdot 2^{-1} + 0.92 \cdot 2^{-1}$

So $\quad 0.62 = 1 \cdot 2^{-1} + 0 \cdot 2^{-2} + 0 \cdot 2^{-3} + (1 \cdot 2^{-1} + 0.92 \cdot 2^{-1})2^{-3}$
$\quad\quad\quad = 1 \cdot 2^{-1} + 0 \cdot 2^{-2} + 0 \cdot 2^{-3} + 1 \cdot 2^{-4} + 0.92 \cdot 2^{-4}$
$\quad\quad\quad = (0.1001)_2$

This may be continued as long as we wish; in general, the binary fraction will be infinite. This is an unfortunate quirk of number base conversion, that finite fractions in one base do not usually have finite forms in another base. [We are familiar with this in such cases as the fraction $\frac{1}{3}$, which as a decimal fraction is nonterminating while in base three it would be $(0.1)_3$.]

The binary expression above is just what we mean by $(0.1001)_2$, and is the equivalent, to four binary digits, of the decimal number (0.62).

There is a systematic way of doing the conversion, expressed in this rule:

To convert a decimal fraction to binary, multiply the fraction (in decimal) by 2. Write down whatever appears to the left of the decimal point, as the first binary digit. Multiply the *fractional* part of the product by 2 again, etc.

Example. $(0.79)_{10}$ *to binary.*

$\quad\quad\quad\quad\quad 0.79$
$\quad\quad\quad\quad\quad\underline{2}$
$\quad\quad\quad\quad\quad 1.58 \quad\quad 0.1$
$\quad\quad\quad\quad\quad\underline{2}$
$\quad\quad\quad\quad\quad 1.16 \quad\quad 0.11$
$\quad\quad\quad\quad\quad\underline{2}$
$\quad\quad\quad\quad\quad 0.32 \quad\quad 0.110$
$\quad\quad\quad\quad\quad\underline{2}$
$\quad\quad\quad\quad\quad 0.64 \quad\quad 0.1100$
$\quad\quad\quad\quad\quad\underline{2}$
$\quad\quad\quad\quad\quad 1.28 \quad\quad 0.11001$, etc.

Since multiplication by 2 can be done mentally, the binary equivalent can be written down quite rapidly.

NUMBER REPRESENTATION

The problem of converting a number which is part integral and part fractional can be handled several ways. The most obvious is to convert the two parts separately:

$$91.42 = 91 + 0.42$$
$$= (1011011)_2 + (0.0110110)_2$$
$$= (1011011.0110110)_2$$

Another way is to convert the entire number as if it were an integer, then multiply, in binary, by the binary equivalent of the required power of ten:

$$91.42 = 9142 \cdot 10^{-2}$$
$$= (10001110110110) \cdot (0.00000010100011)$$
$$= (1011011.0110110)_2$$

Similarly, we can convert the number as if it were entirely fractional, then multiply by the required power of ten:

$$91.42 = (0.9142)(10^2)$$

CONVERSION FROM BINARY TO DECIMAL

The same techniques may be used to reverse the process, except that we must now use the binary representation of decimal ten, and of course all arithmetic must be done in binary. Also, as the decimal digits are developed, they will appear in binary and must be converted to decimal.

Example. $(10110111)_2$ to decimal.

$$(10)_{10} = (1010)_2$$

```
            10010
      1010)10110111
           1010
           ----
            1011
            1010
            ----
              11   remainder = (3)₁₀ = unit's digit
```

```
              1
        1010)10010
             1010
             ----
             1000  remainder = (8)₁₀ = ten's digit
```

```
             0
       1010)1
            1      remainder = (1)₁₀ = hundred's digit
```

So $(10110111)_2 = (183)_{10}$

Example. $(0.1101110)_2$ *to decimal.*

```
    0.1101110
         1010
    11011100
   11011100
 1000.1001100
```
$(1000)_2 = (8)_{10}$, so first decimal digit is 8

```
    0.1001100
         1010
    10011000
   10011000
 0101.1111000
```
$(0101)_2 = (5)_{10}$

```
    0.1111000
         1010
    11110000
   11110000
 1001.0110000
```
$(1001)_2 = (9)_{10}$

So $(0.1101110)_2 = (0.859)_{10}$

RECONVERSION

Suppose we were to convert a decimal fraction to binary, then convert the binary fraction to decimal. Would we get the same decimal fraction? Testing the first example above:

$$(0.62)_{10} = (0.1001)_2$$

```
    0.1001
      1010
    10010
   1001
  101.1010
```
$(101)_2 = (5)_{10}$

```
    0.1010
      1010
    10100
   1010
  110.0100
```
$(110)_2 = (6)_{10}$

We seem to get $(0.62)_{10} = (0.1001)_2 = (0.56)_{10}$?

The problem is that four binary digits cannot carry as much information as two decimal digits. If we had continued the conversion to binary to get seven places:

NUMBER REPRESENTATION

$(0.62)_{10} = (0.1001111)$, then reconversion would have given:

$$\frac{\begin{array}{r}0.1001111 \\ 1010\end{array}}{\begin{array}{r}10011110 \\ 1001111\end{array}}$$
$$\overline{110.0010110} \qquad (110)_2 = (6)_{10}$$

$$\frac{\begin{array}{r}0.0010110 \\ 1010\end{array}}{\begin{array}{r}00101100 \\ 0010110\end{array}}$$
$$\overline{001.1011100} \qquad \text{which rounds off to}$$
$$\qquad\qquad\qquad (010)_2 = (2)_{10}$$

$(0.1001111)_2 = (0.62)_{10}$ as before

The number of binary places necessary to give exact reconversion to decimal may be presented in a table, as illustrated in Table 1.

TABLE 1

NUMBER OF DECIMALS	NUMBER OF BINARY PLACES TO GIVE EXACT RECONVERSION
0	0
1	4
2	7
3	10
4	14
5	17
6	20
7	24
8	27
9	30
10	34

OTHER METHODS

There are other techniques for number base conversion. Some provide short cuts for special uses; others are dictated by equipment design or input format, such as punched cards. The methods presented here are simple and general; they provide a basic technique.

A2.4 Binary Coding of Decimal Digits

Machines which operate in decimal require that each decimal digit be coded in binary. The arithmetic and control circuits then operate on the *groups* of bits which represent the decimal digits.

APPENDIX

There are many ways of "coding" the decimal digits, i.e., of combining several binary digits to represent one decimal digit. All the methods require at least four bits, and involve assigning some value or "weight" to each. There are about five systems in common use, namely the 8-4-2-1, the 2*-4-2-1, the excess-three, the two-out-of-five, and the bi-quinary systems.

TABLE 2

DECIMAL DIGIT	BINARY VARIABLES Weights 8 4 2 1
0	0 0 0 0
1	0 0 0 1
2	0 0 1 0
3	0 0 1 1
4	0 1 0 0
5	0 1 0 1
6	0 1 1 0
7	0 1 1 1
8	1 0 0 0
9	1 0 0 1

The 8-4-2-1 system assigns the same weights as in ordinary binary notation. The coding is simply the binary representation of the decimal digits; see Table 2.

The next two systems share several features which are desirable in design. They have these two characteristics: 1. The nine's complement of a decimal digit can be formed by complementing each binary digit, which is easily done electronically. 2. When two binary coded digits are added in binary, the fifth digit of the sum is one if the sum is ten or greater, zero if less.

The first of these is the 2*-4-2-1 system, the first 2 being starred to remind us that there are two two's. The representations are given in Table 3.

The two characteristics mentioned above may be checked. The nine's complement of seven is two; the representations are respectively 1101 and 0010, which are seen to have binary zeros and ones reversed. Adding two and seven in decimal causes no carry; adding 0010 and 1101 in binary does not. Adding six and five does; adding 1100 and 1011 does.

The other is the excess-three system, so called because it is just like the 8-4-2-1 system but with binary three added to each representation, as Table 4 illustrates.

The two considerations above are also seen to apply. This system

NUMBER REPRESENTATION

TABLE 3

DECIMAL DIGIT	BINARY VARIABLES Weights 2 4 2 1
0	0 0 0 0
1	0 0 0 1
2	0 0 1 0
3	0 0 1 1
4	0 1 0 0
5	1 0 1 1
6	1 1 0 0
7	1 1 0 1
8	1 1 1 0
9	1 1 1 1

has the additional advantage that combinations 0000 and 1111 are illegal. Since these are easy to check for electronically, a simple test of machine reliability is available.

The next system is based on checking machine reliability, to which is sacrificed the cost of an additional binary variable. Sometimes called the two-out-of-five system, it requires that exactly two binary digits be *one* in the representation of each digit. The weights assigned are 0, 1, 2, 3, 6. Each decimal digit can be made up of *exactly* two of these, which provides a simple check of machine operation. There are two ways of coding the digit three; one of these is used for zero.

TABLE 4

DECIMAL DIGIT	BINARY VARIABLES Weights 8 4 2 1 (Three added to each)
0	0 0 1 1
1	0 1 0 0
2	0 1 0 1
3	0 1 1 0
4	0 1 1 1
5	1 0 0 0
6	1 0 0 1
7	1 0 1 0
8	1 0 1 1
9	1 1 0 0

In the machine where the two-out-of-five coding finds widest application, the representations on the drum and in arithmetic registers and the console are different. The two-out-of-five scheme is used on the drum, but the bi-quinary ("two-five") system is used in arithmetic

TABLE 5

DECIMAL	5	0	4	3	2	1	0
0	0	1	0	0	0	0	1
1	0	1	0	0	0	1	0
2	0	1	0	0	1	0	0
3	0	1	0	1	0	0	0
4	0	1	1	0	0	0	0
5	1	0	0	0	0	0	1
6	1	0	0	0	0	1	0
7	1	0	0	0	1	0	0
8	1	0	0	1	0	0	0
9	1	0	1	0	0	0	0

registers and the console. This method requires that each digit be represented by one of two (binary) variables, assigned weights of 5 and 0, and one of five (quinary) variables, assigned weights of 4, 3, 2, 1, and 0. The codings are given in Table 5.

One advantage here seems to be that it can be presented in a very readable form on the console:

```
         0         5
         ●         ●
              0
              ●
              1
              ●
              2
              ●
              3
              ●
              4
              ●
```

Of some historical interest is the fact that the first large electronic (but not stored program) machine, the ENIAC, uses ten binary variables, one for each decimal digit. No other electronic machine has ever been built this way.

Appendix

3 A DATA PROCESSING DIARY*

By Fred Gruenberger

A file maintenance problem was proposed late in September, 1956. It involved a master tape of some 11,000 records of 300 characters each. These would be updated daily by some 2000 to 4000 transactions. Each transaction affected several fields of the corresponding master record (the master records were in payroll number order, one for each man in the plant). Provision was made to handle various corrections to master records each day. Output from each pass included five different reports and a new set of prepunched cards. On these the customers could keypunch the next input information. Such a procedure tends to insure match of input and master tape. A dummy record was written on the master tape with pay number 88888 and identification of IMATESTCASE. Another dummy record, 88889 IMATESTCASEJR, was also used. Together they monitored the system and provided opportunity to apply corrections freely so they could be observed without affecting a real record. TESTCASEJR acted as a buffer, guaranteeing that activity which affected TESTCASE would not reflect in the next record. (Coding errors which apply some action to the record after the one for which they are intended are mighty difficult to find and correct.)

The customers for this application had no experience in punched card work or data processing. They went from pencil and paper to electronics overnight. The transition included installing keypunches to prepare the input data.

The job went into operation December 10, 1956, in parallel. The manual system which had been in operation for years was kept up simultaneously to insure that computer conversion checked out.

Initially, input cards were sorted by payroll number before com-

---

* Reprinted by permission, in slightly altered form, from *Computing News*, published by Jackson W. Granholm, 12805 64th Avenue South, Seattle 88, Wash.

puter processing, and were not edited. Each input card dictated some updating of one field of the master record, and appropriate total fields. Except for corrections to the master record, all the customers were to punch each day was the amount of the activity. This was done on a card from a previous machine pass with identification prepunched.

A new master tape was written each day. The last tape of the year was isolated from tape cycling for use in preparing end-of-year reports.

Near the end of December a logbook was begun in which to record daily events on the job. Excerpts from the log are given here. The job went independent on January 14, 1957.

This log is presented to show some of the interesting ramifications of getting a new application into smooth operation. Little has been written of the specific troubles met in data processing, and of the gay times spent patching mistakes in the wee hours. The log also serves as a valuable reference to detailed decisions made and action taken in the dim past, and may provide an answer to such questions as "How did we get into *this* mess?"

December 29: 12,109 records of input; 15 additions, no deletions; 12,124 records written out. An overflow condition stopped the machine on man number **88888** (input data exceeded capacity of the master record fields); corrected at console by subtracting a large amount from fields in question and noting action. Two output tapes disappeared without being printed. Internal communications seem generally snarled up.

January 3: Pass for 12-29-56 rerun without incident. Some correction cards added so that essential control figures (number of input records, number of additions, number of deletions, number of output records) showed **12109, 25, 7, 12127.**

It was noticed that in some cases input readings of zero were introducing nonzero increments to master records. The trouble was tracked down and corrected.

Trouble noted previously for nonzero increments for case where $X = 1.5y$ seems to have gone away by itself.

January 4: 12127, 60, 0, 12187. All is well. Processed at 3:00 A.M. Started summing pay numbers of cards punched out to give hash total when these cards come back from customers.

January 5: 12187, 21, 37, 12171; processed at 7:00 A.M. Case where $X = 1.5y$ gave trouble again. This time we got a memory dump and made proper corrections.

January 6: Job went on at 3:00 A.M. and promptly collapsed.

Main parameter card had invalid identification. Error discovered when F. wandered in at 1:00 P.M. (this is a Sunday).

Rerun started at 8:00 P.M. Collapsed again due to some data cards with batch numbers not represented in batch parameter cards. The chief customer was notified and started for his office to get missing data.

Rerun again at 11:00 P.M. with complete data. New trouble: 83 tape read errors. Here F. pulled a boner. Changed typewriter address to address of an on-line printer without noting transfer-back address. Transfer made to (actual) 16929 and pass restarted. Precisely one more message came out. The correctness of this procedure should be checked.

January 7: On machine at 9:00 P.M. All went well till the first of five input cards with an invalid month code. This gave sign check at (actual) 8289. F. botched a console patching. Reloaded and restarted. 20 minutes shot. It is imperative that we edit input.

On reaching same point in rerun, *12* (for December) was stored at 0333–0334 and transfer made to 8049. This worked fine and was repeated twice. The last two such errors, though, gave sign check at 8374. Same correction applied with knowledge that two master records were being goofed up. We should examine why they stopped at a different place.

Customers requested that on creation of a new master record it be printed out for inspection.

Pay numbers 88888 and 88889 now have valid suffix so that "invalid suffix" message should disappear.

One report out of balance today.

It seems last three correction cards for #88888 were not processed. No nonmetaphysical explanation leaps to mind.

January 8: Customers decided to pull a stunt. Correction cards for #88888 were inserted so if last three didn't get processed, there would be overflow (correction cards are processed before data cards; correction cards would clear out the totals; the data cards overloaded them). Sure enough: phone call to F. at 12:45 A.M.—overflow. In fact, three successive overflows. Operator subtracted 500 from the field involved and transferred back to the most recent reset-add.

Solution to "last three cards" mystery by G.G.: The correction card type inserted by customers to zero the fields was designed for a different purpose. Hence fields were not zeroed. All is well. Thus the claim that we had not processed the last three cards is false. We are smelling like a rose.

January 9: On at 8:30 P.M. for a special pass—edit the master tape.

Pass collapsed immediately due to our cleverness in writing instructions at same place in memory as the tape input area. Correction made and pass proceeded. However, for some 12,000 master records it produced about 20,000 error messages. This program was debugged?

It was decided that both customers and computer team have been so busy altering master records that we should delete from the tape all activity so far produced and reinsert it as one master correction item, as given by the customers' manual system. Also, it was agreed that our correction card routine should be altered to allow customer correction of two fields with one correction card.

Further, it was agreed that the program should be altered so a correction card which tried to change a total independently of the detail buckets would set off various alarms to document the change extensively.

January 10: The 20,000 error messages from the edit-pass of 1-9-57 were punched out, sorted, then listed on the 407. Most consisted of "for number XXXXX all activity for the year sums to zero." This was a major blunder. Apparently when the first such valid case was found, certain switches in the program were set so that all master records thereafter gave the same message. The list is meaningless.

The other lists seem to be quite accurate.

The most valuable list shows 18 master records which do not crossfoot correctly. Two of these can be accounted for by assuming that we processed data cards punched month *15*. This would not cause machine trouble, and would add the data to one of the total fields. We cannot account for 16 records in which the crossfooted total is lower than the total field. The total may have been altered by correction cards which did not alter the detail fields. All considered, it is not bad that we have only 18 records out of balance internally. These 18 must be well audited.

The report we call the "January 21 Report" was asked for today. It seems simple and straightforward.

Considerable machine trouble today: Card reader giving out repeated checks. Faulty reel of tape. Cards arriving from customers badly warped, causing card jams.

Customers requested 24-hour service on a special report not yet programmed. Although theoretically possible to produce on a crash basis, we declined.

Routine processing today used internal sorting and editing for the first time. Worked like a charm.

January 14: Cards punched 1-3-57 came back from customers today. This was the first batch for which we had a hash total of payroll

A DATA PROCESSING DIARY

numbers. Cards counted and summed on a 407. Card count was off by 5, and hash total of payroll numbers off over 2,000,000.

On today's pass we got a message "unmatched input card bbbbb." Trouble may be this: In the program is a 301 position area reserved for tape input with space for the 300 character record and its record mark. Adjacent to this is the card input area for which the high-order five characters are payroll numbers. If there is an error in tape reading, it is possible for the record to enter memory as a 301 character record with the record mark in the high-order position of card input area.

If this tape reading error occurs, it gives a read/write error signal. Tape rereads and passes read/write check on the second try, but the erroneous record mark is still there.

The program now examines the card image and decides that pay number starting with a record mark is not valid. It picks up this pay number, inserts it in the message, and fires the message. The record mark stops the message cold, and seems to indicate a blank pay number.

This trouble only happens, of course, when there are tape read errors, which are getting rather rare these days. If they do occur, our only protection seems to be either to buffer the two input areas from each other or test for the presence of a record mark in the message.

January 15: Big conference with customers resulted in these conclusions:

1. We should run master tape against payroll records to bring each man's background information up to date.
2. The January 21 Report is now urgent.
3. Hash total control on pay numbers is not needed. We can get control by simpler means.
4. Machine demonstrations will be arranged for the customer personnel.
5. A new program is urgently needed to list specified names from the master tape.

January 16: The program to transfer background information from payroll tapes to master tape was written, punched, assembled, and debugged between 11:45 A.M. and 4:00 P.M. On the machine at 10:00 P.M. Collapsed at the end. An end-of-file procedure was not anticipated in debugging.

The program asked for in item 5 yesterday was written in actual machine language. It ran properly.

Cards to correct December information arrived from the customers at 4:30 P.M.

January 17: Work began on the January 21 Report. Flow charting and programming went on till 1:30 A.M. It's a crowbar program, but it may fly.

Payroll information was transferred without incident.

Regular daily business was processed today by operators, with no intervention on the part of the analysts.

January 18: Cards made on 1-6-57 for the special report were sorted on top five letters of surname and listed. The list shows hundreds of names of the form:

        A S MITH
        P L EWIS
        J A SH
        B J OHNSON

which fall out of sort. These errors come from improper keypunching.

Routine processing today showed an out-of-balance condition for the first time:

    Input   12265
    Additions   32
    Deletions   542
    Output   11765

The input checks with yesterday's output. For each addition a message is printed. There are 32 messages. Probably the trouble lies in the last two figures.

January 19: The January 21 Report was keypunched and assembled at 7:00 P.M. last night. Went on the machine at 12:30 A.M. for debugging.

Real quick collapse. The loops F. had written failed to close. It finally ran at 6:30 A.M. on the fifth try. The report looks fairly good.

January 21: Utter chaos today. The January 21 Report shows figures which are impossible. Something is seriously wrong in the master records.

The first demonstration was given today for customer people. The following took place:

1. Card reader error which would not go away without help from the customer engineer.

2. Sort routine developed false end of file in the middle of a pass and had to be restarted.

A DATA PROCESSING DIARY 467

3. Failure of end-of-file procedure on card reader.
4. A new sickness: names printed out like:

J A SMSMITH
R L JOJONES

In addition, we have not yet accounted for the out-of-balance condition of 1-18-57. Mother told us there would be days like this.

January 22: Glorious recovery. G.G. found two errors in the program transferring payroll information to our tape. Names were inserted in the master records offset from one payroll tape. This accounts for names like SMSMITH and JOJONES. The organization code was at the far end of the master record, not where it belonged. This accounts for a great deal of the trouble of recent dates.

On the machine at 4:00 P.M. with corrected programs. Made six passes to mass-correct all errors and rerun bad reports. Among these was the January 21 Report which now looks very good.

This should teach F. a lesson. We knew yesterday we were in serious trouble. Several small things were awry and one big report was loused up. F.'s reaction was to run in circles, scream, and shout, but at least do *something* to patch. G.G.'s approach was to relax, look for the source of trouble, and correct it. There is no question as to which procedure pays off.

Out of balance of 1-18-57 was finally explained. Procedure for deleting a master record did not work in one case: the last record on tape. In trying to delete #88889, the record count of output became perturbed by one.

January 28: Another demonstration given today: smooth as silk. The regular daily run was moved up to 2:00 P.M. for this purpose. Fifth consecutive daily processing handled by operators only. We are tempted to conclude that the job is now successful.

In Summary: Rereading this diary brings to mind the report at a convention of a committee on debugging techniques. The chairman, new to the business, reported (with a straight face) his conclusion that debugging time on the machine could be materially reduced if programmers could be gotten to make fewer mistakes. There was no rebuttal to this stand.

The conversion job shown here was fairly clean and straightforward. The problem was well defined, and the customers were cooperative and able to learn rapidly. Even so, it took 6 weeks of daily processing to uncover all the troubles and subtle bugs (assuming they are all out now). It is hoped that this account may be of some help to the next man who travels this sort of path.

GLOSSARY

ABSOLUTE CODING: Coding in which all addresses refer to actual machine registers and memory locations.

ACCELERATION TIME: The time which elapses between the interpretation of tape read or write instructions and the time when information can be transferred to or from the tape and high-speed memory.

ACCESS TIME, LATENCY TIME: The time (1) between the instant at which information is called for from storage and the instant at which it is delivered; (2) between the instant at which information is ready for storage and the instant at which it is stored.

ACCUMULATOR: A device containing a register which stores a quantity; when a second quantity is delivered to the device, it forms the sum of the quantity standing in the register and the second quantity, and stores the result in the register. Frequently, the accumulator is involved in other operations upon a quantity in the register such as sensing, shifting, extracting, complementing, etc. Frequently, the accumulator is only a storage register, the actual electronic arithmetic operations being performed in the adder; this fact is usually of no direct importance to the coder.

ACTIVITY: Any information which results in use or modification of the information in a master file.

ACTIVITY RATIO: The fraction of the records in a master file which have activity in a given period.

ADDEND: A number or quantity to be added to another, the augend, to get a result called the sum.

ADDER: A device capable of forming the sum of two quantities delivered to it.

ADDITION RECORD: A record which results in the creation of a new record in the master file being updated.

ADDRESS: A label, name, or number which designates a register, a location, or a device where information is stored; that part of an instruction which specifies the location of an operand.

ADDRESS COMPUTATION: Computer operations which result in the creation or modification of the address part of instructions.

ALPHA-NUMERIC: Characters which may be either letters of the alphabet, numerals, or special symbols.

ANALOG COMPUTER: A computer which represents variables by physical analogies in continuous form such as amount of rotation of a shaft, amount of voltage, etc. Contrasted to digital computer (q.v.); difference sometimes expressed by saying that an analog computer *measures*, whereas a digital computer *counts*.

APPLICATION: The business system or problem to which a computer is applied.

GLOSSARY

ARITHMETIC OPERATIONS: Operations in which numerical quantities form the elements of the calculation, including the fundamental operations of arithmetic: addition, subtraction, multiplication, division.

ARITHMETIC UNIT: That portion of the hardware of a computer where arithmetical and logical operations are performed.

ASSEMBLE: To convert a routine coded in relative form into actual machine instructions with absolute addresses; usually done by the computer under control of an assembly routine. Distinguished from compile (q.v.) by the fact that assembly produces one machine instruction from one relative instruction, where compiling produces (in general) *many* machine instructions from one pseudo instruction.

ASYNCHRONOUS COMPUTER: A computer in which the performance of any operation starts as a result of a signal that the previous operation has been completed. Contrasted with synchronous computer (q.v.).

AUGEND: See Addend.

AUTOMATIC CHECK: See Check.

AUTOMATIC CODING: Any technique of using the computer to assist in the clerical work of coding. See also Relative Coding, Symbolic Coding, Report Generation.

AUTOMATIC DATA PROCESSING (ADP): See Integrated Data Processing.

AUTO-MONITOR: See Monitor.

AUXILIARY STORAGE: A storage device which is capable of holding (usually) larger amounts of information than the main memory (q.v.) of the computer although with slower access.

B-BOX OR B-REGISTER: See Index Register.

BASE: See Number Systems.

BINARY-CODED DECIMAL: Representation of decimal digits by combinations of binary digits. Also used as a convenient abbreviation (BCD) for the representation of *any* character—decimal digit, letter of the alphabet, or special symbol—by combinations of binary digits.

BINARY DIGIT: One of the symbols 0 or 1. A digit in the binary scale of notation. Usually called a bit.

BINARY NUMBER: See Number Systems.

BINARY SEARCH: A technique for reducing the time required to locate a word in an ordered table, by successively cutting in half the area in which the word could be located.

BI-QUINARY NUMBER: See Number Systems.

BIT: Standard abbreviation for binary digit.

BLANK: The character which results in memory when an input record such as a card column which contains no punches is read; the character code which will result in the printing of nothing in a given position. Also called space.

BLOCK: A group of words or characters considered or transported as a unit, particularly with reference to input and output. The term is used sometimes in connection with magnetic tape as a synonym for *record,* or to refer to *grouped* records on tape.

BLOCK DIAGRAM: See Flow Chart.

GLOSSARY

BLOCK SORT: A sorting technique in which the file is "broken down" according to the first character of the key, and the separated parts then sorted one at a time. Frequently used in punched card sorting, less commonly in electronic sorting.

BLOCK TRANSFER: The movement of a group of consecutive words from one area of memory to another.

BOOTSTRAP: A technique for getting the first few instructions into memory when a routine is first loaded; these then bring in the rest of the routine. Usually involves either the execution of a few instructions "manually" from the console, or the use of a special key on the console.

BRANCH: (1) A point in a routine at which one of two or more alternatives is chosen under control of the routine. (2) See Jump.

BREAK POINT: A point in a routine at which special action is taken, such as a stop or a jump, either as the result of the insertion of a special instruction or the setting of a console switch. Usually used in debugging.

BUFFER STORAGE: Facilities linked to: (1) An input device in which information is assembled from external or secondary storage and stored ready for transfer to internal storage. (2) An output device into which information is transmitted from internal storage and held for transfer to secondary or external storage. Computation continues while transfers between buffer storage and secondary or external storage or vice versa take place. (3) Any device which stores information temporarily during data transfers.

CALLING SEQUENCE: A group of parameters associated with a linkage, which provide information to a closed subroutine.

CARD FIELD: A set of card columns fixed as to number and position into which the same information is regularly entered.

CARET: A symbol ($\wedge$) used to indicate the location of a decimal point.

CARRY: (1) A condition occurring during addition when the sum of two digits in the same column equals or exceeds the number base. (2) The digit to be added to the next higher column. (3) The process of forwarding the carry digit.

CATHODE RAY TUBE: A device yielding a visual plot of the variation of several variables by means of a deflected beam of electrons and a phosphorescent screen.

CELL: See Location.

CHANGE RECORD: A record which results in the modification of some of the information in the corresponding master file record.

CHARACTER: One of a set of elementary symbols which may be arranged in ordered groups to express information; these symbols may include the decimal digits zero through nine, the letters A through Z, punctuation symbols, special input and output symbols, and any other symbols which a computer may accept.

CHARACTER READER: A specialized term for an input device which can read printed characters directly without their first being transformed into holes in cards or paper tape or into a coded magnetic form. May operate optically or magnetically, in the latter case reading characters which are printed with a magnetic ink.

GLOSSARY

CHECK: A means of verifying information or computer operations:

(1) Automatic Check: Provision, constructed in hardware, for verifying information transmitted, manipulated, or stored by any unit or device of the computer.

(2) Duplication Check: Duplication of hardware and continuing comparison of results to insure accuracy.

(3) Mathematical Check: A check of an operation making use of mathematical properties of the operation; e.g., checking the multiplication $A \times B = C$ by comparing it with $B \times A = C$.

(4) Parity Check: A redundancy check technique based on an odd or even number of binary one's in some grouping of binary digits. For instance, in the binary representation of a character, a parity bit is made either zero or one, whichever is required to make the number of one's in the character an even number (even parity) or an odd number (odd parity). Whether odd or even parity checking is used depends, usually, on design criteria.

(5) Redundancy Check: A checking technique based on the presence of extra (redundant) information which is used only for checking purposes. Parity checking, check digits, control totals, and hash totals are all examples of redundancy checks.

(6) Validity Check: A checking technique based on known reasonable limits on data or computed results. For instance: a man cannot work 400 hours in one week; there is no day 32 in a month; a man on an hourly classification very seldom has a net week's pay greater than $200.00, etc. Also called a reasonableness check.

CHECK DIGIT(S): One or more digits carried in a word or symbol, often called a self-checking number (q.v.), which are computed from the remaining digits. The check digit(s) is verified at certain points during processing as a check on the remaining digits of the number.

CHECKOUT: See Debugging.

CLEAR (verb): To replace information in a storage device by zero (or blank, in some machines).

CLOCK: In a synchronous computer, the source of the equally spaced pulses which are required for synchronizing computer operations.

CLOSED SUBROUTINE: A subroutine not stored in the main path of the routine. Such a subroutine is entered by a jump operation and provision is made to return control to the main routine at the end of the operation. The instructions related to the entry and re-entry function constitute a linkage. Also called a linked subroutine.

CODE (verb): To write instructions for a computer, whether in absolute or non-machine language. Cf. Program (verb).

CODE (noun): See Routine.

COLLATE: To merge items from two or more similarly sequenced files into one sequenced file, without necessarily including all items from the original files.

COLLATION SEQUENCE: The sequence into which the allowable characters of a computer are ranked.

COMMAND: See Instruction.

COMMON LANGUAGE: A machine-sensible information representation which is common to a related group of data processing machines.

COMPARATOR: A device for making a comparison and, frequently in computers, acting on the result of the comparison.

GLOSSARY 473

COMPARE: To examine the representation of two words, for the purpose of discovering identity or relative magnitude.

COMPILE: To produce a machine-language routine from a routine written in non-machine language by: (1) Selecting appropriate subroutines from a subroutine library, as directed by the instructions or other symbols of the original routine. (2) Supplying the "connective tissue" which combines the subroutines into a workable routine. (3) Translating the subroutines and connective tissue into machine language. The compiled routine is then ready to be loaded into memory and run; i.e., the compiler does not (usually) run the routine it produces. See Assemble. It should be emphasized that a compiler is itself a routine, not a machine—although a machine could be built to do compiling, and may be in the future.

COMPLEMENT: The quantity which is derived from a given quantity by the following rules, where n is the base of the number system used: (1) Complement on n; subtract each digit of the given quantity from $n - 1$, add unity to the least significant digit, and perform all resultant carries. In decimal called ten's complement. (2) Complement on $n - 1$: Subtract each digit of the given quantity from $n - 1$. In decimal called nine's complement.

COMPUTER: Any device capable of accepting information, processing the information, and providing the results of these processes in acceptable form. In this book, the term is always meant to imply a *stored program digital* computer.

COMPUTER LIMITED: On buffered computers, a section of a routine in which the time required for computation exceeds the time required to read and write tapes.

CONDITIONAL JUMP: A jump instruction which is executed only if a certain condition is present in the machine at the time the instruction is executed. The nature of the condition is specified by the operation code of the instruction.

CONNECTOR: In flow charting, a symbol used to indicate the interconnection of two points in the flow chart.

CONSOLE: The part of a computer where most of the external controls over computer operation are exercised, and where most of the indicators of internal operation are located.

CONTROL COUNTER: See Location Counter.

CONTROL FIELD: See Key.

CONTROL PANEL: An interconnection device (usually removable) which employs removable wires to control the operation of computing equipment. Used: (1) On punched card machines, to carry out functions which are under control of the user. (2) On computers, primarily to control input and output functions. Also called plugboard or wiring board.

CONTROL TOTAL: A sum formed by adding together some field from each record in an arbitrary grouping of records; usually has some significance as a number; used for checking machine, program, and data reliability. See also Hash Total.

CONTROL UNIT: That portion of the hardware of a computer which directs a sequence of automatic operations, interprets the coded instructions, and initiates the proper signals to the computer circuits to execute the instructions.

CONVERSION: (1) Changing the form of representation of information, such as from the language of one type of magnetic tape to that of another. (2) The process of changing the information and (sometimes) methods of a data processing operation to a different method. For instance, we speak of conversion from tabulating equipment to computer processing.

CORE STORAGE: A form of high-speed storage in which information is represented by the direction of magnetization of ferromagnetic cores.

COUNTER: A device or technique permitting numbers to be altered by an arbitrary amount. Ordinarily used to determine when a repetitive process has been completed.

CRT: Cathode Ray Tube.

CURRENT INSTRUCTION REGISTER: The control section register which contains the instruction currently being executed after it is brought to the control section from memory. Also called instruction register.

DATA: See Information. (Data is properly plural, the singular form being datum, but in common usage data is often taken as singular.)

DATA PROCESSING: A generic term for all the operations carried out on data according to precise rules of procedure; a generic term for computing in general as applied to business situations.

DATA REDUCTION: The process of transforming masses of raw test or experimentally obtained data, usually gathered by automatic recording equipment, into useful, condensed, or simplified intelligence.

DATING ROUTINE: A routine which computes and/or stores, where needed, a date such as current day's date, expiration date of a tape, etc.

DEBUGGING: The process of determining the correctness of a computer routine, locating any errors in it, and correcting them. Also the detection and correction of malfunctions in the computer itself. See also Diagnostic Routine.

DECELERATION TIME: The time which elapses between completion of reading or writing of a tape record and the time when the tape stops moving.

DECIMAL NUMBER: See Number Systems.

DECISION: The computer operation of determining if a certain relationship exists regarding words in memory or registers, and taking alternative courses of action. Effected by conditional jumps or equivalent techniques.

DECISION BOX: In flow charting, a symbol used to indicate a choice or branching in the information processing path.

DECODING: (1) Internal hardware operations by which the computer determines the meaning of the operation code of an instruction. Also sometimes applied to addresses. (2) In interpretive routines, some subroutines, and elsewhere, an operation by which a routine determines the meaning of parameters.

DELAY-LINE STORAGE: A storage technique in which data is stored by allowing it to travel through some medium such as mercury (acoustic storage).

DELETION RECORD: A record which results in some corresponding record(s) being deleted from a master file.

DIAGNOSTIC ROUTINE: A routine designed to locate a malfunction, either in other routines or in the computer hardware.

DIFFERENCE: See Minuend.

DIGIT: One of the symbols 0, 1, · · ·, 9, and other symbols if necessary, used to designate each of the n quantities smaller than the base n of a scale of numbering.

GLOSSARY

DIGITAL COMPUTER: A computer in which information is represented in discrete form, such as by one of two directions of magnetization of a magnetic core, or by the presence or absence of an electric pulse at a certain point in time. Contrasted to analog computer (q.v.).

DIODE: A circuit element which can pass current in only one direction.

DIRECT INSERT SUBROUTINE: See Open Subroutine.

DIVIDEND: The number or quantity to be divided by another, called the divisor, to get a result called the quotient.

DIVISOR: See Dividend.

DOCUMENT (noun): Any representation of information which is readable by human beings; usually on paper.

DOUBLE PRECISION: Of a quantity: a quantity having twice as many digits as are normally carried in a specific computer word. Often called double length.

DOWN TIME: Time during which a computer is not available for productive work, because of machine failure; contrasted to up time (q.v.).

DUODECIMAL NUMBER: See Number Systems.

DUPLICATION CHECK: See Check.

EAM: Abbreviation for Electric Accounting Machine.

ECHO CHECK: A check in which the information sent to an output device is returned to the information source and compared with the original information to insure accuracy of output.

EDIT: To rearrange information. For instance, editing may involve the deletion of unwanted data, the selection of pertinent data, the insertion of information prior to printing, zero suppression, etc. Also tests for validity (e.g., month 17) and reasonableness (e.g., age 137).

EDP: Electronic Data Processing.

EDPM: Abbreviation for Electronic Data Processing Machine.

ERASE: See Clear. Also used in connection with magnetic recording to describe the removal of all information content from a device, which may be quite different from the state of the device when zeros or blanks are recorded.

EXECUTION: Of an instruction; the set of elementary steps carried out by the computer to produce the result specified by the operation code of the instruction.

EXECUTIVE ROUTINE: A routine which, in some sense, "directs" the operation of other routines. Common examples include routines for handling tape operations, and run location routines.

EXTERNAL STORAGE: Storage facilities removable from the computer itself but holding information in a form acceptable to the computer (magnetic tape, punched cards, etc.).

EXTRACT: To replace the contents of specific parts of a word with the corresponding parts of another word, as determined by some control pattern.

EXTRACTOR: See Filter.

FEASIBILITY STUDY: A preliminary investigation to determine the over-all soundness of applying electronic computers to potential applications.

FIELD: A set of one or more characters which is treated as a whole; a unit of information.

GLOSSARY

FILE (noun): A collection of records; an organized collection of information directed toward some purpose. The records in a file may or may not be sequenced according to a key contained in each record.

FILE MAINTENANCE: The processing of a master file required to handle the non-periodic changes in it. Examples: changes in number of dependents in a payroll file, the addition of new checking accounts in a bank.

FILTER: A word in memory or a register which specifies which parts of another word are to be operated upon. Also called extractor, mask.

FIXED POINT: The decimal point location technique in which the decimal point is not automatically located by the computer or by a routine; used primarily in contrast with floating point (q.v.).

FIXED PROGRAM COMPUTER: See Wired Program Computer.

FIXED WORD LENGTH: Refers to computers in which a computer word always contains the same number of characters. Contrasted to variable word length (q.v.).

FLIP-FLOP: A bi-stable device which may assume a given stable state depending on the pulse history of one or more input points, and having one or more output points. A flip-flop can store one bit, or the result of one decision, for instance.

FLOATING POINT: A form of number representation in which quantities are represented by one number multiplied by a power of the number base. For instance, in floating decimal, 127.6 might be represented as $1.276 \cdot 10^2$. Most useful in engineering and scientific computers where it is often difficult to predict the sizes of computed quantities.

FLOW CHART: A graphical representation of a sequence of operations, using a set of conventional symbols. May be general or detailed.

FORBIDDEN CHARACTER CODE: In the binary coding of characters, a bit code which indicates an error if the code ever occurs.

FORCE: To intervene manually in a routine and change the normal sequence of computer operations.

FORM: A printed or typed document which usually has blank spaces for the insertion of information.

FORMAT: The predetermined arrangement of characters, fields, lines, page numbers, punctuation marks, etc. Refers to input, output, and files.

FOUR ADDRESS INSTRUCTION: See Multiple Address Instruction.

FRAME: A box containing a major portion of a computer.

GARBAGE: Unwanted and meaningless information in memory or on tape. Also called hash.

GATE: A circuit which produces an output which is dependent upon a specified type or the coincidence nature of the input; e.g., an "and" gate produces an output when there is time coincidence of all inputs; an "or" gate produces an output when any one or any combination of input pulses occurs in time coincidence; any gate may contain a number of "inhibit" inputs, in which there is no output under any condition of input if there is time coincidence of an inhibit pulse.

GENERATION: A technique for producing a complete routine from one which is in skeleton form, under control of parameters supplied to a generator routine.

GLOSSARY

GROUPING OF RECORDS: Combining two or more records into one block of information on tape, to decrease the wasted time due to tape acceleration and deceleration and/or to conserve tape space. Also called blocking of records.

HARD COPY: A document produced at the same time that information is transcribed to a form not easily readable by human beings.

HARDWARE: The mechanical, magnetic, electric, and electronic devices from which a computer is constructed.

HASH: See Garbage.

HASH TOTAL: A summation of fields, used for checking purposes, which has no other useful meaning.

HEAD: An assembly of one or more coils of wire and associated pole-pieces, which can record information on a magnetic surface and/or read information from a magnetized surface.

HEXADECIMAL NUMBER: See Number Systems.

HOUSEKEEPING: Operations in a routine which do not directly contribute to the solution of the problem at hand, but which are made necessary by the method of operation of the computer. Examples: loop testing, tape sentinels, record grouping. Also called red tape operations.

IGNORE: A character which is ignored in comparisons.

IMMEDIATE ACCESS: See Random Access Storage.

INDEX REGISTER: A register which contains a quantity which may be used to automatically modify addresses (and for other purposes) under direction of the control section of the computer.

INDIRECT ADDRESSING: See Level of Addressing.

INFORMATION: (Used in specialized sense in computing.) A collection of facts, data, numeric, and alpha-numeric characters, etc., which is processed or produced by a computer.

INITIALIZE: See Loop.

INPUT: Information transferred from auxiliary or external storage into the internal storage of a computer.

INPUT BLOCK: A segment of the internal storage reserved for receiving and/or processing input data. Also called input area or input working storage.

INSTRUCTION: A set of characters which, as a unit, causes a computer to perform one of its operations. Instructions may contain one or more addresses according to the number of references to operands in storage contained in the instruction. (The term instruction is preferred to the terms "command" and "order"; command is reserved for electronic signals; order is reserved for "the order of the characters," etc.)

INSTRUCTION REGISTER: See Current Instruction Register.

INSTRUCTIONAL CONSTANT: A constant written in the form of an instruction; any instruction which is not intended to be executed as an instruction.

INTEGRATED DATA PROCESSING (IDP): (1) (General) Data processing carried out, organized, and directed according to a systems approach. (2) (Special) A collection of data processing techniques built around a common language, in which duplication of clerical operations is minimized. Also called Automatic Data Processing (ADP).

INTERNAL STORAGE: Storage facilities forming an integral physical part of the computer, from which instructions may be executed.

INTERPRET: (1) Refers to an interpretative routine (q.v.). (2) To print at the top of a punched card the information punched in it, using a machine called an interpreter.

INTERPRETIVE ROUTINE: A routine which carries out problem solution by a process of: (1) Decoding instructions written in a pseudo code, and selecting and executing an appropriate subroutine to carry out the functions called for by the pseudo code. (2) Proceeding to the next pseudo instruction. It should be noted that an interpretive routine carries out its functions as it decodes the pseudo code, as contrasted to a compiler, which only prepares a machine-language routine which will be executed later.

ITEM: See Record (noun).

ITEM ADVANCE: In grouping of records, a technique for operating successively on different records in memory.

ITERATION: The technique of repeating a group of computer instructions; one repetition of such a group.

JUMP (verb): To break out of the one-after-the-other sequence of instruction execution employed by many computers. See also Conditional Jump.

JUMP (noun): A jump instruction.

KEY: The field or fields of information by which a record in a file is identified and/or controlled.

KEYBOARD ENTRY AND INQUIRY: A technique whereby the entry into and the interrogation of the contents of a computer's storage may be initiated at a keyboard.

KEY-DRIVEN: Said of any device for translating information into machine-sensible form which requires an operator to depress a key for each character.

LABEL: Exterior label: any visible identification of external storage, such as a paper label attached to a reel of magnetic tape to identify its contents. Interior label: a record magnetically recorded on a tape to identify its contents to a computer routine.

LATENCY TIME: See Access Time.

LEVEL OF ADDRESSING: (1) Zero level addressing: The address part of an instruction *is* the operand, for instance, the addresses of shift instructions, or where the "address" *is* the data (in interpretive or generating systems).

(2) First level addressing: The address of an instruction *is the location in memory* where the operand may be found or is to be stored.

(3) Second level addressing (indirect addressing): The address part of an instruction *is the location in memory where the address* of the operand may be found.

LIBRARY: An organized collection of standard and proven routines and subroutines, which may be incorporated into larger routines.

LINEAR PROGRAMMING: A mathematical technique used in operations research to optimize a business operation subject to given resources and restraints; bears no relation to computer programming.

LINKAGE: A technique for providing a re-entry to the routine from which a closed subroutine was called.

GLOSSARY

LINKED SUBROUTINE: See Closed Subroutine.

LOAD: Broadly speaking, to read information into the computer. More commonly used to refer to the problem of getting the first instructions into the computer.

LOADING ROUTINE: A routine which, once it is itself in memory, is able to bring other information into memory from cards or tape.

LOCATION: A place in memory in which information may be stored; identified by an address. Synonyms: bucket, cell.

LOCATION COUNTER: The control section register which contains the address of the instruction currently being executed. Variously called the instruction counter, program address counter, etc.

LOGICAL DESIGN: (1) The planning of a computer system prior to its detailed engineering design. (2) The synthesizing of a network of elements to perform a specified function. (3) The result of the above, frequently called the logic of the computer.

LOGICAL OPERATIONS: The computer operations which are logical in nature, such as *logical and, logical or, extract,* and *decisions.* This is in contrast with the arithmetic operations such as add, subtract, multiply, and divide.

LOOP: A coding technique whereby a group of instructions is repeated with modification of some of the instructions in the group and/or with modification of the data being operated upon. Usually consist of the following steps:

(1) Loop Initialization: The instructions immediately prior to a loop proper which set addresses, counters, and/or data to their desired initial values.

(2) Loop Computing: Those instructions of a loop which actually perform the primary function of the loop, as distinguished from loop initialization, modification, and testing, which are housekeeping operations.

(3) Loop Modification: Those instructions of a loop which alter instruction addresses, counters, or data.

(4) Loop Testing: Those instructions of a loop which determine when the loop function has been completed.

MACHINE-LANGUAGE CODING: Coding in the form in which instructions are executed by the computer. Contrasted to relative, symbolic, and other nonmachine-language coding.

MACHINE-SENSIBLE: Information represented in a form which can be read by the machine in question. For instance, cards are machine-sensible; handwriting ordinarily is not.

MAGNETIC CORE: See Core Storage.

MAGNETIC DISK: A storage device in which information is recorded on the magnetizable surface of a rotating disk. A magnetic disk storage system is an array of such devices, with associated reading and writing heads which are mounted on movable arms.

MAGNETIC DRUM: A storage device in which information is recorded on the magnetizable surface of a rotating cylinder. Usually implies a complete system consisting of the drum itself, reading and writing heads, and the associated selection and timing circuitry.

MAGNETIC TAPE: A storage system in which information is recorded on the magnetizable surface of a strip of plastic or steel tape.

MAIN MEMORY: Usually the fastest storage device of a computer and the one from which instructions are executed. Contrasted to auxiliary storage (q.v.).

MARK SENSING: A technique for reading special pencil marks on a card and automatically punching the information represented by the marks into the card.

MASK: See Extract, Filter.

MASTER FILE: A file of semipermanent information, which is usually updated periodically.

MATHEMATICAL CHECK: See Check.

MEMORY: Same as storage (q.v.), sometimes, but carries the implication of *internal* memory, i.e., memory from which instructions may be executed.

MEMORY DUMP: A listing of the contents of a storage device, or selected parts of it.

MEMORY FILL (noun): Storage in the areas of memory which are not used by a particular routine, of some pattern of characters which will stop the machine if a routine through error tries to execute instructions from areas which were not intended to contain coding. An aid to debugging.

MEMORY REGISTER: A register which is involved in all transfers of data and instructions in either direction between memory and the arithmetic and control registers. It may be addressed in some machines. Also called distributor, exchange register, high-speed bus.

MERGE (verb): To combine items from two or more similarly sequenced files into one sequenced file, including all items from the original files.

MICROSECOND: One-millionth of a second.

MILLISECOND: One-thousandth of a second.

MINIMUM ACCESS CODING: In machines having nonimmediate-access main memory, a technique of coding which minimizes the time wasted by delays in transfer of data and instructions between memory and other machine components. Also called minimum latency coding.

MINUEND: A number or quantity from which another, the subtrahend, is subtracted to get a result called the difference.

MNEMONIC OPERATION CODES: The writing of operation codes in a symbolic notation which is easier to remember than the actual operation codes of the machine. Must be converted to actual operation codes before execution, which is done as part of an assembly, interpretive, or compiling routine.

MONITOR (verb): To control the operation of a routine during execution by a diagnostic routine, often selectively. Used in debugging.

MULTIPLE ADDRESS INSTRUCTION: An instruction having more than one address, i.e., where more than one operand address may be specified. The term operand is used here to include data to be operated on, instructions, and the results of operations.

One + one address: The first address specifies the operand, the second address specifies the location of the next instruction. This is sometimes referred to as two address instead of one + one address.

Two address: Both the first and second addresses specify operands.

Three address: All three addresses specify operands.

Four address: Three of the addresses specify operands, one specifies the location of the next instruction.

MULTIPLEX: To carry out two or more functions in a computer essentially simultaneously.

MULTIPLICAND: A number or quantity to be multiplied by another, called the multiplier, to get a result called the product.

MULTIPLIER: See Multiplicand.

GLOSSARY

MYLAR: Du Pont's trade name for a polyester film used as a base for magnetic tape.

NONNUMERIC CHARACTER: Any allowable character except a numeric digit.

NORMALIZE: To shift the information in a word until some character, usually the leftmost, contains a nonzero digit.

NUMBER SYSTEMS: The representation of quantities by a positional value system: The general form is

$$N = A_n r^n + A_{n-1} r^{n-1} + \cdots + A_1 r + A_0 + A_{-1} r^{-1} + A_{-2} r^{-2} + \cdots$$

In decimal notation, $r = 10$ and $A_i = 0, 1, \cdots, 9$. r is called the *radix, base,* or *place value* of the system. Commonly used bases:

Base	Name
2	Binary
8	Octal, Octonary
10	Decimal
12	Duodecimal
16	Hexadecimal

The bi-quinary number system employs a *mixed base,* in which the base is alternately 2 and 5.

NUMERIC CHARACTER: Any allowable digit in a machine's number system.

OCTAL NUMBER: See Number Systems.

OFF-LINE (adjective): Operation of input/output and other devices not under direct computer control; most commonly used to designate the transfer of information between magnetic tapes and other media.

ON-LINE (adjective): Operation of an input/output device as a component of the computer, under computer control.

ONE ADDRESS INSTRUCTION: See Single Address Instruction.

ONE + ONE ADDRESS INSTRUCTION: See Multiple Address Instruction.

OPEN SUBROUTINE: A subroutine which is inserted directly into a larger routine where needed. Also called a direct insert subroutine.

OPERAND: Any quantity entering into an operation.

OPERATION CODE: That part of an instruction designating the operation to be performed.

OPERATIONS RESEARCH: The application of scientific methods, techniques, and tools to problems involving the operation of a system so as to provide those in control of the system with optimum solutions to the problems.

OPTIMUM CODING: See Minimum Access Coding.

O.R.: Operations Research.

ORDER: See Instruction.

ORIGIN: In relative coding, the absolute memory address to which addresses in a region are referenced.

OUTPUT: Information transferred from the internal storage of a computer to output devices or external storage.

OUTPUT BLOCK: A segment of the internal storage reserved for output data. Also called output area or output working storage.

OVERFLOW (over capacity): In an arithmetic operation, the generation of a quantity beyond the capacity of the register.

OVERLAY: A technique for bringing routines into high-speed memory from some other form of storage during processing, so that several routines will occupy the same storage locations at different times; used when the total memory requirements for instructions exceed the available main memory.

PACK: To combine several fields, usually into one computer word.

PARALLEL TRANSFER: A system of data transfer in which elements of information are transferred simultaneously over a set of lines.

PARAMETER: A quantity to which arbitrary values may be assigned; used in subroutines and generators to specify item size, decimal point, block arrangement, field length, sign position, etc.

PARITY DIGIT, PARITY BIT: See Check.

PASS: One complete reading of a file.

PATCH: A section of coding inserted into a routine to correct a mistake or alter the routine. Often not inserted into the actual sequence of the routine being corrected, but placed somewhere else, with an exit to the patch and a return to the routine provided.

PERIPHERAL: See Off-line.

PLACE VALUE: See Number Systems.

PLUGBOARD: See Control Panel.

POST MORTEM: A routine which, either automatically or on demand, prints or writes on tape information concerning the contents of certain registers and storage locations at the time the routine stopped, in order to assist in locating a mistake in coding.

PRESELECTION: In buffered computers; a technique in which a spare block of information is read into memory from whichever input tape will next be called upon; determined by inspecting the keys of the last records of each block of working storage.

PROCEDURE: A way of doing something; a written and generally flow-charted description of the processing involved in an application.

PROCEDURES ANALYSIS: See Systems Analysis.

PRODUCT: See Multiplicand.

PROGRAM (verb): To plan the method of attack on a specified and defined problem for computer solution. Distinguished from coding by the fact that coding means writing instructions, whereas programming is symbolized by the drawing of flow charts. Programming is also used to *include* coding. Cf. Code (verb).

PROGRAM (noun): A complete plan of attack on a specific defined problem, including flow charts and a computer routine. Cf. Routine.

PSEUDO INSTRUCTION: A symbolic representation of information to a compiler or interpreter; a group of characters having the same general form as a computer instruction, but never executed by the computer as an actual instruction.

PULSE: A sharp change in the level of some electric variable, usually voltage.

PUNCHED CARD: A piece of lightweight cardboard on which information is represented by holes punched in specific positions.

PUNCHED PAPER TAPE: A strip of paper on which characters are represented by combinations of holes punched across the strip.

GLOSSARY

QUOTIENT: See Dividend.

RADIX: See Number Systems.

RANDOM ACCESS STORAGE: A storage technique in which the time required to obtain information is independent of the location of the information most recently obtained. This strict definition must be qualified by the observation that we usually mean *relatively* random. Thus, magnetic drums are relatively nonrandom access when compared to magnetic cores for main memory, but are relatively random access when compared to magnetic tapes for file storage.

RAPID ACCESS: See Random Access Storage.

RAPID ACCESS LOOP: In drum computers, a small section of memory which has much faster access than the remainder of memory. Also called recirculating loop, revolver.

RAW DATA: Data which has not been processed; may or may not be in machine-sensible form.

READ: To transcribe, usually from input devices or auxiliary storage to main memory.

REAL TIME: Used to describe a problem in which the time requirements are particularly stringent. The term is derived from the process control field and from military applications in which the data processing must "keep up" with a physical process, in a time scale of seconds or less.

RECIRCULATING LOOP: See Rapid Access Loop.

RECORD (verb): To transcribe from one form of storage to another, or to produce a printed document.

RECORD (noun): A collection of fields; the information relating to one area of activity in a data processing activity; files are made up of records. Sometimes called *item*.

RED TAPE: See Housekeeping.

REDUNDANCY CHECK: See Check.

REGION: In relative coding, a group of machine addresses which are all relative to the same origin.

REGISTER: The hardware for temporarily storing information while or until it is used.

RELATIVE CODING: Coding in which all addresses refer to an arbitrarily selected position, or in which all addresses are represented symbolically (in a computable form).

REPORT: An output document prepared by a data processing system.

REPORT GENERATION: A technique for producing complete data processing reports given only a description of the desired content and format of the output reports, and certain information concerning the input file.

RERUN POINT: That stage of a complete run at which all information pertinent to the running of the routine is available to either the routine itself or to a rerun routine in order that a run may be reconstituted. Used for restart procedures if an error occurs or if it is necessary to remove the run from the computer before it is completed.

RESET: To return a location or device to zero or other initial condition.

REVOLVER: See Rapid Access Loop.

REWIND (verb): To return a tape to its beginning.

ROUND-OFF ERROR: The error resulting from deleting the less significant digit or digits of a quantity and applying some rule of correction to the part retained.

ROUTINE: A set of computer instructions which carry out some well-defined function. Cf. Program (noun).

RUN: One routine or several routines automatically linked so that they form an operating unit, during which manual interruptions are not normally required of the computer operator.

RUN BOOK: All material needed to document a computer application, including problem statement, flow charts, coding, and operating instructions.

RUN LOCATOR: A routine which locates the correct run on a program tape, whether initiated by another routine or manually.

SEARCH: To locate a desired word or record in a set of words or records. The set searched may be located in any type of storage: internal, auxiliary, or even (in some cases) external.

SELF-CHECKING NUMBER: One in which an extra checking digit(s) is carried along with the information digits. See Check Digit(s).

SENTINEL: A symbol marking the end of some element of information such as a field, item, block, tape, file, etc. Also called a fence.

SEQUENTIAL ACCESS STORAGE: A storage technique in which the information becomes available in a one-after-the other sequence only, whether all of it is desired or not.

SERIAL STORAGE: See Sequential Access Storage.

SERIAL TRANSFER: A system of data transfer in which elements of information are transferred in succession over a single line.

SERVICE ROUTINE: A routine designed to assist in the actual operation of a computer. Examples: tape correction, tape comparison, run location.

SHIFT (verb): To move information right or left in the arithmetic registers of a computer. In most shifts, information shifted out of an arithmetic register is lost, and zeros are entered at the other end of the register. In other cases, information shifted out of one register enters another register, or enters the other end of the same register. The latter is called a circular, ring, or end-around shift.

SIGN: The symbol which distinguishes positive from negative numbers.

SIGNAL: The output of a circuit, used for control and/or timing of various computer operations.

SIMULATION: In computer programming, the technique of setting up a routine for one computer to make it operate as nearly as possible like some other computer. Used in many other senses in other fields.

SINGLE ADDRESS INSTRUCTION: An instruction having *one* operand address. Cf. Multiple Address Instruction.

SORT (verb): To sequence records according to a key contained in the records. The term "order" is in many ways preferable, but is not in wide usage.

SOURCE DOCUMENT: A document (q.v.) containing data which is eventually processed by a computer.

GLOSSARY

SPACE: See Blank.

STANDBY BLOCK: A technique in which spare input/output blocks of information are always in memory to make more efficient use of buffers.

START-STOP TIME: See Acceleration Time, Deceleration Time.

STORAGE (memory): Any device into which units of information can be transferred, which will hold information, and from which the information can be obtained at a later time.

STORE (verb): To transfer information to a device from which the unaltered information can be obtained at a later time.

STORED PROGRAM COMPUTER: A computer in which the instructions which specify the operations to be performed are stored in the form of coded information in main memory, along with the data currently being operated upon, making possible simple repetition of operations and the modification by the computer of its own instructions.

STRING: A set of records which is in ascending (or descending) sequence according to a key contained in the records.

SUBROUTINE: A small routine which may be incorporated into a larger routine. See Closed Subroutine, Open Subroutine.

SUBTRAHEND: See Minuend.

SUM: See Addend.

SWITCH: In flow charting, a symbol used to indicate a situation where the results of a decision must be used at some later point(s). Also used to describe the same situation in coding, where it may also imply a particular coding technique.

SYMBOLIC CODING: Broadly, any coding system in which symbols other than machine addresses are used. The term is used, unfortunately perhaps, to refer to two rather different types of coding: (1) A relative coding system in which machine instructions are written, but in a much freer form than actual instructions. (2) A method of coding in which addresses are represented by arbitrary symbols which bear no absolute or relative relationship to actual memory locations; in fact, the coding itself may bear little resemblance to machine language.

SYNCHRONOUS COMPUTER: A computer in which all operations are controlled by equally spaced pulses from a clock. Contrasted with asynchronous computer (q.v.).

SYSTEM: (1) An assembly of components united by some form of regulated interaction to form an organized whole. (2) A collection of operations and procedures, men and machines, by which business activity is carried on.

SYSTEMS ANALYSIS: The analysis of a business activity to determine precisely what must be accomplished and how. See System, Systems Approach.

SYSTEMS APPROACH: Looking at the over-all situation rather than the narrow implications of the task at hand; particularly, looking for interrelationships between the task at hand and other functions which relate to it.

TABLE LOOK-UP: A coding technique or an instruction which locates the word (argument) in a table corresponding to a specified word, and, usually, obtains some other word (function) which corresponds to the word located.

TABULATING EQUIPMENT: Used as a generic term to describe the equipment originally devised to carry out data processing based on punched cards.

TALLY: An account of the number of times something has happened.

TAPE LIMITED (adjective): On buffered computers, a section of a routine in which the time required to read and write tapes exceeds the time required for computation.

TEMPORARY STORAGE: An area of working storage not reserved for one use only but used by many sections of a program at different times.

TEST CASE: A set of input data which is intended to determine the correctness of a routine.

THREE ADDRESS INSTRUCTION: See Multiple Address Instruction.

TLU: Table Look-Up.

TRACING: An interpretive diagnostic technique which provides an analysis of each executed instruction and writes it on an output device as each instruction is executed. A *selective tracing* routine provides an analysis of specified instructions only.

TRANSACTION FILE: A file containing current information relating to a data processing activity; it is usually used to update a master file.

TRANSFER (verb): (1) To move information from one storage device to another or from one part of memory to another. (2) Used as synonym for jump ("transfer of control").

TRANSFER OF CONTROL: See Jump.

TRANSFER OF CONTROL CARD: See Transition Card.

TRANSITION CARD: In the loading of a deck of program cards, a card which causes the termination of loading and then initiates the execution of the program.

TRANSLATE: To change information from one form of representation to another without significantly affecting the meaning.

TROUBLE-SHOOT: See Debugging.

TWO ADDRESS INSTRUCTION: See Multiple Address Instruction.

UNCONDITIONAL JUMP: See Jump.

UNPACK: To separate diverse information which has been combined usually into one computer word.

UNWIND: To code explicitly, at length and in full, all the operations of a loop; conserves computer operating time at the expense of memory space. May sometimes be performed automatically by the computer during assembly, compilation, or generation.

UPDATE (verb): To modify a master file according to current information, often that contained in a transaction file, according to a procedure specified as part of a data processing activity.

UP TIME: Time during which a computer is available for productive work; contrasted to down time (q.v.).

VALIDITY CHECK: See Check.

VARIABLE CONNECTOR: See Switch.

VARIABLE WORD LENGTH: Refers to a machine in which the number of characters comprising a computer word is almost completely under the control of the coder. Not usually applied to machines in which there is a very limited form of control, such as half-words or double-length words. Contrasted to fixed word length (q.v.).

GLOSSARY

VERIFY: To check a translation of data from one medium to another by a duplication process.

WIRED PROGRAM COMPUTER: A computer in which the instructions that specify the operations to be performed are specified by the placement and interconnection of wires; the wires are usually held by a removable control panel, allowing flexibility of operation, but the term is also applied to permanently wired machines—which are then called fixed program computers.

WIRING BOARD: See Control Panel.

WORD: A set of characters which is treated by the computer circuits as a unit and transported as such.

WORD LENGTH: The number of characters in a computer word. May be fixed or variable; see Variable Word Length, Fixed Word Length.

WORKING STORAGE: A portion of the internal storage reserved for specific functions such as input and output areas.

WRITE: To transfer information from internal storage to an output device or to auxiliary storage.

ZERO SUPPRESSION: The elimination of nonsignificant zeros to the left of significant digits before printing.

BIBLIOGRAPHY

Books

Alt, Franz L., *Electronic Digital Computers*, Academic Press, New York and London, 1958.

Andree, Richard V., *Programming the IBM 650 Magnetic Drum Computer and Data-Processing System*, Henry Holt and Company, New York, 1958.

Bell, William D., *A Management Guide to Electronic Computers*, McGraw-Hill Book Company, New York, 1957.

Berkeley, Edmund, and Lawrence Wainwright, *Computers, Their Operation and Applications*, Reinhold Publishing Corporation, New York, 1956.

Booth, Andrew D., and Kathleen H. V. Booth, *Automatic Digital Computers* (second edition), Academic Press, New York, and Butterworths Scientific Publications, London, 1953.

Bowden, B. V. (Editor), *Faster than Thought, A Symposium on Digital Computing Machines*, Sir Isaac Pitman and Sons, London, 1953.

Brown, R. Hunt, *Office Automation*, Automation Consultants, New York, 1956.

―――― *Office Automation Applications*, Automation Consultants, New York, 1957.

Bursk, Edward C., and Dan H. Fenn, Jr. (Editors), *Planning the Future Strategy of your Business*, McGraw-Hill Book Company, New York, 1956.

Canning, Richard G., *Electronic Data Processing for Business and Industry*, John Wiley & Sons, New York, 1956.

―――― *Installing Electronic Data Processing Systems*, John Wiley & Sons, New York, 1957.

Chapin, Ned, *An Introduction to Automatic Computers*, D. Van Nostrand Company, Princeton, 1957.

Churchman, C. West, Russell L. Ackoff, and E. Leonard Arnoff, *Introduction to Operations Research*, John Wiley & Sons, New York, 1957.

Courtney, Peggy (Editor), *Business Electronics Reference Guide*, Vol. 4, The Controllership Foundation, New York, 1958.

Craig, Harold F., *Administering a Conversion to Electronic Accounting*, Graduate School of Business Administration, Harvard University Press, Boston, 1955.

Eckert, W. J., and Rebecca Jones, *Faster, Faster: A Simple Description of a Giant Electronic Calculator and the Problems It Solves*, McGraw-Hill Book Company, New York, 1955.

Fairbanks, Ralph W., *Successful Office Automation*, Prentice-Hall, Englewood Cliffs, N. J., 1956.

Forrester, Jay W., *Computer Applications to Management Problems: Strengthening Management for the New Technology*, American Management Association, General Management Series No. 178, New York, 1955.

Gorn, Saul, and Wallace Manheimer, *The Electronic Brain and What it Will Do*, Scientific Research Associates, Chicago, 1956.

Gotlieb, C. C., and J. N. P. Hume, *High Speed Data Processing*, McGraw-Hill Book Company, New York, 1958.

BIBLIOGRAPHY

Grabbe, Eugene M. (Editor), *Automation in Business and Industry*, John Wiley & Sons, New York, 1957.

——, Simon Ramo, and Dean E. Wooldridge (Editors), *Handbook of Automation, Computation and Control;* Volume 1, *Control Fundamentals,* 1958; Volume 2, Computers and Data Processing, 1959; Volume 3, Systems and Components, in preparation, John Wiley & Sons, New York.

Hattery, Lowell H., and George P. Bush (Editors), *Electronics in Management*, The University Press of Washington, D. C., 1956.

Jacobson, Arvid W. (Editor), *Proceedings of the First Conference on Training Personnel for the Computing Machine Field*, Wayne University Press, Detroit, 1955.

Jeenel, Joachim, *Programming for Digital Computers*, McGraw-Hill Book Company, New York, 1959.

Klingman, Herbert F., *Electronics in Business—A Case Study in Planning: Port of New York Authority*, The Controllership Foundation, New York, 1956.

—— (Editor), *Business Electronics Reference Guide*, Vol. 3, The Controllership Foundation, New York, 1956.

—— (Editor), *Electronics in Business: A Descriptive Reference Guide*, The Controllership Foundation, New York, 1955.

Kozmetsky, George, and Paul Kircher, *Electronic Computers and Management Control*, McGraw-Hill Book Company, New York, 1956.

Laubach, Peter B., *Company Investigations of Automatic Data Processing*, Harvard University Press, Boston, 1957.

Lazzaro, Victor (Editor), *Systems and Procedures: A Handbook for Business and Industry*, Prentice-Hall, Englewood Cliffs, N. J., 1959.

Levin, Howard, *Office Work and Automation*, John Wiley & Sons, New York, 1956.

May, Florence A. (Editor), *Electronics in Business: A Descriptive Reference Guide, Supplement No. 1*, The Controllership Foundation, New York, 1956.

McCloskey, Joseph F., and John M. Coppinger, *Operations Research for Management*, Volume 2, The Johns Hopkins Press, Baltimore, 1957.

McCloskey, Joseph F., and Florence N. Trefethen, *Operations Research for Management*, Volume 1, The Johns Hopkins Press, Baltimore, 1954.

McCracken, D. D., *Digital Computer Programming*, John Wiley & Sons, New York, 1957.

Murphy, John S., *Basics of Digital Computers*, John F. Rider, Publisher, New York, 1958.

Neumann, John von, *The Computer and the Brain*, Yale University Press, New Haven, 1958.

Phister, Montgomery, Jr., *Logical Design of Digital Computers*, John Wiley & Sons, New York, 1958.

Richards, R. K., *Arithmetic Operations in Digital Computers*, D. Van Nostrand Company, New York, 1955.

—— *Digital Computer Components and Circuits*, D. Van Nostrand Company, Princeton, 1957.

Ross, H. John, *Integrated Data Processing for Every Office*, Office Research Institute, Miami, 1957.

Smith, Charles V. L., *Electronic Digital Computers*, McGraw-Hill Book Company, New York, 1959.

Smith, J. Sanford, *The Management Approach to Electronic Digital Computers*, Essential Books, Fair Lawn, N. J., 1957.

BIBLIOGRAPHY

Talucci, D. A. (Editor), *The Punched Card Annual of Machine Accounting and Data Processing*, Gille Associates, Detroit.

Wallace, Frank, *Appraising the Economics of Computers*, The Controllership Foundation, New York, 1956.

Weik, Martin H., *A Second Survey of Domestic Electronic Digital Computing Systems*, Office of Technical Services, U. S. Department of Commerce, Washington, 1957.

Wilkes, M. V., *Automatic Digital Computers*, John Wiley & Sons, New York, 1956.

——, D, J. Wheeler, and S. Gill, *The Preparation of Programs for an Electronic Digital Computer* (second edition), Addison-Wesley Press, Boston, 1957.

Williams, R. H., *The Electronic Office* (second edition), Gee and Co., London, 1958.

—— *Automation in the Office*, National Office Management Association, Willow Grove, Pa., 1958.

—— *Electronic Data Processing in Industry: A Casebook of Management Experience*, American Management Association, Special Report No. 3, New York, 1955.

—— *Electronics in the Office*, Office Management Association, London, 1957.

—— *Establishing an Integrated Data-Processing System: Blueprint for a Company Program*, American Management Association, Special Report No. 11, New York, 1956.

—— *An Introduction to the Business Use of Automatic Data Processing Systems*, John Diebold & Associates, New York, 1956.

—— *Introduction to Data Processing*, Haskins and Sells, New York, 1957.

—— *Integrated and Electronic Data Processing in Canada*, The Canadian Institute of Chartered Accountants, Toronto, 1957. (Collection of eight articles which originally appeared in *The Canadian Chartered Accountant*.)

—— *Pioneering in Electronic Data Processing: Company Experience with Electronic Computers*, American Management Association, Special Report No. 9, New York, 1956.

—— *The Uses of Digital Computers*, McGraw-Hill Book Company, New York, 1958. (Reprint of a series of articles from *Control Engineering*.)

Periodicals

The Accountant. Weekly. The City Library, 27–28 Basinghall Street, London E.C. 2, England.

Accounting Research. Quarterly. Cambridge University Press, Bently House, 200 Euston Road, London, N.W. 1, England. Discontinued.

The Accounting Review. Quarterly. American Accounting Association, c/o R. Carson Cox, College of Commerce and Administration, The Ohio State University, Columbus 10, Ohio.

Advanced Management. Monthly. Society for the Advancement of Management, 74 Fifth Avenue, New York 11, N. Y.

The American City. Monthly. The American City Magazine Corp., 470 Fourth Avenue, New York 16, N. Y.

American Gas Association Monthly. Monthly. American Gas Association, Easton, Pa.

Automatic Control. Monthly. Reinhold Publishing Corp., 430 Park Avenue, New York 22, N. Y.

Automatic Data Processing Newsletter. Biweekly. (Part of the Automatic Data Processing Service.) ADP Company, 40 Wall Street, New York 5, N. Y.

492 BIBLIOGRAPHY

The Automatic Office. Monthly. 5057 Woodward Avenue, Detroit 2, Mich.
Automation. Monthly. 6 rue de Liége, Paris 6ème, France.
Banking. Monthly. American Bankers Association, 12 East 36th Street, New York 16, N. Y.
Business Week. Weekly. McGraw-Hill Publishing Co., 330 West 42nd Street, New York 36, N. Y.
The Canadian Chartered Accountant. Monthly. Canadian Institute of Chartered Accountants, 69 Bloor Street East, Toronto 5, Canada.
The Canadian Journal of Accountancy. Quarterly. The Canadian Institute of Certified Public Accountants, C. P. A. Building, 228 Bloor Street West, Toronto, Canada.
Chain Store Age. Monthly, except in March and August, when it is published twice monthly. Lebhar-Friedman Publications, 2 Park Avenue, New York 16, N. Y.
Chemical Processing. Monthly. Putnam Publishing Co., 111 East Delaware Place, Chicago 11, Ill.
The Compleat Programmer. Monthly. Electrodata Division of Burroughs Corp., 460 Sierra Madre Villa, Pasadena 6, Calif.
The Computer Journal. Quarterly. The British Computer Society, Finsbury Court, Finsbury Pavement, London E.C. 2, England.
Computers and Automation. Monthly. Berkeley Enterprises, 815 Washington Street, Newtonville 60, Mass.
Computing News. Bimonthly. 12805-64th Avenue S., Seattle 88, Wash.
Control Engineering. Monthly. McGraw-Hill Publishing Co., 330 West 42nd Street, New York 36, N. Y.
The Controller. Monthly. Controllers Institute of America, 2 Park Avenue, New York 16, N. Y.
The Cost Accountant. Monthly. Institute of Cost and Works Accountants, 63 Portland Place, London W. 1, England.
Cost and Management. Monthly. Society of Industrial and Cost Accountants of Canada, 31 Walnut Street South, Hamilton, Ontario, Canada.
Credit and Financial Management. Monthly. National Association of Credit Men, 229 Fourth Avenue, New York 3, N. Y.
Credit World. Monthly. 375 Jackson Avenue, St. Louis 5, Mo.
Data from Electrodata. Monthly. Electrodata Division of Burroughs Corp., 460 Sierra Madre Villa, Pasadena 6, California.
DATAMATION. Bimonthly. Relyea Publishing Corp., 103 Park Avenue, New York 17, N. Y.
Data Processing Digest. Monthly. Canning, Sisson and Associates, 1140 South Robertson Boulevard, Los Angeles 35, Calif.
Data Processor. Monthly. International Business Machines Corp., 590 Madison Avenue, New York 22, N. Y.
Electrical Engineering. Monthly. 33 West 39th Street, New York 18, N. Y.
Electrical World. Weekly. McGraw-Hill Publishing Co., 330 West 42nd Street, New York 36, N. Y.
Factory Management and Maintenance. Monthly. McGraw-Hill Publishing Co., 330 West 42nd Street, New York 36, N. Y.
The Federal Accountant. Quarterly. The Federal Government Accountants Association, 1523 L Street N. W., Washington 5, D. C.
Fortune. Monthly. Time, 9 Rockefeller Plaza, New York 20, N. Y.

BIBLIOGRAPHY

Harvard Business Review. Bimonthly. Soldiers Field Road, Boston 63, Mass.
IBM Journal of Research and Development. Quarterly. International Business Machines Corp., 590 Madison Avenue, New York 22, N. Y.
The Illinois Certified Public Accountant. Quarterly. The Illinois Society of Certified Public Accountants.
Instruments and Automation. Monthly. Instruments Publishing Co., 845 Ridge Avenue, Pittsburgh 12, Pa.
The Internal Auditor. Quarterly. Institute of Internal Auditors, 120 Wall Street, New York 5, N. Y.
Journal of Accountancy. Monthly. American Institute of Accountants, 270 Madison Avenue, New York 16, N. Y.
Journal of the Association for Computing Machinery. Quarterly. Association for Computing Machinery, 2 East 63rd Street, New York 21, N. Y.
Journal of the Franklin Institute. Monthly. 20th and the Parkway, Philadelphia 3, Pa.
Journal of Industrial Engineering. Bimonthly. American Institute of Industrial Engineers, 225 North Avenue, N. W., Atlanta, Ga.
Journal of Machine Accounting Systems and Management. Monthly (except August). National Machine Accountants Association, 53 West Jackson Boulevard, Chicago 4, Ill.
Management Methods. Monthly. Management Magazines, 22 West Putnam Avenue, Greenwich, Conn.
Management Review. Monthly. American Management Association, 1515 Broadway, New York 36, N. Y.
Management Science. Quarterly. Mr. H. H. Cauvet, 250 North Street, White Plains, N. Y.
The Manager. Monthly. Management Publications, 80 Fetter Lane, London E.C. 4, England.
Modern Office Procedures. Monthly. 812 Huron Road, Cleveland 15, Ohio.
Municipal Finance. Quarterly. Municipal Finance Officers Association of the United States and Canada, 1313 East 60th Street, Chicago 37, Ill.
N.A.A. Bulletin. Monthly. National Association of Accountants, 505 Park Avenue, New York 22, N. Y.
N.A.C.A. Bulletin. Former name of *N.A.A. Bulletin.*
The New York Certified Public Accountant. Monthly. The New York State Society of Certified Public Accountants, 677 Fifth Avenue, New York 22, N. Y.
The Office. Monthly. Office Publications Company, 232 Madison Avenue, New York 16, N. Y.
Office Appliances. Monthly. 600 West Jackson Boulevard, Chicago 6, Ill.
Office Automation News Bulletin. Monthly. Automation Consultants, 155 Fifth Avenue, New York 10, N. Y.
Office Equipment News. Monthly. Wallace Press, 146 Bates Road, Montreal 8, Quebec, Canada.
Office Executive. Monthly. National Office Management Association, Willow Grove, Pa.
Office Management. Monthly. Geyer-McAllister Publications, 212 Fifth Avenue, New York 10, N. Y.
Paperwork Simplification. Quarterly. The Standard Register Co., Dayton 1, Ohio.

494 BIBLIOGRAPHY

Proceedings of the I.R.E. Monthly. The Institute of Radio Engineers, 1 East 79th Street, New York 21, N. Y.

The Programmer. Quarterly. Remington Rand Univac Division of Sperry Rand Corp., 315 Fourth Avenue, New York 10, N. Y. Discontinued.

Scientific American. Monthly. Scientific American, 415 Madison Ave., New York 17, N. Y.

Systems. Bimonthly. 315 Fourth Avenue, New York 10, N. Y.

Systems and Procedures Quarterly. The Systems and Procedures Association of America, 4463 Penobscot Building, Detroit 26, Mich.

Univac Review. Quarterly. Remington Rand Univac Division of Sperry Rand Corporation, 315 Fourth Avenue, New York 10, N. Y.

Conference Proceedings

American Institute of Electrical Engineers, Institute of Radio Engineers, and the Association for Computing Machinery

1952 Eastern Joint Computer Conference. *Review of Input and Output Equipment Used in Computing Systems.*
1953 Eastern Joint Computer Conference. *Information Processing Systems—Reliability and Requirements.*
1954 Western Joint Computer Conference. *Trends in Computers: Automatic Control and Data Processing.*
1954 Eastern Joint Computer Conference. *Design and Application of Small Computers.*
1955 Western Joint Computer Conference.
1955 Eastern Joint Computer Conference. *Computers in Business and Industrial Systems.*
1956 Western Joint Computer Conference.
1956 Eastern Joint Computer Conference. *New Developments in Computers.*
1957 Western Joint Computer Conference. *Techniques for Reliability.*
1957 Eastern Joint Computer Conference. *Computers with Deadlines to Meet.*
1958 Western Joint Computer Conference.
1958 Eastern Joint Computer Conference.
1959 Western Joint Computer Conference. *New Horizons in Computing.*

American Management Association
Annual Electronics Conference and Exhibit. *Electronics in Action: The Current Practicality of Electronic Data Processing,* American Management Association, Special Report No. 22, New York, 1957.

Armour Research Foundation of Illinois Institute of Technology
Computer Applications Symposium. Annual meeting held in Chicago.

Case Institute of Technology
Operations Research, Computers, and Management Decisions. Conference held in Cleveland, in 1957, sponsored by the Operations Research Group, Department of Engineering Administration.

Franklin Institute
Automatic Coding Symposium. Philadelphia, 1957.

The Institution of Electrical Engineers
The Proceedings of the Institution of Electrical Engineers.

BIBLIOGRAPHY

Part B Supplement—1. Convention on Digital-Computer Techniques, London, 1956.

Part B Supplement—2. Convention on Digital-Computer Techniques, London, 1956.

Harvard University, Graduate School of Business Administration (Division of Research)
Automatic Data Processing Conference, Boston, 1955.

Life Office Management Association
Annual meeting held in Chicago. 1956 meeting was devoted largely to computer applications.

The National Association of Bank Auditors and Comptrollers
Automation Symposium, Cleveland, 1957.

National Machine Accountants Association
National meeting, held in various cities.
Western Division sponsors an annual Electronic Business Systems conference.

New York University
Annual Conference on Records Management, New York.

Systems and Procedures Association of America
Annual International Systems Meeting. *Workshop for Management* is the Proceedings of the eighth annual meeting. *Ideas for Management* is the title of subsequent Proceedings.

University of Chicago
Annual Conference on Automation for Senior Officers.

University of Toronto
Proceedings at the Canadian Conference for Computing and Data Processing, June 1958. University of Toronto Press.

Articles

These articles are grouped by chapter, to give a general idea of the primary subject matter covered, and to make the information a little easier to use. It should be noted, however, that in many cases the coverage of an article is considerably broader than the inclusion under one particular chapter might indicate. It will be noted that many more articles are listed for Chapters 1, 20, and 21 than for the others. This is partly because in some of the technical areas little has been published in magazines and journals, but we also wished to reference more material on these chapters because the subject matter covered is in each case somewhat outside the scope of the book. In the case of Chapter 21, in particular (Accounting, Auditing, and Data Protection), the subject matter is outside the scope of *any* book so far published, and we wished to provide references to some of the many articles which have been published.

In general, requests for material from computer manufacturers should be directed to the nearest branch office, not to national headquarters.

Chapter 1 (The Data Processing Problem)

Adams, Charles W., "Processing Business Data," *Control Engineering*, Digital Applications Series No. 6, June 1956.

Angle, Carl, "How TVA Built Its Data Computing Center," *The Office*, November 1958.

BIBLIOGRAPHY

Boardman, L., "What It Means to Integrate Data Processing," *N.A.C.A. Bulletin*, June 1956.

Borchardt, Rudolf, "The Coming Revolution in Information Handling," *Systems and Procedures Quarterly*, August 1957.

Boyer, Paul W., "Commonwealth Edison Starts Electronic Billing," *Electrical World*, March 26, 1956.

Brown, Arthur A., and Leslie G. Peck, "How Electronic Machines Handle Clerical Work," *Journal of Accountancy*, January 1955.

Brown, F. Reese, "The Facts About Operations Research," *Management Methods*, September 1958.

Burch, B. F., Jr., "The Computer in Industry: The Computer at Work on Payrolls," *The Impact of Computers on Office Management*, Office Management Series 136, American Management Association, New York, 1954.

Calhoun, Frank B., "Data Problems of a Grocery Chain," *Computers and Automation*, November 1956.

Carrol, Phil, "Cost Control Through Electronic Data Processing," Society for the Advancement of Management, 1958.

Cronan, Frederick L., "Use of Electronic Computers in Governmental Accounting," *Municipal Finance*, November 1957.

Elliot, J. Douglas, "The Probable Impact of Electronics on Credit and Collection Operation," *Credit World*, February 1957.

Elliot, Paul C., "Integrated Data Processing," *The Accountant*, February 7, 1959.

Fritz, F. H., "Work Simplification Through Data-Processing Equipment," *Cost and Management*, September 1958.

Glendinning, R., "Electronics and Management," *The Accountant*, December 29, 1956.

Greenfield, Harry I., "An Economist Looks at Data Processing," *Computers and Automation*, October 1957.

Hamilton, W. T., "Control by Integrated Data Processing," *The Internal Auditor*, June 1957.

Harris, William B., "The Electronic Business," Part III, The Astonishing Computers, *Fortune*, June 1957.

Howell, Frank S., "Using a Computer to Reconcile Inventory Count to Books," *N.A.C.A. Bulletin*, June 1956.

Lessing, Lawrence P., "Computers in Business," *Scientific American*, January 1954.

Lewis, Daniel C., "An Iron Foundry's Computer Applications," *The Office*, March 1958.

Marlow, F. E., "Processing a Payroll by Computer," *Office Equipment News*, July 1957.

Muns, Frank H., "Using IDP for Inventory Control," *The Controller*, February 1959.

Pleydall, Albert, "Automation and Unemployment," *Office Executive*, January 1957.

Ross, R. R., "Can You Afford the 'Practical' Approach to Electronics?" *Management Methods*, November 1956.

Rule, Leonard, "Electronic Computers," *The Manager*, April 1957.

Salveson, M. E., "Electronic Computers in Business," *The Journal of Industrial Engineering*, March-April, 1958.

———— "High-Speed Operations Research," *Harvard Business Review*, July-August, 1957.

BIBLIOGRAPHY 497

Schmidt, C. W., and R. Bosak, "Production Scheduling and Labor Budgeting with Computers," *Electronic Data Processing in Industry: A Casebook of Management Experience,* American Management Association, New York, 1955.

Schnabel, Harry B., "Insurance Company Adopts EDP," *Office Executive,* March 1958.

Stryker, Perrin, "What Management Doesn't Know Can Hurt," *Fortune,* November 1957.

Thurgood, L. A., "Practical Application of Computers," *The Cost Accountant,* Vol. 37, No. 4, September 1958.

Van Deusen, Edmund L., "The Coming Victory Over Paper," *Fortune,* October 1955.

Worthington, William B., "Application of Electronics to Administrative Systems," *Systems and Procedures Quarterly,* August 1953.

—— "Automated Data Processing," Moore Business Forms, Niagara Falls, N. Y.

—— "Automation Comes to the Office Supply Dealer," *Office Appliances,* January 1957.

—— "Business Week Reports to Readers On: Computers," *Business Week,* June 21, 1958.

—— "Cities Are Discovering a New Office Technology," *The American City,* June 1957.

—— "Computerized Production Control," *Factory Management and Maintenance,* July 1957.

—— "Two-Fold Control by IDP," *Paperwork Simplification,* Fourth Quarter, 1957.

Chapter 2 (Files)

Blumenthal, Sherman, "A Dual Master File System for a Tape Processing Computer," *Journal of the Association for Computing Machinery,* October 1958.

McNamara, Edmond W., "The Filing Problems of Office Automation," *The Office,* December 1958.

Oettinger, Anthony G., "Account Indentification for Automatic Data Processing," *Journal of the Association for Computing Machinery,* July 1957.

Oliver, Foster F., "Preparing for Random Access Equipment for Ordnance Inventory Control," *N.A.A. Bulletin,* January 1959.

Chapter 3 (Flow Charting)

McCracken, D. D., "Flow Charting," Chapter 7 in *Digital Computer Programming,* John Wiley & Sons, New York, 1957.

Pomeroy, Richard W., "Basic Flow Charting Techniques," *Systems and Procedures Quarterly,* August 1957.

Scott, A. E., "Automatic Preparation of Flow Chart Listing," *Journal of the Association for Computing Machinery,* January 1958.

—— "Flow Charts—An Aid to Programming," Chapter 10 in *Programming Univac Fac-Tronic Systems,* Remington Rand Univac Division, Sperry Rand Corp., New York, 1953.

—— *Block Diagramming Techniques,* International Business Machines Corp., Form No. 32-7202-1, New York, 1957.

—— "Flow Process Charting," *Automatic Data Processing Policy Report,* John Diebold and Associates, Cudahy Publishing Co., Chicago, 1956.

BIBLIOGRAPHY

Chapter 4 (The Data Processor)

Abbot, Charles G., "The Anatomy of Electronics," *Office Executive*, January 1958.

Blankenbaker, John, "How Computers Do Arithmetic," *Control Engineering*, Basic Digital Series No. 7, April 1956.

Boehm, George A. W., "The Next Generation of Computers," *Fortune*, March 1959.

Bolles, E. E., and H. L. Engel, "Control Elements in the Computer," *Control Engineering*, Basic Digital Series No. 9, August 1956.

Chase, George C., "History of Mechanical Computing Machinery," *Proceedings of the Association for Computing Machinery*, 1952.

Fowler, Franklin, "The Computer's Memory," *Control Engineering*, May 1956.

Noe, Jerry D., "Data Processing Systems: How They Function," *Control Engineering*, October 1955.

Ridenour, Louis N., "Computer Memories," *Scientific American*, June 1955.

Samuel, Arthur L., "Computing Bit by Bit or Digital Computers Made Easy," *Proceedings of the I.R.E.*, October 1953.

Chapter 5–Chapter 9

Balet, J. W., "Electronic Programming: Programming for an Electronic Computer," *American Gas Association Monthly*, February 1956.

Hopper, Grace Murray, "Programming Business-Data Processors," *Control Engineering*, Digital Application Series No. 8, October 1956.

Mason, Walter R., "The Programming of an Office Computer," *The Office*, April 1957.

Ward, J. B., "Principles of Programming," *Electrical Engineering*, December 1956.

Chapter 10 (Input and Output Devices)

Eldredge, K. R., and F. J. Kamphoefner, "Automatic Input for Business Data-Processing Systems," *Proceedings of the Eastern Joint Computer Conference*, 1956.

Garner, P. W., "Mark Sensing: a Practical Means of Data Recording," *The Cost Accountant*, May 1957.

Gibbons, James, "How Input/Output Units Affect Data-Processor Performance," *Control Engineering*, Digital Application Series No. 13, July 1957.

Hutchinson, J. S., "Choice of Input/Output Media for Computers," *The Cost Accountant*, Vol. 36, No. 8, January 1958.

Rubinoff, Morris, and Ralph H. Beter, "Input and Output Equipment," *Control Engineering*, Basic Digital Series No. 10, November 1956.

———— "Magnetic Ink Character Recognition: The Common Machine Language for Check Handling," *Banking*, August 1956.

———— "Controlling Units at Point-of-Sale," *Chain Store Age*, April 1957.

———— "High Speed Communication Among Data Processing Machines," *Journal of the Franklin Institute*, July 1957.

Chapter 12 (Verifying Program Accuracy)

Blumenthal, Sherman C., "Guideposts for System Design," *Univac Review*, Spring 1958.

McCracken, D. D., "Debugging Computer Programs," *Computers and Automation*, February 1955.

———— "IBM 650 Program Testing Manual," International Business Machines Corp., Form No. 32-7932, New York, 1957.

BIBLIOGRAPHY

Chapter 13 (Advanced Techniques in Magnetic Tape Programming)

Bohrer, R. J., "Variable Record Length Programming Techniques," *The Programmer*, July 1957.

Deutsch, Margaret, "Preselected Standby for Multiple Input," *Univac Review*, Spring 1958.

Holberton, Frances E., "Program Control Techniques," *The Programmer*, September 1956.

Hughes, John H., "Tape File Maintenance," *The Programmer*, July 1957.

Yates, Justin J., and Lawrence Dorf, "A New Technique of Production Run Control," *The Programmer*, April 1957.

Chapter 14 (Machine-Aided Coding)

Hopper, Grace Murray, "Automatic Coding for Digital Computers," *Computers and Automation*, September 1955.

McGee, William C., "Generalization: Key to Successful Electronic Data Processing," *Journal of the Association for Computing Machinery*, January 1959.

Moncreiff, Bruse, "An Automatic Supervisor for the IBM 702," *Proceedings of the Western Joint Computer Conference*, 1956.

Petersen, R. M., "Automatic Coding at G.E.," *Proceedings of the Automatic Coding Symposium*, Franklin Institute, January 1957.

Rossheim, R. J., "The Function of Automatic Programming for Computers in Business Data Processing," *Computers and Automation*, February 1956.

Chapter 15 (Sorting)

Bell, D. A., "The Principles of Sorting," *The Computer Journal*, July 1958.

Canning, Richard G., "How the Four-Tape Sorter Simplifies Storage," *Control Engineering*, February 1957.

Davies, D. W., "Sorting of Data on an Electronic Computer," *Proceedings of the Institution of Electrical Engineers*, Part B Supplement—1. Convention on Digital-Computer Techniques, April 1956.

Demuth, H. B., "A Report on Electronic Data Sorting," Stanford Research Institute, Division of Engineering Research, Menlo Park, Calif.

Friend, E. H., "Sorting on Electronic Computer Systems," *Journal of the Association for Computing Machinery*, July 1956.

Hildebrandt, Paul, and Harold Isbitz, "Radix Exchange—An Internal Sorting Method for Digital Computers," *Journal of the Association for Computing Machinery*, April 1959.

Hosken, J. E., "Evaluation of Sorting Methods," *Proceedings of the Eastern Joint Computer Conference*, 1955.

Isaac, E. J., and R. C. Singleton, "Sorting by Address Calculation," *Journal of the Association for Computing Machinery*, July 1956.

Johnson, Lyle R., and Richard D. Pratt, "An Introduction to the Complete Univac II Sort-Merge System-SESAME," *Univac Review*, Fall 1958.

———, "Sorting Methods for IBM Data Processing Systems," International Business Machines Corp. Form No. F28-8001, New York, 1958.

Chapter 17 (Rerun Techniques)

Eallson, Leonard, "Tape Identification and Rerun Procedures for Tape Data Processing Systems," *Computers and Automation*, April 1956.

——— "Procedure Control for the IBM 705," International Business Machines Corp., Form No. 22-6697-1, New York, 1956.

Chapter 19 (Large Random Access File Storage)

Conway, Ben, "Random Access—Its Meaning and Its Applications," *Office Management*, March 1956.

Dumey, Arnold I., "Indexing for Rapid Random Access Memory Systems," *Computers and Automation*, December 1956.

Hollander, Gerhard L., "Quasi-Random Access Memory Systems," *Proceedings of the Eastern Joint Computer Conference*, 1956.

Jerome, W. L., and L. Hartford, "RAMAC at Work," *Systems and Procedures Quarterly*, November 1957.

Lesser, M. L., and J. W. Haanstra, "The RAMAC Data-Processing Machine: System Organization of the IBM 305," *Proceedings of the Eastern Joint Computer Conference*, 1956.

MacDonald, D. M., "Datafile—a New Tool for Extensive File Storage," *Proceedings of the Eastern Joint Computer Conference*, 1956.

Noyes, T., and W. E. Dickinson, "The Magnetic-Disk, Random-Access Memory," *IBM Journal of Research and Development*, January 1957.

Oliver, Foster F., "Preparing for Random Access Equipment for Ordnance Inventory Control," *N.A.A. Bulletin*, January 1959.

Petersen, W. W., "Addressing for Random-Access Storage," *IBM Journal of Research and Development*, April 1957.

Welsh, H. F., and V. J. Porter, "A Large-Capacity Drum-File Memory System," *Proceedings of the Eastern Joint Computer Conference*, 1956.

———— "The Cost of Inactive Storage," *Data Processing Digest*, July 1957.

———— "Indexing for Random Access Memory Systems," *Data Processor*, April 1957.

———— "Random Access to Data Improves Information Processing," *Automation*, July 1957.

———— 650 Bulletin 11, "650 RAMAC Addressing," International Business Machines Corp., Form No. 32-7935, New York, 1957.

Chapter 20 (Steps in Planning and Programming Computer Applications)

Bagby, Wesley S., "Deciding Upon an Electronic Data-Processing System," *The Controller*, May 1956.

Crichley, William A, "Look Before You Leap," *Chemical Processing*, August 1957.

Dean, Neal J., "Is Automation for You?" *Office Executive*, January 1958.

Diebold, John, "Putting It To Work: Making the Most of Automatic Data Processing," *The Cost Accountant*, July 1958.

———— "False Starts in Office Automation—And How to Avoid Them," *Management Review*, July 1957.

Faulkner, Charles E., "What to Consider When You Buy EDP," *Control Engineering*, November 1956.

James, Peter, "Nine Guideposts in Selecting a Business-Data Processor," *Control Engineering*, January 1958.

Learson, T. V., "Plan Your Computer Installation for Maximum Advantage," *N.A.C.A. Bulletin*, July 1956.

Poland, C. B., III, "Problems of Scheduling a Multiple-Job Electronic Data Processing Machine," *Computing News*, August 15, 1956.

Rowan, T. C., "Psychological Tests and Selection of Computer Programmers," *Journal of the Association for Computing Machinery*, July 1957.

BIBLIOGRAPHY

Rowlands, H. W., "Preparing for Office Automation," *Cost and Management*, February 1957.

Shea, Stevens L., "Organizing for Electronics," *The Accounting Review*, December 1957.

Slater, Robert E., "Conditioning Management for Machine Applications," *Office Executive*, November 1958.

──── "Responsibility of Management as Related to Computers," *Journal of Machine Accounting Systems and Management*, May 1957.

Steele, Forde, "A Check List Giving 12 Steps on How to Get Ready for Automation," *Banking*, October 1956.

Woellner, D. A., "A Computer Development Program," *Journal of Machine Accounting Systems and Management*, February 1956.

──── "Conducting a Feasibility Study," Automatic Data Processing Policy Report, John Diebold and Associates, New York, 1956.

──── "Factors to Consider in a Contract for a Large-Scale Electronic Computing System," *Data Processing Digest*, November 1956.

──── "Forms Design," The Standard Register Company, Dayton, Ohio.

──── "Housing Electronic Equipment," *Office Executive*, July 1958.

──── "How to Prepare Your Office for a Computer Installation," *Office Management*, January 1958.

──── "Staff and Organization and Their Training," *Computing News*, February 15, 1957.

Chapter 21 (Accounting, Auditing, and Data Protection)

Bergstedt, John H., "An Auditor's Viewpoint on Machine Accounting," *Journal of Machine Accounting Systems and Management*, February 1956.

Canning, Richard G., "Electronic Data Processing and the Controller," *The Controller*, April 1956.

Colburn, Dorothy, "The Computer as an Accountant," *Automatic Control*, December 1954.

Conroy, D. S., "The Use of a Computer: Checks and Precautions," *The Cost Accountant*, January 1957.

Elmore, William B., "Some Aspects of Reliability in Electronic Data Processors," *Electronic Data Processing in Industry: A Casebook of Management Experience*, American Management Association, New York, 1955.

Gilmore, R. M., Jr., "Experience in Installing a Large-Scale Electronic Computer," *Workshop for Management*, Management Publishing Corporation, Greenwich, Conn., 1956.

Gregory, Robert H., "Computers and Accounting Systems," *Accounting Research*, January 1955.

Grody, Charles E., "The Internal Auditor and Electronics," *Systems and Procedures Quarterly*, May 1957.

Hamman, Paul E., "The Audit of Machine Records," *The Journal of Accountancy*, March 1956.

Hamming, R. W., "Checking Techniques for Digital Computers," *Control Engineering*, Basic Digital Series No. 13, May 1957.

Jauchem, C. R., "The Importance of Controls in Electronic Data Processing," *The Federal Accountant*, September 1957.

Jones, J. Melvin, "Marginal Checking—An Aid to Preventive Maintenance of Computers," *Computers and Automation*, April 1955.

BIBLIOGRAPHY

Kaufman, Felix, and Leo A. Schmidt, "Auditing Electronic Records," *The Accounting Review*, January 1957.

Keenoy, C. L., "The Impact of Automation on the Field of Accounting," *The Accounting Review*, April 1958.

Lewis, Ralph F., "The CPA Views Mechanized Accounting," *The Controller*, September 1956.

———— "Never Overestimate the Power of a Computer," *Harvard Business Review*, September-October 1957.

McCollum, Ralph C., "Application of Electronic Data Processing to Billing and Accounting in a Public Utility," *Workshop for Management*, Management Publishing Corporation, Greenwich, Conn., 1956.

Margetts, J. W., "The Auditor and the Computer," *The Accountant*, September 6, 1958.

Murray, J. R., "Auditing Electronically Produced Records," *The Canadian Chartered Accountant*, February 1957.

Pelej, Joseph, "How Will Business Electronics Affect the Auditor's Work?" *The Journal of Accountancy*, July 1954.

Schillinger, F. S., "Quality Control for Machines that Think," *Journal of Machine Accounting Systems and Management*, May 1957.

Seitz, Phillip, "Auditing Electronic Data Processing Systems," *The Illinois Certified Public Accountant*, June 1955.

Steele, Allan T., "Office Automation and Auditing Techniques," *The New York Certified Public Accountant*, July 1957.

Toan, A. B., Jr., "Auditing, Control, and Electronics," *The Journal of Accountancy*, May 1955.

Vincent, George O., "Self-Checking Codes for Data Transmission," *Automatic Control*, December 1956.

Ware, Willis H., "Reliability and the Computer," *Proceedings of the Western Joint Computer Conference*, 1957.

Weiss, Harold, "Building Flexibility into Computer Applications," *Journal of Machine Accounting Systems and Management*, April 1958.

———— "Procedure Control for the IBM 705," International Business Machines Corp., Form No. 22–6697-1, New York, 1956.

———— "The Auditor Encounters Electronic Data Processing," Price Waterhouse and Company, published by The International Business Machines Corp., Form No. 32–7489, New York.

———— *IBM 705 Data Processing System, General Information Manual*, International Business Machines Corp., Form No. 222–6769-1, 1958.

INDEX

Abacus, 52
Absolute coding, 261, 262, 469
Acceleration time, 327, 469
Access time, 469
Accounting, 395, 425
Accounts receivable, 156
Accumulator, 49, 469
Activity, 12, 156, 469
Activity ratio, 469
Add instruction, 63, 434
Add to memory instruction, 68, 435
Addend, 469
Adder, 469
Adder-alphabetic error trigger, 66, 179, 434
Addition (in file processing), 13, 21, 156, 469
Address, 60, 61, 78, 96, 106, 172, 230, 260, 263, 369, 431, 469
Address computation, 125, 469
Address sorting, 304
Advancing the rerun point, 348
Aiken, Howard, 52
Airline reservations, 191
Algebraic sign control, 65, 98
Alphabetic addition, 66, 210, 434
Alphabetic error jump instruction, 67, 434, 438
Alphabetization, 98
Alpha-numeric character, 49, 429, 469
Alteration switches, 180
Alternation of tape handlers, 132, 155, 245, 251, 328
American Bankers Association, 1
Analog computer, 469
Analytical Engine, 52
Application, 469
Arabic number system, 445
Arithmetic operations, 470

Arithmetic unit, 44, 51, 470
Assembly routine, 62, 266, 470
Assertion box, *see* Flag
Asynchronous computer, 470
Auditing, 395, 417
Augend, 470
Automatic check, 472
Automatic coding, 260, 261, 470
Automatic-manual switch, 178
Automatic Sequence Controlled Calculator, 52
Auxiliary memory, 45, 50, 250, 429, 470
Auxiliary operation, *see* Off-line operation
Average access time, 16

B-box, *see* Index register
Babbage, Charles, 52
Backspace, 350
Base, of a number system, 446, 470
Base register, *see* Index register
Batch totals, 407
Batching (in file processing), 14, 15, 368
Binary coding of decimal digits, 58, 457, 470
Binary digit, 58, 445
Binary numbers, 53, 58, 178, 181, 234, 429, 444, 470, 481
Binary search, 309, 470
Bi-quinary number system, 52, 403, 460, 481
Bit, *see* Binary digit
Blank, 80, 107, 178, 470
Block, 19, 193, 253, 470
Block buffering, 193, 257
Block diagram, *see* Flow chart
Block sort, 470
Block transfer, 254, 328, 471
Bootstrap, 211, 471

503

504 INDEX

Borrow, 65, 432, 449
Branch, 471
Branch control switches, 180
Breakage, 86
Break point, 471
Breakpoint switches, 180
Bring instruction, 62, 433
Budget forecasting, 3
Buffering, 112, 192, 221, 256, 368, 429, 471

Calling sequence, 171, 276, 471
Card field, 471
Card image, 206
Card reader, 185, 201
Caret, 85, 86, 471
Carriage control, 195, 205
Carry, 65, 432, 448, 471
Casting out nines, 407
Cathode-ray tube, 190, 234, 471
Centralization of control, 395
Changes (in file processing), 13, 21, 471
Channel, 183, 188
Character, 34, 58, 97, 183, 201, 299, 429, 430, 471
Character reading, 6, 194, 471
Check accounting, 1
Check digits, 406, 472
Checkout, *see* Debugging
Choice box, *see* Decision box
Clear, 472
Clerical productivity, 2
Clock, 472
Clock channel, 183
Closed subroutine, 167, 472
Coding, 47, 57, 280, 334, 382, 472
Collate, 472
Collation sequence, 97, 299, 472
Column, 185
Commission calculation, 130
Common language, 6, 472
Comparator, 472
Compare instruction, 96, 437
Comparison, 29, 473
Comparison box, *see* Decision box
Compiler, 218, 220, 262, 275, 278, 280, 296, 473
Complement subtraction, 147, 155, 449, 473
Compute (in loops), 137
Computer, 473

Condition lights, 179
Conditional jump instruction, 96, 97, 180, 473
Conditioning switches, 180
Connector, 29, 31, 473
Console, 177, 188, 473
Control panel, 201, 202, 203, 206, 212, 383, 473, 482
Control total, 330, 355, 407, 473
Control unit, 44, 46, 51, 473
Conversion, 386, 423, 473
Conversion of number systems, 452
Counter, 137, 139, 235, 354, 474
Counter (in indexers), 146, 154, 430
Cross-footing check, 410
Cross-reference listing, 230
Current instruction register, *see* Instruction register
Cyclic conversion, 387

Data discipline, 396
Data protection, 395, 411
Data reduction, 474
DATAC, 48, 429
Dating routine, 249, 474
Debugging, 224, 296, 342, 383, 474
Decapitation, 304
Deceleration time, 474
Decimal point, 64, 86
Decimal point location, 84
Decision box (in flow charting), 30, 31, 121, 474
Decision instruction, 95, 474
Decision making, 7
Decoding, 46, 61, 63, 474
Delay-line storage, 359, 474
Delay tape instruction, 113, 442
Deletion (in file processing), 13, 21, 156, 474
Desk checking, 228, 383
Detailed flow chart, 28, 381
Diagnostic routines, 231, 402, 474
Difference, 474
Difference Engine, 52
Differential memory listing, 235, 236
Digit, 474
Digit selection, 128
Digital computer, 6, 475
Diode, 475
Direct-connected printer, 187
Direct memory buffering, 112, 193, 257

INDEX

Disk storage, see Magnetic disk storage
Display memory button, 179
Divide instruction, 73, 435
Divide overflow, 74, 76, 105, 179, 436
Dividend, 475
Divisor, 475
Document, 6, 198, 475
Dollar edit instruction, 168, 440
Double precision, 475
Down time, 475
DUAL, 278
Duplicated circuits, 403, 472
Dynamic analysis, 236

Echo checking, 404, 475
Eckert, J. P., 53
Economics of computer operation, 398
Edit R instruction, 440
Editing, 58, 80, 110, 168, 199, 202, 203, 210, 219, 330, 343, 440, 462, 475
EDSAC, 53
EDVAC, 53
Effective address, 146, 170, 171, 254, 430
Efficiency of optimization, 365 (exercises)
Electrostatic memory, 46
Eleven-punch, 202
Emergencies, 415
End-around-carry, 450
End-of-file gap, 184, 246
ENIAC, 53
Equal indicator, 96
Equal jump instruction, 96, 437
Erase, 475
Error tape, 352
Estimating computer time, see Time estimating
Evaluation, 392
Exception handling, 199, 239, 337, 399
Excess-three, 458
Exchange sorting, 306
Execute instruction button, 179, 231
Executive routine, 475
Expanding file technique, 22, 156
Expiration date, 415
Expiration plan, 413
Exterior label, 245, 411, 478
External storage, 475
Extract register, 49
Extracting, 106, 431, 475

Father-son technique, 22, 119

Feasibility study, 376, 475
Federal Insurance Contributions Act, see Social Security
Fence, see Sentinel
Fetch instruction, 79, 434
FICA, see Social Security
Field, 218, 475
File, 10, 476
File conversion, 239, 335, 386, 394 (exercises)
File design, 19, 87, 115, 280, 281, 334, 339, 380
File layout, see File design
File maintenance, 293, 333, 461, 476
File record design, see File design
File updating, 461
Filter, 61, 106, 429, 431, 476
Filter register, 49, 51, 106, 108, 429, 431, 432
Final address, 234
Fixed length strings, 315
Fixed point, 476
Fixed record length, 19, 113, 154, 254, 368
Fixed word length, 327, 476
Flag, 33, 121
Flexibility of systems design, 210, 218, 241, 261, 266, 278, 280, 283, 293, 342, 396
Flip-flop, 66, 476
Floating point, 476
Flow chart, 26, 57, 227, 381, 476
FLOW-MATIC, 279
Forbidden character code, 476
Force, 476
Form, 380, 476
Form design, 380
Format, 194, 198, 476
Format chart, see Output format chart
Format control card, 219
FORTRAN, 288
Four-tape merge sorting, 319
Frame, 476
Functional key, 370, 375 (exercises)

Garbage, 476
Gate, 476
Generalized programming, 261, 339
Generator, 218, 220, 289, 328, 476
Grandfather file, 22
Gross flow chart, see Top level flow chart

506 INDEX

Group indication, 293
Grouping, of records, 19, 125, 253, 327, 477

Handwritten coding, 293, 329
Hard copy, 5, 189, 477
Hardware, 477
Hash, see Garbage
Hash total, 355, 408, 462, 477
Head, 21, 49, 181, 350, 359, 477
Header, 255
Heading, 195
Hierarchy of memory, 250
High indicator, 96
High jump instruction, 96, 437
High-speed memory, 45, 51, 250
Hollerith, Herman, 52
Hopper, Grace Murray, 279
Housekeeping, 343, 399, 477
Human relations, 378
Humidity, 412

IBM 701, 53
IBM 705, 218
IDP, see Integrated Data Processing
Ignore, 477
Immediate access storage, see Random access storage
Improper division, see Divide overflow
Increment (in indexers), 146, 148, 154, 430
Independent checking, 226
Index register, 49, 51, 145, 154, 166 (exercises), 170, 252, 328, 429, 432, 477
Indexer, 61, 145, 154, 166 (exercises), 170, 252, 328, 429, 431
Indirect addressing, 132, 258 (exercises), 477
Initial address, 211, 234
Initialization (in loops), 128, 137, 138, 139, 478
Input, 5, 44, 177, 196, 477
Input block, 477
Input/output economics, 221, 342
Input/output files, 18
Input/output subroutines, 203, 216
Inquiry station, see Keyboard entry and inquiry
Insertion, 431
Insertion sorting, 308

Instruction, 45, 47, 56, 60, 260, 431, 433, 477
Instruction register, 49, 51, 62, 63, 432, 477
Instructional constant, 129, 141, 216, 477
Integrated Data Processing, 6, 7, 189, 477
Interior label, 245, 411, 478
Interlacing, 366 (exercises)
Interlock rewind tape instruction, 442
Internal checking, 402
Internal storage, 478
International Business Machines Corporation, 52
Interpreting (of instructions), 46, 61, 63, 113, 232, 237, 262, 276, 478
Interrupted jump instruction, 153, 437
Invariant address, 264, 265
Inventory control, 3, 4, 105, 114, 191
Item, see Record
Item advance, 253, 328, 478
Item layout, see File design
Iteration, 478

Jacquard loom, 52
Jukebox storage, 368
Jump if overflow instruction, 66, 104, 438
Jump if R is minus instruction, 102, 436
Jump if R is not zero instruction, 102, 437
Jump if R is plus instruction, 102, 436
Jump if R is zero instruction, 102, 436
Jump instructions, 96, 147, 436, 478
Jump table, 130

Key, 10, 154, 184, 298, 335, 478
Keyboard entry and inquiry, 190, 338, 410, 478
Keypunch, 185, 384, 478

L register, 49, 51, 62, 432
Label, see Interior label, Exterior label
Label check, 245, 253, 353
Late data, 416
Latency time, 469
Leibnitz, 52
Level of addressing, 135 (exercises), 478
Library of subroutines, 174, 175, 176 (exercises), 275, 478
Limit check, 410
Line image, 206
Line printer, 51, 187, 194, 202

INDEX

Linear programming, 478
Linkage, 167, 170, 478
Load button, 179
Load cards button, 179, 211, 212
Load index instruction, 148, 441
Load tape button, 179
Loading routine, 48, 62, 211, 217, 479
Location, 60, 479
Location counter, 49, 51, 62, 63, 237, 432, 479
Logical *and*, 124 (exercises), 479
Logical decisions, 6, 30, 31, 58, 125, 479
Logical design, 479
Logical *or*, 124 (exercises), 479
Loop, 29, 121, 125, 127, 136, 235, 253, 341, 479
Low indicator, 96
Low jump instruction, 96, 437
LSD, 70, 142

Machine language, 5, 384, 479
Machine-sensible, 479
Macro-coding, 93 (exercises), 297 (exercises)
Magnetic core, 46, 49, 53, 474
Magnetic disk, 21, 479
Magnetic disk storage, 21, 479
Magnetic drum, 46, 49, 359, 368, 479
Magnetic label, *see* Interior label
Magnetic tape, 17, 49, 51, 111, 181, 192, 368, 412, 429, 479
Mail order data processing, 191
Main memory, 46, 479
Maintenance, *see* File maintenance, Preventive maintenance, Program maintenance
Marginal checking, 402
Mark I, 53
Mark sensing, 406, 480
Mask, *see* Filter
Masking of errors, 228
Master file, 11, 115, 156, 256, 372, 461, 480
Material control, 3
Mathematical check, 472
Matrix printer, 187, 190
Mauchly, J. W., 53
Memory, 45, 58, 429, 480
Memory dump, 233, 236, 480
Memory fill, 480
Memory layout, 381

Memory printout, 233, 236
Memory register, 69, 432, 480
Mercury-delay line memory, 46, 53
Merge, 480
Merge sorting, 315, 320
Micro-coding, 93 (exercises)
Microsecond, 480
Millisecond, 480
Minimum access coding, 359, 360, 362, 366 (exercises), 481
Minimum latency coding, *see* Minimum access coding
Minuend, 480
Minus jump instruction, 102, 436
Minus zero, 99
Mnemonic operation codes, 261, 268, 480
Modification (in loops), 137
Modifier (in indexers), 146, 154, 430
Monitor, 61, 237, 480
Monitor switches, 180, 222 (exercises), 237, 431
Multiple address instruction, 480
Multiplex, 480
Multiplicand, 480
Multiplier, 480
Multiply instruction, 69, 435
Mylar, 481

Neumann, John von, 53
New master file, 22
Nine's complement, 449
Nonmachine language coding, 220, 262
Nonnumeric character, 481
Nonzero index jump instruction, 147, 441
Nonzero jump instruction, 102, 437
Normalization, 153, 481
Number systems, 444, 481
Numeric bits, 59, 82
Numeric character, 481

Octal numbers, 234, 446, 481
Off-line operation, 50, 185, 194, 221, 343, 429, 481
Off-line storage, 18
Old master file, 21
One-address instruction, 481, 484
One + one address instruction, 480, 481
On-line operation, 50, 203, 481
On-line storage, 18
Open subroutine, 167, 175, 481
Operand, 481

INDEX

Operating instructions, 388, 389
Operation code, 60, 260, 268, 431, 481
Operations Research, 7, 481
Operator instructions, 203, 245
Optimum coding, see Minimum access coding
Order, 481
Origin, 269, 481
Output, 5, 177, 185, 196, 481
Output block, 481
Output definition form, 291
Output format chart, 199, 200, 205
Output section, 47
Over-all flow chart, see Top level flow chart
Overflow, 65, 179, 482
Overflow jump instruction, 66, 104, 438
Overflow trigger, 66, 74, 105, 179, 238
Overlay, 250, 258 (exercises), 482

Packing, 77, 80, 282, 336, 482
Page numbering, 195, 293
Page skipping, 205
Paper tape, 17, 44, 47, 188, 482
Paperwork reduction, 1
Parallel operation, 239, 386, 461
Parallel transfer, 482
Parameter, 247, 289, 293, 463, 482
Parity checking, 181, 402, 472
Partial word, 106, 124 (exercises)
Pascal, 52
Pass, 270, 299, 318, 482
Patch, 241, 261, 482
Payroll, 4, 11, 26, 87, 102, 244, 299
Peripheral operation, see Off-line operation
Photographic film, 17
Pigeonhole analogy, 60
Place value, 446, 482
Plugboard, see Control panel
Plus jump instruction, 102, 436
Plus zero, 99
Pole piece, 359
Post mortem, 482
Preselection, 257, 482
Presetting, see Initialization
Preventive maintenance, 402
Print instruction, 202, 443
Printing, 187, 199
Probability merge sorting, 320
Procedure, 377, 482

Procedures manual, 390
Process flow chart, see Top level flow chart
Product, 482
Production control, 3
Production scheduling, 3
Program, 47, 482
Program maintenance, 390
Programming, 47, 334
Programming research, 217
Proof figures, 409
Pseudo instruction, 275, 277, 482
Pulse, 482
Punched card, 17, 44, 47, 52, 184, 186, 227, 312, 482
Punched card sorting, 312

Queuing theory, 191
Quotient, 483

R register, 49, 51, 62, 63, 432
Radix, 446, 481, 483
Radix sorting, 310
Raise index and jump instruction, 147, 440
Random access file, 13, 14, 367
Random access storage, 49, 251, 300, 359, 367, 429, 483
Rapid access loop, 363, 483
Raw data, 6, 483
Read, 483
Read instruction, 201, 202, 443
Read tape instruction, 113, 155, 442
Reading head, see Head
Real-time data processing, 190, 483
Reasonableness test, 352, 410, 472
Recirculating loop, see Rapid access loop
Record, 10, 19, 111, 183, 298, 483
Record count, 293, 408, 462
Record grouping, see Grouping, of records
Recording of information, 5
Red tape, see Housekeeping
Redundancy checking, 181, 400, 472, 483
Region, 267, 483
Register, 46, 177, 197, 483
Relative coding, 220, 261, 262, 483
Reliability of computers, 400
Relocatable subroutines, 174, 217, 220, 275
Relocation, 263

INDEX

Remarks (on coding), 240, 269
Repeated arithmetic, 403, 409
Report, 6, 199, 291, 483
Report file, 11
Report generator, 211, 289, 483
Rerun, 249, 347
Rerun point, 348, 483
Reset, 483
Reset and clear button, 178
Reset button, 178
Resetting, 128, 137
Restart, *see* Rerun
Review, 383
Revolver, *see* Rapid access loop
Rewind tape instruction, 442
Rewinding, 184, 245, 412, 484
Rounding, 79, 86
Round-off error, 86, 484
Routine, 47, 62, 246, 484
Run, 27, 244, 247, 251, 252, 329, 334, 380, 484
Run book, 381, 388, 484
Run locator, 247, 484

Sales forecasting, 2
SAP, *see* SHARE Assembly Program
Search, 484
SEESAW, 278
Selection sorting, 302
Self-checking number, 407, 484
Self-loading routine, 211, 212
Sense switch, 180
Sentinel, 23, 142, 158, 245, 255, 325, 484
Sequence checking, 23, 158, 159, 330
Sequence of instruction execution, 433
Sequential access files and storage, 13, 21, 95, 251, 298, 300, 367, 484
Sequential control, 52
Serial transfer, 484
Service routine, 484
Set index and jump instruction, 170, 441
SHARE Assembly Program, 276
Shift all left instruction, 81, 439
Shift all right instruction, 80, 438
Shift left except sign instruction, 81, 439
Shift only R left instruction, 79, 439
Shift only R right instruction, 78, 439
Shift R right and round instruction, 79, 439
Shift register, 49, 51, 82, 431

Shift right except sign instruction, 81, 438
Shifting, 46, 77, 438, 484
Sign, 484
Sign character, 59, 81, 429, 432
Sign character shift, 81
Signal, 484
Simulation, 277, 484
Single address instruction, 484
Single step key, 180
Skeleton flow chart, 34, 41
Social Security, 95
Social Security calculation, 95
Sort generator, 328
Sorting, 14, 18, 98, 117, 156, 195, 227, 289, 295, 298, 339, 342, 373, 484
Source document, 484
Space, 485
Space print instruction, 205, 443
Speed of processing, 397
Sperry Rand Corporation, 53
Sprocket channel, 183
Standardization, 396
Standby block, 256, 257, 485
Start button, 153, 179
Start-stop time, *see* Acceleration time, Deceleration time
Statistics tabulation, 298, 372
Storage, 5, 18, 45, 485
Store, 485
Store index instruction, 148, 441
Store instruction, 63, 434
Stored program computer, 45, 47, 53, 125, 127, 429, 485
Straight line coding, 341
Straight merge sorting, 315
String, 300, 315, 485
String-building, 319
Suboperation code, 60, 82, 431, 432
Suboptimization, 345 (exercises)
Subroutine, 30, 167, 258 (exercises), 275, 278, 485
Subtract from memory instruction, 68, 435
Subtract instruction, 64, 435
Subtrahend, 485
Sum, 485
Switch, 32, 324, 325, 485
Symbolic coding, 262, 273, 485
Synchronous computer, 485
System, 485

INDEX

System flow chart, see Top level flow chart
Systems analysis, 377, 382, 485
Systems approach, 7, 485
Systems design, 283, 334
Systems study, 376

Table look-up, 368, 485
Tabulating equipment, 485
Tally, 486
Tape, see Magnetic tape, Paper tape
Tape allocation, 381
Tape error jump instruction, 438
Tape error trigger, 179, 220
Tape executive routine, 220
Tape handler, 49, 51
Tape librarian, 412
Tape limited, 486
Tape mark, 183
Tape swap, see Alternation of tape handlers
Tape unit, see Tape handler
Techniques development, 217
Teletype, 5
Temporary storage, 486
Ten's complement, 147, 155, 449
Test case, 228, 234, 486
Test data, 385
Testing (in loops), 137
Three-address instruction, 480, 486
Three-way merge sorting, 319
Time, of instruction execution, 359, 429
Time estimating, 333, 342
Top level flow chart, 27, 39, 379
Tracing, 232, 236, 486
Track, 359
Trailer, 255, 258 (exercises), 336, 339
Training, 391
Transaction file, 11, 21, 115, 156, 256, 486
Transfer, 486
Transfer instruction, see Jump instructions
Transfer of control card, see Transition card
Transfer-shift register, see Shift register
Transfer shifting, 82, 431, 432
Transition card, 211, 212, 486
Translate, 486

Trigger, 66, 355
Two-address instruction, 480, 486
Two-out-of-five coding, 458
Two-way merge sorting, 315
Typewriter, 178, 187

Ultrasonic memory, see Mercury-delay line memory
Unconditional jump instruction, 100, 436
Univac I, 53
Unload instruction, 434
Unpack, 486
Unwinding of loops, 162, 486
Up time, 486
Updating, 486
U. S. Census Bureau, 52
Utility programming, 217

Validity check, 472, 486
Variable connector, see Switch
Variable record length, 19, 113, 154, 254, 368, 429
Variable word length, 124 (exercises), 218, 327, 486
Verifier, 385, 405, 487
Volume test, 386

Watson-Watt, Sir Robert, 24
Weighted counts, 407
Whirlwind I, 53
Wilkes, M. V., 53
Wired program computer, 487
Wiring board, see Control panel
Withholding tax, 87, 128
Word, 19, 48, 178, 429, 487
Word count, 211
Word length, 487
Working storage, 206, 254, 325, 487
Write, 487
Write tape instruction, 155, 442
Writing head, see Head

YTD, 29

Zero index jump instruction, 147, 440
Zero jump instruction, 102, 436
Zero suppression, 195, 293, 487
Zone bits, 59, 82

From the Library
RCA Institutes,
New York City